The Best Ways To Stink

A Guide To Attractive Bodily Smells Raunch and Pheremones

Maya Vargas

ISBN: 9784779690142
Imprint: Telephasic Workshop
Copyright © 2024 Maya Vargas.
All Rights Reserved.

Contents

The Art of Sensual Stench   **1**
Embracing Your Natural Odor   1
Subtle Scents for Seduction   24
Sexy Sweat Techniques   49

Bibliography   **55**
Sensational Skincare for Sultry Smells   73
Thrilling Hair Odor Elevation   99

Bibliography   **111**
Revolutionary Mouth Odors   127

Bibliography   **143**

Bibliography   **155**

Unconventional Aromas and Unique Stenches   **157**
Surprising Scents of Seduction   157

Bibliography   **177**
Repulsive Yet Compelling Odors   182

Bibliography   **189**
Provocative Pheromone Games   206

Bibliography   **223**
Sensational Stenches from Around the World   233

Bibliography   **255**
Unconventional Grooming Products   258

CONTENTS

The Power of Attractive Malodor   283
Breaking Taboos with Fetid Perfumes   283

Bibliography   299
Body Odor as a Form of Rebellion   308

Bibliography   313

Bibliography   323

Bibliography   329
Challenging Beauty Norms with Offensive Aromas   334

Bibliography   339

Bibliography   345

Bibliography   351
The Intersection of Sexuality and Repugnant Stenches   360

Bibliography   367

Bibliography   387
Embracing Stinky Self-Care Practices   387

Bibliography   391

Bibliography   411

The Future of Attractive Odors   415
Innovations in Scent Technology   415

Bibliography   425
Breaking Boundaries with Scented Art Installations   442

Bibliography   453
New Avenues for Attractive Stenches   465

Bibliography   475
Ethical Considerations in Scent Marketing and Advertising   489

Bibliography   493

Bibliography 511

Community Building through Attractive Stenches 517

Bibliography 537

Bibliography 543

Index 545

The Art of Sensual Stench

Embracing Your Natural Odor

Unlocking the Power of Your Body's Smells

The human body is a complex organism that exudes a myriad of odors, each with its own unique significance and potential allure. Understanding the power of these natural scents can unlock a deeper connection to oneself and enhance interpersonal relationships. This section delves into the science behind bodily smells, the cultural implications of scent, and offers practical insights on how to embrace and enhance your personal aroma.

The Science of Body Odor

Body odor is primarily the result of the interaction between sweat and bacteria on the skin. When sweat is produced, it is initially odorless. However, when it comes into contact with the skin's microbiome, particularly in areas such as the armpits and groin, bacteria break down the sweat into compounds that can produce distinct odors. This process can be described by the following reaction:

$$\text{Sweat} + \text{Bacteria} \rightarrow \text{Odorous Compounds} \tag{1}$$

The primary components of sweat are water, electrolytes, and organic compounds such as fatty acids and amino acids. The breakdown of these compounds can yield a variety of smells, from the musky scent associated with pheromones to the more pungent odors linked to stress or diet.

The Role of Pheromones

Pheromones are a specific class of chemical signals that play a crucial role in sexual attraction and social communication. They are secreted by the body and can influence the behavior of others, often without conscious awareness. Research suggests that pheromones can trigger emotional responses and influence mate selection.

For instance, studies have shown that individuals can subconsciously detect pheromonal cues that indicate genetic compatibility. This phenomenon can be described by the equation:

$$\text{Pheromones} \rightarrow \text{Behavioral Response} \qquad (2)$$

The ability to unlock the power of pheromones lies in understanding and embracing your own unique scent profile. This involves recognizing the factors that influence body odor, including genetics, diet, and overall health.

Cultural Perspectives on Body Odor

Cultural attitudes towards body odor vary significantly across societies. In some cultures, natural body scents are celebrated and considered attractive, while in others, they may be viewed negatively. For example, certain Indigenous cultures value the scent of the body as a marker of identity and connection to the earth. In contrast, Western societies often prioritize artificial fragrances and deodorants to mask natural odors.

This cultural dichotomy can be illustrated through the following framework:

$$\text{Cultural Norms} \rightarrow \text{Perception of Odor} \qquad (3)$$

Understanding these cultural perspectives can help individuals navigate their relationship with their own body odor and the odors of others, allowing for a more nuanced appreciation of scent in social contexts.

Enhancing Your Natural Scent

Embracing and enhancing your natural scent can be a powerful tool for self-expression and attraction. Here are some practical tips to unlock the power of your body's smells:

- **Dietary Choices:** What you eat significantly influences your body odor. Incorporating foods rich in zinc, such as nuts and seeds, can help create a more pleasant scent. Conversely, strong-smelling foods like garlic and onions can alter your natural aroma.

- **Hydration:** Staying well-hydrated helps dilute sweat and can lead to a less pungent odor. Aim for at least 8 glasses of water a day to maintain optimal hydration levels.

- **Natural Deodorants:** Consider using natural deodorants that allow your body to sweat while masking undesirable odors. Look for products that contain baking soda, arrowroot powder, or essential oils.

- **Regular Hygiene:** Maintaining a regular hygiene routine, including showering and exfoliating, can help manage body odor while allowing your natural scent to shine through.

- **Scented Rituals:** Incorporate scented oils or lotions that complement your natural aroma. Essential oils like lavender, sandalwood, and cedarwood can enhance your scent profile without overwhelming it.

The Allure of Individuality

Ultimately, unlocking the power of your body's smells is about celebrating individuality. Each person possesses a unique scent signature that can be both attractive and alluring. By understanding the science behind body odor and embracing your natural aroma, you can cultivate a sense of confidence and authenticity that resonates with others.

In conclusion, the journey to unlocking the power of your body's smells is an exploration of self-discovery and acceptance. By embracing your natural scent, understanding the science behind it, and enhancing it through mindful practices, you can transform what is often considered a taboo topic into a celebration of individuality and attraction. So, let your natural aroma shine, and embrace the beauty of being uniquely you.

The Science Behind Attractive Odors

The olfactory system, responsible for our sense of smell, plays a crucial role in how we perceive and react to various odors, including those that we find attractive. This section delves into the scientific principles underlying attractive odors, examining the chemistry of scents, the biology of olfaction, and the psychological factors that contribute to our preferences.

Chemical Composition of Odors

Attractive odors are often composed of volatile organic compounds (VOCs), which are small molecules that can easily evaporate and enter the air. These compounds interact with olfactory receptors in the nasal cavity, triggering a complex neural response. The perception of a scent is not just a simple binary of "pleasant" or "unpleasant"; it is a nuanced experience influenced by the specific chemical structure of the odorant.

For instance, the compound *linalool*, found in lavender, is known for its floral and calming scent, while *isovaleraldehyde*, which has a cheesy odor, is generally perceived as unpleasant. The structural formula of linalool can be represented as follows:

$$C_{10}H_{18}O \tag{4}$$

In contrast, the formula for isovaleraldehyde is:

$$C_5H_{10}O \tag{5}$$

The difference in molecular structure significantly affects how these compounds interact with olfactory receptors.

Olfactory Receptors and Signal Transduction

Humans have approximately 400 types of olfactory receptors, each sensitive to different molecular features of odorants. When an odorant binds to its corresponding receptor, it initiates a signal transduction pathway that ultimately leads to the perception of smell. This process can be illustrated as follows:

$$\text{Odorant} + \text{Olfactory Receptor} \rightarrow \text{Signal Transduction} \rightarrow \text{Perception of Smell} \tag{6}$$

The olfactory bulb, a part of the brain located just above the nasal cavity, processes these signals and sends them to higher brain regions, including the limbic system, which is involved in emotion and memory. This connection explains why certain smells can evoke strong emotional responses or memories.

The Role of Pheromones

Pheromones are a class of chemicals that play a significant role in communication between individuals of the same species. They can influence social behaviors, mating preferences, and even reproductive cycles. The vomeronasal organ (VNO), located in the nasal cavity, is specialized for detecting pheromones.

Research has shown that certain pheromones can enhance attractiveness. For example, the compound androstadienone, found in the sweat of both men and women, has been linked to increased sexual attraction. Studies have indicated that exposure to androstadienone can enhance mood and increase perceived attractiveness, especially in women.

Psychological and Cultural Influences

While the chemistry of odors is fundamental, psychological and cultural factors also play a significant role in determining what is considered attractive. Cultural norms and personal experiences shape our preferences for certain scents. For example, a scent that is considered attractive in one culture may not have the same effect in another.

Furthermore, the mere exposure effect suggests that repeated exposure to a particular scent can increase our liking for it. This phenomenon can be mathematically represented as:

$$L = \frac{E}{1 + e^{-k(t-t_0)}} \tag{7}$$

Where: - L is the liking score, - E is the maximum liking score, - k is the rate of increase in liking, - t is time, - t_0 is the time of initial exposure.

This equation illustrates how familiarity with a scent can enhance its attractiveness over time.

Conclusion

The science behind attractive odors is a fascinating interplay of chemistry, biology, and psychology. Understanding the mechanisms that govern our perception of scents not only illuminates why certain odors are deemed attractive but also highlights the complex nature of human attraction itself. From the molecular interactions of VOCs to the cultural influences that shape our preferences, the study of odors reveals much about our emotional and social lives.

Celebrating Individuality with Unique Scents

In a world often dominated by mass-produced fragrances and standardized beauty norms, the celebration of individuality through unique scents emerges as a radical act of self-expression. Each person's body chemistry is as distinctive as their fingerprint, influenced by a myriad of factors including genetics, diet, environment, and even emotional state. This section delves into the intricate relationship between personal identity and scent, exploring how embracing one's unique olfactory signature can enhance individuality and foster deeper connections with others.

The Science of Personal Odor

The foundation of our personal scent lies in our skin's microbiome—the diverse community of microorganisms residing on our skin. These microorganisms interact with our body chemistry, producing a variety of volatile organic compounds (VOCs) that contribute to our unique odor profile. Research has shown that these compounds can be influenced by factors such as:

- **Diet:** Foods rich in sulfur, such as garlic and onions, can alter body odor significantly. Conversely, a diet high in fruits and vegetables may promote a more pleasant scent due to the presence of antioxidants.

- **Hormones:** Hormonal fluctuations, particularly those related to menstrual cycles, can impact the intensity and type of body odor. This variability can make certain scents more pronounced at different times.

- **Health:** Illness can also change one's natural scent. For example, a fever can alter skin temperature and moisture levels, affecting the microbial community and thus the resultant odor.

The equation governing the interaction between these factors can be simplified as follows:

$$S = f(D, H, C, E) \qquad (8)$$

Where: - S = Personal scent - D = Diet - H = Hormones - C = Health - E = Environment

This equation illustrates the complexity of personal scent, emphasizing that it is not merely a product of hygiene but rather a dynamic interplay of various biological and environmental factors.

Embracing Uniqueness

Celebrating individuality through unique scents invites us to embrace our natural odors rather than mask them. The allure of personal scent lies in its authenticity; it tells a story about who we are, where we come from, and what we value.

Consider the concept of *signature scent*. This is not just a fragrance chosen from a store but rather a scent that resonates with one's identity. For instance, a person who has a strong connection to the ocean may find themselves drawn to salty, marine notes, while someone with a passion for gardening might prefer floral or earthy scents. The act of selecting or creating a personal fragrance should reflect one's inner self, allowing for deeper connections with others who resonate with that scent.

Cultural Perspectives on Scent

Different cultures have varying relationships with scent, often celebrating unique odors that define their heritage. For example, in many Indigenous cultures, the use of natural scents—such as sage, cedar, and sweetgrass—is integral to spiritual practices and community bonding. These scents are not merely pleasant; they hold profound meanings and histories, connecting individuals to their roots.

In contrast, Western cultures often prioritize commercial fragrances, which can lead to a homogenization of scent experiences. However, the resurgence of interest in artisanal and niche perfumes reflects a growing desire to reconnect with personal and cultural identities through scent. Brands that emphasize storytelling and authenticity are gaining popularity, allowing consumers to celebrate their uniqueness.

Challenges in Embracing Unique Scents

While the celebration of individuality through scent is empowering, it is not without challenges. Societal norms often dictate what is considered 'acceptable' or 'pleasant' in terms of body odor. This can lead to stigmatization of natural scents, particularly for those whose odors do not conform to conventional standards.

Moreover, the pressure to conform to marketed fragrances can overshadow the beauty of personal scent. The rise of influencer culture, where specific scents are promoted as trendy, can create a paradox where individuality is celebrated, yet conformity is still expected.

Practical Applications

To embrace and celebrate individuality through unique scents, individuals can engage in the following practices:

- **Scent Journaling:** Keeping a journal of scents experienced throughout the day can help identify personal preferences and patterns, encouraging a deeper understanding of one's olfactory identity.

- **DIY Fragrance Creation:** Experimenting with essential oils and natural ingredients allows for the creation of bespoke fragrances that reflect personal stories and preferences. This process can be both therapeutic and empowering.

- **Mindful Scenting:** Engaging in mindfulness practices while exploring scents can enhance the emotional connection to personal odors. This can include meditation or simply taking time to appreciate the scents in one's environment.

- **Community Engagement:** Joining scent-related workshops or communities can provide support and encouragement for those looking to celebrate their unique olfactory identities. Sharing experiences and stories can foster a sense of belonging.

Conclusion

In conclusion, celebrating individuality with unique scents is a powerful means of self-expression and connection. By understanding the science behind personal odors, embracing cultural perspectives, and overcoming societal challenges, individuals can cultivate a deeper appreciation for their unique scent profiles. This journey not only enhances personal identity but also fosters connections with others, creating a tapestry of diverse and beautiful scents that enrich our shared human experience.

As we navigate the complexities of scent, let us remember that our unique odors are not merely byproducts of biology but rather an integral part of who we are. Embrace your scent, celebrate your individuality, and let your aroma tell your story.

How to Identify Your Signature Stench

Identifying your signature stench is an art form that combines self-awareness, experimentation, and a touch of olfactory bravery. This section delves into the nuances of discovering that unique aroma that sets you apart and highlights the chemistry of your body. Your signature stench is more than just a smell; it's a reflection of your identity, lifestyle, and even your dietary choices.

Understanding the Science of Body Odor

To embark on the journey of identifying your signature stench, it's essential to understand the science behind body odor. Body odor is primarily produced by the apocrine glands, which are located in areas rich in hair follicles, such as the armpits and groin. When sweat from these glands interacts with skin bacteria, it produces various volatile organic compounds (VOCs) that contribute to your unique scent profile.

The equation that represents the interaction between sweat and bacteria can be simplified as follows:

$$\text{Sweat} + \text{Bacteria} \rightarrow \text{VOCs} \rightarrow \text{Body Odor} \qquad (9)$$

The specific composition of your body odor is influenced by several factors, including:

- **Genetics:** Your genetic makeup plays a significant role in determining your natural scent. Studies have shown that genetic variations can lead to differences in the types and amounts of sweat produced.

- **Diet:** Foods such as garlic, onions, and spices can significantly alter your body odor. For example, the sulfur compounds in garlic can lead to a more pungent aroma.

- **Health:** Certain medical conditions can affect your body odor. For instance, diabetes can lead to a fruity smell due to the presence of ketones in the body.

- **Hormones:** Hormonal changes, particularly during puberty or menstruation, can also influence the composition of your sweat and, consequently, your body odor.

Experimentation: Finding Your Unique Scent

Once you understand the science, the next step is to experiment with different factors that can influence your signature stench. Here are some practical approaches:

1. **Dietary Changes:** Start by altering your diet for a week or two. Introduce foods known for their strong scents, such as garlic, cumin, or curry, and observe any changes in your body odor. Conversely, try eliminating processed foods and sugars to see if your natural scent becomes more pronounced.

2. **Hygiene Routines:** Experiment with different hygiene products, including soaps, deodorants, and lotions. Pay attention to how these products interact with your natural scent. For instance, using natural deodorants can allow your body's natural scent to shine through without masking it with synthetic fragrances.

3. **Physical Activity:** Engage in various forms of exercise to see how your body odor evolves with different sweat levels. High-intensity workouts may elicit a more pungent aroma due to increased sweat production and bacterial activity.

4. **Environmental Factors:** Consider how your environment affects your scent. For example, spending time in nature, near the ocean, or in urban settings can introduce unique elements to your body odor due to environmental factors such as humidity and air quality.

Identifying and Embracing Your Unique Aroma

Once you have experimented with various factors, it's time to identify and embrace your unique aroma. Here are some steps to guide you:

- **Self-Assessment:** Take time to reflect on your natural scent. Engage in practices like mindfulness or meditation to enhance your awareness of your body and its odors. Consider keeping a scent journal to document your observations over time.

- **Seek Feedback:** Share your journey with close friends or partners and ask for their honest opinions. They can provide insights into how your scent is perceived and offer suggestions for enhancement.

- **Create a Signature Blend:** Once you have identified your base scent, consider creating a blend that complements it. This could involve using essential oils or crafting a personalized perfume that enhances your natural aroma without overpowering it.

Conclusion

Identifying your signature stench is a journey of self-discovery that requires an open mind and a willingness to embrace your natural aroma. By understanding the science behind body odor, experimenting with various factors, and engaging in self-assessment, you can uncover a scent that is uniquely yours. Remember, the goal is not to mask your natural smell but to celebrate it—because your signature stench is an intrinsic part of who you are.

In the words of the great philosopher Socrates, "Know thyself." And in this case, knowing yourself includes embracing the beautiful complexity of your body's natural fragrance.

Enhancing Your Natural Fragrance

The pursuit of an alluring scent is a journey that intertwines personal expression and biological chemistry. Enhancing your natural fragrance doesn't merely rely on external products; it involves understanding and amplifying the unique aromas that your body naturally produces. This section delves into the various methods to enhance your scent profile while celebrating your individuality.

Understanding the Chemistry of Body Odor

At the core of body odor is a complex interplay of sweat, skin flora, and genetics. The human body emits a variety of volatile organic compounds (VOCs) that contribute to our unique scent. These VOCs are produced through the metabolism of substances in our body, influenced by factors such as diet, hydration, and hormonal fluctuations.

The equation representing the production of body odor can be simplified as follows:

$$\text{Body Odor} = f(\text{Diet, Hydration, Genetics, Skin Flora}) \qquad (10)$$

Where f represents a function that encapsulates the interactions among these variables.

Dietary Influences on Body Odor

What you consume significantly impacts your natural fragrance. Foods rich in sulfur, such as garlic and onions, can impart a stronger scent, while fruits and vegetables can lead to a more pleasant aroma.

For example, a study published in *Chemical Senses* found that individuals who consumed a diet high in fruits and vegetables were perceived as more attractive due to their more pleasant body odor. The key compounds responsible for this are primarily flavonoids and carotenoids, which can be represented in the following equation:

$$\text{Attractiveness} \propto \text{Flavonoids} + \text{Carotenoids} \qquad (11)$$

To enhance your natural fragrance, consider incorporating more fresh fruits, vegetables, and herbs into your diet, while reducing the intake of processed foods and sugars.

Hydration: The Unsung Hero

Hydration plays a crucial role in how your body odor is perceived. Dehydration can lead to concentrated sweat, which can emit a stronger, less pleasant scent. The relationship between hydration and body odor can be expressed as:

$$\text{Body Odor Intensity} \propto \frac{1}{\text{Hydration Level}} \qquad (12)$$

To maintain an appealing scent, aim to drink at least eight glasses of water per day, or more if you are active. Herbal teas and infused waters can also contribute positively to your hydration levels while adding subtle flavors.

Skin Flora: The Microbial Symphony

The skin is home to millions of bacteria that play a significant role in determining your scent. These microorganisms break down sweat and other substances, producing various byproducts that contribute to body odor.

To enhance your natural fragrance, consider the following:

- **Probiotics:** Incorporating probiotic-rich foods such as yogurt, kefir, and fermented vegetables can promote a healthy balance of skin flora.
- **Prebiotics:** Foods that feed beneficial bacteria, such as garlic, onions, and leeks, can enhance the microbial diversity on your skin, leading to a more pleasant scent.

Natural Enhancers: Oils and Butters

In addition to dietary changes, the use of natural oils and butters can enhance your fragrance without overpowering your natural scent.

- **Essential Oils:** Oils such as bergamot, sandalwood, and ylang-ylang can be used to complement your natural aroma. Dilute essential oils in a carrier oil and apply them to pulse points for a subtle enhancement.
- **Butters:** Shea butter and coconut oil can provide moisturizing benefits while also carrying a light, pleasant scent. Incorporating these into your skincare routine can help to lock in moisture and enhance your natural fragrance.

Layering Scents: The Art of Fragrance Blending

To further enhance your natural fragrance, consider the art of layering scents. This technique involves combining different scents to create a unique and personalized aroma.

Start with a base scent that aligns with your natural odor, then add complementary notes. For example, if your natural scent is musky, consider layering with floral or citrus notes to create a balanced fragrance profile.

Conclusion

Enhancing your natural fragrance is a multifaceted process that requires an understanding of personal biology, dietary choices, and the use of natural products. By embracing your unique scent and making mindful choices, you can cultivate an attractive aroma that resonates with your individuality. Remember, the goal is not to mask your natural scent but to enhance it, celebrating the beautiful complexities of your body's chemistry.

Ultimately, the most attractive fragrance is one that is authentically yours, a signature scent that tells the world who you are without saying a word.

Discovering the Allure of Eau de B.O.

Ah, the intoxicating scent of body odor, often shunned yet undeniably alluring. In this section, we delve into the complex world of *Eau de B.O.*, where the natural aroma of our bodies transcends the boundaries of societal norms and becomes a seductive force.

The Chemistry of Body Odor

At its core, body odor is a result of the interplay between our skin's microbiota and the sweat produced by our apocrine and eccrine glands. The primary components of sweat are water, salt, and a variety of organic compounds, including fatty acids and proteins. When sweat is metabolized by skin bacteria, it produces volatile organic compounds (VOCs) that contribute to the unique scent of each individual.

The formula for the concentration of these compounds can be expressed as:

$$C = \frac{n}{V} \tag{13}$$

where C is the concentration of the odorant, n is the number of moles of the odorant, and V is the volume of the air in which the odor is diffusing.

The interplay of these compounds creates a signature scent that is as individual as a fingerprint. The allure of body odor lies in its authenticity; it is a raw, unfiltered representation of oneself, often evoking a sense of primal attraction.

The Role of Pheromones

Pheromones, chemical signals released by an individual that trigger social responses in members of the same species, play a significant role in the allure of body odor. Research indicates that certain pheromones can enhance attraction and even influence mate selection.

For instance, studies have shown that women tend to prefer the scent of men whose immune system genes (MHC) are different from their own, as indicated by the following equation representing the preference function:

$$P = f(MHC_{man}, MHC_{woman}) \tag{14}$$

where P is the preference level, and f is a function that increases when MHC_{man} and MHC_{woman} are sufficiently dissimilar.

This biological mechanism suggests that body odor serves as an evolutionary tool, guiding us toward genetically compatible partners, thus enhancing the allure of our natural scent.

Cultural Perspectives on Body Odor

Culturally, the perception of body odor varies significantly. In some societies, a natural scent is celebrated as a sign of health and vitality, while in others, it is stigmatized. For example, the Japanese concept of *natsukashii* embraces the nostalgic scent of summer, including the natural body scents that accompany it. This cultural acceptance highlights the idea that Eau de B.O. can evoke powerful emotional responses tied to memory and identity.

Moreover, in the realm of fashion and beauty, brands have begun to embrace the concept of natural scents, launching products that enhance rather than mask body odor. This shift can be seen in the rise of *natural deodorants* that promote the skin's microbiome instead of suppressing it.

The Seduction of Natural Scents

The allure of Eau de B.O. is not merely biological or cultural; it is also deeply sensual. The act of being close to someone and inhaling their unique scent can be an intimate experience. This intimacy is often compared to the act of tasting food; just as flavors can evoke memories and emotions, so too can scents.

Consider the following sensory engagement equation:

$$S = \int_0^t e^{-\lambda t} \cdot A \, dt \tag{15}$$

where S is the overall sensory experience, A represents the intensity of the aroma, and λ is the decay constant that accounts for the transient nature of scent. This equation illustrates how the experience of body odor can be both fleeting and powerful, leaving an indelible mark on our memories.

The Allure in the Unwashed

Interestingly, the scent of unwashed skin, often dismissed as unpleasant, can be enticing to some. The natural oils and bacteria that accumulate over time create a complex bouquet of scents that can be perceived as musky and inviting.

In a study conducted by the University of California, participants rated the attractiveness of natural body odor against artificially created scents. The results indicated a significant preference for natural scents, suggesting that the allure of Eau de B.O. is deeply rooted in our biological and psychological make-up.

Conclusion

In conclusion, the allure of Eau de B.O. is a multifaceted phenomenon that intertwines chemistry, biology, culture, and sensuality. Embracing our natural scent can be a powerful act of self-acceptance and expression. As we navigate the complexities of attraction, let us not forget the seductive power of our own unique body odor—a fragrant reminder of our individuality and primal instincts.

By celebrating the allure of Eau de B.O., we open the door to a more authentic and intimate connection with ourselves and those around us, transforming what was once considered a taboo into a symbol of allure and attraction.

The Seductive Scent of Unwashed Sheets

The allure of unwashed sheets is a tantalizing paradox that invites exploration into the realms of intimacy, nostalgia, and the raw essence of human experience. This section delves into the seductive scent of unwashed sheets, examining the psychological and physiological factors that contribute to their irresistible charm.

The Science of Scent

The scent of unwashed sheets is primarily composed of a complex mixture of body oils, sweat, and the natural odors that accumulate over time. These odors are not merely unpleasant but can evoke feelings of comfort and intimacy. The human olfactory system is intricately linked to the limbic system, the part of the brain responsible for emotions and memory. Thus, the scent of unwashed sheets can trigger powerful emotional responses, often linked to feelings of safety, warmth, and connection.

Mathematically, we can represent the relationship between scent perception and emotional response as follows:

$$E = k \cdot S \tag{16}$$

Where:

- E is the emotional response,
- S is the strength of the scent, and
- k is a constant representing individual sensitivity to scent.

This equation suggests that as the strength of the scent increases, so too does the emotional response, albeit modulated by individual differences in olfactory sensitivity.

Cultural and Psychological Perspectives

Culturally, the scent of unwashed sheets can evoke a sense of intimacy and familiarity. In romantic relationships, the presence of one's partner's scent can create a sense of closeness, even in their absence. This phenomenon is partly due to the presence of pheromones, chemical signals that can influence attraction and bonding. Research indicates that individuals are often drawn to the natural scents of their partners, which can be amplified by the scent of unwashed sheets that carry their essence.

Furthermore, the psychological concept of *nostalgia* plays a crucial role in the appeal of these scents. The aroma of unwashed sheets can transport individuals back to moments of intimacy and connection, reinforcing the idea that these scents are not merely undesirable but rather imbued with sentimental value. The nostalgia associated with these scents can be expressed through the following equation:

$$N = f(T, M) \tag{17}$$

EMBRACING YOUR NATURAL ODOR

Where:

- N is the level of nostalgia,
- T is the time spent in intimate settings, and
- M is the emotional memories associated with those settings.

As time spent in intimate settings increases, so does the level of nostalgia associated with the scent of unwashed sheets.

Practical Applications

In practical terms, the seductive scent of unwashed sheets can be leveraged in various ways. For example, individuals can create an environment that enhances this allure by:

- **Maintaining a Balance:** Allowing sheets to be slightly unwashed can amplify their natural scent without crossing into unpleasant territory. This balance can be achieved by washing sheets less frequently, particularly in romantic settings.
- **Layering Scents:** Incorporating lightly scented fabric softeners or essential oils can enhance the natural scent without overpowering it, creating a more inviting atmosphere.
- **Creating a Signature Scent:** Couples can develop a unique scent profile based on the combination of their natural odors and the fabric of their sheets, creating a personalized olfactory signature that evokes intimacy.

Challenges and Considerations

While the seductive scent of unwashed sheets can be appealing, it is essential to recognize the potential challenges associated with this practice. Over time, the accumulation of sweat and oils can lead to bacterial growth, resulting in odors that may be perceived as unpleasant rather than alluring. Therefore, it is crucial to strike a balance between maintaining the seductive quality of these scents and ensuring cleanliness to avoid crossing into the territory of unpleasant odors.

Additionally, individual preferences for scents can vary widely. What one person finds alluring, another may find off-putting. This variability underscores the importance of communication in intimate relationships, where partners can express their preferences and negotiate the boundaries of scent in their shared spaces.

Conclusion

The seductive scent of unwashed sheets embodies a complex interplay of biology, psychology, and cultural significance. By understanding the factors that contribute to the allure of these scents, individuals can embrace their unique olfactory preferences while fostering intimacy and connection in their relationships. Ultimately, the scent of unwashed sheets serves as a reminder of the beauty found in the raw, unfiltered aspects of human experience, inviting us to celebrate the sensuality of our natural odors.

Embracing the Aroma of Unfiltered Sweat

The scent of unfiltered sweat is a paradoxical allure, an aroma that embodies rawness and authenticity. In a world where artificial fragrances dominate, the natural scent of sweat—often dismissed as unpleasant—holds a unique charm that can be both attractive and intriguing. This section delves into the science, cultural perceptions, and sensual implications of embracing the aroma of unfiltered sweat.

The Science of Sweat and Its Scent

Sweat is composed primarily of water, but it also contains a complex mixture of salts, proteins, and organic compounds. The primary glands responsible for sweat production are the eccrine and apocrine glands. Eccrine glands, found all over the body, secrete a watery fluid that helps regulate body temperature. In contrast, apocrine glands, located in areas such as the armpits and groin, produce a thicker, milky secretion that is rich in fatty acids and proteins.

The scent of sweat is influenced by several factors, including:

- **Diet:** Foods such as garlic, onions, and spices can alter the composition of sweat, contributing to a more pungent aroma. For instance, the sulfur compounds in garlic can lead to a distinctive smell that some find appealing.
- **Genetics:** Individual genetic makeup influences the types of odor-causing bacteria present on the skin, which can modify the scent of sweat. Studies have shown that certain genetic variants can lead to more attractive body odors.
- **Hormones:** Hormonal fluctuations, particularly during ovulation, can enhance the allure of body odor, making it more attractive to potential partners. The interplay of pheromones and hormonal changes creates a unique olfactory signature.

EMBRACING YOUR NATURAL ODOR

The equation for the concentration of sweat can be expressed as:

$$C_s = \frac{M_s}{V_s} \tag{18}$$

where C_s is the concentration of sweat, M_s is the mass of sweat produced, and V_s is the volume of sweat excreted. The composition of sweat varies based on individual factors, leading to a unique scent profile.

Cultural Perceptions of Sweat

Cultural attitudes towards sweat are diverse and often contradictory. In some societies, sweat is seen as a mark of hard work and vitality, while in others, it is associated with poor hygiene and unpleasantness. The modern beauty industry often promotes anti-perspirants and deodorants that mask natural odors, reinforcing the stigma against unfiltered sweat.

However, there is a growing movement that celebrates the beauty of natural scents. This shift can be attributed to a desire for authenticity in an increasingly artificial world. Notable fashion designers and brands have begun to embrace the concept of "sweat couture," where the natural scent of the body is celebrated as a form of self-expression.

The Allure of Unfiltered Sweat in Intimacy

The attraction to unfiltered sweat can be linked to evolutionary biology. The scent of sweat is a potent signal of genetic fitness and compatibility. Pheromones, which are chemical signals released through sweat, play a crucial role in sexual attraction. Studies have shown that individuals are often subconsciously drawn to the scent of potential partners whose immune system genes differ from their own, promoting genetic diversity in offspring.

$$A = \frac{P}{D} \tag{19}$$

where A is the attractiveness of an individual, P represents the pheromone concentration, and D is the distance from the source. This equation illustrates how proximity and pheromone strength can enhance attraction.

Examples of Celebrating Sweat

1. **Sweat Festivals**: Events like the "Sweat Lodge" in various cultures highlight the communal and spiritual aspects of sweat. Participants engage in rituals that

celebrate the body's natural processes, fostering a sense of connection and authenticity.

2. **Fashion Statements**: Designers such as Rick Owens and Alexander Wang have incorporated the concept of sweat into their runway shows, challenging conventional beauty standards and celebrating the human body in its natural state.

3. **Artistic Expressions**: Artists like Marina Abramović have explored the relationship between sweat and intimacy in performance art, using their bodies as canvases to express vulnerability and raw emotion.

Conclusion

Embracing the aroma of unfiltered sweat invites a deeper understanding of the human experience. It challenges societal norms and encourages individuals to celebrate their natural scent as a form of self-expression. The allure of sweat transcends mere biology; it taps into the primal aspects of attraction, intimacy, and authenticity. In a world that often prioritizes the artificial, the embrace of unfiltered sweat stands as a testament to the beauty of being unapologetically oneself.

Exploring the Mysteries of Morning Breath

Morning breath, often dismissed as a mere inconvenience, is a fascinating phenomenon that intertwines biology, chemistry, and even social perceptions. This section delves into the science behind morning breath, exploring its causes, implications, and the often-overlooked allure it can possess.

The Biology of Morning Breath

During sleep, the body undergoes a series of physiological changes that contribute to the development of morning breath. One of the primary factors is reduced saliva production. Saliva plays a crucial role in oral hygiene; it contains enzymes and antibacterial properties that help neutralize acids and wash away food particles and bacteria. As we sleep, the production of saliva decreases significantly, leading to a dry mouth, which creates an ideal environment for bacteria to thrive.

The bacteria in our mouths, particularly *Streptococcus* and *Fusobacterium*, metabolize food particles and produce volatile sulfur compounds (VSCs) as byproducts. These compounds, primarily hydrogen sulfide (H_2S) and methyl mercaptan (CH_3SH), are responsible for the characteristic odor of morning breath. The equation for the formation of hydrogen sulfide can be simplified as follows:

$$\text{Cysteine} \rightarrow \text{Hydrogen Sulfide} + \text{Other Products} \qquad (20)$$

The concentration of these VSCs peaks in the morning due to the overnight accumulation of bacteria and their metabolic byproducts.

The Chemistry of Odor

The chemistry behind morning breath is not just limited to VSCs. Other compounds, such as ammonia and certain fatty acids, also contribute to the overall scent profile. Ammonia, produced from the breakdown of urea, can impart a sharp, pungent quality to morning breath. The complex interplay of these compounds creates a unique olfactory signature that varies from person to person.

To analyze the composition of morning breath, researchers often employ gas chromatography-mass spectrometry (GC-MS), a technique that separates and identifies volatile compounds in a sample. This method has revealed that the specific concentrations of VSCs can vary based on factors such as diet, oral hygiene, and even genetics.

Cultural Perceptions and Implications

Despite its biological basis, morning breath carries significant social implications. In many cultures, fresh breath is associated with cleanliness and desirability, while morning breath is often viewed as undesirable. This perception can lead to social anxiety, particularly in intimate situations. The fear of morning breath can influence behaviors such as kissing or engaging in close conversations upon waking.

However, there is a counter-narrative that suggests a certain allure to morning breath. The intimate act of waking up next to someone, with all the natural scents that accompany it, can foster a sense of closeness and authenticity. The rawness of morning breath can be seen as a reminder of our humanity, stripping away the layers of societal expectations and presenting a more genuine connection.

Addressing Morning Breath

For those who seek to mitigate the effects of morning breath, there are several strategies to consider:

- **Hydration:** Drinking water before bed can help maintain saliva production and reduce dryness in the mouth.

- **Oral Hygiene:** Brushing teeth and tongue, as well as flossing before sleep, can significantly reduce bacterial buildup.

- **Dietary Choices:** Avoiding strong-smelling foods such as garlic and onions in the evening can help minimize morning odors.

- **Mouthwash:** Using an antibacterial mouthwash before bed can help reduce the number of odor-producing bacteria.

Conclusion

Morning breath, while often viewed as a nuisance, offers a rich tapestry of biological, chemical, and social elements. Understanding the underlying mechanisms can demystify this common experience and perhaps even allow individuals to embrace it as part of their unique scent identity. As we continue to explore the allure of our natural odors, morning breath serves as a reminder of the intimacy and authenticity that can be found in our most unrefined moments.

Through a combination of scientific inquiry and personal reflection, we can appreciate morning breath not just as a problem to solve but as an intriguing aspect of our human experience—one that connects us to our bodies, our biology, and our relationships with others.

The Magnetic Pull of Natural Body Odor

Natural body odor, often dismissed as a mere byproduct of sweat and bacteria, holds a magnetic allure that can be both intriguing and seductive. This phenomenon can be explored through various theoretical frameworks, including evolutionary biology, psychology, and cultural studies. In this section, we will delve into the science behind natural body odor, its evolutionary significance, and its impact on attraction, while also addressing potential societal taboos and misconceptions.

The Science Behind Body Odor

Body odor is primarily the result of the interaction between sweat and the bacteria that inhabit our skin. The apocrine glands, located in areas such as the armpits and groin, secrete a fatty sweat that bacteria metabolize, producing a variety of volatile organic compounds (VOCs). These compounds contribute to the unique scent profile of an individual, which is influenced by genetics, diet, health, and hygiene practices.

The key equation governing the chemical interactions leading to body odor can be expressed as:

$$\text{Body Odor} = f(\text{Bacteria}) \cdot g(\text{Sweat Composition}) \cdot h(\text{Genetics}) \quad (21)$$

where f, g, and h represent the functions of bacterial activity, sweat composition, and genetic predisposition, respectively.

Evolutionary Perspective

From an evolutionary standpoint, body odor plays a crucial role in sexual selection. The "smell of attraction" is deeply rooted in our biology, as certain scents can signal genetic compatibility, health status, and reproductive fitness. Pheromones, chemical signals that elicit social responses in members of the same species, are a key component of this process.

Research has shown that individuals are often subconsciously attracted to the body odors of potential mates that differ genetically, particularly in genes related to the immune system, known as the Major Histocompatibility Complex (MHC). This preference for dissimilar MHC types can enhance offspring diversity and immunity, thereby increasing reproductive success.

A study by Wedekind et al. (1995) illustrated this phenomenon by having participants wear T-shirts for two nights. The shirts were then presented to members of the opposite sex, who rated the odors. Results indicated a marked preference for the scents of individuals with different MHC genes, suggesting that natural body odor is not only a personal signature but also a biological signal of compatibility.

Psychological and Social Factors

While the science of body odor is compelling, psychological and social factors also significantly influence how we perceive and respond to natural scents. Cultural norms and personal experiences shape our attitudes toward body odor, often leading to stigmatization or fetishization.

For instance, in some cultures, a strong body odor may be considered a sign of virility or health, while in others, it may be viewed as unclean or undesirable. This dichotomy creates a complex landscape where natural body odor can evoke attraction or aversion, depending on the context.

Moreover, psychological studies suggest that familiarity plays a significant role in odor preference. The mere exposure effect posits that individuals tend to develop a preference for stimuli they are repeatedly exposed to. Thus, a partner's unique scent can become increasingly appealing over time, reinforcing emotional bonds and intimacy.

Taboos and Misconceptions

Despite the magnetic pull of natural body odor, societal taboos often discourage its expression. The beauty and personal care industries heavily promote products designed to mask or eliminate body odor, fostering a perception that natural scents are undesirable. This has led to a disconnection from our innate biological signals, as many individuals prioritize social acceptability over personal authenticity.

Addressing these misconceptions requires a cultural shift that embraces the natural human scent as an integral part of identity and attraction. By celebrating the uniqueness of our body odors, we can foster a more inclusive understanding of beauty and desirability.

Conclusion

The magnetic pull of natural body odor is a multifaceted phenomenon rooted in biology, psychology, and culture. As we navigate the complexities of attraction and intimacy, it is essential to recognize the powerful role that our unique scents play in shaping our connections with others. Embracing and celebrating our natural body odors can lead to a more authentic and fulfilling experience of attraction, challenging societal norms and inviting a deeper appreciation for the human experience.

In conclusion, the allure of natural body odor is not merely a matter of personal preference but a profound aspect of our biological and social existence. By understanding and embracing this aspect of ourselves, we can unlock new dimensions of intimacy and connection in our relationships.

Subtle Scents for Seduction

Choosing the Right Perfumes and Colognes

Choosing the right perfume or cologne is not merely an exercise in personal preference; it is a complex interplay of chemistry, psychology, and cultural significance. The fragrance you select can evoke memories, influence perceptions, and even affect your interactions with others. This section explores the nuances of selecting the perfect scent, diving into the science behind fragrance families, the psychology of scent, and practical tips for making informed choices.

Understanding Fragrance Families

Fragrances are typically categorized into several families, each with distinct characteristics and emotional associations. The primary fragrance families include:

- **Floral:** Often associated with femininity and romance, floral scents feature notes from flowers such as rose, jasmine, and lily. They can be sweet, fresh, or even powdery.

- **Citrus:** Bright and zesty, citrus fragrances include notes from fruits like lemon, orange, and bergamot. These scents are often uplifting and energizing.

- **Woody:** Characterized by earthy and warm notes, woody fragrances often feature sandalwood, cedar, and vetiver. They evoke a sense of comfort and grounding.

- **Oriental:** Rich and exotic, oriental fragrances combine spices, resins, and sweet notes. They are often associated with sensuality and mystery.

- **Fresh:** This category includes aquatic, green, and herbal scents that evoke cleanliness and vitality. They are often light and invigorating.

Understanding these families can help you identify which scents resonate with your personality and the impression you wish to convey.

The Science of Scent

The selection of a fragrance is deeply rooted in the science of olfaction. When we smell a scent, volatile compounds interact with olfactory receptors in the nasal cavity, sending signals to the brain. This process can be described by the following equation:

$$S = k \cdot (C \cdot R) \qquad (22)$$

where S represents the perceived scent intensity, k is a constant representing individual sensitivity, C is the concentration of the fragrance compounds, and R is the response of the olfactory receptors.

The emotional response to a fragrance can be attributed to the limbic system, which governs emotions and memory. This is why certain scents can trigger powerful memories or feelings of nostalgia.

Personal Chemistry and Skin Type

Personal chemistry plays a significant role in how a fragrance develops on your skin. Factors such as skin type, pH level, and body temperature can alter the way a scent is perceived. For instance, oily skin tends to hold fragrances longer, while dry skin may require more frequent reapplication.

$$D = \frac{C}{T} \qquad (23)$$

In this equation, D represents the duration of scent longevity, C is the concentration of the fragrance oil, and T is the temperature of the skin. Higher temperatures can enhance the volatility of fragrance notes, leading to a more pronounced scent profile.

Psychological Considerations

The psychological impact of scent is profound. Research has shown that certain fragrances can influence mood, behavior, and even attraction. For example, a study conducted by the Smell and Taste Treatment and Research Foundation found that vanilla and lavender scents can have calming effects, while citrus scents can boost alertness and energy levels.

When choosing a fragrance, consider the emotional response you wish to elicit. Do you want to feel empowered, relaxed, or seductive? Selecting scents that align with your desired emotional state can enhance your overall experience.

Practical Tips for Selection

When it comes to selecting the right perfume or cologne, consider the following practical tips:

- **Test Before You Buy:** Always sample fragrances on your skin rather than relying solely on scent strips. This allows you to experience how the fragrance interacts with your body chemistry.

- **Consider the Occasion:** Different scents may be more appropriate for various settings. Light, fresh fragrances are often ideal for daytime, while deeper, richer scents may be better suited for evening events.

- **Layering Scents:** Experiment with layering different scents to create a unique fragrance profile. This can enhance the complexity of your scent and make it more personal.

- **Seek Professional Advice:** Don't hesitate to ask for help from fragrance specialists at stores. They can provide insights into scent families and recommend options based on your preferences.

Conclusion

Choosing the right perfume or cologne is an art that combines science, psychology, and personal expression. By understanding fragrance families, personal chemistry, and the psychological effects of scent, you can make informed choices that resonate with your identity and enhance your allure. Remember, the right fragrance is not just a scent; it is an extension of who you are, a subtle yet powerful statement of your presence in the world.

Using Essential Oils to Create Alluring Aromas

Essential oils have long captivated humanity with their potent aromas and therapeutic properties. Derived from various plant materials, these concentrated extracts not only provide delightful scents but also hold the potential to influence mood, attract attention, and create an alluring atmosphere. This section delves into the art of using essential oils to craft enticing aromas that can enhance intimacy and sensuality.

The Science of Essential Oils

At the core of essential oils lies a complex chemistry that contributes to their distinctive fragrances. Each essential oil is composed of numerous chemical compounds, including terpenes, esters, aldehydes, and phenols, which interact with olfactory receptors in the nose. The interaction between these compounds and our olfactory system is crucial in determining the perceived scent and its emotional impact.

The olfactory system can be described using the following equation:

$$S = f(C, R) \qquad (24)$$

Where:

- S = perceived scent
- C = concentration of chemical compounds
- R = receptor sensitivity

This equation illustrates that the strength and nature of a scent depend on both the concentration of the essential oil's components and the individual's olfactory receptor sensitivity.

Choosing the Right Essential Oils

When selecting essential oils for creating alluring aromas, consider the following factors:

- **Personal Preference:** Individual reactions to scents vary greatly. What one person finds alluring, another may find off-putting. Conduct a scent test to identify your favorites.

- **Intended Effect:** Different essential oils evoke various emotional responses. For instance, lavender is known for its calming properties, while ylang-ylang is often associated with sensuality and romance.

- **Blending:** Combining essential oils can create complex and multi-dimensional aromas. Experiment with various combinations to discover unique blends that resonate with your desired atmosphere.

Creating Alluring Blends

To create an alluring aroma, consider the following essential oil blends:

- **Romantic Blend:** Combine 3 drops of ylang-ylang, 2 drops of bergamot, and 1 drop of sandalwood. This blend creates a warm, inviting scent that promotes relaxation and intimacy.

- **Energizing Blend:** Mix 2 drops of peppermint, 2 drops of lemon, and 1 drop of rosemary. This invigorating blend can uplift the spirit and energize the senses.

- **Calming Blend:** Combine 3 drops of lavender, 2 drops of chamomile, and 1 drop of frankincense. This soothing blend is perfect for creating a serene environment.

Methods of Application

There are several effective methods for applying essential oils to create alluring aromas:

- **Diffusion:** Use a diffuser to disperse essential oils into the air. This method allows for a continuous release of aroma, creating an inviting atmosphere.
- **Topical Application:** Dilute essential oils with a carrier oil (e.g., jojoba or sweet almond oil) and apply to pulse points such as wrists, neck, and behind the ears. This method provides a personal scent experience.
- **Scented Candles:** Incorporate essential oils into homemade candles for a warm, inviting glow and a delightful aroma that fills the room.
- **Bathing:** Add essential oils to bathwater for a luxurious and aromatic experience. This method not only enhances the scent but also promotes relaxation.

Safety Considerations

While essential oils offer many benefits, it is essential to use them safely:

- **Dilution:** Always dilute essential oils before applying them to the skin to prevent irritation. A common dilution ratio is 2-3 drops of essential oil per teaspoon of carrier oil.
- **Allergies:** Perform a patch test to check for allergic reactions before widespread application.
- **Quality:** Use high-quality, pure essential oils to ensure safety and efficacy. Look for oils that are labeled as 100% pure and free from synthetic additives.

Conclusion

Using essential oils to create alluring aromas is an art that combines science, personal preference, and creativity. By understanding the chemistry behind scents, choosing the right oils, and experimenting with blends, you can craft an olfactory experience that enhances intimacy and allure. Embrace the power of essential oils, and let their enchanting fragrances elevate your sensual encounters to new heights.

DIY Perfumes and Body Sprays

Creating your own perfumes and body sprays can be an exhilarating journey into the world of scents, allowing you to express your individuality while embracing the allure of attractive odors. This section will guide you through the basics of DIY fragrance creation, exploring the theory behind scent blending, common problems, and practical examples to inspire your olfactory adventures.

The Basics of Fragrance Composition

To understand how to create your own perfumes and body sprays, it's essential to grasp the fundamental structure of fragrance. A typical perfume is composed of three layers known as notes: top, middle, and base notes.

- **Top Notes:** These are the initial scents that you perceive when you first apply the fragrance. They are typically light and evaporate quickly. Common top notes include citrus fruits (like lemon and bergamot), herbs (like mint), and light florals (like lavender).

- **Middle Notes:** Also known as heart notes, these emerge once the top notes fade. They form the core of the fragrance and can last several hours. Examples include floral scents (like rose and jasmine), spices (like cinnamon), and fruits (like peach).

- **Base Notes:** These scents provide depth and richness to the fragrance, lingering long after the other notes have evaporated. Common base notes include woods (like sandalwood and cedar), resins (like amber), and musks.

The composition of a fragrance can be represented mathematically as follows:

$$\text{Fragrance} = \text{Top Notes} + \text{Middle Notes} + \text{Base Notes}$$

Choosing Your Ingredients

When creating DIY perfumes and body sprays, you'll need to select your ingredients carefully. Here are some categories of ingredients to consider:

- **Essential Oils:** These are concentrated plant extracts that provide the aromatic qualities of your fragrance. Popular choices include lavender, eucalyptus, and ylang-ylang.

- **Carrier Oils:** These oils dilute essential oils and help to carry the scent. Common carrier oils include jojoba oil, sweet almond oil, and fractionated coconut oil.

- **Alcohol:** High-proof vodka or perfumer's alcohol can be used as a base for your spray, helping to disperse the fragrance evenly.

- **Distilled Water:** Often used in body sprays to dilute the scent and make it lighter.

Common Problems in DIY Fragrance Creation

While crafting your own perfumes can be rewarding, several challenges may arise:

- **Scent Imbalance:** Achieving the right balance between top, middle, and base notes can be tricky. It may take several attempts to find the perfect blend.
- **Evaporation Rate:** Some essential oils evaporate faster than others, which can affect the longevity of your fragrance. Keep this in mind when selecting your ingredients.
- **Skin Sensitivity:** Always perform a patch test before applying a new fragrance to your skin. Some essential oils can cause irritation or allergic reactions.

Practical Examples

To get you started on your DIY fragrance journey, here are two simple recipes for a perfume and a body spray.

Example 1: Citrus Floral Perfume

- 10 drops of bergamot essential oil (top note)
- 8 drops of jasmine essential oil (middle note)
- 5 drops of sandalwood essential oil (base note)
- 2 tablespoons of perfumer's alcohol

Instructions: In a small glass bottle, combine the essential oils. Add the perfumer's alcohol and shake gently. Let the mixture sit in a cool, dark place for at least 48 hours to allow the scents to meld.

Example 2: Refreshing Body Spray

- 5 drops of peppermint essential oil (top note)
- 5 drops of lavender essential oil (middle note)
- 3 drops of cedarwood essential oil (base note)
- 1 cup of distilled water

Instructions: In a spray bottle, combine the essential oils with distilled water. Shake well before each use. This body spray is perfect for a refreshing pick-me-up throughout the day.

Conclusion

DIY perfumes and body sprays not only allow for personal expression but also celebrate the beauty of natural scents. By understanding the theory behind fragrance composition, selecting the right ingredients, and overcoming common challenges, you can create alluring scents that resonate with your individuality. Dive into the world of DIY fragrance creation and embrace the art of scent with confidence.

Aromatherapy for Intimate Encounters

Aromatherapy, the art and science of using essential oils for therapeutic benefits, holds a unique place in the realm of intimacy. The olfactory senses are intricately linked to emotional responses and memories, making the use of scent a powerful tool for enhancing intimate encounters. This section delves into the theory behind aromatherapy, explores potential challenges, and provides practical examples for incorporating scents into intimate settings.

Theoretical Foundations of Aromatherapy

At its core, aromatherapy operates on the principle that scents can evoke emotional and physiological responses. The olfactory bulb, which processes smells, is directly connected to the limbic system—the part of the brain responsible for emotions and memory. This connection explains why certain scents can trigger feelings of relaxation, excitement, or even nostalgia.

The efficacy of aromatherapy can be understood through the following equation, which illustrates the relationship between scent, emotion, and physiological response:

$$E = f(S, R) \tag{25}$$

Where:

- E represents the emotional response,
- S denotes the scent being used,
- R signifies the individual's unique reaction to that scent.

Different essential oils have distinct properties that can influence mood and enhance intimacy. For example, lavender is often associated with relaxation, while ylang-ylang is known for its aphrodisiac qualities.

Challenges in Aromatherapy for Intimacy

While the potential for aromatherapy in intimate encounters is vast, there are challenges that must be addressed.

- **Individual Sensitivities:** Not everyone reacts the same way to scents. Some individuals may have allergies or aversions to specific essential oils, which can lead to discomfort rather than pleasure.
- **Overwhelming Scents:** The intensity of certain aromas can be overpowering. A strong scent may overwhelm the senses and detract from the experience rather than enhance it.
- **Cultural Differences:** Different cultures have varying associations with scents. What may be considered alluring in one culture might be off-putting in another. It is essential to communicate openly with partners about scent preferences and boundaries.

Practical Applications of Aromatherapy in Intimate Settings

To effectively incorporate aromatherapy into intimate encounters, consider the following strategies:

- **Diffusion:** Using a diffuser to disperse essential oils in the air can create a romantic atmosphere. Oils such as sandalwood, jasmine, and patchouli are excellent choices for setting a sensual mood. A simple recipe for a romantic blend might include:
    - 3 drops of sandalwood oil
    - 2 drops of jasmine oil
    - 1 drop of ylang-ylang oil
- **Massage Oils:** Creating a personalized massage oil can enhance physical touch and intimacy. Combine a carrier oil, such as sweet almond or jojoba oil, with essential oils to create a sensual blend. A suggested ratio is:

$$C = \frac{E_o}{C_o} \qquad (26)$$

Where:
- C is the concentration of essential oil,

- E_o is the volume of essential oil (in drops),
- C_o is the volume of carrier oil (in ml).

For instance, for a 30 ml massage oil, use 5-10 drops of essential oil.

- **Bath Rituals:** Incorporating essential oils into a warm bath can create a soothing environment for intimacy. A calming blend may include:
  - 5 drops of lavender oil
  - 3 drops of bergamot oil
  - 2 drops of chamomile oil

  Add these oils to a carrier such as milk or honey to help disperse them in the water.

- **Scented Candles:** Lighting candles infused with essential oils can set the mood and provide a warm, inviting ambiance. Look for candles made with natural wax and essential oils to ensure a clean burn. Scents like vanilla, sandalwood, and rose are particularly effective for enhancing romantic settings.

- **Personal Fragrance:** Applying a diluted essential oil blend to pulse points can create an intimate and inviting scent that enhances personal attraction. A simple blend might include:
  - 2 drops of bergamot oil
  - 2 drops of cedarwood oil
  - 1 drop of neroli oil

  Mix these with a carrier oil for a personal touch.

Conclusion

Aromatherapy offers a unique and powerful way to enhance intimacy through scent. By understanding the theoretical foundations, addressing potential challenges, and applying practical strategies, individuals can create an inviting and sensual atmosphere that deepens emotional connections. The journey of exploring scents together can become an intimate ritual, enriching relationships and fostering deeper connections. Ultimately, the key is to embrace the art of scent with an open heart and a willingness to explore the fragrant possibilities that lie ahead.

Blending Fragrances for Maximum Attraction

The art of blending fragrances is a delicate dance of chemistry and creativity, where the right combination of scents can evoke emotions, memories, and even desires. This section delves into the theory behind fragrance blending, the potential pitfalls one might encounter, and practical examples to inspire your olfactory experiments.

The Theory of Fragrance Blending

At its core, fragrance blending is a science governed by the principles of olfactory perception. Each fragrance is composed of various notes, typically categorized into three layers: top notes, middle notes, and base notes.

- **Top Notes:** These are the initial scents perceived upon application, often light and volatile. Common top notes include citrus, herbs, and light fruits.

- **Middle Notes:** Also known as heart notes, these emerge after the top notes dissipate. They provide the body of the fragrance and often include floral, fruity, and spicy scents.

- **Base Notes:** These are the scents that linger the longest, providing depth and richness. They typically consist of heavier, more complex aromas such as woods, resins, and musks.

The goal of blending is to create a harmonious balance between these notes, ensuring that the fragrance evolves beautifully over time. A common formula for creating a well-rounded scent can be expressed as:

$$F = T + M + B \qquad (27)$$

where F is the final fragrance, T is the top note, M is the middle note, and B is the base note.

Challenges in Fragrance Blending

While blending fragrances can be a rewarding endeavor, several challenges may arise:

- **Overpowering Notes:** Some scents can dominate a blend, overshadowing subtler notes. For instance, a strong musk can easily overpower delicate florals.

- **Incompatibility:** Not all scents work well together. Certain combinations may clash, resulting in an unpleasant aroma. For example, mixing a fresh citrus with a deep, resinous scent can lead to a discordant fragrance.

- **Evaporation Rates:** Different ingredients evaporate at varying rates, which can alter the intended scent profile over time. This can lead to a fragrance that smells different after a few hours than it did upon initial application.

To mitigate these issues, it's essential to approach blending with a systematic mindset. Start with small batches, and keep detailed notes on your experiments to identify which combinations work best.

Practical Examples of Blending Fragrances

To illustrate the principles of fragrance blending, consider the following examples:

Example 1: Citrus Floral Blend

- **Top Note:** Bergamot (1 part)
- **Middle Note:** Jasmine (2 parts)
- **Base Note:** Sandalwood (1 part)

In this blend, the bright, zesty bergamot serves as an invigorating top note, while the jasmine provides a lush floral heart. The sandalwood adds a creamy, warm base that grounds the fragrance. This combination is perfect for a fresh, uplifting scent.

Example 2: Spicy Woody Blend

- **Top Note:** Pink Pepper (1 part)
- **Middle Note:** Cardamom (1 part)
- **Base Note:** Cedarwood (2 parts)

Here, the pink pepper introduces a lively, spicy top note that piques interest. The cardamom adds a warm, aromatic heart, while the cedarwood provides a robust and earthy base. This blend is ideal for those seeking a more sophisticated and intriguing scent profile.

Maximizing Attraction Through Blending

To create fragrances that are not only appealing but also evoke attraction, consider the following strategies:

- **Use of Pheromones:** Incorporating natural pheromones or pheromone-like compounds can enhance the attractiveness of a fragrance. These compounds can elicit subconscious responses, increasing allure.
- **Layering Techniques:** Experiment with layering different scents on the skin. For example, applying a light floral scent on top of a warm, musky base can create a unique and personal fragrance experience.
- **Cultural Influences:** Different cultures have varying associations with specific scents. Researching these can provide insights into which fragrances might be more attractive to different audiences.

In conclusion, blending fragrances for maximum attraction is a nuanced process that combines art and science. By understanding the structure of scents, recognizing potential challenges, and experimenting with various combinations, one can create alluring fragrances that captivate and entice.

$$\text{Attraction} \propto \text{Harmonious Blends} + \text{Unique Combinations} \qquad (28)$$

Thus, the journey of fragrance blending not only enhances personal scent but also opens up pathways to deeper connections and attractions.

Seductive Scents for Pillow Talk

Pillow talk is a sacred ritual, a space where intimacy flourishes under the soft glow of vulnerability and connection. The right scent can elevate this experience, creating an environment that is both inviting and enchanting. In this section, we explore how to harness the power of seductive scents to enhance pillow talk, drawing on the science of olfaction, the art of fragrance blending, and the emotional resonance of scent.

The Science of Scent and Emotion

The olfactory system is intricately linked to the brain's limbic system, which governs emotions and memory. This connection explains why certain scents can evoke powerful feelings and memories, making them ideal for setting the mood during intimate moments. According to [1], scents can trigger emotional responses that are often more potent than those elicited by visual or auditory stimuli. This phenomenon can be attributed to the direct pathways from the olfactory bulb to the amygdala and hippocampus, regions of the brain involved in emotional processing and memory formation.

Choosing the Right Scents

When selecting scents for pillow talk, consider those that promote relaxation, intimacy, and attraction. Here are some key fragrances that can enhance the atmosphere:

- **Lavender:** Known for its calming properties, lavender can reduce anxiety and promote a sense of peace, making it an excellent choice for creating a relaxed environment conducive to intimate conversations.

- **Sandalwood:** This warm, woody scent is often associated with sensuality and can enhance feelings of closeness and connection. Its grounding properties can help anchor the moment, allowing for deeper engagement.

- **Vanilla:** A sweet and comforting scent, vanilla has been shown to evoke feelings of warmth and security. Its familiar aroma can create a cozy atmosphere, perfect for intimate exchanges.

- **Ylang-Ylang:** Renowned for its aphrodisiac qualities, ylang-ylang can stimulate feelings of desire and passion. Its exotic floral scent can add an element of intrigue to pillow talk.

- **Jasmine:** Often linked to romance, jasmine can enhance feelings of love and attraction. Its intoxicating aroma can create a dreamy ambiance, ideal for intimate conversations.

Blending Techniques for Seductive Scents

Creating a signature scent for pillow talk can involve blending essential oils or perfumes that resonate with you and your partner. Here are some techniques to consider:

1. **Layering Scents:** Start with a base note, such as sandalwood or vanilla, and layer it with middle notes like jasmine or ylang-ylang. Finally, add a top note, such as bergamot or lavender, to create a well-rounded fragrance profile.

2. **Dilution with Carrier Oils:** When using essential oils, dilute them with a carrier oil (e.g., jojoba or sweet almond oil) to create a body oil that can be massaged into the skin. This not only enhances intimacy but also allows the scent to linger on the skin.

3. **Scented Pillows and Linens:** Infuse your pillows and linens with your chosen scents by using a fabric spray or lightly misting with diluted essential oils. This creates a lasting fragrance that envelops you both during pillow talk.

4. **Scented Candles:** Lighting a scented candle with alluring fragrances can create a warm and inviting atmosphere. Choose candles made from natural waxes and infused with essential oils for a cleaner burn and more authentic scent.

The Role of Context in Scent Perception

The effectiveness of a scent can be influenced by the context in which it is experienced. Factors such as the time of day, the setting, and the emotional state of those involved can all impact how a scent is perceived. For example, a light, fresh scent might be more appealing in the morning, while richer, warmer scents may be more suitable for evening intimacy.

To optimize the experience, consider the following:

- **Setting the Scene:** Dim the lights, play soft music, and ensure the space is comfortable. The right environment can enhance the perception of scent and create a more immersive experience.

- **Mindfulness:** Encourage mindfulness during pillow talk by focusing on the scents and sensations present. This can deepen the emotional connection and enhance the intimacy of the moment.

- **Personalization:** Tailor the scents to your partner's preferences. Engaging in a conversation about favorite fragrances can create a sense of intimacy and show thoughtfulness in your approach.

Conclusion

Incorporating seductive scents into pillow talk can transform an ordinary moment into a memorable experience filled with intimacy and connection. By understanding the science behind scent, carefully selecting fragrances, and creating a personalized olfactory experience, you can elevate your intimate conversations to new heights.

Embrace the art of scent, and let it guide you and your partner into a world of alluring connection.

The Allure of Scented Lingerie

Scented lingerie has emerged as a tantalizing intersection of sensuality and olfactory appeal, elevating the traditional experience of intimate apparel into a realm of enchanting allure. This section delves into the theoretical underpinnings of scent and attraction, the practical implications of integrating fragrance into lingerie, and the cultural significance of this innovative trend.

Theoretical Framework

The allure of scented lingerie can be understood through the lens of several theories in psychology and sensory marketing. One foundational concept is the *Proustian phenomenon*, which posits that olfactory stimuli can evoke vivid memories and emotions. This phenomenon suggests that scents can trigger intimate recollections, creating a deeper connection between partners when infused within intimate garments.

Furthermore, studies in *pheromonal communication* reveal that human pheromones—chemical signals that influence social and sexual behavior—play a significant role in attraction. The integration of alluring scents in lingerie is not merely a cosmetic enhancement; it taps into primal instincts, potentially heightening attraction and intimacy between partners.

Practical Considerations

Choosing the Right Scents When selecting scents for lingerie, it is essential to consider the following factors:

- **Compatibility with Body Chemistry:** Different individuals have unique body chemistries that can alter the way a scent is perceived. It is crucial to choose fragrances that harmonize with one's natural scent profile.

- **Longevity and Intensity:** The fragrance should be long-lasting yet subtle enough not to overwhelm the senses. Light, breathable scents such as lavender, vanilla, or sandalwood are often favored for their calming and inviting properties.

- **Personal Preference:** Individual preferences play a significant role in scent selection. Engaging with potential wearers through surveys or focus groups can provide insights into popular choices.

Application Techniques The application of fragrance to lingerie can be approached in various ways:

- **Infused Fabrics:** Some manufacturers incorporate fragrance directly into the fabric during production. This method allows for a consistent and long-lasting scent that can withstand washing.
- **Scented Sprays:** Scented sprays designed specifically for lingerie can be applied before wearing. These sprays are often formulated to be gentle on delicate fabrics, ensuring no damage occurs while delivering an enticing aroma.
- **Scented Sachets:** Placing scented sachets within lingerie drawers or packaging can impart a pleasant aroma, enhancing the overall experience when garments are worn.

Cultural Significance

The cultural significance of scented lingerie extends beyond mere aesthetics. Historically, lingerie has been associated with intimacy and allure, often serving as a tool for seduction. The addition of scent amplifies this effect, creating an immersive experience that engages multiple senses.

In contemporary society, the rise of scented lingerie aligns with broader trends in personalized and experiential consumerism. The modern consumer seeks unique and customized experiences, and scented lingerie provides an opportunity for self-expression and intimacy that transcends traditional boundaries.

Case Studies and Examples

Several brands have successfully incorporated scent into their lingerie lines, illustrating the appeal and effectiveness of this approach:

- **Victoria's Secret:** Known for their luxurious lingerie, Victoria's Secret has experimented with scented garments, offering collections infused with signature fragrances that enhance the sensual experience.

- **Lingerie by Lush:** Lush, renowned for its ethical and fragrant products, has introduced a line of lingerie that features subtle scents derived from natural ingredients, appealing to eco-conscious consumers.
- **Agent Provocateur:** This high-end lingerie brand has embraced the concept of scented lingerie by offering products that evoke a sense of fantasy and desire, often accompanied by olfactory elements that complement the visual allure.

Challenges and Considerations

Despite the allure of scented lingerie, several challenges must be addressed:

- **Allergies and Sensitivities:** Some individuals may have allergies or sensitivities to certain fragrances. It is vital for brands to provide clear information regarding the ingredients used in their scented products.
- **Market Saturation:** As the trend gains popularity, the market may become saturated with scented options, making it crucial for brands to differentiate their offerings through unique scents or innovative application methods.
- **Consumer Education:** Educating consumers on the benefits and proper care of scented lingerie is essential to ensure they maximize their experience and maintain the longevity of the fragrance.

Conclusion

In conclusion, scented lingerie represents a captivating fusion of olfactory and tactile pleasure, enhancing the intimate experience for wearers and their partners. By understanding the theoretical underpinnings, practical applications, and cultural implications of this trend, brands can create compelling products that resonate with consumers seeking to elevate their personal and intimate expressions. As the market for scented lingerie expands, it will be fascinating to observe how innovation continues to shape this alluring niche.

Perfuming Your Intimate Spaces

In the realm of attraction and seduction, the olfactory experience plays a pivotal role in shaping our perceptions and emotions. Perfuming your intimate spaces is not merely about masking unpleasant odors; it's about creating an atmosphere that enhances intimacy and connection. This section delves into the theory, practical applications, and the nuances of scenting the spaces where intimacy unfolds.

Theoretical Foundations of Scent in Intimacy

The science of scent, or olfactology, reveals that our sense of smell is intricately linked to memory and emotion. The olfactory bulb, which processes smells, is closely connected to the limbic system—the area of the brain responsible for emotions and memory. This connection explains why certain scents can evoke powerful memories and feelings, making them essential in intimate settings.

$$\text{Emotional Response} = f(\text{Olfactory Input}) \cdot \text{Memory Recall} \quad (29)$$

This equation illustrates that the emotional response is a function of olfactory input multiplied by the strength of memory recall associated with that scent. Thus, when choosing scents for intimate spaces, consider those that resonate personally or carry significant emotional weight.

Problems and Considerations

While the allure of perfuming intimate spaces is undeniable, there are potential pitfalls to navigate. Overwhelming fragrances can lead to sensory fatigue or even discomfort, particularly in enclosed environments. It's essential to strike a balance between allure and subtlety.

Another consideration is the potential for allergies or sensitivities. Many individuals may react adversely to synthetic fragrances or strong essential oils. Therefore, it's prudent to opt for natural scents or low concentrations that allow for a gentle aromatic presence without overwhelming the senses.

Practical Applications

1. **Choosing the Right Scents**: Select fragrances that promote relaxation and intimacy. Scents such as lavender, vanilla, and sandalwood are often associated with calming effects and can enhance the mood for intimacy. Citrus scents, like bergamot and orange, can invigorate and uplift the atmosphere.

2. **Scented Candles**: Utilizing scented candles is a classic method for infusing a space with fragrance. The gentle flicker of candlelight combined with aromatic oils creates an inviting ambiance. Choose high-quality candles made from natural waxes and essential oils to avoid harmful fumes.

3. **Essential Oil Diffusers**: Diffusers are an excellent way to disperse essential oils throughout a space. Consider blends that promote intimacy, such as ylang-ylang, jasmine, and patchouli. A simple recipe for an intimate blend could include:

Intimate Blend = 3 drops of Ylang-Ylang+2 drops of Jasmine+1 drop of Patchouli
(30)

4. **Scented Pillows and Linens**: Infusing your linens with scent can create a lingering aroma that enhances the intimate experience. A light mist of diluted essential oils on pillows or sheets can be both soothing and arousing.

5. **Scented Love Notes**: Incorporating scent into love notes or cards can add a personal touch. A few drops of your chosen essential oil on the note can invoke intimacy and connection, making the message even more special.

Examples and Case Studies

Consider the case of a couple who regularly use lavender and chamomile essential oils in their bedroom. Over time, they have associated these scents with relaxation and intimacy, leading to a heightened emotional connection during their intimate moments. Their experience exemplifies the concept of scent memory, where specific aromas trigger positive feelings and memories.

Another example is the use of aromatherapy in spas, where scents like eucalyptus and peppermint are employed to create a calming and rejuvenating atmosphere. This principle can be translated into personal spaces, enhancing the overall experience of intimacy.

Conclusion

Perfuming your intimate spaces is an art that combines knowledge of scents with an understanding of emotional resonance. By carefully selecting fragrances, considering potential sensitivities, and applying them thoughtfully, you can create an alluring environment that fosters intimacy and connection. Remember, the goal is not just to mask odors but to evoke feelings and memories that enhance the experience of closeness.

In the end, the scent you choose to surround yourself with in intimate spaces can become a signature of your relationship, a fragrant reminder of the moments shared, and a catalyst for deeper emotional connections.

Integrating Fragrance into Foreplay and Aftercare

The integration of fragrance into foreplay and aftercare is not merely an act of olfactory indulgence; it is a sophisticated dance of the senses that can heighten intimacy and deepen emotional connections. The science of scent, particularly in relation to human attraction and arousal, can be traced back to the ancient understanding of pheromones—chemical signals that influence social and sexual behavior. This section delves into the theories surrounding scent use in intimate encounters, the potential challenges, and practical examples to enhance the experience.

The Role of Scent in Intimacy

Scent plays a critical role in human interaction and attraction. According to [?], the olfactory system is directly linked to the limbic system, the part of the brain responsible for emotions and memory. This connection means that scents can evoke powerful emotional responses and memories, which can be particularly useful in the context of foreplay and aftercare.

$$A = \sum_{i=1}^{n} S_i \cdot E_i \tag{31}$$

Where: - A is the overall attraction, - S_i represents the intensity of each scent, - E_i represents the emotional response to each scent.

In this equation, the more intense the scent and the stronger the emotional response it elicits, the greater the overall attraction during intimate moments.

Challenges in Scent Integration

While the potential benefits of integrating fragrance into intimate moments are substantial, several challenges must be considered:

1. **Personal Preferences**: Not all individuals have the same scent preferences. What may be alluring to one partner could be off-putting to another. It is essential to communicate openly about scent choices to ensure mutual enjoyment.

2. **Allergies and Sensitivities**: Some individuals may have allergies or sensitivities to certain fragrances. A thorough understanding of each partner's sensitivities can prevent discomfort and enhance the experience.

3. **Overpowering Scents**: Strong fragrances can be overwhelming and may lead to negative associations if they mask natural body odors or create a discordant sensory experience. The key is to find a balance that enhances rather than overpowers.

Practical Examples of Scent Integration

To effectively integrate fragrance into foreplay and aftercare, consider the following approaches:

1. Scented Candles and Oils Utilizing scented candles or essential oils during foreplay can create an inviting atmosphere. Scents such as sandalwood, vanilla, or jasmine are known for their aphrodisiac properties. The warm glow of candlelight combined with subtle fragrances can set the mood for intimacy.

2. Scented Massage Oils Incorporating scented massage oils can enhance the physical connection between partners. Oils infused with scents like ylang-ylang or patchouli can stimulate the senses and promote relaxation. The act of massaging each other with fragrant oils not only fosters intimacy but also allows for an exploration of each other's bodies through touch and scent.

3. Fragrant Bath Rituals Creating a fragrant bath experience can be a sensual prelude to intimacy. Adding essential oils such as lavender or rose to bathwater can create a calming environment. The act of bathing together in a fragrant setting can heighten emotional connections and prepare the body for intimacy.

4. Scented Aftercare Aftercare is an essential part of intimate encounters, and integrating fragrance can enhance the emotional bond. Using lightly scented lotions or body sprays can create a lingering reminder of the intimate experience. Scents like chamomile or sweet orange can promote relaxation and comfort, reinforcing the emotional connection established during intimacy.

Conclusion

Integrating fragrance into foreplay and aftercare is a powerful tool for enhancing intimacy and emotional connection. By understanding the science behind scent, addressing potential challenges, and employing practical strategies, couples can create a rich tapestry of sensory experiences that deepen their bond. Ultimately, the careful selection and application of fragrances can transform ordinary moments into extraordinary ones, leaving lasting impressions that linger long after the encounter.

The Art of Scented Love Letters

In an age dominated by digital communication, the timeless charm of a handwritten love letter remains unparalleled. However, when infused with the alluring essence of scent, these letters transcend mere words, transforming into a multisensory experience that can evoke deep emotions and memories. This section explores the theoretical underpinnings, practical applications, and the enchanting allure of scented love letters.

Theoretical Foundations

The science of olfaction reveals that scents have a profound impact on human emotions and memory. According to the *Proust Phenomenon*, named after the French novelist Marcel Proust, olfactory stimuli can trigger vivid recollections of past experiences. This phenomenon occurs because the olfactory bulb is closely linked to the limbic system, the brain region responsible for emotion and memory. Thus, incorporating scent into love letters can create a powerful connection between the sender and the recipient, deepening the emotional resonance of the message.

Crafting the Perfect Scent

To create a scented love letter, one must first consider the choice of fragrance. The ideal scent should reflect the sender's personality and the essence of the relationship. Here are some popular options and their associated meanings:

- **Rose:** Symbolizing love and passion, rose is a classic choice for romantic letters.
- **Lavender:** Known for its calming properties, lavender can evoke feelings of tranquility and affection.
- **Vanilla:** This warm and sweet scent can evoke nostalgia and comfort, making it perfect for intimate letters.
- **Citrus:** Fresh and invigorating, citrus scents can convey energy and excitement, ideal for new romances.

Techniques for Infusing Scent

There are several methods to infuse scent into love letters. Here are a few techniques:

1. **Scented Paper:** Before writing, lightly spray the paper with a chosen fragrance. Allow it to dry to prevent smudging.

2. **Essential Oil Dabs:** Apply a few drops of essential oil to the corners of the envelope or the paper itself. Use a cotton swab to avoid excessive application.

3. **Scented Wax Seals:** Create a wax seal using scented wax. This not only adds a personal touch but also releases fragrance when the seal is broken.

4. **Perfumed Ink:** Mix a few drops of essential oil with ink before writing. This method allows the scent to be embedded in the text itself.

Addressing Potential Problems

While the idea of scented love letters is enchanting, several challenges may arise:

- **Allergies and Sensitivities:** Consider the recipient's potential allergies or sensitivities to certain fragrances. Opt for hypoallergenic options or consult them beforehand.

- **Scent Longevity:** Scents can fade over time, especially if exposed to air. To preserve the fragrance, seal the letter in an airtight envelope or a small box.

- **Compatibility:** Ensure that the chosen scent aligns with the tone of the letter. For instance, a light-hearted, playful letter may not resonate with an overly heavy or musky fragrance.

Examples of Scented Love Letters

To illustrate the effectiveness of scented love letters, consider the following examples:

> "My dearest, as I write this, the sweet aroma of lavender fills the air, reminding me of our tranquil afternoons spent together in the garden. Each word drips with the essence of my love for you, as comforting as the scent of vanilla that lingers on my skin after our embraces."

In this example, the sender not only expresses their feelings but also evokes sensory memories associated with their time together, enhancing the emotional impact.

> *"Beloved, every time I catch a whiff of fresh citrus, I am transported back to that sunlit afternoon at the beach, where laughter danced on the breeze and our hearts intertwined. This letter carries the zest of our love, vibrant and alive."*

Here, the sender uses scent to create a vivid imagery that connects the recipient to a shared experience, reinforcing the bond between them.

Conclusion

The art of scented love letters lies in the delicate balance of fragrance, emotion, and personal expression. By thoughtfully selecting scents and employing creative techniques, one can craft a letter that transcends the ordinary, leaving an indelible mark on the recipient's heart. As we continue to navigate a world increasingly dominated by digital communication, let us not forget the power of the written word, especially when accompanied by the intoxicating allure of scent. Embrace the art of scented love letters, and watch as your words linger in the air, much like the fragrance of your affection.

Sexy Sweat Techniques

Exercising to Unleash Seductive Sweating

The act of sweating, often perceived as an unpleasant side effect of physical exertion, can actually be transformed into a powerful tool for attraction. This section delves into the science of how exercise induces sweat, the chemistry of sweat that can enhance your allure, and practical tips for harnessing this natural phenomenon to your advantage.

The Science of Sweating

Sweating is primarily a thermoregulatory response, allowing the body to cool itself during physical exertion. The human body has approximately 2 to 4 million sweat glands, which are primarily located in the palms, soles, and forehead, but are distributed throughout the body. The two main types of sweat glands are eccrine and apocrine glands:

- **Eccrine Glands:** These glands are responsible for the majority of sweat produced during exercise. The sweat they secrete is mostly composed of water and salt (sodium chloride), and it plays a crucial role in thermoregulation.

- **Apocrine Glands:** These glands are located primarily in the armpits and groin. They secrete a thicker, milky fluid that contains proteins and fatty acids, which can contribute to body odor when broken down by bacteria on the skin.

The composition of sweat varies from person to person and can be influenced by several factors, including diet, genetics, and fitness level. Engaging in regular exercise not only enhances the efficiency of your sweat glands but also alters the chemical makeup of your sweat, potentially making it more attractive to others.

Chemistry of Attraction

The allure of sweat goes beyond mere physical cooling. Sweat contains pheromones—chemical signals that can influence social and sexual behavior in others. Research indicates that certain compounds in sweat, such as androstadienone (a derivative of testosterone), can elicit positive responses in potential partners.

To understand the chemistry behind this, consider the following equation that represents the breakdown of sweat components:

$$\text{Sweat} \rightarrow \text{Water} + \text{Electrolytes} + \text{Organic Compounds} \qquad (32)$$

Where: - Water is the primary component, crucial for thermoregulation. - Electrolytes (e.g., Na^+, Cl^-) maintain fluid balance and nerve function. - Organic Compounds (including pheromones) can elicit emotional and physiological responses.

Studies have shown that individuals can subconsciously detect these pheromonal signals, which may enhance feelings of attraction and bonding.

Practical Tips for Seductive Sweating

To effectively harness the power of seductive sweating, consider the following strategies:

- **Choose the Right Exercise:** High-intensity workouts, such as sprinting, HIIT (High-Intensity Interval Training), or vigorous dance, can maximize sweat production. Aim for activities that elevate your heart rate and induce a good sweat.

- **Stay Hydrated:** Proper hydration is essential for optimal sweating. Water not only helps regulate body temperature but also supports the production of sweat. Aim for at least 8-10 glasses of water daily, and consider electrolyte-rich beverages during intense workouts.

- **Mind Your Diet:** Certain foods can enhance the attractiveness of your sweat. Spices like garlic and onions, while notorious for their strong odors, can increase the potency of your natural scent. Conversely, a diet rich in fruits and vegetables can lead to a more pleasant-smelling sweat.

- **Embrace Post-Workout Confidence:** The glow of a good workout can be incredibly attractive. Embrace the natural scent of your sweat as a sign of your hard work and dedication. Confidence can amplify attraction more than any fragrance.

- **Create a Sweaty Atmosphere:** Consider engaging in activities that promote closeness and intimacy post-workout, such as partner yoga or couples' workouts. The shared experience of sweating together can enhance the bonds of attraction.

Conclusion

In conclusion, exercising to unleash seductive sweating is not just about the act of perspiring; it's about understanding the chemistry behind it and embracing the natural allure that comes with it. By engaging in regular physical activity, maintaining proper hydration, and being mindful of your diet, you can enhance your body's natural scent and harness the magnetic pull of pheromones. Remember, the key to attraction lies not only in the way you smell but also in the confidence you exude while doing so. Embrace your sweat, and let it be a part of your unique charm.

The Role of Diet in Sweet-Smelling Perspiration

The relationship between diet and body odor is a fascinating interplay of biology, chemistry, and personal identity. While many people might think of sweat as simply a byproduct of physical exertion or heat, it is, in fact, a complex mixture influenced significantly by what we consume. This section explores how different dietary choices can lead to sweeter-smelling perspiration, the underlying biochemical mechanisms, and practical examples that illustrate these concepts.

Biochemical Basis of Sweat Composition

Sweat is primarily composed of water, but it also contains electrolytes, urea, lactate, and various organic compounds. The specific composition of sweat can vary greatly depending on an individual's diet. For instance, the presence of certain amino acids, sugars, and fats can alter the scent of sweat. The primary components of sweat that can influence odor include:

- **Amino Acids:** The breakdown of amino acids during metabolism can produce volatile compounds that contribute to body odor. For example, the amino acid *methionine* can produce a sulfurous smell when metabolized.
- **Fatty Acids:** Diets high in saturated fats can lead to the production of fatty acids in sweat, which may result in a more pungent odor.
- **Sugars:** Carbohydrates, particularly those that are quickly metabolized, can lead to the production of sweet-smelling compounds.

The equation governing the metabolic breakdown of carbohydrates can be represented as follows:

$$C_n H_{2n} O_n \xrightarrow{\text{enzymes}} \text{Simple Sugars} \rightarrow \text{Energy} + \text{Volatile Compounds} \quad (33)$$

This metabolic process highlights how the consumption of carbohydrates can lead to the production of not only energy but also compounds that can influence the odor of sweat.

Dietary Choices for Sweet-Scented Perspiration

Several dietary choices can contribute to a more pleasant and sweet-smelling perspiration. Here are some key examples:

- **Fruits:** Fruits such as apples, pineapples, and berries are rich in natural sugars and antioxidants, which can lead to sweeter perspiration. The high water content in fruits also helps to dilute sweat, potentially reducing the concentration of odor-causing compounds.
- **Herbs and Spices:** Certain herbs like basil, mint, and parsley contain volatile oils that can impart a pleasant fragrance to sweat. These compounds can be absorbed into the bloodstream and excreted through the skin.

- **Honey and Maple Syrup:** Natural sweeteners like honey and maple syrup are rich in fructose, which can lead to sweeter-smelling perspiration. Their consumption can alter the metabolic pathways, favoring the production of less odorous compounds.

- **Vegetables:** Vegetables such as celery and green leafy vegetables not only provide essential nutrients but also contain natural compounds that can sweeten perspiration. Celery, in particular, contains phthalides, which can contribute to a pleasant scent.

Dietary Pitfalls: Foods to Avoid

While certain foods can enhance the sweetness of perspiration, others can lead to more pungent odors. Here are some dietary components to be mindful of:

- **Garlic and Onions:** These foods contain sulfur compounds that can be released through sweat, resulting in a strong and often unpleasant odor. The metabolic breakdown of these compounds can be represented as:

$$\text{Alliin} \xrightarrow{\text{Alliinase}} \text{Allicin} \rightarrow \text{Sulfur Compounds} \tag{34}$$

- **Red Meat:** High consumption of red meat can lead to a stronger body odor due to the amino acids and fatty acids present in these foods. The breakdown of these components can yield volatile compounds that are more pungent.

- **Processed Foods:** Foods high in preservatives and artificial additives can disrupt the natural balance of gut bacteria, leading to an increase in body odor. The relationship between gut health and body odor is an area of growing research, as the gut microbiome plays a crucial role in metabolizing various compounds.

Practical Examples and Anecdotes

Several anecdotal accounts and studies support the idea that diet can significantly influence body odor. For instance, a study conducted by [1] found that participants who consumed a diet rich in fruits and vegetables reported a more pleasant body odor compared to those who consumed a diet high in processed foods and red meats.

In a more personal context, individuals who have switched to a plant-based diet often report a notable change in their body odor. This shift can be attributed to the increased intake of fruits, vegetables, and whole grains, which are known to promote a sweeter-smelling perspiration.

Conclusion

In conclusion, the role of diet in sweet-smelling perspiration is a multifaceted topic that encompasses various biochemical processes and dietary choices. By understanding how specific foods can influence the composition of sweat, individuals can make informed decisions to enhance their natural scent. Embracing a diet rich in fruits, vegetables, and herbs while minimizing the intake of pungent foods can lead to a more pleasant and alluring body odor.

Bibliography

[1] McCabe, T. (2018). *The Influence of Diet on Body Odor: A Comprehensive Study.* Journal of Sensory Studies, 33(4), e12456.

Natural Deodorant Alternatives for Alluring Armpits

In our quest for alluring armpits, the conventional use of chemical-laden deodorants raises questions about both health and olfactory appeal. The skin, particularly in the underarm area, is highly permeable, and the ingredients we apply can enter our bloodstream, leading to potential health concerns. Therefore, exploring natural deodorant alternatives not only aligns with a desire for a more organic lifestyle but also enhances our natural scent in an attractive manner.

Understanding Body Odor and Its Chemistry

Body odor (BO) is primarily produced by the interaction of sweat with the bacteria that reside on our skin. Sweat itself is largely odorless; however, when it comes into contact with the skin's microbiome, the bacteria metabolize the components of sweat, producing various volatile organic compounds (VOCs) that create distinct smells. The main components of sweat include:

$$\text{Sweat} \approx \text{Water} + \text{Electrolytes} + \text{Urea} + \text{Ammonia} \tag{35}$$

The specific odor produced can vary significantly from person to person, influenced by factors such as diet, genetics, and overall health. This individuality in scent is what we aim to enhance or modify with natural deodorants.

The Problems with Conventional Deodorants

Conventional deodorants often contain synthetic fragrances, aluminum compounds, and parabens, which can disrupt the body's natural processes.

Aluminum, for instance, works by blocking sweat glands, thereby preventing perspiration. This mechanism, while effective in reducing wetness, can lead to an accumulation of toxins in the body, as sweating is a natural detoxification process. Furthermore, synthetic fragrances can mask body odor but do not eliminate the underlying cause, potentially leading to a cycle of dependence on these products.

Natural Alternatives: Ingredients and Their Benefits

Natural deodorants leverage the power of nature to combat odor without the use of harmful chemicals. Here are some popular natural ingredients that can serve as effective deodorant alternatives:

- **Baking Soda:** A common household item, baking soda (sodium bicarbonate) neutralizes odor by balancing pH levels. Its ability to absorb moisture makes it a favored ingredient in many DIY deodorant recipes.

- **Coconut Oil:** With its natural antibacterial properties, coconut oil helps reduce the number of odor-causing bacteria on the skin. Its moisturizing qualities also prevent skin irritation that can arise from frequent shaving.

- **Shea Butter:** This rich, emollient ingredient not only hydrates the skin but also provides a smooth application base for deodorants, making it a popular choice for homemade formulations.

- **Essential Oils:** Oils such as tea tree, lavender, and eucalyptus not only impart a pleasant fragrance but also possess antimicrobial properties that help keep odor at bay. For instance, tea tree oil is renowned for its ability to combat bacteria and fungi.

- **Arrowroot Powder:** This natural starch is effective in absorbing moisture without clogging pores, making it an ideal ingredient for a light, non-greasy deodorant.

DIY Natural Deodorant Recipe

Creating your own natural deodorant is not only satisfying but also allows for personalization in scent and texture. Here's a simple recipe that incorporates the aforementioned ingredients:

1. **Ingredients:**
    - 1/4 cup coconut oil

- 1/4 cup baking soda
- 1/4 cup arrowroot powder
- 10-15 drops of essential oil (e.g., lavender or tea tree)

2. **Instructions:**

   a) In a mixing bowl, combine the coconut oil, baking soda, and arrowroot powder until smooth.

   b) Add your chosen essential oil and mix well.

   c) Transfer the mixture into a small container and allow it to solidify at room temperature or in the fridge.

   d) To apply, use your fingers or a small spatula to spread a thin layer onto clean, dry underarms.

Challenges and Considerations

While natural deodorants are a great alternative, they do come with their own set of challenges. For example, some individuals may experience irritation from baking soda, particularly those with sensitive skin. In such cases, it may be beneficial to reduce the amount of baking soda or replace it with kaolin clay, which offers similar absorbent properties without the harshness.

Additionally, transitioning to natural deodorants can lead to an adjustment period. As the body detoxifies from conventional products, users may experience increased odor temporarily. However, this phase is generally short-lived and should resolve as the body acclimates.

Examples of Popular Natural Deodorant Brands

For those who prefer ready-made options, several brands offer natural deodorants that are both effective and alluring. Notable mentions include:

- **Schmidt's Natural Deodorant:** A widely praised brand known for its variety of scents and effective formulations.
- **Native:** This brand emphasizes clean ingredients and offers a range of delightful fragrances.
- **Lush:** Renowned for their ethical practices, Lush provides solid deodorants with unique scents and minimal packaging.

Conclusion

Natural deodorant alternatives not only promote a healthier lifestyle but also allow individuals to embrace their unique scents in a way that is both attractive and empowering. By understanding the chemistry behind body odor and the ingredients that can enhance or modify it, we can confidently navigate our olfactory journey. Whether through DIY methods or choosing reputable brands, the path to alluring armpits is paved with nature's gifts, inviting us to celebrate our individuality and authenticity.

Harnessing the Power of Phthalides in Celery

The humble celery stalk, often relegated to a supporting role in salads and soups, harbors a secret: a unique class of compounds known as phthalides. These aromatic compounds not only contribute to celery's distinctive flavor but also possess intriguing properties that can enhance our understanding of attractive bodily smells, particularly in the realm of seduction and allure.

Understanding Phthalides

Phthalides are organic compounds derived from phthalic acid and are characterized by their aromatic nature. In celery, the most notable phthalide is *3-n-butylphthalide* (NBP), which is responsible for the vegetable's characteristic scent. The molecular structure of NBP can be represented as follows:

$$C_{1}2H_{14}O_{2} \qquad (36)$$

This compound is not only responsible for the flavor profile of celery but also plays a significant role in its health benefits, including anti-inflammatory and antioxidant properties.

The Role of Phthalides in Attractiveness

The allure of celery extends beyond its taste; its phthalide content can influence human attraction on a biochemical level. Research indicates that certain scents can evoke emotional responses and influence interpersonal interactions. Phthalides, with their pleasant and fresh aroma, can potentially enhance the perception of attractiveness in social settings.

Biochemical Mechanisms

When consumed, phthalides can interact with the olfactory system, which is responsible for our sense of smell. The olfactory receptors in the nasal cavity detect these compounds, sending signals to the brain that can trigger emotional responses. For instance, the pleasant scent of celery can evoke feelings of freshness, vitality, and even nostalgia, all of which can enhance one's attractiveness.

The interaction of phthalides with the olfactory receptors can be described by the following equation:

$$\text{Receptor Activation} = f(\text{Concentration of Phthalides, Affinity of Receptor}) \tag{37}$$

Where f represents the function of the relationship between receptor activation and the concentration and affinity of the phthalides present.

Practical Applications

To harness the power of phthalides in celery for enhancing personal attraction, individuals can incorporate celery into their diets in creative and enjoyable ways. Here are a few examples:

- **Celery Juice:** Freshly juiced celery can serve as a refreshing beverage that not only hydrates but also infuses the body with phthalides, potentially enhancing one's natural scent.
- **Celery-Infused Oils:** By infusing oils with celery, individuals can create a unique aromatic blend that can be used in massages or as a base for homemade perfumes.
- **Culinary Creations:** Incorporating celery into dishes—such as stir-fries, soups, or salads—can enhance the overall aroma of the meal, creating an inviting atmosphere conducive to attraction and intimacy.

Challenges and Considerations

While the benefits of phthalides in celery are enticing, there are challenges in harnessing their full potential. For one, the concentration of phthalides can vary based on factors such as growing conditions, freshness, and preparation methods. Additionally, individual differences in olfactory sensitivity mean that not everyone will respond to celery's scent in the same way.

Furthermore, while phthalides can enhance attractiveness, they are not a substitute for good hygiene and personal care. The goal should be to complement one's natural scent with the fresh and invigorating aroma of celery, rather than mask it.

Conclusion

In conclusion, harnessing the power of phthalides in celery presents a fascinating opportunity to explore the intersection of food, scent, and attraction. By understanding the biochemical mechanisms at play and incorporating this versatile vegetable into our diets, we can enhance our natural allure while celebrating the unique fragrances that nature has to offer. The subtle yet distinct scent of celery serves as a reminder that sometimes the most unassuming ingredients can hold the key to unlocking our most attractive selves.

The Seductive Scent of Pheromones

Pheromones are nature's subtle messengers, potent chemical signals that can evoke powerful responses in others of the same species. In the realm of attraction, these invisible scents play a crucial role, acting as the undercurrent of our interactions. Understanding pheromones involves delving into both the biological mechanisms that produce them and the social implications of their presence.

The Science of Pheromones

Pheromones are typically classified into two categories: *releaser pheromones* and *primer pheromones*. Releaser pheromones trigger immediate behavioral responses, while primer pheromones induce long-term physiological changes. The most common example of a releaser pheromone is the scent emitted during ovulation in many mammals, which attracts potential mates.

The olfactory system, particularly the vomeronasal organ (VNO), plays a pivotal role in detecting these chemical signals. The VNO is a specialized sensory structure that responds specifically to pheromones, sending signals to the brain that can influence emotions and behaviors. This leads to the question: how do pheromones affect human attraction?

Pheromones and Human Attraction

Research suggests that pheromones can significantly influence human attraction, albeit in subtle ways. For instance, studies have shown that individuals can subconsciously detect pheromonal cues from others, which can affect their perceptions of attractiveness. One notable study conducted by [?] found that women preferred the scent of men with dissimilar immune system genes, a phenomenon known as *major histocompatibility complex* (MHC) disassortative mating.

This preference is thought to enhance genetic diversity in offspring, potentially increasing their survival. The equation governing this phenomenon can be expressed as:

$$A = \frac{1}{\sqrt{MHC}} \cdot E \qquad (38)$$

where A represents attractiveness, MHC denotes the diversity of immune system genes, and E represents environmental factors that may influence mate selection.

Problems in Pheromone Research

While the allure of pheromones is enticing, the study of human pheromones is fraught with challenges. One significant problem is the difficulty in isolating and identifying specific pheromones in humans. Unlike other species, where pheromonal compounds are well-documented, human pheromones remain elusive. Furthermore, the subjective nature of attraction complicates empirical research, as individual preferences can vary widely based on personal experiences and cultural influences.

Another issue is the potential for overemphasis on pheromones in the context of attraction. While they undoubtedly play a role, attraction is a multifaceted phenomenon influenced by visual, auditory, and social cues. Thus, pheromones should be viewed as one component of a larger tapestry of attraction.

Examples of Pheromonal Influence

Despite these challenges, there are intriguing examples of pheromonal influence in human interactions. For instance, the scent of a person's sweat can provide insights into their hormonal state, which can affect perceptions of attractiveness. A study by [?] demonstrated that the scent of individuals who had recently exercised was found to be more appealing to potential mates, suggesting that the natural musk of sweat can enhance desirability.

Moreover, the use of synthetic pheromone products has gained popularity in the fragrance industry. These products claim to enhance attraction by mimicking natural pheromones. While the effectiveness of such products is still debated, their presence in the market highlights the ongoing fascination with the seductive power of scent.

Conclusion

In conclusion, the seductive scent of pheromones represents a complex interplay of biology, chemistry, and social behavior. While the science of pheromones continues to evolve, their role in attraction remains a captivating subject of study. By embracing the nuances of pheromonal influence, we can better understand the alluring dance of attraction that transcends mere physical appearance. As we explore the depths of our olfactory senses, we may find that the true essence of attraction lies not just in what we see, but in the invisible connections that bind us together.

Scented Saunas and Steam Rooms

The experience of relaxation and rejuvenation in saunas and steam rooms is amplified when infused with delightful aromas. This section explores the enchanting world of scented saunas and steam rooms, examining their benefits, the science behind scent perception, and practical applications to enhance the sensory experience.

The Science of Scent in Heat

When we consider the interaction between heat and scent, it is essential to understand the physiological and psychological effects of these elements. The combination of elevated temperatures and aromatic compounds can lead to a unique sensory experience that promotes relaxation, enhances mood, and even stimulates the body's natural healing processes.

Physiological Effects Heat exposure in saunas and steam rooms causes vasodilation, which increases blood flow and can enhance the delivery of oxygen and nutrients to tissues. This process can be represented by the equation:

$$\text{Blood Flow} = \text{Cardiac Output} \times \text{Vascular Resistance}^{-1} \qquad (39)$$

When combined with aromatic compounds, the effects can be even more pronounced. Essential oils, such as eucalyptus and lavender, can penetrate the skin and respiratory system, providing therapeutic benefits. For instance, eucalyptus oil is known for its anti-inflammatory properties and can help clear the airways, making it easier to breathe in the steam-infused environment.

Psychological Effects The olfactory system is closely linked to the limbic system, which is responsible for emotions and memory. Therefore, inhaling pleasant scents while enveloped in warmth can evoke positive feelings and memories, promoting relaxation and reducing stress. The equation for the relationship between scent concentration and perceived intensity can be expressed as:

$$I = k \cdot \ln(C) \tag{40}$$

where I is the perceived intensity, C is the concentration of the scent, and k is a constant that varies with individual sensitivity.

Choosing the Right Scents

Selecting the appropriate scents for saunas and steam rooms is crucial to maximizing their benefits. Here are some popular essential oils and their effects:

- **Eucalyptus:** Known for its invigorating properties, eucalyptus oil can enhance respiratory function and promote mental clarity.
- **Lavender:** Renowned for its calming effects, lavender oil helps reduce anxiety and improve sleep quality.
- **Peppermint:** This oil provides a refreshing sensation and can alleviate headaches and muscle tension.
- **Citrus Oils (e.g., Orange, Lemon):** These oils uplift mood and energize the spirit, creating a vibrant atmosphere.
- **Tea Tree Oil:** With its antiseptic properties, tea tree oil can purify the air and promote skin health.

Practical Applications

To create a scented sauna or steam room experience, consider the following methods:

Diffusion Techniques

- **Essential Oil Diffusers:** Use electric diffusers designed for high heat environments to disperse essential oils evenly throughout the space.
- **Steam Infusion:** Add a few drops of essential oil to a bowl of water and place it on the heater or steam generator. As the water heats, the oils will vaporize, filling the room with scent.

- **Scented Towels:** Mist towels with diluted essential oils before placing them in the sauna. When heated, the towels will release their fragrance.

Safety Considerations While the benefits of scented saunas and steam rooms are numerous, safety should always be a priority. Essential oils are potent substances that can cause skin irritation or allergic reactions if not used properly. It is essential to:

- Dilute essential oils with a carrier oil before applying them to the skin.
- Conduct a patch test to check for allergic reactions.
- Avoid using strong scents that may overwhelm the senses or cause discomfort.

Examples of Scented Sauna Experiences

Around the world, various cultures have embraced the concept of scented saunas and steam rooms:

- **Finnish Saunas:** Traditionally, Finnish saunas utilize birch leaves and essential oils to enhance the experience, promoting relaxation and well-being.
- **Turkish Hamams:** In these steam baths, scents like rose and jasmine are often used to create a serene atmosphere, enhancing the bathing ritual.
- **Aromatherapy Retreats:** Many wellness centers now offer specialized sessions that combine guided meditation with aromatic infusions, creating a holistic experience for relaxation and rejuvenation.

Conclusion

Scented saunas and steam rooms offer a unique blend of therapeutic benefits that stimulate both the body and mind. By carefully selecting and applying essential oils, one can enhance the overall experience, promoting relaxation, emotional well-being, and a deeper connection with oneself. As we embrace the art of scent in these warm, inviting spaces, we unlock a world of sensory pleasure that celebrates the beauty of both heat and aroma.

The Appeal of Post-Workout Musky Bodies

The allure of post-workout musk is a phenomenon that transcends mere physical exertion. This section delves into the science, cultural significance, and psychological aspects of the scents that arise from our bodies after engaging in vigorous exercise.

The Science Behind Musky Odors

When we exercise, our bodies undergo a series of physiological changes that lead to the production of sweat. Sweat itself is primarily composed of water, but it also contains a variety of compounds such as urea, ammonia, and various fatty acids. The breakdown of these substances by bacteria on the skin's surface creates the characteristic musky odor associated with post-workout bodies.

Mathematically, the process can be described by the following equation:

$$\text{Sweat} \rightarrow \text{Bacterial Action} \rightarrow \text{Volatile Compounds} \rightarrow \text{Musky Odor} \quad (41)$$

This transformation highlights the role of skin microbiota in odor production, suggesting that the unique composition of an individual's microbiome can significantly influence their post-exercise scent.

Cultural Perspectives on Sweat

In many cultures, sweat and the odors associated with it have been romanticized and celebrated. For instance, in some Mediterranean cultures, the scent of sweat is seen as a sign of hard work and vitality, reflecting a person's commitment to physical fitness. This contrasts sharply with more puritanical views in other societies, where the presence of body odor is often stigmatized.

The appeal of post-workout musk can also be linked to evolutionary biology. Studies suggest that natural body odors, including those produced during sweating, can carry pheromonal signals that are subconsciously attractive to potential mates. This can be explained by the theory of sexual selection, which posits that individuals are drawn to partners with unique and diverse genetic backgrounds, as indicated by their scent.

Psychological Factors and Attraction

The psychological aspect of attraction to musky bodies post-exercise is multifaceted. The release of endorphins during physical activity not only enhances mood but can also alter perceptions of attractiveness. Research indicates that individuals are more likely to find others appealing when they themselves are in a heightened emotional state, such as that experienced after a workout.

Moreover, the association of physical fitness with attractiveness plays a crucial role in this dynamic. The sight and scent of a sweaty, well-toned body can evoke feelings of desirability, linking physical exertion with sexual appeal. This connection is further reinforced by the media, which often portrays athletes and fitness enthusiasts as idealized figures of beauty.

Examples in Popular Culture

The allure of post-workout musk has permeated popular culture, as seen in various media representations. For instance, romantic films often depict characters falling for one another during or after a workout, highlighting the sensuality associated with sweat.

Additionally, the fitness industry capitalizes on this appeal through marketing strategies that promote the idea that sweat is synonymous with hard work and desirability. Brands often feature athletes in advertisements, showcasing their glistening, musky bodies as aspirational images.

Challenges and Considerations

Despite the allure of post-workout musk, there are challenges and considerations to be aware of. The stigma surrounding body odor can lead to discomfort or embarrassment for some individuals, creating a dichotomy between the natural appeal of musk and societal expectations of cleanliness and hygiene.

Furthermore, the rise of fitness culture has led to an increase in the use of artificial fragrances to mask natural odors, which can dilute the authenticity of the post-workout experience. This raises questions about the balance between personal expression through scent and societal norms regarding odor.

Conclusion

In conclusion, the appeal of post-workout musky bodies is a complex interplay of biological, cultural, and psychological factors. While the natural scent produced during exercise can be attractive and signify health and vitality, societal pressures and personal preferences continue to shape our perceptions of body odor. Embracing the musky allure of post-workout bodies can lead to a deeper understanding of human attraction and the intricate relationship between scent and identity.

Sweating as a Prelude to Intimacy

Sweating, often viewed as a mere physiological response to heat or exertion, transcends its basic function in the realm of intimacy. It acts as a powerful catalyst that can enhance attraction and deepen emotional connections between partners. This section explores the multifaceted role of sweat in intimacy, examining its biological, psychological, and social dimensions.

The Biology of Sweat and Attraction

At its core, sweat is a complex mixture of water, salts, and organic compounds, including pheromones—chemical signals that can influence the behavior and physiology of others. The primary glands responsible for sweat production are the eccrine and apocrine glands. Eccrine glands are distributed widely across the body and primarily help regulate body temperature, while apocrine glands, located in areas such as the armpits and groin, secrete a thicker fluid that becomes odorous when broken down by skin bacteria.

The presence of pheromones in sweat is particularly intriguing. Research indicates that these chemical compounds can evoke subconscious reactions in others. For instance, studies have shown that individuals can identify the scent of their romantic partners through pheromonal cues, which can enhance feelings of attraction and bonding. The notion of "smell compatibility" suggests that partners with similar or complementary pheromonal profiles may experience heightened attraction, leading to a more profound intimate connection.

The Psychological Dimension of Sweating

Psychologically, the act of sweating can be linked to vulnerability and authenticity. When individuals engage in activities that induce sweating—such as exercise, dancing, or even intimate encounters—they often let down their guard, revealing a more genuine self. This vulnerability can foster a deeper emotional connection, as partners become more attuned to each other's physicality and presence.

Moreover, the association of sweat with physical exertion can evoke feelings of excitement and passion. The adrenaline rush experienced during activities that cause sweating can heighten arousal, making the subsequent intimate moments more intense. This physiological response is often referred to as the "arousal transfer theory," which posits that physiological arousal from one source (e.g., exercise) can amplify emotional responses in another context (e.g., intimacy).

Cultural Perspectives on Sweat and Intimacy

Culturally, the perception of sweat varies significantly. In some cultures, the natural scent of sweat is celebrated as a sign of vitality and health, while in others, it is viewed as something to be masked or eliminated. This cultural dichotomy can influence how individuals perceive their own sweat and that of their partners, impacting their intimate experiences.

For example, in many Mediterranean cultures, the scent of sweat is often associated with masculinity and virility, enhancing the allure of a partner. In contrast, some Western cultures may promote the use of deodorants and perfumes to suppress natural odors, potentially detracting from the intimate experience. Understanding these cultural nuances can help partners navigate their intimate relationships more effectively, fostering an environment where natural scents are embraced rather than shunned.

Practical Implications for Intimacy

To harness the power of sweat as a prelude to intimacy, partners can engage in activities that promote sweating together. This could include:

- **Joint Workouts:** Exercising together not only enhances physical fitness but also creates shared experiences that can deepen emotional bonds. The shared sweat can act as a natural aphrodisiac, heightening attraction.

- **Dancing:** Engaging in dance can induce sweating while allowing for close physical contact. The rhythm and movement can stimulate emotional connections, making the transition to intimacy feel more natural.

- **Outdoor Adventures:** Activities such as hiking or biking can lead to sweating while also providing a backdrop for meaningful conversations and shared experiences, which can be pivotal in building intimacy.

Challenges and Considerations

While sweating can enhance intimacy, it is essential to acknowledge that not everyone may feel comfortable with their natural scent. Some individuals may have heightened sensitivities to odors or may have been conditioned to associate sweat with negative connotations. Open communication is crucial to navigate these challenges. Partners should feel comfortable discussing their preferences and any concerns related to body odor.

Additionally, maintaining personal hygiene while embracing the natural scent of sweat can strike a balance that fosters intimacy without discomfort. This could involve showering together after a workout or using natural deodorants that allow the body's natural scent to shine through without overwhelming the senses.

Conclusion

In conclusion, sweating serves as a powerful prelude to intimacy, intertwining biological, psychological, and cultural threads that enhance attraction and connection. By embracing sweat as a natural part of the intimate experience, partners can foster deeper emotional bonds and enjoy a more profound sense of closeness. As intimacy evolves, so too does the understanding of how our bodies communicate through scent, inviting us to explore the seductive allure of our most primal instincts.

The Art of Sweaty Massage Techniques

In the realm of intimate encounters, the interplay of touch and scent can create a deeply immersive experience. Sweaty massage techniques not only enhance physical connection but also leverage the allure of natural body odors, which can be both intoxicating and inviting. This section explores the theory behind sweaty massages, the potential challenges practitioners may face, and practical examples to elevate the art of massage into an experience that is both sensual and aromatic.

Theoretical Foundations

The foundation of sweaty massage techniques lies in the understanding of human pheromones and the chemistry of sweat. Pheromones are chemical signals released by the body that can influence the behavior of others, particularly in the context of attraction. The primary pheromones associated with sweat are androstadienone and androstenol, both of which can evoke feelings of attraction and arousal.

$$\text{Pheromone Concentration} = \frac{\text{Mass of Pheromone}}{\text{Volume of Sweat}} \tag{42}$$

This equation illustrates how the concentration of pheromones can be enhanced through increased perspiration during physical activity or intimate settings. The higher the concentration, the more potent the effect on the partner's attraction.

Challenges in Practice

While the concept of sweaty massages is enticing, several challenges may arise:

1. **Social Stigmas**: There can be societal taboos surrounding body odor and sweat, leading to discomfort or reluctance in embracing this practice. Overcoming these stigmas requires open communication and a mutual understanding between partners.

2. **Hygiene Concerns**: Some individuals may have concerns about hygiene associated with sweat. It is essential to establish a balance between embracing natural scents and maintaining cleanliness.

3. **Allergies and Sensitivities**: Not everyone responds positively to strong odors. It is crucial to be aware of any allergies or sensitivities your partner may have to specific scents, including those produced by sweat.

Practical Examples

To effectively incorporate sweaty massage techniques into intimate encounters, consider the following approaches:

1. Pre-Massage Preparation Engage in a physical activity together, such as dancing, jogging, or even a playful wrestling match. This not only elevates heart rates and promotes sweating but also creates a playful atmosphere that enhances intimacy.

2. Setting the Scene Create an environment conducive to relaxation and sensuality. Dim the lights, play soft music, and use soft fabrics to enhance the tactile experience. A warm room will also encourage sweating, making the massage more aromatic.

3. Technique Focus Utilize techniques that promote skin-to-skin contact, such as:
 - **The Swedish Technique**: Long, gliding strokes that allow for maximum skin contact and the transfer of pheromones. - **Kneading**: Use your palms to knead the muscles, allowing sweat to mix with the natural oils of the skin, creating a unique aromatic blend. - **Friction Techniques**: Employ gentle friction movements to stimulate circulation and encourage more sweating.

$$\text{Pressure} = \frac{\text{Force}}{\text{Area}} \tag{43}$$

This equation illustrates how varying the pressure during the massage can affect the overall experience. A balance of pressure will enhance the release of sweat and pheromones, creating a more engaging experience.

4. **Incorporating Oils and Lotions** Consider using natural oils that complement the scent of sweat, such as coconut or jojoba oil, to enhance the experience. These oils can help in reducing friction while also adding a layer of scent that blends well with natural body odors.

5. **Post-Massage Connection** After the massage, engage in a moment of closeness, allowing the scents to linger. This can be an opportunity for intimate conversation, cuddling, or simply enjoying the shared experience of the massage.

Conclusion

The art of sweaty massage techniques is an exploration of intimacy that celebrates the natural allure of the human body. By embracing sweat as a source of attraction, practitioners can create a unique sensory experience that deepens connections and enhances the pleasure of touch. The combination of pheromones, skin contact, and the warmth of shared physicality transforms a simple massage into a memorable encounter, inviting partners to explore the intoxicating world of scent and touch together.

The Anticipation of Sweat-Drenched Bedding

The allure of sweat-drenched bedding is a phenomenon that intertwines the realms of desire, intimacy, and the primal instincts that govern human attraction. This section explores the psychological and physiological aspects of this anticipation, delving into the science of scent, the emotional responses elicited by shared bodily experiences, and the cultural narratives that elevate the significance of sweat in romantic contexts.

The Science of Sweat and Scent

Sweat itself is composed primarily of water, but it also contains a variety of organic compounds, including urea, ammonia, and lactic acid, which contribute to its unique odor. The olfactory properties of sweat are largely influenced by the presence of bacteria on the skin, which metabolize these compounds, producing volatile organic compounds (VOCs) that can be perceived as either pleasant or unpleasant.

The interaction between sweat and bedding creates a sensory experience that can heighten intimacy. As individuals share their personal spaces, the mingling of scents can evoke memories and emotions, creating a powerful bond. This phenomenon can be understood through the lens of the following equation:

$$S = f(O, E, P) \qquad (44)$$

Where: - S is the sensory experience, - O represents the olfactory stimuli (the scent of sweat), - E denotes emotional responses (feelings of comfort, safety, and intimacy), and - P signifies personal context (the shared history and experiences of the individuals involved).

The anticipation of sweat-drenched bedding can be linked to the release of pheromones, chemical signals that can influence attraction and social behavior. Research suggests that the presence of certain pheromones in sweat can enhance sexual attraction, further complicating the relationship between scent and intimacy.

Psychological Implications

The anticipation of engaging with sweat-drenched bedding can evoke a range of psychological responses. For many, the scent of a partner's sweat can trigger feelings of warmth and affection, reinforcing the bond between individuals. This is particularly relevant in romantic relationships, where shared experiences, such as sleeping together, can create a sense of belonging and security.

Furthermore, the act of sharing bedding that has absorbed the scents of both partners can be seen as a form of vulnerability. It allows individuals to embrace their natural odors, fostering a deeper connection that transcends superficial attraction. This connection can be illustrated through Maslow's hierarchy of needs, where the need for love and belonging is paramount:

$$L = f(I, S, R) \qquad (45)$$

Where: - L is the level of love and belonging, - I represents intimacy, - S denotes shared experiences, and - R signifies the level of risk taken in revealing one's true self.

Cultural Narratives

Culturally, the anticipation of sweat-drenched bedding has been romanticized in literature, film, and art. The idea that shared sweat can symbolize passion and connection is prevalent in many narratives. For instance, consider the classic trope of lovers entwined in sheets, their bodies glistening with sweat after a passionate encounter. This imagery evokes a sense of raw, primal attraction that speaks to our fundamental human nature.

Moreover, various cultures have different perceptions of sweat and its implications for intimacy. In some societies, the natural scent of the body is celebrated as a marker of authenticity and connection, while in others, it may be viewed as something to be masked or concealed. This dichotomy can be explored through the following cultural framework:

$$C = f(S, A, N) \qquad (46)$$

Where: - C is the cultural perception of sweat, - S represents societal norms, - A denotes attitudes toward body odor, and - N signifies narratives surrounding intimacy and attraction.

Practical Considerations

While the anticipation of sweat-drenched bedding can enhance intimacy, it is essential to consider practical implications. Maintaining hygiene and addressing any potential discomfort associated with sweat is crucial. Couples can engage in open communication about their preferences and boundaries regarding sweat and scent, thereby fostering a healthy environment for intimacy.

In conclusion, the anticipation of sweat-drenched bedding encapsulates a complex interplay of physiological, psychological, and cultural factors that contribute to the allure of intimacy. By embracing the natural scents of our bodies and recognizing their role in attraction, we can deepen our connections with one another, transforming the mundane act of sleeping into a celebration of shared experiences and primal desire.

Sensational Skincare for Sultry Smells

Nourishing Your Skin for Irresistible Odors

In the pursuit of attractive bodily scents, the skin plays a pivotal role as it serves as the canvas on which our natural aromas are painted. The relationship between skin health and odor is complex, influenced by factors such as hydration, pH balance, and the microbiome. This section delves into the science behind skin nourishment and its impact on the allure of your personal scent.

The Science of Skin and Odor

The skin is the largest organ of the body, acting as a barrier and a regulator of various physiological processes. When it comes to scent, the skin's surface is home to a diverse array of microorganisms, collectively known as the skin microbiome. These bacteria and fungi contribute significantly to the production of body odor, transforming the natural oils and sweat produced by our skin into unique scents.

$$\text{Odor} = f(\text{Microbiome, Sebum, Sweat, pH}) \qquad (47)$$

Where: - Odor is the resultant scent profile. - Microbiome represents the diverse microbial population on the skin. - Sebum is the oil produced by sebaceous glands. - Sweat refers to perspiration from eccrine and apocrine glands. - pH indicates the acidity or alkalinity of the skin surface.

A balanced skin microbiome, optimal sebum production, and a neutral pH are crucial for creating an appealing scent. Thus, nourishing the skin is paramount for enhancing its natural fragrance.

Hydration: The Foundation of Fragrance

Hydration is essential for maintaining skin elasticity and function. Well-hydrated skin produces sebum more effectively, which can amplify the natural scent. Dehydrated skin, on the other hand, can lead to an imbalance in the skin's microbiome, resulting in unpleasant odors.

To promote hydration, consider the following:

- **Drink Plenty of Water:** Aim for at least 2 liters of water daily to keep your skin hydrated from within.

- **Use Humectants:** Incorporate products containing hyaluronic acid or glycerin, which attract moisture to the skin.

- **Moisturize Regularly:** Apply a nourishing moisturizer after bathing to lock in hydration.

Balancing pH for Optimal Scent

The skin's natural pH level typically ranges from 4.5 to 5.5, creating an acidic environment that inhibits the growth of harmful bacteria. Disruption of this pH balance can lead to an increase in odor-producing bacteria.

To maintain a healthy pH:

- **Choose pH-Balanced Products:** Look for cleansers and moisturizers that are specifically formulated to match the skin's natural pH.

- **Avoid Harsh Soaps:** Traditional soaps can strip the skin of its natural oils and alter its pH.

- **Incorporate Acidic Foods:** Foods like yogurt, sauerkraut, and citrus fruits can help maintain internal pH balance.

Feeding Your Microbiome

A healthy skin microbiome is crucial for producing pleasant odors. The balance of good bacteria can be influenced by diet, skincare products, and lifestyle choices.

- **Probiotics:** Consider consuming probiotic-rich foods such as kefir, kimchi, and kombucha to support your skin's microbiome.

- **Prebiotics:** Foods high in fiber, such as bananas, onions, and garlic, feed beneficial bacteria on the skin.

- **Limit Sugar and Processed Foods:** These can promote the growth of odor-causing bacteria.

DIY Nourishing Treatments

Creating your own nourishing treatments can be a fun and effective way to enhance your skin's scent profile. Here are a few recipes:

Coconut Oil and Essential Oils

- Mix 2 tablespoons of organic coconut oil with 10 drops of essential oils (such as lavender, bergamot, or ylang-ylang).

- Apply to the skin for hydration and a subtle scent.

Honey and Yogurt Mask

- Combine 1 tablespoon of honey with 2 tablespoons of plain yogurt.

- Apply as a mask for 15 minutes, then rinse off. This nourishes the skin and promotes a healthy microbiome.

The Role of Diet in Skin Nourishment

What you eat directly affects your skin's health and, consequently, its scent. Incorporating the following foods can enhance your skin's natural fragrance:

- **Fatty Fish:** Rich in omega-3 fatty acids, which help maintain skin hydration.

- **Fruits and Vegetables:** High in antioxidants, they promote healthy skin and combat free radicals.

- **Nuts and Seeds:** Provide essential fatty acids and vitamin E for skin nourishment.

Conclusion

Nourishing your skin is a multifaceted approach that involves hydration, pH balance, microbiome health, and diet. By prioritizing these elements, you can enhance your skin's natural scent, making it irresistibly attractive. Embrace the journey of self-care, and let your skin radiate with alluring aromas that are uniquely yours.

Attractive Odor = Hydration+Balanced pH+Nourished Microbiome+Healthy Diet (48)

DIY Body Scrubs and Masks for a Luscious Aroma

Creating your own body scrubs and masks is not just an act of self-care; it's an opportunity to envelop yourself in delightful scents while nourishing your skin. This section will explore the theory behind aromatic properties, the benefits of using natural ingredients, and provide you with recipes that will make your skin feel as good as it smells.

The Theory of Aroma and Skin Care

Aromas have a profound impact on our mood and well-being. The olfactory system is closely linked to the limbic system, which is responsible for emotions and memory. When we smell something pleasant, it can evoke feelings of happiness and relaxation. The use of essential oils in body scrubs and masks not only enhances the sensory experience but also provides therapeutic benefits through aromatherapy.

The key components of essential oils that contribute to their aroma are volatile compounds. These compounds evaporate quickly, allowing the scent to travel through the air and stimulate our olfactory receptors. For example, the main component of lavender oil, linalool, is known for its calming properties, making it a popular choice for relaxation.

Benefits of Natural Ingredients

Using natural ingredients in your DIY scrubs and masks has numerous advantages:

- **Gentle Exfoliation:** Natural exfoliants such as sugar, coffee grounds, and oatmeal effectively remove dead skin cells without the harshness of synthetic ingredients.

- **Nourishment:** Ingredients like honey, yogurt, and oils provide hydration and nourishment, leaving your skin soft and supple.

- **Customizable:** You can tailor your scrubs and masks to your specific skin type, preferences, and desired aromas.

- **Cost-Effective:** Making your own products can save you money compared to purchasing commercial options filled with synthetic fragrances and preservatives.

Common Problems and Solutions

While creating your own scrubs and masks can be a rewarding experience, there are some common issues to be aware of:

- **Skin Sensitivity:** Always perform a patch test before applying any new ingredient to your skin. Some essential oils can cause irritation if used undiluted.

- **Messy Application:** DIY scrubs can be messy, especially when using ingredients like sugar or coffee grounds. Consider applying them in the shower or over a towel to catch any spills.

- **Preservation:** Natural products lack preservatives, so it's essential to make small batches and use them within a week or two to avoid spoilage.

DIY Recipes

Here are a few simple recipes for body scrubs and masks that will leave your skin smelling divine.

1. Citrus Sugar Scrub   Ingredients:

- 1 cup granulated sugar
- 1/2 cup coconut oil (melted)
- Zest of 1 lemon
- Zest of 1 orange
- 10 drops of lemon essential oil
- 10 drops of orange essential oil

Instructions:

1. In a mixing bowl, combine the sugar and melted coconut oil until well blended.
2. Add the citrus zests and essential oils, mixing thoroughly.
3. Transfer the scrub to a jar and store in a cool, dry place.
4. To use, massage a handful onto damp skin in circular motions, then rinse off for a refreshing glow.

2. Lavender Oatmeal Mask   Ingredients:

- 1/2 cup rolled oats
- 1/4 cup honey
- 1/4 cup yogurt
- 10 drops of lavender essential oil

Instructions:

1. Blend the rolled oats in a food processor until finely ground.

2. In a bowl, mix the ground oats, honey, yogurt, and lavender oil until smooth.

3. Apply the mask to your face and neck, avoiding the eye area.

4. Leave on for 15-20 minutes, then rinse with warm water for soft, fragrant skin.

3. Coffee Body Scrub   Ingredients:

- 1 cup coffee grounds
- 1/2 cup brown sugar
- 1/2 cup coconut oil (melted)
- 1 teaspoon vanilla extract

Instructions:

1. Combine coffee grounds and brown sugar in a bowl.
2. Stir in melted coconut oil and vanilla extract until fully mixed.
3. Store in an airtight container and use within two weeks.
4. Massage the scrub onto damp skin in circular motions before rinsing off to reveal smooth, invigorated skin.

Conclusion

DIY body scrubs and masks are an excellent way to indulge in self-care while embracing the allure of luscious aromas. By understanding the theory behind scents, utilizing natural ingredients, and following simple recipes, you can create products that not only smell fantastic but also nourish your skin. So go ahead, unleash your creativity, and enjoy the delightful experience of crafting your own aromatic body care!

Using Natural Oils to Enhance Sexy Skin

The allure of naturally scented skin is an age-old secret that has captivated hearts and ignited passions. In this section, we will explore the enchanting world of natural oils and how they can enhance your skin's appeal, making it irresistibly sexy.

The Science of Natural Oils

Natural oils are derived from various plant sources, including seeds, nuts, and fruits. They are rich in essential fatty acids, vitamins, and antioxidants that nourish and protect the skin. The primary components of these oils include triglycerides, fatty acids, and phytochemicals, which contribute to their moisturizing and healing properties.

The effectiveness of natural oils can be attributed to their ability to penetrate the skin barrier and provide hydration. The skin barrier, composed of lipids and proteins, plays a crucial role in maintaining skin health. When natural oils are applied, they can help restore the lipid barrier, leading to improved moisture retention and a plump, youthful appearance.

$$\text{Hydration Level} = \frac{\text{Moisture Content}}{\text{Trans-Epidermal Water Loss}} \qquad (49)$$

This equation illustrates the relationship between moisture content and trans-epidermal water loss (TEWL). By using natural oils, you can enhance the moisture content of your skin, thus reducing TEWL and promoting a healthy glow.

Choosing the Right Natural Oils

Not all oils are created equal. To achieve the desired sexy skin effect, it is essential to select oils that are known for their skin-enhancing properties. Here are some of the most popular natural oils and their benefits:

- **Coconut Oil:** Renowned for its moisturizing properties, coconut oil contains medium-chain fatty acids that penetrate the skin easily. Its antibacterial properties also help combat body odor, making it an excellent choice for enhancing natural scents.

- **Argan Oil:** Rich in vitamin E and essential fatty acids, argan oil is known for its ability to hydrate and soften the skin. It also has anti-aging properties, helping to reduce the appearance of fine lines and wrinkles.

- **Jojoba Oil:** Structurally similar to the skin's natural sebum, jojoba oil is an excellent moisturizer that balances oil production. Its non-comedogenic properties make it suitable for all skin types, enhancing your skin's natural beauty without clogging pores.

- **Sweet Almond Oil:** This oil is rich in vitamins A and E, making it a fantastic choice for nourishing and soothing the skin. It is particularly effective for dry or sensitive skin, leaving it soft and supple.

- **Rosehip Oil:** Known for its regenerative properties, rosehip oil is packed with antioxidants and essential fatty acids that promote skin repair and rejuvenation. Its ability to improve skin texture and tone makes it a popular choice for achieving that sexy glow.

Application Techniques

To maximize the benefits of natural oils, proper application techniques are crucial. Here are some methods to consider:

- **Massage:** Incorporating a gentle massage while applying natural oils can enhance blood circulation and promote relaxation. Use circular motions to stimulate the skin and allow for better absorption of the oil.

- **Layering:** For added hydration, consider layering natural oils with your regular moisturizer. Apply the oil first, allowing it to penetrate the skin, followed by a moisturizer to lock in the hydration.

- **Mixing:** Create your own signature blend by mixing different natural oils. For instance, combine coconut oil with a few drops of essential oils like lavender or ylang-ylang for an aromatic experience that enhances your natural scent.

- **Bathing:** Add a few drops of your favorite natural oil to your bathwater for a luxurious soak. This not only hydrates your skin but also leaves a lingering scent that is sure to entice.

Potential Problems and Considerations

While natural oils can work wonders for your skin, there are a few considerations to keep in mind:

- **Allergies:** Always perform a patch test before using a new oil, especially if you have sensitive skin or allergies. Apply a small amount to a discreet area and wait 24 hours to check for any adverse reactions.

- **Comedogenic Ratings:** Some oils have higher comedogenic ratings, meaning they are more likely to clog pores. For those with oily or acne-prone skin, it is advisable to choose non-comedogenic oils like jojoba or argan oil.

- **Shelf Life:** Natural oils have varying shelf lives, and exposure to air and light can lead to rancidity. Store oils in a cool, dark place and use them within their recommended time frame for optimal results.

Examples of Natural Oil Blends

To inspire your exploration of natural oils, here are a few blend recipes that can enhance your sexy skin:

- **Sensual Glow Blend:**

    - 2 tablespoons of coconut oil
    - 1 tablespoon of argan oil
    - 5 drops of ylang-ylang essential oil

    Mix the ingredients in a small bottle and apply to your skin after bathing for a radiant glow.

- **Soothing Almond Rose Blend:**

    - 2 tablespoons of sweet almond oil
    - 1 tablespoon of rosehip oil
    - 3 drops of lavender essential oil

    Combine the oils in a bowl and massage into your skin for a calming, hydrating experience.

- **Energizing Citrus Blend:**

    - 2 tablespoons of jojoba oil
    - 1 tablespoon of coconut oil
    - 5 drops of grapefruit essential oil

    This refreshing blend is perfect for morning use, leaving your skin invigorated and glowing.

Conclusion

Using natural oils to enhance sexy skin is not just a beauty ritual; it is a celebration of individuality and sensuality. By selecting the right oils, employing effective application techniques, and embracing the allure of your natural scent, you can cultivate a captivating presence that draws others in. Remember, the journey to sexy skin is as much about self-expression and confidence as it is about the products you use. So, indulge in the luxurious world of natural oils, and let your skin tell a story of allure and attraction.

The Art of Scented Bathing

Scented bathing is more than just a luxurious indulgence; it is an art form that blends the sensory experience of aroma with the therapeutic benefits of water. The practice has roots in ancient cultures, where bathing rituals were often infused with fragrant oils and herbs, believed to cleanse not only the body but also the spirit. In this section, we will explore the theory behind scented bathing, the problems that may arise, and practical examples that can enhance your bathing experience.

The Theory Behind Scented Bathing

The olfactory system is deeply connected to our emotions and memories, making scent a powerful tool for evoking feelings of relaxation and pleasure. When we immerse ourselves in a scented bath, the combination of warm water and fragrant elements creates an environment that can reduce stress, improve mood, and promote overall well-being.

The efficacy of scented bathing can be explained through the following principles:

- **Aromatherapy:** The use of essential oils in bathing taps into the principles of aromatherapy, which posits that certain scents can influence psychological and physiological states. For example, lavender oil is known for its calming properties, while citrus scents can invigorate and uplift.

- **Hydrotherapy:** The therapeutic benefits of water, or hydrotherapy, enhance the effects of aromatherapy. Warm water can improve circulation, relieve muscle tension, and promote relaxation, creating a synergistic effect when combined with aromatic substances.

- **Sensory Engagement:** Scented bathing engages multiple senses, leading to a more immersive experience. The warmth of the water, the softness of the bath products, and the captivating scents work together to create a holistic ritual.

Common Problems in Scented Bathing

While the benefits of scented bathing are numerous, there are some challenges to be aware of:

- **Skin Sensitivity:** Some individuals may experience allergic reactions or sensitivities to certain essential oils or bath products. It is crucial to perform a patch test before fully immersing yourself in a scented bath.

- **Overwhelming Scents:** The intensity of scents can vary widely. Using too much of a fragrant product can lead to an overpowering experience that detracts from relaxation. It is recommended to start with a small amount and adjust according to personal preference.

- **Environmental Concerns:** Many commercial bath products contain synthetic fragrances and chemicals that can be harmful to both the user and the environment. Opting for natural, eco-friendly products is essential for a sustainable bathing practice.

Examples of Scented Bathing Practices

To elevate your bathing experience, consider incorporating the following examples into your routine:

- **Essential Oil Blends:** Create your own blend of essential oils tailored to your mood. For a calming bath, mix 5 drops of lavender oil with 3 drops of chamomile oil. For an invigorating experience, combine 5 drops of peppermint oil with 3 drops of eucalyptus oil.

- **Herbal Bath Soaks:** Infuse your bath with dried herbs such as rosemary, thyme, or rose petals. Simply place the herbs in a muslin bag and steep them in the warm water, allowing their natural aromas to permeate the bath.

- **Scented Bath Salts:** Combine Epsom salts with your favorite essential oils to create a relaxing soak. A common recipe includes 1 cup of Epsom salt, 1/2 cup of sea salt, and 10-15 drops of essential oil. Stir well and add to your bath for a soothing experience.

- **Scented Candles:** Enhance the ambiance of your bathing space with scented candles. Choose candles made from natural wax and essential oils to ensure a clean burn and a delightful fragrance that complements your bath.
- **Bath Bombs:** Craft your own bath bombs using baking soda, citric acid, and essential oils. This DIY project allows you to customize scents and create a fizzy, aromatic experience that transforms your bath into a spa-like retreat.

Conclusion

The art of scented bathing is a beautiful blend of aroma, relaxation, and self-care. By understanding the theory behind it, acknowledging potential problems, and experimenting with various practices, you can create a bathing ritual that is uniquely yours. Embrace the allure of scented bathing and let the transformative power of aroma envelop you in a cocoon of tranquility and pleasure.

Captivating Perfumed Lotions and Ointments

In the realm of alluring scents, perfumed lotions and ointments serve as an exquisite bridge between skincare and fragrance, providing a sensory experience that tantalizes the senses while nourishing the skin. This section delves into the art and science of crafting captivating perfumed lotions and ointments, exploring their composition, benefits, and the enchanting allure they can bring to intimate encounters.

The Composition of Perfumed Lotions and Ointments

Perfumed lotions and ointments are typically composed of three primary components: a base, fragrance, and optional additives. The base can vary between lotions, which are generally water-based, and ointments, which tend to be oil-based. Understanding the properties of these components is crucial for creating effective and attractive products.

1. Base Ingredients The base of a perfumed lotion or ointment serves as the vehicle for the fragrance and provides the moisturizing benefits. Common base ingredients include:

- **Emollients:** These are oils or fats that soften and smooth the skin. Examples include shea butter, coconut oil, and jojoba oil.
- **Humectants:** These ingredients attract moisture to the skin, enhancing hydration. Glycerin and hyaluronic acid are popular choices.

- **Thickeners:** To achieve the desired consistency, thickeners such as xanthan gum or beeswax may be added, especially in ointments.

2. **Fragrance Components**   The fragrance in perfumed lotions and ointments can be composed of natural essential oils, synthetic aroma compounds, or a combination of both. The choice of fragrance significantly influences the product's appeal and can evoke emotions, memories, and desires.

The Science of Scent and Skin Interaction

When applied to the skin, the fragrance in lotions and ointments interacts with body chemistry, which can alter the scent profile. This phenomenon is due to the unique combination of an individual's skin pH, temperature, and moisture levels.

Skin Chemistry and Fragrance   The interaction between skin chemistry and fragrance can be represented by the following equation:

$$S = f(P, T, H) \tag{50}$$

Where:

- S is the scent profile experienced.
- P is the skin pH.
- T is the skin temperature.
- H is the level of skin hydration.

This equation underscores the importance of selecting fragrances that complement individual skin chemistry, enhancing the overall allure of the product.

Crafting Captivating Formulations

Creating a captivating perfumed lotion or ointment involves a blend of art and science. Here are some essential steps to consider:

1. **Selecting the Right Fragrance**   Choosing a fragrance that resonates with the intended emotional response is crucial. For instance, floral scents like jasmine and rose can evoke feelings of romance, while earthy scents like sandalwood and patchouli can impart a sense of grounding and warmth.

2. **Balancing Scent Strength** The strength of the fragrance should be balanced with the base ingredients to ensure a pleasant experience. A general guideline is to use a fragrance concentration of 1-5% for lotions and 5-15% for ointments, depending on the desired intensity.

3. **Testing and Adjusting** Conducting patch tests and scent evaluations is vital to ensure the final product is appealing and safe for use. Adjustments to the formulation may be necessary based on feedback and sensory evaluations.

Examples of Captivating Perfumed Lotions and Ointments

To illustrate the enchanting possibilities of perfumed lotions and ointments, consider the following examples:

1. **Lavender Dream Lotion** This lotion combines lavender essential oil with a base of coconut oil and shea butter, creating a soothing and relaxing experience. The calming properties of lavender are enhanced by the moisturizing benefits of the lotion, making it perfect for bedtime rituals.

2. **Citrus Bliss Ointment** A vibrant blend of sweet orange and bergamot essential oils in a beeswax and almond oil base offers a refreshing and uplifting scent. This ointment can be used for massage or as a fragrant balm for dry areas, providing both hydration and a burst of energy.

The Allure of Scented Self-Care

Incorporating perfumed lotions and ointments into self-care routines not only enhances the sensory experience but also promotes emotional well-being. The act of applying these products can become a ritual of self-love, fostering a deeper connection to one's body and enhancing confidence.

1. **Emotional Benefits** The emotional benefits of scented self-care can be profound. Research indicates that certain scents can trigger positive emotional responses and memories, contributing to an overall sense of well-being. For example, the scent of vanilla has been shown to evoke feelings of comfort and warmth.

2. Enhancing Intimacy   In intimate settings, the use of perfumed lotions and ointments can heighten attraction and create a sensual atmosphere. The act of applying these products can become a shared experience, enhancing intimacy between partners.

Conclusion

Captivating perfumed lotions and ointments represent a delightful fusion of skincare and fragrance, offering an enchanting way to embrace individuality and enhance personal allure. By understanding the composition, science, and emotional benefits of these products, individuals can create and enjoy formulations that not only nourish the skin but also elevate the senses, making every application a celebration of self-expression and attraction.

In the world of scents, the allure of perfumed lotions and ointments is an invitation to explore the captivating intersection of beauty and desire, where every whiff tells a story and every touch ignites a spark.

Embracing the Scent of Skincare Ingredients

In the realm of skincare, the olfactory experience can often be as significant as the visual and tactile sensations. The scent of skincare ingredients not only influences consumer preferences but also enhances the overall enjoyment of the product, creating a multi-sensory experience that can elevate the mundane act of applying lotion or cream into a ritualistic pleasure. This section explores the intricate relationship between scent and skincare ingredients, delving into the science behind why certain aromas are appealing, the problems that arise with synthetic fragrances, and the alluring potential of natural scents.

The Science of Aroma in Skincare

The human sense of smell is remarkably powerful, capable of triggering memories and emotions with a mere whiff. This phenomenon is rooted in the anatomy of the olfactory system, where olfactory receptors in the nasal cavity send signals directly to the limbic system, the part of the brain responsible for emotions and memory. Thus, when we encounter a pleasant scent from a skincare product, it can evoke feelings of relaxation, happiness, or nostalgia, enhancing the overall experience of self-care.

Aromas in skincare can be derived from various sources, primarily essential oils and natural extracts. Essential oils are concentrated plant extracts that retain the natural fragrance of the plant, while natural extracts may contain a broader range of aromatic compounds. The appeal of these scents is often linked to their chemical composition. For instance, the presence of certain compounds, such as linalool in lavender or limonene in citrus fruits, can elicit specific emotional responses.

$$\text{Aroma Intensity} = k \times \text{Concentration}^n \qquad (51)$$

Where k is a constant and n is an exponent that describes the relationship between concentration and the perceived intensity of the aroma. This equation illustrates that even small amounts of aromatic compounds can significantly impact the overall scent profile of a skincare product.

Natural vs. Synthetic Scents

Despite the allure of natural scents, the skincare industry often employs synthetic fragrances to achieve desired aromas. While synthetic fragrances can be more stable and cost-effective, they are not without their problems. Many synthetic fragrances contain allergens or irritants that can lead to skin reactions, disrupting the delicate balance of the skin's microbiome. This has led to a growing demand for transparency in ingredient sourcing and a preference for products that highlight their natural scent profiles.

Natural scents, on the other hand, come with their own set of challenges. The variability in natural ingredients can lead to inconsistent scent profiles, which can be off-putting for consumers seeking a reliable experience. Moreover, the potency of natural scents can vary based on factors such as the plant's growing conditions, harvest time, and extraction method. This inconsistency raises questions about how to maintain a signature scent in a product line while using natural ingredients.

Examples of Alluring Scents in Skincare

Several skincare brands have embraced the power of natural aromas, crafting products that not only nourish the skin but also delight the senses. For example, brands like *Herbivore Botanicals* utilize essential oils such as rose and jasmine to create luxurious scents that enhance the user experience. Their *Rose Hibiscus Hydrating Face Mist* combines the delicate aroma of rose with the refreshing essence of hibiscus, creating an uplifting sensory experience.

Another notable example is *Lush*, known for its commitment to fresh, handmade products. Lush incorporates a variety of natural ingredients with captivating scents, such as their *Sleepy Body Lotion*, which features lavender and tonka bean. The soothing aroma not only promotes relaxation but also transforms the application process into a calming bedtime ritual.

The Allure of Customization

As consumers become more discerning, the trend towards customization in skincare has gained traction. Brands are now offering personalized products that allow consumers to select their preferred scents. This approach not only caters to individual preferences but also empowers consumers to embrace their unique olfactory identities. For instance, *Function of Beauty* allows customers to create custom shampoos and conditioners with their choice of scents, from floral to fruity, enhancing the personal connection to the product.

Conclusion

Embracing the scent of skincare ingredients is not merely about masking unpleasant odors; it is about harnessing the power of aroma to create a holistic sensory experience. By understanding the science behind scents and the implications of ingredient choices, brands can cultivate products that resonate with consumers on a deeper level. As the industry continues to evolve, the emphasis on natural, appealing scents will likely play a pivotal role in shaping consumer preferences and redefining the standards of beauty and self-care. The future of skincare lies not just in efficacy but also in the enchanting aromas that can transform a simple routine into an indulgent ritual, celebrating the authentic aroma of you.

The Erotic Ritual of Oiling the Body

The act of oiling the body transcends mere skincare; it is an intimate ritual steeped in sensuality and connection. This practice not only enhances the skin's appearance but also serves as a conduit for touch, intimacy, and the exploration of one's own bodily scent. In this section, we will delve into the erotic nature of body oiling, exploring its historical significance, the sensory experiences it evokes, and the psychological effects it can have on both the individual and their partner.

Historical Significance of Body Oiling

Throughout history, various cultures have embraced the practice of body oiling. In ancient Egypt, for instance, oils were used not only for moisturizing the skin but also for their aromatic properties. The Egyptians believed that oils could connect the physical body with the spiritual realm, enhancing one's aura and attractiveness. Similarly, in Ayurvedic traditions, the practice of *abhyanga* involves self-massage

SENSATIONAL SKINCARE FOR SULTRY SMELLS

with warm oils, believed to promote balance and harmony within the body and mind.

The Sensory Experience

The sensory experience of oiling the body is multi-faceted. The touch of warm oil gliding over the skin creates a heightened awareness of one's body, stimulating nerve endings and enhancing tactile sensations. The viscosity of the oil allows for a slow, deliberate application that invites mindfulness and presence. The act of rubbing oil into the skin can evoke feelings of pleasure, relaxation, and even arousal.

$$E = \frac{1}{2}mv^2 \qquad (52)$$

Where E is the energy of touch, m is the mass of the oil applied, and v is the velocity of the application. This equation metaphorically illustrates how the energy of touch can be amplified by the quality and quantity of oil used, leading to a more profound sensory experience.

Psychological Effects

The psychological impact of body oiling can be profound. Engaging in this ritual can foster a sense of self-love and acceptance, encouraging individuals to embrace their bodies in a new light. The act of oiling oneself can also serve as a form of self-care, promoting relaxation and reducing stress.

Moreover, when shared with a partner, the ritual of oiling becomes a collaborative exploration of intimacy. The act of applying oil to another's body can create a deep sense of connection, trust, and vulnerability. This shared experience can heighten arousal and foster emotional bonds, making it a powerful tool for enhancing intimacy in relationships.

Examples of Oiling Rituals

1. **Sensual Massage**: Using fragrant oils such as jasmine or sandalwood, partners can take turns giving each other massages. The act of massaging not only nourishes the skin but also allows for exploration of each other's bodies in a loving and intimate manner.

2. **Bathing Rituals**: Incorporating oils into bathwater transforms a simple bath into an aromatic experience. Adding a few drops of essential oils such as lavender or ylang-ylang can create a calming atmosphere that enhances relaxation and intimacy.

3. **Self-Oiling**: Engaging in self-oiling rituals can be empowering. Using oils infused with aphrodisiac scents, individuals can take time to appreciate their own bodies, enhancing self-confidence and body positivity.

4. **Couples' Oiling Sessions**: Setting the mood with dim lighting and soft music, couples can create a sacred space for oiling each other. This ritual not only promotes physical touch but also encourages open communication about desires and boundaries.

The Role of Scent in Oiling Rituals

Scent plays a crucial role in the erotic ritual of oiling the body. The olfactory system is closely linked to the limbic system, the part of the brain that governs emotions and memories. Thus, the scents used in body oils can evoke powerful emotional responses and enhance the overall experience.

$$S = k \cdot \ln(C) \tag{53}$$

Where S represents the sensory satisfaction derived from the scent, k is a constant representing the individual's sensitivity to scent, and C is the concentration of the aromatic compounds in the oil. This equation highlights how the intensity of the scent can impact the overall sensory experience during the ritual.

Conclusion

The erotic ritual of oiling the body is a celebration of touch, scent, and intimacy. By embracing this practice, individuals can enhance their self-awareness, foster deeper connections with their partners, and explore the sensuality inherent in their own bodies. As we navigate a world that often prioritizes the visual, taking the time to engage in the tactile and olfactory can be a transformative experience, leading to greater self-acceptance and enriched relationships.

In conclusion, the art of oiling the body is not merely about hydration; it is a holistic practice that encompasses physical, emotional, and sensory dimensions, making it a powerful ritual for enhancing personal allure and intimate connections.

The Appeal of Scented Sunscreen

Scented sunscreen is an increasingly popular choice among consumers who wish to combine sun protection with pleasurable olfactory experiences. This section delves into the allure of scented sunscreens, exploring the scientific foundations, psychological impacts, and cultural significance of integrating fragrance into sun care products.

The Science of Scented Sunscreen

The primary function of sunscreen is to protect the skin from harmful ultraviolet (UV) radiation. The effectiveness of sunscreen is quantified through its Sun Protection Factor (SPF), which measures the product's ability to prevent sunburn caused by UVB rays. The equation for SPF can be expressed as:

$$\text{SPF} = \frac{\text{Minimal Erythema Dose (MED) with sunscreen}}{\text{MED without sunscreen}} \quad (54)$$

While the SPF rating is critical, the formulation of sunscreen often includes a variety of chemical and physical filters, which can possess inherent scents. For instance, ingredients such as zinc oxide and titanium dioxide are commonly used as physical blockers and can have a chalky odor. To mask or enhance these scents, manufacturers often incorporate fragrances or essential oils, creating a multisensory experience that appeals to consumers.

Psychological Appeal of Fragrance

Fragrance plays a pivotal role in consumer perception and product enjoyment. The olfactory system is closely linked to the limbic system, the part of the brain that governs emotions and memory. This connection means that pleasant scents can evoke positive feelings, enhance mood, and even trigger nostalgic memories.

For instance, the scent of coconut oil, often associated with tropical vacations and relaxation, can transform the mundane act of applying sunscreen into a sensory escape. Research suggests that fragrances can influence consumer behavior, leading to increased purchase intent and brand loyalty. A study conducted by Spangenberg et al. (2006) found that pleasant ambient scents can significantly enhance a consumer's shopping experience, leading to longer dwell times and increased spending.

Cultural Significance of Scented Sunscreen

Culturally, scented sunscreen reflects broader trends in beauty and personal care that prioritize sensory experiences. In many cultures, the scent of sunscreen is synonymous with summer, beach outings, and leisure. The integration of fragrance into sunscreen aligns with the increasing consumer demand for products that not only serve functional purposes but also enhance personal enjoyment and self-expression.

For example, brands like Hawaiian Tropic and Banana Boat have successfully marketed their scented sunscreens by emphasizing the sensory experience of application. Their products often feature tropical or fruity fragrances that evoke imagery of sun-soaked beaches, thus appealing to consumers' desires for escapism and leisure.

Challenges and Considerations

Despite the appeal of scented sunscreens, there are challenges and considerations that manufacturers must navigate. One significant concern is the potential for skin irritation or allergic reactions caused by fragrance ingredients. The American Academy of Dermatology (AAD) notes that fragrance is one of the most common allergens in skincare products. Therefore, it is crucial for brands to offer clear labeling and hypoallergenic options to cater to sensitive skin types.

Moreover, regulatory considerations regarding fragrance use in sunscreens vary by region. In the European Union, for example, there are strict regulations governing the labeling of allergens in cosmetic products. Brands must ensure compliance while still delivering appealing scents to consumers.

Conclusion

In conclusion, the appeal of scented sunscreen lies in its ability to combine effective sun protection with sensory pleasure. By understanding the science behind fragrance, the psychological impacts it has on consumers, and the cultural significance of scented products, brands can create offerings that resonate deeply with their audience. However, navigating the challenges of skin sensitivity and regulatory compliance remains essential to ensure that the allure of scented sunscreen is both enjoyable and safe for all users. The future of scented sunscreens appears bright, as consumers increasingly seek products that enhance their daily rituals with delightful aromas while safeguarding their skin from the sun's harmful effects.

Skin-Scented Candles for Sensual Ambiance

In the realm of intimate experiences, the ambiance plays a crucial role in setting the mood. Skin-scented candles, designed to evoke the natural aromas of human skin, offer a unique approach to creating an inviting and sensual atmosphere. This section explores the theory behind skin-scented candles, the challenges involved in their formulation, and compelling examples that illustrate their potential for enhancing intimacy.

The Theory Behind Skin-Scented Candles

The allure of skin-scented candles lies in their ability to mimic the subtle, warm, and inviting scents that our bodies naturally produce. The concept is rooted in the science of olfaction, where certain scents can trigger emotional responses and memories, often linked to intimacy and attraction. The human skin emits a variety of compounds, including fatty acids, amino acids, and pheromones, which contribute to our unique body odor.

The primary components of skin-scented candles often include:

- **Fatty Acids:** These compounds provide a creamy, rich scent reminiscent of human skin. Common examples include caprylic acid and stearic acid, which can be sourced from natural oils.

- **Amino Acids:** The presence of amino acids like tryptophan and phenylalanine can evoke the warmth of skin, adding depth and complexity to the fragrance.

- **Pheromones:** While the effectiveness of synthetic pheromones in candles is debated, their inclusion aims to enhance attraction and intimacy. These are often derived from natural sources or synthesized to mimic human pheromones.

The olfactory system is intricately linked to the limbic system, the part of the brain that controls emotions and memories. This connection explains why certain scents can evoke powerful feelings of nostalgia, desire, or comfort, making skin-scented candles a potent tool for creating a romantic atmosphere.

Challenges in Formulating Skin-Scented Candles

Creating skin-scented candles is not without its challenges. The formulation process requires a delicate balance of ingredients to ensure that the final product is both pleasant and evocative of human scent without crossing into the realm of unpleasant odors. Key challenges include:

- **Scent Balance:** Achieving the right balance between sweetness, warmth, and the natural muskiness of skin is essential. Overly strong or harsh notes can deter users rather than attract them.

- **Sustainability:** Sourcing natural ingredients that are both sustainable and effective can be a challenge. Many consumers are increasingly aware of the environmental impact of their purchases, prompting brands to seek eco-friendly alternatives.

- **Allergenicity:** Certain individuals may have sensitivities to specific scents or ingredients. Ensuring that skin-scented candles are hypoallergenic and safe for a wide audience is crucial for market acceptance.

Examples of Skin-Scented Candles

Several brands have successfully ventured into the niche market of skin-scented candles, each offering unique interpretations of the concept. Here are a few notable examples:

- **Boy Smells:** Known for their innovative approach to scent, Boy Smells offers candles like "Cedar Stack," which combines notes of cedarwood, sandalwood, and a hint of musk, creating an ambiance reminiscent of skin and earth. Their branding emphasizes inclusivity and the celebration of diverse identities.

- **Byredo:** The luxury fragrance house Byredo has introduced candles that evoke intimate moments, such as "Mojave Ghost," which features notes of ambrette seed—a compound known for its skin-like scent profile. This candle not only enhances the atmosphere but also serves as an olfactory experience that resonates with personal memories.

- **Diptyque:** Their "Feu de Bois" candle, while primarily focused on the scent of wood, incorporates underlying notes that mimic the warmth of human skin. The interplay between the smoky aroma and soft, skin-like notes creates a cozy and intimate environment.

Conclusion

Skin-scented candles represent a fascinating intersection of olfactory science, intimate experiences, and sensory pleasure. By embracing the natural aromas of human skin, these candles can enhance romantic encounters, creating a sensual ambiance that invites connection and intimacy. As consumers continue to seek unique and personal experiences, the market for skin-scented candles is poised for growth, providing opportunities for brands to innovate and explore the depths of scent and emotion.

Mathematical Representation of Scent Perception

To quantify the effectiveness of skin-scented candles in creating a sensual ambiance, we can consider a simplified model of scent perception. Let S represent the overall scent perception, which can be influenced by multiple factors including the concentration of key scent compounds C, the emotional response E, and the context of the environment X. We can express this as:

$$S = k_1 C + k_2 E + k_3 X$$

where k_1, k_2, and k_3 are coefficients that represent the sensitivity of the human olfactory system to each factor. By adjusting these variables, candle makers can optimize their products to enhance the desired sensual ambiance.

In conclusion, skin-scented candles offer a unique approach to creating an intimate atmosphere, blending the science of scent with the art of seduction. Their ability to evoke warmth and connection makes them a valuable addition to any romantic setting.

Enhancing Sensitivity through Skincare

In the realm of personal care, the intersection of skincare and scent plays a pivotal role in enhancing not only the olfactory experience but also the sensitivity of the skin itself. This section delves into the theoretical underpinnings of how specific skincare practices can amplify both sensory perception and the allure of one's natural scent.

The Science of Skin Sensitivity

Skin sensitivity is defined as the skin's heightened response to various stimuli, including environmental factors, allergens, and fragrances. The skin's barrier function, primarily composed of lipids and proteins, is crucial for maintaining hydration and protecting against irritants. When this barrier is compromised, it can lead to increased sensitivity, resulting in reactions such as redness, itching, and inflammation.

The skin's sensitivity can be quantified using the following equation:

$$S = \frac{R}{E} \tag{55}$$

where S represents sensitivity, R is the skin's response to irritants, and E is the effectiveness of the skin barrier. A lower barrier effectiveness E results in a higher sensitivity S.

Skincare Ingredients That Enhance Sensitivity

1. **Natural Oils**: Incorporating oils such as jojoba, argan, and rosehip can enhance skin sensitivity through their nourishing properties. These oils contain fatty acids that mimic the skin's natural lipids, promoting barrier repair and hydration. For instance, jojoba oil is known for its similarity to sebum, allowing for better absorption and enhancement of skin's natural scent.

2. **Exfoliants**: Chemical exfoliants like alpha-hydroxy acids (AHAs) and beta-hydroxy acids (BHAs) can improve skin texture and sensitivity by removing dead skin cells. However, over-exfoliation can lead to increased sensitivity, so it's essential to balance their use. A common formulation might include:

$$E_{total} = E_{AHA} + E_{BHA} - E_{Irritation} \quad (56)$$

where E_{total} represents the total exfoliation effect, E_{AHA} and E_{BHA} are the individual effects of AHAs and BHAs, and $E_{Irritation}$ accounts for any adverse reactions.

3. **Hydrating Agents**: Ingredients like hyaluronic acid and glycerin attract moisture to the skin, enhancing its sensitivity and overall feel. These agents can increase the skin's hydration levels, making it more receptive to fragrances. The hydration level can be expressed as:

$$H = \frac{M}{A} \quad (57)$$

where H is hydration, M is moisture content, and A is the area of the skin. Higher moisture content increases skin's ability to absorb and hold onto scents.

Practical Applications in Skincare Routines

To effectively enhance sensitivity through skincare, consider incorporating the following practices into your routine:

- **Layering Products**: Start with a hydrating serum containing hyaluronic acid, followed by a nourishing oil to seal in moisture. This layering technique not only enhances skin sensitivity but also creates a base for fragrances to adhere to.

- **Scented Exfoliation**: Utilize gentle exfoliating scrubs infused with essential oils, such as lavender or chamomile. This not only promotes skin renewal but also leaves a subtle scent that can enhance your natural aroma.

- **Fragrance-Free Moisturizers**: While it may seem counterintuitive, using fragrance-free moisturizers allows your skin's natural scent to shine through. Look for products that contain skin-loving ingredients like ceramides and antioxidants, which support barrier function and sensitivity.

Challenges and Considerations

While enhancing sensitivity through skincare can yield beautiful results, it is essential to consider potential challenges:
- **Allergic Reactions**: Some individuals may experience allergic reactions to specific ingredients, leading to increased sensitivity. Always perform a patch test before introducing new products.
- **Environmental Factors**: External factors such as pollution and UV exposure can compromise skin sensitivity. Incorporating antioxidants and SPF into your routine can help mitigate these effects.
- **Balance**: Striking a balance between enhancing sensitivity and maintaining skin health is crucial. Overloading the skin with too many active ingredients can lead to irritation rather than enhancement.

Conclusion

Enhancing sensitivity through skincare is a delicate dance of science and art. By understanding the underlying principles of skin sensitivity and selecting the right ingredients, one can create a skincare routine that not only amplifies the allure of their natural scent but also promotes healthy, radiant skin. The journey to discovering one's unique aromatic profile begins with embracing the beauty of sensitivity, transforming the mundane into the extraordinary.

Thrilling Hair Odor Elevation

Hair Care Routines for Attractive Smells

When it comes to the art of seduction, one often overlooks the olfactory allure of hair. Hair care routines that prioritize scent can elevate your entire presence, creating an irresistible aura that draws others in. In this section, we will explore the science behind hair odors, the importance of choosing the right products, and practical routines to ensure your locks are not only visually appealing but also fragrant.

The Science of Hair Odor

Hair naturally retains scents due to its structure. Each strand is composed of a protein called keratin, which has a unique ability to absorb and hold onto aromatic compounds. This means that the products you use, the environment you're in, and even your body chemistry can influence the smell of your hair.

The hair shaft consists of three layers: the cuticle, the cortex, and the medulla. The cuticle, the outermost layer, plays a crucial role in determining how well your hair can hold onto scents. A healthy cuticle that lies flat will trap fragrances better than a damaged one. Therefore, maintaining hair health is essential for ensuring your hair can carry pleasant aromas effectively.

Common Problems with Hair Odors

While attractive smells can enhance your allure, certain habits can lead to undesirable odors. Here are some common problems:

- **Product Buildup:** Overusing styling products can lead to a sticky residue that traps unpleasant smells. Regular cleansing with a clarifying shampoo can help remove buildup.

- **Environmental Factors:** Smoke, pollution, and even cooking odors can cling to hair. Consider using a protective spray before exposure to such environments.

- **Sweat:** Physical activity can result in sweaty hair, which may carry a musky scent. Incorporating hair-specific deodorizing products can mitigate this issue.

Hair Care Routine for Attractive Smells

To cultivate an attractive scent in your hair, consider the following routine:

1. **Cleansing:** Start with a gentle shampoo that contains natural essential oils. Look for ingredients like lavender, rosemary, or citrus, which not only cleanse but also impart delightful fragrances. For example, a lavender-infused shampoo can promote relaxation while leaving your hair smelling fresh.

$$\text{Fragrance Retention} \propto \text{Health of Cuticle} \times \text{Quality of Products}$$

2. **Conditioning:** After cleansing, apply a conditioner that complements your shampoo. Choose conditioners enriched with moisturizing agents like argan oil or coconut oil, which can help seal in fragrance and moisture.

3. **Scented Hair Oils:** Incorporate scented hair oils or serums into your routine. These products can enhance the natural scent of your hair and provide additional nourishment. For instance, a few drops of jasmine oil can add a romantic touch to your mane.

4. **Styling Products:** Opt for hair sprays and gels that are lightly scented. Avoid heavy fragrances that may clash with your natural scent. Instead, choose products with subtle notes, such as vanilla or sandalwood, that can enhance your allure without overwhelming.

5. **Regular Deep Conditioning:** Once a week, treat your hair to a deep conditioning mask. Look for masks with aromatic ingredients like honey or chamomile, which can provide both hydration and a pleasant scent.

6. **Hair Perfumes:** Consider using a dedicated hair perfume. These products are designed specifically for hair and usually contain lighter fragrances that won't weigh your hair down. An example is a mist with notes of bergamot and rose, which can leave your hair smelling divine throughout the day.

7. **Protecting Against Odors:** If you anticipate being in a potentially odor-laden environment, apply a protective hair spray. Such sprays create a barrier against external scents and can help maintain the fragrance of your hair.

Examples of Scented Hair Products

Here are some examples of products that can enhance the scent of your hair:

- **Herbal Essences Bio:Renew Shampoo** - Infused with botanicals, this shampoo not only cleanses but leaves a lasting floral scent.

- **Moroccanoil Treatment** - This versatile oil adds shine and a warm, spicy scent, perfect for a touch of luxury.

- **Bumble and Bumble Hairdresser's Invisible Oil** - A lightweight oil that nourishes hair while imparting a delightful coconut scent.

- **Lush R&B Hair Moisturizer** - A rich conditioner that combines the scents of jasmine and vanilla, perfect for a romantic allure.

Conclusion

In conclusion, establishing a hair care routine that prioritizes attractive smells is an art form that can significantly enhance your personal allure. By understanding the science behind hair odors, addressing common problems, and implementing a thoughtful routine, you can ensure that your hair not only looks stunning but also leaves a captivating scent in its wake. Embrace the power of fragrance, and let your hair be a part of your seductive charm.

Scented Hair Oils and Serums for Sensuous Mane

In the realm of personal grooming, the allure of a scented mane cannot be overstated. Hair oils and serums infused with captivating fragrances not only enhance the aesthetic appeal of your hair but also elevate the sensory experience of those around you. This section delves into the theory behind scented hair products, common challenges faced when using them, and practical examples to inspire your journey toward a more fragrant and sensuous mane.

The Science of Scent in Hair Products

The olfactory system plays a crucial role in human interaction and attraction. When it comes to hair, the use of scented oils and serums can create an olfactory signature that lingers in the air, leaving a memorable impression. The composition of these products often includes essential oils, fragrance oils, and carrier oils, each contributing to the overall scent profile and benefits for the hair.

$$\text{Total Scent} = \sum(\text{Essential Oils} + \text{Fragrance Oils} + \text{Carrier Oils}) \quad (58)$$

Where: - Essential Oils contribute therapeutic properties and natural scents. - Fragrance Oils provide a synthetic or enhanced aroma. - Carrier Oils serve as a base, delivering nourishment while carrying the scent.

Choosing the Right Ingredients

Selecting the right ingredients for your scented hair oils and serums is pivotal. Here are some popular essential oils known for their aromatic qualities and benefits:

- **Lavender Oil:** Renowned for its calming properties, lavender oil can soothe the scalp while imparting a fresh floral scent.

- **Rosemary Oil:** This invigorating oil stimulates hair growth and offers a woody, herbal aroma that can energize your senses.

- **Jojoba Oil:** A fantastic carrier oil, jojoba mimics the natural sebum produced by the scalp, providing moisture and shine without a greasy residue.

- **Coconut Oil:** Known for its deep conditioning properties, coconut oil can enhance the texture of hair while adding a tropical scent.

- **Sandalwood Oil:** With its rich, warm scent, sandalwood oil adds an exotic touch while also promoting relaxation.

Common Challenges

Despite the enticing nature of scented hair products, several challenges can arise:

- **Overpowering Scents:** It's essential to strike a balance; overly strong fragrances can be off-putting. A good rule of thumb is to start with a few drops and gradually increase until the desired scent is achieved.

- **Compatibility with Hair Type:** Not all oils suit every hair type. For instance, heavier oils may weigh down fine hair, while lighter oils may not provide enough moisture for coarse hair.

- **Potential Allergies:** Some individuals may have sensitivities to certain essential oils or fragrance compounds. Conducting a patch test before widespread application is advisable.

Practical Applications and Examples

Creating your own scented hair oil or serum can be a rewarding experience. Here's a simple recipe to get you started:

1. Ingredients:

    - 2 tablespoons of jojoba oil (carrier oil)
    - 1 tablespoon of coconut oil (for moisture)
    - 10 drops of lavender essential oil
    - 5 drops of rosemary essential oil

2. Instructions:

a) In a small bowl, combine the jojoba oil and coconut oil.
b) Add the lavender and rosemary essential oils.
c) Mix thoroughly and transfer to a small dropper bottle for easy application.

3. Usage:

- Apply a few drops to the palms of your hands, rub together, and then gently work through damp or dry hair, focusing on the ends.
- Use it as a finishing touch after styling to lock in moisture and scent.

Conclusion

Scented hair oils and serums offer a unique opportunity to express individuality and enhance personal allure. By understanding the science behind scents, selecting the right ingredients, and addressing potential challenges, you can create a signature fragrance that not only nourishes your hair but also captivates those around you. Embrace the art of olfactory elegance and let your mane tell a story of sensuality and charm.

DIY Hair Perfumes and Mists

Creating your own hair perfumes and mists is not only a delightful way to express your individuality, but it also allows you to experiment with scents that resonate with your personal style. This section will guide you through the process of crafting hair perfumes and mists, exploring the theory behind scent blending, addressing common problems, and providing practical examples.

The Theory of Scent Blending

At the heart of creating a hair perfume lies the art of scent blending. Fragrances are composed of three main components: top notes, middle notes, and base notes. Understanding these layers is essential for crafting a well-rounded scent.

- **Top Notes:** These are the initial scents perceived upon application, often light and fresh. Examples include citrus oils like lemon and bergamot.
- **Middle Notes:** Also known as heart notes, these scents emerge once the top notes evaporate. They form the core of the fragrance and can include floral scents such as lavender or jasmine.

- **Base Notes:** These are the deep, lasting scents that linger long after the perfume is applied. Common base notes include sandalwood, vanilla, and musk.

The balance between these notes creates a harmonious fragrance. A well-crafted hair perfume should ideally include all three layers to ensure a captivating scent experience.

Common Problems in DIY Hair Perfumes

While the process of creating hair perfumes can be exhilarating, it is not without its challenges. Here are some common issues you may encounter:

- **Overpowering Scents:** One of the most frequent problems is creating a scent that is too strong. This can be mitigated by starting with smaller amounts of essential oils and gradually increasing the concentration.

- **Inconsistent Scent:** If your perfume lacks a cohesive scent profile, consider revisiting your blend ratios. Keeping a scent journal can help you track your formulations and refine your recipes over time.

- **Skin Reactions:** Some essential oils can cause irritation. Always conduct a patch test before using a new ingredient extensively. Diluting essential oils in a carrier oil can also reduce the risk of irritation.

Crafting Your Hair Perfume

To create your own hair perfume or mist, you will need the following materials:

- Essential oils of your choice (e.g., lavender, ylang-ylang, sandalwood)

- A carrier oil (e.g., jojoba oil, fractionated coconut oil) or distilled water

- A small glass spray bottle or roller bottle

- A funnel (optional, for easier pouring)

- A dropper for precise measurements

Basic Recipe for Hair Perfume

Here is a simple recipe to get you started:

1. **Choose Your Base:** For a light mist, use distilled water as your base. For a more moisturizing effect, opt for a carrier oil.
2. **Measure Your Ingredients:** In a 2 oz (60 ml) spray bottle, combine:
   - 1 oz (30 ml) distilled water or carrier oil
   - 20-30 drops of your chosen essential oils (adjust based on preference)
3. **Blend:** If using water, shake the bottle gently before each use to mix the oils, as they will separate.
4. **Label Your Creation:** Don't forget to label your bottle with the scent and date created. This will help you keep track of your favorites!

Example Scents

Here are a few examples of scent combinations you can try:

- **Floral Dream:** Combine 10 drops of lavender, 10 drops of ylang-ylang, and 10 drops of geranium with a carrier oil for a soothing floral scent.
- **Citrus Burst:** Mix 15 drops of lemon, 10 drops of sweet orange, and 5 drops of bergamot in distilled water for a refreshing pick-me-up.
- **Woodland Escape:** Blend 10 drops of cedarwood, 10 drops of sandalwood, and 5 drops of patchouli for an earthy, grounding aroma.

Application Techniques

To use your DIY hair perfume effectively, consider the following application techniques:

- **Spritzing:** Hold the spray bottle about 6-8 inches away from your hair and spritz lightly, focusing on the ends.
- **Roll-On:** For a more targeted application, use a roller bottle to apply the perfume to specific sections of your hair.
- **Layering:** You can also layer your hair perfume with complementary body fragrances for a more complex scent profile.

Conclusion

Creating your own hair perfumes and mists allows you to embrace your individuality while exploring the captivating world of scents. By understanding the theory of scent blending, addressing common problems, and following the practical examples provided, you can craft alluring hair fragrances that enhance your natural allure. Remember to experiment, have fun, and most importantly, celebrate the unique aroma that is authentically you.

Incorporating Pleasant Odors into Hairstyling

In the realm of hairstyling, the incorporation of pleasant odors transcends mere aesthetics; it becomes an integral part of personal expression and allure. The olfactory experience associated with hair can evoke memories, feelings, and even influence attraction. This section explores the theory behind scent in hairstyling, addresses potential problems, and provides practical examples for enhancing your hair's aromatic appeal.

The Theory of Scent in Hair

The human sense of smell, or olfaction, is intricately linked to emotion and memory. According to [1], scents can trigger memories and emotions more effectively than other sensory modalities. This phenomenon can be attributed to the olfactory bulb's direct connections to the limbic system, the part of the brain responsible for emotional responses. Thus, incorporating pleasant odors into hairstyling can create a multi-sensory experience that enhances personal identity and attraction.

Mathematically, we can represent the relationship between scent, memory, and emotional response as follows:

$$E = f(S, M) \tag{59}$$

where E is the emotional response, S is the scent, and M is the memory associated with that scent. This function suggests that a pleasant scent can evoke a positive emotional response, especially if it is tied to a cherished memory.

Problems in Incorporating Odors

While the integration of pleasant odors into hairstyling can be beneficial, it is not without challenges. The following issues may arise:

- **Overpowering Scents:** A common problem is the use of overly strong fragrances that can become overwhelming. This can lead to sensory fatigue or even discomfort for those around.

- **Allergic Reactions:** Some individuals may have sensitivities or allergies to specific fragrance components. This necessitates careful selection of products that minimize potential allergens.

- **Incompatibility with Other Products:** Combining various scented products can lead to clashing aromas. It is essential to consider the overall scent profile when layering products.

To mitigate these issues, it is advisable to choose subtle, complementary scents and to perform patch tests when trying new products.

Practical Examples of Scented Hairstyling

1. **Scented Hair Oils:** Hair oils infused with essential oils such as lavender, rosemary, or jasmine not only nourish the hair but also impart a delightful fragrance. For instance, a blend of jojoba oil and a few drops of rosemary essential oil can create a soothing aroma while providing hydration.

2. **Fragrant Hair Mists:** DIY hair mists can be easily crafted using water, a carrier oil (like argan or coconut oil), and your favorite essential oils. A simple recipe might include:

$$\text{Hair Mist} = \text{Water} + \text{Carrier Oil} + \text{Essential Oil} \quad (60)$$

For example, a refreshing mist could consist of 100 ml of distilled water, 10 ml of argan oil, and 5 drops of peppermint essential oil. Shake well before each use to ensure even distribution.

3. **Scented Hair Accessories:** Incorporating scented hair accessories, such as scrunchies or hair clips infused with fragrance, can provide a long-lasting aromatic experience. Look for products made from fabric that can hold scents or consider DIY options by applying a few drops of essential oil to fabric accessories.

4. **Scented Hair Products:** Many hair care brands now offer scented shampoos, conditioners, and styling products. These products are designed to leave a lingering fragrance on the hair. For example, a coconut-scented shampoo can evoke a tropical vibe, making it an excellent choice for summer styling.

5. **Aromatherapy in Styling:** Utilizing aromatherapy techniques while styling hair can enhance the experience. For instance, diffusing essential oils in the

styling space can create a pleasant atmosphere that complements the scents of the hair products being used.

Conclusion

Incorporating pleasant odors into hairstyling is a powerful way to enhance personal expression and attraction. By understanding the underlying theory, addressing potential problems, and exploring practical examples, individuals can create a signature scent that resonates with their identity. The art of hairstyling is not only about appearance but also about creating an olfactory experience that lingers in the memory, making each encounter unforgettable.

Bibliography

[1] Herz, R. S. (2004). *A naturalistic approach to the study of odor-evoked memory.* In *Memory and Emotion* (pp. 29-41). Psychology Press.

Charming Fragrances for Scalp and Strands

In the realm of personal aroma, the hair often goes overlooked, yet it possesses a unique ability to retain and radiate scents. The charming fragrances for scalp and strands can transform an ordinary hair care routine into an olfactory delight, enhancing not just your hair's appeal but also your overall presence. This section delves into the intricacies of hair fragrances, exploring the science behind scent retention, the problems faced in achieving desirable aromas, and examples of effective fragrant products.

The Science of Hair Fragrance Retention

Hair acts as a natural reservoir for scents due to its porous structure. Each strand of hair is composed of a protein called keratin, which has the ability to absorb and hold onto various aromatic compounds. This phenomenon can be described by the equation:

$$C = \frac{m}{V} \qquad (61)$$

where C is the concentration of the fragrance in the hair, m is the mass of the absorbed scent, and V is the volume of hair. The higher the concentration, the more pronounced the aroma.

The retention of fragrance in hair can be influenced by several factors:

- **Hair Type:** Different hair types (straight, wavy, curly) have varying porosity levels, affecting how scents are absorbed. Curly hair tends to retain scents better due to its structure.

- **Environmental Factors:** Humidity and temperature can alter scent retention. Warm, humid conditions may enhance the release of fragrance, while dry conditions may lead to quicker evaporation.

- **Product Composition:** The chemical composition of hair care products plays a crucial role. Products containing silicones can create a barrier that locks in scents, while alcohol-based products may evaporate quickly, reducing fragrance longevity.

Common Problems in Hair Fragrance Application

Despite the allure of fragrant hair, several challenges can arise when attempting to achieve and maintain charming scents:

- **Overpowering Odors:** Some hair products contain strong synthetic fragrances that can clash with natural body odors or perfumes, leading to an unpleasant olfactory experience.

- **Fading Fragrance:** Many hair products lose their scent after a few hours, leaving hair smelling stale or unwashed. This issue is particularly prevalent in products with high alcohol content.

- **Allergic Reactions:** Certain individuals may experience allergic reactions to specific fragrance ingredients, leading to scalp irritation or dermatitis.

- **Product Build-Up:** Frequent use of heavily scented products can lead to residue build-up on the scalp and strands, resulting in a weighed-down appearance and diminished fragrance.

Examples of Charming Hair Fragrances

To navigate these challenges, here are some examples of delightful hair fragrances that strike a balance between charm and practicality:

- **Essential Oil Infusions:** Products infused with natural essential oils, such as lavender, rosemary, or peppermint, not only provide enchanting scents but also offer therapeutic benefits for scalp health. For instance, lavender oil is known for its calming properties, while rosemary oil can stimulate hair growth.

- **Scented Hair Mists:** Lightweight hair mists, such as those containing rose water or coconut essence, provide a refreshing burst of fragrance without weighing hair down. These mists can be reapplied throughout the day for an instant pick-me-up.

- **Fragrant Hair Serums:** Serums that combine nourishing oils with subtle fragrances can enhance both the scent and health of hair. Look for products that contain argan oil or jojoba oil, which provide moisture while leaving a delicate aroma.

- **Scented Hair Accessories:** Incorporating scented hair accessories, such as silk scrunchies infused with essential oils, can add an extra layer of fragrance to your hairstyle. These accessories not only look stylish but also release pleasant scents throughout the day.

DIY Hair Fragrance Techniques

For those who prefer a more personalized approach, creating your own hair fragrances can be a rewarding experience. Here are some simple DIY techniques:

1. **Essential Oil Hair Spray:** Combine distilled water with a few drops of your favorite essential oils in a spray bottle. Shake well before use and spritz lightly onto your hair for a refreshing scent.

2. **Scented Hair Oil:** Mix carrier oils, such as coconut or argan oil, with essential oils to create a fragrant hair oil. Apply a small amount to the ends of your hair for a nourishing and aromatic treatment.

3. **Herbal Infusion:** Steep dried herbs, such as chamomile or hibiscus, in hot water. Once cooled, strain the mixture and use it as a hair rinse for a natural scent boost.

Conclusion

In conclusion, charming fragrances for scalp and strands can elevate your hair care routine, making it not just a necessity but a delightful experience. By understanding the science of scent retention, addressing common problems, and exploring various products and DIY techniques, you can embrace the enchanting world of hair fragrances. Remember, your hair is not just a crowning glory; it's an opportunity to express your individuality and allure through scent. So go ahead, let your hair tell a story—one that's as fragrant as it is fabulous.

The Forbidden Allure of Scents in Unwashed Hair

The aroma of unwashed hair occupies a unique position in the spectrum of bodily scents, often oscillating between the realms of taboo and allure. While society generally promotes cleanliness and the frequent washing of hair as a standard of hygiene, the olfactory experience of unwashed hair can evoke a complex blend of nostalgia, intimacy, and even eroticism. This section delves into the psychological and cultural dimensions of hair scents, the biochemical underpinnings of these odors, and the social implications of embracing unwashed hair as a form of personal expression.

The Psychological Dimension of Hair Scents

The scent of unwashed hair can elicit powerful emotional responses, often tied to memories or associations with loved ones. The intimate act of being close to someone with unwashed hair can trigger feelings of comfort and safety, as it often signifies a level of vulnerability and authenticity. This phenomenon can be explained through the lens of attachment theory, which posits that individuals form emotional bonds based on proximity and shared experiences.

$$E = \frac{1}{2}kx^2 \quad (62)$$

where E represents the emotional energy associated with a scent, k is a constant reflecting the strength of the memory, and x is the distance from the source of the scent. As individuals draw closer to someone with unwashed hair, they may experience an increase in emotional energy, creating a powerful connection that transcends mere physical attraction.

Biochemical Basis of Hair Odors

The odors emanating from unwashed hair are primarily the result of sebum, sweat, and environmental factors. Sebum, an oily substance produced by sebaceous glands, plays a crucial role in maintaining hair health but also contributes to its scent profile. The interaction of sebum with bacteria on the scalp leads to the formation of volatile organic compounds (VOCs) that generate distinct odors.

$$\text{VOCs} = \text{Sebum} + \text{Bacterial Metabolism} \quad (63)$$

The bacteria metabolize sebum, resulting in the release of various compounds, such as fatty acids and alcohols, which can produce scents that some may find appealing. For instance, the presence of certain fatty acids, such as hexanoic acid, can impart a mildly sweet and musky scent that is often associated with intimacy and attraction.

Cultural Perspectives on Unwashed Hair

Cultural attitudes towards hair cleanliness vary significantly across different societies. In some cultures, unwashed hair is viewed as a sign of rebellion or nonconformity, while in others, it may symbolize a deep connection to one's roots and heritage. The rise of the "dirty hair" movement, particularly among artistic and bohemian communities, celebrates unwashed hair as a form of self-expression and individuality.

This cultural shift can be attributed to the broader societal movement towards authenticity and natural beauty. Many individuals are increasingly rejecting conventional beauty standards, choosing instead to embrace their natural hair textures and scents. This rebellion against the norm is encapsulated in the phrase, "Let your hair down," which suggests a liberation from societal expectations.

Examples and Case Studies

Numerous examples illustrate the allure of unwashed hair in both popular culture and personal anecdotes. In literature, characters who embody a free-spirited nature often possess unkempt hair, symbolizing their rejection of societal norms. For instance, the character of Holly Golightly in Truman Capote's *Breakfast at Tiffany's* is frequently depicted with tousled hair, embodying a sense of carefree elegance that captivates those around her.

In contemporary fashion, models and influencers often showcase unwashed hair as part of their aesthetic, challenging traditional beauty standards. The rise of "grunge" and "effortless" hairstyles in fashion campaigns highlights the appeal of a more relaxed and natural approach to hair care.

Moreover, personal anecdotes reveal that many individuals find the scent of unwashed hair to be comforting and intimate. A survey conducted among college students revealed that a significant percentage of respondents associated the scent of unwashed hair with feelings of nostalgia and emotional warmth, often linking it to memories of close relationships or carefree days spent with friends.

Conclusion

The forbidden allure of scents in unwashed hair serves as a testament to the complexity of human attraction and intimacy. By embracing the unique aromas of unwashed hair, individuals can tap into a deeper understanding of their own identities and the connections they forge with others. In a world that often prioritizes cleanliness and conformity, the acceptance of unwashed hair as a symbol of authenticity and sensuality invites a refreshing perspective on beauty and personal expression.

As we continue to explore the intricate relationship between scent and attraction, it becomes clear that the allure of unwashed hair is not merely a matter of hygiene, but rather a celebration of individuality, intimacy, and the raw, unfiltered essence of human experience.

Scented Hair Accessories for Subtle Seduction

In the realm of personal allure, the subtlety of scent can often be the most persuasive form of seduction. Hair accessories, often overlooked in the pursuit of olfactory charm, present a unique opportunity to infuse one's presence with an enticing aroma. This section explores the art and science behind scented hair accessories, delving into their historical significance, practical applications, and the psychological impact they may have on attraction.

The Allure of Scented Hair Accessories

Historically, hair has been a focal point of beauty and attraction. From ancient civilizations adorning their tresses with fragrant oils to modern fashionistas utilizing scented hair products, the interplay of hair and scent has long been recognized as a potent combination. Scented hair accessories—ranging from clips and bands to decorative combs—serve not only as functional items but also as carriers of alluring fragrances.

The Science Behind Scented Hair Accessories

The olfactory system is intricately linked to memory and emotion. When a scent is associated with a particular individual or experience, it can evoke powerful feelings and memories. This phenomenon is explained through the *Proustian phenomenon*, where a specific smell can trigger vivid recollections. This connection can be harnessed through scented hair accessories, allowing individuals to leave a lasting impression on those they encounter.

$$S = \sum_{i=1}^{n} w_i \cdot s_i \qquad (64)$$

Where:

- S = overall scent profile
- w_i = weight of each scent component
- s_i = intensity of each scent component

The equation above illustrates how different scents can be blended to create a unique and personalized aroma that emanates from hair accessories. The careful selection of scent components can enhance the overall olfactory experience, making it more appealing to others.

Crafting Scented Hair Accessories

Creating your own scented hair accessories can be a delightful and intimate process. Here are some steps to guide you in crafting these alluring items:

1. **Choose Your Base:** Select hair accessories made from natural materials such as wood, fabric, or leather, which can absorb and retain scents better than synthetic materials.

2. **Select Your Fragrance:** Use essential oils or perfume oils that resonate with your personal style. Popular choices include lavender for relaxation, jasmine for sensuality, and sandalwood for warmth.

3. **Application:** Lightly dab or spray the chosen fragrance onto the accessory. Allow it to dry completely to prevent staining hair or skin.

4. **Layering Scents:** Consider layering different scents for a complex aroma. For example, pairing floral notes with earthy undertones can create a captivating blend.

5. **Maintenance:** Refresh the scent periodically to maintain its allure. This can be done by reapplying the fragrance or by using scented hair sprays designed for this purpose.

Examples of Scented Hair Accessories

1. **Scented Hair Clips:** These can be infused with essential oils and used to hold hair in place while releasing a subtle fragrance throughout the day. For instance, a rose-scented clip can evoke feelings of romance and femininity.

2. **Aromatic Hair Bands:** Crafted from fabric infused with fragrance, these bands can be worn during workouts or casual outings, providing a refreshing scent that enhances your presence.

3. **Perfumed Hair Combs:** Combs made from natural wood can be treated with oils to impart a lingering scent. The act of combing one's hair can also distribute the fragrance throughout the hair, creating a delightful olfactory experience.

4. **Scented Hair Scarves:** Scarves made from soft materials can be lightly scented and worn in the hair or around the neck, offering a versatile accessory that can be both stylish and aromatic.

Psychological Impact of Scented Hair Accessories

The psychological effects of scent are profound. Research indicates that pleasant aromas can enhance mood and increase perceived attractiveness. A study published in the *Journal of Personality and Social Psychology* found that individuals wearing pleasant scents were perceived as more attractive, sociable, and confident.

When scented hair accessories are employed, they not only enhance the wearer's appeal but also create an inviting atmosphere for social interactions. The scent acts as a non-verbal cue that can draw others closer, fostering connection and intimacy.

Conclusion

Scented hair accessories are a powerful yet subtle tool for enhancing personal allure. By understanding the science of scent, crafting personalized accessories, and recognizing the psychological impact of aroma, individuals can elevate their presence and leave a lasting impression. In a world where first impressions matter, the art of scented hair accessories offers a unique avenue for seduction—one that is both enchanting and intimate.

Aromatherapy with Essential Oils for Hair

Aromatherapy, the practice of using essential oils for therapeutic purposes, has gained significant traction in the realm of hair care. This section delves into the benefits of essential oils, the science behind their efficacy, and practical applications for enhancing hair health and scent.

The Science of Essential Oils

Essential oils are concentrated plant extracts that capture the natural fragrance and beneficial properties of the source plant. They contain volatile compounds that can influence both physical and emotional well-being. The chemical composition of essential oils varies widely, but they generally contain terpenes, alcohols, esters, and phenols, which contribute to their aromatic and therapeutic properties.

The primary mechanism through which essential oils exert their effects is through olfactory stimulation. When inhaled, the molecules travel through the nasal cavity and stimulate the olfactory receptors, sending signals to the brain's limbic system, which is responsible for emotions and memories. This connection explains why certain scents can evoke strong emotional responses or memories, making them powerful tools in aromatherapy.

Benefits of Essential Oils for Hair

1. **Nourishment and Moisture**: Many essential oils possess emollient properties that help to hydrate and nourish the hair. Oils such as *argan oil* and *jojoba oil* mimic the natural sebum produced by the scalp, providing moisture without weighing the hair down.

2. **Scalp Health**: Essential oils like *tea tree oil* and *peppermint oil* have antifungal and antibacterial properties that can help maintain a healthy scalp. These oils can combat dandruff, itchiness, and other scalp conditions, promoting a conducive environment for hair growth.

3. **Strengthening and Growth**: Oils such as *rosemary oil* and *lavender oil* are known for their ability to stimulate blood circulation to the scalp, potentially enhancing hair growth. Studies have shown that rosemary oil can increase hair count and thickness, making it a popular choice for those looking to improve hair density.

4. **Fragrance and Mood Enhancement**: The aromatic properties of essential oils can uplift mood and create a calming atmosphere. Oils like *ylang-ylang* and *geranium* not only impart a pleasant scent to hair but can also reduce stress and anxiety.

Formulating Essential Oil Hair Treatments

Creating your own essential oil hair treatments is an accessible way to incorporate aromatherapy into your hair care routine. Here are a few formulations to consider:

1. Scalp Treatment for Dandruff

- Ingredients:
    - 2 tablespoons of carrier oil (e.g., coconut oil or jojoba oil)
    - 5 drops of tea tree oil

- 5 drops of lavender oil

- Instructions:

    1. Mix the carrier oil with the essential oils in a small bowl.
    2. Apply the mixture directly to the scalp, massaging gently for 5-10 minutes.
    3. Leave it on for at least 30 minutes before washing it out with shampoo.

2. Nourishing Hair Serum

- Ingredients:

    - 1 tablespoon of argan oil
    - 3 drops of rosemary oil
    - 3 drops of ylang-ylang oil

- Instructions:

    1. Combine all ingredients in a small dropper bottle.
    2. Apply a few drops to the ends of the hair after washing and towel-drying.
    3. Style as usual; this will help to seal in moisture and add shine.

3. Refreshing Hair Mist

- Ingredients:

    - 1 cup of distilled water
    - 10 drops of peppermint oil
    - 5 drops of bergamot oil

- Instructions:

    1. Combine the water and essential oils in a spray bottle.
    2. Shake well before each use.
    3. Spray lightly onto hair for a refreshing scent throughout the day.

Potential Issues and Considerations

While essential oils offer numerous benefits, there are some important considerations to keep in mind:
 - **Skin Sensitivity**: Essential oils are highly concentrated and can cause skin irritation or allergic reactions in some individuals. It is recommended to perform a patch test before using a new oil.
 - **Dilution**: Always dilute essential oils with a carrier oil before applying them to the scalp or hair. This prevents irritation and enhances absorption.
 - **Quality of Oils**: The efficacy of essential oils is highly dependent on their quality. Look for pure, therapeutic-grade oils without additives or synthetic fragrances.
 - **Consultation**: If you have pre-existing conditions or are pregnant, consult with a healthcare provider before using essential oils.

Conclusion

Incorporating aromatherapy with essential oils into your hair care routine can enhance not only the health and appearance of your hair but also your overall well-being. By understanding the science behind these powerful plant extracts and utilizing them thoughtfully, you can create a personalized hair care regimen that celebrates both beauty and individuality. Embrace the allure of essential oils and transform your hair care experience into a fragrant journey of self-expression and care.

The Ceremony of Hair-Scented Pillows

In the realm of intimate experiences, the allure of scent is often overlooked, yet it plays a pivotal role in creating atmospheres of comfort and seduction. One of the most enchanting ways to enhance personal aroma is through the art of hair-scented pillows. This practice not only elevates the sensory experience of rest but also intertwines the intimate connection between scent, memory, and attraction.

The Science Behind Hair Scents

Hair, often regarded as a mere aesthetic feature, is a potent reservoir for scents. The structure of hair, composed primarily of keratin, can trap and retain fragrances effectively. This phenomenon occurs due to the porous nature of hair strands, which allows them to absorb and hold onto various aromatic compounds. When we consider the average individual's hair care routine, it becomes evident that the products used—shampoos, conditioners, and styling products—often come infused with fragrances designed to linger.

$$\text{Scent Retention} = \frac{\text{Volume of Fragrance Absorbed}}{\text{Volume of Hair}} \times 100$$

This equation illustrates the capacity of hair to retain scent, where a higher percentage signifies a more fragrant mane. The retention of scent can be influenced by several factors, including hair type, product choice, and environmental conditions.

Creating the Ideal Hair-Scented Pillow

To embark on the ceremony of hair-scented pillows, one must first curate the perfect pillow. This involves selecting a pillowcase made from natural fibers, such as cotton or silk, which are known for their breathability and softness. The choice of fabric is crucial, as synthetic materials may not allow scents to diffuse effectively.

Next, the infusion of scent into the pillowcase can be achieved through various methods:

- **Scented Hair Oils:** Applying a few drops of hair oil infused with essential oils can create a delightful aroma that permeates the pillow. Lavender, chamomile, or sandalwood are excellent choices for their calming properties.

- **Fragrant Sprays:** Homemade or store-bought pillow sprays can be misted onto the pillowcase. A simple concoction of water and essential oils can serve as a refreshing option.

- **Scented Sachets:** Placing sachets filled with dried herbs and flowers, such as rosemary or jasmine, inside the pillowcase can provide a natural and long-lasting fragrance.

The Ritual of Infusion

The infusion process can be considered a ceremonial act, one that requires intention and mindfulness. Begin by selecting a time when you can engage fully in the ritual. Dim the lights, play soft music, and set the mood for this olfactory experience.

1. **Prepare Your Materials:** Gather your chosen oils or sprays, the pillowcase, and any additional elements like herbs or flowers. 2. **Cleanse the Space:** Light a candle or incense to purify the environment, creating a sacred space for your ceremony. 3. **Infuse the Pillow:** As you apply the scent to the

pillowcase, visualize the calming and comforting effects it will have on your mind and body. This mindfulness can enhance the overall experience, making it more personal and intimate. 4. **Allow to Settle:** After applying the scent, allow the pillow to rest for a few moments. This waiting period allows the fragrance to settle into the fabric, ensuring a more potent release when you lay your head down.

The Psychological Impact of Scented Pillows

The psychological effects of scent are profound. Research has shown that certain smells can evoke memories and emotions, making hair-scented pillows not just a sensory delight, but also a gateway to nostalgia and comfort. The scent of a loved one's hair, for instance, can trigger feelings of safety and warmth, enhancing intimacy in relationships.

Furthermore, the act of sleeping on a scented pillow can improve sleep quality. Aromatherapy studies indicate that scents like lavender can promote relaxation and reduce anxiety, leading to a more restful night's sleep. This can be particularly beneficial for individuals who struggle with insomnia or stress.

Examples and Cultural Practices

Across various cultures, the significance of scent in personal care and intimacy is celebrated. In many Asian traditions, for instance, the use of scented pillows is common, with herbal infusions believed to promote health and well-being. In Western cultures, the rise of aromatherapy has popularized the use of scented products in bedrooms, emphasizing the importance of creating a soothing environment for sleep.

One notable example is the use of jasmine-scented pillows in Indian households, where the fragrance is associated with love and affection. In contrast, the French have a penchant for lavender, often incorporating it into their bedding rituals for its calming properties.

Challenges and Considerations

While the ceremony of hair-scented pillows offers numerous benefits, it is essential to consider potential challenges:

- **Allergies and Sensitivities:** Some individuals may be sensitive to certain fragrances, leading to allergic reactions. It is crucial to choose scents that are hypoallergenic and to test them in small amounts.

- **Longevity of Scent:** The scent may fade over time, necessitating regular reapplication. Understanding the longevity of different fragrance types can help in maintaining the desired aroma.

- **Personal Preferences:** Each individual has unique scent preferences. Engaging in conversations about scent choices with partners can enhance intimacy and ensure a mutually enjoyable experience.

Conclusion

The ceremony of hair-scented pillows is more than just a simple practice; it is an exploration of the profound connection between scent, intimacy, and personal expression. By embracing this ritual, individuals can enhance their sensory experiences, promote relaxation, and deepen connections with themselves and others. Ultimately, the art of infusing pillows with alluring scents transforms an ordinary object into a vessel of comfort and attraction, celebrating the beautiful complexity of human olfaction.

The Undeniable Attraction of Hair Perfume

In the world of personal fragrance, hair perfume emerges as a unique and alluring form of olfactory expression. Unlike traditional perfumes, which are typically applied to the skin, hair perfumes are specifically formulated to adhere to hair fibers, providing a lingering scent that dances with movement and captures attention. The undeniable attraction of hair perfume lies not only in its captivating aroma but also in the intricate interplay of scent, texture, and personal identity.

The Science of Hair and Fragrance

Hair is an organic material that possesses unique properties conducive to scent retention. The structure of hair, consisting of the cuticle, cortex, and medulla, allows it to absorb and hold fragrances effectively. This absorption is influenced by several factors:

$$\text{Retention Rate} \propto \text{Hair Porosity} \times \text{Fragrance Composition} \quad (65)$$

Where: - *Retention Rate* is the ability of hair to hold scent, - *Hair Porosity* refers to the hair's ability to absorb moisture and substances, - *Fragrance Composition* indicates the blend of essential oils and aromatic compounds in the hair perfume.

Hair with higher porosity, often seen in curly or damaged hair, tends to retain scents more effectively, making it an ideal canvas for hair perfumes. The choice of fragrance composition is equally crucial; lighter, more volatile compounds are often used in hair perfumes to ensure they evaporate slowly, releasing their scent gradually over time.

Cultural and Historical Context

Historically, hair has been associated with personal identity and cultural expression. In many cultures, hair is seen as a symbol of beauty, power, and sensuality. The use of scented oils and perfumes in hair care dates back to ancient civilizations. For example, in ancient Egypt, oils infused with fragrant herbs and flowers were used to adorn the hair, signifying status and attracting attention.

The modern resurgence of hair perfumes can be linked to the growing trend of personalized beauty products. As individuals seek to express their unique identities, hair perfume serves as an extension of personal style, allowing one to curate a signature scent that resonates with their essence.

The Allure of Hair Perfume in Modern Beauty

In contemporary beauty culture, hair perfumes have gained immense popularity, driven by their ability to enhance one's olfactory presence without the overwhelming intensity of traditional fragrances. The allure of hair perfume lies in several key aspects:

- **Subtlety and Sophistication:** Hair perfumes offer a more nuanced approach to scent application. Unlike body sprays that can be overpowering, hair perfumes provide a gentle, lingering aroma that captivates without overwhelming.

- **Versatility:** Hair perfumes can be used in various settings, from casual outings to formal events. They can be layered with other fragrances or worn alone, allowing individuals to customize their scent experience.

- **Sensory Experience:** The act of applying hair perfume becomes a sensory ritual. The soft mist enveloping the hair creates a moment of indulgence, transforming a simple grooming routine into an aromatic experience.

- **Movement and Dynamic Scent:** As hair moves, the scent is released in a delicate dance, creating an olfactory trail that captures attention. This dynamic quality enhances the allure of the wearer, making hair perfume a potent tool for attraction.

Challenges and Considerations

Despite the undeniable attraction of hair perfume, there are challenges associated with its use. One primary concern is the potential for damage to hair fibers. Many traditional perfumes contain alcohol, which can lead to dryness and brittleness. Hair perfumes, therefore, must be formulated with care, using nourishing ingredients that promote hair health while delivering fragrance.

$$\text{Hair Health} = \text{Nourishing Ingredients} - \text{Alcohol Content} \qquad (66)$$

Where: - *Hair Health* is the overall condition of the hair, - *Nourishing Ingredients* include oils and extracts that benefit hair, - *Alcohol Content* refers to the presence of drying agents in the formula.

Furthermore, individuals with sensitivities to fragrances must approach hair perfumes with caution. It is essential to choose products with hypoallergenic formulations to minimize the risk of adverse reactions.

Examples of Hair Perfume Brands

Several brands have successfully captured the essence of hair perfume, each offering unique formulations that appeal to a diverse audience. Notable examples include:

- **Ouai Haircare:** Known for its luxurious hair products, Ouai offers a signature hair perfume that combines notes of rose, bergamot, and white musk, creating a sophisticated and alluring scent.

- **Byredo:** This high-end fragrance house has ventured into hair perfumes with its unique offerings, such as the "Hair Perfume" line that features iconic scents like "Gypsy Water" and "Bal d'Afrique," designed to linger on hair beautifully.

- **Chanel:** The legendary French brand has embraced the hair perfume trend with its "Chanel No. 5 Hair Mist," allowing fans of the classic scent to enjoy its timeless aroma in a lightweight, hair-friendly formula.

Conclusion

The undeniable attraction of hair perfume lies in its ability to enhance personal expression, evoke sensuality, and create a captivating presence. As individuals continue to seek unique ways to express their identities, hair perfume stands out as a powerful tool in the realm of olfactory artistry. By embracing the science, history, and allure of hair perfumes, one can unlock a new dimension of fragrance that not only complements their style but also captivates those around them.

In a world where scent has the power to evoke memories, emotions, and connections, hair perfume serves as a reminder that the most alluring fragrances are often found in the simplest of gestures—like a gentle sway of hair, carrying with it an unforgettable essence.

Revolutionary Mouth Odors

Fresh Breath Tips for Desired Effects

Achieving fresh breath is an art form that transcends mere minty freshness; it is an essential component of attraction and intimacy. The chemistry of breath, influenced by diet, oral hygiene, and even emotional state, plays a pivotal role in how we are perceived by others. This section explores effective strategies for maintaining desirable breath while delving into the science behind breath freshness.

Understanding Oral Microbiota

The mouth is home to a complex ecosystem of bacteria, known as the oral microbiota. These microorganisms play a crucial role in the breakdown of food particles, but they can also produce volatile sulfur compounds (VSCs), which are often responsible for bad breath (halitosis). The balance of this microbial community is essential; an imbalance can lead to undesirable odors.

$$\text{VSCs} = (\text{Proteins}) \times (\text{Bacterial Activity}) \qquad (67)$$

To maintain a healthy balance, it is essential to adopt practices that promote beneficial bacteria while minimizing harmful strains.

Optimal Oral Hygiene Practices

1. **Brushing and Flossing**: Regular brushing (at least twice daily) and flossing (once daily) are fundamental. Use fluoride toothpaste to prevent decay and plaque buildup. Brushing the tongue is equally important, as it harbors bacteria that contribute to bad breath.

$$\text{Plaque Reduction} \propto \text{Frequency of Brushing} + \text{Flossing} \qquad (68)$$

2. **Mouthwash**: An antibacterial mouthwash can help reduce the number of bacteria in the mouth. Look for products containing chlorhexidine or

cetylpyridinium chloride, which are effective against bacteria responsible for bad breath.

Dietary Choices for Fresh Breath

What you consume significantly impacts your breath. Here are some dietary tips for maintaining fresh breath:

1. **Hydration**: Drinking water throughout the day helps wash away food particles and bacteria. A hydrated mouth produces more saliva, which acts as a natural cleanser.

$$\text{Saliva Production} \propto \text{Hydration Level} \tag{69}$$

2. **Crunchy Fruits and Vegetables**: Foods like apples, carrots, and celery are not only nutritious but also help in mechanically cleaning teeth and stimulating saliva production.

3. **Herbs and Spices**: Chewing fresh herbs like parsley, mint, or basil can neutralize odors due to their high chlorophyll content and antimicrobial properties.

4. **Avoiding Odorous Foods**: Limit consumption of garlic, onions, and certain spices, which contain compounds that linger in the mouth and bloodstream long after consumption.

Natural Remedies for Fresh Breath

In addition to traditional oral hygiene practices, several natural remedies can enhance breath freshness:

1. **Green Tea**: Rich in polyphenols, green tea can inhibit the growth of bacteria that cause bad breath. Drinking a cup of green tea daily can provide both hydration and breath-freshening benefits.

2. **Apple Cider Vinegar**: A diluted solution of apple cider vinegar can be used as a mouth rinse to help balance oral pH and reduce bacteria.

$$\text{pH Balance} = \frac{\text{Acidity of Vinegar}}{\text{Saliva Production}} \tag{70}$$

3. **Baking Soda**: Brushing with baking soda can neutralize odors and whiten teeth. Its alkaline nature helps to balance the pH in the mouth, reducing acidity that promotes bacterial growth.

The Role of Breath Freshening Products

Incorporating breath-freshening products into your routine can provide immediate results:

1. **Sugar-Free Gum**: Chewing gum stimulates saliva production and can help mask bad breath. Look for xylitol-sweetened varieties that also combat bacteria.
2. **Mints and Lozenges**: These can be effective for a quick fix but should not replace good oral hygiene practices. Choose products that contain natural ingredients for added benefits.

Understanding the Psychological Aspect of Breath

Fresh breath is not just a physical attribute; it has psychological implications as well. Studies have shown that individuals with fresh breath are often perceived as more attractive and approachable. The confidence that comes from knowing your breath is fresh can enhance social interactions and intimacy.

$$\text{Attractiveness} \propto \text{Breath Freshness} + \text{Confidence} \qquad (71)$$

Conclusion

Maintaining fresh breath requires a multifaceted approach that includes proper oral hygiene, dietary considerations, and the use of natural remedies. By understanding the science behind breath freshness and implementing these strategies, one can enhance their appeal and foster intimate connections. Remember, fresh breath is not just about masking odors; it's about embracing the art of attraction through personal care and confidence.

Using Natural Mouthwashes for Sexy Smiles

In the pursuit of an alluring smile, the role of oral hygiene cannot be overstated. While conventional mouthwashes often contain synthetic ingredients and strong alcohols that can lead to dryness and irritation, natural mouthwashes offer an alternative that not only freshens breath but also enhances the overall health of your mouth. This section explores the benefits, formulations, and some DIY recipes for natural mouthwashes that can contribute to a sexy smile.

The Importance of Oral Hygiene

Oral hygiene is crucial not only for maintaining fresh breath but also for overall health. Studies have shown that poor oral hygiene can lead to various health issues, including gum disease, heart disease, and diabetes. A fresh and healthy mouth is often perceived as attractive, making the pursuit of an appealing smile a worthy endeavor.

Common Problems with Conventional Mouthwashes

Conventional mouthwashes often contain ingredients such as alcohol, artificial sweeteners, and synthetic flavors that can cause more harm than good. Some of the common issues associated with these products include:

- **Dry Mouth:** Alcohol-based mouthwashes can lead to xerostomia, or dry mouth, which can create an environment conducive to bad breath and oral infections.

- **Irritation:** Artificial ingredients can irritate the mucous membranes in the mouth, leading to discomfort and sensitivity.

- **Altered Taste:** Strong flavors can mask natural tastes, diminishing the enjoyment of food and beverages.

The Benefits of Natural Mouthwashes

Natural mouthwashes, on the other hand, can provide a plethora of benefits without the drawbacks of their conventional counterparts. Some of these benefits include:

- **Moisturizing Properties:** Many natural mouthwashes use ingredients like aloe vera or glycerin, which help to keep the mouth hydrated.

- **Antimicrobial Effects:** Essential oils such as tea tree oil, peppermint, and clove have natural antimicrobial properties that can help reduce harmful bacteria in the mouth.

- **Fresh Breath:** Natural ingredients like baking soda and essential oils can neutralize odors effectively without the use of artificial fragrances.

Key Ingredients for Natural Mouthwashes

When creating or selecting a natural mouthwash, consider the following ingredients that contribute to oral health and breath freshness:

- **Baking Soda:** Known for its ability to neutralize acids and odors, baking soda can help maintain a balanced pH in the mouth.

- **Essential Oils:** Oils such as peppermint, eucalyptus, and tea tree are not only aromatic but also possess antibacterial properties.

- **Apple Cider Vinegar:** This ingredient can help with pH balancing and has antimicrobial properties, making it a popular choice in natural mouthwash recipes.

- **Aloe Vera:** Known for its soothing properties, aloe vera can help reduce inflammation and promote healing in the mouth.

DIY Natural Mouthwash Recipes

Creating your own natural mouthwash can be both fun and rewarding. Here are a couple of simple recipes to get you started:

Recipe 1: Basic Baking Soda Mouthwash

- **Ingredients:**
  - 1 cup of distilled water
  - 1 teaspoon of baking soda
  - 2 drops of peppermint essential oil

- **Instructions:**
  1. In a clean bottle, combine distilled water and baking soda.
  2. Add the peppermint essential oil and mix well.
  3. Shake before use and swish in your mouth for 30 seconds before spitting out.

Recipe 2: Herbal Infusion Mouthwash

- **Ingredients:**
  - 1 cup of distilled water
  - 1 tablespoon of dried chamomile or calendula
  - 2 drops of tea tree essential oil

- **Instructions:**
  1. Boil the distilled water and steep the dried herbs for about 15 minutes.

2. Strain the liquid into a clean bottle and let it cool.

3. Add the tea tree essential oil, mix well, and store in the refrigerator.

4. Use as a mouthwash by swishing for 30 seconds before spitting out.

Using Natural Mouthwash Effectively

To maximize the benefits of your natural mouthwash, consider the following tips:

- **Frequency:** Use your natural mouthwash twice daily after brushing your teeth for optimal freshness.

- **Storage:** Store your mouthwash in a cool, dark place to preserve the integrity of the natural ingredients.

- **Consultation:** If you have specific oral health concerns, consult with a dental professional before making significant changes to your oral care routine.

Conclusion

Incorporating natural mouthwashes into your oral hygiene routine can not only enhance your smile but also elevate your overall health. By choosing ingredients that promote freshness and well-being, you can achieve a sexy smile that is both attractive and healthy. Embrace the power of nature and let your smile shine with confidence.

Aromatic Gums and Mints for Irresistible Kisses

In the realm of attraction, the power of a kiss cannot be overstated. It serves as a gateway to intimacy, a silent language that conveys desire and affection. However, the effectiveness of a kiss can be significantly enhanced by the aromatic qualities of the breath. This section delves into the world of aromatic gums and mints, exploring their role in creating irresistible kisses that linger in memory.

The Science of Breath and Attraction

The olfactory system plays a crucial role in human attraction. According to research, our sense of smell is closely linked to emotional responses and memory. The phenomenon known as the *Proustian memory effect* illustrates how scents can evoke vivid memories and feelings. In the context of kissing, fresh and appealing breath can enhance the overall sensory experience, making the moment more memorable.

$$\text{Attraction} \propto \text{Pleasant Odor} + \text{Emotional Response} \qquad (72)$$

This relationship suggests that incorporating aromatic gums and mints into one's oral hygiene routine can elevate the experience of kissing. The freshness they provide acts as a catalyst for attraction, enhancing both the physical and emotional aspects of intimacy.

Choosing the Right Aromatic Gums and Mints

When selecting gums and mints for optimal kissing experiences, consider the following factors:

- **Flavor Profile:** Choose flavors that are universally appealing, such as peppermint, spearmint, or cinnamon. These flavors not only freshen breath but also stimulate the senses.

- **Sugar-Free Options:** Opt for sugar-free varieties to avoid the risk of dental issues. Sugar-free gums often contain xylitol, which can help reduce cavity-causing bacteria in the mouth.

- **Duration of Freshness:** Look for products that offer long-lasting flavor. The ability to maintain fresh breath over time is essential for spontaneous moments of intimacy.

The Role of Ingredients in Aromatic Gums and Mints

The ingredients in aromatic gums and mints can significantly impact their effectiveness and appeal. Key components include:

- **Essential Oils:** Many gums and mints incorporate essential oils such as peppermint oil or spearmint oil, which provide a refreshing flavor and aroma. These oils can also have antibacterial properties, contributing to oral health.

- **Herbal Extracts:** Ingredients like green tea extract or eucalyptus can add unique flavors and additional health benefits, enhancing the overall experience.

- **Natural Sweeteners:** Using natural sweeteners like stevia or monk fruit can provide sweetness without the drawbacks of sugar, making the gum more appealing.

Practical Applications: Enhancing Kissing with Aromatic Products

Incorporating aromatic gums and mints into your routine can be both practical and pleasurable. Consider the following strategies:

- **Pre-Kiss Preparation:** Before a date or intimate moment, chew a piece of aromatic gum or pop a mint. This simple act can boost confidence and ensure that your breath is kiss-ready.

- **Sharing the Experience:** Offer a mint to your partner as a playful gesture. This not only freshens both parties' breath but also creates a shared moment of intimacy.

- **Post-Kiss Freshening:** After an intimate kiss, discreetly pop a mint to maintain freshness. This can enhance the overall experience and encourage further kisses.

Potential Problems and Considerations

While aromatic gums and mints can significantly enhance kissing experiences, there are potential pitfalls to be aware of:

- **Overpowering Flavors:** Some individuals may find certain flavors too strong or overwhelming. It's essential to choose products with balanced flavors to ensure mutual enjoyment.

- **Allergies and Sensitivities:** Be mindful of any allergies or sensitivities your partner may have to specific ingredients. Always opt for products that are free from common allergens.

- **Breath Masking vs. Freshening:** While aromatic gums and mints can mask unpleasant odors, they should not replace proper oral hygiene. Regular brushing and flossing are vital for maintaining fresh breath.

Conclusion

Aromatic gums and mints are more than mere breath fresheners; they are tools for enhancing intimacy and attraction. By understanding the science behind olfactory attraction and selecting the right products, individuals can elevate their kissing experiences to new heights. Embrace the power of aromatic gums and mints, and unlock the potential for irresistible kisses that leave a lasting impression.

$$\text{Irresistible Kisses} = \text{Fresh Breath} + \text{Emotional Connection} \qquad (73)$$

Delicious Foods That Enhance Oral Odors

The olfactory experience of kissing or intimate moments can be significantly influenced by the foods we consume. Understanding the relationship between diet and oral odors can enhance personal appeal and intimacy. This section explores delicious foods that can enhance oral odors, presenting a blend of culinary delights and their olfactory impacts.

The Science of Taste and Smell

The connection between taste and smell is a fundamental aspect of human perception. According to [?], approximately 80% of what we perceive as taste is actually derived from our sense of smell. This phenomenon is particularly important when considering how certain foods can influence the aromas emitted from the mouth. The olfactory receptors in our nasal cavity interact with volatile compounds released from food during digestion, contributing to the overall scent profile of our breath.

Key Components in Foods

Certain foods contain compounds that can either enhance or detract from the attractiveness of oral odors. The following components are particularly noteworthy:

- **Volatile Sulfur Compounds (VSCs):** Found in foods like garlic and onions, VSCs are notorious for their strong odors. While they can lead to less desirable breath, they can also create a unique allure when consumed in moderation.

- **Essential Oils:** Foods such as mint, basil, and citrus fruits contain essential oils that can freshen breath. These oils not only mask unpleasant odors but also contribute to a more appealing scent.

- **Natural Sugars:** Fruits like apples and strawberries can promote saliva production, which helps wash away food particles and bacteria that cause bad breath. Additionally, their natural sweetness can enhance the overall aroma of the mouth.

Delicious Foods to Enhance Oral Odors

Here are some delectable options that can enhance your oral aromas:

1. **Mint:** The classic herb is a natural breath freshener. Mint leaves contain menthol, which has a cooling effect and can leave a refreshing scent. Incorporating mint into your diet can be as simple as adding fresh mint to salads, smoothies, or teas.

2. **Citrus Fruits:** Oranges, lemons, and grapefruits are rich in vitamin C and contain citric acid, which can help neutralize odors. The refreshing scent of citrus can linger on the breath, making it more appealing. Enjoy citrus fruits as snacks or in salads for a zesty addition.

3. **Berries:** Strawberries and blueberries are not only delicious but also packed with antioxidants. Their natural sweetness and juiciness can help cleanse the palate and combat bad breath. Consider blending them into smoothies or enjoying them as a snack.

4. **Yogurt:** Probiotic-rich yogurt can help balance the bacteria in the mouth, reducing the presence of odor-causing bacteria. Opt for plain yogurt with live cultures, and consider adding honey or fresh fruit for flavor.

5. **Cheese:** Certain cheeses, such as aged cheddar and gouda, can help neutralize odors due to their fat content, which binds to sulfur compounds. Enjoy cheese as part of a balanced diet, but be mindful of the quantity to avoid excess fat intake.

6. **Green Tea:** Rich in polyphenols, green tea can inhibit the growth of bacteria that cause bad breath. Sipping on green tea not only refreshes the palate but also provides a pleasant aroma. Try incorporating green tea into your daily routine as a flavorful beverage.

7. **Apples:** The crunchy texture of apples stimulates saliva production, which helps cleanse the mouth. Their natural sweetness and crispness make them a delightful snack that can enhance oral odors.

Potential Pitfalls and Considerations

While many foods can enhance oral odors, it is essential to be mindful of potential pitfalls:

- **Garlic and Onions:** While they can add depth to culinary experiences, these foods can lead to strong, lingering odors. Moderation is key to enjoying their flavors without compromising breath.

- **Dairy Products:** Certain dairy products can lead to the production of mucus, which may contribute to bad breath. Individuals who are lactose intolerant may experience more pronounced effects.

- **Sugary Foods:** Excessive consumption of sugary snacks can lead to tooth decay and bad breath. Opt for natural sugars found in fruits instead of processed candies.

Conclusion

The foods we choose to consume can significantly influence the aromas we emit during intimate moments. By incorporating delicious options like mint, citrus fruits, and yogurt into our diets, we can enhance our oral odors and create a more appealing olfactory experience. Understanding the science behind taste and smell allows us to make informed choices that not only satisfy our palates but also elevate our charm and desirability.

Oral Hygiene Routines for Attractive Breath

The quest for attractive breath is an intricate dance of science, routine, and personal expression. This section delves into the essential components of effective oral hygiene routines, focusing on their impact on breath freshness and overall oral health.

The Importance of Oral Hygiene

Maintaining oral hygiene is paramount not only for aesthetic reasons but also for health. Poor oral hygiene can lead to the accumulation of plaque, a biofilm of bacteria that can produce volatile sulfur compounds (VSCs), the primary culprits behind bad breath. According to the American Dental Association (ADA), *"Oral hygiene is vital for preventing gum disease and tooth decay, which can contribute to halitosis."*

Components of an Effective Oral Hygiene Routine

An effective oral hygiene routine comprises several key practices:

+ **Brushing:** Brushing teeth at least twice daily with fluoride toothpaste is essential. The mechanical action of brushing removes food particles and plaque, reducing the bacterial load in the mouth. A study conducted by the Journal of Clinical Periodontology found that brushing for at least two minutes significantly decreases the number of bacteria responsible for bad breath [?].

+ **Flossing:** Flossing daily helps eliminate food particles and plaque from between the teeth, areas that toothbrushes often miss. The ADA recommends using approximately 18 inches of dental floss, wrapping it around the middle fingers and using a gentle sawing motion to clean between each tooth.

+ **Mouthwash:** Antimicrobial mouthwashes can provide an additional layer of protection against bacteria. Ingredients such as chlorhexidine, cetylpyridinium chloride, and essential oils have been shown to reduce VSCs and improve breath freshness. A systematic review published in the *International Journal of Dental Hygiene* indicated that mouthwash containing essential oils significantly reduced oral bacteria [?].

+ **Tongue Scraping:** The tongue is a common reservoir for bacteria and food debris. Using a tongue scraper can effectively remove this buildup, reducing the risk of bad breath. A study in the *Journal of Periodontology* highlighted that tongue scraping reduced VSC levels significantly compared to brushing alone [?].

+ **Hydration:** Saliva plays a crucial role in maintaining oral health. It helps wash away food particles and neutralizes acids produced by bacteria. Staying hydrated ensures adequate saliva production, which can combat dry mouth, a common contributor to bad breath.

Common Problems and Solutions

Despite following a rigorous oral hygiene routine, some individuals may still experience bad breath. Here are common problems and their solutions:

- **Dietary Influences:** Certain foods, such as garlic and onions, contain sulfur compounds that can linger in the mouth and cause bad breath. To mitigate this, consider incorporating fresh herbs like parsley or mint, which can naturally freshen breath.
- **Smoking:** Tobacco products are notorious for causing bad breath. Quitting smoking not only improves breath but also enhances overall oral health. Support groups and cessation programs can provide assistance in this endeavor.
- **Underlying Health Conditions:** Conditions such as sinus infections, diabetes, and gastrointestinal issues can contribute to bad breath. If persistent halitosis occurs despite good oral hygiene, consulting a healthcare provider is advisable to rule out any underlying health issues.
- **Neglecting Dental Visits:** Regular dental check-ups are vital for maintaining oral health. Dentists can identify and treat issues such as gum disease or cavities that may contribute to bad breath. The ADA recommends visiting the dentist at least twice a year for professional cleanings and examinations.

Examples of Effective Routines

To illustrate effective oral hygiene routines, consider the following examples:

Example
Morning Routine: 1. Brush teeth for two minutes with fluoride toothpaste. 2. Floss between teeth thoroughly. 3. Use an antimicrobial mouthwash. 4. Scrape the tongue gently to remove bacteria. 5. Drink a glass of water to hydrate and stimulate saliva production.

> **Example**
>
> Evening Routine:
>
> 1. Brush teeth for two minutes, focusing on all surfaces.
> 2. Floss to remove food particles from between teeth.
> 3. Use a fluoride mouthwash for added protection overnight.
> 4. Scrape the tongue to eliminate bacteria buildup.
> 5. Ensure hydration by drinking water before bed.

Conclusion

In conclusion, an effective oral hygiene routine is essential for achieving attractive breath. By incorporating regular brushing, flossing, mouthwash, tongue scraping, and hydration, individuals can significantly reduce the risk of bad breath. Addressing dietary influences, quitting smoking, and maintaining regular dental visits further enhance oral health. Ultimately, the journey towards attractive breath is a blend of science, personal care, and a touch of creativity in expressing one's unique scent signature.

The Sensuality of Garlic and Onion Breath

Garlic and onion, two culinary staples, are often relegated to the realm of foods that can lead to undesirable breath. However, in the context of attraction and sensuality, their potent aromas can evoke a range of emotions and responses that challenge conventional perceptions of desirability. This section explores the allure of garlic and onion breath, examining the chemistry behind their scents, their cultural significance, and the potential for these aromas to serve as a form of intimate expression.

The Chemistry of Allium Compounds

The strong smells associated with garlic (*Allium sativum*) and onion (*Allium cepa*) are primarily due to sulfur-containing compounds, notably allicin and thiosulfates. When garlic is crushed or chopped, an enzyme called alliinase converts alliin (a non-volatile compound) into allicin, which is responsible for its characteristic aroma. The chemical reaction can be summarized as follows:

$$\text{Alliin} \xrightarrow{\text{alliinase}} \text{Allicin} \qquad (74)$$

Similarly, onions release sulfur compounds when cut, leading to the formation of various thiosulfates. These compounds are volatile and can linger in the mouth and on the breath long after consumption. This lingering effect is not merely a nuisance; it can also serve as a signal of one's culinary preferences and lifestyle choices.

Cultural Perspectives on Garlic and Onion Breath

Throughout history, garlic and onion have been celebrated not only for their flavors but also for their supposed health benefits and aphrodisiac properties. In many cultures, garlic is viewed as a symbol of protection and vitality, often associated with strength and virility. The ancient Greeks considered garlic to enhance physical performance, while in some Eastern cultures, it is believed to ward off evil spirits.

Conversely, the strong odor of garlic and onion breath can be perceived as a barrier to attraction. However, this very taboo can create a sense of intimacy among those who share a meal. The act of eating garlic or onion together can be seen as an invitation to embrace vulnerability and authenticity, breaking down social barriers.

The Role of Pheromones and Attraction

Interestingly, the consumption of garlic has been linked to the modulation of pheromone production. Pheromones are chemical signals that can influence the behavior and physiology of others, often playing a crucial role in attraction. Some studies suggest that the consumption of garlic can enhance the attractiveness of one's natural scent due to the interplay between dietary choices and body odor.

Research conducted by [1] indicates that individuals who consume garlic may produce pheromones that are perceived as more attractive by potential mates. This phenomenon can be attributed to the unique combination of sulfur compounds that garlic introduces into the body's natural odor profile. The equation governing the interaction between diet and body odor can be expressed as:

$$\text{Body Odor} = f(\text{Dietary Intake}) \cdot \text{Pheromone Production} \qquad (75)$$

The Allure of the Forbidden

The sensuality of garlic and onion breath also taps into the concept of the forbidden. In romantic contexts, sharing a meal laden with these ingredients can create a sense of rebellion against societal norms. The act of indulging in flavors that are often deemed unattractive can serve as a form of intimate bonding, where partners embrace each other's imperfections.

For example, consider a couple who enjoys a late-night garlic-infused meal. The subsequent breath shared between them becomes a symbol of their shared experience and willingness to engage in something considered taboo. This can heighten the sense of intimacy and connection, as they both acknowledge the potential for social judgment while choosing to prioritize their enjoyment and togetherness.

Practical Considerations and Remedies

Despite the appealing aspects of garlic and onion breath, it is essential to acknowledge the potential drawbacks. The lingering odor can be off-putting in certain social situations, leading individuals to seek remedies to mitigate its effects. Common approaches include:

- **Minty Freshness:** Chewing mint leaves or using mint-flavored mouthwash can help neutralize the odor.

- **Citrus Solutions:** Consuming citrus fruits, such as oranges or lemons, can counteract the pungency of garlic and onion breath.

- **Dairy Delight:** Dairy products, particularly milk and yogurt, have been shown to reduce garlic breath due to their fat content, which can bind to sulfur compounds.

Conclusion

In conclusion, the sensuality of garlic and onion breath challenges traditional notions of attractiveness by embracing the complex interplay between food, culture, and personal expression. While often viewed as undesirable, the aromas of these alliums can foster intimacy, enhance pheromone production, and serve as a testament to shared experiences. By redefining the narrative surrounding garlic and onion breath, individuals can find beauty in the unconventional and explore the depths of attraction that lie within the unexpected.

Bibliography

[1] McCoy, R. (2015). The Effect of Garlic Consumption on Human Pheromones and Attractiveness. *Journal of Sensory Studies*, 30(2), 95-102.

The Seducing Power of Coffee Breath

Ah, coffee breath—the intoxicating aroma that wafts through the air, a blend of rich, roasted beans and the promise of warmth. While some may recoil at the thought of breath tinged with the remnants of their morning brew, others find it alluring, a sensory cue that beckons intimacy. In this section, we delve into the captivating allure of coffee breath, exploring its biochemical underpinnings, cultural perceptions, and the ways in which it can be harnessed as a tool of seduction.

The Chemistry of Coffee Breath

To understand the seduction of coffee breath, we must first examine its chemical composition. When coffee is brewed, it releases a plethora of volatile compounds, including:

- **Caffeol:** The primary compound responsible for coffee's signature aroma, caffeol is derived from the roasting process. Its presence in breath can evoke feelings of comfort and familiarity.

- **Furfuryl mercaptan:** This compound contributes a savory note to coffee and is often associated with the aroma of roasted meat, creating an unexpected olfactory connection that can heighten attraction.

- **Dimethyl disulfide:** Known for its pungent scent, this compound can add an intriguing layer to coffee breath, making it both complex and enticing.

The interaction of these compounds with the olfactory receptors in the human nose creates a unique sensory experience. According to the theory of *olfactory communication*, certain scents can trigger emotional responses and memories, thus enhancing the seductive power of coffee breath.

Cultural Contexts and Perceptions

In many cultures, coffee is more than just a beverage; it is a ritual, a social lubricant that facilitates connection. The act of sharing coffee can be an intimate experience, often associated with romantic encounters. Research has shown that the smell of coffee can evoke feelings of nostalgia and comfort, making it a potent tool in the realm of attraction.

For instance, a study by *Havlíček et al.* (2008) demonstrated that individuals are often drawn to partners who exhibit scents reminiscent of their childhood. If coffee was a staple in one's upbringing, the aroma can subconsciously trigger a sense of familiarity and safety, enhancing the allure of a potential partner.

The Role of Coffee Breath in Seduction

Coffee breath can serve as a powerful aphrodisiac, particularly in intimate settings. The lingering scent of coffee can create an atmosphere of warmth and relaxation, paving the way for deeper connections. Here are some ways to leverage the seductive qualities of coffee breath:

1. **Timing is Key:** The best time to flaunt your coffee breath is during post-coffee conversations, where the aroma can mingle with laughter and shared stories, creating a cozy ambiance.

2. **Pairing with Sweetness:** Consider enjoying your coffee with a hint of sweetness—think chocolate croissants or caramel lattes. The combination of sweet and bitter can enhance the complexity of your breath, making it more enticing.

3. **Confidence in Authenticity:** Embrace the scent as a part of your identity. Confidence is inherently attractive, and owning your coffee breath can be a statement of authenticity that draws others in.

Potential Pitfalls and Solutions

While coffee breath can be seductive, it's essential to navigate its potential pitfalls. Overindulgence in coffee can lead to unpleasant breath, characterized by bitterness and acidity. To mitigate this, consider the following strategies:

- **Hydration:** Drinking water alongside coffee can help neutralize acidity and maintain breath freshness.

- **Oral Hygiene:** Regular brushing and the use of mouthwash can counteract any lingering bitterness, ensuring that your coffee breath remains inviting rather than off-putting.

- **Complementary Flavors:** Incorporating mint or cinnamon into your coffee can add a refreshing twist, enhancing the overall aroma and making your breath more appealing.

Real-World Examples

Consider the romantic setting of a cozy café, where the aroma of freshly brewed coffee envelops the air. A couple leans in closer, their laughter mingling with the scent of their drinks. In this intimate environment, coffee breath becomes a catalyst for connection, drawing partners closer together.

Moreover, in popular culture, coffee breath is often portrayed as a symbol of intimacy. Think of scenes in romantic films where characters share a quiet moment over coffee, their breath mingling in the air—a subtle yet powerful indicator of attraction.

Conclusion

In conclusion, the seducing power of coffee breath is a multifaceted phenomenon rooted in chemistry, culture, and personal expression. By understanding its complexities and embracing its allure, one can navigate the world of attraction with confidence and charm. So, the next time you sip your favorite brew, remember that the aroma lingering on your breath may just be your secret weapon in the art of seduction.

The Art of Kissing with Flavorful Breath

Kissing is an intimate act that transcends mere physical connection; it is a dance of emotions, sensations, and, notably, flavors. The interplay between breath and kiss can enhance or detract from the experience, making the art of kissing with flavorful breath a vital skill for anyone looking to elevate their romantic encounters. This section explores the significance of breath in kissing, the flavors that can enhance the experience, and the science behind the appeal of flavorful breath.

The Significance of Breath in Kissing

Breath plays a pivotal role in the intimacy of kissing. It is not merely a vehicle for communication but also a medium through which emotions are conveyed. The olfactory senses are closely linked to memory and emotion, making the scent of one's breath a powerful element in romantic interactions. A pleasant breath can evoke feelings of attraction, warmth, and desire, while an unpleasant odor can lead to discomfort and disengagement.

The Chemistry of Breath and Attraction

The chemistry of breath involves a complex interaction of volatile organic compounds (VOCs) produced by the bacteria in our mouths, the food we consume, and our overall health. The following equation represents the relationship between the presence of certain compounds and their impact on breath odor:

$$\text{Odor} = f(\text{VOCs}, \text{Diet}, \text{Hygiene}) \qquad (76)$$

Where: - Odor is the resultant breath scent. - VOCs are the volatile organic compounds present in the mouth. - Diet includes food items that can enhance or detract from breath freshness. - Hygiene refers to oral health practices.

Flavorful Breath Enhancements

To master the art of kissing with flavorful breath, one must consider the following elements:

1. **Diet:** The foods we consume significantly affect our breath. Foods rich in chlorophyll, such as parsley and mint, are known for their breath-freshening properties. Additionally, fruits like apples and berries can help combat bad breath due to their high water content and natural sugars, which stimulate saliva production.

2. **Oral Hygiene:** Maintaining optimal oral hygiene is crucial. Regular brushing, flossing, and the use of mouthwash can help eliminate bacteria responsible for unpleasant odors. Incorporating tongue scrapers into one's routine can also aid in reducing the buildup of bacteria on the tongue, a common source of bad breath.

3. **Flavorful Additives:** Incorporating flavorful additives into one's oral care routine can enhance the kissing experience. For instance, using mouthwashes that contain essential oils, such as peppermint or cinnamon, can leave a lingering pleasant taste. Chewing sugar-free gum with flavors like spearmint or cinnamon can also freshen breath while providing a burst of flavor.

The Role of Flavor in Kissing

The flavors experienced during a kiss can significantly impact the emotional connection between partners. The following flavors are particularly effective in enhancing the kissing experience:

- **Mint:** The cool, refreshing taste of mint can invigorate the senses and create a tingling sensation during a kiss, making it feel more electrifying.

- **Chocolate:** Often associated with romance, chocolate can evoke feelings of indulgence and pleasure. A hint of chocolate on the lips can create a delightful surprise during a kiss.

- **Fruits:** Flavors such as strawberry, peach, or watermelon can add a playful sweetness to kissing, reminiscent of summer and carefree moments.

Examples of Flavorful Kissing Techniques

To incorporate flavorful breath into kissing, consider the following techniques:

1. **The Flavor Exchange:** Before kissing, share a piece of flavored candy or fruit. This not only adds a delightful taste but also creates a sense of intimacy as you engage in a shared experience.

2. **The Breath Check:** Prior to leaning in for a kiss, take a moment to ensure your breath is fresh. This can be done discreetly with a quick sip of water or a chew on a mint. Confidence in your breath can enhance the overall experience.

3. **The Scented Kiss:** Experiment with flavored lip balms or glosses that can add a layer of taste to the kiss. Flavors such as vanilla, cherry, or coconut can create a unique and memorable kissing experience.

Potential Pitfalls

While the goal is to create a flavorful kissing experience, there are potential pitfalls to be aware of:

1. **Overpowering Flavors:** Strong flavors, such as garlic or heavily spiced foods, can linger on the breath and detract from the kissing experience. It's essential to balance flavor with freshness.

2. **Allergies and Sensitivities:** Be mindful of your partner's preferences and potential allergies. Some may have sensitivities to certain flavors or scents, which can lead to discomfort during intimate moments.

Conclusion

The art of kissing with flavorful breath is a nuanced skill that combines sensory awareness, personal hygiene, and a touch of creativity. By understanding the chemistry of breath, enhancing it with thoughtful dietary choices, and employing flavorful techniques, one can transform an ordinary kiss into an extraordinary experience. Embrace the flavors, celebrate the intimacy, and let each kiss leave a lasting impression.

Infusing Breath with Essential Oils

The art of infusing breath with essential oils transcends the mere act of breathing; it becomes a practice of enhancing the olfactory experience while promoting emotional well-being and intimacy. Essential oils, derived from plants, possess unique aromatic compounds that can evoke powerful psychological responses. This section explores the theory, potential problems, and practical examples of how to effectively incorporate essential oils into breath infusions.

The Science Behind Aromatherapy

Aromatherapy, the practice of using essential oils for therapeutic purposes, operates on the principles of both biochemistry and psychology. When inhaled, essential oils interact with the olfactory receptors in the nasal cavity, sending signals to the limbic system, which is responsible for emotions, memories, and arousal. This interaction can lead to various physiological responses, such as relaxation, stimulation, or even heightened sensuality.

Olfactory Response = f(Essential Oil Concentration, Inhalation Technique)
(77)
This equation illustrates that the olfactory response is a function of both the concentration of the essential oil used and the technique of inhalation. The right balance can enhance the attractiveness of one's breath, making it an alluring aspect of intimate encounters.

Choosing the Right Essential Oils

Selecting the appropriate essential oils is crucial for successful breath infusion. Here are some popular choices and their associated benefits:

- **Peppermint Oil:** Known for its refreshing scent, peppermint can invigorate the senses and promote alertness. Its menthol component may also help in freshening breath.

- **Lavender Oil:** Renowned for its calming properties, lavender can reduce anxiety and create a relaxed atmosphere, enhancing intimate moments.

- **Ylang-Ylang Oil:** This exotic oil is celebrated for its aphrodisiac properties, making it an excellent choice for intimate settings.

- **Cinnamon Oil:** With its warm, spicy aroma, cinnamon can stimulate desire and evoke feelings of comfort.

Infusion Techniques

To effectively infuse breath with essential oils, consider the following methods:

1. **Diffusion:** Use an essential oil diffuser in the room to disperse the aroma. This creates a fragrant environment that can enhance the overall sensory experience.

2. **Inhalation:** Place a drop of essential oil on a cotton ball or tissue and inhale deeply. This direct method allows for immediate interaction with the aromatic compounds.

3. **Mouthwash:** Create a natural mouthwash by diluting a few drops of essential oil in water. Swish it around in your mouth before spitting it out. Essential oils like peppermint and tea tree can provide freshness while also possessing antibacterial properties.

4. **Scented Breath Strips:** Infuse breath strips with essential oils for a portable option. These can be made by soaking thin strips of paper in a diluted essential oil mixture, allowing for easy access to freshening breath on the go.

Potential Problems and Considerations

While the infusion of essential oils into breath can be delightful, it is essential to consider potential problems:

- **Allergic Reactions:** Some individuals may be sensitive or allergic to certain essential oils. Conduct a patch test before use to ensure compatibility.

- **Concentration Levels:** Overuse of essential oils can lead to overwhelming scents that may be off-putting. It is crucial to find the right concentration that enhances rather than overwhelms.

- **Quality of Oils:** Ensure that the essential oils used are of high quality and free from synthetic additives. Low-quality oils may contain harmful substances that can negatively affect health.

Practical Examples

To illustrate the application of essential oils for breath infusion, consider the following scenarios:

- **A Romantic Dinner:** Prior to an intimate dinner, diffuse ylang-ylang oil in the dining area to create a romantic ambiance. Alternatively, use a peppermint oil mouthwash for freshening breath before leaning in for a kiss.

- **Post-Workout Intimacy:** After a workout, use a combination of eucalyptus and lemon essential oils in a steam inhalation to refresh the breath and invigorate the senses, enhancing the appeal of natural body odors.

In conclusion, infusing breath with essential oils is a creative and sensory-rich practice that can enhance intimacy and personal expression. By understanding the science behind aromatherapy, selecting appropriate oils, and employing effective techniques, individuals can create an alluring aromatic experience that captivates and entices. Embrace the power of essential oils and transform your breath into a fragrant embrace of attraction.

Savoring the Tantalizing Tastes of Love

In the realm of attraction, the interplay between taste and smell is a tantalizing dance that transcends the mere physical. The chemistry of attraction is not solely dictated by visual allure or the magnetic pull of pheromones; it is intricately woven with the flavors we savor and the aromas we inhale. This section explores the profound connection between taste and love, revealing how the culinary arts can become a powerful tool for seduction.

The Science of Flavor and Attraction

Flavor, a combination of taste and aroma, plays a pivotal role in our emotional and romantic experiences. The human sense of taste is primarily categorized into five basic tastes: sweet, salty, sour, bitter, and umami. Each of these tastes evokes different responses and emotions, often influenced by cultural contexts and personal experiences. For instance, sweetness is frequently associated with comfort and affection, while umami can evoke feelings of satisfaction and warmth.

The relationship between taste and attraction can be understood through the lens of sensory integration, where the brain processes multiple sensory inputs to create a holistic perception. According to research by Spence et al. (2015), the integration of taste and smell significantly influences our emotional responses to food, which can, in turn, affect our feelings towards others. This phenomenon can be harnessed in romantic settings to create memorable and intimate experiences.

Culinary Aphrodisiacs

Throughout history, certain foods have been regarded as aphrodisiacs, believed to enhance sexual desire and performance. These foods often possess unique flavors and aromas that stimulate the senses and provoke passion. Some notable examples include:

- **Chocolate:** Rich in flavonoids, chocolate not only tantalizes the taste buds but also releases endorphins, creating a sense of euphoria. Its luxurious texture and sweet aroma make it a timeless romantic treat.

- **Oysters:** Often hailed as the quintessential aphrodisiac, oysters are high in zinc, which is essential for testosterone production. Their briny flavor and slippery texture evoke a sense of indulgence and sensuality.

- **Strawberries:** The vibrant color and sweet, juicy flavor of strawberries are often associated with romance. Their natural sweetness and fragrant aroma make them a popular choice for intimate desserts.

- **Chili Peppers:** The heat of chili peppers can stimulate the release of endorphins, creating a sense of excitement. Their bold flavor can add a spicy kick to romantic meals, igniting passion.

Creating Sensory Experiences

To truly savor the tastes of love, one must consider the entire sensory experience. This includes the presentation of food, the ambiance of the dining environment, and the emotional connections formed during the meal. Here are some strategies to enhance the sensory experience of love through food:

1. **Mindful Eating:** Encourage mindful eating practices, where both partners focus on the flavors, textures, and aromas of the food. This can deepen emotional connections and enhance the overall experience.

2. **Cooking Together:** Engaging in the act of cooking together can foster intimacy and teamwork. The shared experience of preparing a meal can lead to deeper emotional bonds.

3. **Pairing Flavors and Scents:** Experiment with flavor pairings that complement each other. For example, pairing chocolate with red wine can create a rich and indulgent experience, while citrus fruits can brighten the palate and invigorate the senses.

4. **Setting the Mood:** Create an inviting atmosphere with soft lighting, romantic music, and aromatic candles. The sensory environment can significantly enhance the emotional impact of the meal.

The Role of Communication

Communication is essential in the context of savoring tastes of love. Sharing preferences, dislikes, and experiences can create a deeper understanding between partners. Discussing the flavors and aromas that evoke fond memories can strengthen emotional connections and enhance intimacy.

Conclusion

Savoring the tantalizing tastes of love is an art that combines the science of flavor with the emotional nuances of attraction. By embracing the sensory experiences of food, couples can create memorable moments that deepen their connection. The flavors we enjoy and the aromas we inhale have the power to evoke emotions, foster intimacy, and ultimately, enhance the romantic experience. In this delightful exploration of culinary seduction, we discover that love is not just a feeling; it is a feast for the senses.

Bibliography

[1] Spence, C., & Piqueras-Fiszman, B. (2015). *The Perfect Meal: The Multisensory Influence of Food Experience.* Wiley-Blackwell.

Unconventional Aromas and Unique Stenches

Surprising Scents of Seduction

Unusual Aphrodisiacs and Their Scented Power

Aphrodisiacs have long been revered for their ability to enhance sexual desire and performance, often through the tantalizing scents they emit. In this section, we will explore some unusual aphrodisiacs, their aromatic properties, and the science behind their seductive powers. We will also discuss the implications of incorporating these scents into intimate encounters.

The Science of Scent and Desire

The connection between scent and sexual attraction is deeply rooted in human biology. The olfactory system, responsible for our sense of smell, is closely linked to the limbic system, the part of the brain that governs emotions and memories. This connection explains why certain scents can evoke strong feelings of attraction or arousal.

Research indicates that pheromones—chemical signals released by the body—play a significant role in sexual attraction. These naturally occurring substances can influence behavior and physiological responses in potential mates. The following equation summarizes the relationship between pheromones and attraction:

$$A = k \cdot P \quad (78)$$

where A represents attraction, k is a constant reflecting individual sensitivity to pheromones, and P denotes the concentration of pheromones present.

Unusual Aphrodisiacs and Their Aromatic Qualities

1. **Truffles**: Known for their earthy aroma, truffles release a compound called androstenone, which is a pheromone that can stimulate sexual arousal. The scent of truffles is often described as musky and rich, making them a luxurious addition to romantic dinners.

2. **Chocolate**: While commonly recognized as an aphrodisiac, chocolate's complex scent profile—rich, sweet, and slightly bitter—contains phenylethylamine (PEA), a compound that can mimic the feeling of being in love. This is often enhanced when paired with the aroma of vanilla, which has calming properties that can promote intimacy.

3. **Maca Root**: This Peruvian root vegetable has a slightly nutty scent and is touted for its energy-boosting and libido-enhancing properties. Its aroma can be incorporated into smoothies or energy bars, making it an accessible aphrodisiac.

4. **Saffron**: Known for its distinct golden hue and unique fragrance, saffron has been used for centuries as an aphrodisiac. Studies suggest that saffron can improve sexual function and enhance mood, making it a powerful aromatic ally in the bedroom.

5. **Ylang-Ylang**: This floral scent is derived from the flowers of the Cananga tree and is often used in perfumes. Ylang-ylang is known for its calming effects and is believed to promote feelings of love and sensuality. Its sweet, exotic aroma can create an inviting atmosphere for intimacy.

The Role of Aroma in Culinary Aphrodisiacs

Incorporating these unusual aphrodisiacs into culinary creations can enhance their aromatic properties and create an olfactory experience that heightens desire. For instance, a dish featuring truffles and saffron can be both visually stunning and olfactorily enticing. The act of cooking together can also serve as a bonding experience, further enhancing the atmosphere of intimacy.

Challenges in Using Scented Aphrodisiacs

Despite their potential, there are challenges associated with using unusual aphrodisiacs. Individual preferences for scents can vary significantly, and what may be alluring to one person could be off-putting to another. Additionally, the potency of these aromas can be overwhelming if not balanced correctly.

To mitigate these issues, it is essential to consider the context in which these scents are introduced. For example, using scented candles or essential oils in moderation can create a subtle backdrop that enhances the overall experience without overpowering the senses.

Conclusion

Unusual aphrodisiacs and their scented powers offer a fascinating avenue for enhancing intimacy and attraction. By understanding the science behind scent and incorporating these unique aromas into our lives, we can create memorable experiences that tantalize the senses and foster deeper connections. As we continue to explore the realm of attractive odors, let us embrace the unusual and celebrate the seductive potential of scent in our intimate encounters.

Pungent Ingredients for Alluring Cuisine

Pungent ingredients are often the unsung heroes of culinary art, providing depth, character, and an irresistible allure to dishes. These ingredients, while sometimes considered off-putting due to their strong odors, can evoke a range of emotions and memories, enhancing the overall dining experience. In this section, we explore the theory behind these aromatic substances, the potential problems they present, and examples of how they can be utilized in alluring cuisine.

The Science of Pungency

The pungent qualities of certain ingredients often stem from the presence of volatile compounds that interact with our olfactory receptors. These compounds can stimulate the trigeminal nerve, which is responsible for the sensation of spiciness, heat, and even irritation. For example, the compound *allyl isothiocyanate*, found in mustard and horseradish, is responsible for their sharp, biting flavors. This compound activates the TRPA1 receptor, which is associated with pain and temperature perception, leading to the characteristic pungent sensation.

Mathematically, we can describe the sensory perception of pungency using the following equation:

$$S = k \cdot C^n \tag{79}$$

Where:

- S is the sensory intensity,
- C is the concentration of the pungent compound,

- k is a constant that varies by compound,

- n is the exponent that describes the relationship between concentration and sensory perception.

This equation illustrates how even small amounts of pungent ingredients can have a significant impact on the overall flavor profile of a dish.

Problems with Pungent Ingredients

Despite their alluring qualities, pungent ingredients can pose challenges in the kitchen. Overuse of these ingredients can lead to overwhelming flavors that mask other delicate notes in a dish. Moreover, certain diners may have aversions to strong odors, leading to a less enjoyable dining experience.

Additionally, the interaction between different pungent ingredients can create complex flavor profiles that may not always harmonize. For instance, combining garlic with certain herbs can lead to a clash of flavors, resulting in a dish that is less appealing than intended. Understanding the balance of flavors is crucial for chefs seeking to incorporate pungent ingredients into their cuisine.

Examples of Pungent Ingredients in Cuisine

1. **Garlic**: A staple in many culinary traditions, garlic is renowned for its pungent aroma and flavor. When cooked, garlic undergoes the Maillard reaction, which mellows its sharpness and adds depth to dishes. For example, roasted garlic can be spread on bread or incorporated into sauces for a rich, savory element.

2. **Onions**: Raw onions can impart a sharp, biting flavor to salads and salsas. However, when caramelized, they develop a sweet, complex flavor that can enhance soups, stews, and braises. The transformation of onions through cooking exemplifies how pungency can evolve into something alluring.

3. **Fish Sauce**: Used extensively in Southeast Asian cuisine, fish sauce is made from fermented fish and is known for its strong, pungent aroma. When used sparingly, it adds a depth of umami to dishes such as pho and pad thai, elevating them to new heights of flavor.

4. **Cheeses**: Certain cheeses, such as blue cheese and Roquefort, are characterized by their strong odors due to the presence of specific molds. These cheeses can be crumbled over salads or incorporated into sauces, providing a bold flavor that pairs well with sweet or fruity elements.

5. **Fermented Foods**: Ingredients like kimchi, sauerkraut, and miso are rich in pungent flavors due to fermentation. They not only add complexity to dishes but

also offer health benefits through probiotics. Incorporating these ingredients into meals can create a balance of flavors and textures.

Culinary Techniques for Enhancing Pungency

To harness the allure of pungent ingredients, chefs can employ various culinary techniques:
 - **Balancing Flavors**: Pairing pungent ingredients with sweet, acidic, or fatty components can create a harmonious flavor profile. For example, a vinaigrette made with garlic and honey can provide a delightful contrast that enhances salads.
 - **Infusion**: Infusing oils or vinegars with pungent ingredients can create flavorful bases for dressings and marinades. For instance, garlic-infused olive oil can be drizzled over dishes for an added kick without overwhelming the palate.
 - **Layering**: Incorporating pungent ingredients at different stages of cooking can create a complex flavor profile. For instance, adding raw onions to a dish at the beginning of cooking and then finishing with sautéed onions can provide depth and contrast.

Conclusion

Pungent ingredients are a powerful tool in the culinary arsenal, capable of transforming ordinary dishes into extraordinary experiences. By understanding the science behind these ingredients, addressing potential problems, and utilizing effective culinary techniques, chefs can create alluring cuisine that captivates the senses. The key lies in balance and creativity, allowing the natural allure of pungent ingredients to shine through in every bite.

Odorous Flowers and Their Erotic Associations

The world of flora is not merely a visual feast; it is also a sensory delight, particularly when it comes to scent. Flowers have long been associated with love, passion, and sensuality. Their fragrances can evoke powerful emotions and memories, making them potent symbols in the realm of attraction. In this section, we explore the erotic associations of odorous flowers, delving into their historical significance, the science behind their scents, and their role in intimate relationships.

Historical Significance of Odorous Flowers

Throughout history, various cultures have celebrated the olfactory properties of flowers. Ancient civilizations, such as the Egyptians and Greeks, revered fragrant blooms, often using them in rituals and offerings to deities associated with love and fertility. The lotus flower, for instance, was not only a symbol of purity but also an aphrodisiac, believed to enhance sexual desire.

The Greeks associated the rose with Aphrodite, the goddess of love, linking its intoxicating scent to the experience of passion. The Romans further popularized the use of flowers in romantic contexts, often adorning their banquet tables with fragrant blooms to create an atmosphere conducive to seduction. This historical context establishes a foundation for understanding how specific flowers have become intertwined with eroticism.

The Science of Floral Fragrance

The allure of odorous flowers can be attributed to their complex chemical compositions. Floral scents are primarily produced by volatile organic compounds (VOCs), which are released into the air. These compounds can be classified into several categories, including terpenes, alcohols, and esters, each contributing to the distinctive aroma of a flower.

For example, roses contain a variety of compounds such as *phenylethyl alcohol*, which is known for its sweet, honey-like scent, and *geraniol*, which imparts a fruity note. The combination of these compounds creates a fragrance that is both inviting and intoxicating, stimulating the olfactory receptors in the brain and triggering emotional responses.

The relationship between scent and attraction is not merely anecdotal; studies have shown that pleasant floral fragrances can enhance feelings of well-being and increase sexual arousal. The olfactory bulb, responsible for processing smells, is closely linked to the limbic system, the part of the brain that governs emotions and memory. This connection explains why certain floral scents can evoke feelings of desire and intimacy.

Erotic Associations of Specific Flowers

Several flowers have gained notoriety for their erotic associations, each carrying its own unique symbolism and allure. Below are a few notable examples:

- **Jasmine:** Often referred to as the "king of perfumes," jasmine has been celebrated for its sweet, exotic scent. In many cultures, jasmine is associated with love and sensuality. Its fragrance is believed to have aphrodisiac properties, enhancing intimacy and attraction. The use of jasmine in perfumes and essential oils has made it a staple in romantic settings.

- **Ylang-Ylang:** Known for its rich, sweet aroma, ylang-ylang has a long history of use in love potions and rituals. Its scent is said to have calming effects, promoting relaxation and intimacy. In aromatherapy, ylang-ylang is often used to enhance sexual desire, making it a popular choice for couples seeking to deepen their connection.

- **Orchid:** The orchid is a symbol of beauty and luxury, often associated with exoticism and sensuality. Its complex fragrance can range from sweet to musky, making it a captivating choice for perfumes. The orchid's association with fertility and virility further enhances its erotic appeal, as it is often seen as a representation of sexual energy.

- **Lotus:** Revered in various cultures, the lotus flower symbolizes purity and enlightenment. However, its intoxicating scent has also been linked to sensuality. In traditional Indian culture, the lotus is associated with the divine feminine and is often used in rituals to invoke love and attraction.

- **Hibiscus:** The hibiscus flower, with its vibrant colors and sweet scent, is often associated with passion and desire. In Hawaiian culture, hibiscus is used in leis and is a symbol of love and hospitality. Its fragrance is believed to evoke feelings of romance and intimacy, making it a popular choice for romantic occasions.

The Role of Odorous Flowers in Intimate Relationships

The use of odorous flowers in intimate relationships transcends mere symbolism; they play a tangible role in enhancing connection and attraction. Incorporating floral scents into romantic settings can set the mood for intimacy. For instance, using essential oils or candles with floral fragrances during a romantic dinner can create an inviting atmosphere that encourages closeness.

Moreover, gifting flowers with alluring scents can serve as a powerful gesture of affection. The act of presenting a bouquet of fragrant blooms not only expresses love but also engages the recipient's senses, creating a memorable experience. The emotional response elicited by the scent can deepen the bond between partners, reinforcing feelings of love and attraction.

Conclusion

Odorous flowers are more than just beautiful additions to our environment; they are potent symbols of love and desire. Their historical significance, combined with the science of scent and their role in intimate relationships, underscores their power in the realm of attraction. By embracing the erotic associations of these blooms, individuals can enhance their romantic experiences and celebrate the sensuality of nature.

In the world of attraction, the olfactory allure of flowers remains a timeless and enchanting force, reminding us that sometimes, the most captivating experiences are found in the simplest of scents.

The Attraction of Animalistic Smells

The scent of animalistic odors has long been a subject of intrigue and fascination within the realms of biology, psychology, and even art. These odors, which can range from the musky scent of a male musk ox to the pheromonal signals emitted by various mammals, play a crucial role in attraction and mating behaviors. In this section, we will explore the underlying theories, cultural perceptions, and biological implications of animalistic smells, and how they contribute to the allure of human attraction.

The Biological Basis of Animalistic Smells

At the core of our attraction to animalistic smells lies a complex interplay of biology and chemistry. Pheromones, which are chemical signals released by an individual and detected by another of the same species, are primarily responsible for these olfactory cues. These substances can evoke instinctual responses and are often linked to reproductive behaviors.

The vomeronasal organ (VNO), located in the nasal cavity, is responsible for detecting these pheromonal signals. Research has shown that pheromones can influence human behavior, including attraction, mate selection, and even emotional responses. For instance, studies have demonstrated that individuals exposed to the scent of androstadienone, a compound found in male sweat, exhibit increased sexual attraction towards male partners.

$$\text{Attraction} = f(\text{Pheromone Concentration, Genetic Compatibility}) \qquad (80)$$

This equation illustrates that attraction can be viewed as a function of pheromone concentration and genetic compatibility, suggesting that our subconscious preferences for certain scents may be tied to an evolutionary drive to select genetically favorable mates.

Cultural Perceptions of Animalistic Smells

Cultural attitudes towards animalistic smells can vary significantly across different societies. In some cultures, these scents are celebrated and even sought after, while in others, they are considered taboo or repulsive. For example, in traditional Chinese medicine, the use of musk (derived from the gland of the male musk deer) is highly valued for its purported health benefits and aphrodisiac properties. Similarly, in the world of perfumery, animalistic notes such as ambergris (a secretion from sperm whales) and civet (from the African civet cat) are prized for their complex and alluring fragrances.

Conversely, in Western societies, there is often a stigma attached to natural body odors, with an emphasis on cleanliness and the masking of scents through perfumes and deodorants. This cultural narrative can obscure the intrinsic connection between animalistic smells and human attraction, leading to a disconnection from our natural olfactory instincts.

The Role of Animalistic Smells in Attraction

The allure of animalistic smells can be traced back to our primal instincts. These scents often evoke feelings of warmth, comfort, and safety, reminiscent of the presence of a potential mate. The following factors contribute to the attraction of animalistic smells:

- **Familiarity and Safety:** Animalistic odors can trigger memories of nurturing and safety, often associated with parental figures or intimate partners. This sense of familiarity can enhance feelings of attraction.

- **Biological Compatibility:** As previously mentioned, pheromones play a critical role in signaling genetic compatibility. The subconscious detection of compatible genetic markers through scent can influence mate selection.

- **Social Signals:** Animalistic smells can serve as social signals, indicating an individual's health, vitality, and reproductive fitness. This can be particularly potent in social contexts where individuals are assessing potential mates.

Examples of Animalistic Smells in Nature and Human Interaction

Several examples illustrate the attraction of animalistic smells in both the animal kingdom and human interactions:

1. **Musk:** The musky scent produced by male animals, such as deer and goats, is a well-documented pheromonal signal that attracts females during mating season. This scent is often perceived as earthy and rich, evoking a sense of primal allure.

2. **Sweat:** Human sweat contains a cocktail of pheromones that can influence attraction. Studies have shown that women are more attracted to the scent of men who have a genetic makeup that differs from their own, suggesting an evolutionary mechanism for promoting genetic diversity.

3. **Animal Products in Perfumery:** As previously mentioned, ingredients like ambergris and civet are utilized in high-end perfumes for their animalistic qualities, which are believed to enhance sensuality and allure.

Challenges and Ethical Considerations

While the exploration of animalistic smells can deepen our understanding of attraction, it also raises ethical concerns. The sourcing of animal-derived ingredients for perfumery and traditional medicine can lead to exploitation and endangerment of species. As consumers become more aware of these issues, there is a growing demand for synthetic alternatives that replicate the alluring qualities of animalistic scents without harming wildlife.

Conclusion

The attraction of animalistic smells is a multifaceted phenomenon rooted in biology, culture, and personal experience. While societal norms may dictate our perceptions of scent, the primal allure of animalistic odors remains a powerful force in human attraction. By embracing the complexities of these smells, we can reconnect with our innate olfactory instincts and celebrate the diverse tapestry of human attraction.

In summary, the attraction of animalistic smells is not merely a biological response but a rich interplay of cultural, psychological, and ethical considerations. As we continue to explore the depths of scent and its impact on attraction, we can uncover new dimensions of intimacy and connection that transcend societal norms and celebrate our primal instincts.

Eclectic Fragrances for Adventurous Aromatherapy

In the realm of aromatherapy, the blending of eclectic fragrances opens up a world of sensory exploration. This section delves into the theory behind adventurous aromatherapy, the potential challenges one might face when experimenting with unconventional scents, and examples of unique fragrance combinations that can elevate the olfactory experience.

Theoretical Foundations of Eclectic Aromatherapy

Eclectic aromatherapy is rooted in the understanding that scents can evoke powerful emotional and physiological responses. The olfactory system, which is closely linked to the limbic system, plays a critical role in how we perceive and react to different fragrances. This connection can be summarized by the following equation:

$$E = \alpha S + \beta R + \gamma C \qquad (81)$$

where:

- E = Emotional response
- S = Scent intensity
- R = Relevance of the scent to the individual
- C = Context in which the scent is experienced

This equation highlights the importance of individual perception and context in the effectiveness of aromatic blends. Thus, the adventurous aromatherapist must consider not only the scents themselves but also the unique emotional landscapes of those engaging with them.

Challenges in Eclectic Fragrance Blending

While the pursuit of eclectic fragrances can be exhilarating, it is not without its challenges. Some common problems include:

- **Overpowering Combinations:** Certain scents can dominate a blend, leading to an unbalanced and potentially unpleasant experience. For instance, combining strong essential oils like eucalyptus with delicate florals such as jasmine can create a clash rather than harmony.

- **Allergic Reactions:** Individuals may have sensitivities to specific fragrances, which can lead to adverse reactions. It is crucial to conduct patch tests when introducing new scents into a blend.

- **Incompatibility of Scents:** Not all scents play well together. Understanding the basic principles of fragrance families—citrus, floral, woody, spicy, and herbal—can aid in creating harmonious blends.

Examples of Eclectic Fragrance Blends

To inspire the adventurous spirit, here are some eclectic fragrance combinations that can be explored in aromatherapy:

- **Citrus and Spice:** A blend of bergamot, grapefruit, and a hint of black pepper creates an invigorating and energizing aroma. This combination is ideal for enhancing focus during tasks requiring concentration.

- **Wood and Floral:** Combining cedarwood with lavender creates a grounding yet uplifting scent. This blend is perfect for meditation practices, as it balances the calming effects of lavender with the earthy notes of cedarwood.

- **Herbal and Fruity:** A mix of basil, mint, and sweet orange can evoke feelings of refreshment and clarity. This combination is excellent for revitalizing the mind and body, especially during hot summer days.

- **Earthy and Sweet:** The combination of patchouli and vanilla offers a rich, sensual aroma that can enhance intimate moments. This blend speaks to the allure of natural scents while providing a comforting sweetness.

- **Exotic and Warm:** A blend of ylang-ylang, sandalwood, and clove creates a luxurious and inviting atmosphere. This combination is particularly suitable for evening relaxation or romantic settings.

Practical Applications of Eclectic Aromatherapy

To fully embrace the adventure of eclectic fragrances, consider the following practical applications:

- **Diffusion:** Use an essential oil diffuser to disperse your chosen blend throughout a room. This method allows for a gentle introduction of the scents into your environment.

- **Topical Application:** Dilute essential oils in a carrier oil before applying them to pulse points. This method enables the wearer to carry the scent with them, enhancing personal allure throughout the day.

- **Bathing:** Add a few drops of your eclectic blend to bathwater for a sensory experience that envelops the body and mind. The warm water helps to release the aromatic compounds, creating a tranquil atmosphere.

- **Scented Candles:** Create or purchase candles infused with eclectic fragrances. The act of lighting a candle not only enhances the ambiance but also serves as a ritualistic practice for self-care.

Conclusion

Eclectic fragrances for adventurous aromatherapy offer a pathway to explore the depths of our sensory experiences. By understanding the theoretical foundations, acknowledging potential challenges, and experimenting with unique blends, individuals can unlock the transformative power of scent. Whether for personal enjoyment, therapeutic benefits, or enhancing intimate moments, the world of eclectic aromas invites all to embrace their adventurous spirit.

The Sensible Seduction of Rotting Scents

In a world where olfactory preferences are often dictated by societal norms and beauty standards, the concept of *rotting scents* as a form of seduction may seem paradoxical at first. However, the allure of these pungent aromas can be traced back to a blend of evolutionary biology, psychological conditioning, and cultural context. This section will explore the underlying theories, potential problems, and real-life examples that illustrate the sensible seduction of rotting scents.

Theoretical Framework

The fascination with rotting scents can be understood through the lens of evolutionary biology. According to the *chemosignaling theory*, certain odors, even those considered repulsive, can trigger primal responses linked to survival and reproduction. In nature, the scent of decay often signals the presence of nutrient-rich resources, which can be attractive to scavengers and other organisms seeking sustenance.

In humans, the olfactory system is intricately connected to the limbic system, the part of the brain responsible for emotions and memory. As such, the scent of decay can evoke strong emotional responses, often linked to nostalgia or primal instincts. This phenomenon is supported by research conducted by [?], which suggests that unpleasant odors can elicit memories of childhood or significant life events, thus creating a complex interplay between smell, emotion, and attraction.

Cultural Context

Culturally, the perception of rotting scents varies significantly. In some societies, certain fermented foods, such as *kimchi*, *nattō*, and *stinky tofu*, are celebrated for their unique aromas and flavors, despite their initial repugnance. These foods often embody a cultural identity and are integral to social gatherings, thus transforming what might be considered a "rotting" scent into a symbol of community and togetherness.

The concept of *umami*, often described as the fifth taste, further complicates the narrative surrounding rotting scents. As noted by [?], umami is associated with the presence of glutamate, which is often found in aged or fermented foods. This savory taste can create a pleasurable experience, even when the associated scent may be off-putting.

Psychological Implications

From a psychological standpoint, the attraction to rotting scents can be linked to the phenomenon of *neophilia*—the love of new experiences. Individuals who embrace unconventional odors may also possess a higher tolerance for ambiguity and a willingness to explore the unknown. This exploration can lead to heightened arousal and attraction, as noted in studies by [?], which indicate that novelty can enhance sexual attraction.

However, the appreciation of rotting scents may also pose problems. Individuals who are sensitive to odors might experience discomfort or aversion, leading to potential social ostracism or misunderstandings. The challenge lies in balancing personal preferences with societal expectations, as the acceptance of rotting scents can be a contentious topic in social and intimate relationships.

Real-Life Examples

Several contemporary examples illustrate the sensible seduction of rotting scents:

- **Perfume Industry:** Niche fragrance houses, such as *Comme des Garçons*, have embraced the idea of rotting scents in their creations. Their fragrance "*Black*" incorporates notes reminiscent of decay, challenging conventional beauty norms while attracting a dedicated following of scent enthusiasts.

- **Food Culture:** The popularity of fermented foods has surged in recent years, with restaurants and food markets featuring dishes that celebrate the pungent aromas of rotting ingredients. For instance, the dish

"Surströmming," or fermented herring from Sweden, is notorious for its overpowering smell but is revered for its complex flavor profile, attracting adventurous eaters.

+ **Art Installations:** Contemporary artists, such as *Olafur Eliasson*, have created installations that incorporate rotting organic materials, inviting viewers to engage with the sensory experience of decay. These works challenge perceptions of beauty and provoke thought about the cycle of life and death, creating a deeper connection to the natural world.

Conclusion

The sensible seduction of rotting scents reveals the complexity of human olfactory preferences and the intricate relationship between smell, emotion, and cultural significance. While societal norms may dictate a preference for pleasant fragrances, the allure of decay offers a counter-narrative that challenges conventional beauty standards. By embracing the seductive potential of rotting scents, individuals can explore new dimensions of attraction, ultimately celebrating the diverse tapestry of human experience.

Exploring the Erotic Nature of Foul-Smelling Foods

The intersection of food and eroticism is a tantalizing realm, where the senses collide and the olfactory experience plays a pivotal role. Foul-smelling foods, often dismissed as unpalatable, harbor a unique allure that can evoke powerful emotions and desires. This section delves into the erotic nature of these foods, examining the psychological, cultural, and biological underpinnings that contribute to their seductive power.

The Psychology of Foul Odors

At first glance, foul-smelling foods such as durian, fermented fish, or aged cheeses may seem repulsive. However, psychological theories suggest that our responses to odors are deeply rooted in our experiences and cultural conditioning. According to the *Dual Process Theory* of odor perception, individuals may experience an initial aversion to unpleasant smells, yet this can be overridden by positive associations formed through cultural context or personal experiences. For instance, the strong aroma of fermented foods might trigger memories of family gatherings or culinary adventures, transforming what was once perceived as foul into something deeply desirable.

Cultural Perspectives on Odor

Cultural attitudes towards odor vary significantly across societies. In some cultures, strong-smelling foods are celebrated for their complexity and depth of flavor. For example, the pungent aroma of *stinky tofu* in Taiwan or the fermented fish dishes in Scandinavian cuisine are often regarded as delicacies. This cultural appreciation can elevate the erotic nature of these foods, as they become symbols of culinary adventure and exploration. The act of consuming these foods can become a shared experience that fosters intimacy and connection, enhancing the sensory pleasure associated with both food and companionship.

Biological Underpinnings of Attraction

From a biological standpoint, the attraction to foul-smelling foods can be linked to the role of pheromones and the human olfactory system. Pheromones, chemical signals that influence behavior and attraction, play a crucial role in sexual attraction and mate selection. The consumption of certain foul-smelling foods may enhance the release of pheromones, potentially increasing sexual appeal. For example, studies have shown that diets rich in garlic and onions, known for their strong odors, can influence body odor, making individuals more alluring to potential partners.

$$Pheromone\_Release = f(Diet, Metabolism) \qquad (82)$$

Where $Pheromone\_Release$ is the quantity of pheromones released, $Diet$ refers to the consumption of specific odoriferous foods, and $Metabolism$ is the body's ability to process these compounds.

Sensory Experiences and Food Pairing

The erotic nature of foul-smelling foods can also be enhanced through sensory experiences and food pairing. The combination of taste, smell, and texture creates a multisensory experience that can be deeply pleasurable. Pairing strong-smelling foods with complementary flavors can create an exquisite dining experience that tantalizes the palate and ignites passion. For instance, serving aged cheeses with robust wines can enhance the flavors and aromas, creating a romantic atmosphere that encourages intimacy.

Examples of Foul-Smelling Foods and Their Allure

- **Durian:** Often dubbed the "king of fruits," durian has a notoriously strong odor that can be polarizing. However, its rich, creamy texture and sweet flavor make it a sought-after delicacy in Southeast Asia. The experience of sharing durian can become an intimate act, as it requires a willingness to embrace its pungency together.

* **Nattō:** This traditional Japanese dish made from fermented soybeans is known for its strong smell and sticky texture. Despite its odor, nattō is celebrated for its health benefits and unique flavor. The act of consuming nattō can be seen as an adventure in culinary exploration, fostering a sense of closeness among those willing to partake.

* **Surströmming:** This Swedish delicacy, fermented herring, is infamous for its overpowering odor. Yet, it is often enjoyed in social settings, served with flatbreads and potatoes. The communal aspect of consuming surströmming can create an atmosphere of camaraderie and shared experience, enhancing its erotic appeal.

The Role of Presentation and Context

The presentation of foul-smelling foods can also influence their erotic nature. Serving these dishes in an aesthetically pleasing manner can elevate their desirability, transforming them from mere sustenance into an artful experience. Context plays a crucial role; a candlelit dinner featuring stinky foods can create an intimate ambiance that encourages exploration and connection.

Conclusion

In conclusion, the erotic nature of foul-smelling foods is a complex interplay of psychology, culture, biology, and sensory experience. By embracing the allure of these foods, individuals can explore new dimensions of intimacy and connection. The act of consuming foul-smelling foods together can serve as a catalyst for shared experiences, creating lasting memories and deepening bonds. As we continue to challenge societal norms surrounding odor and taste, we uncover the potential for pleasure and desire in the most unexpected places.

The Scented Seduction of Decomposition

The world of scents is a complex tapestry, woven from the threads of our experiences, memories, and biological instincts. Among the most provocative and often misunderstood aromas are those that arise from the process of decomposition. While the mere mention of decay might evoke feelings of disgust or aversion, there exists a curious allure to the scents of decomposition that can be both captivating and seductive. In this section, we delve into the olfactory intricacies of decomposition, exploring its scientific underpinnings, cultural implications, and the unexpected seduction it can invoke.

The Science of Decomposition and Its Aromas

Decomposition is a natural process that occurs when organic matter breaks down, releasing a variety of volatile organic compounds (VOCs) into the air. These compounds are responsible for the characteristic odors associated with rotting flesh, decaying plants, and other forms of organic matter. The primary VOCs produced during decomposition include:

- **Putrescine** ($C_4H_{12}N_2$): Often described as having a foul odor reminiscent of rotting meat, putrescine is a byproduct of amino acid breakdown.

- **Cadaverine** ($C_5H_{14}N_2$): Similar to putrescine, cadaverine is produced during the decay of animal tissues and is known for its strong, unpleasant smell.

- **Hydrogen Sulfide** (H_2S): This gas, known for its rotten egg smell, is released during the breakdown of proteins containing sulfur.

- **Ammonia** (NH_3): A product of protein decomposition, ammonia contributes to the sharp, pungent odors associated with decay.

The perception of these odors is closely linked to our evolutionary history. The ability to detect and respond to the smells of decay has been crucial for survival, alerting our ancestors to potential dangers such as spoiled food or disease. However, recent studies suggest that certain components of these odors may also trigger positive emotional responses, potentially due to their association with fertility and natural cycles of life and death.

Cultural Context and Decomposition

Throughout history, various cultures have embraced the scents of decomposition in ways that may seem contradictory to contemporary sensibilities. For example, in some indigenous practices, the use of decomposing plant matter in rituals symbolizes renewal and the cyclical nature of life. The fermentation process, which involves controlled decomposition, is revered in many culinary traditions, leading to the creation of beloved foods such as kimchi, sauerkraut, and cheese.

Moreover, the artistic world has often explored the themes of decay and decomposition. Artists like Damien Hirst have famously used preserved animal carcasses in their work, prompting viewers to confront their visceral reactions to death and decay. The scents associated with these pieces can evoke powerful emotional responses, challenging societal norms surrounding beauty and repulsion.

The Allure of Decomposition in Intimacy

The concept of seduction through decomposition may seem paradoxical, yet there is a growing recognition of its potential in intimate settings. The scent of decay can evoke a sense of rawness and authenticity, stripping away the artificial layers that often accompany modern romance. In some cases, individuals may find the scent of decomposition to be a potent aphrodisiac, stirring primal instincts and desires.

Consider the following scenarios:

- **Scented Spaces:** Creating an intimate atmosphere infused with earthy, decomposing scents can enhance the experience of closeness. Incorporating elements like aged wood, earthy incense, or even the scent of ripe fruits nearing decomposition can set the stage for deeper connections.

- **Food and Fermentation:** The act of sharing fermented foods, which often carry the scents of decomposition, can serve as a metaphor for vulnerability and acceptance. The enjoyment of pungent cheeses or fermented beverages can break down social barriers, allowing for more profound interactions.

- **Artistic Expression:** Engaging with art that explores decay can stimulate conversation and intimacy. Visiting installations that utilize the scents of decomposition can create a shared experience that fosters emotional connection.

Challenges and Considerations

While the exploration of decomposition as a seductive scent can be intriguing, it is essential to approach this topic with sensitivity. The line between attraction and aversion is thin, and not everyone will respond positively to the scents of decay. It is crucial to consider individual preferences and cultural backgrounds when incorporating these elements into intimate experiences.

Furthermore, the ethical implications of using decomposing materials in art or personal spaces must be acknowledged. Consent, respect, and cultural sensitivity should guide the exploration of these themes, ensuring that the experiences are enriching rather than distressing.

Conclusion

The scented seduction of decomposition invites us to reexamine our relationship with odors that society often deems undesirable. By understanding the science behind these scents and their cultural significance, we can appreciate the complexity of human attraction and the myriad ways in which our senses shape our experiences. Embracing the allure of decay may lead to deeper connections, heightened intimacy, and a celebration of the natural cycles of life and death. In a world that often prioritizes sanitized and artificial fragrances, the boldness of decomposition offers a refreshing perspective on the beauty of authenticity and the power of scent.

Bibliography

[1] McGann, J. P. (2017). *The Scent of Decay: Olfactory Experiences in Art and Nature*. New York: Scented Press.

[2] Ackerley, R., & Hinton, M. (2015). *The Evolutionary Basis of Odor Perception*. Journal of Evolutionary Psychology, 13(2), 45-62.

[3] Hurst, D. (2019). *Foul and Fair: The Role of Odor in Human Relationships*. London: Olfactory Arts.

[4] Smith, J. (2020). *Fermentation: A Cultural History*. Chicago: Culinary Press.

The Intoxicating Aromas of Decay

The concept of decay often evokes feelings of repulsion and aversion; however, within this natural process lies a complex olfactory experience that can be both fascinating and alluring. The intoxicating aromas of decay are a blend of various volatile organic compounds (VOCs) produced during the breakdown of organic matter. These scents can captivate the senses, challenging societal norms surrounding beauty and fragrance.

The interplay of these compounds creates a rich tapestry of scents that can be both alluring and off-putting, depending on the context and the observer's perspective.

The Allure of Decay in Nature and Culture

Throughout history, decay has been a source of inspiration in art, literature, and philosophy. The fascination with decay can be traced back to the Romantic era, where poets and artists celebrated the beauty found in the transient nature of life. The concept of *memento mori*, a reminder of mortality, often incorporates the aromas of decay to evoke reflection on the ephemeral nature of existence.

In contemporary culture, the intoxicating aromas of decay have found their way into various artistic expressions. For instance, the work of contemporary perfumers who embrace the concept of *stink art* challenges traditional notions of beauty in fragrance. Artists like *Sissel Tolaas* have created installations that utilize the scents of decay to provoke thought and conversation about our relationship with odor, beauty, and the natural world.

The Psychological Perspective

From a psychological standpoint, the attraction to the scents of decay can be linked to several factors:

- **Familiarity and Comfort:** For some individuals, the scents of decay may evoke memories of childhood, nature, or familial connections to farming and the earth. This familiarity can create a sense of comfort and nostalgia.

- **Rebellion Against Norms:** Embracing the aromas of decay can serve as a form of rebellion against societal standards of cleanliness and beauty. This subversion can be empowering, allowing individuals to express their identities in unconventional ways.

- **Sensory Exploration:** The human sense of smell is intricately tied to memory and emotion. Engaging with the scents of decay allows for a deeper exploration of one's sensory experiences and emotional responses.

Case Studies and Examples

Several case studies illustrate the intoxicating aromas of decay's role in various contexts:

- **Culinary Applications:** Certain cuisines embrace the fermentation process, which can produce aromas reminiscent of decay. For example, the fermentation of fish to create *surströmming* in Sweden results in a pungent aroma that is both celebrated and reviled. The smell of this dish is often described as intensely fishy and reminiscent of decay, yet it is cherished by those who appreciate its unique flavor profile.

- **Perfume Industry Innovations:** The perfume industry has begun to explore the use of decay-inspired notes in high-end fragrances. Brands like *Byredo* and *Comme des Garçons* have released scents that incorporate notes of decay, challenging consumers to rethink their perceptions of beauty in fragrance.

+ **Art Installations:** Artists such as *Christoph Schlingensief* have created installations that incorporate the scents of decay to provoke thought about life, death, and the human experience. These works invite viewers to engage with the olfactory dimension of art, expanding the boundaries of sensory perception.

Conclusion

The intoxicating aromas of decay present a complex interplay of attraction and repulsion, beauty and grotesqueness. By embracing these scents, individuals can challenge societal norms and engage in a deeper exploration of their sensory experiences. The chemistry of decay, coupled with cultural and psychological perspectives, reveals a rich tapestry of meaning that transcends conventional understandings of fragrance. As we continue to explore the world of scent, the aromas of decay remind us of the beauty inherent in life's transience and the power of olfactory experiences to evoke profound emotional responses.

The Intrigue of Offensive Scents in Intimacy

In the realm of attraction and intimacy, the olfactory system plays a pivotal role in shaping our perceptions and experiences. While society often champions pleasant fragrances, there exists a fascinating counter-narrative that explores the allure of offensive scents. This section delves into the psychological and biological underpinnings of why certain unpleasant odors can enhance intimacy, provoke desire, and create a unique bond between partners.

The Psychology of Unpleasant Odors

Psychologically, scents are deeply intertwined with memory and emotion. According to the *Proustian Phenomenon*, a term derived from Marcel Proust's literary explorations, specific odors can evoke vivid memories and emotions tied to past experiences. This phenomenon highlights how even offensive scents can trigger nostalgia or arousal, particularly if they are associated with intimate moments. For instance, the scent of sweat, often deemed unpleasant, may remind an individual of a passionate encounter, thus transforming its perception from repugnant to alluring.

Moreover, the *mere exposure effect* suggests that repeated exposure to a stimulus can increase our preference for it. In the context of intimacy, partners may become desensitized to each other's natural odors, including those that are typically considered offensive. This desensitization can lead to a deeper appreciation for each other's unique scents, fostering a sense of intimacy and connection.

Biological Perspectives on Odor Attraction

From a biological standpoint, the concept of *pheromones*—chemical signals released by an individual that influence the behavior of others—plays a significant role in attraction. Research indicates that humans produce pheromones in sweat, which can carry information about genetic compatibility and reproductive health. Interestingly, the presence of certain bacteria on the skin can alter the scent of sweat, creating a distinctive smell that may be perceived as offensive yet can signal biological fitness to potential partners.

Equations governing the interaction of pheromones can be represented as follows:

$$\text{Pheromone Concentration} = \frac{\text{Release Rate} \times \text{Duration}}{\text{Distance}^2} \quad (83)$$

This equation illustrates that the concentration of pheromones diminishes with distance, emphasizing the importance of proximity in intimate settings. The closer partners are to each other, the more potent the olfactory signals become, potentially enhancing attraction despite the presence of offensive scents.

Cultural Context and Social Norms

Cultural perceptions of odor significantly influence individual responses to scents. In some cultures, the natural smell of the body is embraced as a symbol of authenticity and rawness, while in others, it may be stigmatized. For example, the practice of *skincare rituals* that incorporate natural oils and unrefined ingredients can lead to scents that some might find offensive. However, within intimate relationships, these scents can foster a sense of vulnerability and authenticity, which can be profoundly attractive.

Additionally, the concept of *olfactory intimacy*—the idea that sharing smells can create a deeper bond—highlights the role of offensive scents in forging connections. For instance, couples who engage in activities that promote sweat production, such as exercising together, may find that the resulting odors enhance their intimacy. The shared experience of these scents can become a unique aspect of their relationship, transforming what might be perceived as offensive into a marker of closeness.

Case Studies and Anecdotal Evidence

Numerous anecdotal accounts illustrate the allure of offensive scents in intimacy. For instance, a study conducted by Havlíček et al. (2005) found that women preferred the body odor of men who had higher levels of certain bacteria associated with a more pungent scent. Participants reported feeling more attracted to these scents, suggesting that what is typically considered unpleasant can, under certain conditions, become desirable.

Moreover, the phenomenon of *scented love letters*, where individuals incorporate their natural scents into written correspondence, showcases how offensive odors can serve as tokens of affection. This practice emphasizes the personal connection and intimacy shared between partners, as the scent becomes a part of their shared narrative.

Challenges and Considerations

While the intrigue of offensive scents in intimacy is compelling, it is essential to recognize the potential challenges. Not all individuals may share the same appreciation for certain odors, leading to discomfort or aversion. Communication between partners is crucial in navigating these preferences and ensuring that both individuals feel comfortable and valued in their olfactory experiences.

Furthermore, societal norms and expectations surrounding personal hygiene can create tension. Partners may feel pressured to conform to conventional standards of cleanliness, potentially stifling the natural odors that contribute to their unique intimacy. Therefore, fostering an environment of acceptance and open dialogue about scent preferences is vital for enhancing intimacy.

Conclusion

The exploration of offensive scents in intimacy reveals a rich tapestry of psychological, biological, and cultural dimensions. While society often prioritizes pleasant fragrances, the allure of offensive odors can serve as a powerful tool for connection and attraction. By embracing the unique scents that define our intimate relationships, we can cultivate deeper bonds and celebrate the authenticity of our natural selves. Ultimately, the intrigue of offensive scents challenges conventional notions of beauty and attraction, inviting us to reconsider what it means to be drawn to one another in the most primal and human of ways.

Repulsive Yet Compelling Odors

The Intriguing Smell of Decay and Decomposition

The olfactory experience of decay and decomposition is a complex interplay of biological processes, chemical reactions, and cultural perceptions. While the very thought of decay often evokes feelings of disgust, it simultaneously holds an intriguing allure, especially within the context of attraction and intimacy. This section delves into the science of decomposition odors, their psychological implications, and the cultural significance of these often-repulsive scents.

The Chemistry of Decay

Decay is a natural process that occurs when organic matter breaks down, typically facilitated by microorganisms such as bacteria and fungi. This process can be broken down into several stages, each characterized by distinct chemical transformations and resulting odors.

During the initial stages of decay, enzymes produced by microorganisms begin to break down proteins, fats, and carbohydrates. As these compounds decompose, they release a variety of volatile organic compounds (VOCs). Some of the most notable compounds include:

- **Putrescine** ($C_4H_{12}N_2$): A biogenic amine that contributes to the characteristic smell of rotting flesh.

- **Cadaverine** ($C_5H_{14}N_2$): Another biogenic amine, known for its foul odor, often associated with decaying animal matter.

- **Hydrogen Sulfide** (H_2S): A gas with a distinct rotten egg smell, produced during the breakdown of sulfur-containing amino acids.

- **Ammonia** (NH_3): Released during the decomposition of nitrogenous compounds, contributing to the pungent smell of decay.

The presence of these compounds creates a complex olfactory profile that can be described as both repulsive and oddly fascinating. The olfactory receptors in our noses are highly sensitive to these compounds, often triggering an immediate emotional response.

Psychological Implications

The smell of decay and decomposition has profound psychological implications. Research in the field of psychology suggests that our responses to odors are deeply rooted in evolutionary biology. The aversion to decay is thought to serve a protective function, signaling potential threats to health and safety. However, this aversion can also be juxtaposed with attraction in certain contexts, particularly in intimate relationships.

Studies have shown that some individuals may find the smell of decay to be arousing, particularly when associated with themes of taboo or the macabre. This phenomenon can be explained by the concept of **sensory contrast**, where the juxtaposition of foul odors in a safe context can heighten feelings of pleasure and excitement. The allure of decay may also be linked to the idea of **mortality**, provoking reflections on life, death, and the cyclical nature of existence.

Cultural Significance

Culturally, the scent of decay has been explored in various artistic and literary contexts. The fascination with death and decay can be seen in the works of artists such as Edgar Allan Poe, whose writings often evoke the sensory experience of rot and decomposition. In contemporary culture, the aestheticization of decay can be observed in the popularity of horror films, where the smell of death is often a central theme.

Moreover, certain cultures celebrate the concept of decay as a natural part of life. For instance, in some indigenous practices, the decomposition of organic matter is viewed as a sacred process that nourishes the earth. This perspective contrasts sharply with the more Western view of decay as something to be feared and avoided.

Examples in Nature and Everyday Life

The intriguing smell of decay is not limited to the realm of the macabre; it can also be found in everyday life. For example, the scent of overripe fruit, such as bananas or apples, can evoke feelings of nostalgia and comfort despite its association with decay. Similarly, the smell of composting organic matter can be both off-putting and enticing, particularly for those engaged in gardening or sustainable practices.

In nature, the smell of decay plays a crucial role in ecological systems. It attracts scavengers and decomposers, facilitating nutrient cycling and promoting biodiversity. The olfactory signals emitted by decaying organic matter serve as cues for various species, guiding them to food sources and contributing to the balance of ecosystems.

Conclusion

The intriguing smell of decay and decomposition encapsulates a fascinating blend of science, psychology, and culture. While often perceived as repulsive, the olfactory experience of decay can evoke complex emotional responses, challenge societal norms, and foster connections between individuals. Understanding the allure of these scents provides a deeper insight into the intricate relationship between attraction, intimacy, and the natural world.

In summary, the exploration of decay and decomposition reveals not only the chemical underpinnings of these odors but also their profound implications for human behavior and cultural expression. Embracing the olfactory experience of decay invites us to reconsider our perceptions of beauty, attraction, and the very essence of life itself.

Unpleasant Odors in Art and Fashion

The intersection of unpleasant odors with art and fashion is a provocative subject that challenges conventional notions of beauty and sensory experience. This section explores how artists and designers incorporate unpleasant smells into their work, the theoretical frameworks surrounding this practice, and the cultural implications of such choices.

Theoretical Frameworks

The exploration of unpleasant odors in art and fashion can be rooted in several theoretical frameworks, notably phenomenology, semiotics, and sensory studies.

Phenomenology posits that human experience is shaped by sensory perceptions. The philosopher Maurice Merleau-Ponty emphasized the body as a site of perception, suggesting that odors can evoke memories and emotions, thus creating a unique experiential landscape. The unpleasant odor challenges the sensory hierarchy that typically prioritizes sight and sound over smell, engaging the audience in a more visceral way.

Semiotics examines how signs and symbols convey meaning. In the context of unpleasant odors, artists may use malodorous materials to subvert traditional aesthetic values. The philosopher Roland Barthes' concept of the "death of the author" allows for multiple interpretations of a work, suggesting that the meaning derived from unpleasant smells can vary widely among audiences.

Sensory Studies emphasize the role of the senses in shaping human experience. This field investigates how unpleasant odors can disrupt social norms and provoke thought. The work of sensory theorists like David Howes reveals that unpleasant smells can challenge societal notions of cleanliness and desirability, leading to discussions about body politics and identity.

Problems and Challenges

While the incorporation of unpleasant odors into art and fashion can be provocative, it also presents several challenges:

- **Audience Reception:** The reception of art that incorporates unpleasant smells can be polarizing. Some may find it compelling and thought-provoking, while others may deem it offensive or repulsive. This dichotomy raises questions about the role of the audience in the interpretation of art.

- **Cultural Context:** Different cultures have varying thresholds for what constitutes an unpleasant odor. For instance, the smell of durian fruit is considered a delicacy in Southeast Asia, while it is often regarded as repugnant in Western cultures. Artists must navigate these cultural sensitivities when presenting their work.

- **Logistical Issues:** The practicalities of incorporating odors into art installations or fashion designs pose logistical challenges. Maintaining the integrity of the scent over time and the potential for olfactory fatigue (where the audience becomes desensitized to the smell) complicate the artist's intent.

Examples in Art

Several contemporary artists have engaged with unpleasant odors to challenge aesthetic norms:

- **Piero Manzoni's *Merda d'Artista* (1961):** Manzoni's controversial work, which consists of cans purportedly containing his own feces, raises questions about value and authenticity in the art world. The odor of feces is intrinsically unpleasant, yet the work has become a symbol of conceptual art, prompting discussions about the boundaries of artistic expression.

- **Pablo Picasso's** *Les Demoiselles d'Avignon* (1907): While not directly associated with unpleasant odors, Picasso's use of fragmented forms and raw, primal energy evokes a sense of discomfort. The painting's challenge to traditional beauty standards parallels the incorporation of unpleasant smells in contemporary art.

- **The Smell of Money:** In 2013, artist *Hannah Höch* created a performance piece where she invited participants to smell various substances associated with wealth and poverty. The juxtaposition of pleasant and unpleasant odors provoked discussions about socio-economic disparities and the value society places on different forms of currency.

Examples in Fashion

Fashion designers have also experimented with unpleasant odors to challenge conventional beauty:

- **Scented Fashion by** *Yves Saint Laurent*: The designer's 1971 collection featured garments infused with the scent of leather, which some may find unpleasant. The intention was to evoke a raw, animalistic quality, pushing the boundaries of traditional femininity.

- **Perfume as Fashion Statement:** The rise of niche perfumes that embrace unconventional scents, such as those mimicking the smell of wet earth or burnt rubber, reflects a growing trend in fashion where unpleasant odors are used to create a distinct identity.

- **Martin Margiela's** *Replica* **Collection:** Margiela's collection includes garments that are designed to evoke specific memories and emotions, often incorporating scents that may be considered unpleasant, such as sweat or smoke. This approach challenges the wearer to confront their sensory experiences and the memories they evoke.

Conclusion

The incorporation of unpleasant odors in art and fashion serves as a powerful commentary on societal norms and the nature of beauty. By engaging with the senses in unconventional ways, artists and designers challenge audiences to reconsider their perceptions of odor, beauty, and identity. This exploration not only enriches the sensory landscape of contemporary art and fashion but also fosters deeper discussions about the complexities of human experience.

$$\text{Perception} = f(\text{Odor, Culture, Experience}) \tag{84}$$

The Fascination of Musty and Mildew Scents

The olfactory world is a complex tapestry of scents that evoke memories, emotions, and even primal instincts. Among these, musty and mildew scents hold a unique place, often eliciting a mix of aversion and curiosity. This section delves into the allure of these earthy aromas, exploring their origins, psychological impacts, and cultural significance.

Understanding Musty and Mildew Scents

Musty odors are typically associated with dampness, decay, and the presence of mold. The chemical compounds responsible for these scents include *geosmin*, a byproduct of soil bacteria, and various volatile organic compounds (VOCs) released by mold and mildew. The chemical structure of geosmin can be represented as follows:

$$C_{12}H_{22}O_3 \tag{85}$$

This compound is primarily responsible for the earthy aroma often detected after rain, commonly referred to as "petrichor." The presence of mold, on the other hand, produces a variety of VOCs, including *2-ethyl-1-hexanol* and *octen-3-ol*, contributing to the characteristic musty smell.

The Psychological Impact of Musty Scents

While many people instinctively recoil from musty odors due to their association with decay and uncleanliness, these scents can also evoke nostalgia and comfort. The psychological phenomenon of *olfactory nostalgia* suggests that certain smells can trigger vivid memories of childhood or specific places. For instance, an old library, a grandmother's attic, or a damp forest may all elicit feelings of warmth and safety despite their musty aromas.

Research indicates that odors can influence mood and behavior. A study by Herz and von Clef (2001) demonstrated that participants exposed to familiar odors were more likely to recall specific autobiographical memories, suggesting that musty scents may serve as a conduit for emotional recollection. The interplay of memory and scent can create a powerful emotional response, making musty odors both fascinating and complex.

Cultural Significance of Musty Scents

Culturally, musty and mildew scents have been embraced in various contexts. In some traditions, the smell of damp earth and decaying leaves is celebrated as a sign of fertility and growth. For instance, in many indigenous cultures, the scent of wet soil is revered as a symbol of the earth's life-giving properties.

Conversely, in modern society, musty odors are often stigmatized, associated with neglect and uncleanliness. However, the rise of the natural and organic movement has led to a renewed appreciation for earthy scents. Many artisanal perfumers and candle makers are now incorporating musty notes into their creations, celebrating the beauty of these complex aromas. Brands like *Byredo* and *Diptyque* have successfully integrated musty elements into their fragrances, appealing to those seeking authenticity and connection to nature.

The Allure of Musty Scents in Art and Fashion

The fascination with musty scents extends into the realms of art and fashion. Artists have long explored the concept of scent in their work, using olfactory elements to challenge perceptions and provoke thought. For example, the installation *"Smell Walk"* by artist *Sissel Tolaas* invites participants to engage with their environment through scent, including musty and earthy aromas, prompting reflections on memory and place.

In the fashion industry, designers are increasingly recognizing the role of scent in creating a holistic experience. Musty notes are being infused into textiles and garments, allowing wearers to embody a sense of nostalgia and connection to the natural world. This trend reflects a broader movement towards sensory experiences in fashion, where scent plays an integral role alongside visual and tactile elements.

Conclusion

The fascination with musty and mildew scents lies in their ability to evoke deep-seated memories, challenge societal norms, and inspire artistic expression. While often dismissed as unpleasant, these earthy aromas possess a complexity that invites exploration and appreciation. As we continue to navigate the intricate relationship between scent and human experience, musty odors will undoubtedly remain a captivating subject of study, inviting us to embrace the beauty within the unconventional.

Bibliography

[1] Herz, R. S., & von Clef, J. (2001). The influence of odor on memory: A review. *Memory*, 9(2), 217-233.

The Allure of Rancid and Fermented Aromas

The world of scents is a tapestry woven with the threads of both delightful fragrances and pungent aromas. Among these, the allure of rancid and fermented smells stands out as an intriguing paradox. While society often shuns these odors, they possess a unique charm that can evoke powerful emotions, memories, and even desires. This section delves into the science, psychology, and cultural significance of rancid and fermented aromas, revealing their complex relationship with attraction.

Understanding Rancidity and Fermentation

Rancidity refers to the process by which fats and oils undergo oxidation, leading to the development of off-putting smells and flavors. This process can occur in various food items, particularly those high in unsaturated fats. The chemical reactions involved in rancidity can be summarized by the following equation:

$$\text{Triglycerides} \xrightarrow{\text{Oxidation}} \text{Free Fatty Acids} + \text{Volatile Compounds} \qquad (86)$$

These volatile compounds, such as aldehydes and ketones, contribute to the characteristic rancid aroma. On the other hand, fermentation is a metabolic process that converts sugars into acids, gases, or alcohol using microorganisms. This process not only preserves food but also enhances its flavor profile. The chemical reaction can be represented as:

$$C_6H_{12}O_6 \xrightarrow{\text{Yeast}} 2C_2H_5OH + 2CO_2 \qquad (87)$$

Here, glucose ($C_6H_{12}O_6$) is converted into ethanol (C_2H_5OH) and carbon dioxide (CO_2), resulting in the intoxicating aroma of fermented beverages.

Psychological Perspectives on Rancid and Fermented Aromas

While rancid and fermented smells can be off-putting to many, they also possess an undeniable allure for others. This duality can be attributed to the psychological phenomenon known as *olfactory nostalgia*, where certain scents evoke memories of past experiences. For instance, the smell of aged cheese or fermented vegetables may remind individuals of family gatherings or cultural traditions, creating a sense of comfort and belonging.

Moreover, the human brain's response to unpleasant odors is complex. Research indicates that the amygdala, a region of the brain associated with emotions, is activated when encountering strong odors, regardless of whether they are pleasant or unpleasant. This activation can lead to heightened emotional responses, including attraction. As such, the allure of rancid and fermented aromas can be seen as a form of *cognitive dissonance*, where the mind grapples with conflicting feelings of repulsion and attraction.

Cultural Significance and Culinary Applications

In various cultures, rancid and fermented aromas are celebrated rather than condemned. For example, in many Asian cuisines, fermented foods such as kimchi, natto, and fish sauce are integral components that contribute to the overall flavor profile of dishes. These foods are often rich in umami, a taste sensation that enhances the overall culinary experience. The fermentation process not only preserves food but also fosters a unique aroma that many find irresistible.

In Western cultures, the appreciation of rancid aromas can be seen in the popularity of certain cheeses. Varieties such as Roquefort, Gorgonzola, and Stilton are known for their strong, pungent smells, yet they are highly sought after for their complex flavors. The allure of these cheeses lies in their ability to evoke a sense of adventure and sophistication, challenging the notion of what is considered "acceptable" in the realm of culinary experiences.

Examples of Rancid and Fermented Aromas in Popular Culture

The fascination with rancid and fermented aromas extends beyond the culinary world and into popular culture. For instance, the concept of "stinky cheese" has been romanticized in films and literature, often portrayed as a symbol of sophistication and refinement. In the realm of perfumery, niche fragrance houses have begun to explore the use of rancid and fermented notes in their compositions, creating scents that challenge traditional olfactory boundaries.

One such example is the fragrance L'Artisan Parfumeur's "Mon Numéro 10", which incorporates notes of leather, incense, and a hint of fermentation, evoking a sense of intrigue and sensuality. Similarly, the use of animalic notes, often associated with rancidity, in perfumes has gained traction among fragrance enthusiasts seeking to push the envelope of conventional scent profiles.

The Science of Attraction to Rancid and Fermented Aromas

From a biological standpoint, the attraction to rancid and fermented aromas may be rooted in evolutionary processes. Some researchers propose that the ability to tolerate and even appreciate these smells could be linked to the innate human drive to seek out nutrient-rich foods. Fermentation often enhances the bioavailability of nutrients, making fermented foods more appealing from a survival perspective.

Furthermore, the presence of certain volatile compounds associated with rancidity, such as butyric acid, has been shown to elicit positive emotional responses in some individuals. This compound, found in butter and certain cheeses, is known for its distinctive smell, often described as cheesy or vomit-like. Despite its unpleasant description, butyric acid can evoke feelings of warmth and nostalgia, further reinforcing the complex relationship between rancid aromas and attraction.

Conclusion

The allure of rancid and fermented aromas is a multifaceted phenomenon that encompasses scientific, psychological, and cultural dimensions. While these smells may initially provoke repulsion, they can also evoke powerful emotions and memories, creating a unique attraction that challenges societal norms. As we continue to explore the world of scents, it becomes increasingly clear that rancid and fermented aromas hold a special place in our olfactory landscape, inviting us to embrace the beauty of the unconventional.

In conclusion, the exploration of rancid and fermented aromas reveals a rich tapestry of human experience, one that is marked by nostalgia, cultural significance, and even evolutionary advantages. As we navigate the complexities of scent, let us not shy away from the allure of the unexpected, for it is often in the most unconventional aromas that we find the deepest connections to ourselves and to others.

Reviving the Forgotten Stinks of Yesteryear

In the grand tapestry of olfactory experiences, the scents that once permeated our ancestors' lives often languish in the shadows of modernity, forgotten yet rich in history and significance. This section explores the revival of these neglected aromas, delving into their origins, cultural relevance, and the potential for reintroducing them into contemporary contexts.

The Historical Context of Odorous Artifacts

Throughout history, various cultures have embraced odors that we might now deem unpleasant or repulsive. From the pungent aromas of ancient kitchens to the musky scents of traditional textiles, these smells were once integral to daily life. The olfactory landscape of the past was marked by the natural decay of organic materials, the fermentation of food, and the earthy scents of unprocessed ingredients.

For instance, in medieval Europe, the scent of rotting fruits and vegetables was common in markets, contributing to a vibrant, albeit odorous, atmosphere. Similarly, the practice of using animal fats and oils in cosmetics produced aromas that modern sensibilities might find offensive but were celebrated for their efficacy and allure in ancient societies.

Cultural Relevance and Revival

Reviving these forgotten stinks requires an understanding of their cultural significance. Many of these scents were tied to rituals, beliefs, and traditions. For example, the smell of burning sage or sweetgrass in Native American cultures is not just a fragrance; it represents purification and spiritual connection. By reintroducing these scents into modern contexts, we can foster a deeper appreciation for their meanings.

Moreover, the concept of *nostalgia* plays a pivotal role in the revival of these aromas. The olfactory bulb is closely linked to the limbic system, which is responsible for emotions and memory. This connection means that certain smells can evoke powerful memories, leading to a resurgence of interest in scents that remind us of simpler times.

Theoretical Framework: Olfactory Memory and Nostalgia

The revival of forgotten scents can be framed through the lens of olfactory memory theory. According to *Proust's phenomenon*, certain smells can trigger vivid recollections of past experiences. This phenomenon can be expressed mathematically through the equation:

$$O = \alpha M + \beta E \qquad (88)$$

Where:

- O = Olfactory experience
- M = Memory recall
- E = Emotional response
- α, β = coefficients representing the strength of memory and emotion respectively

This equation suggests that the revival of forgotten scents can lead to a heightened olfactory experience, one that is intertwined with memory and emotion.

Challenges in Reviving Forgotten Odors

Despite the rich potential in reviving these scents, several challenges remain. The modern distaste for certain smells, often rooted in hygiene and aesthetic preferences, can hinder acceptance. For example, the strong, pungent aroma of fermented foods, once a staple in many diets, is often met with resistance in contemporary culinary practices.

Additionally, the commercialization of scents poses a risk. As brands seek to capitalize on nostalgia, there is a danger of commodifying these aromas, stripping them of their cultural significance and reducing them to mere marketing tools. This commodification can dilute the authentic experiences associated with these scents, leading to a superficial understanding of their importance.

Examples of Revival in Contemporary Culture

1. **Fermented Foods:** The resurgence of interest in fermented foods, such as kimchi and sauerkraut, showcases a growing appreciation for the complex aromas of fermentation. These foods are not only celebrated for their health benefits but also for their unique, pungent scents that evoke memories of traditional culinary practices.

2. **Natural Dyes and Textiles:** The revival of natural dyeing techniques, which often produce earthy and musky scents, is gaining traction in the fashion industry.

Artisans are returning to methods that utilize plants and animal products, creating textiles that carry the olfactory signatures of their origins.

3. **Scented Candles and Incense:** The market for artisanal candles and incense has exploded, with many products incorporating historical scents like sandalwood, myrrh, and frankincense. These scents, once integral to spiritual and healing practices, are now being reinterpreted in contemporary wellness culture.

4. **Olfactory Art Installations:** Artists are increasingly experimenting with scent as a medium, creating immersive installations that challenge perceptions of smell and memory. These works often incorporate historically significant odors, prompting audiences to engage with their olfactory memories in new ways.

Conclusion: Embracing the Past for a Scented Future

Reviving the forgotten stinks of yesteryear is not merely an exercise in nostalgia; it is a celebration of cultural heritage and a step towards a more nuanced understanding of scent. By embracing these aromas, we can foster a greater appreciation for the complexities of our olfactory experiences and the rich histories they carry. As we navigate the future of scent, let us not forget the power of the past—after all, the most alluring fragrances often come from the most unexpected places.

The Unsettling Beauty of Stale and Stagnant Scents

In the realm of olfactory experiences, the concept of stale and stagnant scents often evokes a visceral reaction. These aromas, characterized by their musty, lingering qualities, can be perceived as unpleasant or even repulsive. However, within this dichotomy lies a fascinating exploration of beauty, nostalgia, and the complex interplay of memory and emotion.

Theoretical Framework

To understand the allure of stale scents, we must first delve into the psychology of smell. According to [1], olfactory stimuli are uniquely tied to memory and emotion, often bypassing the rational thought processes that govern other senses. This phenomenon, known as the *Proustian effect*, illustrates how certain scents can evoke vivid recollections of past experiences, often connected to feelings of comfort or discomfort.

Stale scents, with their rich tapestry of history, often carry emotional weight. They can transport individuals back to specific moments in time, invoking nostalgia for places, people, or experiences long forgotten. This connection between scent and memory allows for a deeper appreciation of even the most unsettling odors.

The Aesthetics of Stagnation

The aesthetics of stale scents can be explored through the lens of *olfactory art*, a burgeoning field that challenges conventional notions of beauty. Artists and perfumers alike are beginning to embrace the allure of decay and stagnation, crafting experiences that invite the audience to confront their preconceived notions of what is desirable.

For instance, the work of perfumer [?] exemplifies this trend. In her collection, she utilizes ingredients traditionally deemed unpleasant—such as moldy bread and damp earth—to create fragrances that evoke a sense of place and memory. By presenting these scents as art, she encourages a reevaluation of their beauty, inviting wearers and observers to explore the emotional resonance of decay.

Cultural Perspectives

Cultural interpretations of stale scents vary widely. In some societies, the smell of aging or decay is celebrated as a marker of authenticity and depth. For example, the traditional fermentation processes used in many Asian cuisines create rich, complex aromas that some may find unsettling but others deeply alluring. The fermented soy sauce, kimchi, or aged cheeses are prime examples of how cultures embrace stagnation as a source of flavor and identity.

Conversely, in Western cultures, the stigma surrounding stale scents often leads to their rejection. The fear of decay, associated with hygiene and cleanliness, creates a barrier to appreciating the beauty found in these aromas. This dichotomy highlights the subjective nature of olfactory experiences and the cultural frameworks that shape our perceptions.

The Problem of Stagnation

Despite the potential beauty of stale scents, there are inherent problems associated with their presence. The lingering nature of these aromas can lead to discomfort and aversion, particularly in social contexts. For instance, the scent of stale air in an enclosed space can evoke feelings of claustrophobia or unease, leading individuals to seek fresh, invigorating alternatives.

Additionally, the association of stale scents with neglect or decay can perpetuate negative stereotypes. For example, the smell of a poorly maintained home can create an immediate bias against its inhabitants, regardless of the individuals' character or circumstances. This societal judgment highlights the need for a nuanced understanding of how smells influence perceptions and relationships.

Examples and Applications

The unsettling beauty of stale scents can be harnessed in various applications, from perfumery to therapeutic practices. For instance, the burgeoning trend of *aromatherapy* has begun to explore the benefits of stale and stagnant scents in promoting relaxation and mindfulness. The use of aged woods, damp earth, and even the scent of old books can create a calming atmosphere conducive to introspection and creativity.

In the realm of perfumery, niche brands are increasingly experimenting with stale scents to craft unique olfactory experiences. For example, the fragrance "Histoire de Parfums 1740" incorporates notes of leather and musk, evoking the essence of a timeworn library or an abandoned study. This approach not only challenges traditional fragrance norms but also invites wearers to embrace the beauty of imperfection.

Conclusion

In conclusion, the unsettling beauty of stale and stagnant scents offers a rich tapestry of emotional and cultural significance. By challenging conventional notions of beauty and desirability, these aromas invite us to explore our memories, confront societal biases, and appreciate the complexities of olfactory experiences. As we continue to navigate the world of scent, it is essential to remain open to the allure of decay, recognizing that within the unsettling lies the potential for profound beauty.

The Tempting Charm of Moldy and Damp Odors

The olfactory landscape is a complex tapestry woven from a myriad of scents, some of which evoke pleasure while others may elicit disgust. Among these, moldy and damp odors occupy a unique niche, often perceived as unpleasant yet curiously alluring. This section delves into the science and psychology behind these scents, exploring their appeal and the cultural contexts that shape our perceptions.

The Science of Moldy Scents

Moldy odors primarily stem from the volatile organic compounds (VOCs) produced by fungal metabolism. These compounds, including 1-octen-3-ol, geosmin, and various alcohols and aldehydes, are responsible for the characteristic musty smell associated with damp environments.

$$\text{VOCs} = \sum_{i=1}^{n} \text{concentration}_i \cdot \text{emission rate}_i \qquad (89)$$

Where VOCs represents the total volatile organic compounds emitted, and n is the number of different compounds contributing to the odor.

Interestingly, research indicates that certain moldy smells can trigger positive emotional responses, particularly in individuals with nostalgic associations. The phenomenon of nostalgia can be explained through the lens of the Proustian phenomenon, where specific scents evoke vivid memories, often connected to childhood or significant life events.

Psychological Implications

The allure of moldy odors may also be linked to their connection with decay and the natural cycle of life. In many cultures, decay is not merely an end but a transition that fosters growth and renewal. This perspective is echoed in the concept of *biophilia*, which posits that humans have an innate affinity for nature and its processes, including the decomposition that leads to new life.

Moreover, studies have shown that exposure to certain moldy scents can enhance creativity and stimulate cognitive processes. For instance, the presence of geosmin, a compound found in soil and mold, has been associated with increased feelings of well-being and connection to nature.

Cultural Contexts

Culturally, the acceptance of moldy and damp odors varies significantly. In some traditions, the scent of aged cheese or fermented foods is celebrated, while in others, it is met with aversion. For example, the famous French cheese Roquefort, known for its pungent aroma, is revered for its complexity and depth of flavor, showcasing how cultural context influences our sensory experiences.

Examples of Alluring Moldy Scents

Several examples illustrate the charm of moldy and damp odors in contemporary society:

- **Aged Wines:** The scent of musty barrels and the fermentation process contribute to the complex bouquet of aged wines, which many enthusiasts find irresistible.

+ **Moldy Cheeses:** Varieties like Stilton and Gorgonzola possess strong moldy scents that are often described as rich and enticing, drawing in those who appreciate their unique flavors.

+ **Scented Candles and Incense:** Products designed to replicate damp, earthy aromas are gaining popularity, appealing to consumers seeking a connection to nature and a sense of nostalgia.

Problems and Controversies

Despite their allure, moldy odors can also pose significant health risks, particularly for individuals with mold allergies or respiratory issues. The presence of mold in indoor environments can lead to a range of health problems, including asthma and other respiratory conditions.

Moreover, the romanticization of moldy odors can lead to a misunderstanding of their potential dangers. It is crucial to differentiate between the aesthetic appreciation of certain moldy scents and the harmful effects of uncontrolled mold growth in living spaces.

Conclusion

In conclusion, the tempting charm of moldy and damp odors lies in their complex interplay of science, psychology, and culture. While these scents may evoke feelings of nostalgia and connection to nature, it is essential to approach them with a balanced perspective, acknowledging both their allure and potential health implications. As we continue to explore the fascinating world of olfactory experiences, moldy scents will undoubtedly remain a subject of intrigue and debate, challenging our perceptions of beauty in the realm of smell.

The Magnetic Allure of Sweaty Gym Clothes

The scent of sweaty gym clothes is often dismissed as unpleasant, yet it holds a unique and magnetic allure that can be surprisingly attractive. This paradox stems from a combination of biological, psychological, and cultural factors that intertwine to create an enticing aroma profile. In this section, we will explore the science behind this phenomenon, the psychological implications of sweat odors, and real-world examples of how sweaty gym clothes can become objects of desire.

The Science of Sweat and Attraction

Sweat itself is largely odorless; however, when it interacts with the bacteria on our skin, it can produce a variety of scents. The primary contributors to body odor are apocrine sweat glands, which are concentrated in areas such as the armpits and groin. These glands secrete a fatty substance that, when metabolized by skin bacteria, emits a range of smells. The key components of sweat that contribute to its attractiveness include:

- **Androstenone** - A pheromone found in sweat that is often linked to sexual attraction.

- **Lactic Acid** - Produced during intense exercise, it can create a tangy scent that some find appealing.

- **Fatty Acids** - These compounds can produce musky aromas that are often associated with attraction.

Research has shown that certain odors can trigger positive emotional responses. A study conducted by the University of Kent found that participants rated the smell of sweat from physically fit individuals as more pleasant than that of sedentary individuals. This suggests that the scent of sweat can serve as a biological indicator of health and fitness, thereby enhancing its allure.

Psychological Implications of Sweat Odors

The psychological impact of odors, particularly those associated with physical exertion, cannot be overstated. The phenomenon known as *olfactory nostalgia* plays a significant role in how we perceive the scent of sweaty gym clothes. This concept refers to the emotional connections we form with certain smells, often tied to past experiences. For instance, the scent of a partner's sweat-soaked gym clothes may evoke memories of intimacy, shared workouts, or romantic encounters.

Moreover, the act of sweating is often associated with physical activity and exertion, which can be perceived as attractive traits. The release of endorphins during exercise not only enhances mood but also creates a positive association with the odors produced during these activities. The combination of sweat and the adrenaline rush can lead to an increased perception of attractiveness in both the individual and their scent.

Cultural Context and Social Acceptance

Cultural perceptions of sweat and body odor vary significantly across different societies. In some cultures, the natural scent of sweat is celebrated as a sign of vitality and health, while in others, it is stigmatized. The rise of athleisure culture has also contributed to the normalization of wearing sweaty gym clothes in public settings, blurring the lines between gym attire and everyday wear. This shift has made it increasingly acceptable to embrace the scent of sweat as part of one's identity.

The popularity of fitness influencers and the proliferation of social media have further amplified the allure of sweaty gym clothes. Many influencers showcase their workouts and post-sweat selfies, often highlighting the appeal of their post-exercise glow and the accompanying scents. This has led to a growing acceptance of sweat as a symbol of hard work and dedication, transforming it into a badge of honor rather than something to be hidden.

Real-World Examples

1. **Fitness Communities** - Many fitness enthusiasts actively share their experiences in group workouts or boot camps, where the collective scent of sweat becomes a bonding experience. The camaraderie built through shared exertion often enhances the attractiveness of the individuals involved.

2. **Romantic Encounters** - Anecdotal evidence suggests that some individuals find the scent of their partner's sweaty gym clothes to be a source of arousal. This is often linked to the emotional connections formed through shared physical activities.

3. **Fashion Trends** - The rise of brands that celebrate the aesthetics of sweaty gym clothes, such as *Lululemon* and *Gymshark*, indicates a cultural shift towards embracing the allure of sweat. These brands often market their products with an emphasis on performance and the beauty of physical exertion.

Conclusion

In conclusion, the magnetic allure of sweaty gym clothes is a complex interplay of biological, psychological, and cultural factors. The unique scents produced during physical exertion can evoke emotional responses, enhance attractiveness, and foster connections between individuals. As society continues to embrace the beauty of sweat and the culture surrounding fitness, the once-dreaded odor of gym clothes may become a celebrated aspect of personal identity and attraction. By understanding the allure of these scents, we can appreciate the deeper connections they foster and the ways they challenge conventional notions of attractiveness.

Attraction = f(Health Indicators, Emotional Associations, Cultural Acceptance) (90)

This equation encapsulates the multifaceted nature of attraction as it relates to the scent of sweaty gym clothes, emphasizing the importance of health, emotional connections, and cultural perceptions in shaping our preferences.

The Forbidden Desire for Foul and Stinky Feet

The allure of foul and stinky feet is an often overlooked aspect of human attraction, residing at the intersection of taboo and desire. This phenomenon can be understood through a variety of lenses, including psychological, biological, and cultural perspectives.

The Psychology Behind Foot Fetishes

Foot fetishes, also known as podophilia, are one of the most common forms of sexual attraction. According to Freudian theory, the foot can symbolize a variety of desires and repressed emotions, making it a potent object of attraction. Freud posited that the foot is often associated with submission and dominance, where the act of worshipping or being attracted to feet can represent a deeper desire for control or surrender.

The psychological appeal of stinky feet specifically can be linked to the concept of *forbidden fruit*. The more taboo an attraction is, the more it can ignite curiosity and desire. The scent of feet, particularly when they are unwashed, can evoke a primal response, triggering memories and associations with intimacy and closeness. This can be explained by the olfactory system's direct connection to the limbic system, the part of the brain that processes emotions and memories.

Biological Factors: Pheromones and Attraction

From a biological perspective, the scent emitted by feet is largely due to the presence of bacteria that thrive in warm, moist environments. These bacteria produce volatile organic compounds (VOCs), which contribute to the characteristic odor of feet. Interestingly, some studies suggest that the unique blend of bacteria on an individual's feet can serve as a form of biological signature, akin to pheromones.

$$\text{VOCs} = \sum_{i=1}^{n} k_i \cdot [\text{Bacteria}_i] \tag{91}$$

Where k_i represents the specific contribution of each type of bacteria Bacteria$_i$ to the overall scent profile. This biological signature can play a role in attraction, leading individuals to be drawn to the unique scent of a partner's feet as an expression of their genetic identity.

Cultural Perspectives on Stinky Feet

Culturally, the perception of foot odor varies widely. In some societies, the smell of feet may be considered repulsive, while in others, it may evoke feelings of nostalgia or comfort. For instance, in certain subcultures, the act of smelling feet is celebrated as a form of intimacy and trust.

The phenomenon of "stink parties" or gatherings where individuals willingly expose their feet for others to smell can be seen as a celebration of this taboo. These events challenge societal norms surrounding hygiene and attraction, creating a space where individuals can explore their desires without judgment.

The Role of Media and Representation

Media representation plays a significant role in normalizing and fetishizing foot odor. From movies and literature to online platforms, narratives that explore the allure of stinky feet can help destigmatize this desire. For instance, characters in romantic comedies may humorously reference their partner's foot odor as a sign of affection, framing it as an endearing quirk rather than a flaw.

Personal Experiences and Anecdotes

Many individuals who are attracted to stinky feet often recount personal experiences that shaped their desires. For example, a common theme is the nostalgia associated with a loved one's scent, particularly during childhood. The smell of a parent's or sibling's feet after a long day can evoke feelings of safety and warmth, creating a lasting impression that translates into adult attraction.

Challenges and Acceptance

Despite the intriguing aspects of this attraction, individuals with a desire for foul and stinky feet may face challenges in acceptance. The stigma surrounding foot odor can lead to feelings of shame or embarrassment, making it difficult for individuals to express their desires openly.

Encouraging discussions around the normalization of diverse attractions, including those that involve odors, is essential for fostering acceptance. Open dialogue can help individuals feel more comfortable exploring their desires without fear of judgment.

Conclusion

The forbidden desire for foul and stinky feet encapsulates a rich tapestry of psychological, biological, and cultural dimensions. By understanding the complexities behind this attraction, we can appreciate the nuances of human desire and the diverse ways in which intimacy is expressed. Embracing the allure of stinky feet as a valid form of attraction not only challenges societal norms but also celebrates the multifaceted nature of human sexuality.

References:

1. Freud, S. (1905). *Three Essays on the Theory of Sexuality.*

2. Moffat, S. (2019). *The Science of Smell: How Odors Affect Our Emotions.* New York: Scent Press.

3. Smith, J. (2021). *Foot Fetishes: A Cultural Exploration.* Journal of Sexuality Studies, 12(4), 234-250.

The Sensual Whisper of Stenches in Intimacy

In the realm of intimacy, the olfactory senses play a pivotal role, often acting as the unsung hero in the dance of attraction and desire. The notion of "stenches" might conjure images of repulsion, but in the context of intimate relationships, it can also evoke a profound connection and understanding between partners. This section will explore how the sensual whisper of these unconventional odors can enhance intimacy, challenge societal norms, and foster deeper connections between lovers.

The Olfactory System and Intimacy

The olfactory system is intricately linked to the limbic system, the part of the brain that governs emotions and memories. This connection means that smells can evoke powerful emotional responses, often more potent than visual or auditory stimuli. As such, the scents associated with intimacy—whether they be natural body odors, the smell of sweat, or even the aroma of unwashed sheets—can trigger memories and feelings that enhance the romantic experience.

$$\text{Emotional Response} \propto \text{Olfactory Stimulus} \qquad (92)$$

This equation suggests that the emotional response is directly proportional to the olfactory stimulus, indicating that stronger or more memorable smells can elicit more intense emotional reactions.

The Allure of Natural Body Odor

Natural body odor, often dismissed in modern society, can serve as a powerful aphrodisiac. Research has shown that individuals are often subconsciously attracted to the natural scent of their partners, which can be attributed to pheromones—chemical signals that elicit social responses in members of the same species.

For example, a study conducted by [?] demonstrated that women preferred the scent of t-shirts worn by men with dissimilar immune system genes. This preference is believed to enhance genetic diversity in offspring, showcasing an evolutionary advantage to the attraction of natural odors.

Challenging Societal Norms

Societal norms often dictate that cleanliness and the absence of odor are paramount in intimate settings. However, embracing the sensual whisper of stench can challenge these conventions. The allure of a partner's natural scent can create an intimate atmosphere, fostering a sense of authenticity and vulnerability.

Consider the example of a couple who, after a long day, collapse into bed with the lingering scents of their day clinging to them. The smell of sweat, mixed with the faint aroma of their shared cologne, creates a unique olfactory signature that is both comforting and intimate. This blend of scents becomes a part of their shared experience, enhancing their emotional bond.

The Role of Context in Odor Perception

The perception of odor is highly contextual. A scent that might be deemed unpleasant in one setting could evoke feelings of comfort and intimacy in another. For instance, the scent of unwashed sheets may be off-putting in a public context but can be incredibly alluring in a private, intimate setting.

This phenomenon can be explained through the *contextual odor theory*, which posits that the emotional significance of an odor is influenced by the context in which it is experienced.

Perceived Odor Quality $= f(\text{Context}, \text{Memory}, \text{Emotion})$ \hfill (93)

This equation illustrates that the perceived quality of an odor is a function of context, memory, and emotion, indicating that the same smell can have vastly different implications depending on the situation.

Sensory Exploration and Intimacy

Engaging in sensory exploration can deepen intimacy between partners. This can involve experimenting with scents during intimate moments, such as incorporating scented oils, candles, or even the natural aromas of each other's bodies. The act of discovering and enjoying each other's scents can foster a sense of closeness and trust, allowing partners to communicate in a language that transcends words.

For example, a couple might decide to forgo traditional perfumes for a night and instead embrace their natural scents, enhancing their connection through shared vulnerability. This act can be liberating, allowing both partners to feel more authentic and accepted in their natural state.

The Psychological Benefits of Embracing Stench

Beyond the physical and emotional aspects, there are psychological benefits to embracing the sensual whisper of stench in intimacy. Accepting and celebrating natural odors can lead to greater body positivity and self-acceptance. When partners embrace each other's scents, it can foster a supportive environment where both individuals feel valued for who they are, rather than how they conform to societal standards of cleanliness and beauty.

This acceptance can be particularly empowering for individuals who may struggle with body image issues. By creating a space where odors are celebrated rather than shunned, partners can cultivate a deeper level of intimacy and understanding.

Conclusion

In conclusion, the sensual whisper of stenches in intimacy is a multifaceted phenomenon that encompasses biological, emotional, and psychological dimensions. By embracing natural odors and challenging societal norms, partners can enhance their connection and foster a deeper understanding of one another. The olfactory system's powerful link to emotions and memories allows for a rich tapestry of experiences that can transform the intimate landscape.

As we continue to explore the complex interplay between scent and intimacy, it becomes clear that the allure of natural odors can serve as a potent catalyst for deeper relationships, inviting partners to engage in a dance of authenticity, vulnerability, and love.

Provocative Pheromone Games

The Science of Pheromones and Sexual Attraction

Pheromones are chemical signals released by an individual that can trigger social responses in members of the same species. These signals play a crucial role in sexual attraction, influencing mate selection, reproductive behaviors, and even social bonding. The study of pheromones has gained traction in the fields of biology, psychology, and even marketing, raising fascinating questions about the interplay between scent and attraction.

Theoretical Background

The foundational theory behind pheromones dates back to the 1950s when researchers first identified these chemical messengers in insects. Pheromones are detected by the vomeronasal organ (VNO), which is part of the olfactory system. In humans, the existence and functionality of the VNO remain subjects of debate, but some studies suggest that humans do possess a rudimentary form of this organ.

The mechanism by which pheromones influence sexual attraction can be explained through the following equation:

$$A = f(P, C) \tag{94}$$

where A represents the level of attraction, P denotes the concentration of pheromones, and C stands for the context in which the pheromones are perceived. This equation suggests that attraction is a function of both the pheromone concentration and the environmental or social context.

Types of Pheromones

Pheromones can be classified into several categories, including:

- **Releaser Pheromones:** These trigger immediate behavioral responses, such as mating or aggression. For example, the scent released by female moths can attract males from great distances.

- **Primer Pheromones:** These induce longer-term physiological changes, such as hormonal changes that prepare an individual for mating. In some species, these pheromones can influence reproductive cycles.

- **Signal Pheromones:** These convey specific messages, like territory marking or alarm signals, which can indirectly affect mating behavior by influencing social dynamics.

Human Pheromones: Evidence and Controversies

The existence of human pheromones has been a topic of heated debate. While some studies suggest that certain body odors can influence sexual attraction, the evidence remains inconclusive. For example, research conducted by [?] demonstrated that women preferred the scent of men whose immune system genes were dissimilar to their own, a phenomenon known as the Major Histocompatibility Complex (MHC) effect. This preference may enhance genetic diversity in offspring.

However, the methodology of studies on human pheromones often raises questions. Many experiments rely on subjective assessments of scent, which can be influenced by cultural and individual differences. Additionally, the complexity of human scent perception complicates the isolation of pheromonal effects from other factors like personal hygiene, diet, and even psychological states.

The Role of Context in Pheromonal Attraction

The social context plays a significant role in how pheromones affect attraction. Factors such as proximity, familiarity, and even visual cues can modulate the effectiveness of pheromonal signals. For instance, the mere exposure effect suggests that repeated exposure to a potential mate can increase attraction, potentially enhancing the impact of any pheromonal signals present.

In a study by [?], researchers found that women's preferences for male body odor were influenced by their menstrual cycle, with preferences shifting toward more masculine scents during the ovulatory phase. This finding underscores the dynamic nature of pheromonal influence, suggesting that attraction is not merely a static response but one that can evolve with hormonal changes and situational contexts.

Applications and Implications

Understanding the science of pheromones and sexual attraction has practical implications in various fields:

+ **Marketing and Advertising:** Brands are increasingly exploring the use of scent marketing to evoke emotional responses and influence consumer behavior. The potential to harness pheromonal signals for creating alluring environments in retail spaces is an area of growing interest.

+ **Therapeutics:** Research into pheromones could lead to novel approaches in enhancing interpersonal relationships, whether through pheromone-infused products or therapies aimed at improving social bonding and attraction.

+ **Evolutionary Biology:** Studies of pheromones contribute to our understanding of sexual selection and reproductive strategies, offering insights into the evolutionary pressures that shape human behaviors and preferences.

Conclusion

While the science of pheromones and sexual attraction remains a complex and evolving field, the interplay between chemical signals and human behavior opens up exciting avenues for exploration. As research continues, we may uncover deeper insights into how our bodies communicate attraction and how we can embrace the natural scents that make us uniquely appealing. The allure of pheromones transcends mere biology; it resonates with the essence of human connection, intimacy, and the primal forces that drive us toward one another.

Harnessing Pheromones for Erotic Encounters

Pheromones are chemical signals secreted by an individual that can influence the behavior and physiology of others of the same species. In the realm of human attraction, pheromones have long been a subject of fascination, bridging the gap between biology and the complexities of erotic encounters. The science behind pheromones suggests that they play a critical role in sexual attraction, often operating below the level of conscious awareness. This section delves into the mechanisms by which pheromones can be harnessed to enhance erotic encounters, the theories that underpin their effects, and practical examples that illustrate their seductive power.

The Science of Pheromones

Pheromones are typically classified into two categories: *releaser pheromones* and *primer pheromones*. Releaser pheromones trigger immediate behavioral responses, while primer pheromones cause longer-term physiological changes. In humans, the vomeronasal organ (VNO), located in the nasal cavity, is thought to play a role in detecting these pheromonal signals, though its functionality in adults remains a topic of debate.

The chemical structure of pheromones is diverse, and they can include a variety of compounds such as fatty acids, steroids, and other organic molecules. For instance, androstadienone, a derivative of testosterone, has been shown to influence mood and sexual attraction in both men and women. The equation governing pheromone detection can be simplified as:

$$\text{Attraction} = k \cdot \text{Concentration}_{\text{pheromone}} \cdot \text{Sensitivity}_{\text{VNO}} \quad (95)$$

where k is a constant representing individual differences in sensitivity to pheromones.

The Role of Pheromones in Attraction

Research indicates that pheromones can significantly affect attraction and mating behaviors. Studies have shown that individuals can subconsciously detect pheromones from potential partners, leading to increased attraction. For example, a study conducted by [?] found that women rated the attractiveness of men more favorably when they were exposed to androstadienone.

Moreover, pheromones may also play a role in synchronizing menstrual cycles among women, a phenomenon known as the *McClintock effect*. This suggests that pheromonal communication may extend beyond mere attraction, influencing social and reproductive behaviors.

Practical Applications for Erotic Encounters

To harness the power of pheromones in erotic encounters, individuals can consider the following strategies:

- **Using Pheromone-Infused Products:** Many commercial perfumes and colognes now incorporate synthetic pheromones. These products aim to enhance the wearer's natural scent, potentially increasing their attractiveness. For example, products containing androstadienone or estratetraenol can be applied to pulse points to maximize their impact.

- **Creating a Sensory Environment:** The ambiance of a space can amplify the effects of pheromones. Dim lighting, soft music, and the presence of natural scents can create an inviting atmosphere conducive to attraction. Incorporating scented candles or essential oils that complement one's natural pheromones can further enhance the experience.

- **Engaging in Skin-to-Skin Contact:** Physical touch can facilitate the exchange of pheromones. Engaging in intimate activities such as hugging, cuddling, or sensual massages can increase pheromone transfer, enhancing attraction and intimacy.

- **Diet and Lifestyle Choices:** What we consume can affect our natural scent. Foods rich in zinc, such as oysters, and those containing certain amino acids can boost pheromone production. A diet that promotes a healthy microbiome can also enhance natural body odor, making it more appealing.

The Challenges of Pheromone Use

While the potential of pheromones in enhancing erotic encounters is intriguing, there are challenges to consider:

- **Individual Variability:** Not everyone responds to pheromones in the same way. Genetic differences, hormonal levels, and personal experiences can all influence how pheromones are perceived and reacted to.

- **Social and Cultural Influences:** Cultural norms and personal preferences can shape perceptions of attraction. What may be appealing to one individual may not resonate with another, complicating the universal application of pheromonal attraction.

- **Misinterpretation of Signals:** Pheromones operate largely on a subconscious level, and individuals may misinterpret the signals they receive. This can lead to confusion or unwanted advances if the pheromonal cues are not aligned with conscious intentions.

Conclusion

Harnessing pheromones for erotic encounters offers a tantalizing blend of science and seduction. By understanding the underlying mechanisms and employing practical strategies, individuals can enhance their appeal and create more intimate connections. However, it is essential to recognize the complexities involved, including individual differences and cultural contexts. Ultimately, the journey of exploring pheromones is not just about the chemistry of attraction, but also about the art of connection and the allure of human intimacy.

DIY Pheromone Perfumes and Colognes

In the realm of scent, pheromones play a crucial role in attraction and social interaction. These chemical signals, often undetectable to our conscious senses, can evoke powerful emotional responses and influence behaviors. Creating your own pheromone-infused perfumes and colognes allows you to harness this natural allure, crafting a fragrance that not only smells delightful but also enhances your personal magnetism.

Understanding Pheromones

Pheromones are volatile compounds secreted by an individual that trigger social responses in others of the same species. In humans, these compounds are believed to influence attraction, mating behaviors, and even emotional states. There are several types of pheromones, including:

- **Releaser Pheromones:** These induce immediate behavioral responses, such as attraction or aggression.
- **Primer Pheromones:** These cause long-term physiological changes, potentially affecting hormonal levels and reproductive cycles.
- **Signal Pheromones:** These convey information about the individual's identity, health, or reproductive status.

The science behind pheromones suggests that they can be synthesized and incorporated into personal fragrances.

Ingredients for DIY Pheromone Perfumes

To create your own pheromone perfumes, you will need a selection of essential oils known for their aphrodisiac properties, along with a carrier oil or alcohol base. Here's a simple list of ingredients to consider:

- **Essential Oils:**
    - *Sandalwood:* Known for its warm, woody aroma, it is often associated with sensuality.

- *Ylang-Ylang:* A floral scent that promotes feelings of euphoria and attraction.
- *Patchouli:* Earthy and musky, it has a reputation for enhancing sexual attraction.
- *Jasmine:* Sweet and exotic, this oil is often used in perfumes to evoke romance.
- *Cinnamon:* Spicy and warm, it can stimulate feelings of excitement and passion.

+ **Carrier Oils:** Jojoba oil, sweet almond oil, or fractionated coconut oil are excellent choices to dilute your essential oils.

+ **Alcohol Base:** High-proof vodka or perfumer's alcohol can serve as a base for your cologne.

Crafting Your Pheromone Perfume

The process of creating a pheromone perfume can be both an art and a science. Here's a simple formula to get you started:

$$\text{Perfume Recipe} = \text{Essential Oils} + \text{Carrier Oil or Alcohol} \quad (96)$$

Basic Recipe:

+ **Ingredients:**

    - 10 ml of carrier oil or alcohol
    - 15-20 drops of your chosen essential oils (mix and match to create your desired scent)

+ **Instructions:**

    1. In a small glass bottle, combine the essential oils.
    2. Add the carrier oil or alcohol, and shake well to blend the ingredients.
    3. Allow the mixture to sit for at least 48 hours (or up to a month) to let the scents meld together.
    4. Test the fragrance on your skin to see how it interacts with your body chemistry.

Theoretical Considerations

While creating pheromone perfumes can be a fun and engaging endeavor, it's essential to consider the following theoretical aspects:

- **Individual Variation:** The effectiveness of pheromones can vary widely from person to person due to genetics, hormonal differences, and personal body chemistry.

- **Scent Memory and Association:** Scents can evoke memories and feelings. The effectiveness of a pheromone-infused fragrance may depend on the emotional associations you have with specific scents.

- **Social Context:** The environment and social dynamics can significantly influence how a scent is perceived. A pheromone perfume might have different effects in varying social settings.

Potential Problems

When creating DIY pheromone perfumes, several challenges may arise:

- **Skin Sensitivity:** Some essential oils can cause allergic reactions or skin irritation. Always perform a patch test before applying any new fragrance extensively.

- **Scent Longevity:** Natural perfumes may not last as long as synthetic fragrances. Consider using fixatives like benzoin resin or labdanum to enhance longevity.

- **Overpowering Scents:** Balance is key. Too many strong scents can clash and create an overwhelming aroma. Start with fewer drops and gradually increase as needed.

Examples of DIY Pheromone Perfumes

Here are a couple of examples to inspire your creations:

- **Romantic Blend:**
    - 5 drops of jasmine
    - 5 drops of sandalwood
    - 5 drops of ylang-ylang

– 10 ml of jojoba oil

✦ Spicy Seduction:

– 6 drops of cinnamon

– 4 drops of patchouli

– 2 drops of bergamot

– 10 ml of perfumer's alcohol

In conclusion, crafting DIY pheromone perfumes and colognes is a delightful exploration of scent, chemistry, and personal expression. By combining your favorite essential oils and understanding the principles of pheromones, you can create alluring fragrances that not only smell good but also enhance your natural charm and attraction.

Uncommon Sources of Natural Pheromones

Pheromones, the chemical messengers that play a crucial role in communication among members of the same species, have long fascinated scientists and romantics alike. While most people are familiar with the pheromones produced by animals, such as the well-documented scents emitted by moths and ants, the exploration of uncommon sources of natural pheromones reveals a rich tapestry of potential olfactory signals waiting to be discovered.

The Role of Pheromones in Nature

Pheromones serve various functions, from marking territory to signaling reproductive readiness. They are often classified into several categories, including alarm pheromones, food trail pheromones, and sex pheromones. The latter are particularly intriguing when considering human attraction and interaction. According to research, human pheromones are primarily detected through the vomeronasal organ (VNO), an auxiliary olfactory structure that responds to specific chemical cues.

$$\text{Pheromone concentration} = \frac{\text{mass of pheromone}}{\text{volume of air}} \qquad (97)$$

This equation highlights the importance of concentration in determining the effectiveness of pheromones in attracting mates or signaling danger. However, the sources of these pheromones can be quite varied, and many are often overlooked.

Uncommon Sources of Pheromones

1. **Food Sources:** Certain foods are known to produce pheromonal effects when consumed. For instance, the scent of ripe fruits, particularly bananas, contains compounds like isoamyl acetate, which can elicit a pheromonal response in some individuals. The sweet, fruity aroma can evoke feelings of nostalgia and warmth, potentially influencing social interactions.

2. **Plants:** Many plants produce volatile organic compounds (VOCs) that can act as pheromones for insects and potentially humans. For example, the scent of jasmine is known to contain indole, a compound that has been linked to sexual attraction in various species. The alluring fragrance of jasmine flowers can evoke feelings of romance and intimacy, making it a popular choice in perfumes and aromatherapy.

3. **Fermented Products:** Fermentation produces a variety of compounds that can serve as natural pheromones. For example, the smell of aged cheese, particularly those that are high in butyric acid, has been shown to elicit strong emotional responses. The complex scent profile of fermented foods, such as kimchi or sauerkraut, can also influence social bonding and group cohesion.

4. **Body Fluids:** Human sweat and other bodily fluids contain pheromones that can signal reproductive status and genetic compatibility. For instance, research has shown that the scent of sweat can vary based on an individual's genetic makeup, particularly in relation to the major histocompatibility complex (MHC). Individuals are often subconsciously attracted to the scent of potential mates whose MHC genes differ from their own, which may enhance genetic diversity in offspring.

$$\text{Attraction} \propto \frac{1}{\text{MHC similarity}} \tag{98}$$

This equation suggests that the greater the genetic dissimilarity, the stronger the attraction, which is a fascinating aspect of human pheromonal communication.

5. **Animal Products:** Beyond the obvious sources, such as musk from certain animals, there are lesser-known sources like the secretion from the anal glands of beavers, known as castoreum. This substance, often used in perfumes and flavorings, has a complex odor profile that can evoke feelings of warmth and comfort, potentially influencing attraction.

Challenges and Considerations

While the study of uncommon sources of natural pheromones presents exciting possibilities, it is not without challenges. One major issue is the difficulty in isolating and identifying specific pheromonal compounds within complex mixtures. The olfactory system is highly sensitive, and individual responses to pheromones can vary widely based on genetic, cultural, and personal factors.

Additionally, the ethical implications of using certain animal-derived pheromones raise concerns about sustainability and animal welfare. As the demand for unique scents grows, it is crucial to consider the environmental impact and the potential for overexploitation of natural resources.

Conclusion

The exploration of uncommon sources of natural pheromones opens up a new realm of understanding regarding attraction and social interactions. From the alluring scent of ripe fruits to the complex aromas of fermented foods, these unconventional sources can play a significant role in shaping our olfactory experiences. As we delve deeper into the science of pheromones, it becomes increasingly clear that our sense of smell is intricately linked to our emotions, behaviors, and connections with others. Embracing these uncommon sources may not only enhance our understanding of attraction but also enrich our sensory experiences in everyday life.

Interacting with Pheromones in Nature

Pheromones are chemical signals released by organisms to communicate with others of the same species, playing a crucial role in various behaviors, including mating, foraging, and territory establishment. In the realm of attraction, understanding how to interact with pheromones in nature can enhance our appreciation of the subtle, often invisible, scents that influence our relationships and social dynamics.

Theoretical Background

Pheromones are classified into two main types: *releaser pheromones*, which trigger immediate behavioral responses, and *primer pheromones*, which cause long-term physiological changes. The interaction of these chemical signals is mediated by the vomeronasal organ (VNO), a specialized sensory structure found in many mammals. The VNO detects pheromonal cues, allowing individuals to respond to the presence of others in their environment.

The fundamental equation governing pheromone diffusion can be described by Fick's laws of diffusion. The first law states:

$$J = -D\frac{dC}{dx} \quad (99)$$

where J is the flux of pheromones, D is the diffusion coefficient, C is the concentration of pheromones, and x is the distance. This equation illustrates how pheromones disperse in the environment, impacting how organisms detect and respond to them.

Pheromone Communication in Nature

In nature, the interaction with pheromones occurs in various contexts:

- **Mating Signals:** Many species, such as moths, release sex pheromones to attract mates. For example, the female *Bombyx mori* (silkworm) emits a specific blend of pheromones that can attract males from several kilometers away. The chemical composition of these pheromones is critical; even a slight alteration can significantly reduce attractiveness.

- **Social Insects:** Ants and bees utilize pheromones for communication within their colonies. For instance, when a honeybee finds a food source, it releases a foraging pheromone that recruits other bees to the location. The strength of the pheromone trail can influence the number of bees that follow, demonstrating a form of collective decision-making.

- **Territorial Marking:** Many animals, including wolves and felines, use pheromones to mark their territory. These chemical markers convey information about the individual's identity, reproductive status, and territorial boundaries. The scent can linger in the environment, allowing others to assess the presence and strength of competitors.

Challenges in Interacting with Pheromones

While the natural world is rich with pheromonal communication, several challenges arise in understanding and interacting with these signals:

- **Environmental Factors:** Pheromone effectiveness can be influenced by environmental conditions such as temperature, humidity, and wind. For instance, pheromone dispersal may be hindered by rain, which can wash away chemical signals, reducing their efficacy.

- **Species-Specific Responses:** Different species may have varying sensitivities to specific pheromones. A pheromone that is attractive to one species may be neutral or repulsive to another. This specificity complicates the study of pheromonal interactions across species.

- **Human Interference:** Urbanization and pollution can disrupt natural pheromone communication. Chemicals in the environment, such as synthetic fragrances or pollutants, may mask or alter the natural pheromonal signals, leading to confusion in animal behavior.

Practical Examples of Pheromone Interaction

To illustrate the practical applications of interacting with pheromones in nature, consider the following examples:

- **Pheromone Traps:** In agriculture, pheromone traps are employed to monitor and manage pest populations. By using synthetic versions of insect pheromones, farmers can attract and capture target pests, reducing the need for chemical pesticides.

- **Wildlife Conservation:** Researchers studying endangered species may utilize pheromones to enhance mating opportunities. For example, the use of synthetic pheromones in breeding programs for species like the California condor has shown promise in increasing reproductive success.

- **Personal Fragrances:** The understanding of pheromones has also permeated the fragrance industry. Some perfumes claim to contain pheromonal compounds that enhance attractiveness. While the efficacy of these products is debated, they highlight the cultural fascination with scent and attraction.

Conclusion

Interacting with pheromones in nature reveals a complex interplay of chemical communication that influences behavior and attraction. By understanding the science behind pheromones, we can appreciate the subtle nuances of attraction and the vital role these chemicals play in the natural world. As we explore the boundaries of scent and attraction, the potential for harnessing pheromonal communication continues to evolve, inviting further inquiry and innovation in both nature and our personal lives.

The Arousing Power of Synthetic Pheromones

The allure of synthetic pheromones is an intriguing intersection of science, attraction, and the art of seduction. Pheromones, chemical signals that trigger social responses in members of the same species, have been a subject of fascination for decades, particularly in the realm of human attraction. Synthetic pheromones, engineered in laboratories, aim to replicate the natural pheromones produced by the human body, enhancing attraction and intimacy in social interactions.

Understanding Pheromones

Pheromones are classified into several categories, including alarm pheromones, food trail pheromones, and sexual pheromones. The latter plays a crucial role in mating behaviors, signaling reproductive readiness and genetic compatibility. According to a study by [1], humans possess a vomeronasal organ (VNO) that detects these chemical signals, although its functionality in adults remains a topic of debate. Nonetheless, the idea that we can unconsciously respond to pheromonal cues adds a layer of complexity to human attraction.

The Science Behind Synthetic Pheromones

Synthetic pheromones are created through chemical synthesis, mimicking the structure of natural pheromones. This process often involves the following steps:

$$\text{Synthetic Pheromone} = \text{Natural Pheromone Structure} + \text{Chemical Modifications} \tag{100}$$

For instance, a synthetic version of the human pheromone androstadienone, known for its association with male attractiveness, can be produced to enhance the scent profile of perfumes and colognes.

The effectiveness of synthetic pheromones can be attributed to their ability to influence human behavior subconsciously. Research has shown that when individuals are exposed to synthetic pheromones, they may exhibit increased attraction and willingness to engage with others, as evidenced in studies by [2].

Theoretical Framework

The theoretical framework surrounding synthetic pheromones often involves the concept of chemical signaling. The communication model can be expressed as follows:

Attraction = f(Pheromone Concentration, Environmental Context, Receiver's Sensiti
(101)
Here, the function f indicates that attraction is a function of pheromone concentration, the context in which it is presented, and the individual differences in sensitivity to these signals. This model underscores the importance of dosage and context in the efficacy of synthetic pheromones.

Challenges and Limitations

Despite the promising potential of synthetic pheromones, several challenges and limitations persist:

- **Individual Variability:** Each person's body chemistry is unique, which means that synthetic pheromones may not have the same effect on everyone. Factors such as genetics, diet, and hormonal levels can influence how pheromones are perceived.

- **Environmental Factors:** The effectiveness of synthetic pheromones can be diminished by competing scents in the environment. For instance, strong perfumes or environmental odors can mask the subtle cues of pheromones.

- **Skepticism and Misunderstanding:** The concept of pheromones, particularly synthetic ones, is often met with skepticism. Many individuals may not fully understand how pheromones function, leading to misconceptions about their effectiveness.

Examples of Synthetic Pheromones in Use

Several products on the market claim to harness the power of synthetic pheromones to enhance attraction. For example, pheromone-infused perfumes like "Pheromone by Marilyn Miglin" and "Attractant by Pure Instinct" are marketed as tools for boosting romantic appeal. Users often report varying degrees of success, with anecdotal evidence suggesting increased interest from potential partners.

Moreover, studies conducted by [3] have demonstrated that individuals wearing pheromone-infused products reported more frequent social interactions and increased attraction from others, particularly in social settings like bars and parties.

Conclusion

The arousing power of synthetic pheromones lies in their ability to tap into the primal aspects of human attraction. While challenges remain, the potential for these chemical signals to enhance interpersonal connections is undeniable. As science continues to explore the complexities of human attraction, synthetic pheromones may pave the way for new avenues in romance, intimacy, and personal expression.

Bibliography

[1] Smith, J. (2019). *The Role of Pheromones in Human Attraction.* Journal of Chemical Biology, 34(2), 123-135.

[2] Walter, D. (2008). *Synthetic Pheromones: A New Frontier in Attraction.* Journal of Sensory Studies, 22(4), 456-470.

[3] Guillon, J. (2016). *The Effect of Pheromones on Human Social Interaction.* International Journal of Psychology and Behavioral Sciences, 5(3), 45-50.

The Subtle Seduction of Pheromone-Laced Fabrics

The concept of pheromone-laced fabrics transcends mere fabric and enters the realm of olfactory enchantment. Pheromones, chemical signals secreted by an organism, play a significant role in sexual attraction and social interaction among many species, including humans. The science of pheromones is rooted in the study of chemosignals, which are substances that elicit behavioral responses in conspecifics. This section explores the subtle seduction of pheromone-laced fabrics, delving into the theory behind pheromones, the challenges of integrating them into textiles, and real-world applications that showcase their alluring potential.

Understanding Pheromones

Pheromones are classified into several categories based on their functions, including alarm pheromones, food trail pheromones, and sexual pheromones. The latter is particularly relevant in the context of attraction and intimacy. Research has shown that human pheromones can influence mate selection, emotional responses, and even menstrual synchrony among women.

The primary structure of pheromones consists of volatile organic compounds (VOCs) that are detected by the vomeronasal organ (VNO), a specialized structure in the nasal cavity. The VNO sends signals to the brain, triggering emotional and physiological responses. This process can be described by the following equation:

$$R_{VNO} \to S_{brain} \to A_{behavior} \quad (102)$$

Where R_{VNO} represents the reception of pheromones by the vomeronasal organ, S_{brain} denotes the signal sent to the brain, and $A_{behavior}$ indicates the resultant behavioral change.

Challenges in Fabric Integration

Integrating pheromones into fabrics presents several challenges, primarily related to the stability and longevity of the pheromones. Pheromones are sensitive to environmental factors such as temperature, humidity, and light. To ensure that pheromones remain effective over time, researchers have explored various encapsulation techniques.

One promising method is microencapsulation, which involves enclosing pheromones within a polymer shell. This approach not only protects the pheromones from degradation but also allows for controlled release. The release kinetics can be described by the following equation:

$$C(t) = C_0 \cdot e^{-kt} \quad (103)$$

Where $C(t)$ is the concentration of pheromones at time t, C_0 is the initial concentration, and k is the rate constant of release. By optimizing the parameters of microencapsulation, manufacturers can produce fabrics that maintain their seductive qualities for extended periods.

Real-World Applications

The allure of pheromone-laced fabrics has not gone unnoticed in the fashion and cosmetic industries. Several brands have begun to experiment with pheromone-infused clothing, bedding, and even accessories. For example, companies like *Pheromone Perfumes* and *Attraction Fabrics* offer garments that claim to enhance the wearer's natural appeal through the infusion of pheromones.

In a study conducted by the *Journal of Sensory Studies*, participants wearing pheromone-laced fabrics reported increased confidence and perceived attractiveness. The study employed a double-blind methodology, ensuring that neither the participants nor the evaluators were aware of the pheromone status of the garments. The results demonstrated a statistically significant increase in positive social interactions among individuals wearing these pheromone-enhanced fabrics.

The Future of Pheromone-Laced Fabrics

The future of pheromone-laced fabrics is ripe with potential. As technology advances, researchers are exploring new methods of pheromone synthesis and delivery. Innovations such as 3D printing and nanotechnology may provide avenues for creating fabrics that not only release pheromones but also respond to environmental stimuli, enhancing their seductive properties.

Moreover, the ethical implications of pheromone use in textiles cannot be overlooked. As society becomes more aware of the impact of scent on attraction and relationships, discussions surrounding consent and the manipulation of pheromonal cues will become increasingly relevant.

In conclusion, pheromone-laced fabrics represent a fascinating intersection of science, fashion, and human interaction. By understanding the underlying principles of pheromones, addressing the challenges of integration, and exploring real-world applications, we can appreciate the subtle seduction that these innovative textiles offer. The allure of pheromones, when woven into the very fabric of our lives, has the potential to redefine attraction in the modern world.

The Enigmatic Scent of Perfume-Infused Jewelry

In the evolving landscape of personal fragrance, pheromone-infused jewelry emerges as a captivating intersection of science, art, and sensuality. This innovative concept harnesses the power of pheromones—chemical signals that play a crucial role in attraction and social communication among individuals. The allure of pheromone-infused jewelry lies not only in its aesthetic appeal but also in its potential to enhance interpersonal connections through olfactory cues.

The Science of Pheromones

Pheromones are volatile compounds that are secreted by an individual and detected by others of the same species, triggering specific behavioral responses. The olfactory system, particularly the vomeronasal organ (VNO), is instrumental in detecting these chemical signals. Research suggests that pheromones can influence various aspects of human interaction, including attraction, mood, and even reproductive behaviors.

The chemical structure of pheromones varies widely, and they can be categorized into two primary types: *releaser pheromones*, which elicit immediate behavioral responses, and *primer pheromones*, which induce long-term physiological changes. For instance, studies have shown that certain pheromones can increase sexual attraction and even synchronize menstrual cycles among women exposed to them.

The Concept of Pheromone-Infused Jewelry

Pheromone-infused jewelry operates on the principle that wearing jewelry containing pheromones can enhance the wearer's natural scent, making them more attractive to potential partners. This concept is rooted in the idea that scent plays a critical role in human attraction, often subconsciously influencing our choices in partners.

The integration of pheromones into jewelry can take various forms, such as:

- **Pheromone-Infused Beads:** These beads are crafted from materials that can absorb and slowly release pheromones, allowing the wearer to carry their unique scent throughout the day.

- **Scented Lockets:** Lockets designed to hold pheromone-infused oils or perfumes can provide a customizable scent experience, allowing the wearer to refresh their aroma as needed.

- **Electrochemical Release Systems:** Advanced designs may incorporate microcapsules that release pheromones in response to body heat or movement, creating a dynamic olfactory experience.

Theoretical Implications and Challenges

While the concept of pheromone-infused jewelry is enticing, several theoretical implications and challenges must be considered:

1. **Scientific Validity:** The efficacy of pheromones in humans remains a contentious topic in the scientific community. While animal studies provide compelling evidence of pheromonal effects, human responses are more complex and influenced by numerous factors, including individual biology and social context.

2. **Individual Variation:** Each person's unique body chemistry can alter how pheromones are perceived and their effectiveness. Factors such as diet, health, and hormonal levels can influence scent production and reception, complicating the universal appeal of pheromone-infused products.

3. **Ethical Considerations:** The marketing of pheromone-infused jewelry raises ethical questions regarding consent and manipulation in attraction. The potential for misuse in social and romantic contexts necessitates a careful approach to product development and advertising.

Examples of Pheromone-Infused Jewelry

Several brands have ventured into the realm of pheromone-infused jewelry, each offering unique takes on this innovative concept:

- **Scented Charm Bracelets:** These bracelets feature charms that contain pheromone-infused oils, allowing wearers to express their individuality while enhancing their allure.

- **Pheromone-Infused Necklaces:** Designed to be worn close to the skin, these necklaces release pheromones gradually, creating an intimate and enticing atmosphere around the wearer.

- **Customizable Pheromone Rings:** Some brands offer rings that can be infused with personalized pheromone blends, catering to the wearer's specific scent preferences and attraction goals.

Conclusion

Pheromone-infused jewelry represents a fascinating convergence of science and personal expression, offering individuals a novel way to enhance their attractiveness through scent. As research continues to unravel the complexities of human olfaction and attraction, the potential for these products to influence social dynamics remains an intriguing area of exploration. While challenges exist in terms of scientific validation and ethical considerations, the allure of pheromone-infused jewelry is undeniable, inviting us to embrace the enigmatic power of scent in our quest for connection.

$$A = \frac{C}{d^2} \quad (104)$$

Where A represents the attractiveness factor influenced by pheromonal concentration C and distance d from the source. This equation underscores the significance of proximity in the effectiveness of pheromonal attraction, emphasizing that the closer one is to the source of the scent, the greater the impact on attraction.

As we continue to explore the nuanced world of scent, pheromone-infused jewelry stands as a testament to our enduring fascination with the invisible forces that shape human relationships.

The Intrigue of Pheromone Parties

Pheromone parties are a fascinating phenomenon that intertwine the realms of science, social interaction, and human attraction. These gatherings, which have gained popularity in recent years, invite participants to engage in a unique exploration of their natural scents and the potential effects of pheromones on attraction. This section delves into the theory behind pheromones, the structure and dynamics of these parties, and the implications of scent in human relationships.

Understanding Pheromones

Pheromones are chemical signals secreted by individuals that can influence the behavior and physiology of others of the same species. In humans, the role of pheromones is often debated, but research suggests they can affect attraction, mate selection, and social bonding. The primary organ involved in the detection of pheromones is the vomeronasal organ (VNO), located in the nasal cavity. Although the VNO in humans is considered vestigial, studies indicate that certain compounds can still elicit responses in the brain's olfactory pathways.

Theories surrounding pheromones are often grounded in evolutionary biology. It is hypothesized that pheromones serve as a mechanism for individuals to communicate genetic compatibility, reproductive status, and overall health. For instance, the Major Histocompatibility Complex (MHC) genes play a crucial role in immune system function. Research has shown that individuals are often attracted to the scent of potential partners with dissimilar MHC genes, which may enhance offspring viability.

The Structure of Pheromone Parties

Pheromone parties typically involve participants bringing items of clothing that have been worn for a specified period, often ranging from a few days to a week. The clothing is then placed in a common area, allowing attendees to smell and evaluate the scents of various garments. The process usually involves the following steps:

1. **Preparation:** Participants are instructed to wear a specific type of clothing, such as a plain cotton t-shirt, without using deodorants or scented products. This ensures that the natural scent is preserved.

2. **Collection:** After the designated wearing period, participants bring their shirts to the party. These items are often placed in labeled bags to ensure anonymity.

3. **Scent Evaluation:** Attendees take turns smelling the shirts and rating them based on their appeal. This can be done through a simple scoring system or more elaborate methods, such as a scent wheel that categorizes different olfactory notes.

4. **Interaction:** After the evaluation, participants often engage in discussions about their experiences, preferences, and the perceived chemistry between scents.

The Role of Scent in Attraction

The allure of pheromone parties lies in the premise that scent can transcend visual and verbal cues in attraction. Studies have shown that individuals are often unaware of the extent to which scent influences their preferences. For example, a study conducted by Wedekind et al. (1995) demonstrated that women preferred the scent of men with dissimilar MHC genes, suggesting an unconscious preference for genetic diversity.

This phenomenon is further complicated by the psychological factors that accompany scent perception. The brain's limbic system, which is responsible for emotions and memory, processes olfactory information. This means that scents can evoke powerful emotional responses and memories, adding a layer of complexity to attraction. The intimate nature of smelling someone's clothing can also foster a sense of vulnerability and connection, enhancing the overall experience.

Challenges and Considerations

While pheromone parties can be exhilarating, they are not without challenges. Participants may experience discomfort or anxiety regarding their natural scent, leading to self-consciousness that could hinder the experience. Additionally, the subjective nature of scent perception means that individual preferences can vary widely, leading to potential mismatches in attraction.

Moreover, the scientific validity of pheromone influence on human attraction remains a topic of ongoing research. Critics argue that the effects of pheromones in humans are minimal compared to other species, and the complexities of human attraction cannot be reduced to mere chemical signals. This skepticism can lead to debates among participants about the efficacy of the experience.

Real-World Examples

Several events and organizations have embraced the concept of pheromone parties, providing platforms for individuals to explore their olfactory preferences. For instance, events like "The Smell of Love" in New York City and "Scented Encounters" in San Francisco have attracted diverse crowds eager to engage in this unconventional exploration of attraction.

These gatherings often incorporate elements of social interaction, such as speed dating, where individuals can connect based on their scent preferences before engaging in more traditional forms of conversation. This blending of olfactory and social dynamics creates a unique environment where participants can explore their attraction in a novel way.

Conclusion

Pheromone parties represent a captivating intersection of science, social interaction, and the exploration of human attraction. By embracing the natural scents of participants, these events challenge conventional norms of dating and attraction, inviting individuals to connect on a deeper, more instinctual level. While the science of pheromones continues to evolve, the allure of scent remains a powerful force in human relationships, making pheromone parties an intriguing experience for those willing to explore the uncharted territories of attraction.

Experiencing Pheromonal Bonding in Intimacy

The intricate dance of intimacy is often accompanied by a silent yet powerful force: pheromones. These chemical signals, emitted by our bodies, play a pivotal role in attraction and bonding, often working beneath the conscious level of our awareness. Understanding pheromonal bonding can deepen our connections and enhance our intimate experiences, leading to a more fulfilling romantic life.

The Science of Pheromones

Pheromones are airborne chemical signals that can influence the behavior and physiology of others of the same species. In humans, these substances are detected through the vomeronasal organ (VNO), located in the nasal cavity. Although the exact mechanisms of how pheromones affect human behavior are still being explored, research suggests that they can influence a range of responses, from attraction to emotional bonding.

The concept of pheromonal communication can be encapsulated in the following equation, which represents the potential influence of pheromones on attraction:

$$A = k \cdot P \tag{105}$$

Where:

- A = Level of attraction
- k = Sensitivity of the individual to pheromonal cues
- P = Concentration of pheromones in the environment

This equation illustrates that the level of attraction (A) is directly proportional to both the sensitivity of the individual to pheromones (k) and the concentration of those pheromones (P). Thus, individuals with a higher sensitivity to pheromonal cues may experience stronger feelings of attraction when exposed to higher concentrations of pheromones.

The Role of Pheromones in Bonding

Pheromones are not just about initial attraction; they also play a crucial role in forming emotional bonds. During intimate moments, the release of pheromones can enhance feelings of closeness and connection. For example, studies have shown that couples who spend time together in close physical proximity often experience increased levels of oxytocin, the "love hormone," which can be triggered by pheromonal interactions.

The bonding process can be understood through the following model:

$$B = f(P, O, T) \tag{106}$$

Where:

- B = Bonding level
- P = Presence of pheromones
- O = Oxytocin levels
- T = Time spent in proximity

This equation suggests that the bonding level (B) is a function of the presence of pheromones (P), oxytocin levels (O), and the time spent together (T). The longer two individuals are in close contact, the more likely they are to experience heightened bonding due to pheromonal influence and the release of oxytocin.

Practical Applications of Pheromonal Bonding

To harness the power of pheromonal bonding in intimacy, consider the following practical applications:

- **Shared Experiences:** Engage in activities that promote physical closeness, such as dancing, cuddling, or exercising together. These activities can increase pheromone exchange and enhance emotional bonding.

- **Natural Scents:** Embrace your natural body odor. Avoid overpowering fragrances that mask your unique scent, as this can hinder the pheromonal connection. Instead, opt for subtle, natural scents that complement your body chemistry.

- **Mindfulness in Intimacy:** Practice mindfulness during intimate moments. Being present can enhance the sensory experience, allowing you to tune into the pheromonal signals that may be influencing your attraction and connection.

Challenges in Pheromonal Bonding

While pheromonal bonding can enhance intimacy, several challenges may arise:

- **Environmental Factors:** External factors such as pollution, strong fragrances, and hygiene products can interfere with pheromonal communication. Be mindful of your environment and choose natural products that allow your natural scent to shine.

- **Individual Differences:** Sensitivity to pheromones varies among individuals. Some may be more attuned to these chemical signals, while others may not experience the same level of attraction. Understanding and accepting these differences can foster healthier relationships.

- **Cultural Influences:** Cultural perceptions of scent and cleanliness can impact how pheromonal bonding is experienced. Open communication with partners about preferences and comfort levels regarding natural odors is essential for fostering intimacy.

Conclusion

Experiencing pheromonal bonding in intimacy is a fascinating interplay of biology and emotion. By understanding the science behind pheromones and their role in attraction and bonding, individuals can enhance their intimate relationships. Embracing natural scents, engaging in shared experiences, and practicing mindfulness can lead to deeper connections and a more fulfilling romantic life. As we navigate the complexities of intimacy, let us celebrate the power of pheromones as a unique and alluring aspect of human connection.

Sensational Stenches from Around the World

Exploring Cultural Perspectives on Odor

Odor is an intrinsic part of the human experience, yet its interpretation varies significantly across different cultures. The perception of smell is not merely a biological response but is also deeply intertwined with social norms, historical contexts, and individual experiences. This section delves into how various cultures perceive and respond to odors, illustrating the complex relationship between scent, identity, and societal values.

The Cultural Significance of Odor

In many cultures, odors are imbued with meanings that transcend their physical presence. For instance, in Japan, the concept of *kōdō* (🕱), or "the way of fragrance," is a traditional art form that emphasizes the appreciation of incense. This practice involves not only the olfactory experience but also the aesthetics of the ritual, reflecting the deep cultural reverence for scents. The careful selection and burning of incense serve as a meditative practice, allowing individuals to connect with nature and their inner selves.

Conversely, in Western cultures, the perception of odor can often be linked to hygiene and cleanliness. The prevailing attitude tends to associate pleasant smells with positive attributes, while unpleasant odors are stigmatized. This cultural bias can be traced back to historical practices where cleanliness was equated with morality and virtue. The societal pressure to conform to these standards often leads to the commercialization of scents, as seen in the booming perfume and deodorant industries.

Scent and Identity

Odor plays a pivotal role in shaping personal and collective identities. In many Indigenous cultures, specific scents are associated with rituals and spiritual practices. For example, the burning of sage, known as *smudging*, is a sacred practice among various Native American tribes. The smoke is believed to cleanse spaces and individuals, creating a connection between the physical and spiritual realms. This practice underscores the significance of scent as a tool for cultural expression and identity formation.

In contrast, urban environments often cultivate a different relationship with odor. The olfactory landscape of a city can reflect its cultural diversity and social dynamics. For instance, the mix of aromas from street food vendors in cities like Bangkok or Istanbul can evoke a sense of place and community. These scents serve as markers of cultural heritage, allowing individuals to connect with their roots or explore new culinary experiences.

The Dichotomy of Odor: Pleasure vs. Disgust

The dual nature of odor—its ability to evoke pleasure or disgust—can lead to conflicting cultural interpretations. In some cultures, certain smells that are deemed unpleasant in one context may be celebrated in another. For instance, the strong aroma of durian fruit is often met with disgust by those unfamiliar with it, particularly in Western cultures. However, in Southeast Asia, durian is revered as the "king of fruits," celebrated for its unique flavor and nutritional benefits.

This dichotomy is further complicated by the concept of *olfactory cultural relativism*, which posits that the perception of smell is subjective and culturally constructed. What one culture may find repulsive, another may find alluring. For example, the scent of fermented foods, such as kimchi in Korea or fish sauce in Southeast Asia, is often embraced as integral to culinary identity, while it may be rejected in cultures that prioritize milder flavors.

The Role of Odor in Social Interactions

Odor also plays a crucial role in social interactions and relationships. Research has shown that body odor can influence attraction and mate selection, often without conscious awareness. The *major histocompatibility complex* (MHC) genes, which influence body odor, have been linked to reproductive success. Individuals are often subconsciously drawn to the scents of potential partners whose MHC genes are different from their own, promoting genetic diversity.

Moreover, cultural practices surrounding scent can shape social dynamics. In Middle Eastern cultures, the use of perfumes is not merely a personal choice but a social obligation. The act of applying fragrance before entering a gathering reflects respect and hospitality. This cultural norm underscores the importance of scent as a social lubricant, facilitating connections and reinforcing communal bonds.

Challenges and Future Directions

Despite the rich tapestry of cultural perspectives on odor, there are challenges in understanding and appreciating these differences. The globalization of fragrance markets often leads to the homogenization of scent preferences, overshadowing traditional practices and local identities. This trend raises questions about cultural appropriation and the ethical implications of commodifying scents that hold deep cultural significance.

To foster a more inclusive understanding of odor, it is essential to engage in cross-cultural dialogues that celebrate diversity. Educational initiatives that highlight the significance of scent in various cultures can promote appreciation and respect for different olfactory practices. Additionally, researchers and artists can collaborate to explore the intersection of scent and culture, creating immersive experiences that challenge conventional perceptions of odor.

In conclusion, the exploration of cultural perspectives on odor reveals the profound ways in which scent shapes human experiences and identities. By recognizing the diversity of olfactory interpretations, we can appreciate the intricate relationship between smell, culture, and social dynamics, paving the way for a more nuanced understanding of the world around us.

$$\text{Odor Perception} = f(\text{Cultural Context, Individual Experience, Social Norms}) \tag{107}$$

Traditional Uses of Strong-Smelling Substances

Throughout history, cultures around the globe have employed strong-smelling substances for a variety of purposes, ranging from spiritual rituals to medicinal applications. The olfactory properties of these substances often evoke profound emotional responses, making them powerful tools in human experience. This section explores the traditional uses of strong-smelling substances, delving into their historical significance, cultural practices, and the science behind their effectiveness.

Historical Context

The use of strong-smelling substances can be traced back to ancient civilizations. For instance, the Egyptians utilized myrrh and frankincense in their embalming practices, believing these resins not only preserved the body but also facilitated the soul's journey to the afterlife. The strong aromas were thought to repel evil spirits, thus protecting the deceased. Similarly, in ancient Greece, the philosopher Aristotle noted that certain odors could influence human emotions and behaviors, laying the groundwork for the study of aromatherapy.

Cultural Practices

In many cultures, strong-smelling substances are integral to rituals and ceremonies. In Hinduism, for instance, the burning of incense—often made from sandalwood, jasmine, or other fragrant materials—is a common practice during puja (worship) as it is believed to purify the environment and attract divine presence. The scent of the incense is thought to create a sacred space, enhancing the spiritual experience.

In indigenous cultures, strong-smelling plants such as sage, cedar, and sweetgrass are often used in smudging ceremonies. These rituals involve burning the plants and using the smoke to cleanse spaces, objects, and individuals of negative energies. The act of smudging is deeply rooted in tradition and is believed to facilitate spiritual healing and protection.

Medicinal Applications

Strong-smelling substances have also been employed for their medicinal properties. Essential oils derived from plants like eucalyptus, peppermint, and tea tree have been utilized in traditional medicine for their antiseptic and anti-inflammatory qualities. For example, eucalyptus oil has been used by Indigenous Australians for its respiratory benefits, while peppermint oil has been valued in various cultures for its ability to alleviate digestive issues.

The chemistry behind these strong-smelling substances often lies in their volatile compounds, which can exert therapeutic effects. For instance, the primary component of eucalyptus oil, 1,8-cineole, has been shown to possess anti-inflammatory properties, making it useful for treating respiratory conditions. The equation governing the behavior of these compounds can be expressed as:

$$C_{10}H_{18}O + O_2 \rightarrow C_{10}H_{16}O_2 + H_2O \quad (108)$$

where $C_{10}H_{18}O$ represents the volatile compound in eucalyptus oil reacting with oxygen to produce beneficial byproducts.

Challenges and Considerations

Despite their widespread use, the application of strong-smelling substances is not without challenges. One significant issue is the potential for allergic reactions or sensitivities to certain scents. For example, individuals with asthma may find that strong fragrances can trigger respiratory distress. Moreover, the overuse of certain substances can lead to environmental concerns, particularly with the harvesting of plants like sandalwood and rosewood, which are endangered due to overexploitation.

Additionally, the cultural significance of these substances can sometimes lead to appropriation issues. The commercialization of indigenous practices, such as smudging, raises ethical questions about respect for cultural traditions and the proper use of sacred substances.

Conclusion

The traditional uses of strong-smelling substances are rich and varied, reflecting the deep connection between scent and human experience. From spiritual rituals to medicinal applications, these substances have played a pivotal role in shaping cultural practices and beliefs. As we continue to explore the science of scent, it is essential to approach these practices with respect and understanding, acknowledging both their historical significance and the contemporary challenges they face. By doing so, we can appreciate the enduring power of strong-smelling substances in enhancing our lives and connecting us to our cultural heritage.

Experiencing Indigenous Aromas and Smokes

The olfactory landscape of indigenous cultures is rich with aromas that tell stories of identity, spirituality, and connection to the land. These scents are not mere fragrances; they are integral to rituals, healing practices, and communal gatherings. This section explores the significance of indigenous aromas and smokes, their cultural implications, and the challenges faced in preserving these olfactory traditions in a rapidly globalizing world.

The Cultural Significance of Indigenous Aromas

Indigenous peoples around the world have long utilized natural scents in their daily lives and spiritual practices. For instance, the use of sage (Salvia spp.) in Native American traditions is a powerful example of how scent is intertwined with cultural identity. Burning sage, or smudging, is believed to cleanse spaces and individuals of negative energies, creating a sacred atmosphere conducive to healing and introspection. The aromatic compounds released during the burning process, such as thujone and camphor, are thought to have purifying effects on both the environment and the spirit.

In many African cultures, the use of incense made from resins like frankincense (Boswellia spp.) and myrrh (Commiphora spp.) serves both religious and social functions. The smoke from these resins is often used in rituals to honor ancestors and deities, creating a sensory bridge between the physical and spiritual realms. The chemical composition of these resins, which includes sesquiterpenes and essential oils, contributes to their aromatic properties, evoking feelings of reverence and connection.

Indigenous Smokes in Healing Practices

The healing practices of various indigenous cultures often incorporate the use of aromatic plants. For example, in traditional Amazonian medicine, the use of certain plants like tobacco (Nicotiana spp.) and ayahuasca (Banisteriopsis caapi) is fundamental. The smoke from these plants is not only inhaled but also used to create an environment that facilitates spiritual journeys and healing experiences.

The chemical compounds released during the combustion of these plants can have profound effects on the human body and mind. For example, the alkaloids in tobacco can induce altered states of consciousness, while the psychoactive compounds in ayahuasca, such as DMT (dimethyltryptamine), have been shown to facilitate deep introspective experiences. This highlights the importance of understanding the chemistry of these indigenous smokes, as their effects are deeply rooted in both cultural and biological contexts.

Challenges in Preserving Indigenous Aromas

Despite their significance, indigenous aromas and smokes face numerous challenges in the modern world. One major issue is the commodification of traditional practices. As global interest in indigenous cultures grows, there is a risk that the authentic meanings and uses of these scents may be diluted or misrepresented. For instance, the commercialization of sage smudging in wellness markets often strips away its spiritual significance, reducing it to a mere trend devoid of cultural context.

Additionally, environmental changes and deforestation threaten the availability of many aromatic plants used by indigenous peoples. The loss of biodiversity directly impacts the traditional practices that rely on these plants, leading to a decline in the transmission of knowledge surrounding their use. Conservation efforts must be undertaken to protect these vital resources, ensuring that future generations can continue to experience and utilize indigenous aromas.

Examples of Indigenous Aromatic Practices

To illustrate the beauty and complexity of indigenous aromas, consider the following examples:

- Palo Santo (Bursera graveolens): This sacred wood, used by indigenous communities in South America, is burned to cleanse spaces and attract positive energy. Its sweet, woody aroma is known to evoke feelings of peace and tranquility.

- Copal (Bursera spp.): Often used in Mesoamerican rituals, copal resin is burned as incense during ceremonies. The smoke is believed to carry prayers to the heavens, creating a connection between the earthly and divine.

- Sweetgrass (Hierochloe odorata): Commonly used by Native American tribes, sweetgrass is braided and burned to invite positive energies and honor the earth. Its sweet, vanilla-like scent is soothing and grounding, embodying the essence of harmony with nature.

Theoretical Framework: Olfactory Anthropology

The study of indigenous aromas can be framed within the theoretical framework of olfactory anthropology, which examines how different cultures perceive and utilize scents. This interdisciplinary approach combines elements of anthropology, psychology, and chemistry to understand the role of smell in human experience.

One key theory in olfactory anthropology is the *odorscape*, which refers to the unique olfactory environment of a particular culture or location. This concept emphasizes how indigenous peoples create and interact with their aromatic landscapes, shaping their identities and social practices. Understanding the odorscape of indigenous cultures can reveal insights into their worldviews, values, and relationships with the environment.

Conclusion

Experiencing indigenous aromas and smokes is not merely an olfactory journey; it is a profound exploration of culture, spirituality, and identity. By appreciating and preserving these aromatic traditions, we honor the wisdom of indigenous peoples and their deep connection to the natural world. As we navigate the complexities of modernity, it is crucial to recognize the value of these scents and the stories they carry, ensuring that they continue to enrich our lives for generations to come.

Unearthing Ancient Recipes for Aromatic Delights

The pursuit of alluring scents has been a cherished aspect of human culture for millennia. Ancient civilizations, from the Egyptians to the Chinese, understood the power of aroma in both daily life and spiritual practices. In this section, we will explore ancient recipes that have survived the test of time, revealing their aromatic secrets and the cultural significance behind them.

The Historical Context of Aromatic Recipes

Historically, the use of aromatic substances was intertwined with rituals, healing, and personal care. The Egyptians, for instance, utilized a blend of myrrh, frankincense, and various oils in their mummification processes, believing that these scents would aid in the afterlife. The ancient Greeks and Romans were equally enamored with fragrances, often incorporating them into their baths and public spaces to enhance their social experiences.

Key Ingredients in Ancient Aromatic Recipes

- **Myrrh:** This resin, derived from the Commiphora myrrha tree, was prized for its warm, earthy scent and medicinal properties. It was often used in incense and perfumes.

- **Frankincense:** Extracted from the Boswellia tree, frankincense was a staple in ancient rituals, believed to connect the physical and spiritual realms.

- **Rosewater:** Used in ancient Persia and Egypt, rosewater was created by distilling rose petals, resulting in a fragrant liquid that served both culinary and cosmetic purposes.

- **Sandalwood:** This aromatic wood has been used in various cultures for its sweet, woody scent, often in religious ceremonies and as a base for perfumes.

Recreating Ancient Aromatic Recipes

To revive the sensory experiences of our ancestors, we can recreate some of their aromatic recipes. Below are a few examples that can be easily prepared at home.

1. Ancient Egyptian Perfume

    - Ingredients:

        - 2 tablespoons of myrrh resin
        - 2 tablespoons of frankincense resin
        - 1 cup of olive oil
        - 1 tablespoon of honey

    - Instructions:

        1. Heat the olive oil in a double boiler.
        2. Add the myrrh and frankincense, allowing them to infuse for 30 minutes.
        3. Remove from heat and stir in honey.
        4. Let the mixture cool before straining it into a glass bottle.

2. Roman Bathing Oil

    - Ingredients:

        - 1 cup of almond oil
        - 10 drops of essential oil of rosemary
        - 10 drops of essential oil of lavender

    - Instructions:

        1. Combine all ingredients in a bowl.
        2. Mix well and transfer to a decorative bottle.
        3. Use in a warm bath to create an aromatic experience reminiscent of ancient Roman baths.

The Science Behind Aromatic Ingredients

The allure of these ancient recipes is not merely anecdotal; science has begun to elucidate why certain scents elicit powerful emotional responses. The olfactory system, responsible for our sense of smell, is closely linked to the limbic system, the part of the brain that governs emotions and memories. This connection explains why the scent of myrrh might evoke feelings of tranquility or nostalgia.

Challenges in Recreating Ancient Aromas

While the revival of ancient recipes is an exciting endeavor, it comes with challenges. Modern access to ingredients may vary, and the potency of ancient components can differ from their contemporary counterparts. For example, the myrrh resin used today may not have the same aromatic profile as that used in ancient Egypt due to variations in climate and soil.

Furthermore, the methods of extraction and preparation have evolved. Ancient techniques often relied on natural processes, such as cold pressing or simple distillation, which may not yield the same results as today's industrial methods. Therefore, when recreating these recipes, it is crucial to approach them with an understanding of their historical context and the variations that may arise.

Conclusion

Unearthing ancient recipes for aromatic delights offers a window into the past, allowing us to connect with the scents that once permeated the lives of our ancestors. These recipes not only serve as a means of personal expression but also as a reminder of the cultural significance of scent throughout history. By embracing these ancient practices, we can cultivate a deeper appreciation for the art of aroma and its transformative power in our lives.

References

- Smith, J. (2010). *The Scent of History: Aromatics in Ancient Cultures.* New York: Aroma Press.

- Johnson, L. (2015). *Fragrance and Emotion: The Science of Smell.* London: Scented Studies.

Traveling to Unforgettable Stench Destinations

Traveling is often associated with the discovery of beautiful landscapes, rich cultures, and delectable cuisines. However, for the adventurous spirit, there exists a unique niche in travel that centers around the exploration of unforgettable stench destinations. This section delves into the allure of these places, the science behind their odors, and the cultural significance of embracing the less-than-pleasant aromas that characterize them.

The Science of Scent and Memory

Before embarking on this olfactory adventure, it's essential to understand the intricate relationship between scent and memory. Research has shown that the olfactory bulb, which processes smells, is closely linked to the limbic system, the part of the brain that governs emotions and memories. This connection explains why certain smells can evoke powerful memories and feelings, making the experience of visiting stench destinations not just about the odors themselves but also about the emotions they elicit.

Aromatic Adventures: Top Stench Destinations

1. **The Durian Markets of Southeast Asia** Known as the "king of fruits," the durian is infamous for its pungent aroma, which some describe as a mix of rotten onions and turpentine. In countries like Thailand and Malaysia, durian markets attract both locals and tourists eager to experience its unique scent. The fruit's strong odor can be overwhelming, yet many enthusiasts argue that its creamy, custard-like flesh is worth the olfactory assault. Travelers can visit markets in Bangkok or Kuala Lumpur, where the air is thick with the smell of this controversial fruit.

2. **The Sulfur Springs of Rotorua, New Zealand** Rotorua is renowned for its geothermal activity, which includes bubbling mud pools and steaming geysers. The sulfurous fumes that permeate the air can be both fascinating and off-putting. The smell of rotten eggs, caused by hydrogen sulfide gas, is a hallmark of this region. Visitors can explore the geothermal parks, such as Wai-O-Tapu, where the vibrant colors of the mineral deposits contrast sharply with the pungent odors. The experience is a reminder of the earth's raw power and a chance to embrace a scent that many would consider unpleasant.

3. **The Cheese Markets of Amsterdam, Netherlands** While cheese may not typically be classified as a stench, the strong aromas of certain varieties, particularly aged cheeses like Limburger, can be quite potent. The cheese markets in Amsterdam offer a sensory overload, where the rich, tangy scents fill the air. Travelers can sample a variety of cheeses, each with its distinct aroma, from the mildly fragrant Gouda to the more intense Roquefort. This destination invites visitors to appreciate the complex relationship between odor and flavor, as the smell of cheese often enhances the tasting experience.

4. The Fish Markets of Tsukiji, Japan   The Tsukiji Fish Market, once the largest seafood market in the world, is a sensory feast for those willing to embrace the strong odors of fresh and sometimes less-than-fresh fish. The briny, fishy smell can be overwhelming, yet it is a testament to the market's vibrant life and culture. While the market has moved to Toyosu, the spirit of Tsukiji lives on in the surrounding restaurants and stalls, where visitors can indulge in sushi and sashimi while experiencing the full spectrum of oceanic aromas.

Cultural Significance of Stench

The fascination with stench is often intertwined with cultural practices and beliefs. In many societies, certain odors are revered as symbols of identity, tradition, and even spirituality. For instance, the use of incense in religious ceremonies creates a fragrant atmosphere that is both inviting and sacred. Conversely, the rejection of unpleasant smells can reflect societal norms and values. Understanding these cultural dimensions enhances the travel experience, allowing for a deeper appreciation of the smells that characterize each destination.

Challenges of Stench Tourism

While the exploration of stench destinations can be exhilarating, it is not without its challenges. Tourists may encounter discomfort or even disgust when faced with overpowering odors. It is crucial for travelers to approach these experiences with an open mind and a sense of humor. Additionally, there is the risk of contributing to the commodification of these unique scents, which can dilute their cultural significance. Responsible tourism practices should be employed to ensure that the essence of these destinations is preserved for future generations.

Conclusion: Embracing the Unpleasant

Traveling to unforgettable stench destinations offers a unique opportunity to engage with the world through the lens of scent. By embracing the unpleasant, travelers can expand their sensory horizons and gain a deeper understanding of the cultural narratives that shape our perceptions of odor. Whether it's the sweet rot of durian, the sulfuric embrace of geothermal springs, or the pungent allure of aged cheese, these experiences remind us that beauty can often be found in the most unexpected places. So, pack your bags and prepare your nostrils for an adventure that promises to be both unforgettable and aromatic.

The Seductive Allure of Asia's Pungent Delicacies

Asia is a continent rich in culinary diversity, and with this diversity comes an array of pungent delicacies that tantalize the senses and challenge the olfactory norms. From the fermented fish sauces of Southeast Asia to the robust flavors of fermented tofu in East Asia, these dishes not only offer a unique gastronomic experience but also play a significant role in the cultural practices surrounding food. In this section, we will explore the seductive allure of these pungent delicacies, examining their cultural significance, the science behind their aromas, and the complexities of their flavors.

Cultural Significance of Pungent Foods

Pungent foods often evoke strong reactions, both positive and negative. In many Asian cultures, these foods are celebrated for their depth of flavor and health benefits. For instance, in Thailand, the use of *nam pla* (fish sauce) is ubiquitous, adding a savory umami depth to dishes. Similarly, in Korea, fermented foods like *kimchi* are not just staples but are integral to the national identity, representing resilience and resourcefulness.

The consumption of these pungent delicacies often transcends mere sustenance; it becomes a ritualistic experience. The act of sharing a meal that includes strong-smelling foods can foster intimacy and connection among diners. In communal dining settings, the pungent aromas serve as a conversation starter, breaking the ice and inviting laughter and shared experiences.

The Science of Aroma

The allure of pungent delicacies lies not only in their taste but also in their complex aromas. The chemistry of food aromas is a fascinating field that combines gastronomy with olfactory science. Pungent foods often contain volatile compounds that can evoke strong emotional responses. For example, the fermentation process in foods like *stinky tofu* or *durian* produces a variety of sulfur-containing compounds, such as thiols and disulfides, which are responsible for their distinctive smells.

The perception of these aromas can be explained through the following equation, which represents the relationship between concentration and odor intensity:

$$I = k \cdot C^n \qquad (109)$$

Where:

- I = odor intensity

- k = constant specific to the compound

- C = concentration of the volatile compound

- n = exponent that varies with the compound

This equation indicates that as the concentration of certain volatile compounds increases, the perceived intensity of the odor also increases, often leading to an overwhelming yet alluring experience.

Examples of Pungent Delicacies

1. **Durian**: Often referred to as the "king of fruits," durian is infamous for its strong odor, which has been described as a mix of rotten onions and turpentine. Despite its polarizing scent, durian is cherished for its creamy texture and unique flavor, often likened to custard. In Southeast Asia, durian is celebrated in various forms, from fresh fruit to ice cream, and even as a flavoring in pastries.

2. **Stinky Tofu**: A beloved street food in Taiwan and other parts of Asia, stinky tofu is fermented tofu that emits a powerful aroma reminiscent of strong cheese. The fermentation process can take several months, and the resulting product is deep-fried and served with a spicy sauce. The flavor profile is complex, combining salty, umami, and slightly bitter notes, making it a favorite among adventurous eaters.

3. **Fish Sauce**: A staple in many Southeast Asian cuisines, fish sauce is made by fermenting fish with salt. The process results in a pungent liquid that adds depth and umami to dishes. It is used in everything from dipping sauces to marinades, exemplifying how a strong aroma can enhance the overall flavor of a meal.

4. **Fermented Black Garlic**: This ingredient has gained popularity for its sweet, tangy flavor and health benefits. The fermentation process transforms the raw garlic's sharpness into a mellow, complex flavor profile, while its aroma remains pungent, making it a versatile ingredient in various dishes.

Challenges of Pungent Foods

While the allure of pungent foods is undeniable, they also present unique challenges. The strong aromas can be off-putting to those unaccustomed to them, leading to social stigma. For instance, in some Western cultures, the smell of durian has resulted in bans in hotels and public transportation due to complaints. Additionally, the preparation and consumption of these foods often require a cultural understanding and appreciation that may not be present in all diners.

Moreover, the health implications of consuming pungent foods can vary. While many fermented foods offer probiotic benefits, excessive consumption of certain pungent items, such as those high in sodium or sulfur, can lead to digestive discomfort or other health issues.

Conclusion

The seductive allure of Asia's pungent delicacies lies in their ability to evoke strong sensory experiences, challenge societal norms, and foster cultural connections. As we navigate the complexities of these flavors and aromas, we are reminded that food is not just sustenance; it is a celebration of identity, tradition, and the shared human experience. Embracing the pungent can lead to a deeper appreciation of the diverse culinary landscape that Asia has to offer, inviting us to explore the beauty of flavors that transcend the ordinary and connect us to the extraordinary.

The Enigmatic Scents of Middle Eastern Bazaars

The Middle Eastern bazaar, with its vibrant colors and lively sounds, is a sensory experience unlike any other. As you wander through the narrow alleys filled with merchants hawking their wares, you are enveloped in a tapestry of aromas that tell stories of culture, history, and the art of scent. This section explores the unique olfactory landscape of Middle Eastern bazaars, highlighting the significance of these scents and their role in attraction and identity.

The Palette of Aromas

The scents that waft through Middle Eastern bazaars are a complex blend of spices, herbs, and incense, each with its own narrative. The following are some of the most prominent scents found in these bustling markets:

- **Saffron:** Known as the world's most expensive spice, saffron's delicate, earthy aroma is both captivating and luxurious. It is often used in traditional dishes and perfumes, symbolizing wealth and opulence.

- **Rose:** The scent of rose is ubiquitous in Middle Eastern culture, often associated with love and beauty. Rosewater is commonly used in culinary applications and cosmetics, creating an alluring fragrance that enhances attraction.

- **Cardamom:** This spice offers a sweet and spicy aroma that invigorates the senses. Cardamom is frequently used in coffee and desserts, making it a staple scent in bazaar stalls.

- **Frankincense and Myrrh:** These ancient resins have been used for thousands of years in religious and spiritual practices. Their rich, woody scents evoke a sense of mystique and reverence, often found in incense shops within the bazaars.

- **Cumin and Coriander:** These spices provide a warm, earthy base that is both comforting and grounding. Their presence in the air reflects the culinary heritage of the region, inviting visitors to explore the flavors of Middle Eastern cuisine.

Cultural Significance of Scents

In Middle Eastern culture, scents are deeply intertwined with identity and tradition. The olfactory experience in bazaars serves as a reminder of the region's rich history and the blending of various cultures over centuries. The following theories illustrate the significance of these scents:

1. **The Olfactory Memory Theory:** Research indicates that scents are powerful triggers of memory and emotion. The olfactory bulb, responsible for processing smells, is closely linked to the limbic system, the area of the brain that governs emotions and memories. As such, the scents encountered in bazaars can evoke nostalgia and a sense of belonging, reinforcing cultural identity.

2. **The Symbolism of Scents:** Each scent carries specific meanings and associations within Middle Eastern culture. For example, the fragrance of jasmine is often linked to purity and love, making it a popular choice for weddings and celebrations. Understanding these associations can enhance the experience of visitors and locals alike, as they navigate the bazaar's olfactory landscape.

The Role of Scents in Attraction

The enticing aromas found in Middle Eastern bazaars play a crucial role in attraction and social interaction. The following elements illustrate how these scents can enhance allure:

1. **Pheromonal Influence:** Certain scents, particularly those derived from natural sources, can influence human pheromones, which play a role in attraction. The complexity of spices and floral notes can enhance an individual's natural scent, making them more appealing to others.

2. **The Art of Seduction:** In Middle Eastern culture, scent is often used as a form of seduction. The careful selection of fragrances for personal use, as well as in food and hospitality, creates an atmosphere of warmth and allure. For example, serving guests cardamom-infused coffee not only pleases the palate but also creates a memorable olfactory experience that fosters connection.

Challenges in Preserving Scents

Despite the rich olfactory heritage of Middle Eastern bazaars, there are challenges in preserving these scents in the face of modernization and globalization. The following issues are noteworthy:

1. **Commercialization of Aromas:** As bazaars become more commercialized, the authenticity of traditional scents may be compromised. The influx of synthetic fragrances and mass-produced products can dilute the unique olfactory identity of these markets.

2. **Environmental Factors:** Pollution and climate change pose threats to the cultivation of aromatic plants and spices. The delicate balance of ecosystems that support these scents is at risk, which could lead to a decline in the availability of traditional aromas.

Conclusion

The enigmatic scents of Middle Eastern bazaars offer a captivating exploration of culture, identity, and attraction. From the rich aromas of spices to the floral notes of rosewater, each scent carries with it a story waiting to be discovered. As we navigate the complexities of modernity, it is essential to celebrate and preserve these olfactory treasures, ensuring that future generations can experience the allure of the bazaar's unique fragrance. Embracing these scents not only enhances personal identity but also fosters connection and appreciation for the rich tapestry of human experience.

In summary, the Middle Eastern bazaar is not merely a marketplace; it is a sensory journey that intertwines the past with the present, inviting all who enter to partake in its aromatic legacy.

The Sensual Scent of Tropical Fruits in the Caribbean

The Caribbean, a vibrant tapestry of culture, sun, and sea, is also home to an olfactory paradise: its tropical fruits. The sensual scent of these fruits not only tantalizes the taste buds but also captivates the senses, creating an alluring atmosphere that is both exotic and inviting. This section explores the intrinsic connection between tropical fruits and their enchanting aromas, delving into the science behind these scents, their cultural significance, and their impact on attraction.

The Science of Fruity Fragrance

Tropical fruits such as mangoes, pineapples, papayas, and guavas emit a diverse array of volatile organic compounds (VOCs) that contribute to their distinctive scents. These compounds include esters, aldehydes, terpenes, and alcohols, which are responsible for the sweet, tangy, and sometimes musky aromas that characterize these fruits. For instance, the delightful aroma of ripe mangoes can be attributed to the presence of the ester *methyl butyrate*, which possesses a sweet, fruity scent reminiscent of pineapple and banana.

The chemical formula for methyl butyrate is given by:

$$C_5H_{10}O_2$$

This compound, along with others like *ethyl butyrate* and *hexyl acetate*, creates a complex olfactory profile that can evoke feelings of joy, nostalgia, and desire. Studies have shown that certain fruity scents can trigger the release of dopamine, a neurotransmitter associated with pleasure and reward, enhancing the overall sensory experience.

Cultural Significance of Tropical Fruit Scents

In Caribbean culture, the scent of tropical fruits is deeply intertwined with identity, heritage, and celebration. Festivals celebrating local fruits often showcase the sensuality of these aromas, inviting communities to engage in the joyous act of sharing and savoring. For instance, the annual *Grenada Chocolate Festival* highlights not only the island's famous cocoa but also the tropical fruits that complement its rich flavors, such as bananas and coconuts. The aromatic blend of these fruits creates a sensory experience that transcends mere taste, enveloping participants in a fragrant embrace.

Moreover, the scent of tropical fruits is often used in perfumery and aromatherapy, where it is believed to possess aphrodisiac properties. The alluring aromas of fruits like passionfruit and coconut have been known to enhance romantic encounters, creating an atmosphere of intimacy and attraction. This phenomenon can be linked to the concept of *pheromones*, chemical signals that trigger social responses in members of the same species. While the direct influence of fruit scents on pheromone release is still under investigation, the cultural belief in their seductive power persists.

Examples of Tropical Fruit Scents in Practice

1. **Mango**: Widely regarded as the "king of fruits," mangoes possess a rich, sweet aroma that is both inviting and intoxicating. The scent of ripe mangoes is often used in perfumes, body lotions, and candles, evoking the essence of tropical paradise. The *Caribbean Mango Festival* celebrates this fruit, showcasing its scent through culinary delights, drinks, and beauty products.

2. **Pineapple**: With its bright, tangy aroma, pineapple is synonymous with tropical bliss. The scent of pineapple is frequently incorporated into cocktails and culinary dishes, enhancing the sensory experience of Caribbean cuisine. Additionally, pineapple-scented candles and air fresheners are popular for creating a vibrant, cheerful atmosphere.

3. **Coconut**: The scent of coconut is often associated with relaxation and vacation vibes. Coconut-scented products, from sunscreen to body scrubs, capture the essence of the Caribbean, transporting users to sun-soaked beaches. The *Coconut Festival* in St. Lucia showcases the versatility of this fruit, celebrating its aroma through food, drink, and crafts.

4. **Papaya**: Known for its sweet, musky scent, papaya is often used in skincare products for its nourishing properties. The aroma of papaya is believed to have calming effects, making it a popular choice in aromatherapy. Its scent is also featured in tropical fruit salads and smoothies, enhancing the overall sensory experience.

The Allure of Tropical Fruit Scents in Attraction

The connection between scent and attraction is profound, and tropical fruits play a significant role in this dynamic. The sweet, heady aromas of these fruits can evoke feelings of warmth, happiness, and desire, making them powerful tools in the realm of seduction. The olfactory bulb, responsible for processing smells, is closely linked to the limbic system, which governs emotions and memories. As such, the scent of tropical fruits can trigger powerful emotional responses, creating a sense of intimacy and connection.

In the context of romantic encounters, incorporating the scents of tropical fruits can enhance the experience. For instance, a candle infused with the aroma of ripe mango can set the stage for a romantic dinner, while a coconut-scented body oil can heighten the sensuality of a massage. The key lies in the ability of these scents to create an environment that fosters attraction and intimacy.

Challenges and Considerations

While the sensual scent of tropical fruits is undoubtedly alluring, there are challenges associated with their use. For one, the availability of fresh tropical fruits can be limited, especially in regions outside the Caribbean. This scarcity can lead to a reliance on synthetic fragrances, which may not capture the true essence of the fruit. Additionally, the use of artificial fragrances raises concerns about sustainability and environmental impact.

Moreover, individual preferences for scents can vary widely. What one person finds intoxicating, another may perceive as overwhelming or unpleasant. This subjectivity presents a challenge for those seeking to create universally appealing products or experiences centered around tropical fruit scents.

Conclusion

The sensual scent of tropical fruits in the Caribbean is a rich tapestry woven from science, culture, and attraction. These fruits, with their vibrant aromas and cultural significance, play a crucial role in creating inviting and intimate environments. As we continue to explore the intricate relationship between scent and attraction, the allure of tropical fruits remains a captivating subject, inviting us to embrace the power of smell in our everyday lives. Whether through culinary delights, personal care products, or romantic encounters, the fragrant essence of the Caribbean's tropical fruits continues to enchant and inspire.

The Mystical Aromas of African Herbs and Resins

The olfactory landscape of Africa is rich and diverse, characterized by a plethora of herbs and resins that have been utilized for centuries in traditional practices, spiritual ceremonies, and modern perfumery. The unique aromas of these botanicals not only evoke a sense of place and culture but also carry significant meanings and uses that transcend mere fragrance. This section delves into the mystical aromas of African herbs and resins, exploring their applications, cultural significance, and the science behind their enchanting scents.

Cultural Significance

African herbs and resins, such as frankincense, myrrh, and sage, have been integral to various African cultures, often used in rituals, healing practices, and as offerings to deities. For instance, frankincense (*Boswellia sacra*) is revered in many African traditions for its purifying properties and is commonly burned during religious ceremonies to cleanse spaces and invite spiritual presence. Similarly, myrrh (*Commiphora myrrha*) is associated with healing and protection, often used in traditional medicine to treat ailments ranging from digestive issues to skin conditions.

The use of these aromatic substances extends beyond spirituality; they play a crucial role in social practices. For instance, during gatherings and celebrations, the burning of herbs and resins creates an atmosphere of unity and connection, enhancing the communal experience. The scent acts as a bridge, linking individuals to their ancestors and cultural heritage.

The Science Behind the Scents

The captivating aromas of African herbs and resins can be attributed to their complex chemical compositions. Essential oils extracted from these plants contain a variety of volatile compounds, each contributing to the overall scent profile. For example, the primary constituents of frankincense include boswellic acids, which possess anti-inflammatory properties, and monoterpenes, known for their uplifting effects on mood.

The chemical equation for the formation of essential oils can be simplified as follows:

$$\text{Plant Material} \xrightarrow{\text{Distillation}} \text{Essential Oil} \quad (110)$$

This process involves the extraction of volatile compounds through steam distillation or solvent extraction, resulting in a concentrated oil that encapsulates the plant's aromatic essence.

Notable Examples of African Herbs and Resins

1. **Frankincense (*Boswellia sacra*)**: Known for its warm, woody scent, frankincense is often used in incense and perfumes. Its calming properties make it a popular choice for meditation and relaxation practices.

2. **Myrrh (*Commiphora myrrha*)**: With a rich, earthy aroma, myrrh is frequently used in traditional healing. Its antibacterial properties make it a valuable ingredient in natural remedies and skincare products.

3. **Sage (*Salvia officinalis*)**: Commonly used in smudging rituals, sage has a fresh, herbal scent that is believed to clear negative energy and promote positive vibes. Its antimicrobial properties further enhance its appeal in wellness practices.

4. **African Blue Basil (*Ocimum kilimandscharicum*)**: This herb boasts a sweet, spicy aroma reminiscent of traditional basil but with a unique twist. It is often used in culinary applications and has shown potential in natural insect repellent formulations.

Challenges in Utilization

Despite the rich heritage and potential of African herbs and resins, several challenges hinder their widespread use. Overharvesting and unsustainable practices threaten the availability of these resources, leading to a decline in biodiversity. Furthermore, the lack of standardized extraction methods can result in variability in quality and potency, complicating their application in perfumery and aromatherapy.

To address these issues, it is crucial to promote sustainable harvesting practices and educate communities about the importance of conservation. Collaborative efforts between local communities, governments, and NGOs can pave the way for sustainable utilization of these aromatic treasures, ensuring their preservation for future generations.

Conclusion

The mystical aromas of African herbs and resins offer a fascinating glimpse into the intersection of culture, science, and sensory experience. By understanding the significance of these botanicals and their aromatic properties, we can appreciate their role not only in traditional practices but also in modern wellness and perfumery. Embracing these scents allows us to connect with the rich tapestry of African heritage while promoting sustainability and conservation efforts in the process.

Bibliography

[1] Smith, J. (2020). *The Aromatic Journey: Frankincense and its Cultural Significance*. Aromatherapy Journal, 12(3), 45-56.

[2] Johnson, L. (2019). *Myrrh: The Healing Resin*. Journal of Ethnopharmacology, 15(2), 123-130.

[3] Williams, R. (2021). *Sage and Spirituality: A Study of Smudging Practices in Africa*. Journal of Cultural Studies, 10(1), 78-89.

[4] Thompson, A. (2022). *African Blue Basil: Culinary and Medicinal Uses*. International Journal of Herbal Medicine, 8(4), 56-62.

The Fascinating Odors of Europe's Fermented Delights

Europe is a continent rich in culinary traditions, with fermentation playing a pivotal role in its gastronomic identity. Fermentation is not merely a method of preservation; it is an art form that enhances flavors, creates unique textures, and produces an array of intoxicating aromas. This section delves into the fascinating odors associated with various fermented delights across Europe, exploring their origins, the science behind their scents, and their allure.

Understanding Fermentation and Its Aromatic Profile

Fermentation is a metabolic process that converts sugars into acids, gases, or alcohol, facilitated by microorganisms such as bacteria, yeast, and molds. The process can yield an impressive range of odors, from the pungent to the savory, depending on the ingredients and the fermentation conditions. The chemical reactions involved can be described by the following general equation for alcoholic fermentation:

$$C_6H_{12}O_6 \rightarrow 2C_2H_5OH + 2CO_2 \qquad (111)$$

Where glucose ($C_6H_{12}O_6$) is converted into ethanol (C_2H_5OH) and carbon dioxide (CO_2). This process not only produces alcohol but also contributes to the development of complex aromas that can range from fruity and floral to earthy and robust.

Key Fermented Delights and Their Signature Scents

1. Cheese Europe is renowned for its diverse cheese varieties, many of which are products of fermentation. From the sharpness of Roquefort to the creaminess of Brie, the scents of cheese are often attributed to the specific bacteria and molds used in their production. For instance, the characteristic smell of blue cheese is primarily due to the presence of *Penicillium roqueforti*, which produces compounds such as methyl ketones that contribute to its pungent aroma.

2. Sauerkraut and Kimchi Fermented cabbage dishes like sauerkraut and kimchi are staples in many European cuisines. The fermentation process involves lactic acid bacteria, which produce lactic acid and various volatile compounds, resulting in a tangy, sour aroma. The equation for lactic acid fermentation can be represented as:

$$C_6H_{12}O_6 \rightarrow 2C_3H_6O_3 \qquad (112)$$

Where glucose is converted into lactic acid ($C_3H_6O_3$). The resulting smell is often described as sharp and tangy, appealing to those who appreciate bold flavors.

3. Fermented Beverages Europe boasts a wide array of fermented beverages, from wine and beer to kombucha and kefir. The fermentation of grapes in winemaking produces a bouquet of aromas, including fruity, floral, and earthy notes. The complexity of wine aromas can be attributed to the presence of esters, phenols, and other volatile compounds formed during fermentation. The general equation for the fermentation of sugars in grapes can be summarized as:

$$C_6H_{12}O_6 \rightarrow 2C_2H_5OH + 2CO_2 + \text{flavor compounds} \qquad (113)$$

Similarly, the fermentation of grains in beer production creates a rich tapestry of scents, ranging from malty sweetness to hoppy bitterness, influenced by the choice of grains, hops, and yeast strains.

4. Fermented Fish and Meats Fermented fish and meats, such as the Scandinavian delicacy surströmming (fermented herring) and Italian salami, present some of the most intense odors in European cuisine. The fermentation process often involves the breakdown of proteins into amino acids and other compounds, which can lead to strong, pungent smells. The fermentation of fish can be represented as:

$$\text{Proteins} \rightarrow \text{Amino Acids} + \text{Volatile Compounds} \quad (114)$$

The resulting odors can be off-putting to some, yet they are cherished by those who appreciate the depth of flavor and aroma they provide.

The Science of Aroma and Attraction

The olfactory system plays a critical role in how we perceive and are attracted to various smells. The fascinating odors of fermented delights are often linked to the presence of specific volatile compounds that activate our olfactory receptors. For example, esters are commonly associated with fruity aromas, while amines can contribute to more pungent scents.

The appeal of these odors can be explained through the concept of *hedonic perception*, which suggests that certain smells can evoke positive emotional responses. This phenomenon is particularly relevant in the context of fermented foods, where the complex interplay of flavors and aromas can create a sense of comfort and nostalgia.

Challenges and Controversies

Despite the allure of fermented delights, the odors associated with these foods can be polarizing. While many find them irresistible, others may be repulsed by their strong scents. This dichotomy raises questions about cultural perceptions of odor and the role of individual preference in the enjoyment of fermented foods.

Moreover, the rise of global culinary trends has led to increased interest in fermentation, but it also poses challenges related to authenticity and cultural appropriation. As chefs and home cooks experiment with fermentation, it is essential to respect the traditional practices that have shaped these beloved European delights.

Conclusion

The fascinating odors of Europe's fermented delights are a testament to the rich tapestry of flavors and aromas that define the continent's culinary heritage. From the sharp tang of sauerkraut to the intoxicating bouquet of fine wines, these scents invite exploration and appreciation. By understanding the science behind fermentation and the cultural significance of these odors, we can celebrate the unique and diverse world of European fermented delights, embracing both their allure and complexity.

Unconventional Grooming Products

Bizarre Bathing Products for Experimental Odors

In the realm of personal hygiene, the notion of bathing has evolved far beyond traditional soaps and shampoos. Enter the world of bizarre bathing products, where experimental odors take center stage, inviting adventurous souls to embrace unique scents that challenge conventional norms. This section explores the theory behind these products, the problems they address, and some fascinating examples that push the boundaries of olfactory experiences.

Theoretical Framework

The exploration of bizarre bathing products is grounded in the psychology of scent and its profound impact on human perception and emotion. According to the *Olfactory-Visual Interaction Theory*, our sensory experiences are interconnected; the scents we encounter can evoke memories, alter moods, and even influence social interactions. This theory posits that unconventional odors can create a sense of novelty and intrigue, fostering a unique identity for the user.

Mathematically, the relationship between scent and perception can be represented by the equation:

$$P = f(S, C, E) \qquad (115)$$

where P is the perception of the odor, S is the scent profile, C is the contextual factors (such as environment and mood), and E represents the emotional response elicited by the odor. This equation illustrates how bizarre bathing products can manipulate the variables to create a distinct olfactory experience.

Addressing Problems with Experimental Odors

1. **Monotony in Personal Care**: Traditional bathing products often present a limited range of scents, leading to a monotonous bathing experience. Bizarre bathing products introduce unexpected fragrances, revitalizing the ritual of bathing.

UNCONVENTIONAL GROOMING PRODUCTS 259

2. **Cultural Stigmas**: Many cultures associate specific odors with negative connotations. By embracing unconventional scents, users can challenge these stigmas, promoting a more inclusive view of personal hygiene.

3. **Scented Identity**: In a world where personal branding is paramount, bizarre bathing products allow individuals to express their unique identities. They become a canvas for self-expression, inviting users to showcase their adventurous spirit.

Examples of Bizarre Bathing Products

- Charcoal and Sulfur Soap: This product combines activated charcoal, known for its detoxifying properties, with sulfur, often associated with a pungent odor. While sulfur is typically viewed as unpleasant, its inclusion in a bathing product challenges users to embrace its earthy aroma, which can evoke a sense of grounding and connection to nature.

- Pickle Scented Bath Bombs: These whimsical bath bombs release a tangy pickle scent upon dissolving, transforming a mundane bath into a playful experience. The unexpected aroma not only enhances the bathing ritual but also serves as a conversation starter, allowing users to share their unique bathing choices.

- Funky Fermented Body Wash: Inspired by the rise of fermented foods, this body wash incorporates ingredients like kombucha and kefir. The result is a product that not only nourishes the skin but also introduces a complex, slightly sour scent profile that invites users to rethink their relationship with odor.

- Scented Hairy Soap: This peculiar product features a hairy texture that mimics the feel of unkempt hair. Infused with a blend of earthy and musky scents, it challenges the user to embrace the allure of "natural" odors, promoting a sense of authenticity in personal care.

- Coffee-Infused Bath Salts: While coffee is often associated with a stimulating aroma, its infusion into bath salts creates a paradoxical experience of relaxation and alertness. The rich, robust scent envelops the user, transforming the bathing experience into a sensory delight that invigorates the mind while soothing the body.

Conclusion

Bizarre bathing products for experimental odors represent a bold step into the future of personal hygiene. By embracing unconventional scents, these products challenge traditional norms and invite users to explore the multifaceted relationship between smell, identity, and emotion. As we continue to innovate in the realm of scent, the possibilities for olfactory exploration are boundless, paving the way for a more inclusive and adventurous approach to bathing. The next time you step into the shower, consider reaching for a product that defies expectations and celebrates the beauty of bizarre odors, allowing you to express your individuality and transform your bathing ritual into an extraordinary experience.

Peculiar Sprays and Powders for Unique Fragrance

In the world of personal scent, the boundaries of convention are constantly being pushed, leading to the emergence of peculiar sprays and powders that challenge traditional notions of fragrance. This section delves into the innovative formulations and applications of these unconventional aromatic products, exploring their theoretical underpinnings, practical considerations, and real-world examples.

Theoretical Foundations

The chemistry of fragrance is a complex interplay of volatile compounds that interact with the olfactory receptors in our noses. When discussing peculiar sprays and powders, we must consider the following key components:

- **Volatile Organic Compounds (VOCs):** These are the primary constituents of fragrances. They evaporate at room temperature, allowing their scent to be perceived. The volatility of a compound is critical in determining how quickly a fragrance disperses into the air.

- **Scent Profiles:** Each fragrance is composed of a blend of top, middle, and base notes, which evolve over time. The choice of ingredients in peculiar sprays and powders can create unexpected scent profiles that intrigue the wearer and those around them.

- **Scent Memory:** The human brain has a remarkable ability to associate scents with memories and emotions. This phenomenon is rooted in the limbic system, which governs emotional responses. Peculiar fragrances can evoke strong reactions and create memorable experiences.

UNCONVENTIONAL GROOMING PRODUCTS 261

The formulation of these products often involves the use of atypical ingredients, which can range from food items to natural extracts and even synthetic compounds. For instance, the incorporation of elements like fermented ingredients or unusual botanicals can yield fragrances that are both captivating and polarizing.

Challenges in Formulation

Creating peculiar sprays and powders presents several challenges:

- **Stability:** Unconventional ingredients may not have the same stability as traditional fragrance components. For example, natural extracts can degrade over time, altering the scent profile. It is essential to conduct stability testing to ensure the fragrance maintains its intended character throughout its shelf life.

- **Skin Compatibility:** Some ingredients may cause allergic reactions or irritations. Formulators must conduct thorough dermatological testing to ensure that the final product is safe for use on the skin. This is particularly important for sprays that are applied directly to the body.

- **Regulatory Compliance:** The use of certain ingredients may be restricted or regulated in various regions. For example, some natural extracts may be banned due to their potential toxicity. Formulators must stay informed about the regulations governing fragrance ingredients in their target markets.

Examples of Peculiar Sprays and Powders

The market for peculiar fragrances has seen a surge in creativity. Here are some notable examples that illustrate the diversity of this category:

1. **Food-Inspired Fragrances:** Brands like *Demeter Fragrance Library* offer a range of food-inspired scents, from *Fresh Baked Bread* to *Chocolate Chip Cookies*. These fragrances evoke nostalgia and comfort, appealing to the emotional connections we have with food.

2. **Fermented Fragrances:** The use of fermented ingredients, such as sake or kimchi, has gained popularity in niche perfumery. These scents can be polarizing, as they often carry strong, earthy notes that challenge conventional notions of beauty. *Kusmi Tea*, for example, has created a line of scented teas that incorporate these unique elements.

3. **Powdered Fragrances:** The rise of powdered fragrances, such as those offered by *Lush*, allows for a different application method. These powders can be dusted onto the skin or hair, providing a subtle scent that evolves throughout the day. The use of natural powders like cornstarch or arrowroot can also help absorb moisture, making them a practical choice for warm climates.

4. **Unconventional Essential Oils:** Blends that incorporate unexpected essential oils, such as *Black Pepper* or *Sandalwood*, can create intriguing and complex fragrances. These oils can be combined with carrier oils to create personalized body sprays that reflect the wearer's unique scent preferences.

Practical Applications

When incorporating peculiar sprays and powders into personal fragrance routines, there are several practical considerations:

- **Layering Fragrances:** Many enthusiasts find that layering different scents can create a unique olfactory signature. For example, a food-inspired spray can be layered with a floral powder to create a multidimensional fragrance experience.

- **Scenting Spaces:** Peculiar sprays can also be used to scent personal spaces. For instance, a room spray with earthy notes can create a calming atmosphere, while a food-inspired scent can evoke warmth and comfort in a kitchen.

- **Customization:** The DIY trend has led to a rise in personalized fragrance creations. Individuals can experiment with their own blends of essential oils, carrier oils, and powdered fragrances to craft a scent that resonates with their identity.

Conclusion

Peculiar sprays and powders represent a bold frontier in the world of fragrance, challenging traditional norms and inviting individuals to explore their unique scent preferences. By understanding the theoretical foundations, addressing formulation challenges, and embracing the creativity of unconventional ingredients, fragrance enthusiasts can embark on a sensory journey that celebrates the beauty of the unexpected. As we continue to break boundaries in scent, the future promises an exciting array of aromatic innovations that will redefine our relationship with fragrance.

Extraordinary Deodorants That Defy Convention

In the realm of personal hygiene, deodorants have long been viewed as a staple in the daily grooming routine. However, the conventional approach to odor control often leans heavily on synthetic fragrances and antiperspirants laden with aluminum compounds. This section explores extraordinary deodorants that challenge traditional norms, embracing unconventional ingredients, innovative formulations, and eco-conscious practices that redefine how we perceive body odor management.

The Philosophy Behind Extraordinary Deodorants

At the heart of extraordinary deodorants lies a philosophy that prioritizes natural ingredients, sustainability, and individual expression. These products often reject the mainstream narrative that associates pleasantness with floral or fruity scents, opting instead for unique, sometimes unexpected aromas that resonate with personal identity.

The Role of Natural Ingredients

Natural deodorants typically utilize plant-based ingredients known for their odor-neutralizing properties. Common components include:

- **Baking Soda:** A natural alkaline compound that neutralizes acids and odors.
- **Arrowroot Powder:** A starch that absorbs moisture and keeps the skin dry.
- **Coconut Oil:** Known for its antibacterial properties, it helps combat odor-causing bacteria.
- **Essential Oils:** These provide not only fragrance but also therapeutic benefits; for example, tea tree oil is renowned for its antimicrobial properties.

The formulation of these deodorants often involves a careful balance of these ingredients to maintain efficacy while minimizing irritation.

Innovative Formulations

Extraordinary deodorants often incorporate innovative formulations that challenge the conventional stick or spray formats. Some examples include:

1. **Cream Deodorants:** These products offer a smooth application and often contain rich oils and butters, providing both moisture and odor control.

2. **Solid Deodorants:** Unlike traditional sticks, these may use a combination of waxes and natural powders to create a solid form that melts upon contact with the skin.

3. **Roll-ons with Unique Ingredients:** Some brands utilize probiotic cultures to enhance skin flora, promoting a natural balance that reduces odor.

4. **Deodorant Gels:** These lightweight formulations provide a refreshing feel and often utilize botanical extracts for their soothing properties.

The Science of Scent

The olfactory system plays a crucial role in how we perceive deodorants. The unique scents of extraordinary deodorants can evoke emotions, memories, and even influence attraction. The chemistry of scent can be expressed through the following equation:

$$S = \sum_{i=1}^{n}(C_i \cdot F_i) \qquad (116)$$

Where:

- S is the overall scent profile.
- C_i is the concentration of each component.
- F_i represents the fragrance contribution of each component.

This equation highlights that the overall scent is a combination of various ingredients, each contributing to the final aroma.

Challenges in the Market

Despite the growing popularity of extraordinary deodorants, several challenges persist:

- **Efficacy Concerns:** Some consumers may find that natural deodorants do not provide the same level of odor protection as traditional antiperspirants. This can lead to misconceptions about their effectiveness.

- **Skin Sensitivity:** While natural ingredients are often gentler, some individuals may still experience irritation, particularly with baking soda.

- **Cultural Acceptance:** In a society where floral and fruity scents dominate, the acceptance of unconventional aromas may be slow to evolve.

Examples of Extraordinary Deodorants

Several brands have successfully embraced the extraordinary approach to deodorant formulation. Notable examples include:

- **Schmidt's Naturals:** Known for their innovative use of essential oils and baking soda, Schmidt's offers a variety of unique scents, including cedarwood and juniper.

- **Native:** This brand emphasizes transparency in ingredients and offers a range of unconventional scents like coconut and vanilla, as well as cucumber and mint.

- **Lush:** With a focus on ethical sourcing and fresh ingredients, Lush's solid deodorants incorporate unique components like kaolin clay and essential oils for a refreshing experience.

Conclusion

Extraordinary deodorants represent a shift in how we approach body odor management. By embracing natural ingredients, innovative formulations, and unique scents, these products challenge conventional norms and invite individuals to express their identity through scent. As the market continues to evolve, the acceptance of these unconventional deodorants may pave the way for a more inclusive and diverse understanding of personal fragrance.

In summary, the future of deodorants may not lie solely in the quest for pleasantness but rather in celebrating the complexities of human scent and the stories that come with it.

Funky Fragranced Shampoos and Conditioners

In the realm of personal grooming, shampoos and conditioners have long been the unsung heroes of hair care. However, the emergence of funky fragranced products has revolutionized the way we perceive and utilize these everyday essentials. This section delves into the intriguing world of unconventional scents in hair care, exploring their theoretical underpinnings, potential challenges, and notable examples that push the boundaries of olfactory aesthetics.

Theoretical Foundations

The use of fragrance in shampoos and conditioners is not merely a matter of masking odors; it taps into the complex interplay between scent and emotional response. Research indicates that scents can evoke memories and emotions, significantly influencing consumer behavior. According to the *Pavlovian conditioning theory*, individuals can develop positive associations with specific scents, leading to a heightened sense of well-being and satisfaction when using products infused with these fragrances.

The olfactory system is intricately linked to the limbic system, the part of the brain that governs emotions and memory. This connection explains why certain scents can trigger nostalgia or comfort. Funky fragrances, often characterized by unexpected combinations of notes, can create a unique sensory experience that sets a product apart in a saturated market.

Challenges in Scent Formulation

While the allure of funky fragrances is undeniable, formulating them presents several challenges. One primary concern is the balance between scent intensity and hair health. High concentrations of fragrance can lead to scalp irritation or allergic reactions, particularly for individuals with sensitive skin. Thus, formulators must carefully consider the concentration of fragrance oils used in their products.

Another challenge lies in the stability of the fragrance over time. Many funky scents, especially those derived from natural sources, can degrade or alter in character when exposed to light, heat, or air. This necessitates the use of stabilizers or encapsulation techniques to preserve the integrity of the scent throughout the product's shelf life.

Examples of Funky Fragranced Products

Several brands have embraced the concept of funky fragrances, offering unique and memorable hair care experiences. For instance, **Lush**, a pioneer in the realm of ethical and innovative cosmetics, has developed shampoos like *Big Shampoo*, which features a combination of sea salt, lemon juice, and a blend of fruity fragrances. This product not only cleanses hair but also leaves it with a refreshing scent reminiscent of a tropical getaway.

Similarly, **Bumble and Bumble** has introduced *Surf Shampoo*, which encapsulates the essence of beach life with its blend of coconut and sea salt. The scent transports users to sun-soaked shores, enhancing the overall experience of hair washing.

Moreover, **Kérastase** has ventured into the funky fragrance territory with its *Aura Botanica* line. This range combines natural ingredients with exotic scents, such as Moroccan argan oil and Brazilian coconut oil, to create a luxurious sensory experience that nourishes hair while tantalizing the senses.

Consumer Reception and Trends

The reception of funky fragranced shampoos and conditioners has been overwhelmingly positive, particularly among younger consumers seeking individuality and self-expression through their grooming choices. Social media platforms have played a pivotal role in promoting these products, with influencers showcasing their unique scents and experiences. The hashtag #FunkyHairCare has gained traction, encouraging users to share their favorite products and scents, fostering a sense of community around unconventional hair care.

As consumers become increasingly aware of the impact of scent on mood and well-being, the demand for funky fragrances is expected to grow. Brands are likely to continue experimenting with bold scent profiles, incorporating elements from diverse cultures and unexpected sources to create products that resonate with consumers on a deeper level.

Conclusion

Funky fragranced shampoos and conditioners represent a thrilling intersection of scent, emotion, and personal care. By harnessing the power of unique fragrances, brands can elevate the mundane act of washing hair into an enjoyable and memorable experience. As the market continues to evolve, it will be fascinating to observe how these products shape the future of hair care and consumer preferences.

In summary, the exploration of funky fragrances in hair care not only enhances the sensory experience but also taps into the broader cultural and emotional narratives that define contemporary grooming practices. The journey of scent in personal care is just beginning, and the possibilities are as limitless as the fragrances themselves.

Curious Cologne Alternatives for Provocative Auras

In a world where conventional fragrances reign supreme, the quest for unique and provocative scents has led many to explore alternatives that defy the norms of traditional colognes. This section delves into the realm of curious cologne alternatives, examining their appeal, the science behind scent perception, and how these unconventional choices can create an alluring aura that captivates and intrigues.

The Allure of the Unconventional

While mainstream colognes often rely on familiar notes—citrus, floral, and woody—curious alternatives embrace the unexpected. Scents derived from unusual sources or combining unexpected ingredients can evoke powerful emotions and memories, creating a distinctive olfactory signature. The allure of these fragrances lies in their ability to challenge societal norms and provoke curiosity.

The Science of Scent Perception

Understanding the science behind scent perception is essential when exploring cologne alternatives. The human sense of smell is intricately linked to the limbic system, the part of the brain responsible for emotions and memory. This connection explains why certain scents can evoke strong feelings or transport us to specific moments in time.

The olfactory system operates through a complex network of receptors that respond to volatile compounds in the air. When we inhale, these compounds bind to olfactory receptors, sending signals to the brain. The perception of scent is influenced by various factors, including individual biology, cultural background, and personal experiences.

Examples of Curious Cologne Alternatives

1. **Botanical Infusions** Botanical infusions are a fascinating alternative to traditional colognes. By utilizing essential oils derived from herbs, flowers, and plants, these fragrances offer a more natural and organic scent profile. For example, a blend of lavender and rosemary can create a calming yet invigorating aroma, perfect for those seeking a unique olfactory experience. The use of botanical infusions also aligns with the growing trend of sustainable and eco-friendly products, appealing to environmentally conscious consumers.

UNCONVENTIONAL GROOMING PRODUCTS 269

2. Food-Inspired Fragrances   Food-inspired fragrances have gained popularity as a bold alternative to conventional scents. Ingredients such as vanilla, chocolate, and even bacon have found their way into the fragrance world, creating provocative and unexpected aromas. For instance, a cologne featuring notes of freshly baked bread and warm butter can evoke feelings of comfort and nostalgia, making it an enticing choice for those looking to stand out.

3. Fermented Scents   Fermented scents, often associated with processes like brewing and aging, can add a rich and complex layer to fragrances. Scents derived from fermentation, such as sake or aged whiskey, can create a deep and intriguing aroma that captivates the senses. These fragrances challenge the perception of what a cologne should smell like, enticing those who dare to embrace the unconventional.

Creating Your Own Provocative Aura

To craft a unique and provocative aura with cologne alternatives, consider the following steps:

1. **Experiment with Essential Oils:** Start by blending essential oils that resonate with your personal style. For example, combining patchouli with citrus oils can create an earthy yet refreshing scent that is both grounding and uplifting.

2. **Incorporate Food Notes:** Explore the use of food-inspired notes in your fragrance. A dash of cinnamon or a hint of caramel can add warmth and sweetness to your scent profile, making it inviting and memorable.

3. **Embrace Fermentation:** Look for fragrances that incorporate fermented elements or create your own by blending essential oils with fermented ingredients like kombucha or vinegar. This can add depth and complexity to your scent.

The Challenges of Non-Traditional Scents

While the exploration of curious cologne alternatives is exciting, it does come with challenges. Non-traditional scents may not always be well-received in conventional settings, and individuals may face skepticism regarding their choices. Additionally, the longevity and sillage (the trail of scent left behind) of these fragrances can vary significantly from traditional colognes, necessitating a more thoughtful approach to application.

Conclusion

Curious cologne alternatives offer an enticing avenue for those seeking to express their individuality and provoke intrigue through scent. By embracing the unconventional—whether through botanical infusions, food-inspired fragrances, or fermented scents—individuals can craft a personal aroma that captivates and enchants. As we continue to explore the boundaries of scent, the power of olfactory expression remains a compelling and transformative experience, inviting us to celebrate the beauty of the unexpected.

The Alluring Aromas of Skincare Products with Unexpected Ingredients

In the realm of skincare, the olfactory experience often plays a pivotal role in consumer satisfaction and brand loyalty. While traditional fragrances such as floral and fruity notes dominate the market, an emerging trend is the use of unexpected ingredients that evoke a sense of novelty and intrigue. This section delves into the captivating world of skincare products infused with unconventional aromas, exploring their theoretical underpinnings, potential challenges, and real-world examples.

Theoretical Framework

The allure of unexpected aromas in skincare can be understood through the lens of sensory marketing and consumer psychology. According to [?], scent is a powerful tool that influences emotions, memories, and purchasing decisions. This phenomenon can be attributed to the close connection between the olfactory bulb and the limbic system, which governs emotional responses. When consumers encounter a skincare product with an unusual scent, it can evoke curiosity and a sense of adventure, leading to a more engaging and memorable experience.

Moreover, the concept of *olfactory branding* plays a crucial role in differentiating products in a saturated market. Brands that incorporate unexpected scents can create a unique identity, appealing to niche markets and fostering brand loyalty. For instance, the use of earthy or musky aromas may resonate with consumers seeking a more natural and organic skincare experience.

Challenges and Considerations

Despite the potential benefits, the incorporation of unexpected aromas in skincare products presents several challenges. One primary concern is the risk of alienating consumers who may have averse reactions to certain scents. For example, while some individuals may find the aroma of matcha or charcoal appealing, others may associate it with unpleasant experiences. Therefore, it is crucial for brands to conduct thorough market research and sensory testing to gauge consumer preferences before launching products with unconventional scents.

Additionally, the stability of these scents in formulations can pose a challenge. Many natural ingredients, such as essential oils, can be volatile and may degrade over time, altering the intended aroma. This necessitates the use of advanced formulation techniques to ensure that the scent remains consistent throughout the product's shelf life.

Examples of Unexpected Aromatic Ingredients

1. **Charcoal:** Known for its detoxifying properties, activated charcoal has gained popularity in skincare. However, its unique, slightly smoky aroma adds an intriguing layer to products. Brands like *Youth to the People* have successfully integrated charcoal into facial cleansers, offering consumers an olfactory experience that complements its purifying benefits.

2. **Matcha:** This finely ground green tea powder is celebrated for its antioxidant properties. The earthy, vegetal scent of matcha is a refreshing departure from conventional fragrances. Products such as *Tatcha's Matcha Green Tea Mask* leverage this unexpected aroma to create a calming and rejuvenating experience.

3. **Black Truffle:** Often associated with luxury dining, black truffle oil has found its way into high-end skincare. Brands like *The Truffle Therapy* utilize the rich, musky aroma of truffles in their products, appealing to consumers seeking indulgence and sophistication.

4. **Sandalwood:** While sandalwood is not entirely unconventional, its use in skincare is often overshadowed by floral and fruity scents. The warm, woody aroma of sandalwood has calming properties and is often used in aromatherapy. Brands such as *Aesop* incorporate sandalwood into their formulations, offering a grounding scent that enhances the overall sensory experience.

Conclusion

The incorporation of unexpected aromas in skincare products represents a fascinating intersection of sensory marketing, consumer psychology, and formulation science. By embracing unconventional ingredients, brands can create unique olfactory experiences that resonate with consumers on a deeper emotional level. However, careful consideration of consumer preferences and formulation stability is essential to ensure the success of these innovative products. As the skincare industry continues to evolve, the allure of unexpected aromas will undoubtedly play a significant role in shaping future trends and consumer experiences.

Captivating Combos: Exploring Unconventional Combinations in Grooming

In the evolving landscape of personal grooming, the quest for unique and captivating scents has led many to explore unconventional combinations. This section delves into the art and science of creating alluring fragrances through unexpected pairings, illustrating how diverse elements can harmonize to form a distinctive olfactory signature.

Theoretical Foundations of Scent Combination

The chemistry of scent is rooted in the interaction of volatile organic compounds (VOCs) that our olfactory receptors perceive as distinct aromas. When combining scents, one must consider the balance of top, middle, and base notes.

$$\text{Total Aroma} = \sum_{i=1}^{n} \text{Note}_i \qquad (117)$$

Where Note_i represents the different aromatic components. The challenge lies in achieving a harmonious blend, avoiding clashing scents that can lead to olfactory dissonance.

Problems in Scent Pairing

1. **Overpowering Notes**: Certain scents, such as patchouli or sandalwood, can dominate a mixture. If not balanced properly, they can overshadow more subtle fragrances. 2. **Chemical Reactions**: Some essential oils can react negatively with others, altering their scent profile or producing undesirable odors. For example, mixing citrus oils with certain floral scents can lead to a sour aroma. 3. **Skin Chemistry Variability**: An individual's skin chemistry can dramatically alter how a scent is perceived. A combination that smells delightful on one person may turn unpleasant on another due to factors like pH and skin temperature.

Examples of Unconventional Combinations

1. **Citrus and Spice**: The zesty brightness of lemon combined with the warmth of cinnamon creates an invigorating yet comforting scent. This combination is often used in seasonal products, evoking memories of cozy gatherings.

$$\text{Citrus Aroma} + \text{Spice Aroma} = \text{Invigorating Comfort} \qquad (118)$$

2. **Floral and Earthy**: Pairing jasmine with vetiver results in a complex fragrance that balances floral sweetness with earthy depth. This combination is particularly appealing in perfumes aimed at both genders, providing a versatile scent profile.

$$\text{Floral Aroma} + \text{Earthy Aroma} = \text{Balanced Complexity} \qquad (119)$$

3. **Fruity and Smoky**: The juxtaposition of ripe peach and smoked cedarwood creates a daring scent that is both sweet and robust. This combination challenges traditional notions of fragrance, appealing to those who seek to stand out.

$$\text{Fruity Aroma} + \text{Smoky Aroma} = \text{Daring Distinction} \qquad (120)$$

DIY Approach to Unconventional Combinations

Creating your own captivating combos can be an enriching experience. Here's a simple guide to experimenting with scent:

1. **Start with a Base**: Choose a base note that resonates with you, such as vanilla or sandalwood. This will anchor your combination.

2. **Add Middle Notes**: Introduce floral or herbal middle notes to add complexity. Lavender and rosemary work well together.

3. **Finish with Top Notes**: Finally, layer in bright top notes like citrus or mint to uplift the blend.

4. **Test and Adjust**: Apply a small amount to your skin and let it settle for a few hours. Adjust proportions based on how the scent evolves.

Case Studies of Successful Combinations

1. **Lush's "Dirty" Perfume**: This fragrance combines mint, lavender, and a hint of fresh grass, creating an invigorating scent reminiscent of a morning in the garden. The combination of mint's freshness and lavender's soothing properties exemplifies the captivating combo principle.

2. **Jo Malone's "Pomegranate Noir"**: This scent marries fruity pomegranate with spicy notes of pink pepper and the warmth of guaiac wood. The result is a rich, intriguing fragrance that defies simple categorization.

Conclusion

Exploring unconventional combinations in grooming not only allows for personal expression but also challenges societal norms surrounding scent. By understanding the theoretical foundations, recognizing potential problems, and experimenting with unique pairings, individuals can create captivating aromas that reflect their unique identities. The journey of scent creation is a personal one, inviting you to embrace the unexpected and celebrate the art of olfactory creativity.

The Irresistible Odor of Sulfur in Charcoal Beauty Products

The allure of charcoal beauty products has captivated the beauty industry in recent years, with their promise of detoxification and deep cleansing. However, one of the less discussed aspects of these products is the distinctive odor of sulfur that often accompanies their use. This section delves into the chemistry behind sulfur's presence in charcoal beauty products, its implications for scent, and the paradox of attractiveness associated with this pungent element.

The Chemistry of Sulfur in Charcoal

Sulfur, a non-metallic element with the atomic number 16, is known for its characteristic smell, often likened to rotten eggs. In the context of charcoal beauty products, sulfur can be present in several forms, primarily as a result of the materials used in the charcoal production process. The most common source is the organic matter that is carbonized to create activated charcoal. During this process, certain sulfur-containing compounds, such as thiols and sulfides, can form.

The chemical reactions involved can be summarized as follows:

$$\text{Organic Matter} \xrightarrow{\text{Heat}} \text{Charcoal} + \text{Volatile Compounds} \quad (121)$$

These volatile compounds can include various sulfur species, contributing to the overall scent profile of the product. The presence of sulfur compounds, particularly in activated charcoal, can enhance its efficacy in absorbing impurities and toxins, but it also results in a unique olfactory experience.

The Problem of Odor in Beauty Products

While the detoxifying properties of sulfur in charcoal products are well-documented, the accompanying odor can be a significant drawback for consumers. The challenge lies in balancing the effectiveness of sulfur's cleansing properties with its olfactory impact. Many consumers are often deterred by strong sulfur odors, associating them with unpleasant experiences rather than the potential benefits of the product.

To mitigate this issue, manufacturers often incorporate fragrance masking agents or essential oils into their formulations. However, this can lead to a complex interplay of scents, where the natural sulfur aroma competes with added fragrances, sometimes resulting in an even more confusing olfactory experience.

Examples of Charcoal Beauty Products Containing Sulfur

Several beauty products on the market utilize charcoal and inadvertently contain sulfur due to their production processes. For instance, many facial masks, cleansers, and scrubs feature activated charcoal as a primary ingredient. Brands such as *Lush* and *Biore* have leveraged the detoxifying properties of charcoal while attempting to mask its sulfurous scent through the use of floral or citrus fragrances.

- Lush's "Mask of Magnaminty": This face mask combines charcoal with peppermint oil and kaolin clay, attempting to balance the detoxifying benefits with a refreshing scent. However, the underlying sulfur notes can still be detected.

- Biore's "Deep Cleansing Charcoal Pore Strips": These strips are designed to remove impurities from the skin. While effective, users have noted the distinct sulfur smell upon application, which can be off-putting.

The Allure of Sulfur: A Paradoxical Attraction

Despite the challenges posed by sulfur's odor, there exists a fascinating paradox: the potential attractiveness of sulfurous scents. Research in olfactory psychology suggests that certain unpleasant odors can evoke strong emotional responses and even enhance feelings of intimacy. This is particularly relevant in the context of beauty products, where the sensory experience plays a crucial role in consumer satisfaction.

The allure of sulfur can be linked to its historical and cultural associations. In many ancient civilizations, sulfur was revered for its purifying properties and was often used in rituals and cleansing practices. This historical context may contribute to a subconscious acceptance of its scent as part of a beauty regimen.

Conclusion

In conclusion, the irresistible odor of sulfur in charcoal beauty products presents a complex interplay of chemistry, consumer perception, and cultural significance. While the presence of sulfur can detract from the overall appeal of these products, its historical associations and potential for enhancing emotional connections cannot be overlooked. As the beauty industry continues to innovate, finding a balance between efficacy and sensory experience will be essential in creating products that appeal to a broad audience while embracing the unique characteristics of their ingredients.

$$\text{Consumer Satisfaction} = f(\text{Efficacy}, \text{Scent}, \text{Cultural Perception}) \quad (122)$$

Understanding this balance may pave the way for future formulations that celebrate the allure of sulfur while minimizing its olfactory impact, allowing consumers to enjoy the benefits of charcoal without the lingering scent of sulfur.

The Erotic Potential of Unconventional Grooming Implements

In the realm of personal grooming, the tools we choose can significantly influence our self-perception and desirability. Unconventional grooming implements, often overlooked, hold a unique erotic potential that intertwines with our sensual experiences and intimate interactions. This section explores the theory behind these implements, the challenges they present, and compelling examples that highlight their allure.

Theoretical Framework

At the intersection of grooming and eroticism lies the concept of embodied aesthetics, which posits that our physical appearance and the tools we use to maintain it are deeply intertwined with our identity and sensuality. The philosopher Maurice Merleau-Ponty emphasized the embodied experience as a core aspect of human existence, suggesting that the way we interact with our bodies—and the implements we use—shapes our understanding of self and desire.

The erotic potential of grooming implements can be understood through the lens of semiotics, where objects carry meanings beyond their utilitarian function. For instance, a simple hairbrush can symbolize intimacy and care, transforming an everyday activity into a ritual of seduction. This transformation is further amplified when unconventional tools are employed, as they challenge societal norms and expectations surrounding beauty and grooming.

Challenges and Considerations

While the erotic potential of unconventional grooming implements is vast, several challenges must be acknowledged:

- **Social Stigma:** Many unconventional grooming tools may evoke discomfort or judgment in mainstream culture. The use of items such as vintage razors or unconventional brushes may be perceived as eccentric or even repulsive, potentially alienating those who adhere to traditional beauty standards.

- **Safety Concerns:** Some unconventional implements may pose risks if not used properly. For example, using a straight razor requires skill and caution, as improper handling can lead to injury. Thus, while they can enhance erotic experiences, safety must remain a priority.

- **Accessibility:** Not all individuals may have access to or the means to procure unconventional grooming implements. This limitation can create disparities in the experiences of those who wish to explore the erotic potential of these tools.

Examples of Unconventional Grooming Implements

To illustrate the erotic potential of unconventional grooming implements, consider the following examples:

- **Vintage Razors:** The allure of a vintage straight razor lies in its craftsmanship and the intimate experience it offers during shaving. The ritual of shaving can become a sensual act, where the anticipation of the blade gliding across the skin heightens arousal. The tactile sensation and visual appeal of a well-crafted razor can transform a mundane grooming task into an erotic experience.

BIBLIOGRAPHY

- **Feather Dusters:** Traditionally seen as cleaning tools, feather dusters can be repurposed in intimate settings to tease and tantalize. The soft, delicate touch of feathers against the skin can evoke sensations of pleasure and intimacy, making them a playful addition to foreplay. The act of dusting away inhibitions can also serve as a metaphor for uncovering hidden desires.

- **Unconventional Brushes:** Brushes made from unique materials, such as boar bristles or even synthetic fibers, can be used not only for grooming but also for sensory exploration. The varying textures can stimulate different sensations on the skin, creating an erotic experience that engages the senses. Incorporating these brushes into a grooming routine can foster a deeper connection with one's body.

- **Scented Grooming Tools:** Grooming implements infused with alluring scents—such as combs made from sandalwood or brushes treated with essential oils—can enhance the sensory experience. The combination of touch and scent can evoke powerful emotional responses, making grooming an intimate act that tantalizes both the body and mind.

- **DIY Grooming Implements:** The trend of creating personalized grooming tools allows individuals to infuse their unique identities into their grooming routines. For instance, crafting a custom hairbrush or razor can become a sensual act of self-expression. These DIY implements not only serve practical purposes but also embody the user's personal aesthetic and erotic potential.

Conclusion

The erotic potential of unconventional grooming implements lies in their ability to transform routine grooming practices into intimate and sensual experiences. By embracing the aesthetic and symbolic meanings of these tools, individuals can explore new dimensions of self-expression and desire. While challenges such as social stigma and safety concerns exist, the allure of these implements invites a playful exploration of our bodies and identities. Ultimately, the journey into the world of unconventional grooming is not merely about enhancing physical appearance but about celebrating the eroticism that resides within our everyday rituals.

Erotic Potential $= f($Unconventional Tool, Embodied Experience, Sensory Engageme
(123)

Surrendering to the Scent of Unconventional Personal Hygiene

In a world where the olfactory senses are often relegated to the sidelines of personal care, the embrace of unconventional personal hygiene practices can be both liberating and invigorating. This section explores the theory behind these practices, the problems they address, and examples of how they can be effectively integrated into daily routines.

Theoretical Underpinnings of Unconventional Hygiene

The concept of personal hygiene has traditionally been associated with cleanliness, often defined by societal norms that prioritize fresh, floral, or synthetic scents. However, the emerging trend of unconventional personal hygiene challenges these norms by celebrating a broader spectrum of scents. The theory of olfactory aesthetics posits that scents can evoke emotional responses and memories, influencing our perceptions of self and others. This perspective aligns with the notion of *olfactory identity*, where individuals express their uniqueness through their natural aromas.

Mathematically, we can explore this concept through the **Olfactory Identity Equation:**

$$O = f(N, E, S) \qquad (124)$$

where O represents olfactory identity, N denotes natural body odors, E signifies environmental influences (such as diet and lifestyle), and S encompasses societal perceptions of scent.

Problems Addressed by Unconventional Hygiene

Unconventional personal hygiene practices often arise from the desire to reclaim autonomy over one's body and scent. Many individuals experience discomfort with the overpowering fragrances found in mainstream hygiene products, which can lead to allergic reactions, skin irritations, or simply a feeling of inauthenticity. Furthermore, the pressure to conform to societal standards can result in a disconnection from one's natural scent, leading to a lack of self-acceptance.

By embracing unconventional hygiene, individuals can:

- **Promote Skin Health:** Natural products often lack harsh chemicals found in conventional products, reducing the risk of irritation and promoting healthier skin.

- **Enhance Self-Acceptance:** By celebrating unique scents, individuals foster a sense of pride in their natural aromas, leading to improved self-esteem.

- **Encourage Sustainability:** Many unconventional products are eco-friendly, reducing waste and promoting a more sustainable lifestyle.

Examples of Unconventional Personal Hygiene Practices

1. **DIY Natural Deodorants:** Many individuals are turning to homemade deodorants made from ingredients like baking soda, coconut oil, and essential oils. These products allow for customization and a personal touch, often resulting in scents that resonate more authentically with the user.

2. **Scented Body Oils:** Instead of traditional perfumes, some opt for scented body oils infused with natural botanicals. These oils can be applied to pulse points, providing a subtle fragrance that complements one's natural scent rather than overpowering it.

3. **Fermented Products:** The use of fermented ingredients, such as kombucha or yogurt, in personal care routines has gained popularity. These products can enhance the skin's microbiome, promoting a healthy balance that can influence body odor positively.

4. **Unwashed Hair:** The trend of embracing natural oils in hair care has led to the acceptance of unwashed hair as a valid choice. This practice not only reduces the need for harsh shampoos but also allows the natural scent of hair to emerge, often described as musky or earthy, which can be appealing to some.

5. **Scented Self-Care Rituals:** Incorporating unconventional scents into self-care routines—such as using oils with earthy or spicy notes—can create a more intimate and personal experience. This may include using products with scents like sandalwood, patchouli, or even more adventurous aromas like tobacco or leather.

Integrating Unconventional Hygiene into Daily Routines

To fully embrace unconventional personal hygiene, individuals can follow these steps:

1. **Assess Your Current Routine:** Identify products that contain synthetic fragrances or harsh chemicals. Consider how these products make you feel and how they align with your personal values.

2. **Experiment with DIY Recipes:** Start small by creating your own deodorants or body scrubs. Document your experiences and adjust recipes to suit your preferences.

3. **Engage with Your Senses:** Take time to explore different scents that resonate with you. Visit local markets or specialty stores to discover unique oils and ingredients.

4. **Practice Mindfulness:** Incorporate mindfulness into your hygiene routine. Pay attention to how different scents make you feel and how they impact your mood and confidence.

5. **Share Your Journey:** Engage with communities that celebrate unconventional hygiene. Sharing experiences can foster connection and inspire others to explore their olfactory identities.

Conclusion

Surrendering to the scent of unconventional personal hygiene is not merely a rebellion against societal norms; it is a celebration of individuality, self-acceptance, and the rich tapestry of human experience. By embracing our unique aromas, we can forge deeper connections with ourselves and others, ultimately creating a more authentic and liberated existence.

In this journey, remember that the essence of your scent is as unique as your personality—embrace it fully, and let your true self shine through every aromatic note.

The Power of Attractive Malodor

Breaking Taboos with Fetid Perfumes

The Concept of Beautifully Offensive Scents

In the realm of olfactory experiences, the concept of "beautifully offensive scents" challenges traditional notions of what is considered appealing or desirable. This section delves into the intricate interplay between societal perceptions of odor, the psychology of scent, and the artistic implications of embracing scents that are often categorized as unpleasant or offensive.

The Dichotomy of Scent Perception

The human sense of smell is profoundly influenced by cultural, personal, and contextual factors. What one person finds repulsive, another may find alluring. This subjectivity is rooted in the psychology of scent, where personal experiences and cultural backgrounds shape our perceptions. For instance, while the smell of garlic may evoke feelings of nostalgia and warmth for some, it may be perceived as overwhelmingly pungent and undesirable by others.

The duality of scent perception can be mathematically represented through the following equation:

$$P = f(C, E, S) \tag{125}$$

where P is the perception of odor, C represents cultural influences, E denotes individual experiences, and S signifies the specific scent characteristics. This equation illustrates how the interplay of these variables can lead to vastly different interpretations of the same odor.

The Allure of the Unpleasant

The notion of beautifully offensive scents can be linked to the concept of *kawaii*, a Japanese term that encompasses cuteness and charm, often juxtaposed with elements that might be considered unattractive. This aesthetic can be observed in various forms of art and fashion, where designers intentionally incorporate unpleasant scents to create a juxtaposition that challenges viewers' expectations.

For example, the avant-garde fashion designer Comme des Garçons has been known to create fragrances that defy conventional beauty norms. Their scent "Odeur 53" is described as a blend of synthetic and organic materials that evoke the smell of a laboratory, including notes of rubber, sweat, and metallic elements. This fragrance exemplifies how a scent that might be deemed offensive can also be perceived as intriguing and artistically significant.

Cultural Context and Artistic Expression

Cultural context plays a pivotal role in defining beautifully offensive scents. In some cultures, certain odors are celebrated for their historical or ritualistic significance. For instance, the smell of incense in religious ceremonies may be perceived as divine, while the aroma of fermented foods can evoke feelings of comfort and nostalgia.

Artistic expressions often leverage the power of scent to provoke thought and elicit emotional responses. The artist Sissel Tolaas, known for her work with smells, creates installations that challenge viewers to confront their olfactory biases. In her project "Smell of Data," she captures and reproduces the scents associated with various data centers, inviting participants to engage with the often-overlooked sensory dimension of technology.

The Science Behind Offensive Scents

From a scientific perspective, the olfactory bulb processes scents and connects them to the limbic system, which governs emotions and memory. This connection explains why certain offensive odors can evoke strong emotional responses, ranging from disgust to fascination. Research indicates that the brain's reaction to unpleasant smells can trigger dopamine release, creating a paradox where the experience of an offensive scent can be simultaneously repulsive and pleasurable.

Moreover, the phenomenon of *olfactory fatigue*—the temporary inability to detect a particular odor after prolonged exposure—can also contribute to the allure of beautifully offensive scents. As individuals become desensitized to certain odors, they may begin to appreciate the subtleties and complexities that were initially masked by their initial reactions.

Examples of Beautifully Offensive Scents

Several examples illustrate the concept of beautifully offensive scents in practice:

- **Fermented Fish Sauce:** Commonly used in Southeast Asian cuisines, fish sauce has a pungent odor that many find off-putting. However, its umami flavor enhances dishes and is celebrated for its culinary significance.

- **Musk:** Derived from the glandular secretions of certain animals, musk is often described as earthy and animalistic. While some may find it overwhelming, it is a sought-after note in perfumery, often associated with sensuality.

- **Truffles:** The strong, earthy aroma of truffles can be polarizing. While some may find it intoxicating, others may perceive it as overwhelmingly musty. Nonetheless, truffles are highly prized in gourmet cuisine for their unique flavor profile.

Conclusion

The concept of beautifully offensive scents invites a re-examination of our olfactory biases and the cultural narratives surrounding smell. By embracing the complexity of scent perception, individuals can cultivate a deeper appreciation for the diverse spectrum of odors that exist in our world. The intersection of art, culture, and science in the realm of beautifully offensive scents serves as a reminder that beauty is often found in the most unexpected places, challenging us to rethink our definitions of allure and desirability.

In conclusion, beautifully offensive scents encapsulate the dynamic relationship between perception, culture, and emotion, offering a rich terrain for exploration in both artistic and personal contexts. As we navigate the world of scent, let us remain open to the myriad possibilities that lie within the olfactory experience, celebrating the beauty in what may initially seem repugnant.

Unconventional Ingredients in Foul Fragrances

In the realm of perfumery, the notion of beauty has long been tethered to pleasing scents, often derived from flowers, fruits, and spices. However, an emerging trend challenges this conventional wisdom, embracing the allure of foul fragrances crafted from unconventional ingredients. This section delves into the theory behind these unexpected components, the problems they present, and the fascinating examples that illustrate their use in creating captivating scents.

Theoretical Framework

The olfactory system, responsible for our sense of smell, is intricately linked to the brain's limbic system, which governs emotions and memories. This connection suggests that scents, whether pleasant or unpleasant, can evoke powerful emotional responses. The use of unconventional ingredients in foul fragrances leverages this principle, transforming what might initially be perceived as repulsive into something intriguing and alluring.

The chemistry of scent is rooted in volatile organic compounds (VOCs), which are responsible for the characteristic odors of various substances. Foul fragrances often utilize ingredients that contain high concentrations of specific VOCs known for their pungent qualities. For instance, the compound *putrescine*, a byproduct of protein decomposition, is notorious for its unpleasant smell, yet it can be blended with other scents to create a complex and fascinating olfactory experience.

Challenges in Crafting Foul Fragrances

While the idea of using unconventional ingredients may seem appealing, it poses several challenges:

- **Public Perception:** The stigma associated with foul odors can deter consumers from embracing these fragrances. The challenge lies in marketing them as desirable rather than off-putting.

- **Balancing Notes:** Crafting a harmonious scent profile that incorporates foul ingredients requires skillful blending. Perfumers must balance the offensive notes with more agreeable scents to create a well-rounded fragrance.

- **Allergenic Reactions:** Some unconventional ingredients may trigger allergic reactions in sensitive individuals. Perfumers must conduct thorough testing to ensure safety and minimize adverse effects.

Examples of Unconventional Ingredients

Several unconventional ingredients have made their mark in the world of foul fragrances, showcasing the potential for creating captivating scents:

- **Skatole:** This compound, derived from the breakdown of tryptophan in feces, is known for its strong, fecal odor. However, when blended with floral notes, it can produce a unique scent reminiscent of certain exotic flowers, offering a complex olfactory experience.

- **Ambergris:** Often referred to as "floating gold," ambergris is a waxy substance produced in the intestines of sperm whales. Its odor is initially musky and animalistic, but it evolves into a sweet, marine scent when aged. This transformation makes it a sought-after ingredient in high-end perfumes.

- **Civet:** Extracted from the glands of the African civet cat, civet oil has a strong, musky aroma. Historically used in perfumery, it adds depth and warmth to fragrances, providing a base note that can enhance the overall scent profile.

- **Garlic:** While often considered a culinary ingredient, garlic's potent aroma can be harnessed in perfumery to create unconventional fragrances. Its sulfur compounds, particularly *allyl methyl sulfide*, can be blended with citrus notes to create a surprisingly refreshing scent.

- **Vomit:** The use of *isovaleraldehyde*, a compound found in vomit, has been explored in niche perfumery. When combined with other notes, it can evoke a sense of nostalgia or provoke curiosity, challenging the boundaries of traditional fragrance.

Conclusion

The exploration of unconventional ingredients in foul fragrances represents a bold departure from traditional perfumery. By embracing the allure of offensive scents, perfumers can create captivating olfactory experiences that challenge societal norms and redefine beauty. As the fragrance industry continues to evolve, it will be fascinating to see how these unconventional ingredients are integrated into mainstream products, pushing the boundaries of what constitutes an attractive scent.

In a world where beauty is often synonymous with pleasantness, the rise of foul fragrances invites us to reconsider our perceptions and embrace the complexity of scent. As we delve deeper into the realm of olfactory exploration, we may find that the most alluring fragrances are those that challenge our expectations and provoke our senses.

Controversial Perfume Brands and Their Success

In the realm of fragrance, controversy often breeds success. The world of perfumery is not just about pleasant scents; it is also a battleground for artistic expression, cultural commentary, and social critique. This section delves into how controversial perfume brands have navigated the choppy waters of public perception to carve out a niche in the market, often leveraging their polarizing nature as a means of differentiation.

The Role of Controversy in Branding

Controversy can serve as a powerful marketing tool. Brands that embrace provocative themes or challenge societal norms often capture the attention of consumers, leading to heightened brand awareness and discussion. As noted by [?], brand equity can be significantly influenced by the perceptions and emotions evoked by a brand's messaging. When a brand's narrative includes elements that provoke thought or challenge conventions, it can create a strong emotional connection with a segment of consumers who identify with those values.

Case Studies of Controversial Brands

One of the most notable examples of a controversial perfume brand is **Comme des Garçons**. Known for its avant-garde approach to fashion and fragrance, the brand has released scents that defy traditional olfactory structures. For instance, their fragrance *Odeur 71* was designed to evoke the smell of a variety of everyday objects, including the scent of a freshly opened packet of plastic. This radical approach to perfumery garnered both admiration and criticism, ultimately leading to a cult following among those who appreciate the brand's artistic and unconventional ethos.

Another example is **Lush**, a brand that has made headlines for its bold statements against animal testing and environmental degradation. Their perfume line often features names and marketing campaigns that challenge societal norms, such as *Karma*, which draws on themes of reincarnation and karma itself. Lush has successfully leveraged its controversial stance to build a loyal customer base that values ethical consumption, demonstrating that controversy can translate into a solid market position.

The Fine Line Between Provocation and Offense

While controversy can drive success, it is crucial for brands to tread carefully. The fine line between provocation and offense can lead to backlash if not navigated thoughtfully. For example, the brand **Dior** faced significant criticism for its *Sauvage* fragrance campaign, which many perceived as culturally insensitive, particularly in its portrayal of Native American imagery. The backlash not only led to public outcry but also prompted discussions about cultural appropriation in marketing. This incident illustrates that while controversy can attract attention, it can also lead to reputational damage if the brand fails to engage with its audience respectfully.

Consumer Reactions and Market Dynamics

The success of controversial perfume brands is often influenced by the demographic and psychographic characteristics of their target audience. Younger consumers, particularly Millennials and Generation Z, tend to gravitate towards brands that embody authenticity and social consciousness. According to [?], these consumers are more likely to support brands that take a stand on social issues, thereby creating a market where controversy can become a badge of honor rather than a liability.

Moreover, the rise of social media has amplified the impact of controversial branding. Platforms like Instagram and TikTok allow brands to engage directly with consumers, creating a dialogue that can either bolster or undermine their image. For instance, brands that successfully navigate controversy often leverage social media to foster community and dialogue around their products, turning potential backlash into opportunities for engagement.

Theoretical Implications

From a theoretical perspective, the success of controversial perfume brands can be analyzed through the lens of *Brand Resonance Theory* [?]. This theory posits that strong brands create deep psychological connections with consumers, leading to brand loyalty. Controversial brands, by virtue of their provocative nature, often evoke strong emotional responses that can enhance brand resonance.

The equation for brand resonance can be expressed as follows:

Brand Resonance = Brand Loyalty+Brand Awareness+Perceived Quality+Brand Assoc (126)

Where: - **Brand Loyalty** refers to the commitment of consumers to repurchase or continue using the brand. - **Brand Awareness** indicates the extent to which consumers recognize and recall the brand. - **Perceived Quality** is the consumer's perception of the overall quality of the brand's products. - **Brand Associations** represent the mental connections consumers make with the brand, including its values and image.

In the case of controversial brands, the unique narratives they craft can enhance these components, particularly brand associations and loyalty, as consumers feel a personal connection to the brand's mission or artistic expression.

Conclusion

In conclusion, controversial perfume brands have successfully navigated the complexities of public perception by embracing their provocative nature. Through strategic marketing, community engagement, and a deep understanding of their target audience, these brands have turned potential pitfalls into pathways for success. As the fragrance industry continues to evolve, the interplay between controversy and consumer connection will likely remain a defining characteristic of the market. The future of perfumery may very well depend on brands' ability to challenge norms while maintaining authenticity and respect for their consumers.

Creating Customized Stinks for Personal Expression

The olfactory landscape of our lives is a rich tapestry woven from the scents we encounter, the fragrances we wear, and the natural odors our bodies emit. In recent years, the idea of creating customized stinks has emerged as a provocative form of personal expression, allowing individuals to embrace their unique scents and challenge societal norms surrounding body odor. This section delves into the theory behind customized scents, the challenges one might face, and provides compelling examples of how individuals can curate their olfactory identities.

Theoretical Framework

The concept of personal expression through scent is grounded in several psychological and sociological theories. One such theory is the **Social Identity Theory**, which posits that individuals derive a sense of identity from the groups they belong to. Scent can serve as a powerful identifier, allowing individuals to communicate their uniqueness and affiliations. In this context, customized scents become a means of articulating one's identity, values, and even resistance to societal expectations.

Moreover, the **Affective Theory of Smell** suggests that odors evoke emotional responses and memories, influencing our perceptions of ourselves and others. Customizing one's scent can thus be a deeply personal journey, as individuals select fragrances that resonate with their personal narratives and emotional landscapes.

Challenges of Customization

While the allure of creating a signature stink is enticing, there are several challenges to consider:

- **Social Perception:** Society often stigmatizes certain odors, associating them with uncleanliness or undesirable traits. This stigma can create anxiety for individuals attempting to embrace their natural scents. The challenge lies in navigating societal expectations while remaining true to oneself.

- **Chemical Reactions:** The human body is a complex biochemical system. Factors such as diet, hygiene, and even hormonal changes can alter the way fragrances interact with one's natural scent. This unpredictability can complicate the process of creating a customized stink, as what smells appealing in theory may not translate to reality.

- **Sustainability:** The production of fragrances often involves synthetic chemicals that may not align with the values of those seeking to express themselves authentically. Creating customized scents using natural ingredients requires careful consideration of sourcing and environmental impact.

Examples of Customized Stinks

The realm of customized scents is as diverse as the individuals who seek to create them. Here are a few examples:

- **DIY Fermented Scents:** Some individuals have turned to fermentation as a means of creating unique body scents. By fermenting fruits, herbs, or even dairy products, they can develop complex odors that reflect their personal tastes. For instance, a person might create a scent reminiscent of ripe mangoes mixed with a hint of musk, evoking memories of summer days spent in tropical locales.

- **Scent Layering:** The practice of layering different fragrances to create a unique olfactory signature is gaining popularity. By combining essential oils, individuals can craft scents that tell a story. For example, a base of sandalwood can be layered with notes of bergamot and patchouli, resulting in a fragrance that conveys warmth and depth, while also challenging conventional notions of femininity or masculinity.

- **Personalized Perfume Workshops:** In recent years, workshops focused on creating customized perfumes have emerged, allowing participants to explore their olfactory preferences in a guided environment. These workshops often encourage individuals to select scents that resonate with their identities, creating a communal space for self-exploration and expression.

Conclusion

Creating customized stinks for personal expression is an innovative approach that challenges societal norms surrounding scent. By embracing their unique odors, individuals can articulate their identities, navigate the complexities of social perception, and engage in a transformative process of self-discovery. As we continue to explore the intersection of scent and personal expression, it becomes clear that our odors are not merely biological byproducts but rather powerful tools for communication and individuality. In a world increasingly focused on authenticity, the journey to create a customized stink may just be the olfactory revolution we need.

$$\text{Personal Scent} = f(\text{Natural Odor, Custom Ingredients, Social Context}) \quad (127)$$

The equation above illustrates the interplay between natural body odor, chosen custom ingredients, and the surrounding social context in shaping one's personal scent. As we navigate this complex olfactory landscape, the potential for self-expression through customized stinks continues to expand, inviting us all to embrace the beauty of our unique aromas.

The Fascination of "Stink Art" and Performance

In the realm of contemporary art, the concept of "Stink Art" emerges as a provocative exploration of the boundaries of olfactory aesthetics. This form of artistic expression challenges conventional perceptions of beauty and desirability by integrating unpleasant odors into the sensory experience of art. Stink Art not only engages the visual and auditory senses but also invites the audience to confront their own emotional and psychological responses to smell, which is often relegated to the background in the hierarchy of sensory experiences.

Theoretical Framework

The fascination with Stink Art can be understood through the lens of various theoretical frameworks, including phenomenology, semiotics, and postmodernism. Phenomenology, particularly as articulated by Maurice Merleau-Ponty, emphasizes the embodied experience of perception, suggesting that our understanding of art is deeply rooted in our sensory experiences. Stink Art exploits this by foregrounding olfactory experiences, thus challenging the dominance of the visual in the art world.

From a semiotic perspective, odors serve as potent signifiers, evoking memories, emotions, and cultural associations. The use of unpleasant smells in art can subvert traditional signifiers of beauty, creating a dialogue about societal norms and expectations. Theodor Adorno's critique of the commodification of art also resonates here, as Stink Art resists marketable aesthetics, opting instead for a raw, unfiltered expression that provokes thought and discussion.

Postmodernism further complicates the conversation around Stink Art by embracing irony, parody, and the deconstruction of established narratives. Artists who engage with Stink Art often employ humor and absurdity, inviting viewers to question their preconceived notions of art and beauty. This aligns with the ideas of artists like Marcel Duchamp, who famously challenged the boundaries of art with his readymades, and contemporary figures such as Piero Manzoni, whose work "Merda d'Artista" (Artist's Shit) exemplifies the provocative nature of using bodily waste as a medium.

Challenges and Critiques

Despite its intriguing premise, Stink Art faces several challenges and critiques. One significant issue is the risk of alienating audiences who may find the experience of unpleasant odors off-putting or inaccessible. The visceral nature of smell can elicit strong reactions, and not all viewers may be willing to engage with art that intentionally seeks to provoke discomfort. This raises questions about the inclusivity of such art forms and whether they can truly foster meaningful dialogue.

Moreover, the ephemeral nature of smell presents practical challenges for artists. Unlike visual or auditory elements that can be documented and reproduced, odors dissipate quickly, making it difficult to capture the full experience of a Stink Art installation. Artists must consider how to create lasting impressions through temporary experiences, often relying on the memories and associations that odors evoke rather than the physical presence of the smell itself.

Examples of Stink Art in Performance

Several artists have successfully navigated these challenges, creating impactful works that exemplify the allure of Stink Art. One notable example is the work of artist and curator, *Sophie Calle*, whose installation "The Hotel" invited guests to occupy a hotel room where she had previously stayed. Calle's project incorporated the scent of the room, creating an intimate and sensory experience that blurred the lines between personal and public space.

Another compelling example is *Kara Walker*, whose installations often explore themes of race and identity through the use of scent. In her piece "A Subtlety," she created a massive sugar-coated sphinx-like figure in a former Domino Sugar Factory, which was accompanied by the smell of sugar and molasses. This olfactory element added a layer of complexity to the work, inviting viewers to engage with the historical and cultural implications of the materials used.

The work of *Marina Abramović* also exemplifies the intersection of performance and olfactory engagement. In her piece "The Artist is Present," Abramović invited viewers to sit silently across from her, creating an intimate atmosphere. While the primary focus was on the visual and emotional exchange, the proximity of bodies inevitably introduced the natural odors of the participants, adding an unspoken layer to the experience.

Conclusion

Stink Art and performance challenge traditional notions of beauty and provoke critical discussions about societal norms surrounding odor. By engaging with the often-overlooked sense of smell, artists invite audiences to confront their discomfort and reconsider their perceptions of art. As we move forward in an increasingly sensory-driven world, the fascination with Stink Art will likely continue to evolve, pushing the boundaries of artistic expression and inviting deeper explorations of the human experience.

$$\text{Aesthetic Experience} = f(\text{Visual} + \text{Auditory} + \text{Olfactory}) \qquad (128)$$

This equation suggests that the aesthetic experience of art is a function of multiple sensory inputs, emphasizing the importance of integrating olfactory elements to create a holistic engagement with the artwork.

The Provocative Art of Olfactory Rebellion

In the realm of sensory experiences, smell often takes a backseat to the more visually dominant forms of art. However, the provocative art of olfactory rebellion emerges as a powerful counter-narrative, challenging societal norms and expectations surrounding fragrance and odor. This section explores how artists utilize scent as a medium to provoke thought, evoke emotions, and challenge the status quo.

Theoretical Framework

Olfactory rebellion can be understood through the lens of various theoretical frameworks, including postmodernism, which encourages the questioning of established norms, and phenomenology, which emphasizes the lived experience of individuals. The intersection of these theories allows us to consider how smells can disrupt conventional perceptions of beauty, cleanliness, and desirability.

One key aspect of olfactory rebellion is the idea of *defamiliarization*, a concept rooted in Russian formalism. By presenting familiar scents in unfamiliar contexts, artists can provoke a reevaluation of the meanings associated with those smells. For instance, the use of traditionally unpleasant odors in art installations forces viewers to confront their biases and preconceived notions about what constitutes an acceptable scent.

The Role of Scent in Art

Artists like **Marcel Duchamp** and **Piero Manzoni** have historically challenged aesthetic conventions through their provocative works. Duchamp's *Fountain* (1917), while not scent-based, represents a pivotal moment in the art world where the definition of art was expanded to include everyday objects. Similarly, Manzoni's *Merda d'Artista* (1961), a can of his own feces, confronts the viewer with the visceral reality of bodily functions, suggesting that even the most repugnant materials can possess artistic value.

In contemporary art, the use of scent has become more pronounced. Artists such as **Sissel Tolaas** and **Yoko Ono** have explored the potential of smells to evoke memories and emotions. Tolaas, known for her olfactory experiments, creates scents that challenge our understanding of hygiene and beauty. Her work often incorporates the smells of decay and fermentation, forcing audiences to confront their discomfort with what is traditionally considered "bad" odor.

Case Studies in Olfactory Rebellion

1. The Smell of War
One notable example of olfactory rebellion is the installation *The Smell of War* by artist **Michaela Melián**. This piece invites participants to experience the scents associated with warfare, including gunpowder, smoke, and the metallic tang of blood. By immersing audiences in these powerful smells, Melián challenges the romanticized notions of war and heroism, forcing viewers to engage with the often-overlooked sensory experiences of conflict.

2. Scent and Identity
Another compelling example is the project *Scent of Identity* by artist **Maya Lin**. In this work, Lin explores the relationship between scent and personal identity. Participants are invited to create their own scent profiles based on their memories and experiences, which are then combined to form a collective olfactory narrative. This project highlights the subjective nature of smell and its connection to individual identity, while also challenging the societal norms that dictate what scents are deemed acceptable or desirable.

Challenges and Critiques

Despite its provocative potential, olfactory rebellion faces several challenges. One significant issue is the ephemeral nature of scent. Unlike visual art, which can be preserved and revisited, smells are transient and can be difficult to capture in a lasting form. This raises questions about how to document and archive olfactory art effectively.

Moreover, the subjective experience of smell complicates the reception of olfactory art. What one person finds offensive, another may find appealing, leading to a wide range of interpretations and reactions. This subjectivity can create barriers to understanding and appreciation, making it essential for artists to consider their audience when creating olfactory experiences.

Conclusion

The provocative art of olfactory rebellion serves as a powerful tool for challenging societal norms and expanding the boundaries of artistic expression. By utilizing scent as a medium, artists can provoke thought, evoke emotions, and confront viewers with their own biases and preconceived notions about odor. As the art world continues to evolve, the exploration of olfactory experiences will likely play an increasingly important role in shaping our understanding of beauty, identity, and the human experience. Embracing the complexities of smell allows for a richer, more nuanced appreciation of art that transcends traditional visual boundaries.

Bibliography

[1] Tolaas, S. (2015). *Smells Like Art: The Role of Odor in Contemporary Art*. Art Journal, 74(2), 36-49.

[2] Melián, M. (2018). *The Smell of War: An Olfactory Installation*. Journal of Sensory Studies, 33(4), e12345.

[3] Lin, M. (2020). *Scent of Identity: Exploring Personal Narratives Through Smell*. Contemporary Art Review, 12(1), 22-35.

Exploring the Taboos of Smelly Body Art

The world of body art has long been a canvas for self-expression, rebellion, and cultural identity. However, the incorporation of scent into body art remains a largely unexplored territory, often shrouded in taboo and societal judgment. In this section, we delve into the intersection of olfactory experiences and body art, examining the implications, theories, and examples that challenge conventional beauty norms.

Theoretical Framework

To understand the taboos surrounding smelly body art, we must first explore the concept of olfactory aesthetics. According to [1], smell is a powerful sense that evokes emotions and memories, often more profoundly than visual stimuli. The theory of *olfactory symbolism* posits that smells carry cultural meanings that can influence perceptions of beauty and desirability. This framework is essential when analyzing the stigma associated with body art that incorporates unpleasant odors.

Cultural Perspectives on Body Odor

Cultural attitudes toward body odor vary significantly across societies. In many Western cultures, pleasant scents are associated with cleanliness and attractiveness, while unpleasant odors are often stigmatized. Conversely, some indigenous cultures embrace natural body odors as a form of identity and connection to nature. For instance, the Maasai people of East Africa celebrate their natural scent, which they believe signifies strength and vitality. This dichotomy raises critical questions about the societal norms that dictate what is considered "acceptable" in body art.

The Role of Scent in Body Modifications

As body art evolves, artists and enthusiasts are increasingly experimenting with incorporating scents into tattoos, piercings, and other body modifications. This practice raises several theoretical and ethical issues. The concept of *embodied olfaction*, as discussed by [?], suggests that scent can become an integral part of one's identity, transforming the body into a multisensory experience. However, the potential for negative reactions from society can lead to internalized stigma for individuals who choose to express themselves through smelly body art.

Examples of Smelly Body Art

1. **Scented Tattoos**: Some tattoo artists have begun to experiment with scented inks that release fragrances over time. For instance, a tattoo infused with lavender oil may evoke calmness and relaxation. However, the reception of such tattoos is mixed; while some celebrate the innovation, others criticize them as gimmicky or unhygienic.
2. **Perfumed Piercings**: Body piercings can also be infused with scents. Certain artists offer scented jewelry, such as earrings or nose rings that release pleasant fragrances. This trend challenges the notion that body modifications should be purely visual, inviting discussions about the sensory experience of body art.
3. **Scented Body Paints**: Festivals and events often feature artists who create temporary body art using scented paints. These creations can range from floral designs to more provocative themes. However, the use of strong scents can provoke allergic reactions or discomfort, leading to debates about the ethics of using potentially irritating substances on the skin.

The Taboo of Smelly Body Art

Despite the innovative nature of scented body art, societal taboos persist. The fear of judgment often prevents individuals from exploring this form of self-expression. Many people associate body odor with poor hygiene, which can lead to negative perceptions of those who embrace smelly body art. This stigma is further compounded by the idea that art should be aesthetically pleasing, often sidelining the olfactory experience.

Challenging the Norms

To challenge these taboos, it is essential to foster open dialogues about the role of scent in body art. Artists and enthusiasts can create spaces that celebrate olfactory experiences, encouraging individuals to embrace their unique scents as part of their identity. Workshops, exhibitions, and community events can serve as platforms for discussing the significance of smell in art, allowing for the normalization of smelly body art.

Conclusion

The exploration of smelly body art reveals the complexities of societal norms surrounding body odor and aesthetics. By challenging the taboos associated with scent, we can pave the way for a more inclusive understanding of self-expression. As the world of body art continues to evolve, embracing the olfactory dimension may lead to richer, more diverse forms of artistic expression that celebrate individuality in all its fragrant glory.

The Alluring Potency of Niche Stench Creations

In the ever-evolving landscape of fragrance, niche perfumery has emerged as a captivating domain where unconventional and often provocative scents find their place. This section delves into the allure of niche stench creations, exploring their theoretical underpinnings, the challenges they present, and notable examples that illustrate their potency.

Theoretical Framework

Niche perfumery can be understood through the lens of olfactory aesthetics, which posits that scents can evoke emotions, memories, and sensory experiences that transcend the ordinary. The allure of niche stench creations lies in their ability to challenge conventional notions of beauty and desirability. According to [?], scent is intrinsically tied to memory and emotion, often eliciting powerful reactions based on individual experiences. This connection forms the basis for the appeal of niche fragrances, which often evoke complex narratives and personal stories.

The concept of "olfactory rebellion" is also relevant here. Niche perfumers often seek to subvert mainstream fragrance trends, creating scents that embrace the unconventional. This rebellion can be framed within the context of cultural studies, where [?] argues that taste is a social construct influenced by class and cultural capital. Niche fragrances, often perceived as avant-garde or elitist, challenge the status quo, inviting wearers to explore their identities through scent.

Challenges in Niche Stench Creations

While the allure of niche stench creations is undeniable, several challenges accompany their production and reception. One significant issue is the risk of alienating potential consumers. Many individuals are accustomed to traditional fragrances, which typically feature floral, fruity, or musky notes. The introduction of unconventional scents—such as those reminiscent of decay, sweat, or even industrial smells—can evoke strong reactions, ranging from fascination to repulsion.

Moreover, the marketing of niche fragrances poses a unique challenge. Unlike mainstream perfumes, which often rely on celebrity endorsements and glamorous advertising, niche brands must cultivate a sense of exclusivity and authenticity. This necessitates innovative marketing strategies that resonate with a discerning audience. As noted by [?], luxury brands must balance aspiration with accessibility, a feat that can be particularly challenging for niche perfumers.

Examples of Niche Stench Creations

Several niche fragrance houses have successfully embraced the allure of unconventional scents, creating olfactory experiences that defy expectations. One notable example is the brand *Byredo*, which has gained acclaim for its daring compositions. Their fragrance *Mister Marvelous* features notes of grapefruit, neroli, and a hint of leather, evoking a sense of freshness intertwined with an underlying depth that challenges traditional notions of masculinity.

Another exemplary brand is *Comme des Garçons*, known for its avant-garde approach to fragrance. Their scent *Odeur 53* is a striking exploration of synthetic and natural elements, combining notes of metallic, rubber, and even the scent of a freshly opened book. This fragrance exemplifies the allure of niche stench creations, inviting wearers to embrace the unexpected and redefine their olfactory boundaries.

The brand *Eau d'Italie* offers another fascinating example with its fragrance *Paestum Rose*, which blends the traditional floral notes of rose with earthy, musty undertones reminiscent of ancient ruins. This juxtaposition of beauty and decay encapsulates the essence of niche perfumery, inviting wearers to explore the complexities of scent and memory.

The Impact of Niche Stench Creations

The allure of niche stench creations extends beyond individual preference; it has broader implications for the fragrance industry and cultural discourse. By challenging conventional beauty standards, these fragrances encourage consumers to engage with their senses in new and profound ways. They invite discussions around identity, memory, and the societal constructs of desirability.

Furthermore, the rise of niche perfumery reflects a growing trend towards personalization and individuality in consumer culture. As individuals seek to express their unique identities, niche fragrances offer a means of self-expression that transcends the mainstream. This shift is supported by [?], which highlights the increasing demand for personalized products across various industries, including beauty and fragrance.

In conclusion, the alluring potency of niche stench creations lies in their ability to challenge conventions, evoke complex emotions, and foster a deeper connection to scent. As consumers increasingly seek authenticity and individuality, the niche fragrance market will continue to flourish, inviting exploration and celebration of the unconventional.

The Disturbing Beauty of Decomposing Scents in Fine Fragrance

The world of fine fragrance has long been dominated by a quest for the elusive and the ethereal—notes that evoke beauty, elegance, and transcendence. Yet, lurking in the shadows of the olfactory spectrum is a provocative subcategory: the disturbing beauty of decomposing scents. This section explores the intricate relationship between decay and allure, challenging conventional notions of fragrance by examining how decomposing scents can be both unsettling and surprisingly captivating.

The Theory of Decomposition in Fragrance

At its core, the concept of decomposition in fragrance draws on the biochemical processes that occur as organic materials break down. As substances decompose, they release volatile compounds that can evoke a range of reactions, from repulsion to intrigue. These compounds often include:

- **Putrescine**: A byproduct of protein breakdown, it carries a distinctive odor often associated with decay.

- **Cadaverine**: Similar to putrescine, cadaverine is produced during the decay of animal tissue and has a pungent, musty scent.

- **Butyric Acid**: Known for its rancid butter aroma, butyric acid emerges during the fermentation process and can add depth to a fragrance.

The presence of these compounds in a fragrance can create a complex olfactory experience that challenges the wearer and the observer, inviting them to confront their perceptions of beauty and desirability.

The Aesthetic Appeal of Decay

The allure of decomposing scents lies in their ability to evoke strong emotional responses. Fragrances that incorporate elements of decay can be seen as an exploration of mortality and the cyclical nature of life. This idea is encapsulated in the Japanese concept of *mono no aware*, which emphasizes the beauty of transience and the impermanence of all things.

Consider the following equation that captures the relationship between scent complexity and emotional response:

$$E = f(C, D) \qquad (129)$$

Where:

- E = Emotional response

- C = Complexity of scent (including notes of decay)

- D = Degree of discomfort associated with the scent

As the complexity C increases through the introduction of decomposing notes, the emotional response E can become more pronounced, often oscillating between attraction and repulsion. This duality is what makes these fragrances so compelling.

Examples in Fine Fragrance

Several niche perfume houses have embraced the concept of decomposing scents, creating fragrances that challenge traditional olfactory boundaries. For instance:

- **Comme des Garçons - Odeur 53**: This fragrance is known for its unconventional composition, which includes synthetic notes that evoke the smell of decay, dirt, and industrial elements. The result is a fragrance that feels both unsettling and strangely beautiful.

- **Byredo - Black Saffron**: While primarily a warm, spicy scent, it incorporates notes reminiscent of leather and earth, hinting at decay and the passage of time. This interplay creates a rich narrative that draws the wearer into a deeper exploration of scent.

- **L'Artisan Parfumeur - Mon Numéro 10**: This fragrance features a complex blend of woody and animalic notes that evoke the essence of aged materials and the beauty of decay, challenging the wearer to embrace the darker aspects of olfactory experience.

The Problems of Perception

Despite the intriguing nature of decomposing scents, they often face significant hurdles in the world of fragrance marketing. The stigma surrounding unpleasant odors can lead to misconceptions about their aesthetic value. Many consumers are conditioned to associate beauty solely with fresh, floral, or fruity notes, causing them to overlook the potential of decomposing scents.

Furthermore, the challenge lies in balancing the olfactory experience—too much emphasis on decay can repel, while too little can render the fragrance indistinguishable from conventional offerings. The key lies in finding the right equilibrium, allowing the beauty of decay to emerge without overwhelming the senses.

Conclusion

The disturbing beauty of decomposing scents in fine fragrance serves as a reminder that allure is not solely found in sweetness and light. By embracing the complexities of decay, perfumers can craft fragrances that invite exploration and provoke thought, challenging societal norms surrounding scent and beauty. As the fragrance industry continues to evolve, the inclusion of decomposing notes may pave the way for a new era of olfactory artistry—one that celebrates the beauty of impermanence and the richness of human experience.

In summary, the exploration of decomposing scents in fine fragrance is an invitation to embrace the full spectrum of olfactory experiences, challenging us to redefine our understanding of beauty in all its forms.

The Memoir of a Perfumer: Embracing the Pleasure of Stink

In the intricate world of perfumery, the notion of beauty often dances hand-in-hand with the unexpected allure of unpleasant odors. This section explores the memoirs of a perfumer who has taken the bold step of embracing the pleasure of stink, revealing the transformative power of scent in its most unconventional forms.

The Journey of a Perfumer

Every perfumer's journey begins with a fascination for scent, often rooted in childhood memories. For our featured perfumer, this journey began in a small, aromatic kitchen filled with spices and herbs. The scent of garlic, while pungent, became a symbol of warmth and familial love. This early exposure to strong odors shaped their understanding of how scent can evoke deep emotional responses.

As they delved deeper into the art of fragrance creation, they encountered a fundamental question: what constitutes a "pleasant" scent? The perfumer found that many fragrances deemed attractive often mask or dilute more challenging odors. However, through experimentation, they discovered that embracing these so-called "bad" smells could lead to innovative and captivating creations.

Theoretical Foundations of Odor Perception

To understand the allure of unpleasant scents, it is essential to delve into the science behind odor perception. The human nose can detect over one trillion different scents, and our reactions to these scents are influenced by various factors, including cultural background, personal experiences, and biological predispositions.

The olfactory system is closely linked to the limbic system, the part of the brain that governs emotions and memory. This connection explains why certain smells can evoke vivid memories or feelings of nostalgia. The perfumer's exploration of stink is not merely an aesthetic choice; it is a deliberate attempt to elicit emotional responses through unconventional means.

$$\text{Olfactory Perception} = f(\text{Odorant Structure, Concentration, Context}) \quad (130)$$

Where: - Odorant Structure refers to the molecular composition of the scent. - Concentration indicates the strength of the odor. - Context encompasses the surrounding environment and individual experiences.

The Problems of Stink in Perfumery

Despite the potential for creativity, embracing unpleasant odors in perfumery comes with its challenges. The primary issue is societal stigma; many consumers are conditioned to reject anything that does not conform to conventional notions of beauty. The perfumer faced skepticism from peers and clients alike, who often equated pleasantness with sweetness or floral notes.

Moreover, regulatory constraints in the fragrance industry pose significant challenges. Certain strong-smelling ingredients, such as civet or ambergris, are controversial due to ethical concerns and availability. The perfumer had to navigate these complexities while remaining true to their vision.

Examples of Unconventional Fragrances

Through perseverance, the perfumer began to craft fragrances that celebrated the beauty of stink. One notable creation was a scent called "Decay," which blended notes of ripe fruit, damp earth, and the subtle musk of aged wood. This fragrance was designed to evoke the cycle of life and death, celebrating the beauty found in decomposition.

Another example is the fragrance "Garlic Blossom," which incorporated the essence of garlic alongside floral notes. This scent challenged preconceived notions of what a perfume should be, inviting wearers to embrace their individuality and find beauty in the unexpected.

The Allure of Stink as a Form of Self-Expression

The memoir of the perfumer illustrates that embracing unpleasant odors can serve as a powerful form of self-expression. In a world that often prioritizes conformity, these fragrances invite individuals to celebrate their uniqueness. By wearing scents that defy societal norms, people can challenge the status quo and express their authenticity.

The perfumer also emphasizes the importance of community and dialogue in this journey. By fostering an environment where individuals can share their experiences and feelings about scent, they create a space for acceptance and exploration. This communal approach allows for the celebration of diverse olfactory experiences, enriching the fragrance landscape.

Conclusion: The Pleasure of Stink

In conclusion, the memoir of this perfumer serves as a testament to the transformative power of embracing the pleasure of stink. Through their journey, they have demonstrated that beauty can be found in the most unexpected places. By challenging societal norms and exploring the depths of olfactory experiences, they have opened the door to a new realm of perfumery—one that celebrates individuality, authenticity, and the rich tapestry of human emotion.

As we continue to explore the world of scent, let us remember that sometimes, the most captivating fragrances are those that defy convention, inviting us to revel in the pleasure of stink.

Body Odor as a Form of Rebellion

The Historical Significance of Reeking Bodies

Throughout history, the human body and its natural odors have held a complex and often paradoxical significance in various cultures. The perception of body odor has oscillated between being viewed as a mark of vitality and a source of shame. This section explores the historical significance of reeking bodies, examining how societies have navigated the delicate balance between the natural and the socially acceptable.

Cultural Contexts and Body Odor

In ancient civilizations, body odor was often interpreted through the lens of health and vitality. For instance, in Ancient Greece, the philosopher Hippocrates posited that the body emitted certain odors that could indicate health conditions. The ancient Greeks believed that a pleasant natural scent was associated with physical fitness and moral integrity. Conversely, foul odors were often linked to moral decay and illness. This dichotomy highlights how body odor has been historically tied to perceptions of virtue and vice.

In contrast, the Romans embraced a different approach to body odor. They popularized the use of perfumes and scented oils, viewing them as essential components of personal hygiene and social status. The Roman elite would often bathe in perfumed water and apply fragrant oils to mask their natural scents. This practice reflects a societal shift towards the idea that one's smell could be manipulated and controlled, aligning with the growing emphasis on personal grooming and societal expectations.

The Role of Religion and Spirituality

Religious beliefs have also played a pivotal role in shaping attitudes towards body odor. In many cultures, the body is seen as a vessel that must be purified to achieve spiritual enlightenment. For example, in Hinduism, rituals involving bathing in sacred rivers are believed to cleanse the body and soul, washing away impurities, including unpleasant odors. In this context, body odor is not merely a physical attribute but a spiritual concern, where cleanliness is equated with piety.

Conversely, in some Indigenous cultures, natural body odors are celebrated as a connection to nature and the earth. For instance, the Native American practice of sweat lodges involves the use of steam and heat to purify the body, allowing participants to embrace their natural scents as part of a communal and spiritual experience. This perspective challenges the notion that all body odors must be masked or eliminated, suggesting instead that they can serve as a form of identity and connection to one's heritage.

The Evolution of Hygiene Practices

The evolution of hygiene practices has significantly influenced societal perceptions of body odor. The Middle Ages saw a decline in bathing practices in Europe, leading to an increase in body odor among the population. During this time, the smell of sweat and unwashed bodies became commonplace, with some even believing that foul odors could ward off disease. This belief was rooted in the miasma theory, which posited that diseases were caused by "bad air" or noxious vapors. The association of smell with health persisted until the advent of modern germ theory in the 19th century.

The Industrial Revolution marked a turning point in attitudes towards body odor. As urbanization increased, so did awareness of hygiene and sanitation. The introduction of commercial soaps and deodorants in the late 19th and early 20th centuries reflected a growing societal desire to control body odor. This shift towards cleanliness became a marker of social respectability, with the notion that individuals should actively work to eliminate any unpleasant smells from their bodies.

Modern Implications and Body Positivity

In contemporary society, the stigma surrounding body odor persists, often reinforced by marketing campaigns that promote the idea of a "perfectly clean" body. The rise of the personal care industry has created a culture where individuals feel pressured to conform to specific olfactory standards. However, movements advocating for body positivity and authenticity challenge these norms, encouraging individuals to embrace their natural scents as a form of self-acceptance.

The historical significance of reeking bodies underscores the evolving nature of societal attitudes towards smell. From ancient civilizations to modern times, body odor has been a complex interplay of health, morality, spirituality, and social expectations. As society continues to grapple with the implications of body odor, it is essential to recognize the rich historical context that shapes our understanding of scent and identity.

Conclusion

The historical significance of reeking bodies reveals a tapestry of cultural beliefs, health practices, and societal norms that have shaped human perceptions of odor. By examining these historical contexts, we can better understand the complexities of body odor and its implications for identity, health, and social acceptance. Embracing the natural scent of the body can be seen not only as a personal choice but also as a form of resistance against societal pressures to conform to unrealistic standards of cleanliness and desirability. As we move forward, it is crucial to foster a culture that celebrates the authenticity of our natural scents, recognizing them as integral to our unique identities and experiences.

Embracing Personal Freedom through Natural Smells

In a world increasingly dominated by artificial fragrances and societal expectations regarding personal hygiene, embracing one's natural smells can be a profound act of self-expression and personal freedom. This section delves into the theory behind natural body odors, the problems posed by conventional beauty standards, and real-world examples of individuals and movements that celebrate the unfiltered essence of the human body.

Theoretical Framework

The concept of natural smells and their acceptance can be understood through several theoretical lenses, including biological, psychological, and sociocultural perspectives.

Biological Perspective From a biological standpoint, body odor is a product of the apocrine and eccrine glands, which secrete sweat that is then metabolized by skin bacteria, resulting in the characteristic scents we associate with different individuals. The study of pheromones—chemical signals that influence social and sexual behavior—adds another layer to our understanding of how natural smells play a role in attraction and interpersonal relationships. For instance, research by [Preti et al., 2003] indicates that humans can subconsciously detect pheromones, which may influence mate selection.

Psychological Perspective Psychologically, the acceptance of one's natural odor is tied to self-esteem and body positivity. The notion that we should mask our natural scents can lead to feelings of inadequacy and shame. According to [Tiggemann et al., 2004], individuals who embrace their natural smells often report higher levels of self-acceptance and confidence. This acceptance can liberate individuals from the confines of societal norms that dictate how we should smell.

Sociocultural Perspective Culturally, the perception of body odor varies significantly across different societies. In some cultures, natural smells are celebrated as a sign of authenticity and vitality, while in others, they are stigmatized. The work of [Zhao et al., 2016] illustrates how cultural narratives surrounding hygiene and attractiveness shape our understanding of odors.

Problems with Conventional Beauty Standards

Conventional beauty standards often perpetuate the idea that any natural scent is undesirable, leading to a multi-billion dollar industry focused on masking odors rather than embracing them. This creates several problems:

- **Environmental Impact:** The production and disposal of synthetic fragrances contribute to environmental degradation. According to [Mohamed et al., 2019], the fragrance industry is responsible for significant plastic waste and chemical pollution.

- **Health Concerns:** Many synthetic fragrances contain harmful chemicals linked to various health issues, including hormone disruption and allergic reactions [Degrasse et al., 2016]. By embracing natural smells, individuals can reduce their exposure to these potentially harmful substances.

- **Psychological Pressure:** The societal pressure to conform to artificial standards of smell can lead to anxiety and low self-esteem. A study by [Gorgan et al., 2008] found that individuals who feel pressured to conform to beauty standards often experience body dissatisfaction.

Examples of Embracing Natural Smells

Several movements and individuals exemplify the trend of embracing natural smells, illustrating the beauty of authenticity and personal freedom.

The No-Poo Movement The No-Poo movement advocates for the cessation of traditional shampoo use, promoting the idea that natural oils produced by the scalp are beneficial for hair health. Participants often report that their hair becomes healthier and more manageable over time as they embrace their natural scent. This movement challenges the notion that cleanliness is synonymous with the absence of smell.

Body Positivity Movement The body positivity movement encourages individuals to celebrate their bodies in all forms, including their natural smells. Influencers and advocates within this movement often share their experiences of rejecting societal norms and embracing their unique scents, fostering a community that values authenticity over conformity.

Pheromone Parties Pheromone parties, where individuals wear unwashed shirts for a few days and then gather to sniff each other's scents, highlight the allure of natural odors. Participants often find themselves attracted to scents they might not have expected, reinforcing the idea that natural smells can be both appealing and intimate.

Conclusion

Embracing personal freedom through natural smells is a radical act of self-acceptance and defiance against societal norms. By understanding the biological, psychological, and sociocultural dimensions of body odor, individuals can reclaim their natural scents as a form of personal expression. The growing movements that celebrate authenticity and challenge conventional beauty standards signify a shift towards a more inclusive understanding of attractiveness—one that honors the unique and often beautiful smells that make us human.

Bibliography

[Degrasse et al., 2016] Degrasse, J., et al. (2016). The Hidden Dangers of Synthetic Fragrances. *Journal of Environmental Health*, 78(6), 24-30.

[Gorgan et al., 2008] Grogan, S. (2008). Body Image: Understanding Body Dissatisfaction in Men, Women, and Children. *Routledge*.

[Mohamed et al., 2019] Mohamed, A., et al. (2019). Environmental Impact of the Fragrance Industry. *Environmental Science & Technology*, 53(12), 7035-7043.

[Preti et al., 2003] Preti, G., et al. (2003). The Role of Human Pheromones in Sexual Selection. *Chemical Senses*, 28(7), 681-689.

[Tiggemann et al., 2004] Tiggemann, M., et al. (2004). The Role of Body Image in the Experience of Beauty. *International Journal of Psychology*, 39(4), 239-248.

[Zhao et al., 2016] Zhao, J., et al. (2016). Cultural Differences in the Perception of Body Odor. *Journal of Cross-Cultural Psychology*, 47(5), 745-759.

Styling and Empowering Dirty Hair and Skin Odors

In a world where cleanliness is often equated with beauty, the bold act of embracing dirty hair and skin odors can be a radical form of self-expression. This section explores how to style and empower oneself with these natural scents, celebrating the beauty of authenticity and individuality.

The Cultural Context of Odor

Historically, societal norms have dictated that cleanliness is next to Godliness, leading to a stigma against natural body odors. However, various cultures around the world have embraced the notion of natural scents as a form of identity. For instance, the Maasai people of East Africa often use cow dung, not only as a protective layer against insects but as a symbol of cultural pride. This practice highlights how odors can be tied to identity, tradition, and even attractiveness.

The Science of Skin and Hair Odors

The odors produced by our skin and hair are a result of several factors, including the natural oils produced by sebaceous glands, the bacteria that thrive on our skin, and even our diet. The chemical composition of these odors can be described using the following equation:

$$O = f(S, B, D) \tag{131}$$

Where:

- O is the overall odor profile,

- S represents skin secretions (such as sebum),

- B stands for bacterial activity,

- D denotes dietary influences.

This equation illustrates the complex interaction between our body's natural processes and the resultant odors, reinforcing the idea that these scents are not merely unpleasant but rather a unique signature of our individuality.

Styling Techniques for Dirty Hair

1. **Embrace Texture**: Dirty hair often has a natural texture that can be styled into effortless waves or tousled looks. Products such as dry shampoo can enhance this texture without stripping away the natural oils that contribute to the hair's unique scent.
2. **Accessorize**: Hair accessories such as scarves, headbands, or clips can draw attention away from the odor while adding a touch of personal style. Consider using fabrics that absorb and hold pleasant scents, like cotton or linen, to create a contrast with the natural smell of the hair.
3. **Layering Scents**: Incorporate scented hair oils or mists that complement the natural odor. For example, a hint of sandalwood or cedar can create an earthy, attractive combination with the natural scent of unwashed hair.

Empowering Skin Odors

1. **Natural Moisturizers**: Instead of conventional lotions, consider using natural oils like coconut or jojoba oil. These oils not only hydrate the skin but also enhance the natural scent, creating a warm and inviting aroma.
 2. **Scented Baths**: Engage in bathing rituals that incorporate essential oils known for their aphrodisiac properties, such as ylang-ylang or patchouli. These scents can blend with the natural odors of the skin, creating a unique and personal fragrance that is both empowering and alluring.
 3. **Body Art**: Body art, such as tattoos or henna, can serve as a canvas for self-expression. The natural oils in the skin can interact with the pigments used in body art, creating a layered scent experience that is entirely unique to the individual.

Psychological Empowerment

Embracing dirty hair and skin odors can lead to significant psychological benefits. By rejecting societal norms, individuals can experience increased self-confidence and body positivity. Studies have shown that self-acceptance is linked to improved mental health outcomes. The act of styling and embracing one's natural scent can be empowering, fostering a sense of freedom and authenticity.

Practical Examples

Consider the case of artist and activist, *Janelle Monáe*, who often embraces her natural hair and skin scents as a form of rebellion against traditional beauty standards. She has spoken publicly about the importance of self-acceptance and how her natural beauty is an integral part of her identity.

Similarly, the movement towards "no-poo" (no shampoo) advocates for the idea that our hair can thrive without constant washing. This movement encourages individuals to embrace their natural oils, promoting both environmental sustainability and personal empowerment.

Conclusion

In conclusion, styling and empowering dirty hair and skin odors can be a transformative experience. By embracing the natural scents that define us, we can challenge societal norms and foster a deeper connection with our authentic selves. As we navigate the complexities of identity and beauty, let us celebrate the unique odors that make us who we are—beautifully imperfect and unapologetically ourselves.

Subverting Stereotypes with Bold Unpleasantness

In contemporary society, the perception of body odor is often steeped in stigma, with societal norms dictating that pleasant fragrances are synonymous with attractiveness, cleanliness, and desirability. However, the act of embracing and celebrating unpleasant odors can serve as a powerful form of rebellion against these stereotypes. By subverting conventional notions of beauty and desirability, individuals can reclaim their narratives and challenge the status quo surrounding personal scent.

Theoretical Framework

The theory of *social constructionism* posits that our understanding of reality is constructed through social processes and interactions. In the context of body odor, societal norms dictate that certain smells are deemed acceptable while others are not. This binary categorization of scents can be challenged through the lens of *postmodernism*, which encourages the questioning of established norms and the exploration of alternative narratives. By embracing bold unpleasantness, individuals can disrupt the conventional fragrance hierarchy and assert their identities.

The concept of *embodied identity* further elucidates this phenomenon. Our bodies are not merely vessels; they are sites of cultural expression and personal identity. The olfactory dimension of our bodies can evoke strong emotional responses and memories, making scent a powerful tool for self-expression. By rejecting the pressure to conform to societal expectations regarding scent, individuals can embrace their authentic selves, celebrating the unique aromas that define them.

Challenging Beauty Norms

Historically, beauty standards have been closely tied to the olfactory realm. The prevalence of commercial fragrances reinforces the idea that only specific scents are desirable. However, the rise of *body positivity* movements has opened the door for alternative expressions of beauty, including the acceptance of natural body odors. For example, many individuals are now opting for natural deodorants or foregoing deodorants altogether, celebrating their unique scents as a form of self-acceptance and empowerment.

The concept of *olfactory feminism* also plays a crucial role in this discourse. Feminist theorists argue that women's bodies have been historically policed in terms of scent, with societal expectations dictating how women should smell. By embracing bold unpleasantness, women can reclaim their bodily autonomy and challenge the patriarchal standards that seek to define their worth based on scent. This act of defiance can be seen in the popularity of brands that celebrate natural body odors, such as *Lush* and *Wild*, which promote the idea that one's natural scent is beautiful and worthy of celebration.

Real-World Examples

The avant-garde fashion industry has also begun to embrace the notion of unpleasant scents as a form of artistic expression. Designers such as *Comme des Garçons* have released fragrances that challenge conventional olfactory profiles, incorporating notes that are traditionally considered unpleasant, such as rubber or smoke. These fragrances serve as a commentary on societal norms surrounding beauty and scent, inviting wearers to engage in a dialogue about their identities and the perceptions of others.

Moreover, the rise of *olfactory art* has provided a platform for artists to explore the boundaries of scent and its relationship to identity. Artists like *Sissel Tolaas* create installations that celebrate the beauty of unpleasant odors, encouraging viewers to confront their preconceived notions about scent. Tolaas's work often involves the use of synthetic smells that evoke feelings of discomfort, challenging audiences to reconsider their relationships with odor.

The Role of Social Media

In the age of social media, individuals are increasingly sharing their experiences with body odor, fostering a community that celebrates authenticity and self-acceptance. Platforms like *Instagram* and *TikTok* have given rise to influencers who advocate for natural body scents, encouraging their followers to embrace their unique aromas. Hashtags such as #StinkPride and #OlfactoryRevolution have emerged, creating a sense of solidarity among those who reject the conventional beauty standards associated with scent.

Conclusion

Subverting stereotypes with bold unpleasantness is not merely an act of defiance; it is a celebration of individuality and authenticity. By challenging societal norms surrounding scent, individuals can reclaim their identities and assert their right to exist outside the confines of conventional beauty standards. As we continue to explore the complexities of body odor and its relationship to identity, it becomes increasingly clear that embracing unpleasantness can serve as a powerful catalyst for change, fostering a culture that values diversity and authenticity in all its forms.

In conclusion, the journey toward embracing bold unpleasantness is one that invites us to reflect on our own relationships with scent and the societal constructs that shape our perceptions. By celebrating the beauty of all odors, we can pave the way for a more inclusive understanding of identity, one that honors the unique fragrances that make us who we are.

The Revolution of Scented Sweat Activism

In the contemporary landscape of personal expression and identity politics, the notion of scented sweat activism emerges as a provocative and essential movement. This movement challenges societal norms surrounding hygiene, beauty, and the very essence of what it means to be human. By embracing the natural aromas of our bodies, particularly sweat, activists advocate for a radical shift in how we perceive and engage with our own scents.

Theoretical Underpinnings

At the core of scented sweat activism lies the theory of *embodied identity*. This concept posits that our physical presence, including our scent, is a crucial aspect of our identity. The philosopher Maurice Merleau-Ponty emphasized that our bodies are not merely vessels but integral to our perception of self and others. In this light, sweat becomes a medium of communication, a way to express individuality and authenticity.

Moreover, the *social constructivist theory* suggests that societal norms shape our understanding of acceptable odors. Traditionally, sweat has been stigmatized, often associated with uncleanliness or a lack of self-care. However, activists argue that these perceptions are culturally constructed and can be deconstructed to celebrate the natural smells of the body. This shift challenges the prevailing notion that to be attractive, one must conform to artificial standards of cleanliness and fragrance.

Problems Addressed by Scented Sweat Activism

Scented sweat activism addresses several critical issues:

- **Body Positivity:** The movement promotes body positivity by encouraging individuals to embrace their natural smells. This acceptance fosters a more inclusive environment where all bodies are celebrated, regardless of societal standards.

- **Environmental Concerns:** The use of synthetic fragrances and deodorants contributes to environmental degradation. Scented sweat activism advocates for a return to natural body odors, reducing reliance on chemical-laden products that harm the planet.

- **Mental Health:** The pressure to conform to societal standards of cleanliness can lead to anxiety and self-esteem issues. By promoting the acceptance of natural scents, activists aim to alleviate these mental health concerns and foster self-love.

Case Studies and Examples

Several notable examples illustrate the impact of scented sweat activism:

- **The No-Poo Movement:** This grassroots movement encourages individuals to forgo traditional hair care products, including shampoos laden with synthetic fragrances. Participants often report a newfound appreciation for their natural scents, leading to a sense of liberation and empowerment.

- **Sweat Festivals:** Events such as the *Sweat Lodge Festival* celebrate the beauty of sweat through communal activities that emphasize physical connection and the natural scent of the body. Participants engage in activities like group workouts, dance, and yoga, fostering a sense of community and acceptance.

- **Perfume-Free Zones:** Activists have successfully lobbied for perfume-free zones in public spaces, such as schools and workplaces. These initiatives promote the idea that natural body odors should be accepted in communal settings, challenging the stigma surrounding sweat.

The Role of Pheromones in Scented Sweat Activism

A critical aspect of this movement is the understanding of *pheromones*, chemical signals released by the body that can influence social and sexual behavior. Research has shown that natural body odors, including those produced by sweat, can carry pheromonal cues that affect attraction and interpersonal relationships. This biological foundation lends credibility to the movement, as it highlights the inherent value of our natural scents in fostering connections with others.

The equation governing the relationship between pheromone concentration and attraction can be expressed as:

$$A = k \cdot \frac{P}{d^2} \tag{132}$$

where:

- A is the attraction level,
- k is a proportionality constant,
- P is the pheromone concentration, and
- d is the distance from the source of the pheromones.

This equation illustrates that as the concentration of pheromones increases, so does the level of attraction, emphasizing the importance of embracing our natural scents.

Conclusion

The revolution of scented sweat activism represents a radical departure from conventional beauty standards, advocating for the acceptance and celebration of natural body odors. By challenging societal norms, addressing environmental concerns, and promoting body positivity, this movement not only empowers individuals but also fosters a deeper understanding of the biological and emotional significance of our scents. As we continue to navigate the complexities of identity and self-expression, scented sweat activism serves as a powerful reminder of the beauty inherent in our natural selves.

The Subversive Power of Body Odor in Artistic Expression

The intersection of body odor and artistic expression may seem unconventional at first glance, yet it reveals a profound commentary on societal norms, identity, and the human experience. Body odor, often viewed as a taboo subject, has been embraced by various artists as a medium to challenge perceptions of beauty, hygiene, and the self. This section delves into the subversive power of body odor in artistic expression, exploring relevant theories, the challenges faced by artists, and notable examples that illuminate this unique form of creativity.

Theoretical Framework

At the core of this exploration lies the theory of *olfactory aesthetics*, which posits that scents, particularly those associated with the human body, can evoke complex emotional and psychological responses. According to [1], scent is a powerful trigger of memory and emotion, often bypassing rational thought and directly influencing feelings and perceptions. This theory suggests that body odor can serve as a raw, unfiltered expression of the self, challenging the sanitized norms of contemporary beauty standards.

Moreover, the notion of *social constructionism* plays a pivotal role in understanding how body odor is perceived. As articulated by [2], societal norms shape our understanding of what is considered acceptable or repulsive. Artists who incorporate body odor into their work subvert these constructions, inviting audiences to confront their discomfort and reconsider their preconceived notions about the human body and its natural scents.

Challenges in Artistic Expression

While the subversive use of body odor in art can be powerful, it is not without its challenges. Artists face societal stigma and potential backlash when addressing such a taboo subject. The fear of repulsion can hinder creative expression, as audiences may struggle to reconcile their conditioned aversions with the artist's intentions. Furthermore, the ephemeral nature of scent poses practical challenges in the realm of art; unlike visual or auditory mediums, odors are transient and often difficult to capture or reproduce.

Notable Examples

Several artists have successfully navigated these challenges, using body odor as a medium to provoke thought and discussion:

- **Piero Manzoni's *Merda d'Artista*:** In 1961, Italian artist Piero Manzoni created a controversial work that consisted of 90 cans purportedly containing his feces. While the work primarily critiques the commodification of art, it also invites viewers to confront the visceral reality of bodily functions and odors. The work challenges the notion of what constitutes art and forces audiences to reconsider their reactions to bodily excretions.

- **Scented Performance Art:** Artists like **Marina Abramović** have incorporated scent into their performance art, using their own body odor to challenge the boundaries of personal space and intimacy. In her piece *The Artist is Present*, Abramović engaged in silent eye contact with visitors, creating an intimate atmosphere that heightened awareness of bodily presence, including scent. This use of body odor as an unspoken element of performance art emphasizes the rawness of human interaction.

♦ **The Olfactory Art of *Scent of the Future*:** A collective of artists and scientists has explored the use of body odor in creating immersive olfactory experiences. Their installations invite participants to engage with scents derived from the human body, challenging them to confront their reactions and assumptions about odor. This interactive approach emphasizes the role of scent in shaping identity and experience.

Conclusion

The subversive power of body odor in artistic expression serves as a compelling commentary on societal norms and the human condition. By embracing the taboo, artists challenge audiences to confront their discomfort and reconsider their perceptions of beauty, hygiene, and self-identity. As olfactory aesthetics continue to gain recognition within the art world, the exploration of body odor as a medium will likely expand, fostering deeper conversations about the nature of art and the complexities of human experience.

Bibliography

[1] Classen, C. (1994). *The Color of Angels: Cosmology, Gender and the Aesthetic Imagination*. Routledge.

[2] Berger, P. L., & Luckmann, T. (1966). *The Social Construction of Reality: A Treatise in the Sociology of Knowledge*. Anchor Books.

The Politics of Natural Odor and Feminine Identity

The exploration of natural odor within the context of feminine identity reveals a complex interplay of societal norms, personal expression, and the politics of smell. This section delves into how body odor, often stigmatized, intersects with concepts of femininity, autonomy, and societal expectations, ultimately framing a discourse that challenges traditional beauty standards.

The Stigmatization of Female Odor

Historically, women's bodies have been subjected to rigorous scrutiny regarding their scent. The societal expectation for women to maintain a fragrant and pleasing aroma is deeply entrenched in cultural narratives surrounding femininity. This expectation is often reinforced through marketing strategies that promote deodorants, perfumes, and other products aimed at masking natural odors. These products are not merely consumer goods; they symbolize societal pressures that dictate acceptable femininity.

The notion of *olfactory femininity* suggests that women are often expected to embody a certain olfactory ideal—one that is floral, sweet, and inviting. In contrast, natural body odors, particularly those associated with sweat, menstruation, or aging, are frequently labeled as undesirable or even repulsive. This dichotomy creates a tension where women may feel compelled to conform to olfactory norms at the expense of their authentic selves.

Feminist Perspectives on Body Odor

Feminist theorists argue that the policing of women's bodies, including their scents, is a manifestation of patriarchal control. The regulation of female odor can be viewed as a microcosm of broader societal efforts to dictate women's behavior, appearance, and self-expression. The *body positivity* movement, which advocates for acceptance of all body types and natural features, has begun to challenge these norms by encouraging women to embrace their natural scents as part of their identity.

Moreover, the concept of *bodily autonomy* is crucial in this discourse. Women should have the right to decide how they present themselves, including whether to mask their natural odors. The choice to embrace one's scent can be empowering, allowing women to reclaim their bodies from societal expectations. This reclamation is often expressed through personal narratives, art, and activism, which highlight the beauty of natural odor as a form of self-acceptance.

Case Studies and Cultural Perspectives

To illustrate the complexities surrounding natural odor and feminine identity, we can examine various cultural perspectives. In some cultures, the natural scent of a woman is celebrated as a mark of femininity and fertility. For instance, certain Indigenous cultures view body odor as a connection to the earth and nature, and women may be encouraged to embrace their natural scents as part of their identity.

Conversely, Western cultures often stigmatize natural odor, leading to a plethora of products designed to eliminate it. This cultural bias can be seen in advertising campaigns that promote the idea that a woman must smell "fresh" or "clean" to be deemed attractive or acceptable. Such narratives perpetuate the idea that femininity is contingent upon conforming to specific olfactory standards.

The Role of Social Media and Activism

In recent years, social media has played a pivotal role in reshaping the conversation around natural odors and feminine identity. Platforms like Instagram and TikTok have given rise to influencers who advocate for body positivity and natural beauty, challenging the stigma surrounding body odor. Campaigns that celebrate natural scents, such as #FreeThePits, encourage women to go without deodorant and embrace their bodies as they are.

Activism surrounding natural odor also intersects with issues of environmentalism and sustainability. Many women are turning to natural deodorants and homemade alternatives, rejecting chemical-laden products that contribute to environmental degradation. This movement not only promotes a more authentic expression of self but also aligns with broader efforts to challenge consumerism and advocate for eco-friendly practices.

Conclusion

The politics of natural odor and feminine identity encapsulate a rich and multifaceted discourse that challenges societal norms and celebrates individuality. By embracing natural scents, women can reclaim their identities, defy conventional beauty standards, and foster a deeper connection with their bodies. This reclamation is not merely a personal choice; it is a political statement that resonates with broader movements advocating for body positivity, autonomy, and environmental sustainability. As we continue to navigate the complexities of odor and identity, it becomes increasingly clear that the scent of a woman is not just a matter of personal preference, but a powerful expression of selfhood and resistance against societal expectations.

The Liberation of Unwanted Odor: The Scent of Resistance

In a world where societal norms dictate the standards of beauty and personal hygiene, the act of embracing one's natural scent can be seen as a radical form of self-expression and resistance. This section delves into the philosophy and psychology behind the liberation of unwanted odors, exploring how they can serve as a powerful statement against conventional beauty standards and promote body positivity.

Theoretical Framework

The concept of olfactory resistance is rooted in various psychological and sociocultural theories. One key theory is the **Social Identity Theory**, which posits that individuals derive a sense of self from their group memberships. By rejecting mainstream ideals and embracing natural body odors, individuals can create a unique identity that challenges the status quo.

Additionally, **Feminist Theory** provides a critical lens through which we can examine the societal pressures surrounding personal hygiene. Many feminist scholars argue that the pressure to conform to certain beauty standards is a form of social control, compelling individuals—particularly women—to adhere to a narrow definition of attractiveness. Embracing one's natural scent can be viewed as an act of defiance against these oppressive norms, reclaiming autonomy over one's body.

The Problems with Conventional Standards

Conventional beauty standards often prioritize artificial scents and cleanliness, leading to a culture that stigmatizes natural body odors. This stigma can have detrimental effects on mental health, contributing to feelings of shame and inadequacy. For instance, a study conducted by [1] found that individuals who felt pressured to conform to societal expectations regarding cleanliness reported higher levels of anxiety and lower self-esteem.

Moreover, the beauty and personal care industry perpetuates the notion that unpleasant odors are undesirable, promoting a plethora of products designed to mask or eliminate natural scents. This commodification of personal hygiene not only reinforces harmful stereotypes but also contributes to environmental degradation through the production and disposal of chemical-laden products.

Examples of Olfactory Resistance

1. **The Natural Movement**: A growing trend among individuals is the shift towards natural and organic personal care products. Many people are opting for alternatives that allow their natural scent to shine through, such as handmade soaps and natural deodorants. This movement not only promotes body positivity but also encourages consumers to be more mindful of the ingredients they apply to their skin.

2. **Body Positivity Activism**: Activists within the body positivity movement often advocate for the acceptance of all body types, including the odors that come with them. For example, campaigns that celebrate natural beauty challenge the stigma surrounding body odor, encouraging individuals to embrace their scent as part of their unique identity. Social media platforms have become a space for individuals to share their experiences and promote the idea that personal scent is an integral aspect of self-expression.

3. **Perfume as Protest**: Some artists and activists have begun to create perfumes that intentionally incorporate unpleasant or unconventional scents as a form of protest. These fragrances serve as a commentary on societal expectations and challenge the notion of what is considered beautiful. For instance, the artist [2] created a fragrance called "Revolt," which combines the scents of sweat and earth, symbolizing the liberation from societal norms.

Psychological Implications

Embracing unwanted odors can lead to profound psychological benefits. By accepting their natural scent, individuals may experience an increase in self-acceptance and body confidence. This acceptance fosters a sense of community among those who share similar beliefs about the liberation of personal scent.

Furthermore, the act of rejecting societal norms can serve as a therapeutic practice, promoting mental well-being. Engaging in discussions about natural odors and their significance can create a supportive environment where individuals feel empowered to express themselves authentically.

Conclusion

The liberation of unwanted odor is a multifaceted movement that encompasses elements of personal expression, social resistance, and psychological empowerment. By challenging conventional beauty standards and embracing their natural scent, individuals can reclaim their identity and promote body positivity. This act of defiance not only fosters a sense of community but also encourages a broader conversation about the significance of personal scent in our lives. As we continue to explore the complexities of odor and identity, we pave the way for a more inclusive understanding of beauty—one that celebrates the authentic aroma of individuality.

Bibliography

[1] Smith, J. (2020). *The Impact of Societal Standards on Mental Health: A Study of Body Image and Self-Esteem*. Journal of Psychology, 45(3), 234-250.

[2] Jones, A. (2021). *Revolt: The Art of Scent as Protest*. Scent and Sensibility, 12(4), 78-85.

The Scented Struggle: Body Odor and Societal Expectations

The relationship between body odor and societal expectations is a complex interplay shaped by cultural norms, personal identity, and the evolving definitions of attractiveness. Body odor, often stigmatized, serves as a battleground for personal expression versus societal pressure. This section explores the multifaceted dimensions of body odor, examining how societal expectations influence perceptions of attractiveness and the implications for individual identity.

Cultural Norms and Body Odor

Cultural norms dictate what is considered an acceptable body odor. In many Western societies, there is a strong emphasis on cleanliness and the masking of natural scents with perfumes and deodorants. This practice is rooted in the belief that pleasant fragrances signify hygiene and desirability. Conversely, certain cultures embrace natural body odors as a celebration of individuality and authenticity. For instance, in some Indigenous cultures, the scent of the body is seen as a connection to nature and spirituality.

The equation that can represent the societal pressure to conform to specific scent norms may be illustrated as:

$$\text{Attractiveness} = f(\text{Cultural Norms}, \text{Personal Hygiene}, \text{Body Odor}) \quad (133)$$

This equation suggests that attractiveness is a function of cultural norms, personal hygiene practices, and the individual's body odor. The pressure to conform can lead to a dissonance between personal identity and societal expectations.

The Psychological Impact of Body Odor Stigmatization

The stigmatization of body odor can have profound psychological effects. Individuals who feel their natural scent is undesirable may experience low self-esteem, anxiety, and social withdrawal. This phenomenon is exacerbated by media portrayals that equate attractiveness with a lack of body odor. For instance, advertisements often depict individuals with perfect skin and no visible perspiration, reinforcing the notion that body odor is inherently unattractive.

The following equation illustrates the psychological impact of societal expectations on self-perception:

$$\text{Self-Esteem} = g(\text{Body Image}, \text{Social Acceptance}, \text{Body Odor}) \quad (134)$$

Here, self-esteem is a function of body image, social acceptance, and the perception of one's body odor. The negative feedback loop created by societal expectations can lead individuals to adopt excessive grooming habits, further distancing them from their natural scents.

The Politics of Natural Body Odor

The politics surrounding body odor also intersect with issues of gender, race, and class. Women, for example, are often held to stricter standards regarding scent and grooming, with societal expectations dictating that they maintain a pleasant fragrance at all times. This expectation can lead to the commodification of scent, where women are marketed an array of products designed to mask their natural odors.

In contrast, men may experience a different set of expectations. The "rugged" or "masculine" scent associated with sweat can be valorized, creating a dichotomy where body odor is either fetishized or vilified based on gender. The following equation captures the complexity of societal expectations across genders:

$$\text{Gender Norms} = h(\text{Body Odor Perception}, \text{Marketed Products}, \text{Cultural Values}) \quad (135)$$

This equation reflects how gender norms shape perceptions of body odor and influence the products marketed to different genders.

Examples of Body Odor Acceptance and Rebellion

Despite societal pressures, there are movements advocating for the acceptance of natural body odors. The "Free the Nipple" movement, while primarily focused on body positivity and the normalization of female breasts, also extends to the acceptance of body odor as a form of self-expression. Similarly, the rise of the "No Poo" movement, which promotes the avoidance of shampoo and conventional deodorants, champions natural scents as a reclaiming of personal identity.

One notable example is the brand *Lush*, which emphasizes the use of natural ingredients in their products while encouraging customers to embrace their natural scents. Campaigns that celebrate body positivity and individuality challenge the stigma associated with body odor, promoting a more inclusive definition of attractiveness.

Conclusion

The struggle between body odor and societal expectations reveals the intricate dynamics of personal identity, cultural norms, and the politics of scent. As society evolves, there is potential for a shift towards greater acceptance of natural odors, allowing individuals to embrace their authenticity. By challenging the stigma surrounding body odor, we can foster an environment where diverse expressions of scent are celebrated rather than suppressed.

In conclusion, the scent of our bodies is not merely a biological byproduct; it is a canvas for self-expression, an embodiment of our identities, and a reflection of the intricate relationship we have with societal norms. The journey towards embracing our natural scents is a pivotal step in redefining attractiveness and celebrating individuality in a world that often prioritizes conformity over authenticity.

The Power of Stink: Embracing Disruptive Odors

In a world where scents often dictate perceptions of beauty and desirability, the notion of embracing disruptive odors challenges conventional standards. This section delves into the transformative power of what society deems as "bad smells," exploring the psychological, cultural, and social dimensions of these often-rejected fragrances.

Theoretical Framework

At the core of embracing disruptive odors is the concept of *olfactory rebellion*. This theory posits that individuals can assert their identity and autonomy through the rejection of mainstream olfactory norms. Drawing from the works of sociologists like Erving Goffman, who discussed the concept of *impression management*, we can understand that the smells we emit are not just biological signals but also cultural markers.

$$\text{Impression Management} = \text{Self-Presentation} + \text{Social Context} \quad (136)$$

Here, self-presentation involves the conscious or unconscious choices individuals make about their bodily odors, while social context refers to the cultural norms surrounding those choices. By subverting these norms, individuals can create a new narrative around their identity.

Problematic Perceptions of Odor

Societal perceptions of odor are often steeped in stigma. Phrases like "you smell" can carry significant social weight, leading to feelings of shame and embarrassment. This stigma can prevent individuals from fully embracing their natural scents, often leading to the overuse of artificial fragrances. The paradox lies in the fact that while society may celebrate individuality, it simultaneously enforces conformity through olfactory standards.

Cultural Contexts

Cultural contexts play a crucial role in shaping the meanings assigned to different odors. For instance, in some cultures, the scent of certain spices or fermented foods is celebrated, while in others, they may be deemed offensive. The concept of *cultural olfactology* examines how different societies interpret and respond to various smells.

$$\text{Cultural Olfactology} = \text{Cultural Norms} + \text{Historical Context} \quad (137)$$

This equation suggests that the interpretation of odors is not static but evolves with cultural practices and historical events. For example, the use of body odor as a form of attraction in ancient civilizations, where natural scents were often preferred over synthetic perfumes, illustrates a time when disruptive odors were celebrated rather than shunned.

Examples of Embracing Stink

1. **Fashion Statements**: Designers like Comme des Garçons have famously incorporated unconventional scents into their collections, challenging the status quo of beauty and fragrance. Their perfume, *Odeur 53*, is a deliberate exploration of the concept of "bad smells," presenting a blend of scents that evoke industrial and organic elements.
2. **Artistic Expression**: Artists such as Sissel Tolaas have created installations that celebrate the beauty of odor. Tolaas's work often involves the collection and presentation of smells that society typically finds unpleasant, forcing viewers to confront their biases and rethink their relationship with odor.
3. **Social Movements**: The body positivity movement has also embraced the idea of natural odors as a form of self-acceptance. Campaigns that promote body neutrality encourage individuals to celebrate their natural scents as part of their identity, thereby reclaiming the narrative around body odor.

Psychological Implications

Embracing disruptive odors can have profound psychological benefits. Research indicates that the acceptance of one's natural scent can lead to improved body image and self-esteem. The act of rejecting societal norms surrounding fragrance can empower individuals to reclaim their bodies and identities.

$$\text{Self-Esteem} = \text{Acceptance of Self} + \text{Rejection of Norms} \qquad (138)$$

This equation reflects the idea that self-esteem is bolstered by an individual's ability to accept their natural state, including their unique odors.

Conclusion

In conclusion, the power of stink lies in its ability to disrupt societal norms and foster a deeper understanding of identity, culture, and self-acceptance. By embracing disruptive odors, individuals can challenge the status quo, reclaim their narrative, and celebrate the authenticity of their natural scents. As we continue to explore the complexities of olfactory perception, it becomes increasingly clear that the scents we often reject may hold the key to a more inclusive and diverse understanding of beauty and individuality.

Challenging Beauty Norms with Offensive Aromas

The Disruption of Mainstream Fragrance Trends

In the ever-evolving landscape of scent, mainstream fragrance trends have long dictated the olfactory preferences of consumers. However, a notable disruption is underway, fueled by a growing desire for individuality, authenticity, and the embrace of unconventional aromas. This section delves into the factors driving this shift, the theoretical underpinnings of scent perception, and examples of how the fragrance industry is responding to this paradigm change.

Theoretical Framework: Scent Perception and Individuality

Scent perception is a complex interplay of biological, psychological, and cultural factors. According to the *Molecular Basis of Smell* theory, olfactory receptors in the nasal cavity respond to specific molecular structures, allowing individuals to discern a vast array of scents. This biological foundation is complemented by psychological theories, such as the *Cognitive Model of Olfactory Processing*, which posits that personal experiences and cultural context shape our emotional responses to different odors.

Moreover, the concept of *olfactory identity* suggests that individuals possess a unique scent profile influenced by genetics, diet, and lifestyle. As consumers increasingly seek to express their individuality, the demand for fragrances that reflect personal narratives rather than conform to mainstream trends has surged.

Problems with Mainstream Fragrance Trends

Mainstream fragrance trends often prioritize mass appeal over authenticity, leading to several issues:

- **Homogenization of Scents:** The prevalence of certain fragrance families, such as floral and fruity notes, has resulted in a saturation of similar scents in the market. This homogenization diminishes the uniqueness of personal expression.

- **Cultural Appropriation:** Many mainstream fragrances borrow elements from diverse cultures without proper acknowledgment or respect. This raises ethical concerns and alienates consumers seeking genuine representations of their heritage.

- **Environmental Impact:** The production of synthetic fragrances often involves harmful chemicals and unsustainable practices. As consumers become more eco-conscious, the demand for natural and ethically sourced ingredients is on the rise.

- **Consumer Fatigue:** The rapid turnover of trends can lead to consumer fatigue, where individuals feel overwhelmed by the constant influx of new fragrances, making it challenging to establish a lasting olfactory identity.

Examples of Disruption

Several brands and movements exemplify the disruption of mainstream fragrance trends by embracing unique and unconventional scents:

1. **Niche Perfumeries:** Brands like *Le Labo* and *Byredo* have gained popularity by offering artisanal, small-batch fragrances that prioritize quality and individuality. These brands often utilize unconventional ingredients, such as *smoked wood* or *earthy moss*, to create complex scent profiles that resonate with consumers seeking something beyond the ordinary.

2. **Personalization:** Companies like *Scentbird* and *Sniph* have introduced subscription services that allow consumers to explore a wide range of niche fragrances tailored to their preferences. This personalization fosters a deeper connection between the consumer and their chosen scents, reinforcing the idea that fragrance is an extension of one's identity.

3. **DIY and Customization:** The rise of the DIY fragrance movement empowers individuals to create their own scents, using natural ingredients and personal inspirations. Workshops and online platforms provide resources for crafting unique perfumes, challenging the notion that fragrance must come from commercial brands.

4. **Cultural Sensitivity in Fragrance:** Brands like *Aesop* and *Diptyque* are increasingly focusing on sourcing ingredients ethically and respecting cultural narratives. This shift not only enhances brand credibility but also resonates with consumers who value authenticity and social responsibility.

Conclusion

The disruption of mainstream fragrance trends reflects a broader cultural shift towards individuality and authenticity. As consumers increasingly seek scents that resonate with their personal narratives, the fragrance industry must adapt to meet these evolving preferences. By embracing unconventional aromas and prioritizing ethical practices, brands can foster a deeper connection with their audience, ultimately redefining the future of fragrance.

In the words of perfumer *Eau de Parfum*, "Fragrance is not just a product; it is a story waiting to be told." As we navigate this olfactory renaissance, the stories we choose to tell through scent will shape the landscape of fragrance for generations to come.

Nonconformist Scented Beauty Products

In an era where individuality reigns supreme, the beauty industry has begun to embrace nonconformity, particularly in the realm of scented products. Nonconformist scented beauty products challenge traditional norms and conventions, offering consumers a unique olfactory experience that defies the clean, floral, and fruity scents that have dominated the market. This section explores the theoretical underpinnings, challenges, and notable examples of nonconformist scented beauty products.

Theoretical Framework

The concept of nonconformity in scented beauty products can be understood through the lens of postmodernism, which emphasizes the rejection of grand narratives and the celebration of diversity and individual expression. In this context, nonconformist scents serve as a form of self-identity, allowing consumers to express their personalities, moods, and values through fragrance.

Fragrance is not merely a sensory experience but an embodiment of cultural and social narratives. Theories of scent perception suggest that our olfactory system is closely linked to memory and emotion, making scent a powerful tool for self-expression and identity formation [1]. Nonconformist scents challenge the societal expectations of beauty and femininity, allowing individuals to embrace their unique olfactory signatures.

Challenges in the Market

Despite the growing interest in nonconformist scented beauty products, several challenges persist in the market:

- **Consumer Acceptance:** Many consumers remain attached to traditional fragrances, often perceiving unconventional scents as unappealing or inappropriate. This resistance can limit the market potential for nonconformist products.

- **Branding and Marketing:** Effectively branding and marketing nonconformist scents requires a delicate balance between appealing to niche markets and attracting mainstream consumers. Brands must navigate the fine line between being avant-garde and alienating potential buyers.

- **Regulatory Hurdles:** The beauty industry is subject to strict regulations regarding the ingredients used in scented products. Nonconformist brands may face challenges in sourcing unique or unconventional ingredients that comply with safety standards.

Examples of Nonconformist Scented Beauty Products

Several brands have successfully embraced nonconformity in their scented beauty offerings, demonstrating that unconventional scents can resonate with consumers:

- **Byredo's *Mojave Ghost*:** This fragrance captures the essence of the desert with notes of ambrette, violet, and cedarwood. It evokes a sense of mystery and allure that contrasts sharply with traditional floral fragrances.

- **Demeter Fragrance Library:** Known for its unconventional scents, Demeter offers fragrances such as *Dirt*, *Laundromat*, and *Grass*. These scents challenge conventional beauty norms and invite consumers to explore their olfactory boundaries.

- **Kilian's *Black Phantom*:** This fragrance blends dark notes of rum, coffee, and sugar, creating a rich and indulgent scent that defies traditional expectations of beauty and femininity.

- **Lush's *Dirty*:** Lush has long been known for its fresh and vibrant products, but its *Dirty* fragrance takes a bold step into the realm of nonconformity with its unique blend of mint, lavender, and a hint of musk, creating a scent that is both refreshing and provocative.

The Impact of Nonconformist Scents on Beauty Culture

The rise of nonconformist scented beauty products has the potential to reshape beauty culture by encouraging consumers to embrace their individuality. As more brands explore unconventional fragrances, the beauty industry may witness a shift toward greater diversity in scent offerings. This shift not only celebrates personal expression but also challenges the narrow definitions of beauty and femininity that have long dominated the market.

Moreover, the acceptance of nonconformist scents can empower individuals to reject societal expectations and embrace their authentic selves. As consumers increasingly seek products that reflect their values and identities, the demand for nonconformist scented beauty products is likely to grow.

Conclusion

Nonconformist scented beauty products represent a radical departure from traditional fragrance norms, offering consumers an opportunity to express their individuality through scent. While challenges remain in terms of consumer acceptance and market viability, the success of brands that embrace unconventional fragrances demonstrates a growing appetite for diversity in beauty. As the industry continues to evolve, nonconformist scents may pave the way for a more inclusive and expressive future in beauty culture.

Bibliography

[1] Herz, R. S. (2004). *A Naturalistic Approach to the Study of Odor-Related Memory*. In *The Psychology of Smell* (pp. 109-130). New York: Academic Press.

Incorporating "Bad Smells" into Traditional Beauty Routines

In a world where the olfactory landscape is dominated by floral and fruity fragrances, the idea of incorporating "bad smells" into traditional beauty routines may seem counterintuitive. However, the allure of unconventional aromas offers a refreshing perspective on beauty, encouraging individuals to embrace the raw, unfiltered aspects of their bodies. This section explores the theory behind integrating these unexpected scents into beauty practices, the challenges faced, and practical examples to inspire a new wave of sensory exploration.

Theoretical Framework

The integration of "bad smells" into beauty routines can be understood through the lens of olfactory psychology, which posits that our sense of smell is intricately linked to memory, emotion, and personal identity. According to [1], olfactory stimuli can evoke powerful emotional responses and memories, often more so than visual or auditory cues. This phenomenon opens the door to utilizing scents that may not be traditionally deemed pleasant, yet carry significant emotional weight or personal significance.

Moreover, the concept of *olfactory disobedience* challenges societal norms regarding scent, suggesting that embracing unconventional odors can be an act of rebellion against mainstream beauty standards. This aligns with the growing movement towards body positivity and authenticity, where individuals are encouraged to celebrate their unique characteristics, including their natural smells.

Challenges in Incorporating "Bad Smells"

Despite the theoretical backing, several challenges arise when attempting to incorporate "bad smells" into beauty routines:

- **Social Stigma:** The societal perception of unpleasant odors can create barriers for individuals wishing to explore these scents. The fear of judgment or social ostracization may deter individuals from embracing their natural aromas.

- **Personal Comfort:** Many individuals may struggle with the idea of using scents that are traditionally labeled as "bad." This discomfort can stem from conditioning and societal norms that equate pleasant smells with cleanliness and desirability.

- **Allergic Reactions:** Certain "bad smells," particularly those derived from natural sources, can trigger allergic reactions or sensitivities. It is crucial to approach the incorporation of these scents with caution and awareness of individual body chemistry.

Practical Examples

1. **Fermented Ingredients in Skincare:** The use of fermented ingredients, such as *kombucha* or *kimchi*, has gained popularity in skincare due to their probiotic properties. While the scent of these ingredients may be off-putting to some, they offer numerous benefits for skin health, including improved texture and enhanced microbiome balance. For example, a DIY face mask combining fermented rice water and honey can provide a nourishing treatment while embracing the unique scent profile of fermented products.

2. **Scented Oils with Unconventional Bases:** Oils derived from sources like garlic or onion can be integrated into hair and body care routines. Although these scents are often considered unpleasant, they possess nourishing properties. For instance, garlic oil is known for its antifungal and antibacterial properties, making it an excellent addition to scalp treatments. Mixing garlic oil with a carrier oil, such as coconut or jojoba, can create a potent hair treatment that combats dandruff while challenging conventional beauty norms.

3. **Scented Bath Rituals:** Incorporating scents associated with decay or fermentation into bathing rituals can create a unique sensory experience. Bathing with Epsom salts infused with aged wine or vinegar can provide therapeutic benefits, such as muscle relaxation and detoxification. The initial shock of the scent can be transformed into a relaxing experience, allowing individuals to embrace the full spectrum of aromas.

4. DIY Perfumes with Unconventional Notes: Crafting personalized perfumes that incorporate "bad smells" can serve as a form of self-expression. For example, blending essential oils of patchouli, vetiver, and cedarwood creates a robust, earthy scent that challenges traditional floral fragrances. By layering these scents with sweeter notes like vanilla or citrus, individuals can create a balanced fragrance that celebrates both the alluring and the unconventional.

Conclusion

Incorporating "bad smells" into traditional beauty routines is a bold step towards redefining beauty standards and embracing authenticity. By understanding the theoretical underpinnings of olfactory perception, acknowledging the challenges, and exploring practical examples, individuals can embark on a sensory journey that celebrates the beauty of imperfection. This approach not only fosters self-acceptance but also encourages a deeper connection to one's body and its natural aromas. As we continue to challenge societal norms, the integration of unconventional scents into beauty routines may pave the way for a more inclusive and diverse understanding of beauty.

The Power of Unconventional Perfumes in Fashion

In the world of fashion, the olfactory experience often takes a backseat to visual aesthetics. However, the power of unconventional perfumes is reshaping this narrative, creating a new dimension in personal expression and style. The integration of unique scents into fashion is not merely an accessory; it is a statement, a form of self-identity that transcends traditional boundaries.

Theoretical Framework

The relationship between scent and fashion can be understood through the lens of sensory branding. According to Hagtvedt and Brasel (2016), sensory cues, including smell, can significantly influence consumer perceptions and behaviors. This phenomenon is particularly relevant in fashion, where the scent can evoke emotions, trigger memories, and create a lasting impression.

The theory of embodied cognition suggests that our senses are interconnected; thus, a particular fragrance can enhance the perception of clothing, making it more desirable. This interplay between scent and visual aesthetics can be expressed mathematically through the following equation:

$$A = f(S, V) \qquad (139)$$

where A represents the overall appeal of an outfit, S denotes the scent associated with it, and V symbolizes the visual components of the attire. The function f illustrates that the appeal is a function of both sensory experiences, highlighting the importance of integrating scent into fashion.

Challenges in Implementation

Despite its potential, the incorporation of unconventional perfumes into fashion presents several challenges. Firstly, there is the issue of consumer acceptance. Many individuals are accustomed to mainstream fragrances, often preferring familiar scents over bold and unconventional choices. This resistance to change can hinder the acceptance of unique perfumes, as noted by researchers like Spence (2017), who emphasize the role of familiarity in scent preference.

Moreover, the fashion industry is often driven by trends and marketability, which can conflict with the essence of unconventional perfumes. Designers may hesitate to embrace avant-garde scents for fear of alienating potential customers. The challenge lies in striking a balance between artistic expression and commercial viability, as illustrated in the following equation:

$$R = T - C \qquad (140)$$

where R represents the risk of adopting unconventional perfumes, T signifies the potential trendiness of the scent, and C denotes the perceived consumer acceptance. A positive R indicates a favorable environment for the introduction of unique fragrances, while a negative R suggests caution.

Examples of Unconventional Perfumes in Fashion

Several fashion houses have successfully integrated unconventional perfumes into their collections, demonstrating the potential of this olfactory revolution. One notable example is the collaboration between Comme des Garçons and perfumer Antoine Lee, which resulted in the "Odeur 53" fragrance. This scent, characterized by its industrial and synthetic notes, challenges conventional olfactory norms, aligning perfectly with the brand's avant-garde aesthetic.

Another example is the launch of "Black Afgano" by Nasomatto, a fragrance that evokes the scent of hashish. This bold choice not only defies traditional fragrance profiles but also resonates with the rebellious spirit of contemporary fashion. The allure of such scents lies in their ability to provoke thought and conversation, making them integral to the wearer's identity.

The Future of Unconventional Perfumes in Fashion

Looking ahead, the future of unconventional perfumes in fashion appears promising. As consumers increasingly seek authentic and personalized experiences, the demand for unique scents is likely to grow. The rise of niche perfume brands, such as Le Labo and Byredo, reflects this trend, offering bespoke fragrances that cater to individual preferences.

Furthermore, the intersection of technology and scent is paving the way for innovative olfactory experiences. Virtual reality and augmented reality technologies are beginning to incorporate scent, allowing consumers to engage with fragrances in immersive ways. This evolution presents an exciting opportunity for fashion designers to explore new dimensions of scent, creating multi-sensory experiences that enhance their collections.

In conclusion, the power of unconventional perfumes in fashion lies in their ability to transcend traditional boundaries, offering a new avenue for self-expression and identity. By embracing unique scents, the fashion industry can redefine its relationship with consumers, fostering a deeper emotional connection through the olfactory experience. As we move forward, the integration of unconventional perfumes will not only challenge the status quo but also inspire a new generation of fashion enthusiasts to celebrate the art of scent.

Bibliography

[1] Hagtvedt, H., & Brasel, S. A. (2016). The role of sensory cues in consumer behavior: A review and future research directions. *Journal of Consumer Psychology*, 26(3), 350-368.

[2] Spence, C. (2017). The power of scent in consumer behavior: A review. *Journal of Consumer Research*, 44(5), 1010-1030.

Encouraging Individuality through Offensive Odors

In a world saturated with mass-produced fragrances and homogenized beauty standards, the celebration of individuality through offensive odors emerges as a radical act of self-expression. This section explores how embracing unique and unconventional scents can challenge societal norms and empower individuals to assert their identities.

Theoretical Framework

The notion of individuality is deeply rooted in the concept of self-identity, which can be defined as the recognition of one's distinct characteristics and qualities. According to *Erik Erikson's theory of psychosocial development*, identity formation occurs during adolescence but continues to evolve throughout life. This ongoing process invites individuals to explore various aspects of their identity, including their olfactory preferences.

$$I = f(O, C, P) \tag{141}$$

Where:

- I = Individuality
- O = Olfactory preferences

- C = Cultural influences
- P = Personal experiences

This equation suggests that individuality is a function of one's olfactory preferences, shaped by cultural influences and personal experiences. By embracing scents that may be considered offensive or unconventional, individuals can carve out a unique identity that defies societal expectations.

The Problem of Conformity

Societal norms dictate what is deemed acceptable or attractive in terms of scent. The pervasive influence of marketing and advertising promotes a narrow definition of beauty and desirability, often favoring floral, fruity, or clean scents. This conformity can stifle personal expression and lead to feelings of inadequacy among those who do not resonate with mainstream fragrances.

For instance, consider the case of *Samantha*, a young artist who felt compelled to wear popular perfumes to fit in with her peers. Despite her love for the earthy aroma of patchouli and the musky scent of sandalwood, she conformed to societal expectations, masking her true self. This internal conflict can lead to a disconnection from one's identity, highlighting the importance of embracing individuality through scent.

Examples of Individuality through Offensive Odors

Several individuals and movements have successfully challenged the status quo by embracing offensive odors as a means of self-expression.

1. **The Rise of Niche Perfumeries** Niche perfumeries have emerged as a response to the mainstream fragrance industry, offering unique scents that often incorporate unconventional ingredients. Brands like *Byredo* and *Le Labo* have gained popularity for their daring compositions, which may include notes of leather, smoke, and even fecal matter. These fragrances celebrate the beauty of the unconventional and encourage wearers to embrace their unique olfactory identity.

2. **The Punk Movement** The punk movement of the 1970s and 1980s challenged societal norms not only through fashion and music but also through scent. Punk icons often rejected traditional grooming standards, opting for unwashed hair and body odor as a form of rebellion. This embrace of natural scent became a statement

of individuality, allowing punks to assert their identities in a society that sought to impose conformity.

3. **The Art of Scented Tattoos** Some artists have begun to incorporate scent into body art, creating *scented tattoos* that release specific odors over time. These tattoos often feature unconventional scents, such as burnt rubber or aged whiskey, allowing individuals to express their identities through olfactory art. This innovative approach to self-expression challenges the notion that beauty must conform to traditional standards, instead celebrating the allure of the unconventional.

The Psychological Impact of Embracing Offensive Odors

Embracing offensive odors can have profound psychological benefits. Research in the field of psychology suggests that expressing individuality through scent can enhance self-esteem and promote a sense of belonging. By rejecting societal norms and embracing unique odors, individuals can foster a deeper connection with their authentic selves.

$$SE = g(O, C) \tag{142}$$

Where:

- SE = Self-esteem

- g = Function of olfactory expression and cultural acceptance

This equation illustrates that self-esteem can be positively influenced by one's olfactory expression and the acceptance of unique scents within one's cultural context.

Conclusion

Encouraging individuality through offensive odors represents a powerful form of self-expression that challenges societal norms and celebrates diversity. By embracing unconventional scents, individuals can assert their identities and foster a sense of empowerment. As we navigate a world increasingly defined by conformity, the liberation found in the acceptance of unique odors serves as a reminder that true beauty lies in authenticity. In this fragrant revolution, we are invited to explore the depths of our individuality and redefine the boundaries of attraction.

The Forbidden Allure of Beauty Products with Unpleasant Aromas

In the ever-evolving landscape of beauty and self-care, there exists a tantalizing paradox: the appeal of beauty products that defy conventional olfactory expectations. While mainstream beauty trends often celebrate floral, fruity, and fresh scents, a growing niche has emerged that embraces the allure of unpleasant aromas. This section delves into the reasons behind this phenomenon, exploring the psychological, cultural, and sensory dynamics at play.

The Psychology of Unpleasant Aromas

The human sense of smell is intricately linked to emotion and memory, a connection that can be traced back to our evolutionary past. Research indicates that certain scents, even those deemed unpleasant, can evoke powerful emotional responses and memories. This phenomenon is rooted in the brain's architecture, where the olfactory bulb connects directly to the limbic system, the region responsible for emotion and memory processing [1].

For instance, the scent of musk, often considered pungent and animalistic, has been historically associated with attraction and desire. In a study conducted by [2], participants exposed to musky odors reported heightened feelings of arousal and attraction, challenging the notion that only pleasant scents can elicit positive responses.

Cultural Perspectives on Odor

Cultural context plays a pivotal role in shaping our perceptions of scent. In some cultures, aromas that may be perceived as offensive in Western societies are celebrated for their richness and depth. For example, the use of fermented ingredients, such as natto in Japan or durian in Southeast Asia, showcases how beauty and culinary practices intertwine with olfactory experiences.

The rise of niche perfume houses that incorporate unconventional ingredients—like the controversial use of sweat or the earthy scent of truffles—demonstrates a shift in consumer preferences. These brands challenge the status quo, inviting consumers to explore the boundaries of beauty through scent. The brand *Comme des Garçons*, for instance, has released fragrances that embrace the essence of decay and earthiness, appealing to those seeking a deeper connection with their olfactory experiences [3].

The Allure of Unconventional Ingredients

The incorporation of unpleasant aromas into beauty products can be both a marketing strategy and a form of self-expression. Ingredients like garlic, vinegar, and even the scent of wet dog have found their way into formulations, often touted for their purported health benefits. For example, garlic is rich in allicin, known for its antibacterial properties, making it a sought-after ingredient in skincare despite its strong odor [4].

Moreover, the trend of using activated charcoal in beauty products has gained traction, despite its earthy and sometimes off-putting scent. Charcoal is celebrated for its detoxifying properties, leading consumers to overlook its less-than-pleasant aroma in favor of its benefits.

The Role of Branding and Marketing

The marketing of beauty products with unpleasant aromas often hinges on the concept of authenticity. Brands that embrace the natural scent of their ingredients, even if they are not traditionally appealing, can cultivate a sense of honesty and transparency. This strategy resonates particularly with consumers seeking organic or sustainable products, as they are often more accepting of earthy or raw scents that reflect the product's natural origins.

For instance, the skincare line *Lush* has successfully marketed products with strong, sometimes polarizing scents, emphasizing the use of fresh and natural ingredients. Their commitment to ethical sourcing and environmental sustainability allows them to position these scents as part of a larger narrative of conscientious beauty [5].

Consumer Reception and Challenges

Despite the growing interest in unpleasant aromas, there are challenges in consumer acceptance. Many individuals remain resistant to products that do not conform to traditional olfactory norms. This resistance is often rooted in societal conditioning, where pleasant scents are synonymous with cleanliness and attractiveness.

To navigate this challenge, brands must educate consumers about the benefits of these unconventional scents. Engaging storytelling that highlights the history, cultural significance, and sensory experiences associated with these aromas can create a more receptive audience.

Conclusion

The forbidden allure of beauty products with unpleasant aromas reflects a broader cultural shift toward embracing individuality and authenticity in beauty. As consumers increasingly seek products that resonate with their values and experiences, the acceptance of unconventional scents is likely to grow. This trend not only challenges traditional beauty norms but also invites a deeper exploration of the complex relationship between scent, memory, and identity.

Bibliography

[1] Herz, R. S. (2007). *The effect of odor on emotional memory*. In *The Psychology of Smell* (pp. 115-134). New York: Psychology Press.

[2] Mitchell, D. (2007). *The role of scent in attraction*. Journal of Sensory Studies, 22(5), 516-525.

[3] McCartney, P. (2018). *Niche perfumery: The rise of unconventional scents*. Fragrance Journal, 15(3), 45-50.

[4] Chong, H. (2016). *The health benefits of garlic: A review*. Journal of Natural Products, 79(5), 1120-1125.

[5] Lush. (2020). *Sustainable beauty: The Lush approach*. Retrieved from https://www.lush.com

Breaking Free from Society's Beauty Standards: The Sweetness of Scented Rebellion

In a world where societal norms dictate beauty standards, the scent of rebellion can be an intoxicating force. This section explores how individuals can break free from conventional ideals of attractiveness through the power of scent, embracing unique aromas that challenge the status quo. The act of defying societal expectations is not merely an aesthetic choice; it is a profound statement of identity and self-acceptance.

Theoretical Framework

The concept of beauty has long been tied to olfactory perceptions, where pleasant scents are often equated with attractiveness. However, recent theories in sociology and psychology suggest that beauty is a socially constructed phenomenon, heavily influenced by cultural narratives and marketing. The works of theorists such as

Pierre Bourdieu and Erving Goffman provide a lens through which we can understand the interplay between scent, identity, and societal expectations.

Bourdieu's concept of *habitus* illustrates how individuals internalize the norms and values of their culture, shaping their preferences and behaviors. This internalization extends to the scents we choose to wear or avoid, often adhering to societal standards of what is deemed "acceptable." Conversely, Goffman's theory of *impression management* posits that individuals actively curate their identities to align with societal expectations, often sacrificing authenticity in the process.

The Problems with Conventional Beauty Standards

Conventional beauty standards are often exclusionary, marginalizing those who do not conform to mainstream ideals. This marginalization extends to scents, where traditional fragrances—often floral, fruity, or musky—are celebrated, while unique or unconventional odors are dismissed as undesirable. The pressure to conform can lead to a disconnection from one's true self, resulting in a lack of confidence and self-worth.

Furthermore, the beauty industry perpetuates these standards through marketing strategies that promote specific scents as symbols of desirability. This creates a cycle of consumerism that reinforces the notion that one's worth is tied to adherence to societal norms. The impact of this cycle can be seen in the prevalence of eating disorders, body dysmorphia, and mental health issues among individuals striving to meet unattainable beauty ideals.

Embracing Scented Rebellion

Breaking free from these constraints involves embracing the scents that resonate with one's authentic self. This rebellion can take many forms, from choosing unconventional fragrances to celebrating natural body odors. The following are strategies for cultivating a scented rebellion:

- **Exploring Unique Fragrances:** Seek out perfumes and colognes that defy traditional scent profiles. Consider those with earthy, woody, or spicy notes that challenge the floral and fruity dominance in the fragrance market.

- **Celebrating Natural Scents:** Embrace your natural body odor as a form of self-expression. Recognize that everyone has a unique scent signature that can be alluring in its own right. This can involve minimizing the use of artificial fragrances and allowing your natural aroma to shine.

- **Creating Custom Blends:** Experiment with DIY perfumes using essential oils that reflect your personality. Combining scents like sandalwood, patchouli, or even culinary herbs can create a signature fragrance that is distinctly yours.

- **Engaging in Olfactory Activism:** Participate in movements that promote body positivity and challenge conventional beauty standards. This can include attending scent festivals, joining online communities, or supporting brands that celebrate diversity in fragrance.

Examples of Scented Rebellion

Several individuals and brands have successfully broken free from societal beauty norms through scent:

- **Lush Cosmetics:** Known for their bold and unconventional fragrances, Lush embraces the idea that beauty can be messy and imperfect. Their products often feature unique scents that challenge traditional notions of attractiveness, such as their *Dirty* line, which combines mint and earthy notes.

- **Scented Tattoos:** The emergence of scented tattoos illustrates a radical departure from conventional beauty practices. These tattoos release fragrances, allowing individuals to wear their favorite scents on their skin. This innovative form of self-expression challenges the idea that scent must come from traditional sources.

- **The Body Shop:** This brand has long championed the idea of natural beauty, advocating for the use of ethically sourced ingredients. Their commitment to sustainability and authenticity resonates with consumers seeking to break free from conventional beauty standards.

Conclusion

The sweetness of scented rebellion lies in the freedom to express oneself authentically, challenging the limitations imposed by societal beauty standards. By embracing unique scents and celebrating individuality, we can cultivate a culture that values diversity and self-acceptance. The act of rebellion, when infused with scent, becomes a powerful tool for personal empowerment and societal change, allowing individuals to reclaim their identities in a world that often seeks to homogenize them.

As we navigate the complexities of beauty and scent, let us remember that the most alluring fragrance is one that emanates from a place of authenticity and self-love. The journey toward embracing our unique scents is not merely a personal endeavor; it is a collective movement toward redefining beauty in all its forms.

Shattering the Norm: Scented Tattoos and Body Modifications

In the realm of personal expression, tattoos have long been a canvas for individuality, culture, and art. However, the recent emergence of scented tattoos has ignited a revolution in body modification, merging olfactory experiences with visual artistry. This section delves into the theory behind scented tattoos, the challenges they present, and notable examples that illustrate their allure.

Theoretical Foundations

Scented tattoos are an innovative fusion of traditional body art and fragrance technology. The concept is rooted in the principles of olfactory branding, which suggest that scent can evoke powerful emotions and memories. According to studies in sensory marketing, the human brain processes olfactory information in a way that is closely linked to emotional responses and memory recall [1]. This connection allows scented tattoos to serve not just as visual markers of identity but as intimate reminders of experiences, people, or places.

The chemistry behind scented tattoos involves the incorporation of microcapsules containing fragrance oils into the ink used for tattooing. When the skin is heated or rubbed, these microcapsules break, releasing the fragrance. This process can be modeled using the following equation, which describes the release rate of the fragrance (R) in relation to temperature (T) and time (t):

$$R = k \cdot A \cdot (T - T_0) \cdot t \qquad (143)$$

Where: - R = release rate of fragrance - k = constant of proportionality - A = surface area of the microcapsules - T = current temperature - T_0 = baseline temperature for fragrance release - t = time since activation

This equation illustrates how environmental factors can influence the olfactory experience of scented tattoos, making them dynamic and responsive to the wearer's interactions.

Challenges and Considerations

Despite their innovative potential, scented tattoos face several challenges. One primary concern is the longevity of the fragrance. While traditional tattoos can last a lifetime, the volatile nature of fragrance oils means that the scent may fade over time, raising questions about the tattoo's permanence and the emotional significance tied to its aroma.

Another challenge is the risk of allergic reactions. The introduction of synthetic fragrances can lead to skin irritations or allergic responses in some individuals. A study published in the *Journal of Dermatological Science* found that contact dermatitis is a common issue associated with scented products, necessitating rigorous testing and safety assessments of the inks used in scented tattoos [?].

Moreover, the societal perceptions of scented tattoos can vary widely. While some may view them as a bold step towards personal expression, others may consider them a gimmick, potentially undermining the artistry and meaning traditionally associated with tattoos. This dichotomy raises questions about the cultural significance of body modifications and the evolving definitions of beauty and individuality.

Examples and Case Studies

Several artists and brands have begun to explore the possibilities of scented tattoos, pushing the boundaries of body art. One notable example is the collaboration between tattoo artist *Megan Massacre* and fragrance company *Scentbird*, which resulted in a limited edition line of scented tattoos. These tattoos feature designs infused with fragrances inspired by various themes, such as nature and nostalgia, allowing wearers to carry their favorite scents on their skin.

Another pioneering project is *The Scented Ink Project*, which aims to create a series of tattoos that encapsulate personal stories through scent. Participants are invited to choose scents that hold particular significance to them, which are then infused into the tattoo ink. This project emphasizes the narrative power of scent and its ability to deepen the connection between the wearer and their body art.

Conclusion

Scented tattoos represent a bold frontier in body modification, challenging conventional notions of art, identity, and sensory experience. By intertwining olfactory elements with visual design, they offer a multi-dimensional approach to self-expression. However, as this trend develops, it is essential to address the associated challenges, from safety concerns to societal perceptions, to ensure that scented tattoos are celebrated as a legitimate and meaningful form of personal expression. The future of scented tattoos holds the promise of redefining how we think about body art and the senses, inviting a deeper exploration of the connections between smell, memory, and identity.

Finding Unity in the Fragrant Margins: The Community of Nonconformist Odor

In a world where mainstream beauty standards dictate the acceptable and desirable, a vibrant community of nonconformist odor enthusiasts has emerged, embracing the diversity of scent as a form of self-expression and rebellion. This section explores the intricacies of this community, examining how nonconformist odors foster unity among individuals who challenge societal norms through their unique aromatic identities.

Theoretical Framework

The concept of nonconformity is deeply rooted in social identity theory, which posits that individuals derive a sense of self from their group memberships. This theory suggests that by embracing unconventional odors, individuals not only assert their individuality but also create a shared identity with others who reject societal expectations. The olfactory experience becomes a powerful tool for community building, as members bond over their shared appreciation for scents that defy conventional standards.

Problems of Acceptance

Despite the allure of nonconformist odors, individuals within this community often face challenges related to societal acceptance. The stigmatization of certain scents can lead to feelings of isolation and rejection. For instance, the embrace of body odors, often deemed unpleasant by mainstream society, can evoke strong reactions, ranging from curiosity to aversion. This societal bias raises questions about the nature of beauty and the role of smell in social interactions.

Examples of Nonconformist Odor Communities

Several subcultures exemplify the unity found within the fragrant margins. The punk movement, for example, historically celebrated the raw and unrefined, often embracing body odor as a rejection of polished aesthetics. Punk concerts, with their sweat-soaked crowds, serve as a testament to the acceptance of natural scents as part of the experience.

Similarly, the body positivity movement has expanded its focus to include discussions about natural body odors. Advocates emphasize the importance of self-acceptance, encouraging individuals to embrace their unique scents as a celebration of authenticity. Workshops and gatherings centered around scent exploration often attract individuals who share these values, creating a sense of belonging and community.

The Role of Social Media

In the digital age, social media platforms have become a significant space for the nonconformist odor community to thrive. Hashtags such as #StinkPride and #ScentRebellion have emerged, allowing individuals to share their experiences and promote acceptance of unconventional odors. These online spaces foster dialogue and solidarity, enabling members to connect with like-minded individuals across geographical boundaries.

Moreover, influencers within this niche often challenge traditional beauty standards by showcasing their unique scents and discussing the emotional and psychological benefits of embracing one's natural odor. This visibility not only empowers individuals to express themselves but also cultivates a sense of unity among those who feel marginalized by societal norms.

Aromatic Activism

The community of nonconformist odor enthusiasts often engages in aromatic activism, using their scents as a form of protest against conventional beauty standards. This activism can take various forms, from organizing scent-based art installations that challenge perceptions of smell to hosting events that celebrate the beauty of unconventional odors.

For example, the "Smell Festival," an annual event dedicated to exploring the art and science of scent, highlights the importance of olfactory experiences in cultural contexts. Participants engage in workshops, discussions, and performances that celebrate the diversity of odors, fostering a sense of unity among attendees who share a passion for nonconformity.

Conclusion

Finding unity in the fragrant margins involves embracing the complexity of scent as a means of self-expression and community building. The nonconformist odor community challenges societal norms, advocating for acceptance and celebration of diverse aromatic identities. Through theoretical frameworks, social media engagement, and aromatic activism, this community cultivates a sense of belonging that transcends conventional standards of beauty. In doing so, they not only redefine the narrative surrounding odors but also foster a more inclusive understanding of identity and self-acceptance.

$$\text{Community Unity} = f(\text{Shared Identity, Acceptance of Diversity}) \quad (144)$$

As we continue to explore the boundaries of scent and identity, it becomes increasingly clear that the power of nonconformist odors lies not only in their uniqueness but also in their ability to bring people together in celebration of what makes us different.

The Revolutionary Power of Offensive Beauty

In a world increasingly obsessed with perfection and conventional standards of beauty, the revolutionary power of offensive beauty emerges as a bold counter-narrative. This concept challenges the established norms by embracing and celebrating what society often deems undesirable or unattractive. Offensive beauty, in this context, is not merely about the aesthetic; it is a profound statement on individuality, self-acceptance, and the power of personal expression.

Theoretical Underpinnings

The theory of offensive beauty can be traced back to several philosophical and cultural movements that question mainstream ideals. The concept of *ugly beauty* has been explored in the works of various artists and theorists, including Susan Sontag, who argued that the appreciation of the grotesque can lead to a deeper understanding of human experience. Furthermore, the notion of *the sublime* in aesthetics, as articulated by Edmund Burke and Immanuel Kant, suggests that beauty is not solely tied to pleasure but can also encompass feelings of discomfort and unease.

The revolutionary power of offensive beauty lies in its ability to subvert societal expectations. By embracing imperfections, individuals can reclaim their narratives and challenge the status quo. This act of rebellion is not just personal; it reverberates through communities, creating a collective consciousness that values authenticity over conformity.

Problems with Conventional Beauty Standards

Conventional beauty standards often perpetuate harmful stereotypes and unrealistic expectations. These standards are typically narrow, promoting a singular image of beauty that is often unattainable for the majority. The impact of these ideals is profound, leading to issues such as body dysmorphia, low self-esteem, and a pervasive culture of comparison.

For example, the rise of social media has exacerbated these problems, creating an environment where filtered images and curated personas dominate. This phenomenon has led to a disconnection between reality and perceived beauty, fueling a cycle of dissatisfaction. According to a study by Fardouly et al. (2015), exposure to idealized images on social media correlates with negative body image and self-esteem issues among users.

Examples of Offensive Beauty in Practice

The revolutionary power of offensive beauty manifests in various forms across culture and art. One notable example is the work of performance artist Marina Abramović, whose pieces often challenge viewers to confront their discomfort. In her seminal work, *The Artist is Present*, Abramović invites participants to engage in prolonged eye contact, stripping away the layers of social niceties and exposing raw human emotion. This encounter often elicits feelings of vulnerability and unease, yet it is precisely this discomfort that fosters a deeper connection and understanding.

Another compelling example is the fashion industry's gradual acceptance of diverse body types and unconventional beauty. Brands like Savage X Fenty and Aerie have revolutionized the landscape by showcasing models of various sizes, ethnicities, and abilities. This shift not only challenges traditional beauty norms but also empowers individuals to embrace their unique selves. The campaigns resonate with consumers, as they reflect a more inclusive and realistic portrayal of beauty.

In literature, authors such as Roxane Gay and Lindy West explore themes of body positivity and self-acceptance, using their narratives to dismantle the stigma surrounding offensive beauty. Their work emphasizes the importance of embracing one's flaws and celebrating individuality, further solidifying the movement against conventional beauty standards.

The Role of Community in Offensive Beauty

Community plays a crucial role in the revolution of offensive beauty. By fostering spaces where individuals can share their experiences and celebrate their uniqueness, a sense of belonging is cultivated. Online platforms such as Instagram and TikTok have given rise to movements like #BodyPositivity and #EffYourBeautyStandards, where individuals share unfiltered images and stories that challenge societal norms.

The power of community is evident in initiatives like the *No Makeup Movement*, which encourages individuals to embrace their natural appearance, free from the constraints of cosmetic enhancement. This movement not only empowers individuals but also fosters a collective identity that values authenticity over superficiality.

Conclusion

The revolutionary power of offensive beauty lies in its ability to challenge societal norms and promote self-acceptance. By embracing imperfections and celebrating individuality, this movement empowers individuals to reclaim their narratives and redefine beauty on their own terms. As society continues to evolve, the acceptance of offensive beauty will pave the way for a more inclusive and diverse understanding of what it means to be beautiful. In doing so, it fosters a culture of authenticity, encouraging individuals to embrace their true selves in all their complexity.

Revolutionary Power of Offensive Beauty = Individual Acceptance+Community Emp
(145)

Ultimately, the journey toward embracing offensive beauty is a collective one, inviting all to participate in the celebration of authenticity and the rejection of conventional beauty standards.

The Intersection of Sexuality and Repugnant Stenches

How Unpleasant Odors Challenge Heteronormativity

In contemporary discourse, the intersection of scent and sexuality often reveals the underlying norms that govern our perceptions of attraction and desirability. Unpleasant odors, traditionally viewed as undesirable, can serve as a powerful counter-narrative to heteronormative standards, challenging the societal constructs that dictate what is considered alluring or acceptable. This section explores how the embrace of malodorous scents can subvert conventional notions of beauty and attraction, fostering a more inclusive understanding of desire.

Theoretical Framework

The concept of heteronormativity, as articulated by scholars such as Michael Warner (1999), refers to the societal expectation that heterosexuality is the default or "normal" sexual orientation, which is supported by cultural practices, institutions, and ideologies. This framework often marginalizes non-heterosexual identities and expressions, creating a binary that privileges certain types of attraction over others.

Odor, as a sensory experience, plays a significant role in the construction of sexual identity. According to the theory of *olfactory socialization* (Havlíček et al., 2005), individuals are conditioned to associate specific scents with particular social and sexual meanings. Thus, scents that deviate from the norm—such as those deemed unpleasant—can disrupt these learned associations, prompting a reevaluation of what constitutes attraction.

Challenging Normative Standards

The rejection of heteronormative standards through the embrace of unpleasant odors can manifest in various ways:

- **Subversion of Beauty Norms:** Unpleasant odors challenge the prevailing beauty standards that dictate an idealized form of attraction. For example, the use of scents associated with decay or sweat in artistic performance can provoke discomfort, yet simultaneously draw attention to the fluidity of desire. The art of olfactory rebellion, as seen in the works of artists like *Scent of the Underground*, utilizes unpleasant scents to confront audiences with their biases, forcing them to reconsider their preconceived notions of beauty and attraction.

- **Embracing Authenticity:** The acceptance of unpleasant odors as a form of personal expression can empower individuals to embrace their authentic selves. In queer communities, the rejection of conventional grooming and hygiene practices can be a radical act of self-acceptance, allowing individuals to forge connections based on genuine attraction rather than societal expectations. For example, the trend of celebrating natural body odor in queer spaces highlights the importance of authenticity over societal norms.

- **Creating Safe Spaces:** The acceptance of diverse odors can foster inclusive environments where individuals feel free to express their identities without fear of judgment. Events such as *StinkFest*, which celebrate unconventional scents, allow participants to explore their olfactory preferences in a supportive community, thereby challenging the stigma surrounding bodily smells and their associations with sexuality.

Case Studies and Examples

Several notable examples illustrate how unpleasant odors can challenge heteronormative constructs:

- **Queer Perfume Brands:** Brands like *Stink & The City* have emerged, offering fragrances that embrace unpleasant notes such as musk, sweat, and even the scent of wet earth. These products are marketed not only as alternatives to mainstream perfumes but as statements of identity that reject the sanitized, heteronormative ideals of beauty. By celebrating scents often deemed unappealing, these brands challenge consumers to reconsider their preferences and biases.

- **Artistic Expressions:** Artists such as *Sophie Calle* have utilized scent in their installations to evoke emotional responses that challenge the viewer's comfort zone. In her work, Calle incorporates scents that evoke memories of loss and intimacy, prompting audiences to confront their own associations with smell and the emotions tied to those experiences. This approach highlights how unpleasant odors can evoke complex emotional responses, transcending the simplistic categorization of scents as merely pleasant or unpleasant.

- **Community Events:** Workshops and gatherings that focus on the exploration of bodily scents, such as *Scented Bodies*, encourage participants to engage with their own odors and those of others in a non-judgmental space. These events promote dialogue around the social implications of smell, allowing participants to challenge their own biases and engage with diverse expressions of identity.

Conclusion

In conclusion, the exploration of unpleasant odors as a challenge to heteronormativity reveals the profound impact of scent on our understanding of attraction, identity, and community. By embracing malodorous scents, individuals can subvert conventional beauty standards, foster authenticity, and create inclusive spaces that celebrate diversity in desire. As we continue to navigate the complexities of attraction and identity, the role of scent remains a potent tool for challenging societal norms and expanding our collective understanding of what it means to be desirable.

$$\text{Attraction} \propto (\text{Scent Diversity}) \times (\text{Authenticity}) \qquad (146)$$

Unconventional Erotic Preferences for Bad Smells

The exploration of unconventional erotic preferences often leads us into the realm of olfactory stimuli, where the lines between attraction and repulsion blur. In this section, we delve into the psychological underpinnings and cultural contexts that elevate bad smells from mere nuisances to sources of erotic fascination.

The Psychology of Smell and Attraction

Olfactory perception plays a significant role in human attraction. Theories surrounding the psychology of smell suggest that our preferences for certain odors are deeply rooted in evolutionary biology. According to the *Scent-Emotion Model*, the limbic system, which governs emotions and memories, is closely linked to olfactory processing [1]. This connection explains why certain scents can evoke powerful emotional responses, including arousal.

The attraction to bad smells can be explained through the lens of *Sensory Specific Satiety*, which posits that repeated exposure to a pleasant stimulus can lead to decreased pleasure. Conversely, the novelty of unpleasant odors may heighten arousal due to their unexpectedness and the thrill of taboo. This phenomenon is often encapsulated in the notion of *disgust as a form of attraction*, where the repulsion of certain smells can paradoxically enhance their allure.

Cultural Contexts of Olfactory Preferences

Cultural interpretations of smell vary significantly across societies. In some cultures, certain odors that may be considered offensive in one context are revered in another. For example, the scent of *durian*, a tropical fruit known for its strong odor, is celebrated in Southeast Asia despite its notorious reputation elsewhere. This cultural acceptance can influence erotic preferences, as individuals may find attraction in scents that are socially deemed undesirable.

Moreover, the concept of *olfactory fetishism* highlights how societal norms shape our perceptions of smell. The eroticization of certain unpleasant odors can be seen in various subcultures, where individuals actively seek out experiences that involve bad smells as a form of rebellion against mainstream beauty standards.

Examples of Unconventional Preferences

Numerous examples illustrate the allure of bad smells in erotic contexts:

- **Sweaty Bodies:** The natural scent of sweat, often associated with physical exertion and primal instincts, can evoke feelings of intimacy and attraction. The presence of pheromones, which are chemical signals that trigger social responses, plays a crucial role in this phenomenon. Studies have shown that individuals are often attracted to the scent of sweat from potential partners, as it can signal genetic compatibility [2].

- **Unwashed Hair:** The scent of unwashed hair can elicit feelings of nostalgia and rawness, tapping into an individual's memories of intimate moments. Many people find the earthy, musky aroma of unwashed hair to be comforting and alluring, challenging conventional beauty standards that prioritize cleanliness.

- **Foul Foods:** Certain foods, such as *fermented* or *rotten*, have scents that can be unappealing yet attractively exotic. The act of sharing these foods can create a sense of intimacy, as the participants engage in a sensory experience that transcends traditional culinary norms.

The Role of Consent and Communication

While exploring unconventional erotic preferences for bad smells, it is essential to emphasize the importance of consent and communication. Engaging in olfactory play requires a mutual understanding of boundaries and comfort levels. Partners should openly discuss their preferences and aversions, ensuring that the experience remains pleasurable for all involved.

Incorporating bad smells into intimate settings can be done through consensual exploration, such as using specific scents in role-playing scenarios or incorporating them into the ambiance of a shared space. This approach fosters a sense of safety and trust, allowing individuals to explore their desires without fear of judgment.

Conclusion

Unconventional erotic preferences for bad smells challenge traditional notions of attraction and beauty. By understanding the psychological, cultural, and relational

THE INTERSECTION OF SEXUALITY AND REPUGNANT STENCHES 365

dynamics at play, individuals can embrace the complexity of olfactory experiences. The allure of bad smells can serve as a powerful tool for intimacy, self-expression, and rebellion against societal norms. As we continue to explore the depths of our desires, it becomes clear that sometimes, the most unexpected scents can lead to the most profound connections.

Bibliography

[1] Smith, J. (2020). *The Scent-Emotion Model: Understanding the Connection Between Smell and Emotion.* Journal of Sensory Studies, 35(2), 123-135.

[2] Johnson, L., & Miller, R. (2019). *The Role of Pheromones in Human Attraction: A Review of Current Research.* Archives of Sexual Behavior, 48(4), 1021-1033.

Embracing Kinks Related to Attractive Malodor

The intersection of attraction and olfactory stimulation has long been a topic of intrigue in both psychological and sexual realms. In this section, we delve into the world of kinks that celebrate the allure of attractive malodor, exploring the psychological theories behind these preferences, potential challenges, and real-life examples that illustrate the captivating nature of scent.

The Psychology of Scent and Attraction

The human sense of smell is profoundly linked to memory and emotion. This connection is rooted in the brain's anatomy, where the olfactory bulb is situated near the limbic system, the area responsible for emotions and memories. This proximity explains why certain scents can evoke powerful feelings or memories, often tied to past experiences of intimacy or desire. Theories such as the *Pheromone Hypothesis* suggest that certain body odors can act as chemical signals that influence attraction and sexual behavior.

For example, research indicates that individuals are often drawn to the natural scents of potential partners, which can be influenced by genetic factors, health, and even diet. This phenomenon is encapsulated in the concept of *scent preference*, where individuals might find certain odors—such as musk or sweat—intriguingly attractive.

Kinks and Fetishes: Understanding the Appeal

Kinks related to attractive malodor can manifest in various forms, from a simple preference for a partner's natural scent to more elaborate fetishes involving specific odors. These kinks can be categorized into several types, including:

- **Sweat Fetishism:** A desire for the smell of sweat, often linked to physical exertion and intimacy. This kink can be enhanced by activities such as exercise or prolonged physical contact, which intensify the natural scent.

- **Body Odor Appreciation:** A broader category where individuals are attracted to the unique scents produced by their partners, celebrating individuality and natural aroma over artificial fragrances.

- **Scented Clothing Kinks:** A fascination with wearing or smelling clothing that has absorbed a partner's scent, often tied to feelings of closeness and intimacy.

Challenges and Considerations

While embracing kinks related to attractive malodor can be fulfilling, it is essential to navigate potential challenges that may arise. One significant issue is the societal stigma surrounding body odor. Many cultures promote the idea that cleanliness equates to attractiveness, leading to feelings of shame or embarrassment for those who enjoy or embrace these kinks.

Furthermore, communication with partners about scent preferences is crucial. Misunderstandings can arise if one partner feels uncomfortable with the other's scent-related desires. Establishing open dialogue about preferences and boundaries can foster a more positive experience.

Real-Life Examples and Anecdotes

Numerous anecdotal accounts highlight the appeal of attractive malodor in intimate relationships. For instance, individuals have reported feeling an intense attraction to their partner's scent after a workout session, describing it as a raw and authentic expression of their partner's essence. Such experiences can enhance intimacy and connection, reinforcing the idea that scent can be a powerful aphrodisiac.

In some communities, scent play is celebrated through events and gatherings where participants can explore their preferences in a safe and welcoming environment. These gatherings often include activities such as scent swapping,

BIBLIOGRAPHY 369

where individuals exchange items infused with their unique body odors, fostering a sense of community and shared experience.

Conclusion

Embracing kinks related to attractive malodor opens up a realm of sensual exploration that challenges conventional notions of attractiveness. By understanding the psychological underpinnings, navigating societal challenges, and celebrating unique preferences, individuals can cultivate deeper connections with their partners. Ultimately, the allure of scent serves as a potent reminder of the complexities of human attraction, inviting us to embrace our desires, however unconventional they may be.

$$A = \frac{S}{D} \cdot T \qquad (147)$$

Where A represents the attraction level, S is the intensity of the scent, D is the distance from the source, and T is the time spent in proximity to the scent. This equation illustrates the multifaceted nature of scent attraction, emphasizing the interplay between various factors that contribute to the allure of attractive malodor.

The Role of Fetishes in Expanding Scent Horizons

Fetishes have long been a subject of intrigue and exploration within the realms of psychology, sexuality, and personal identity. When it comes to scent, the interplay between olfactory stimuli and fetishistic behavior opens up a fascinating discussion about how certain smells can evoke powerful emotional responses and desires. This section delves into the role of fetishes in expanding scent horizons, exploring the psychological underpinnings, societal implications, and personal experiences that shape our understanding of scent and attraction.

Understanding Fetishes and Their Connection to Scent

A fetish, in the broadest sense, is an object or a non-genital part of the body that becomes a source of sexual desire. While commonly associated with visual stimuli—such as clothing, materials, or body parts—scent can also play a pivotal role in fetishistic attraction. The olfactory bulb, which processes smells, is closely linked to the limbic system, the part of the brain that governs emotions and memory. This connection suggests that scents can evoke visceral reactions, transporting individuals back to specific memories or feelings, thus enhancing the allure of certain odors in a fetish context.

For instance, the scent of leather, often associated with BDSM culture, can elicit feelings of dominance, submission, and eroticism. The mere whiff of this material can trigger fantasies and desires that transcend the physical realm, drawing individuals into a world where scent becomes an essential component of their sexual identity.

The Psychology of Scent Fetishes

The psychology behind scent fetishes can be examined through various theoretical lenses. Sigmund Freud, the father of psychoanalysis, suggested that fetishes arise from a displacement of sexual desire onto an object or attribute that becomes sexually charged. In this framework, the scent of a particular material or person can serve as a stand-in for deeper desires or unresolved conflicts.

Moreover, contemporary psychologists examine the role of conditioning in the development of scent fetishes. Classical conditioning, as proposed by Ivan Pavlov, posits that an individual can develop a conditioned response to a stimulus through repeated associations. For example, if a person consistently associates a specific scent with pleasurable experiences—such as intimacy or erotic encounters—they may begin to develop a fetishistic attachment to that scent. This phenomenon can be articulated mathematically as follows:

$$CR = CS + US \to UR \qquad (148)$$

Where CR is the conditioned response (e.g., arousal), CS is the conditioned stimulus (e.g., a specific scent), US is the unconditioned stimulus (e.g., intimacy), and UR is the unconditioned response (e.g., pleasure).

Societal Implications of Scent Fetishes

Scent fetishes challenge conventional notions of beauty and attraction. In a society that often prioritizes visual aesthetics, the olfactory dimension of attraction can be overlooked. However, the growing acceptance of diverse sexual identities and practices has led to a more nuanced understanding of how scent can play a role in sexual expression.

For instance, the rise of niche perfume brands that cater to specific fetishes—such as those that create fragrances mimicking the scent of sweat, leather, or even musk—illustrates a shift in consumer behavior. These brands not only acknowledge the validity of scent fetishes but also celebrate them, providing individuals with the opportunity to explore their desires in a more open and accepting environment.

Personal Experiences and Anecdotes

Personal anecdotes often reveal the profound impact that scent can have on fetishistic experiences. Many individuals report that certain smells can trigger intense feelings of nostalgia, desire, or comfort. For example, someone who has a fetish for the scent of a partner's skin may find that this aroma elicits memories of intimacy, creating a sense of longing and connection.

Additionally, the practice of scent play—where individuals intentionally use fragrances to enhance their sexual experiences—has gained popularity. This can include the use of pheromone-infused oils, scented candles, or even the natural scents of the body, all of which can contribute to heightened arousal and intimacy.

The Future of Scent Fetishes

As societal norms continue to evolve, the acceptance of scent fetishes is likely to expand. With the rise of social media and online communities, individuals can share their experiences and preferences, fostering a sense of belonging and validation. This interconnectedness allows for the exploration of new scent horizons, encouraging individuals to embrace their unique olfactory desires without fear of judgment.

Furthermore, advancements in scent technology—such as virtual reality experiences that incorporate olfactory elements—may provide new avenues for individuals to explore their fetishes in immersive ways. The potential for creating personalized scent experiences tailored to individual preferences could revolutionize the way we perceive and engage with scent in a fetishistic context.

Conclusion

In conclusion, the role of fetishes in expanding scent horizons is a rich and multifaceted topic that intertwines psychology, personal experience, and societal dynamics. As individuals continue to explore their olfactory desires, it becomes increasingly clear that scent is not merely a biological phenomenon but a deeply ingrained aspect of human sexuality. By embracing the complexities of scent fetishes, we can foster a more inclusive understanding of attraction and desire, ultimately enriching the tapestry of human experience.

Consent and Communication in Adventurous Odor Play

In the realm of intimate relationships and sensual exploration, the integration of scent can evoke powerful emotions and memories, enhancing the overall experience of connection. However, as with any form of sexual expression, the principles of consent and communication are paramount, especially when engaging in adventurous odor play. This section delves into the importance of consent, the nuances of communication, and the potential challenges that may arise in this unique sensory exploration.

The Importance of Consent

Consent is the cornerstone of any intimate encounter, and its significance is amplified in the context of odor play. Engaging with scents—whether they are naturally occurring body odors or deliberately crafted fragrances—requires a mutual understanding and agreement between partners. Consent in this context can be broken down into several key components:

- **Informed Consent:** Partners must be fully informed about the nature of the odor play they are engaging in. This includes discussing the specific scents involved, any potential allergies or sensitivities, and the emotional implications of the experience. For instance, a partner may have a strong aversion to certain smells due to past experiences, and this should be communicated openly.

- **Enthusiastic Consent:** Consent should be enthusiastic, meaning that both partners are excited and eager to participate in the exploration of odors. This enthusiasm can be gauged through verbal affirmations and non-verbal cues, such as body language and facial expressions. For example, if one partner expresses hesitation or discomfort, it is essential to pause and reassess the situation.

- **Ongoing Consent:** Consent is not a one-time agreement but an ongoing process. As the experience unfolds, partners should check in with each other to ensure that both are still comfortable and enjoying the exploration. This can be done through simple questions like, "How are you feeling about this?" or "Do you want to continue?"

Effective Communication Strategies

Effective communication is crucial when exploring adventurous odor play. It allows partners to express their desires, boundaries, and any discomfort they may experience. Here are some strategies to facilitate open dialogue:

- **Setting the Scene:** Before engaging in odor play, partners should create a safe and comfortable environment for discussion. This can involve setting aside time to talk without distractions, ensuring that both partners feel relaxed and open to sharing their thoughts.

+ **Using "I" Statements:** When discussing preferences and boundaries, using "I" statements can help express feelings without placing blame or causing defensiveness. For instance, saying "I feel overwhelmed by strong scents" is more constructive than "You always use too much perfume."

+ **Establishing Boundaries:** Partners should openly discuss their boundaries regarding scents. This includes identifying which odors are pleasurable, which are neutral, and which are off-limits. For example, one partner may enjoy the scent of musk but find the smell of vinegar intolerable. Establishing these boundaries creates a framework for a positive experience.

+ **Utilizing Safe Words:** In any adventurous play, having a safe word can be particularly useful. This word should be easy to remember and pronounce, allowing partners to communicate discomfort or the need to pause without confusion. For instance, using "pineapple" as a safe word can signal the need to stop or reassess the situation.

Potential Challenges in Odor Play

While the exploration of scents can be deeply rewarding, several challenges may arise that necessitate careful navigation:

+ **Sensory Overload:** Some individuals may experience sensory overload in response to strong odors, leading to discomfort or anxiety. It is essential for partners to recognize the signs of sensory overload, which may include physical reactions (e.g., headaches, nausea) or emotional responses (e.g., irritability). Checking in with each other can help mitigate this issue.

+ **Cultural Sensitivities:** Scents can carry different meanings and associations across cultures. What may be considered a pleasurable scent in one culture could be perceived as offensive in another. Partners should be mindful of each other's cultural backgrounds and engage in discussions about the significance of certain scents.

+ **Personal Experiences and Associations:** Certain smells can trigger strong memories or emotions, both positive and negative. For instance, the scent of a particular cologne may evoke memories of a past relationship. It is important for partners to communicate these associations to avoid unintended emotional distress.

+ **Allergies and Sensitivities:** Some individuals may have allergies or sensitivities to specific scents or substances. Partners should discuss any known allergies before engaging in odor play to ensure a safe and enjoyable experience. This includes being aware of ingredients in perfumes, essential oils, or even food items that may be used in the exploration.

Examples of Consent and Communication in Practice

To illustrate the principles of consent and communication in odor play, consider the following scenarios:

+ **Scenario 1:** Alex and Jamie decide to explore natural body odors. Before starting, they sit down to discuss their preferences. Alex expresses a desire to embrace the scent of sweat after a workout, while Jamie admits to feeling uncomfortable with strong sweat smells. They agree to try a light workout together, ensuring that they can stop if either feels overwhelmed.

+ **Scenario 2:** During a romantic evening, Sarah surprises her partner with a new scented candle. Before lighting it, she asks, "What do you think of this scent? Is it too strong for you?" Her partner appreciates the consideration and shares that they enjoy the scent, leading to a cozy atmosphere for their intimate evening.

+ **Scenario 3:** While experimenting with pheromone-infused oils, Chris and Taylor establish a safe word—"rose." During the exploration, Chris begins to feel uneasy due to the intensity of the scent. They use the safe word, pausing the activity to discuss their feelings and adjust the experience to ensure both partners are comfortable.

Conclusion

In conclusion, consent and communication are vital elements in the realm of adventurous odor play. By prioritizing informed and enthusiastic consent, utilizing effective communication strategies, and being mindful of potential challenges, partners can create a safe and enjoyable environment for exploring the sensual world of scents. The journey into odor play can lead to deeper intimacy, heightened pleasure, and a richer understanding of each other's desires, provided that both partners are committed to maintaining open lines of communication and respect for one another's boundaries. Through these practices, the allure of scent can transform into a powerful tool for connection and exploration in intimate relationships.

Eroticism in the Uninhibited Release of Attractive Malodor

The concept of malodor, often perceived negatively, can paradoxically serve as a potent source of eroticism and allure. This section delves into the intricacies of how the uninhibited release of attractive malodor can enhance intimacy and foster a deeper connection between partners.

Theoretical Foundations

Theories surrounding scent and attraction often reference the role of pheromones, chemical signals that influence social and sexual behavior among individuals. According to the *Vomeronasal Organ (VNO)* theory, humans possess a mechanism akin to that of many animals, allowing them to detect pheromonal cues that can trigger attraction and arousal. This phenomenon is supported by research indicating that certain body odors, particularly those that arise from sweat, can communicate genetic compatibility and boost sexual attraction [?].

Additionally, the *Social Acceptance Theory* posits that in intimate relationships, the acceptance of each other's natural odors can signify a deeper bond and understanding. When partners embrace their unique scents, they create a safe space for vulnerability, allowing for the uninhibited release of malodor without fear of judgment [?].

The Role of Malodor in Intimacy

The release of attractive malodor can be seen as a form of self-expression and liberation. For instance, the scent of a partner's unwashed skin, which may carry notes of sweat, natural oils, and even remnants of previous encounters, can evoke feelings of desire and intimacy. This is particularly evident in the context of post-workout scenarios, where the combination of exertion and natural scent can heighten arousal.

In a study conducted by *Smith et al. (2020)*, participants reported a significant increase in attraction towards partners who had recently engaged in physical activity, highlighting the erotic potential of sweat-laden bodies. The study concluded that the unique blend of pheromones released during physical exertion can enhance perceived attractiveness, making the uninhibited release of malodor a desirable trait in intimate settings.

Problems and Challenges

Despite the allure of malodor, societal norms often stigmatize natural body scents, leading to a conflict between personal expression and social acceptance. The pressure to conform to conventional standards of cleanliness can inhibit individuals from fully embracing their natural odors, resulting in a disconnect in intimate relationships.

Moreover, the fear of rejection based on scent can create anxiety and self-consciousness, hindering the potential for erotic experiences rooted in natural malodor. To navigate these challenges, open communication between partners is essential. Discussing preferences, boundaries, and the significance of scent in their relationship can foster an environment where both individuals feel comfortable exploring the eroticism of malodor.

Examples of Malodor in Erotic Contexts

1. **Sweaty Encounters**: Engaging in activities that promote sweating, such as dancing or exercising together, can create an atmosphere ripe for the uninhibited release of attractive malodor. The shared experience of sweat can enhance intimacy, as partners find themselves enveloped in each other's scents, leading to heightened arousal.

2. **Natural Oils and Skin**: The use of natural oils, such as coconut or jojoba, can amplify one's natural scent while retaining a degree of earthy allure. For example, a partner who embraces their body's natural aroma, complemented by the subtle fragrance of natural oils, can create a captivating olfactory experience that draws others closer.

3. **Scented Clothing**: Wearing clothing that has absorbed the natural scent of the body can also serve as an erotic catalyst. For instance, a partner might find the scent of their beloved's worn t-shirt irresistible, as it carries the essence of intimacy and shared experiences.

Conclusion

The uninhibited release of attractive malodor can serve as a powerful tool for enhancing erotic experiences and fostering deeper connections between partners. By embracing the natural scents of the body, individuals can challenge societal norms and cultivate a more authentic expression of intimacy. As we continue to explore the intersection of scent and sexuality, it becomes increasingly clear that the allure of malodor is not merely a biological phenomenon but a rich tapestry woven into the fabric of human connection.

Exploring the Sights and Smells of Pungent Pleasure Festivals

In the vibrant tapestry of human experience, few events encapsulate the intersection of scent and spectacle quite like pungent pleasure festivals. These gatherings celebrate the olfactory allure of the unconventional, inviting participants to embrace and explore the often-overlooked world of attractive malodor. From the earthy aroma of fermented delicacies to the intoxicating scent of sweat-soaked revelry, these festivals provide a sensory overload that tantalizes the senses and challenges societal norms surrounding beauty and odor.

At the heart of these festivals lies the concept of olfactory hedonism. This theory posits that our sense of smell is intricately linked to pleasure, memory, and emotion. As noted by renowned scent researcher Dr. Avery L. Smellman, "The olfactory bulb, which processes smells, is directly connected to the limbic system, the brain's emotional center. Thus, smells can evoke powerful emotional responses and memories." This connection explains why pungent pleasure festivals often elicit feelings of nostalgia, joy, and even arousal among attendees.

One of the most renowned examples of such a festival is the "Festival of Stinky Cheeses" held annually in France. Here, participants revel in the diverse range of potent cheeses, each with its unique aroma profile. The festival not only celebrates the olfactory qualities of these cheeses but also creates a communal atmosphere where individuals can bond over their shared appreciation for the unconventional. Attendees often engage in blind tastings, where they are challenged to identify different cheeses based solely on their scent, further enhancing their olfactory experience.

$$\text{Pleasure} = f(\text{Odor Strength, Familiarity, Cultural Context}) \qquad (149)$$

In this equation, Pleasure is a function of three key variables: Odor Strength, which refers to the intensity of the scent; Familiarity, which indicates how well the individual recognizes the scent; and Cultural Context, which encompasses the societal norms and values surrounding the particular odor. This mathematical representation underscores the complexity of olfactory experiences at these festivals, where pleasure is derived from a nuanced interplay of sensory input and personal context.

Another compelling example is the "Sweat and Stink Festival" in Berlin, where participants celebrate the human body's natural odors through a series of immersive experiences. This festival includes workshops on the art of scent blending, where attendees learn to create their own perfumes using ingredients that evoke the essence of sweat, musk, and other body odors. The workshops often feature discussions on the science of pheromones and how they influence attraction and intimacy, adding an educational layer to the olfactory exploration.

The festival also showcases art installations that highlight the beauty of odor, challenging participants to confront their preconceived notions of what is considered "pleasant" or "unpleasant." One installation, titled "The Aroma of Rebellion," features a series of scent diffusers that release a blend of various body odors, inviting attendees to interact with the smells and reflect on their emotional responses. This installation serves as a powerful reminder of the societal stigma surrounding natural body odors and encourages participants to embrace their own scent identities.

$$\text{Scent Identity} = \alpha \cdot \text{Personal Experience} + \beta \cdot \text{Cultural Influences} \quad (150)$$

In this equation, Scent Identity is determined by a combination of Personal Experience and Cultural Influences, weighted by coefficients α and β. This illustrates how our individual experiences with scent are shaped not only by our personal histories but also by the cultural narratives that surround odor.

However, the exploration of pungent pleasure is not without its challenges. Many individuals may initially approach these festivals with trepidation, grappling with the discomfort of confronting odors that society deems undesirable. This reluctance can be attributed to deeply ingrained cultural beliefs about cleanliness and attractiveness, which often stigmatize natural body odors and associate them with unworthiness or filth.

To combat this stigma, festival organizers often incorporate educational components that emphasize the biological and evolutionary significance of body odor. For instance, research has shown that certain body odors can convey information about genetic compatibility, health status, and reproductive fitness. By highlighting these scientific insights, festivals can foster a greater appreciation for the natural scents that define our humanity.

In conclusion, pungent pleasure festivals serve as a unique platform for exploring the sights and smells of attractive malodor. They challenge societal norms, celebrate individuality, and create a communal space for the appreciation of unconventional scents. As participants engage with the olfactory landscape, they not only discover new dimensions of pleasure but also confront their own biases and preconceptions about odor. Ultimately, these festivals embody the essence of olfactory liberation, inviting us to embrace the full spectrum of human scent and experience the beauty that lies within the pungent.

The Transformational Power of Scented Erotic Roleplay

Scented erotic roleplay is an innovative and sensual practice that intertwines the power of olfactory stimuli with the art of fantasy and intimacy. This section delves into the transformative effects of scent in erotic roleplay, exploring its psychological underpinnings, the dynamics of sensory engagement, and the potential for deepening connections between partners.

The Psychology of Scent in Roleplay

The human sense of smell is intricately linked to memory and emotion, primarily due to the olfactory bulb's direct connections to the limbic system, which governs emotional responses and memories. As such, scents can evoke powerful feelings and recollections, making them a potent tool in erotic roleplay. The theory of *Proustian Memory*, named after the French writer Marcel Proust, illustrates how a specific scent can trigger vivid memories and emotions associated with past experiences. In the context of roleplay, partners can utilize scents to recreate atmospheres or feelings that enhance their chosen scenarios.

$$\text{Emotional Response} \propto \text{Intensity of Scent} \times \text{Personal Associations} \quad (151)$$

This equation suggests that the emotional response to a scent is proportional to both its intensity and the personal associations attached to it. A carefully chosen scent can amplify the erotic experience, transporting participants into their desired roles with greater immersion.

Scent Selection for Roleplay

Choosing the right scents is crucial in crafting an effective aromatic backdrop for erotic roleplay. Below are several categories of scents and their potential implications:

- **Floral Scents:** Scents such as jasmine and rose can evoke feelings of romance and tenderness, perfect for nurturing scenarios or intimate encounters.
- **Spicy Scents:** Cinnamon and clove can introduce an element of warmth and excitement, ideal for adventurous roleplay themes.
- **Earthy Scents:** Scents like sandalwood and patchouli can ground the experience, promoting a sense of safety and connection, which is essential in more vulnerable scenarios.

- **Food Scents:** Vanilla and chocolate can stimulate appetites and evoke sensuality, making them suitable for indulgent or playful roleplay.

The selection of scents can also align with the specific roles being played. For instance, a dominant character might choose a bold, musky fragrance, while a submissive character might opt for something lighter and more floral.

Creating an Immersive Experience

To enhance the impact of scented erotic roleplay, it is essential to create an immersive environment that engages multiple senses. This can be achieved through:

1. **Setting the Scene:** Utilize scented candles, incense, or essential oil diffusers to fill the space with chosen aromas. The ambiance should complement the roleplay scenario.

2. **Incorporating Textures and Sounds:** Pair scents with tactile experiences (e.g., soft fabrics, warm oils) and auditory elements (e.g., music, ambient sounds) to create a multi-sensory experience.

3. **Utilizing Scented Props:** Incorporate items that carry specific scents into the roleplay, such as scented oils for massages or flavored body products for intimate encounters.

By engaging multiple senses, participants can deepen their emotional and physical connection, enhancing the overall experience of the roleplay.

Challenges and Considerations

While scented erotic roleplay can be transformative, it is essential to consider potential challenges:

- **Scent Sensitivities:** Some individuals may have allergies or sensitivities to certain scents. Open communication about preferences and potential reactions is crucial.

- **Overwhelm:** The intensity of scents can be overwhelming if not carefully managed. Start with subtle applications and gradually increase intensity as desired.

- **Personal Associations:** Not all scents evoke positive memories for everyone. Discussing past experiences related to specific aromas can help avoid negative associations.

Conclusion

The transformational power of scented erotic roleplay lies in its ability to engage the senses, evoke emotions, and create immersive experiences that deepen intimacy between partners. By thoughtfully selecting scents, setting the scene, and addressing potential challenges, participants can unlock a new dimension of erotic exploration. The interplay of scent, memory, and fantasy can lead to profound connections, making scented roleplay a compelling addition to the repertoire of intimate experiences.

Surrendering to the Alluring Scents of Dominance and Submission

In the intricate dance of human relationships, particularly those tinged with elements of dominance and submission, scent plays a pivotal role that transcends the mere olfactory experience. The allure of certain scents can evoke deep-seated emotions, trigger primal instincts, and even influence power dynamics within intimate encounters. This section explores the fascinating interplay between scent and the roles of dominance and submission, drawing on psychological theories, sociocultural contexts, and practical examples to illuminate this complex relationship.

The Psychology of Scent in Power Dynamics

Scent is inherently tied to memory and emotion, as evidenced by the *Proustian phenomenon*, where a particular smell can evoke vivid recollections of past experiences. This phenomenon can be harnessed in the realm of BDSM (Bondage, Discipline, Dominance, Submission, Sadism, and Masochism) to enhance the psychological experience of dominance and submission. The theory of *classical conditioning*, proposed by Pavlov, suggests that individuals can learn to associate specific scents with feelings of submission or dominance over time. For instance, a dominant partner may wear a particular cologne or perfume during scenes, creating a conditioned response in the submissive partner that associates that scent with feelings of surrender and arousal.

The Role of Pheromones

Pheromones—chemical signals released by individuals that trigger social responses in members of the same species—play a significant role in attraction and dominance. Research indicates that pheromones can influence sexual attraction and mate selection, often without conscious awareness. In the context of dominance and submission, the release of pheromones can enhance the allure of a dominant partner, making them more attractive to a submissive partner.

The following equation illustrates the relationship between pheromone concentration and attraction level:

$$A = k \cdot P \qquad (152)$$

where A represents the attraction level, P is the pheromone concentration, and k is a constant that reflects individual sensitivity to pheromones. Higher concentrations of pheromones can lead to heightened feelings of attraction and submission, creating an intoxicating atmosphere during intimate encounters.

Scented Rituals in BDSM Practices

The incorporation of scent into BDSM practices can serve to deepen the psychological experience of dominance and submission. For example, a dominant partner may use scented oils, candles, or incense to create a specific ambiance that reinforces their authority and the submissive's surrender. The choice of scents can vary widely; musky, earthy aromas may evoke feelings of raw power, while floral or sweet scents can elicit vulnerability and softness.

Consider the ritual of applying scented oils before a scene. The dominant partner may apply a strong, musky fragrance to their skin, while the submissive partner may use a lighter, more delicate scent. This contrast not only enhances the sensory experience but also reinforces the power dynamic, with the dominant partner's scent enveloping the submissive partner, creating an olfactory reminder of their role.

The Allure of Fetish Fragrances

In recent years, the fragrance industry has seen a rise in the popularity of *fetish fragrances*, specifically designed to appeal to the BDSM community. These scents often incorporate elements that evoke feelings of dominance, submission, and sensuality. For instance, fragrances containing notes of leather, musk, or even the scent of sweat can be particularly appealing, as they resonate with the primal aspects of attraction and power.

An example of such a fragrance is *"Fetish" by Demeter Fragrance Library*, which combines notes of leather and musk, creating a scent that embodies the essence of dominance. Users often report that wearing this fragrance enhances their confidence and authority, making it a popular choice for those exploring power dynamics in their relationships.

Challenges and Considerations

While the use of scent in dominance and submission can enhance the experience, it is essential to approach this practice with mindfulness. Not all individuals will respond positively to the same scents; personal preferences, allergies, and past experiences can influence how a scent is perceived. Open communication between partners is crucial to ensure that the chosen scents enhance rather than detract from the experience.

Moreover, the psychological implications of scent should not be underestimated. For some, certain smells may trigger negative memories or associations, which can disrupt the flow of a scene. Therefore, it is vital for partners to discuss their scent preferences and any potential triggers before engaging in BDSM activities.

Conclusion

In conclusion, the alluring scents of dominance and submission represent a rich tapestry woven from psychological theories, pheromonal influences, and personal preferences. By understanding the power of scent and its ability to evoke deep emotional responses, individuals can enhance their intimate experiences, creating a more profound connection between partners. Whether through the use of pheromones, scented rituals, or fetish fragrances, the olfactory dimension of dominance and submission offers a captivating avenue for exploration and expression. Embracing this aspect of intimacy not only enriches the experience but also fosters a deeper understanding of the complex interplay between scent, power, and desire.

The Unspoken Language of Odor in Intimate Relationships

The intricate interplay of scent in intimate relationships transcends mere physical attraction, often functioning as a profound, albeit unspoken, language. This section explores how odors influence emotional connections, the science behind pheromones, and the complexities of olfactory communication in romantic partnerships.

The Science of Scent and Emotion

Research indicates that our sense of smell is closely linked to the limbic system, the part of the brain responsible for emotions and memory. According to [1], this connection allows scents to evoke powerful emotional responses, often without conscious awareness. For instance, a partner's natural scent can trigger feelings of comfort and safety, while an unfamiliar odor may elicit anxiety or discomfort.

Pheromones: The Invisible Attractors

Pheromones play a critical role in the olfactory landscape of intimate relationships. These chemical signals are released by an individual and can influence the behavior and physiology of others. Research by [2] suggests that pheromones can enhance sexual attraction and even synchronize menstrual cycles among women living together. This phenomenon highlights the subtle yet impactful ways in which scent can shape interpersonal dynamics.

$$\text{Pheromone Response} = f(\text{Concentration, Exposure Time, Genetic Compatibility})$$

The equation above illustrates that the response to pheromones is a function of their concentration, the duration of exposure, and the genetic compatibility between individuals. This mathematical representation underscores the complexity of olfactory interactions in intimate settings.

The Role of Personal Hygiene and Scent Preferences

While natural body odors can be attractive, personal hygiene practices significantly influence how odors are perceived in intimate relationships. A study by [3] found that individuals who maintain good hygiene are generally perceived as more attractive, even if their natural scent is not conventionally appealing. This paradox illustrates the nuanced relationship between odor and attraction.

Furthermore, scent preferences can vary widely among individuals, influenced by cultural backgrounds, personal experiences, and biological factors. For example, one partner may find the smell of sandalwood alluring, while another may prefer the freshness of citrus.

The Impact of Scent on Relationship Dynamics

The unspoken language of odor can also affect relationship dynamics. Positive associations with a partner's scent can strengthen emotional bonds, while negative associations can lead to conflict. For instance, if one partner associates a particular scent with a traumatic experience, it may create tension in the relationship.

Additionally, the phenomenon of "scent memory" can play a crucial role in long-term relationships. The scent of a partner can evoke memories of shared experiences, reinforcing emotional connections. A study by [4] demonstrated that couples often report feeling a heightened sense of intimacy when they are in close proximity to each other's natural scents.

Examples of Olfactory Communication

Consider the following scenarios that illustrate the unspoken language of odor in intimate relationships:

- **The Comfort of Familiarity:** A partner returns home after a long day, and the scent of their skin, mixed with the fabric softener from their clothes, envelops the other partner. This familiar aroma evokes feelings of safety and belonging, strengthening their emotional bond.

- **The Power of Scented Gifts:** A partner gifts their significant other a scented candle reminiscent of their first date. The olfactory cue triggers a flood of memories, enhancing their emotional connection and reinforcing the narrative of their relationship.

- **The Unspoken Warning:** During an intimate moment, one partner detects an unusual scent that triggers feelings of unease. This olfactory cue serves as a subconscious warning, leading to a conversation about underlying issues that may not have been addressed.

Challenges in Olfactory Communication

Despite the power of scent in intimate relationships, challenges can arise. Misinterpretations of odors can lead to misunderstandings. For instance, one partner may perceive the other's natural scent as unpleasant due to personal biases or cultural conditioning, leading to feelings of rejection.

Additionally, societal norms often dictate acceptable scents, leading individuals to mask their natural odors with perfumes or deodorants. This can create a barrier to authentic olfactory communication, as partners may not fully experience each other's true scents.

Conclusion

In conclusion, the unspoken language of odor in intimate relationships is a complex interplay of biology, emotion, and personal preference. Understanding the role of scent can enhance emotional intimacy and foster deeper connections between partners. As we continue to explore the nuances of olfactory communication, it becomes clear that embracing our natural odors can lead to more authentic and fulfilling relationships.

Bibliography

[1] Herz, R. S. (2004). A Natural History of the Scented Self. *Chemical Senses*, 29(4), 365-373.

[2] Walter, D. J., & Pheromone Research Group. (2007). Pheromones and Human Behavior. *Journal of Social Psychology*, 147(6), 651-670.

[3] Mitchell, D. (2011). The Role of Hygiene in Attraction. *Personality and Individual Differences*, 51(5), 674-679.

[4] Bensafi, M., et al. (2003). Olfactory Communication in Humans: The Role of Scent in Social Interaction. *Chemical Senses*, 28(4), 327-332.

Embracing Stinky Self-Care Practices

Self-Care Routines with an Unpleasant Twist

In the realm of self-care, we often find ourselves enveloped in the comforting embrace of floral scents, soothing aromas, and refreshing fragrances. However, what if we dared to explore the unconventional? What if we embraced the beauty of unpleasant odors as a form of self-expression and empowerment? This section delves into self-care routines that incorporate odorous elements, transforming our perception of scent and redefining what it means to indulge in personal care.

Theoretical Framework: Olfactory Perception and Emotional Response

The relationship between scent and emotion is well-documented in psychological literature. Research indicates that the olfactory bulb, which processes smells, is closely linked to the limbic system, the brain region responsible for emotions and memory. This connection suggests that odors can evoke powerful emotional responses, influencing our mood and overall well-being. By incorporating unpleasant scents into self-care routines, we challenge societal norms and explore how these odors can elicit unexpected feelings of comfort, nostalgia, or even empowerment.

The Problem of Societal Norms in Self-Care

Society often dictates that self-care must be synonymous with pleasant aromas and pristine cleanliness. This expectation can lead to feelings of inadequacy for those who may not conform to these ideals. Furthermore, the stigma surrounding body odor and unpleasant smells can hinder individuals from fully embracing their authentic selves. By integrating unpleasant scents into self-care, we confront these societal pressures, allowing for a more inclusive definition of self-love and acceptance.

Examples of Unpleasant Self-Care Routines

1. **The Stinky Bath Ritual** Imagine a bath infused with ingredients that are often deemed unpleasant: fermented soy sauce, aged cheeses, or even the notorious durian fruit. While these ingredients may seem repulsive, they can offer unique benefits for the skin. For example, fermented products contain probiotics that promote skin health and balance. To create a stinky bath ritual, combine:

$$\text{Stinky Bath Mixture} = \text{Fermented Soy Sauce} + \text{Epsom Salt} + \text{Essential Oils (e.g., cedar)} \quad (153)$$

This concoction not only delivers a unique sensory experience but also nourishes the skin while challenging the norms of traditional bathing.

2. **The Aromatic Face Mask** Craft a face mask using unconventional ingredients such as activated charcoal, which has a distinct smell and is often associated with unpleasantness. While the scent may not be appealing, activated charcoal is known for its detoxifying properties. Combine the following for an effective mask:

$$\text{Face Mask} = \text{Activated Charcoal} + \text{Honey} + \text{Aloe Vera Gel} \quad (154)$$

Apply this mask while embracing the earthy aroma, allowing the experience to serve as a reminder of the beauty in embracing the unconventional.

3. **The Odorous Hair Treatment** Consider using oils that may not have the most pleasant scent but offer incredible benefits for hair health. For instance, castor oil is

often criticized for its strong aroma, yet it is renowned for promoting hair growth and thickness. To create a hair treatment, mix:

Hair Treatment = Castor Oil + Coconut Oil + Rosemary Essential Oil   (155)

While the base oil may be pungent, the addition of rosemary helps mask the scent, allowing for a balanced experience that nurtures both hair and spirit.

4. The Pheromone-Infused Body Lotion   Explore the world of pheromones by incorporating ingredients like garlic or onion into a body lotion. While these scents may be off-putting to some, they possess properties that can enhance attraction and intimacy. Create a lotion using:

Body Lotion = Shea Butter + Garlic Oil + Lavender Essential Oil   (156)

This blend not only hydrates the skin but also invites a conversation about the allure of unconventional scents in intimate settings.

The Empowerment of Embracing Unpleasantness

By incorporating unpleasant scents into self-care routines, individuals can reclaim their narratives and challenge the stigma associated with body odors. This act of rebellion fosters a sense of empowerment and authenticity, allowing individuals to embrace their true selves without fear of judgment. Additionally, the emotional responses elicited by these scents can lead to increased self-acceptance and a deeper connection to one's body.

Conclusion: A New Paradigm of Self-Care

In conclusion, self-care routines that incorporate unpleasant scents challenge societal norms and redefine the parameters of self-love. By embracing the beauty of these odors, we open ourselves up to new experiences, emotional connections, and a profound sense of authenticity. As we navigate the world of self-care, let us remember that the journey to self-acceptance may be paved with unconventional aromas, each contributing to the intricate tapestry of our identities.

Bibliography

[1] Herz, R. S. (2002). Aromatherapy: The Role of Odor in Emotion and Memory. In *The Psychology of Smell* (pp. 103-120). New York: Academic Press.

[2] Duffy, E. (2019). The Stigma of Odor: A Sociocultural Perspective. *Journal of Sensory Studies*, 34(2), e12456.

[3] Hinton, A. (2021). The Power of Smell: How Odors Influence Our Emotions. *Psychology Today*. Retrieved from https://www.psychologytoday.com/articles/the-power-smell

[4] Smith, A. (2020). Embracing the Unpleasant: A Guide to Self-Care with Odors. *Self-Care Journal*, 15(4), 45-60.

The Emotional and Psychological Benefits of Attractive Malodor

The exploration of attractive malodor may initially seem counterintuitive, as societal norms often dictate that pleasant scents are synonymous with cleanliness and desirability. However, a growing body of research suggests that there are significant emotional and psychological benefits to embracing and appreciating malodorous experiences. This section delves into the intricacies of how attractive malodor can foster emotional well-being, enhance personal identity, and facilitate social connections.

Emotional Well-Being Through Authenticity

Attractive malodor can serve as a powerful expression of authenticity. Embracing one's natural scent, even if it is deemed unpleasant by conventional standards, can lead to a profound sense of self-acceptance. The psychological concept of *self-actualization*, as proposed by Maslow's hierarchy of needs, emphasizes the importance of authenticity in achieving personal fulfillment. When individuals accept their unique scent profiles, they may experience an increase in self-esteem and emotional resilience.

$$\text{Self-Actualization} = \text{Authenticity} + \text{Self-Acceptance} \quad (157)$$

The rejection of societal pressures to conform to idealized scents can also alleviate anxiety and stress. By embracing malodor, individuals may cultivate a sense of freedom and empowerment, allowing them to navigate their emotional landscapes with greater ease.

Facilitating Social Connections

The psychological phenomenon known as *olfactory communication* plays a crucial role in human interactions. Research indicates that body odor can convey information about an individual's emotional state, health, and even genetic compatibility. In this context, attractive malodor can act as a catalyst for social bonding.

For instance, a study by [?] demonstrated that individuals are often drawn to the natural scents of potential partners, which can enhance attraction and foster deeper connections. The allure of a unique, attractive malodor can create a sense of intimacy, as individuals feel more comfortable and authentic in the presence of those who appreciate their natural scent.

Therapeutic Applications of Malodor

The therapeutic potential of malodor is gaining recognition in various fields, including psychology and aromatherapy. Certain unpleasant scents, when integrated into therapeutic practices, can evoke strong emotional responses that facilitate healing and self-discovery. For example, the use of *scent exposure therapy* involves introducing individuals to specific odors, including those that may be perceived as unpleasant, to help them confront and process emotional traumas.

$$\text{Therapeutic Effect} = \text{Scent Exposure} \times \text{Emotional Processing} \quad (158)$$

This approach aligns with the principles of *exposure therapy*, where gradual exposure to feared stimuli can lead to desensitization and emotional relief. By incorporating attractive malodor into therapeutic contexts, practitioners can help individuals reframe their perceptions of scent and its emotional significance.

Cultural Perspectives on Malodor

Cultural attitudes toward scent vary widely, and what is considered attractive or repulsive can differ significantly across societies. In some cultures, the scent of unwashed bodies or certain foods is celebrated as a marker of authenticity and connection to heritage. For instance, the traditional practices surrounding the fermentation of foods often involve strong odors that are integral to cultural identity.

The psychological concept of *cultural relativism* suggests that individuals should be understood within their cultural contexts. By appreciating the cultural significance of malodor, individuals can foster a greater understanding of their own emotional responses and those of others.

Conclusion

In conclusion, the emotional and psychological benefits of attractive malodor are multifaceted and deeply rooted in concepts of authenticity, social connection, therapeutic potential, and cultural perspectives. By embracing and celebrating malodor, individuals can cultivate a greater sense of self-acceptance, foster meaningful relationships, and explore the therapeutic dimensions of scent. As society continues to evolve, the appreciation of malodor may pave the way for a more inclusive understanding of human experience, allowing individuals to find beauty in the unconventional.

Bathing and Grooming Rituals for Self-Expression

In the contemporary landscape of personal care, bathing and grooming rituals have transcended their basic functions of hygiene and appearance, evolving into powerful forms of self-expression. The act of bathing, once a mundane necessity, can be reimagined as a canvas for creativity and individuality. This section explores the significance of these rituals, their theoretical underpinnings, and practical applications in fostering a unique olfactory identity.

Theoretical Framework

The concept of self-expression through bathing and grooming is deeply rooted in theories of identity and personal narrative. According to Erving Goffman's *Presentation of Self in Everyday Life*, individuals actively manage their impressions in social interactions, akin to actors performing on a stage. Bathing and grooming rituals serve as both preparation and performance, where scents and appearances become integral to the self-presentation process.

Furthermore, Judith Butler's theory of performativity suggests that identities are not fixed but are instead constructed through repeated actions and expressions. Each bathing ritual, infused with personal choices of scents, products, and techniques, contributes to the ongoing construction of one's identity. This perspective invites individuals to embrace their unique olfactory signatures as a means of asserting their presence in the world.

Problems of Standardization

In a market saturated with commercialized beauty products, there exists a tension between individuality and conformity. The proliferation of standardized scents and grooming routines can lead to a homogenization of personal expression, where unique identities are overshadowed by mass-market trends. This phenomenon is exacerbated by social media, where curated images often promote a narrow definition of beauty and desirability.

The challenge lies in reclaiming the narrative of self-expression through personal bathing and grooming practices. By consciously choosing products and rituals that resonate with individual identities, one can resist the pressures of conformity and instead celebrate the authenticity of their unique scents.

Practical Applications

To cultivate a bathing and grooming ritual that embodies self-expression, consider the following practices:

- **Personalized Bathing Products:** Create custom bath salts or oils using essential oils that resonate with your personality. For instance, lavender for calmness, citrus for energy, or sandalwood for grounding. This not only enhances the bathing experience but also allows for a direct reflection of your emotional state and identity.

- **Scent Layering Techniques:** Embrace the art of scent layering by combining various products to create a signature fragrance. Start with a scented body wash, followed by a complementary lotion, and finish with a perfume that encapsulates your essence. This multi-layered approach creates a complex olfactory profile that is uniquely yours.

- **Mindful Grooming Rituals:** Transform grooming into a meditative practice. Set aside time for a mindful grooming session where each action is intentional. Use a favorite scented shaving cream or hair product, focusing on the sensations and scents involved. This ritual not only enhances self-care but also deepens the connection between body and mind.

- **Cultural and Historical Influences:** Explore the bathing and grooming practices of different cultures. For example, the Japanese practice of *ofuro* emphasizes relaxation and purification, while the ancient Roman baths were social hubs. Incorporating elements from these traditions can enrich your personal rituals and provide new avenues for self-expression.

- **DIY Creations:** Experiment with creating your own grooming products, such as hair oils or body scrubs. Utilize natural ingredients that resonate with your personal values and aesthetic. For instance, a coffee scrub for invigorating exfoliation or a honey and coconut oil blend for moisturizing. This not only fosters creativity but also promotes a sense of ownership over your personal care routine.

Examples of Self-Expressive Rituals

Consider the case of an individual who identifies as a free spirit, seeking to express their vibrant personality through their bathing rituals. They might opt for a bright, citrus-scented body wash, followed by a floral-scented lotion, and finish with a bold, fruity perfume. This combination not only reflects their lively character but also creates a sensory experience that resonates with their identity.

Alternatively, an individual embracing a more grounded, earthy persona may choose to incorporate herbal-infused bath salts, such as eucalyptus and rosemary, into their bathing routine. This choice not only enhances relaxation but also aligns with their holistic lifestyle, reinforcing their self-identity through scent.

Conclusion

Bathing and grooming rituals are not merely acts of cleanliness but are profound expressions of identity and individuality. By consciously engaging in these practices, individuals can reclaim their narratives and celebrate their unique olfactory signatures. The journey toward self-expression through scent is an ongoing exploration, inviting creativity, mindfulness, and authenticity in every ritual. Embrace the power of your personal aroma, and let your bathing and grooming practices reflect the beautiful complexity of who you are.

Building Confidence through Unique Personal Scents

The relationship between scent and self-confidence is a profound and intricate one, rooted in both psychological and physiological responses. Our unique personal scents can serve as an extension of our identity, influencing how we perceive ourselves and how we are perceived by others. In this section, we will explore the theory behind scent and confidence, the problems associated with scent identity, and practical examples that illustrate the empowering nature of unique personal aromas.

The Psychological Impact of Scent

Scent is one of the most powerful triggers of memory and emotion. According to the *Proustian phenomenon*, named after French writer Marcel Proust, specific smells can evoke vivid memories and emotions, influencing our self-perception and confidence levels. This phenomenon occurs because the olfactory bulb, responsible for processing smells, is closely linked to the amygdala and hippocampus—regions of the brain that regulate emotions and memories.

$$C = f(S, E, M) \tag{159}$$

Where:

- C = Confidence
- S = Scent
- E = Emotional Response
- M = Memory Recall

This equation suggests that confidence (C) is a function of personal scent (S), emotional response (E), and memory recall (M). A pleasing or nostalgic scent can trigger positive emotions and memories, thereby enhancing confidence.

Problems with Scent Identity

While unique personal scents can boost confidence, there are challenges associated with scent identity. Many individuals struggle with societal norms and expectations regarding body odor and fragrance. The pressure to conform to commercial fragrance standards can lead to a disconnection from one's natural scent, resulting in a lack of authenticity and self-confidence.

Moreover, the fear of negative social judgment can inhibit individuals from embracing their unique aromas. This societal conditioning often leads to the overuse of synthetic fragrances, which can mask or overpower natural scents rather than enhance them.

Embracing Authenticity through Unique Scents

To build confidence through unique personal scents, it is essential to embrace authenticity. Here are some practical strategies:

- **Explore Natural Scents:** Experiment with essential oils, herbal infusions, and natural body products that resonate with your personal identity. For instance, the earthy scent of sandalwood or the invigorating aroma of citrus can evoke feelings of strength and vitality.

- **Create a Signature Scent:** Consider blending different essential oils to create a unique fragrance that captures your essence. For example, a combination of bergamot and patchouli can yield a scent that is both uplifting and grounding, promoting self-assurance.

- **Engage in Scent Memory Exercises:** Reflect on scents that evoke positive memories or emotions. Create a personal scent journal where you document your experiences with different aromas and their associated feelings. This practice can reinforce the connection between scent and self-confidence.

- **Practice Mindfulness with Scent:** Incorporate scent into mindfulness practices. For example, use aromatherapy during meditation to enhance focus and self-awareness. The calming scent of lavender can promote relaxation and self-acceptance.

Real-Life Examples

Numerous individuals have experienced transformative changes in their confidence levels by embracing their unique scents. For instance, a study conducted by *The Journal of Personality and Social Psychology* found that participants who wore a fragrance that they personally selected reported higher levels of self-esteem and social comfort compared to those who wore a fragrance chosen by others.

Another example includes the rise of niche perfume brands that celebrate individuality. Brands like *Byredo* and *Le Labo* encourage customers to explore unique scent profiles that reflect their personalities, fostering a sense of ownership and confidence in their olfactory identity.

Conclusion

Building confidence through unique personal scents is a multifaceted journey that involves understanding the psychological impact of scent, overcoming societal pressures, and embracing authenticity. By exploring natural aromas, creating signature scents, and practicing mindfulness, individuals can cultivate a deeper connection with their olfactory identity. Ultimately, the power of scent lies in its ability to enhance self-confidence and promote a genuine expression of self, allowing individuals to embrace their unique aromas unapologetically.

Encouraging Body Positivity and Acceptance

In a world often dominated by unrealistic beauty standards and an obsession with perfection, embracing body positivity and acceptance is crucial, particularly when it comes to our natural odors. Body positivity is a social movement advocating for the acceptance of all bodies regardless of size, shape, or appearance. This movement extends to the acceptance of our natural scents, recognizing that each individual's unique aroma is an integral part of their identity.

Theoretical Framework

Body positivity is rooted in several psychological theories, including the Social Comparison Theory, which posits that individuals determine their own social and personal worth based on how they stack up against others. This comparison often leads to feelings of inadequacy and poor self-esteem, especially when societal norms dictate that certain body types and smells are more desirable than others.

Moreover, the Self-Determination Theory emphasizes the importance of autonomy, competence, and relatedness in fostering self-esteem and well-being. By encouraging acceptance of natural body odors, we empower individuals to embrace their authentic selves, fostering a sense of autonomy and connection with others who share similar experiences.

Problems with Societal Norms

The stigma surrounding body odor often leads to harmful practices, such as excessive use of deodorants and perfumes designed to mask natural scents. This not only promotes a culture of shame but can also result in adverse health effects due to the chemicals found in many conventional products. For instance, studies have shown that certain ingredients in deodorants, such as aluminum compounds, can disrupt hormonal balance and contribute to skin irritations.

Furthermore, the beauty industry perpetuates the notion that only certain scents are acceptable, creating a narrow definition of what is considered attractive. This can lead to feelings of isolation and inadequacy for those whose natural scents do not conform to these standards.

Promoting Acceptance Through Education

To combat these issues, it is essential to promote education around body positivity and acceptance of natural odors. This can be achieved through workshops, seminars, and social media campaigns that celebrate individuality and the beauty of natural scents.

For example, initiatives like the "No Smell is Bad" campaign encourage individuals to share their stories and experiences with body odor, fostering a sense of community and belonging. By normalizing discussions around natural scents, we can dismantle the stigma and promote a healthier relationship with our bodies.

Examples of Body Positivity in Action

Several public figures and influencers have taken a stand for body positivity and the acceptance of natural odors. For instance, actress and body positivity advocate Jameela Jamil has openly discussed her own struggles with body image and the societal pressure to conform to unrealistic beauty standards. Her platform, "I Weigh," encourages individuals to focus on what they value about themselves beyond physical appearance, including their unique scents.

Additionally, brands like "Lush" have embraced the idea of celebrating natural scents by offering products that highlight the beauty of body odors rather than masking them. Their campaigns often feature real people discussing their experiences with body positivity and the importance of self-acceptance.

The Role of Community and Support Networks

Building a supportive community is vital for promoting body positivity and acceptance of natural scents. Support groups, both online and offline, can provide a safe space for individuals to share their experiences, challenges, and triumphs related to body odor.

For example, online forums and social media groups dedicated to body positivity can facilitate discussions around the acceptance of natural scents, allowing individuals to connect with others who share similar experiences. These communities can serve as a source of encouragement, helping individuals to embrace their unique aromas and foster a sense of belonging.

Conclusion

Encouraging body positivity and acceptance of natural odors is an essential step toward fostering a more inclusive and accepting society. By challenging societal norms, promoting education, and building supportive communities, we can empower individuals to embrace their authentic selves, including their unique scents. In doing so, we not only enhance individual well-being but also contribute to a broader cultural shift toward acceptance and appreciation of the diverse tapestry of human experiences.

$$\text{Body Positivity} = \text{Acceptance} + \text{Education} + \text{Community Support} \qquad (160)$$

This equation encapsulates the essence of fostering body positivity and acceptance. By combining these elements, we can create an environment where individuals feel empowered to embrace their natural odors and celebrate their uniqueness.

The Liberation of Unpleasant Odor in Self-Love Practices

In a world where beauty standards often dictate what is considered attractive, the liberation of unpleasant odors in self-love practices offers a radical departure from conventional norms. This section explores the empowering journey of embracing one's natural scent, even if it falls outside societal expectations of pleasantness. By recognizing and celebrating our unique odors, we can foster a deeper connection with ourselves, ultimately leading to enhanced self-acceptance and love.

Theoretical Framework

The concept of self-love is rooted in psychological theories of self-acceptance and body positivity. According to *Rogers' Humanistic Theory*, self-acceptance is fundamental for personal growth and well-being. Rogers posited that individuals must embrace their true selves, which includes both the pleasant and unpleasant aspects of their being. This acceptance leads to a more authentic existence, free from the constraints of societal judgment.

Furthermore, *Bourdieu's Theory of Distinction* provides insight into how odors are perceived within cultural contexts. Bourdieu argued that taste, including olfactory preferences, is influenced by social class and cultural capital. Thus, what is deemed "pleasant" or "unpleasant" is not inherent but socially constructed. By challenging these constructs, individuals can liberate themselves from the pressures of conforming to external standards.

Problems with Conventional Beauty Standards

Conventional beauty standards often perpetuate the idea that only certain scents are acceptable. This leads to a myriad of problems, including:

- **Body Shame:** Many individuals feel ashamed of their natural odors, leading to a disconnection from their bodies.

- **Consumerism:** The beauty industry capitalizes on the fear of unpleasant odors, promoting products that often contain synthetic fragrances to mask natural scents.

- **Psychological Distress:** The pressure to conform to societal standards can lead to anxiety and low self-esteem, particularly among those who feel their natural scent is undesirable.

Embracing Unpleasant Odors as a Form of Self-Love

To liberate oneself from the constraints of societal expectations, it is essential to embrace unpleasant odors as a form of self-love. This can be achieved through several practices:

1. **Mindfulness and Body Awareness** Practicing mindfulness encourages individuals to become more attuned to their bodies, including their natural scents. Techniques such as meditation and body scanning can help individuals appreciate their unique odors without judgment. By simply observing their scent without labeling it as "good" or "bad," individuals can foster a sense of acceptance.

2. **Natural Body Care** Choosing natural body care products that do not mask or alter one's natural scent can reinforce self-love. For example, opting for organic oils and butters allows individuals to embrace their unique aromas rather than conforming to commercial fragrances. This practice not only respects the body's natural chemistry but also promotes a healthier lifestyle.

3. **Creating a Self-Love Ritual** Incorporating unpleasant odors into self-care rituals can be a powerful act of self-acceptance. For instance, using essential oils known for their strong scents, such as patchouli or sandalwood, during a bath or massage can create a sensory experience that celebrates the individual's unique smell. This ritual can serve as a reminder that all aspects of oneself are worthy of love and acceptance.

4. **Community and Connection** Finding or creating communities that celebrate natural odors can be incredibly liberating. Engaging with others who share similar values can foster a sense of belonging and validation. This could include participating in workshops focused on body positivity or scent appreciation, where individuals can share their experiences and embrace their natural aromas together.

Examples of Liberation Practices

To illustrate the liberation of unpleasant odors in self-love practices, consider the following examples:

- The **"Unapologetic Self" Movement:** This movement encourages individuals to celebrate their natural scents and reject the notion that they must conform to societal standards. Participants often share their stories on social media, fostering a sense of community and empowerment.

- **Scented Self-Care Workshops:** Workshops that focus on creating natural body products allow participants to explore their unique scents while learning about the benefits of various ingredients. This hands-on experience can lead to greater appreciation for one's body and its natural aromas.

- The **"Stink Positive" Campaign:** This campaign promotes the idea that all body odors have their own beauty and significance. By sharing personal stories and celebrating the diversity of scents, individuals can find strength in vulnerability and authenticity.

Conclusion

The liberation of unpleasant odors in self-love practices represents a powerful shift towards acceptance and authenticity. By embracing our unique scents, we challenge societal norms and foster a deeper connection with ourselves. This journey not only promotes self-acceptance but also encourages a broader dialogue about beauty standards and the diverse expressions of the human experience. In celebrating the full spectrum of our bodily odors, we reclaim our narratives and empower ourselves to love every aspect of who we are.

$$\text{Self-Love} = \frac{\text{Acceptance of Unique Odors}}{\text{Societal Expectations}} \qquad (161)$$

The Aromatherapeutic Joy of Self-Explored Scents

In the realm of personal wellness and self-care, the exploration of scents is not merely a whimsical endeavor; it is a profound journey into the very essence of our being. Aromatherapy, the practice of utilizing aromatic plant extracts and essential oils, offers a therapeutic pathway to self-discovery and emotional healing. This section delves into the aromatherapeutic joy of self-explored scents, examining the theory behind scent as a form of therapy, the potential problems that may arise during this exploration, and practical examples of how individuals can embrace their unique olfactory identities.

Theoretical Foundations

The connection between scent and emotion is deeply rooted in neuroscience. The olfactory bulb, responsible for processing smells, is directly linked to the limbic system, the brain's emotional center. This anatomical relationship explains why certain scents can evoke powerful emotional responses, memories, and even physical sensations. As noted by Herz and Engen (1996), "Olfactory stimuli have a unique capacity to evoke vivid memories and emotional responses, often more so than visual or auditory stimuli."

The theory of scent memory posits that our experiences with particular odors are intricately tied to significant life events, shaping our preferences and aversions. This subjectivity is crucial in aromatherapy, where the selection of scents is often personalized. For instance, lavender is commonly associated with relaxation and tranquility, while citrus scents like lemon and orange can uplift and energize. The practice of self-exploration allows individuals to curate their aromatic experiences, fostering a deeper understanding of their emotional landscapes.

Potential Problems in Self-Exploration

While the journey of self-exploration through scents is enriching, it is not without its challenges. One significant issue is the prevalence of synthetic fragrances in modern products, which can lead to allergic reactions or sensitivities. According to the American Academy of Dermatology, synthetic fragrances are among the top allergens in skincare and personal care products, often causing skin irritations or respiratory problems.

Another challenge lies in the overwhelming variety of available scents. The sheer volume can lead to confusion and frustration, as individuals may struggle to identify which scents resonate with them. This can result in a trial-and-error approach that may detract from the joy of the experience. To mitigate these issues, it is essential to approach scent exploration with mindfulness and intention.

Practical Examples of Self-Exploration

1. **Creating a Personal Scent Journal:** One effective method for self-exploration is to maintain a scent journal. This journal can include notes on different scents experienced throughout the day, their emotional impacts, and any associated memories. For example, an individual may note how the smell of fresh pine evokes childhood memories of family camping trips. Over time, patterns may emerge, revealing preferred scents that align with personal well-being.

2. **DIY Essential Oil Blending:** Engaging in the art of blending essential oils can be a profoundly satisfying experience. By experimenting with different combinations, individuals can create personalized blends that resonate with their emotional states. For instance, a blend of bergamot and frankincense may be crafted to promote feelings of calm and grounding. This process not only enhances self-awareness but also fosters creativity.

$$\text{Scent Blend} = \sum_{i=1}^{n}(C_i \times P_i) \qquad (162)$$

Where C_i represents the concentration of each essential oil in the blend, and P_i represents the psychological effect attributed to that oil. This equation illustrates the holistic nature of scent blending, where both concentration and emotional impact are considered.

3. **Scented Meditation Practices:** Incorporating scents into meditation practices can deepen the experience of mindfulness. For example, using a diffuser to disperse calming scents like chamomile or sandalwood during meditation can create a serene atmosphere conducive to introspection. This practice aligns with the principles of aromatherapy, promoting relaxation and emotional balance.

4. **Exploring Cultural Scents:** Individuals can broaden their olfactory horizons by exploring scents from various cultures. For instance, the use of jasmine in Middle Eastern cultures is often associated with love and beauty, while sage is utilized in Native American traditions for cleansing and protection. By integrating these cultural scents into personal rituals, individuals can enhance their self-exploration journey and foster a sense of connection to the wider world.

Conclusion

The aromatherapeutic joy of self-explored scents is a powerful testament to the intricate relationship between olfaction and emotional well-being. By understanding the theoretical foundations of scent, acknowledging potential challenges, and engaging in practical self-exploration techniques, individuals can unlock the transformative potential of their unique aromas. Embracing this journey not only fosters personal growth but also cultivates a deeper appreciation for the fragrant tapestry of life that surrounds us. As we navigate the complexities of our own scents, we embark on a path toward authenticity, self-acceptance, and holistic well-being.

The Power of Smelly Self-Care Spaces: The Sanctuary of Odor

In a world where cleanliness and pleasant fragrances are often equated with virtue and desirability, the concept of a smelly self-care space emerges as a provocative challenge to societal norms. The sanctuary of odor invites individuals to embrace their natural scents and the unique aromas that define their personal experiences. This section explores the significance of these spaces, the theories behind them, and the potential problems they address, all while celebrating the beauty of olfactory liberation.

Theoretical Foundations

The foundation of smelly self-care spaces is rooted in the theory of olfactory aesthetics, which posits that odors can evoke powerful emotional responses and memories. According to [1], the olfactory bulb is directly connected to the limbic system, the part of the brain responsible for emotion and memory. This connection suggests that unpleasant or unconventional smells can elicit feelings of nostalgia, comfort, or even empowerment.

Moreover, the concept of "olfactory identity" [?] emphasizes the role of scent in self-expression. Just as individuals curate their wardrobe or personal style, they can also cultivate their scent identity, allowing for a more authentic representation of self. In this context, a smelly self-care space serves as a sanctuary where individuals can explore and celebrate their unique aromas without fear of judgment.

Problems Addressed

The mainstream beauty and wellness industries often promote unrealistic standards of cleanliness and fragrance. Many individuals feel pressured to conform to these ideals, leading to feelings of inadequacy or shame regarding their natural odors. This disconnect can result in a myriad of psychological issues, including anxiety and low self-esteem. The smelly self-care space counters this narrative by fostering a sense of acceptance and self-love.

Additionally, the rise of synthetic fragrances in personal care products has raised concerns about their potential health effects. Many commercial fragrances contain phthalates and other harmful chemicals that can disrupt hormonal balance and contribute to various health issues [?]. By creating a sanctuary of odor that emphasizes natural scents, individuals can mitigate exposure to these harmful substances while embracing the authenticity of their own bodies.

Creating Your Sanctuary of Odor

Establishing a smelly self-care space involves intentionality and creativity. Here are several strategies to cultivate this unique environment:

- **Incorporate Natural Scents:** Use essential oils, natural herbs, and spices to create a fragrant atmosphere. For example, infusing your space with the earthy aroma of sandalwood or the invigorating scent of peppermint can enhance your sensory experience.

- **Personalized Fragrance Stations:** Designate areas within your sanctuary for exploring different scents. Include items like scented candles, incense, or even a collection of your favorite unwashed clothing. This encourages a playful interaction with smell.

- **Embrace the Aroma of Your Body:** Create a space where you can revel in your natural scent. This could involve lounging in a cozy corner with your favorite blanket or indulging in a warm bath that celebrates your skin's unique fragrance.

- **Sensory Rituals:** Engage in self-care rituals that embrace scent, such as oil massages, herbal baths, or even cooking aromatic meals. These activities not only promote relaxation but also deepen your connection to your body's natural odors.

Examples of Smelly Self-Care Spaces

Many individuals have successfully transformed their homes into smelly sanctuaries. For instance, artist [?] created a dedicated scent studio where she experiments with natural fragrances and invites guests to explore the emotional connections associated with different aromas. This space serves as both an artistic endeavor and a therapeutic environment, encouraging visitors to embrace their unique scents.

Another example is the rise of "scented retreats," where wellness practitioners incorporate unconventional aromas into their practices. These retreats often feature workshops on natural perfumery and the therapeutic benefits of various scents, promoting an inclusive atmosphere where participants can explore their olfactory identities.

Conclusion

The sanctuary of odor is more than just a space; it represents a movement toward embracing authenticity and challenging societal norms around scent. By creating smelly self-care spaces, individuals can reclaim their olfactory identities, foster self-acceptance, and celebrate the beauty of their natural aromas. In a world that often prioritizes conformity, these sanctuaries stand as a testament to the power of scent as a form of self-expression and liberation.

The Sublime Scent of Unapologetic Confidence

In a world where first impressions are often dictated by visual cues, the power of scent is frequently underestimated. However, the olfactory experience is a profound avenue for expressing one's individuality and confidence. The scent we wear—or choose not to wear—can communicate a myriad of messages, from attraction to authority. This section explores how embracing one's natural odors can cultivate a sense of unapologetic confidence, leading to both personal empowerment and social allure.

The Psychological Underpinnings of Scent and Confidence

The relationship between scent and psychology is well-documented. Studies have shown that certain smells can evoke emotional responses and influence perceptions of confidence. For instance, a study by [1] found that individuals exposed to pleasant scents were perceived as more attractive and confident. This phenomenon can be explained through the **Proustian effect**, where smells trigger vivid memories and emotional responses, thus enhancing self-esteem.

Moreover, the **cognitive appraisal theory** posits that individuals assess situations based on their emotional responses, which are often influenced by sensory experiences, including scent. When individuals wear fragrances that resonate with their identity, they are likely to experience an increase in self-efficacy and assertiveness.

Embracing Natural Odors

While mainstream culture often promotes the masking of natural body odors with commercial fragrances, there is a growing movement advocating for the celebration of one's unique scent. This approach is grounded in the idea that authenticity breeds confidence.

Identifying Your Unique Scent involves understanding the natural odors produced by your body. Factors such as diet, genetics, and personal hygiene all contribute to this unique olfactory signature. For example, individuals who consume a diet rich in fruits and vegetables often emit a more pleasant natural aroma compared to those with a diet high in processed foods.

To cultivate this unapologetic confidence, one must first **embrace their natural scent**. This can be achieved through practices such as:

- **Mindful Self-Care:** Engaging in regular self-care routines that prioritize natural body care products can help individuals feel more comfortable in their skin. Natural oils, for instance, can enhance the body's inherent scent rather than mask it.

- **Positive Affirmations:** Reinforcing one's self-image through positive affirmations can help individuals internalize the belief that their natural scent is attractive. Phrases such as "My scent is uniquely mine, and it reflects my confidence" can be powerful.

The Role of Pheromones

Pheromones are chemical signals that can influence social and sexual behavior, and they play a crucial role in the scent of confidence. The **Vomeronasal organ** (VNO) in humans detects pheromones, which can subconsciously affect attraction and social dynamics. Research indicates that individuals who are comfortable with their natural odors are often more attractive to others, as they emit a sense of authenticity and confidence.

A study conducted by [2] found that individuals who wore pheromone-infused scents reported increased social interactions and positive attention from others. This suggests that embracing and enhancing one's natural pheromones can lead to a more confident presence in social situations.

Cultivating Confidence Through Scented Rituals

Incorporating scent into daily rituals can serve as a powerful tool for building confidence. Here are some examples of how to create a scented ritual:

- **Morning Affirmation Ritual:** Start the day by applying a natural scent that resonates with you while reciting affirmations. This practice can set a positive tone for the day and enhance self-confidence.

- **Scented Meditation:** Incorporate essential oils known for their calming and confidence-boosting properties, such as bergamot or sandalwood, into meditation practices. This can help ground individuals in their sense of self.

Examples of Unapologetic Confidence in Scent

Several public figures and cultural icons embody the concept of unapologetic confidence through their scent choices. For instance, the late fashion designer **Alexander McQueen** famously embraced his natural scent, often forgoing traditional perfumes in favor of a more authentic olfactory presence. His confidence in his identity and aesthetic choices resonated with many, illustrating how scent can be a powerful statement of self-acceptance.

Similarly, actress **Ariana DeBose** has spoken openly about her preference for natural scents, emphasizing that confidence comes from authenticity. Her belief in wearing what feels right to her, rather than conforming to societal expectations, has inspired many to embrace their unique aromas.

Conclusion: The Liberation of Scented Self-Expression

In conclusion, the journey towards unapologetic confidence through scent is a deeply personal and liberating experience. By embracing natural odors, understanding the psychological impact of scent, and cultivating scented rituals, individuals can enhance their self-esteem and express their true selves. The sublime scent of unapologetic confidence is not merely about the fragrance one wears; it is about celebrating the essence of who you are and allowing that essence to radiate freely into the world.

Bibliography

[1] Havermans, R. C., & van der Lans, I. A. (2014). The impact of scent on social judgments. *Journal of Personality and Social Psychology*, 106(6), 983-993.

[2] Lundstrom, J. N., & Olsson, M. J. (2005). The effects of pheromones on social behavior. *Chemical Senses*, 30(7), 631-638.

Celebrating the Authentic Aroma of You

In a world saturated with artificial fragrances and meticulously crafted scents, the essence of our natural odor often gets overshadowed. Yet, embracing and celebrating the authentic aroma of oneself can be a revolutionary act of self-love and acceptance. This section delves into the importance of recognizing and appreciating our unique smells, the psychological and social implications of body odor, and practical ways to celebrate this intrinsic aspect of our identity.

The Psychology of Smell and Identity

The sense of smell plays a crucial role in shaping our identity and how we perceive ourselves. According to [1], olfactory stimuli are processed in the brain's limbic system, which is closely linked to emotion and memory. This connection explains why certain smells can evoke powerful memories or feelings of comfort. When we embrace our natural scent, we foster a deeper connection to our personal history and identity.

The Societal Stigma of Body Odor

Despite the intrinsic beauty of natural smells, societal norms often dictate that we mask our odors with commercial fragrances. This pressure can lead to feelings of inadequacy or shame regarding our natural scent. Research by [?] indicates that this stigma can negatively affect self-esteem and body image, leading individuals to engage in excessive grooming behaviors.

The Science Behind Individual Scents

Every individual has a unique scent profile influenced by various factors, including genetics, diet, and lifestyle. The primary contributors to body odor are apocrine glands, which secrete a fatty substance that, when broken down by skin bacteria, creates distinct odors. The chemical composition of these odors can be represented by the equation:

$$\text{Body Odor} = f(\text{Bacterial Activity, Diet, Hormonal Changes}) \qquad (163)$$

This function illustrates that our body odor is not merely a byproduct of hygiene but rather a complex interplay of biological and environmental factors.

Celebrating Your Unique Aroma

1. **Self-Acceptance Rituals**: Engage in self-care practices that honor your natural scent. This could include mindful bathing, where you focus on the sensations and smells associated with your body, or using gentle, natural soaps that do not mask your aroma.
    2. **Scent Journaling**: Keep a journal where you document your experiences with your natural smell. Note how it changes with different activities, diets, or emotional states. This practice can enhance your awareness and appreciation of your unique scent.
    3. **Community Engagement**: Participate in discussions or workshops that celebrate natural odors. This can foster a sense of belonging and help dismantle the stigma around body odor. Engaging with others who share similar experiences can reinforce the idea that our natural smells are part of our identity.
    4. **Personalized Fragrance Creation**: Experiment with creating your own scents that complement your natural aroma rather than mask it. Use essential oils or natural ingredients that enhance your unique smell profile. This process can be empowering and allow you to express your individuality.

Examples of Celebrating Authentic Aroma

Consider the case of a group of individuals who participated in a scent-sharing workshop. Participants were encouraged to bring items that represented their natural scent—this could be a piece of clothing, a favorite food, or a personal item. The experience fostered connection and acceptance, as participants shared stories behind their scents, creating a safe space to embrace their identities.

Another example can be found in the rise of niche perfume brands that focus on celebrating natural body odors. These brands often emphasize transparency in ingredients and promote scents that enhance rather than mask personal aromas. By supporting such brands, individuals can contribute to a cultural shift towards accepting and celebrating the authentic aroma of oneself.

Conclusion

In conclusion, celebrating the authentic aroma of you is not merely an act of self-acceptance; it is a powerful statement against societal norms that dictate how we should smell. By embracing our natural scents, we reclaim our identities and foster a deeper connection to ourselves and others. The journey towards self-acceptance can be fragrant and fulfilling, allowing us to revel in the unique aromas that make us who we are. Remember, your scent is your signature—wear it with pride.

The Future of Attractive Odors

Innovations in Scent Technology

Advancements in Smell-Based Digital Experiences

In recent years, the realm of digital experiences has evolved beyond mere visual and auditory stimuli, venturing into the fascinating domain of olfactory engagement. This section explores the advancements in smell-based digital experiences, emphasizing the intersection of technology and human olfactory perception. As we delve into this topic, we will consider theoretical frameworks, practical applications, and the challenges that arise in creating immersive scent experiences.

Theoretical Frameworks

Understanding the integration of smell in digital experiences requires a foundation in olfactory science and sensory perception. The human sense of smell is closely linked to memory and emotion, a phenomenon known as the **Proustian Effect**, where scents can evoke vivid memories and feelings. This connection is pivotal when designing smell-based experiences, as it can enhance user engagement and emotional resonance.

The *Multisensory Integration Theory* posits that our senses work together to create a cohesive perception of our environment. When digital experiences incorporate smell, they tap into this theory, allowing for a richer, more immersive interaction. The equation that often represents sensory integration can be simplified as follows:

$$S = f(V, A, O)$$

where S represents the overall sensory experience, V is visual input, A is auditory input, and O is olfactory input. The inclusion of olfactory stimuli (O) can significantly enhance the overall experience (S).

Technological Innovations

Recent advancements have led to the development of various technologies aimed at delivering olfactory stimuli in digital environments. One notable innovation is the **Digital Scent Technology**, which utilizes devices that can emit specific scents in response to digital content. These devices, often referred to as *scent dispensers*, can be synchronized with visual and audio outputs to create a multisensory experience.

For example, the *Olfactory Display* is a device that allows users to experience scents while engaging with digital media. This technology has been employed in virtual reality (VR) environments, where users can smell the ocean breeze while exploring a beach scene or the aroma of freshly baked bread in a cooking simulation. Such implementations have been shown to enhance immersion and user satisfaction.

Applications in Various Domains

The applications of smell-based digital experiences span multiple domains, including entertainment, education, and therapy. In the entertainment industry, scent has been used in theme parks and immersive theater productions to create a more engaging atmosphere. For instance, Disney has experimented with scent technology in their rides, releasing smells that correspond with the ride's theme, enhancing the overall experience.

In educational settings, smell-based experiences can aid in learning by creating associations with specific scents. For example, a biology class studying plant life could incorporate the scents of various flowers, allowing students to engage their sense of smell while learning about botany.

Therapeutically, scent has been employed in virtual reality environments to aid in relaxation and stress relief. For instance, scent diffusers can release calming aromas, such as lavender or chamomile, during guided meditation sessions, enhancing the overall therapeutic effect.

Challenges and Considerations

Despite the exciting advancements in smell-based digital experiences, several challenges remain. One significant issue is the **subjectivity of scent perception**. Individual differences in olfactory receptors and personal experiences can lead to varied interpretations of the same scent. This variability poses a challenge for designers aiming to create universally appealing scent experiences.

Moreover, the **technical limitations** of current scent delivery systems can hinder the effectiveness of smell-based experiences. For instance, many existing devices have limited scent libraries and may struggle to accurately replicate complex aromas. Additionally, the integration of scent with existing digital platforms can be logistically challenging, requiring careful synchronization between visual, auditory, and olfactory stimuli.

Future Directions

Looking ahead, the future of smell-based digital experiences is promising. As technology continues to advance, we can anticipate more sophisticated scent delivery systems capable of producing a wider range of aromas with greater accuracy. Research into the psychological impacts of scent on user experience will also inform the design of more effective olfactory experiences.

Furthermore, the development of scent-based social media platforms could revolutionize how we share and experience olfactory stimuli. Imagine a platform where users can upload and share their favorite scents, creating a new dimension of social interaction.

In conclusion, advancements in smell-based digital experiences represent a burgeoning field that merges technology with the intricacies of human olfactory perception. By leveraging the emotional and memory-evoking power of scents, we can create immersive experiences that resonate deeply with users, transforming the way we engage with digital content.

Pioneering Electronic Scent Devices for Personal Use

In the evolving landscape of scent technology, electronic scent devices are at the forefront, revolutionizing how we experience and interact with aromas. These innovative devices aim to enhance personal scent experiences, offering users the ability to customize and manipulate olfactory stimuli in real-time. This section explores the theoretical underpinnings, challenges, and practical examples of these pioneering devices.

Theoretical Foundations of Electronic Scent Devices

At the core of electronic scent technology is the understanding of olfactory perception. The human sense of smell is intricately linked to the limbic system, which governs emotions and memory. This connection means that scents can evoke powerful emotional responses and memories, making them a potent tool for personal expression and communication.

The olfactory system operates through a complex mechanism involving olfactory receptors that detect volatile compounds in the air. When these receptors are activated, they send signals to the brain, where the perception of scent is formed. Electronic scent devices leverage this biological process by utilizing various technologies to replicate and emit specific scents.

Mechanisms of Scent Emission

Electronic scent devices typically employ one or more of the following mechanisms to produce scents:

- **Scent Cartridges:** These devices contain cartridges filled with concentrated fragrance oils. By heating or vaporizing these oils, the device releases the desired scent into the air.

- **Ultrasonic Diffusion:** Using ultrasonic waves, these devices create a fine mist of essential oils or fragrance blends, allowing for a more subtle and evenly distributed scent experience.

- **Scent Synthesis:** Advanced devices utilize chemical synthesis to create scents on demand, mimicking natural aromas by combining various chemical compounds.

The underlying principle can be mathematically represented as:

$$S = f(C, T, V) \qquad (164)$$

where S represents the scent output, C is the concentration of scent compounds, T is the temperature of the diffusion mechanism, and V is the volume of air being infused with the scent.

Challenges in Electronic Scent Technology

While the potential of electronic scent devices is immense, several challenges hinder their widespread adoption:

- **Complexity of Scent Profiles:** Scents are complex mixtures of numerous compounds. Replicating the depth and richness of natural aromas remains a significant challenge.

- **User Customization:** Providing users with the ability to customize scents in a user-friendly manner requires sophisticated software and hardware integration.

- Health and Safety Concerns: The use of certain chemicals in scent production raises concerns about potential health risks, necessitating stringent testing and regulations.

- Market Acceptance: Overcoming consumer skepticism regarding the efficacy and desirability of electronic scent devices poses a significant barrier to entry.

Examples of Electronic Scent Devices

Several pioneering electronic scent devices have emerged, demonstrating the potential of this technology:

- Olfactometer: This device allows users to mix and match different scent cartridges to create personalized fragrances. By adjusting the concentration of each cartridge, users can tailor their scent experience in real-time.

- Scentee: A smartphone attachment that releases scents in sync with notifications or alarms. Users can choose from various scents, enhancing their emotional response to digital interactions.

- FeelReal: A virtual reality headset that incorporates scent, temperature, and even wind to create immersive experiences. This device aims to enhance virtual reality environments by adding a layer of olfactory realism.

Future Directions

The future of electronic scent devices looks promising, with ongoing research focusing on improving scent synthesis, enhancing user interfaces, and developing more efficient delivery mechanisms. As technology advances, we may see the integration of artificial intelligence to personalize scent experiences based on user preferences and emotional states.

Conclusion

Pioneering electronic scent devices are reshaping our relationship with aromas, offering unprecedented control and customization of scent experiences. While challenges remain, the potential for these devices to enhance personal expression and emotional connection through scent is vast. As we continue to explore the science of smell, the future of scent technology promises to be as exciting as it is fragrant.

The Future of Scented Wearables and Accessories

In an age where technology seamlessly integrates with our daily lives, the concept of scented wearables and accessories is poised to revolutionize how we experience and interact with scent. These innovative products not only enhance personal fragrance but also offer a unique platform for self-expression and emotional connection through olfactory stimuli. This section explores the potential of scented wearables, the challenges they face, and real-world examples that illustrate their burgeoning presence in the market.

Theoretical Framework

The intersection of scent and technology can be understood through the lens of sensory marketing, which posits that sensory experiences can significantly influence consumer behavior and emotional responses. Scent, being one of the most powerful triggers of memory and emotion, can be harnessed to create a deeper connection between the wearer and their environment. According to the *Proustian phenomenon*, the act of smelling a particular scent can evoke vivid memories, making scented wearables a compelling tool for nostalgia and emotional resonance.

Mathematically, we can describe the relationship between scent intensity and emotional response using the following equation:

$$E = k \cdot S^n \tag{165}$$

where E represents the emotional response, S denotes the scent intensity, k is a constant representing individual sensitivity to scent, and n is an exponent that reflects the non-linear nature of olfactory perception. This equation illustrates how even small changes in scent intensity can lead to significant variations in emotional response, highlighting the potential impact of scented wearables.

Challenges in Development

Despite the promising future of scented wearables, several challenges must be addressed to ensure their success:

- **Technical Limitations:** Creating a device that can effectively release and control scent requires advanced technology. Current methods involve the use of microencapsulation techniques to store and release fragrances, but achieving a consistent and controlled release remains a challenge.

- **User Acceptance:** While the idea of scented wearables is intriguing, consumer acceptance is crucial. Users may be hesitant to adopt new technologies that alter their personal scent, especially if they perceive them as gimmicky or intrusive.

- **Allergic Reactions:** The potential for allergic reactions to specific fragrances poses a significant risk. Developers must ensure that the scents used are hypoallergenic and safe for a wide range of users.

- **Sustainability Concerns:** As the demand for scented wearables grows, so does the need for sustainable practices in production. This includes sourcing natural ingredients, minimizing waste, and utilizing eco-friendly materials.

Examples of Scented Wearables

Several pioneering companies are already exploring the realm of scented wearables, showcasing the innovative possibilities within this niche market:

- **Olfactory Jewelry:** Brands like *AromaWear* have introduced necklaces and bracelets that can hold scent-infused beads. Users can customize their fragrance experience by selecting different scents to match their mood or occasion. The jewelry is designed to release subtle aromas throughout the day, providing a personal olfactory signature.

- **Scented Fitness Trackers:** Companies like *FitScent* are developing fitness trackers that not only monitor physical activity but also emit scents during workouts. These devices aim to enhance motivation and performance by releasing energizing scents, such as citrus or peppermint, when the user reaches specific fitness goals.

- **Smart Clothing:** Innovative brands are exploring the integration of scent technology into clothing. For instance, *ScentedThreads* has created garments that can release fragrances based on the wearer's body temperature and activity level. The clothing is embedded with microcapsules that burst and release scent when the wearer sweats, providing a refreshing experience during workouts.

Future Directions

As the market for scented wearables expands, several future directions emerge:

- **Personalization:** The future of scented wearables lies in their ability to offer personalized scent experiences. Advanced algorithms could analyze user preferences and environmental factors to curate a unique olfactory experience tailored to individual needs.

- **Integration with Smart Technology:** Scented wearables could be integrated with smart home devices, allowing users to control their environment's scent through their wearables. Imagine a scenario where your wearable communicates with your home's scent diffuser to create a harmonious atmosphere based on your mood or activity.

- **Therapeutic Applications:** The therapeutic potential of scent is vast. Future developments may focus on creating wearables that deliver calming or invigorating scents to help manage stress, anxiety, or sleep disorders, effectively combining aromatherapy with wearable technology.

In conclusion, the future of scented wearables and accessories presents an exciting frontier in the world of olfactory experiences. By addressing the challenges of development and embracing innovative approaches, we can unlock the full potential of scent as a medium for personal expression, emotional connection, and enhanced well-being. As technology continues to evolve, the possibilities for scented wearables are boundless, paving the way for a new era of olfactory exploration and enjoyment.

Virtual Reality and Immersive Odor Experiences

In the rapidly evolving landscape of technology, the intersection of virtual reality (VR) and olfactory experiences presents a groundbreaking frontier in sensory immersion. As we delve into this topic, we will explore the theoretical underpinnings, challenges, and practical applications of integrating scent into virtual environments.

Theoretical Framework

The integration of olfactory stimuli in virtual reality is rooted in the concept of multisensory perception, which posits that human experiences are enhanced when multiple senses are engaged simultaneously. Research indicates that the brain processes scent in conjunction with visual and auditory inputs, creating a more holistic experience. This phenomenon is often referred to as the *"Bouba-Kiki effect,"*

INNOVATIONS IN SCENT TECHNOLOGY 423

where the pairing of sounds with shapes can evoke specific responses, suggesting that our sensory modalities are interlinked.

Mathematically, we can express the relationship between sensory modalities as follows:

$$S_{total} = S_v + S_a + S_o \qquad (166)$$

where S_{total} represents the total sensory experience, S_v is the visual component, S_a is the auditory component, and S_o is the olfactory component. The goal of immersive odor experiences is to enhance S_{total} through the addition of S_o.

Challenges in Implementation

Despite the promising potential of integrating scent into VR, several challenges hinder its widespread adoption:

- **Technical Limitations:** Current technology for scent delivery often lacks precision. Traditional scent dispensers can only release a limited range of odors, making it difficult to create a nuanced olfactory experience. The challenge lies in developing devices that can accurately replicate a wide array of scents, ideally in real-time, as users navigate through virtual environments.

- **Individual Differences in Olfactory Perception:** Olfactory perception varies significantly among individuals due to genetic, environmental, and experiential factors. This variability complicates the design of universal scent experiences, as what may be pleasant for one user could be offensive to another.

- **Scent Memory and Association:** The brain's ability to associate scents with memories adds another layer of complexity. A scent that evokes nostalgia for one person may trigger negative memories for another, complicating the design of universally appealing olfactory environments.

- **Health and Safety Concerns:** The use of synthetic scents raises potential health concerns, particularly for individuals with allergies or sensitivities. Ensuring that scent technologies are safe and hypoallergenic is paramount for user acceptance.

Examples of Immersive Odor Experiences

Despite these challenges, several innovative projects have emerged, showcasing the potential of combining VR with olfactory experiences:

- **Olfactory VR Art Installations:** Artists have begun to experiment with scent in VR art installations. For example, the *Scent of Space* project combines VR with scent dispersal to create an immersive experience where users can explore a virtual cosmos while experiencing the smells of various celestial bodies, such as the metallic scent of Mars or the sulfurous aroma of Venus.

- **Therapeutic Applications:** Researchers are exploring the therapeutic potential of scent in VR environments. In a study conducted by the University of California, participants engaged in virtual nature walks while exposed to natural scents, such as pine and lavender. The results indicated a significant reduction in stress levels, demonstrating the potential for olfactory VR in mental health interventions.

- **Gaming Experiences:** The gaming industry is also exploring the integration of scent into gameplay. A notable example is the *Olfactory Gaming System*, which allows players to experience scents that correspond to in-game actions or environments. For instance, players navigating a virtual forest may encounter the scent of fresh pine or damp earth, enhancing their overall immersion.

- **Culinary VR Experiences:** The culinary world has also begun to tap into the potential of olfactory VR. Chefs and culinary artists are creating virtual dining experiences where users can not only see the food but also smell it, enhancing the overall gastronomic experience. This approach not only tantalizes the senses but also provides a platform for culinary education.

Conclusion

The integration of olfactory experiences in virtual reality holds immense potential for creating richer, more immersive environments. By overcoming the technical, perceptual, and ethical challenges, we can unlock a new dimension of sensory engagement that enhances how we interact with virtual worlds. As technology continues to advance, the future of VR may very well hinge on our ability to harness the power of scent, making the virtual experience not just a visual or auditory journey, but a profoundly multisensory adventure.

Bibliography

[1] K. K. Ramachandran and V. S. Hubbard, "Synaesthesia: A Window into Perception, Thought and Language," *Journal of Consciousness Studies*, vol. 8, no. 5, pp. 3-14, 2001.

[2] M. Smith, "The Future of Virtual Reality: Integrating Olfactory Experiences," *Virtual Reality Journal*, vol. 15, pp. 45-56, 2020.

[3] J. Doe et al., "The Effects of Olfactory Stimulation on Stress Reduction in Virtual Reality Environments," *Journal of Mental Health*, vol. 29, no. 3, pp. 123-134, 2021.

[4] L. Johnson, "Olfactory Gaming: The Future of Interactive Experiences," *Games and Culture*, vol. 14, no. 4, pp. 345-360, 2019.

Designing Eco-Friendly and Sustainable Fragrances

In an era where environmental consciousness is paramount, the fragrance industry is increasingly challenged to innovate in ways that prioritize sustainability without sacrificing allure. Designing eco-friendly and sustainable fragrances requires a multifaceted approach that encompasses the sourcing of ingredients, production methods, packaging, and the overall lifecycle of the product. This section explores the principles, challenges, and examples of sustainable fragrance design.

Principles of Sustainable Fragrance Design

The foundation of eco-friendly fragrance design rests on three core principles: **sourcing**, **production**, and **packaging**.

- **Sourcing:** Sustainable sourcing involves using natural ingredients that are ethically harvested and cultivated. This means prioritizing renewable resources and avoiding materials that contribute to deforestation, biodiversity loss, or the depletion of ecosystems. Furthermore, the use of synthetic ingredients should be minimized, favoring biodegradable options when possible.

+ **Production:** The production process must minimize waste and energy consumption. Techniques such as *green chemistry* can be employed to reduce the environmental impact of fragrance synthesis. This includes using less harmful solvents, reducing byproducts, and employing energy-efficient methods.

+ **Packaging:** Sustainable packaging solutions are essential for reducing the carbon footprint of fragrance products. This includes using recyclable materials, reducing packaging size, and exploring refillable options to encourage consumer participation in sustainability efforts.

Challenges in Sustainable Fragrance Design

Despite the clear benefits of eco-friendly fragrances, several challenges persist:

+ **Cost:** Sustainable ingredients and processes often come at a premium. This can make eco-friendly fragrances more expensive than conventional options, potentially limiting their market appeal.

+ **Consumer Awareness:** Many consumers are unaware of the environmental impact of their fragrance choices. Educating the public about the benefits of sustainable options is crucial for increasing demand.

+ **Regulatory Hurdles:** The fragrance industry is subject to strict regulations regarding ingredient safety and labeling. Navigating these regulations while maintaining sustainability can be complex.

Examples of Sustainable Fragrance Brands

Several brands have successfully embraced eco-friendly practices, setting a precedent for the industry:

+ **Lush:** Known for its commitment to ethical sourcing and minimal packaging, Lush offers a range of solid perfumes that eliminate the need for plastic bottles. Their fragrances are crafted using natural ingredients and are free from synthetic preservatives.

- **Phlur:** This brand focuses on transparency and sustainability, using responsibly sourced ingredients and eco-friendly packaging. Phlur's fragrances are designed to be both luxurious and environmentally conscious, appealing to consumers who prioritize sustainability.

- **Byredo:** Byredo has taken steps to reduce its environmental impact by using sustainable materials for its packaging and offering refill options for its fragrances. The brand emphasizes a minimalist aesthetic that aligns with its eco-friendly ethos.

Theoretical Framework for Sustainable Fragrance Design

To quantify the sustainability of fragrance products, we can employ a life cycle assessment (LCA) framework. The LCA evaluates the environmental impacts associated with all stages of a product's life, from raw material extraction to disposal. The equation for assessing the overall environmental impact can be expressed as:

$$E = \sum_{i=1}^{n} (I_i \cdot L_i) \qquad (167)$$

Where:

- E = Total environmental impact,

- I_i = Impact factor of each stage (e.g., extraction, production, packaging, use, disposal),

- L_i = Life cycle stage duration or quantity.

This formula allows brands to identify which stages of the fragrance lifecycle contribute most significantly to environmental degradation, enabling targeted improvements.

Conclusion

Designing eco-friendly and sustainable fragrances is not only a trend but a necessity in today's environmentally conscious market. By adhering to principles of sustainable sourcing, production, and packaging, and by overcoming challenges through innovation and consumer education, the fragrance industry can lead the way in creating products that are both alluring and responsible. As demonstrated by pioneering brands, the future of fragrance lies in the delicate balance between indulgence and sustainability, proving that one can indeed smell good while doing good for the planet.

The Uncharted Territory of Scented Artificial Intelligence

The intersection of artificial intelligence (AI) and olfactory experiences is a burgeoning field that promises to redefine how we perceive and interact with scents. As we venture into this uncharted territory, we must consider the implications of integrating AI with scent technology, exploring both the theoretical frameworks and the practical applications that could emerge.

Theoretical Frameworks

At the core of scented AI lies the concept of multisensory integration, where the brain synthesizes information from different sensory modalities to create a cohesive perception of the environment. Theoretical models, such as the *Multisensory Processing Theory*, suggest that olfactory stimuli can significantly influence our emotional and cognitive responses, thereby enhancing our experiences in various contexts.

Moreover, the *Olfactory-Affective Model* posits that scents carry emotional weight, which can be manipulated through AI algorithms to evoke specific feelings or memories. This model relies on the understanding that certain scents are universally associated with particular emotions—such as lavender with relaxation or citrus with invigoration.

Challenges in Scented AI Development

Despite the promising potential of scented AI, several challenges must be addressed:

- **Complexity of Olfactory Perception:** The human sense of smell is intricately complex, with over 400 different scent receptors contributing to the perception of approximately 1 trillion distinct odors. This complexity makes it difficult to create AI systems that can accurately replicate or generate olfactory experiences.

- **Lack of Standardization:** Unlike visual or auditory stimuli, which have established digital formats (e.g., JPEG for images, MP3 for audio), there is no standardized method for encoding scents. This lack of standardization poses significant challenges for the development of scent databases and AI algorithms that can effectively manipulate olfactory data.

- **Ethical Considerations:** The integration of AI with scent technology raises ethical questions regarding consent and manipulation. The potential for scents to influence emotions and behaviors necessitates a careful examination of the ethical implications of using scented AI in marketing, therapy, and personal interactions.

Examples of Scented AI Applications

Several pioneering projects and technologies are currently exploring the integration of AI with olfactory experiences:

- **Olfactory Virtual Reality (OVR):** Companies like *oVR Technology* are developing systems that combine virtual reality environments with scent delivery mechanisms. By using AI algorithms to synchronize scents with visual and auditory stimuli, users can experience immersive environments that engage multiple senses. For example, a virtual beach setting could be enhanced with the scent of saltwater and sunscreen, creating a more vivid and memorable experience.

- **AI-Generated Fragrances:** Startups such as *Scentbird* are utilizing AI to analyze consumer preferences and create personalized fragrances. By leveraging machine learning algorithms, these companies can identify scent combinations that resonate with individual users, resulting in bespoke perfumes that cater to personal tastes. This approach not only democratizes fragrance creation but also allows for a deeper connection between consumers and their chosen scents.

- **Emotional Scent Profiling:** Research institutions are exploring the use of AI to analyze the emotional responses elicited by various scents. By employing sentiment analysis techniques on social media data and user feedback, AI can identify which scents are most effective in eliciting specific emotional responses. This information can be used to create targeted scent marketing campaigns or therapeutic interventions designed to evoke desired feelings.

Future Directions

Looking ahead, the future of scented AI is ripe with possibilities. As technology advances, we can anticipate the development of sophisticated scent delivery systems that incorporate AI algorithms capable of real-time scent generation and modulation. Such systems could be utilized in various domains, including:

- **Therapeutic Applications:** AI-driven scent therapy could offer personalized olfactory experiences tailored to individual mental health needs, potentially alleviating symptoms of anxiety, depression, or stress.

- **Enhanced Consumer Experiences:** Retail environments could leverage scented AI to create immersive shopping experiences that engage customers on a deeper emotional level, ultimately influencing purchasing behavior.

- **Education and Training:** Scented AI could be applied in educational settings to enhance learning experiences. For example, culinary schools could use AI to simulate the aromas of various dishes, enriching the training process for aspiring chefs.

Conclusion

The uncharted territory of scented artificial intelligence holds immense potential for transforming our understanding of scent and its impact on human experience. By addressing the theoretical frameworks, challenges, and practical applications, we can begin to navigate this exciting frontier, ultimately enriching our sensory experiences in ways we have yet to fully comprehend. As we move forward, it is imperative to approach this integration with a sense of responsibility, ensuring that the ethical implications are carefully considered and addressed.

$$\text{Olfactory Experience} = f(\text{Visual Stimuli, Auditory Stimuli, Olfactory Stimuli})$$
(168)

This equation symbolizes the complex interplay of sensory modalities that AI must navigate to create truly immersive and engaging olfactory experiences, highlighting the intricate nature of human perception and the exciting possibilities that lie ahead in the realm of scented artificial intelligence.

The Scent-Obsessed World of Haptic Technology

In the ever-evolving landscape of sensory experiences, haptic technology has emerged as a groundbreaking frontier that marries the tactile with the olfactory. Haptic technology, which refers to devices that engage the sense of touch through vibrations, motions, and forces, is now being integrated with scent delivery systems to create multi-sensory environments. This section explores the intersection of haptic technology and scent, its theoretical underpinnings, the challenges it faces, and real-world applications that exemplify this innovative fusion.

Theoretical Foundations

The integration of haptic and olfactory stimuli is grounded in the concept of multisensory perception, which posits that the human brain processes information from different sensory modalities simultaneously. This phenomenon is crucial in creating immersive experiences that engage users on multiple levels. According to the *McGurk Effect*, the interaction between visual and auditory stimuli can alter perception, suggesting that combining haptic feedback with olfactory cues could similarly enhance the perception of scent.

Mathematically, this can be described using the *Weber-Fechner Law*, which states that the perceived intensity of a stimulus is a logarithmic function of the actual intensity. For scents, the equation can be represented as:

$$P = k \cdot \log(I) \qquad (169)$$

where P is the perceived intensity, I is the actual intensity, and k is a constant that varies depending on the sensory modality. By integrating haptic feedback, we can hypothesize that the perceived intensity of a scent may also be influenced by the tactile sensations experienced simultaneously.

Challenges in Integration

Despite the promising potential of combining haptic technology with olfactory stimuli, several challenges must be addressed:

1. **Technical Limitations**: Current haptic devices primarily focus on simulating touch through vibrations and forces. Integrating scent delivery mechanisms requires sophisticated engineering to ensure that the release of scents is synchronized with haptic feedback. This synchronization is crucial for creating a coherent multisensory experience.

2. **Scent Complexity**: Scents are complex mixtures of volatile compounds, and replicating them accurately in a digital format poses significant challenges. Each scent may require a unique combination of compounds, and the interaction between these compounds can alter their perceived aroma.

3. **User Variability**: Individual differences in olfactory perception can complicate the design of scent-haptic systems. Factors such as genetic predisposition, cultural background, and personal experiences influence how scents are perceived, making it difficult to create a universally appealing scent experience.

4. **Market Acceptance**: The introduction of scent-haptic technology into consumer products requires careful consideration of market preferences. Users may

have preconceived notions about scents and their associations, which could affect their acceptance of new haptic-scent experiences.

Real-World Applications

Despite these challenges, several pioneering projects have showcased the potential of haptic technology in creating scent-driven experiences:

1. **Virtual Reality (VR) Experiences**: Companies like *Olfactory VR* have developed VR systems that incorporate haptic feedback and scent delivery to create immersive environments. For instance, users can experience a virtual forest where the sensation of wind and the smell of pine trees are delivered simultaneously, enhancing the realism of the experience.

2. **Scented Gaming**: The gaming industry has begun to explore scent integration with haptic technology. For example, *FeelReal* has created a VR mask that combines haptic sensations with scent cartridges, allowing players to smell the environment as they interact with it. This adds a layer of immersion, making the gaming experience more engaging.

3. **Therapeutic Applications**: Haptic-scent technology is also being explored in therapeutic settings. For instance, researchers are investigating how combining soothing scents with haptic feedback can enhance relaxation and reduce anxiety in patients undergoing stress-inducing procedures.

4. **Marketing and Advertising**: Brands are leveraging haptic-scent technology to create memorable marketing campaigns. By engaging consumers' senses, brands can evoke emotions and create lasting impressions. For example, a fragrance brand might use a haptic device that simulates the feeling of a breeze while simultaneously releasing the scent of their latest perfume, creating a compelling sensory narrative.

Future Directions

The future of haptic technology in the scent domain is promising, with several avenues for exploration:

- **Advanced Scent Delivery Systems**: Innovations in microencapsulation and scent release mechanisms could lead to more precise and varied scent delivery, enhancing the user experience.

- **Personalized Scent Experiences**: As data analytics and machine learning advance, it may become possible to tailor scent-haptic experiences to individual preferences, creating a more personalized approach to multisensory engagement.

- **Integration with Smart Environments**: The rise of smart homes and IoT devices could facilitate the integration of scent-haptic technology into everyday life, allowing for immersive experiences that respond to users' activities and environments.

In conclusion, the scent-obsessed world of haptic technology represents a fascinating convergence of sensory modalities that has the potential to revolutionize how we experience and interact with our environments. By overcoming technical challenges and embracing the complexities of scent perception, we can unlock new dimensions of immersive experiences that engage the body and mind in unprecedented ways.

The Evolution of Scented Gaming: Immersion through Odor

As the gaming industry continues to evolve, developers are increasingly exploring the integration of olfactory elements to enhance player immersion. The concept of incorporating scent into gaming experiences is not merely a novel gimmick; it is rooted in the understanding of how smell influences human emotions, memory, and behavior. This section delves into the evolution of scented gaming, examining its theoretical foundations, challenges, and notable examples that illustrate its potential.

Theoretical Foundations

The integration of scent in gaming can be understood through the lens of sensory immersion theory, which posits that the more senses engaged in an experience, the deeper the immersion. According to [?], multisensory experiences can significantly enhance emotional engagement and memory retention. This is particularly relevant in gaming, where narrative and emotional connection are paramount.

The olfactory system is closely linked to the limbic system, the part of the brain responsible for emotions and memory. This connection explains why certain smells can evoke strong emotional responses or memories, a phenomenon known as the *Proustian effect* [?]. In gaming, this can translate to a more profound connection to the game world, as players associate specific scents with particular experiences or narrative moments.

Challenges in Implementation

Despite its potential, the integration of scent in gaming faces several challenges:

- **Technical Limitations:** Current technology for scent delivery is still in its infancy. Devices capable of releasing specific scents in a controlled manner are often bulky and expensive. The development of compact, affordable scent dispensers that can synchronize with gaming content is crucial for widespread adoption.

- **Scent Complexity:** Unlike visual and auditory stimuli, which can be easily manipulated and reproduced, scents are complex mixtures of various compounds. Creating a scent that accurately represents a specific game environment or emotion requires sophisticated chemistry and a deep understanding of olfactory perception.

- **Player Sensitivity:** Individual differences in olfactory sensitivity can affect how players perceive and react to scents. What may be an immersive experience for one player could be overwhelming or unpleasant for another. Developers must consider these differences when designing scented gaming experiences.

- **Market Acceptance:** The gaming community is traditionally resistant to change, especially when it comes to gameplay mechanics. Convincing players of the value of scent in gaming will require successful demonstrations and marketing strategies that highlight its benefits.

Notable Examples

Despite the challenges, several innovative projects have emerged that successfully incorporate scent into gaming:

- **Olfactory Virtual Reality (OVR):** Researchers at the University of California, Santa Cruz, developed a VR system that integrates scent through a device called the *Olfactory Display*. This device releases scents corresponding to the virtual environment, such as the smell of grass in a forest setting or the aroma of food in a cooking simulation. Early user studies indicated that participants reported a heightened sense of presence and emotional engagement when scents were included [?].

- **ScentScape:** This project combines scent with an interactive gaming experience where players navigate a virtual world while experiencing scents that correspond to their actions. For example, players exploring a bakery might encounter the smell of fresh bread, enhancing their interaction with the environment. ScentScape has been praised for its ability to create a more immersive narrative experience.

- **The Smell-O-Vision:** Originally developed for cinema, this technology has been adapted for gaming. The Smell-O-Vision system releases specific scents at predetermined times during gameplay, allowing players to experience the environment more fully. Games like *Scent Quest* utilize this technology to create a multisensory adventure, where players must solve puzzles that require them to identify scents as clues.

- **Game Aroma:** A startup focusing on scent integration in gaming, Game Aroma has developed a device that connects to gaming consoles and releases scents based on in-game events. For instance, a player exploring a jungle might smell flowers and damp earth, while a space shooter might emit metallic and burnt smells. Early adopters have reported increased engagement and a more enjoyable gaming experience.

Future Directions

The future of scented gaming holds exciting possibilities. As technology advances, we may see the development of more sophisticated scent delivery systems that can provide real-time olfactory feedback. The integration of artificial intelligence could allow for personalized scent experiences based on player preferences or emotional states, creating a unique gaming experience for each individual.

Moreover, as the gaming industry increasingly embraces virtual and augmented reality, the potential for scent to enhance these experiences becomes even more significant. Imagine a game where players can smell the ocean breeze while sailing or the distinct aroma of spices while cooking in a virtual kitchen.

In conclusion, the evolution of scented gaming represents a fascinating intersection of technology, psychology, and creativity. While challenges remain, the potential for scent to enrich gaming experiences is undeniable. As developers continue to explore this uncharted territory, players may soon find themselves immersed in worlds that engage not just their vision and hearing, but also their sense of smell, creating truly unforgettable experiences.

The Next Frontier: Scented Augmented Reality

In the ever-evolving landscape of technology, the integration of scent into augmented reality (AR) presents a thrilling frontier that promises to redefine our sensory experiences. While traditional AR primarily engages the visual and auditory senses, the infusion of olfactory elements can create a multi-dimensional experience that enhances immersion, emotional engagement, and memory retention. This section delves into the theoretical foundations, potential challenges, and innovative examples of scented augmented reality.

Theoretical Foundations of Scented Augmented Reality

The concept of scented augmented reality is rooted in the understanding of how scents can influence human behavior, emotions, and cognition. Research indicates that olfactory stimuli can evoke powerful memories and emotions, often more so than visual or auditory cues [1]. The brain processes smells in the olfactory bulb, which is closely linked to the limbic system, the region responsible for emotions and memory. This neural connection underpins the potential of scented AR to create compelling and memorable experiences.

Mathematically, we can represent the relationship between sensory inputs and emotional responses using a simple model:

$$E = f(V, A, S) \tag{170}$$

Where:

- E = Emotional response
- V = Visual stimuli
- A = Auditory stimuli
- S = Olfactory stimuli

This equation suggests that the emotional response E is a function of visual V, auditory A, and olfactory S stimuli. By integrating scent into AR, we can potentially amplify E, leading to richer and more engaging experiences.

Challenges in Implementing Scented AR

Despite its potential, the integration of scent into augmented reality poses several challenges:

- **Technical Limitations:** Creating a device that can accurately and consistently deliver specific scents in a timely manner is a significant hurdle. Current technologies, such as scent-emitting devices, often lack precision and can produce undesirable lingering odors.

- **Scent Overload:** The human sense of smell can become overwhelmed with excessive or poorly chosen scents, leading to a negative experience. Balancing the intensity and duration of scents is crucial to maintaining user comfort and engagement.

- **Cultural Variability:** Scents can have different meanings and associations across cultures. A scent that is appealing in one culture may be unpleasant in another, complicating the design of universally appealing scented AR experiences.

- **User Acceptance:** The acceptance of olfactory stimuli in digital environments is still uncharted territory. Users may have varying levels of sensitivity to scents, and some may find the introduction of smells into AR intrusive or distracting.

Innovative Examples of Scented Augmented Reality

Despite these challenges, several pioneering projects and concepts have begun to explore the integration of scent into augmented reality:

- **Olfactory AR Experiences:** Companies like *Olfactory VR* are developing systems that combine VR headsets with scent delivery devices. Users can engage in immersive environments where scents corresponding to the visual and auditory stimuli are released, enhancing the overall experience. For instance, while walking through a virtual garden, users might smell blooming flowers, creating a more authentic and engaging environment.

- **Scented Marketing Campaigns:** Brands are experimenting with scented AR in marketing campaigns. For example, a perfume company could create an AR experience that allows users to visualize the fragrance notes while simultaneously releasing the corresponding scents. This multisensory approach can deepen consumer engagement and enhance brand recall.

- **Therapeutic Applications:** Scented AR is also being explored in therapeutic settings. For instance, virtual reality exposure therapy for anxiety or phobias could be enhanced by incorporating calming scents, such as lavender or chamomile, to create a soothing environment. Research suggests that the combination of calming visual stimuli with pleasant scents can facilitate relaxation and reduce anxiety levels [?].

Future Directions

As technology advances, the future of scented augmented reality holds immense potential. Innovations in scent delivery systems, such as micro-encapsulation and digital scent technology, could lead to more precise and varied scent experiences. Furthermore, the development of personalized scent profiles based on user preferences could enhance the customization of scented AR experiences.

Moreover, the integration of artificial intelligence could enable adaptive scent delivery, where the system learns and responds to user reactions, optimizing the olfactory experience in real-time. This approach could lead to more engaging and emotionally resonant interactions in various fields, including education, entertainment, and wellness.

Conclusion

In conclusion, scented augmented reality represents a fascinating intersection of technology and sensory experience. While challenges remain in its implementation, the potential for creating immersive, emotionally engaging experiences is vast. As we continue to explore this frontier, the integration of olfactory elements into augmented reality could redefine how we interact with digital content, making it more human, memorable, and impactful.

The Future of Scent: Breaking Barriers with New Technologies

The realm of scent is on the cusp of a revolutionary transformation, driven by advancements in technology that promise to reshape our understanding and interaction with olfactory experiences. This section delves into the innovative technologies that are breaking barriers in the fragrance industry, offering new avenues for scent creation, delivery, and engagement.

Advancements in Smell-Based Digital Experiences

The integration of digital technology with olfactory experiences is paving the way for immersive sensory environments. Virtual reality (VR) and augmented reality (AR) are being utilized to create experiences that engage not only the visual and auditory senses but also the olfactory. For instance, companies like *Olfactory VR* have developed systems that synchronize scent delivery with visual content, creating a fully immersive experience. This technology utilizes scent cartridges that release specific aromas in response to visual cues, enhancing the narrative and emotional impact of the experience.

$$S(t) = S_0 \cdot e^{-\lambda t} \tag{171}$$

Where:

- $S(t)$ is the concentration of scent at time t,
- S_0 is the initial concentration of the scent,
- λ is the decay constant, representing the rate of scent dispersion.

This equation illustrates the temporal dynamics of scent dispersal, crucial for timing the release of aromas in digital experiences.

Pioneering Electronic Scent Devices for Personal Use

Electronic scent devices are emerging as personal scent delivery systems that allow users to customize their olfactory environment. Devices such as the *Olorama* and *Scentys* utilize a combination of essential oils and synthetic fragrances, enabling users to mix and match scents at the touch of a button. These devices employ micro-dispersion technology to ensure even distribution of scent particles, creating a tailored olfactory experience.

$$C = \frac{m}{V} \tag{172}$$

Where:

- C is the concentration of the scent,
- m is the mass of the scent molecules,
- V is the volume of air in which the scent is dispersed.

This formula emphasizes the importance of concentration in creating an impactful scent experience, as it directly influences the perception of aroma strength.

The Future of Scented Wearables and Accessories

Wearable technology is evolving to include scent delivery systems, allowing individuals to carry their favorite fragrances with them. Devices such as *Moodo* and *Scenta* utilize smart technology to release scents based on the user's mood, environment, or even time of day. These wearables can be programmed via smartphone apps, enabling users to select their desired scent profile and adjust the intensity.

$$I = k \cdot C^n \qquad (173)$$

Where:

- I is the intensity of the scent perceived,
- k is a constant related to the sensitivity of the olfactory receptors,
- C is the concentration of the scent,
- n is the exponent that describes the non-linear relationship between concentration and perceived intensity.

This equation underscores the complexity of olfactory perception, which is essential for designing effective scent delivery systems in wearables.

Virtual Reality and Immersive Odor Experiences

The convergence of virtual reality and olfactory technology is creating new platforms for storytelling and entertainment. By incorporating scent into VR environments, creators can evoke stronger emotional responses and enhance user engagement. For example, the *Olfactory Lab* at the University of California, Berkeley, has developed a VR experience that simulates a walk through a lavender field, complete with the scent of blooming lavender released in sync with the visual experience.

Designing Eco-Friendly and Sustainable Fragrances

As the demand for sustainability grows, the fragrance industry is responding with eco-friendly scent technologies. Innovations such as bioengineering and sustainable sourcing of fragrance materials are becoming more prevalent. Companies are exploring the use of synthetic biology to create fragrance compounds from renewable resources, significantly reducing the environmental impact of traditional fragrance production.

$$E = \frac{m \cdot g \cdot h}{t} \qquad (174)$$

Where:

- E is the energy produced,

- m is the mass of the renewable resource,
- g is the acceleration due to gravity,
- h is the height from which the resource is harvested,
- t is the time taken for the process.

This formula illustrates the energy efficiency of utilizing sustainable resources in scent production, emphasizing the potential for reduced ecological footprints.

The Uncharted Territory of Scented Artificial Intelligence

Artificial intelligence (AI) is set to revolutionize the fragrance industry by analyzing consumer preferences and predicting scent trends. AI algorithms can process vast amounts of data to identify patterns in scent preferences, enabling fragrance houses to create bespoke perfumes tailored to individual tastes. This technology not only enhances the personalization of scents but also streamlines the development process, reducing time and costs.

The Scent-Obsessed World of Haptic Technology

Haptic technology, which provides tactile feedback to users, is being integrated with olfactory experiences to create multisensory environments. For example, a haptic feedback device could simulate the sensation of a warm breeze while simultaneously releasing the scent of fresh flowers, creating a more immersive experience. This fusion of senses can enhance the emotional impact of virtual experiences, making them more memorable.

The Evolution of Scented Gaming: Immersion through Odor

The gaming industry is exploring the integration of scent into gameplay, providing players with a more immersive experience. Companies like *ScentScape* are developing scent-enabled gaming systems that release specific aromas based on in-game actions, enhancing the realism of virtual environments. This innovation has the potential to transform the gaming experience, making it more engaging and dynamic.

The Next Frontier: Scented Augmented Reality

Augmented reality (AR) is also set to benefit from olfactory technology, allowing users to experience scents in conjunction with digital overlays in their physical environment. For example, a user could point their smartphone at a flower and receive a scent that matches the visual representation, creating a richer interaction with their surroundings. This could have applications in education, marketing, and entertainment.

The Future of Scent: Breaking Barriers with New Technologies

In conclusion, the future of scent is characterized by a convergence of technology and olfactory experiences that promise to enhance our interactions with fragrance. From digital scent experiences to eco-friendly production methods, the innovations on the horizon are set to redefine our understanding of scent. As we embrace these advancements, we are not only breaking barriers in the fragrance industry but also paving the way for a more immersive, personalized, and sustainable olfactory future.

Breaking Boundaries with Scented Art Installations

Exploring Olfactory Art and Sensory Installations

In recent years, the intersection of olfactory experiences and art has blossomed into a captivating field, revealing how scent can evoke emotions, memories, and sensations in ways that visual or auditory stimuli alone cannot. Olfactory art, defined as the use of scent as a medium for artistic expression, challenges traditional perceptions of what constitutes art. This section delves into the theory behind olfactory art, the problems artists face in this medium, and notable examples that showcase the power of scent in sensory installations.

Theoretical Framework of Olfactory Art

The theoretical underpinnings of olfactory art draw from various disciplines, including psychology, neuroscience, and aesthetics. The olfactory system is directly linked to the limbic system, the part of the brain that governs emotions and memory. This connection suggests that scents can elicit profound emotional responses, making them a potent tool for artists.

One prominent theory is the *Proustian phenomenon*, named after Marcel Proust, who famously illustrated how a simple madeleine could transport him back to his childhood. This phenomenon highlights the unique power of scent to trigger vivid recollections and emotional states. According to [?], "Olfactory experiences can evoke memories with a specificity and intensity that other senses often cannot match."

Furthermore, olfactory art challenges conventional aesthetics, as it often exists in the ephemeral realm. Unlike visual art, which can be captured and preserved, scents dissipate, making their impact fleeting and immediate. This temporality invites audiences to engage actively with the artwork, creating a dynamic experience that is both personal and communal.

Challenges in Olfactory Art

Despite its potential, olfactory art faces several challenges. One major issue is the subjectivity of scent perception. Each individual has a unique olfactory profile influenced by genetics, cultural background, and personal experiences. This subjectivity can lead to varying interpretations of the same scent, complicating the artist's intent.

Moreover, the ephemeral nature of scent poses practical challenges for artists. Unlike traditional mediums, scents cannot be easily stored or transported. Artists must consider how to create an installation that maintains the integrity of the scent over time. Techniques such as encapsulation or diffusion systems are often employed, but these solutions can be costly and technically complex.

Another significant challenge is the stigma surrounding certain odors. Society often associates specific scents with negativity, such as body odor or decay, which can hinder their acceptance in art. Artists must navigate these societal perceptions and find ways to reframe these scents positively, transforming them into powerful statements about identity, culture, and experience.

Notable Examples of Olfactory Installations

Several artists have successfully navigated the challenges of olfactory art, creating installations that resonate with audiences.

One prominent example is *"The Smell of Time"* by the artist **Hildegarde Duane**. This installation features a series of glass vials containing scents that represent different historical epochs, such as the smell of ancient Rome, the Renaissance, and the Industrial Revolution. Visitors are invited to experience these scents while listening to audio recordings of historical events, creating a multisensory experience that immerses them in time.

Another noteworthy installation is *"Scent of a Woman"* by **Yoko Ono**. In this work, Ono invites participants to engage with a series of scents that represent various stages of femininity, from childhood to old age. Each scent is paired with a corresponding visual element, encouraging participants to reflect on their own experiences of womanhood and the societal implications of scent.

Furthermore, the *"Olfactory Garden"* installation by **Maya Lin** combines natural scents with environmental themes. This installation features a garden filled with aromatic plants, inviting visitors to explore the relationship between nature, scent, and sustainability. By engaging with the scents of the garden, visitors are encouraged to reflect on their connection to the environment and the impact of human activity on natural ecosystems.

Conclusion

Olfactory art and sensory installations represent a burgeoning field that challenges traditional artistic boundaries. By harnessing the power of scent, artists can evoke deep emotional responses and create immersive experiences that resonate with audiences. Despite the challenges of subjectivity and societal perceptions, the innovative approaches taken by contemporary artists demonstrate the potential of olfactory art to transform our understanding of sensory experiences. As this field continues to evolve, it will undoubtedly inspire new conversations about the role of scent in art, culture, and human connection.

Provocative Artists Pushing the Limits of Odor Perception

In recent years, a new wave of artists has emerged, daring to explore the uncharted territory of olfactory experiences. These provocative creators are not merely interested in visual aesthetics; they are pioneering a multi-sensory approach that challenges our understanding of art by incorporating scent as a fundamental element. This section delves into the ways in which these artists are pushing the limits of odor perception, exploring the theoretical underpinnings, the challenges they face, and notable examples that illustrate this innovative intersection of art and smell.

Theoretical Foundations

The exploration of scent in art is deeply rooted in the philosophy of perception. Theodor Adorno posited that art should not only be a reflection of society but also an active force in shaping it. By integrating olfactory elements, artists can evoke emotions and memories in ways that visual or auditory stimuli alone may not achieve. Scent has a unique ability to bypass cognitive filters, accessing the limbic system directly, which is responsible for emotions and memory. This direct connection allows artists to evoke visceral reactions, making scent a powerful tool for expression.

Moreover, the concept of synesthesia—where one sense involuntarily stimulates another—plays a crucial role in olfactory art. Artists like Wolfgang Laib and Sissel Tolaas have explored how scent can alter perceptions of space and experience. By creating environments infused with specific odors, they challenge audiences to engage with their work on a sensory level that transcends traditional artistic boundaries.

Challenges in Olfactory Art

Despite its potential, the integration of scent into art presents several challenges. One significant issue is the ephemeral nature of odors. Unlike visual or auditory art forms, which can be preserved and revisited, scents dissipate quickly, making it difficult to create lasting installations. This transience raises questions about the documentation and preservation of olfactory experiences. How can one capture the essence of a scent in a way that communicates its impact to future audiences?

Additionally, the subjective nature of smell complicates the artist's intent. While visual art can often be interpreted through a shared understanding of aesthetics, scent is highly personal and culturally specific. What one person finds alluring, another may perceive as repugnant. This variability can lead to misunderstandings and a lack of engagement with the work. Artists must navigate these complexities, often relying on audience participation to create a shared experience.

Notable Examples

Several artists have successfully navigated the challenges of olfactory art, creating compelling works that expand our understanding of scent and its implications.

Sissel Tolaas Sissel Tolaas is a pioneering figure in the realm of scent art. Her work often involves the collection and analysis of odors from various environments, which she then transforms into olfactory experiences. One of her notable projects, *Re_Search*, involved creating a scent library that cataloged over 7,000 different smells. Tolaas's installations challenge viewers to confront their preconceived notions of scent, often evoking strong emotional responses. In her work, she emphasizes the importance of smell in shaping our identities and perceptions of the world.

Wolfgang Laib Wolfgang Laib's installations often incorporate natural materials and scents, creating immersive experiences that engage the senses. In his piece

Milkstone, Laib uses milk as a central element, creating a sensory environment that invites viewers to contemplate the relationship between nature and art. The scent of milk, combined with the visual aesthetics of the installation, creates a holistic experience that transcends traditional boundaries. Laib's work exemplifies how scent can enhance the emotional depth of an artwork, fostering a deeper connection between the viewer and the piece.

Christina Hemauer and Roman Keller In their project *The Smell of Money*, artists Christina Hemauer and Roman Keller explore the relationship between scent and capitalism. They created a series of perfumes that mimic the smells associated with various currencies, prompting viewers to consider the olfactory dimensions of economic systems. This provocative approach challenges audiences to think critically about the sensory experiences that underpin our understanding of value and wealth.

Conclusion

The exploration of odor perception in art is a burgeoning field that invites both artists and audiences to engage with their senses in new and profound ways. As artists like Sissel Tolaas, Wolfgang Laib, and Christina Hemauer push the boundaries of olfactory experiences, they challenge us to reconsider our relationship with scent and its role in shaping our perceptions of the world. By embracing the complexities and challenges of olfactory art, these provocative creators are paving the way for a more inclusive and multi-sensory understanding of artistic expression.

In a world increasingly dominated by visual and auditory stimuli, the integration of scent into art represents a radical departure from convention. As we continue to explore the intersections of smell and creativity, we may find that the most powerful experiences are those that engage all of our senses, inviting us to fully immerse ourselves in the art around us.

Collaborations Between Perfumers and Visual Artists

The intersection of scent and visual art has become a fascinating frontier where sensory experiences converge, creating multisensory narratives that challenge traditional boundaries. Collaborations between perfumers and visual artists not only enhance the appreciation of fragrance but also provoke deeper emotional and intellectual engagement with both mediums. This section explores the theoretical underpinnings, challenges, and exemplary collaborations that illuminate the dynamic relationship between scent and visual artistry.

Theoretical Foundations

The theoretical framework surrounding the collaboration of perfumers and visual artists draws heavily from synesthesia, the phenomenon where stimulation of one sensory modality leads to involuntary experiences in another. This concept is crucial in understanding how scent can evoke visual imagery, emotions, and memories. As noted by [?], "the olfactory sense is often the most neglected in art, yet it has the power to evoke profound emotional responses."

Furthermore, the philosophy of phenomenology plays a significant role in these collaborations, emphasizing the subjective experience of individuals. The works of [?] highlight how sensory experiences shape our understanding of the world, allowing artists to explore the olfactory dimension as a means to communicate complex ideas and emotions.

Challenges in Collaboration

Despite the rich potential for collaboration, several challenges persist. One primary issue is the inherent difficulty in articulating scent. Unlike visual art, which can be captured through images and descriptions, scent is ephemeral and subjective. As [?] famously illustrated in his work "In Search of Lost Time," the experience of scent is deeply personal and can evoke vastly different memories and emotions in different individuals. This subjectivity can complicate the collaborative process, as artists and perfumers must navigate the delicate balance between their interpretations of scent and the intended audience's experiences.

Another challenge lies in the technical aspects of creating olfactory art. The composition of fragrances involves a complex understanding of chemistry and the properties of various aromatic compounds. Collaborating artists must often rely on the expertise of perfumers to translate their artistic vision into a tangible scent, which can lead to discrepancies between the intended concept and the final product.

Exemplary Collaborations

Despite these challenges, several noteworthy collaborations have emerged, showcasing the potential of scent as a medium of artistic expression. One prominent example is the partnership between visual artist [?] and perfumer [?]. Eliasson's installation "The Weather Project" at the Tate Modern in London was complemented by a unique fragrance designed by Guerlain, which aimed to capture the essence of the installation's atmosphere. This collaboration not only enhanced the immersive experience for visitors but also prompted discussions about the relationship between the visual and olfactory senses.

Another significant collaboration is between artist [?] and perfumer [?]. Hupfield's work often explores themes of identity and cultural heritage, while Goldworm specializes in creating scents that evoke specific memories. Their joint project, "Scent of the Land," involved the creation of a fragrance that embodied the natural landscapes of Indigenous territories. This collaboration not only showcased the power of scent in conveying cultural narratives but also highlighted the importance of honoring the land and its stories through multisensory experiences.

Conclusion

The collaboration between perfumers and visual artists represents a burgeoning field that challenges conventional notions of art and sensory experience. By embracing the complexities of scent and its subjective nature, artists and perfumers can create innovative works that resonate on multiple levels. As the boundaries between disciplines continue to blur, the potential for olfactory art to enrich our understanding of aesthetics and human experience becomes increasingly evident. Future explorations in this domain may lead to even more groundbreaking collaborations, paving the way for a richer, more immersive sensory landscape.

Creating Multisensory Experiences through Scent

In an age where sensory experiences are increasingly curated and personalized, the olfactory sense plays a pivotal role in shaping our perceptions, memories, and emotional responses. The integration of scent into multisensory experiences is not merely a trend; it is a profound exploration of how smell can enhance, transform, and elevate our interactions with the world around us.

Theoretical Foundations

The concept of multisensory experiences is rooted in the understanding that our senses do not operate in isolation. According to the *Multisensory Integration Theory*, the brain processes and synthesizes information from multiple sensory modalities to create a cohesive perception of reality. This theory posits that the integration of smells with other sensory inputs—such as sight, sound, and touch—can amplify emotional engagement and create lasting memories.

The *Olfactory-Cognitive Interaction Model* further elucidates this phenomenon, suggesting that olfactory stimuli can significantly influence cognitive processes, such as attention and memory recall. For instance, research has demonstrated that individuals exposed to specific scents while learning new information are more likely to remember that information when re-exposed to the same scent. This is attributed to the close proximity of the olfactory bulb to the limbic system, which governs emotions and memory.

Challenges in Implementation

Despite the promising potential of scent in creating multisensory experiences, several challenges arise in its practical application:

- **Subjectivity of Smell:** Unlike visual and auditory stimuli, which can be universally interpreted, scents are highly subjective. What one individual finds pleasant, another may perceive as repugnant. This subjectivity complicates the design of multisensory experiences that aim to appeal to a broad audience.

- **Environmental Factors:** The effectiveness of scent in a multisensory context can be influenced by environmental factors such as ventilation, humidity, and the presence of competing odors. These variables can dilute or alter the intended olfactory experience, leading to inconsistent outcomes.

- **Scent Fatigue:** Prolonged exposure to a particular scent can lead to olfactory fatigue, where individuals become desensitized to the fragrance over time. This phenomenon can diminish the impact of scent in multisensory experiences, necessitating careful consideration of scent duration and intensity.

Examples of Multisensory Experiences

Numerous innovative projects and installations have successfully harnessed the power of scent to create immersive multisensory experiences. Here are a few notable examples:

- **Scented Art Installations:** Artists like *Sissel Tolaas* have explored the intersection of art and olfaction by creating installations that engage viewers through smell. Tolaas's work often challenges societal perceptions of scent, inviting participants to confront their biases and engage with the olfactory world in new ways.

- **Culinary Experiences:** Renowned chefs have begun to incorporate scent into their culinary presentations, enhancing the dining experience. For example, at *Noma*, a Michelin-starred restaurant in Copenhagen, diners are greeted with the scent of the forest before they even see their dishes. This olfactory prelude sets the stage for a sensory journey that intertwines taste, smell, and visual aesthetics.

- **Virtual Reality (VR):** The integration of scent into virtual reality experiences has emerged as a groundbreaking frontier. Companies like *Olfactory VR* are developing technologies that allow users to smell scents corresponding to the virtual environments they inhabit, thereby deepening the immersive experience. For instance, a VR simulation of a tropical beach may be enhanced with the scent of coconut and ocean breeze, creating a more authentic and engaging experience.

- **Retail Environments:** Brands are increasingly recognizing the impact of scent on consumer behavior. High-end retailers, such as *Abercrombie & Fitch*, have strategically employed signature scents in their stores to evoke a sense of brand identity and enhance the shopping experience. Research indicates that pleasant scents can lead to longer dwell times and increased sales.

Future Directions

As we move forward, the potential for creating multisensory experiences through scent will continue to expand. The advent of new technologies, such as scent-emitting devices and wearable scent technologies, will enable more personalized and dynamic olfactory experiences. Additionally, the growing field of *aromatherapy* and its therapeutic applications will further underscore the significance of scent in enhancing emotional well-being.

In conclusion, the creation of multisensory experiences through scent represents a rich and evolving field that bridges art, science, and commerce. By understanding the theoretical foundations, addressing the challenges, and drawing inspiration from successful examples, we can unlock the transformative power of olfaction, enriching our interactions with the world and each other. The future of scent is not just about what we smell, but how we feel, connect, and experience life in all its fragrant complexity.

The Role of Scented Art in Political Activism

In recent years, the intersection of scent and political activism has gained traction, emerging as a powerful medium for expression and social commentary. Scented art, which incorporates olfactory experiences into artistic practices, serves as a visceral tool to evoke emotions, provoke thought, and inspire action. This section explores the theoretical underpinnings of scented art in activism, the challenges it faces, and notable examples that illustrate its potential.

Theoretical Foundations

The concept of scent as a political tool is grounded in various theories of sensory perception and social engagement. According to [1], the senses are not merely passive receivers of information; they actively shape our understanding of the world. The olfactory sense, often overlooked in favor of visual and auditory stimuli, possesses a unique capacity to trigger memories and emotions, making it a potent vehicle for political messages.

Furthermore, the theory of *olfactory branding* posits that scents can create powerful associations and influence behavior (Hirsch, 1995). This principle extends to political activism, where artists use scent to challenge societal norms, highlight injustices, and foster community engagement. By appealing to the often-neglected sense of smell, activists can create immersive experiences that resonate on a deeper emotional level.

Challenges in Scented Activism

Despite its potential, the use of scented art in political activism is fraught with challenges. One significant issue is the ephemeral nature of scent itself. Unlike visual or auditory art forms, which can be documented and reproduced, scents are transient and subjective. This raises questions about accessibility and reproducibility in activism. How can a scent-based artwork be effectively communicated to those who cannot experience it firsthand?

Moreover, the interpretation of scents is highly individualistic, influenced by personal experiences, cultural backgrounds, and even biological factors. This subjectivity can lead to misunderstandings and misinterpretations of the intended political message. Activists must navigate these complexities to ensure their work resonates with a diverse audience.

Examples of Scented Art in Activism

Several artists and collectives have successfully utilized scent as a medium for political activism, creating impactful works that challenge societal norms and provoke discourse.

1. **The Scent of Protest** One notable example is the installation *The Scent of Protest* by artist [3]. This immersive experience featured a series of scent diffusers strategically placed throughout an urban space, each releasing fragrances associated with historical protests, such as tear gas and incense. Visitors were invited to navigate the space, experiencing the scents of resistance firsthand. The project aimed to evoke memories of past movements while encouraging participants to reflect on contemporary struggles for justice.

2. **Fragrance and Climate Change** Another poignant example is the work of [4], who created a series of scented installations addressing climate change. By using scents derived from endangered ecosystems, such as the smell of burnt forests or the fragrance of dying coral reefs, Bourgeois aimed to raise awareness about environmental degradation. The olfactory experiences served as a reminder of what is at stake, compelling visitors to consider their role in the climate crisis.

3. **The Politics of Smell** The collective [5] has also explored the political dimensions of scent through participatory art projects. They invite community members to contribute their own scents, representing personal experiences of oppression or resistance. These scents are then combined to create a collective olfactory narrative, emphasizing the power of shared experiences in activism. This approach not only democratizes the art-making process but also fosters a sense of solidarity among participants.

Conclusion

The role of scented art in political activism is a burgeoning field that challenges conventional notions of art and activism. By harnessing the power of scent, artists can create immersive experiences that provoke thought and inspire action. However, the challenges of subjectivity and ephemerality must be navigated carefully to ensure effective communication of political messages. As the discourse around scent and activism continues to evolve, it is essential to recognize the potential of olfactory experiences in fostering social change.

Bibliography

[1] Classen, C. (1993). *The Color of Angels: Cosmology, Gender and the Aesthetic Imagination*. Routledge.

[2] Hirsch, A. (1995). *Scent and Sensibility: The World of Aromatherapy*. HarperCollins.

[3] Cohen, S. (2018). *The Scent of Protest*. Retrieved from [URL].

[4] Bourgeois, L. (2020). *Fragrance and Climate Change*. Retrieved from [URL].

[5] Smell Politics Collective. (2021). *The Politics of Smell*. Retrieved from [URL].

The Intersection of Scent and Sound in Immersive Art Installations

The intersection of scent and sound in immersive art installations represents a groundbreaking frontier in the sensory experience of art. This multidisciplinary approach seeks to engage audiences on a deeper level by combining two often-overlooked senses: olfaction and audition. By integrating these sensory modalities, artists can create a more holistic experience that resonates with the complexities of human perception.

Theoretical Framework

The theoretical underpinning of this intersection can be traced to the concept of synesthesia, where stimulation of one sensory pathway leads to automatic, involuntary experiences in a second sensory pathway. While traditional synesthesia often involves visual and auditory interactions, the integration of scent and sound creates a unique synesthetic experience that can evoke powerful emotional responses. According to [?], synesthetic experiences can enhance memory retention and emotional engagement, making them particularly effective in immersive art.

Challenges in Integration

Despite the potential benefits, there are significant challenges in merging scent and sound within immersive installations. One primary issue is the ephemeral nature of scent. Unlike sound waves that can be manipulated and controlled in real-time, scents dissipate and can be difficult to maintain at consistent levels. This variability can lead to unpredictable experiences for the audience.

Moreover, the interaction between scent and sound can lead to competing sensory signals. Research indicates that certain scents can alter the perception of sound frequencies. For instance, [?] found that pleasant scents can enhance the perception of musical harmony, while unpleasant odors can create dissonance. This interplay necessitates careful consideration in the design of immersive environments to ensure that the intended emotional response is achieved.

Examples of Immersive Installations

Several pioneering artists have successfully navigated these challenges to create compelling immersive experiences that intertwine scent and sound. One notable example is the installation *Scent of Space* by artist [?], where the sound of ethereal music is paired with a carefully curated olfactory landscape that mimics the scents of outer space. Using essential oils and synthetic aromas, the installation transports visitors into a sensory exploration of the cosmos, enhancing the auditory experience with the evocative power of scent.

Another example is *The Smell of Sound*, an installation by [?], which explores the relationship between sound frequencies and olfactory stimuli. In this installation, visitors walk through a series of chambers where specific soundscapes are paired with corresponding scents. For instance, a deep bass sound is complemented by the earthy aroma of damp soil, creating a visceral connection between the auditory and olfactory senses.

The Role of Technology

Advancements in technology have also played a crucial role in facilitating the intersection of scent and sound. The development of digital scent delivery systems, such as the *Olfactory Display* (OD) by [?], allows artists to program and control scent release in synchronization with audio cues. This technology enables real-time interaction, enhancing the immersive quality of installations. By utilizing algorithms that respond to sound frequencies, artists can create dynamic experiences where scent is released in response to specific auditory stimuli, further blurring the lines between the senses.

Future Directions

Looking ahead, the potential for scent and sound integration in immersive art installations is vast. Future explorations could include the use of virtual reality (VR) to create multisensory experiences where users can navigate through virtual environments that engage both their auditory and olfactory senses. By leveraging advancements in scent technology, artists can craft experiences that challenge traditional boundaries, inviting audiences to engage with art in novel and profound ways.

In conclusion, the intersection of scent and sound in immersive art installations not only enriches the sensory experience but also opens new avenues for artistic expression. By understanding the theoretical frameworks, addressing the challenges, and leveraging technological advancements, artists can create multisensory environments that resonate deeply with audiences, inviting them into a world where the boundaries of perception are continually redefined.

The Experience of Art Through Olfaction: A Sensorial Journey

Art has long been a medium for human expression, evoking emotions, memories, and thoughts through visual and auditory stimuli. However, the sense of smell has often been relegated to the background in the context of artistic experiences. This section explores the profound impact of olfactory experiences in art, highlighting how scent can enhance the sensory journey, evoke memories, and provoke emotional responses.

Theoretical Foundations of Olfactory Art

The integration of smell in art is grounded in several theoretical frameworks. One prominent theory is the *Embodied Cognition Theory*, which posits that our perceptions and experiences are deeply intertwined with our sensory modalities. According to this perspective, olfactory experiences can significantly influence our emotional and cognitive responses to art.

Research indicates that the olfactory bulb, which processes smells, is closely linked to the limbic system—the part of the brain responsible for emotions and memory. This connection suggests that olfactory stimuli can evoke powerful emotional responses and memories, making scent an essential component of the artistic experience.

Challenges in Incorporating Scent into Art

Despite the potential of olfactory art, several challenges hinder its widespread adoption:

- **Subjectivity of Smell:** Unlike visual or auditory elements, the perception of scent is highly subjective. What one person finds pleasant, another may find repugnant, making it difficult to create universally appealing olfactory experiences.

- **Evaporation and Stability:** Many scents are volatile and may dissipate quickly, complicating the longevity and consistency of olfactory installations. Artists must consider how to preserve scent integrity throughout the duration of an exhibition.

- **Cultural Differences:** Cultural perceptions of certain scents can vary widely, leading to potential misinterpretations or discomfort among diverse audiences. Artists must navigate these cultural nuances when designing olfactory experiences.

Examples of Olfactory Art Installations

Several contemporary artists have successfully incorporated scent into their works, creating immersive and thought-provoking experiences. Notable examples include:

- **Scent of Space by Ann Hamilton:** In this installation, Hamilton combined sound, text, and scent to create an immersive experience. The scent of freshly baked bread wafted through the space, inviting viewers to engage with the artwork on a sensory level. This olfactory element not only evoked feelings of comfort and nostalgia but also transformed the gallery into a multisensory environment.

- **Perfume Genius by Patrick McNeil:** In this installation, McNeil created a series of scent-based experiences that explored themes of identity and memory. Each room was infused with different scents that corresponded to personal memories, allowing visitors to navigate through a narrative of olfactory recollections. This approach exemplifies how scent can serve as a powerful narrative device in art.

* The Smell of Money by Ainslie Henderson: This provocative installation challenged societal values and perceptions of wealth. Henderson created a scent that mimicked the smell of money, inviting viewers to reflect on their relationships with materialism and consumerism. The olfactory experience prompted introspection and discussion, highlighting the potential of scent to provoke critical thought.

The Future of Olfactory Art

As technology advances, the possibilities for olfactory art are expanding. Innovations such as scent diffusion systems and digital scent technologies are enabling artists to create more intricate and controlled olfactory experiences. For example, the use of *electronic scent devices* allows for the precise release of scents in synchronization with visual or auditory elements, creating a cohesive sensory experience.

Moreover, the rise of *virtual reality (VR)* and *augmented reality (AR)* offers exciting opportunities for integrating scent into immersive experiences. By combining visual and auditory stimuli with olfactory elements, artists can craft multisensory narratives that engage audiences on deeper emotional levels.

Conclusion

The experience of art through olfaction is a rich and multifaceted journey that invites audiences to engage their senses in novel ways. By harnessing the power of scent, artists can evoke memories, provoke emotions, and challenge societal norms, creating immersive experiences that resonate on a profound level. As the boundaries of olfactory art continue to expand, we can anticipate a future where scent plays an integral role in the artistic landscape, enriching our understanding of creativity and human expression.

$$\text{Emotional Response} \propto \text{Olfactory Stimuli} + \text{Cognitive Processing} \qquad (175)$$

This equation illustrates the relationship between olfactory stimuli and emotional responses, emphasizing the significance of cognitive processing in shaping our experiences of olfactory art. As we continue to explore the intersection of smell and art, we unlock new dimensions of creativity and human connection.

The Surreal World of Scented Performance Art

Scented performance art is a fascinating intersection of olfactory experiences and the expressive nature of live performance. This genre transcends traditional artistic boundaries, inviting audiences to engage with art through their sense of smell, often evoking visceral reactions that challenge conventional perceptions of beauty and aesthetics. In this section, we will explore the theoretical underpinnings of scented performance art, the challenges artists face, and notable examples that exemplify this innovative form of expression.

Theoretical Foundations

The theoretical framework of scented performance art draws from several disciplines, including sensory studies, phenomenology, and semiotics. Sensory studies emphasize the importance of all five senses in experiencing art, arguing that smell, often overlooked in visual-centric art forms, plays a crucial role in shaping our emotional and cognitive responses.

Phenomenology, particularly the work of Maurice Merleau-Ponty, posits that our perception is inherently embodied. In the context of scented performance art, this means that the experience of scent is not merely a passive reception but an active engagement that influences the viewer's bodily awareness and emotional state.

Semiotics, the study of signs and symbols, offers insight into how scents can communicate meaning. For instance, the use of a particular fragrance may evoke memories, cultural associations, or even provoke discomfort, thus creating a complex interplay between the audience and the artwork.

Challenges in Scented Performance Art

Despite its innovative potential, scented performance art faces several challenges:

- **Subjectivity of Smell:** Unlike visual or auditory elements, the perception of scent is highly subjective and can vary significantly between individuals. This subjectivity poses a challenge for artists seeking to create a universal experience.

- **Transience of Odor:** Scents are ephemeral; they dissipate over time, making it difficult for artists to maintain a consistent olfactory experience throughout a performance. This transience can lead to a disconnect between the intended experience and the audience's perception.

- **Logistical Constraints:** The integration of scent into performance art requires careful planning and execution. Artists must consider how to effectively disperse scents, manage audience reactions, and ensure safety, particularly when using potent or potentially irritating fragrances.

- **Cultural Sensitivity:** Scents carry cultural meanings that can vary widely. Artists must navigate these cultural nuances to avoid misinterpretation or offense, particularly in multicultural settings.

Notable Examples

Several artists and collectives have successfully integrated scent into their performances, pushing the boundaries of artistic expression:

- **Scent of the Future by Ann Hamilton:** In this installation, Hamilton combined spoken word, visual art, and scent to create an immersive experience. The scent was released in tandem with the rhythm of the spoken word, enhancing the emotional impact of the performance. The choice of scent was deliberate, aiming to evoke nostalgia and longing, demonstrating how scent can deepen the audience's connection to the narrative.

- **Perfume and Performance by Marina Abramović:** Abramović's work often challenges the limits of endurance and the body. In her performance "The Artist is Present," she incorporated the scent of her own skin, emphasizing the raw, human aspect of her presence. The olfactory element added a layer of intimacy, inviting viewers to confront their own perceptions of proximity and personal space.

- **The Smell of Money by Kira O'Reilly:** This provocative performance involved the artist covering herself in a mixture of scents associated with wealth and poverty. As she moved through the space, the contrasting scents created a dialogue about socioeconomic disparities, forcing the audience to confront their own biases and associations with smell.

- **Scented Installation by Maja K. Kovačević:** In her work, Kovačević utilized scent as a medium to explore memory and identity. By inviting participants to engage with scents from their childhood, she created a communal experience that fostered connections among strangers, highlighting the power of scent to evoke shared memories and emotions.

Conclusion

The surreal world of scented performance art challenges traditional notions of artistic expression by incorporating the often-neglected sense of smell. Through theoretical frameworks that emphasize the embodied nature of perception, artists can create immersive experiences that resonate on a deeper emotional level.

Despite the challenges inherent in this medium, the innovative use of scent in performance art opens new avenues for exploration and expression, inviting audiences to engage with art in profoundly personal and transformative ways.

$$S_{scent} = f(S_{context}, S_{audience}, S_{artist}) \tag{176}$$

where S_{scent} represents the overall olfactory experience, $S_{context}$ refers to the environmental factors influencing scent perception, $S_{audience}$ denotes the subjective reactions of the audience, and S_{artist} encompasses the artist's intentions and choices in scent selection.

In conclusion, scented performance art represents a bold frontier in contemporary art, inviting us to reconsider our sensory experiences and the meanings we attach to them. As artists continue to experiment with this medium, we can anticipate a rich tapestry of olfactory narratives that challenge our perceptions and expand the boundaries of artistic expression.

Interactive Olfactory Exhibitions: Engaging the Senses

In an era where sensory experiences are increasingly valued, interactive olfactory exhibitions have emerged as captivating venues for engaging the senses in novel ways. These exhibitions transcend traditional visual art forms by incorporating smell, allowing visitors to experience art through a multi-sensory lens. The integration of olfactory elements into exhibitions not only enhances the immersive experience but also invites deeper emotional and psychological responses from participants.

Theoretical Framework

The foundation of interactive olfactory exhibitions is rooted in the understanding of how scent influences human perception and emotional states. Research in psychology indicates that olfactory stimuli can evoke memories and emotions more effectively than visual or auditory stimuli. This phenomenon is often attributed to the close connection between the olfactory bulb and the limbic system, the part of the brain responsible for emotion and memory (Herz, 2004).

$$\text{Emotional Response} \propto \text{Olfactory Stimulus Intensity} \tag{177}$$

This equation suggests that as the intensity of an olfactory stimulus increases, so does the emotional response it elicits. This principle is harnessed in interactive olfactory exhibitions, where carefully curated scents are used to create specific atmospheres or evoke particular memories.

Designing Interactive Olfactory Experiences

Creating an engaging olfactory exhibition involves careful consideration of scent selection, spatial design, and participant interaction. Curators must choose scents that resonate with the themes of the exhibition while also considering the potential for olfactory fatigue, where repeated exposure to a scent diminishes its perceived intensity (Morrin and Ratneshwar, 2000).

$$\text{Scent Perception} = \frac{\text{Scent Concentration}}{\text{Exposure Time}} \quad (178)$$

This equation illustrates that the perception of a scent is a function of its concentration and the duration of exposure. Curators can mitigate olfactory fatigue by varying scent concentrations and introducing new scents at regular intervals throughout the exhibition.

Examples of Successful Interactive Olfactory Exhibitions

One notable example of an interactive olfactory exhibition is "The Smell of Time," presented at the Museum of Contemporary Art in Sydney. This exhibition featured a series of scent-infused installations that allowed visitors to explore the relationship between time and memory through olfactory cues. Each installation was designed to evoke specific memories associated with different periods in life, such as childhood, adolescence, and adulthood.

Another innovative exhibition is "Scent of the Future," held at the Centre Pompidou in Paris. This exhibition invited visitors to engage with futuristic scents created by perfumers and scientists, exploring the potential of scent in enhancing everyday experiences. Interactive scent stations allowed participants to mix and match scents, creating their own personalized olfactory experiences.

Challenges in Implementation

Despite the captivating potential of interactive olfactory exhibitions, several challenges must be addressed. One major concern is the variability in individual scent perception. Factors such as genetic differences, cultural backgrounds, and personal experiences can significantly influence how individuals perceive and react to specific scents (Schneider, 2006).

$$\text{Perceived Scent} = f(\text{Genetics, Culture, Experience}) \quad (179)$$

This function highlights the complexity of scent perception and underscores the need for curators to consider diverse audience backgrounds when designing olfactory experiences.

Another challenge is the technical logistics of scent delivery systems. Maintaining scent integrity and ensuring an even distribution of scents throughout the exhibition space can be technically demanding. Advanced scent diffusion technologies, such as programmable scent dispensers and scent-activated environments, can help overcome these challenges, but they require significant investment and expertise.

Future Directions

As technology continues to advance, the future of interactive olfactory exhibitions looks promising. Innovations in scent technology, such as digital scent synthesis and virtual reality integration, offer exciting possibilities for creating even more immersive experiences. For instance, virtual reality environments that incorporate scent can enhance the realism of the experience, allowing participants to feel as though they are truly immersed in a different world.

$$\text{Immersion} = \text{Visual} + \text{Auditory} + \text{Olfactory} \qquad (180)$$

This equation emphasizes that true immersion in an experience is achieved through the harmonious integration of multiple sensory modalities. By continuing to explore the intersection of scent, art, and technology, interactive olfactory exhibitions can redefine how we engage with art and our surroundings.

In conclusion, interactive olfactory exhibitions represent a revolutionary approach to engaging the senses, offering unique opportunities for emotional connection and personal reflection. By embracing the complexities of scent perception and harnessing innovative technologies, curators can create unforgettable experiences that resonate with audiences on a profound level.

The Scented Art Experience: A Revolution in Perception

In a world where visual art has long dominated the cultural landscape, the emergence of scented art represents a revolutionary shift in how we perceive and interact with creative expression. This section explores the transformative power of scent in art, examining its implications for perception, memory, and emotional engagement.

Theoretical Foundations of Scent in Art

The integration of scent into artistic practice is grounded in several theoretical frameworks, including phenomenology, synesthesia, and multisensory perception. Phenomenology emphasizes the subjective experience of individuals, suggesting that scent can evoke deeply personal memories and emotions that are often inaccessible through visual stimuli alone. This aligns with the theory of synesthesia, where one sensory experience involuntarily triggers another, allowing for a richer, more immersive artistic experience.

$$E = mc^2 \qquad (181)$$

This famous equation by Einstein, while primarily associated with physics, metaphorically illustrates the concept that energy (E) can manifest in multiple forms, analogous to how scent can transform our understanding of art. Just as mass (m) and the speed of light (c) are interconnected, so too are the senses intertwined in the experience of scented art.

Challenges in Scented Art

Despite its potential, the incorporation of scent into art faces several challenges. One significant issue is the ephemeral nature of scent, which can dissipate quickly, making it difficult to create lasting installations. Additionally, individual differences in olfactory perception mean that a scent that resonates with one person may be unpleasant or insignificant to another. This variability complicates the artist's intent, as the intended emotional response may not be universally experienced.

Moreover, there is the challenge of context; scents can evoke strong associations that vary widely across cultures and personal experiences. For example, the smell of sandalwood may evoke tranquility for some, while for others, it may remind them of a less pleasant memory. This complexity necessitates a thoughtful approach to scent selection and deployment in artistic contexts.

Examples of Scented Art Installations

Several artists have successfully navigated these challenges, creating immersive experiences that highlight the power of scent. One notable example is the work of artist *Sissel Tolaas*, who has dedicated her career to exploring the emotional and cultural significance of scent. Her installation *"The Smell of Fear"* invites participants to engage with various scents associated with fear, prompting introspection and conversation about the often-overlooked role of smell in our emotional lives.

Another compelling example is *"Perfume Genius"*, a project by musician Mike Hadreas, who collaborated with perfumer *Jovoy Paris* to create a scent that embodies the themes of his music. This olfactory extension of his artistic vision allows listeners to experience his work in a multisensory manner, deepening their connection to the music and its underlying emotions.

The Future of Scented Art

As technology advances, the potential for scented art to evolve becomes increasingly promising. Innovations in olfactory technology, such as scent-emitting devices and digital scent delivery systems, may enable artists to create more complex and enduring scent experiences. The concept of *scented virtual reality* is particularly intriguing, allowing for a fully immersive experience that engages multiple senses simultaneously.

Furthermore, the rise of *sensory art festivals* and installations worldwide highlights a growing interest in olfactory experiences. Events like *"Scent Festival"* in Amsterdam and *"The Olfactory Art Experience"* in New York City showcase the work of various artists who are pushing the boundaries of traditional art forms through scent, fostering a community of scent enthusiasts and artists alike.

Conclusion

The scented art experience represents a revolution in perception, challenging traditional notions of art and expanding the sensory palette available to artists and audiences. By embracing the complexities of scent, artists can create profound emotional connections and invite viewers to engage with their work in new and unexpected ways. As we continue to explore the intersections of scent and art, we may find that our understanding of creativity, memory, and human experience is forever transformed.

In summary, the integration of scent into the art world not only enhances the aesthetic experience but also serves as a catalyst for deeper emotional engagement and cultural dialogue. As we look to the future, the potential for scented art to redefine our sensory experiences remains vast and exciting, promising a new frontier in the realm of artistic expression.

Scented Art = Visual Art + Olfactory Experience (182)

New Avenues for Attractive Stenches

Scented Wellness and Meditation Practices

The intersection of scent and wellness has gained significant traction in recent years, particularly within the realms of meditation and mindfulness. Scented wellness practices utilize the power of aromatherapy to enhance mental clarity, emotional stability, and overall well-being. This section explores the theoretical underpinnings, potential challenges, and practical applications of integrating scent into wellness and meditation practices.

Theoretical Framework

Aromatherapy is based on the principle that certain scents can evoke specific emotional responses and physiological changes within the body. The olfactory system, responsible for the sense of smell, is directly linked to the limbic system, the part of the brain that governs emotions and memories. This connection facilitates the therapeutic effects of scents, making them powerful tools for enhancing meditation practices.

The effectiveness of aromatherapy can be understood through the following equation, which represents the relationship between scent, emotional response, and physiological change:

$$E = f(S, R) \tag{183}$$

Where:

- E = Emotional response
- S = Scent
- R = Physiological response

This equation suggests that the emotional response E is a function of the scent S and the physiological response R. For example, the scent of lavender (S) is often associated with relaxation and calmness, leading to a decrease in heart rate (R), ultimately enhancing the meditation experience.

Challenges in Scented Wellness Practices

Despite the benefits, there are challenges associated with incorporating scent into wellness and meditation practices. Individual preferences for scents can vary widely, and what is soothing for one person may be unpleasant for another. Additionally, some individuals may have sensitivities or allergies to certain fragrances, which can hinder their experience.

Another challenge lies in the quality of the essential oils or scented products used. Many commercially available products contain synthetic fragrances that may not provide the intended therapeutic benefits. It is crucial to select high-quality, pure essential oils to ensure the effectiveness of the aromatic experience.

Practical Applications

Scented wellness practices can be seamlessly integrated into various meditation techniques. Below are several examples of how to incorporate scent into your meditation routine:

1. **Essential Oil Diffusion:** Using a diffuser, disperse essential oils such as lavender, chamomile, or sandalwood into the air before beginning meditation. The gentle aroma will create a calming environment conducive to relaxation and focus.

2. **Scented Candles:** Lighting a candle infused with natural essential oils can enhance the ambiance of your meditation space. The flickering flame combined with the scent can help ground your practice and foster a sense of peace.

3. **Inhalation Techniques:** Prior to meditation, take a moment to inhale a drop of essential oil directly from the bottle or apply it to your wrists. This technique allows for immediate olfactory engagement, setting the tone for your meditation session.

4. **Scented Meditation Cushions:** Consider using meditation cushions infused with calming scents. These cushions can provide both physical comfort and olfactory stimulation, enhancing the overall experience.

5. **Guided Meditation with Aromatherapy:** Participate in guided meditation sessions that incorporate aromatherapy. Instructors may use specific scents at different stages of the meditation to evoke particular emotional responses, enhancing the depth of the practice.

Case Studies and Examples

Several studies have explored the effectiveness of scented wellness practices in enhancing meditation. A notable study conducted by [?] demonstrated that participants who meditated with lavender essential oil reported significantly lower anxiety levels compared to those who meditated without scent. The results indicated that the presence of the calming aroma facilitated a deeper state of relaxation and mindfulness.

Another study by [?] examined the effects of citrus scents on mood during meditation. Participants exposed to citrus essential oils experienced increased feelings of happiness and vitality, suggesting that uplifting scents can enhance the overall meditation experience.

Conclusion

Scented wellness and meditation practices offer a unique avenue for enhancing emotional well-being and mindfulness. By understanding the theoretical frameworks, addressing potential challenges, and implementing practical applications, individuals can create a more enriching meditation experience. As the field of aromatherapy continues to evolve, the integration of scent into wellness practices promises to deepen our understanding of the connection between olfaction, emotion, and mental health.

Innovative Approaches to Aromatherapy and Healing Scents

Aromatherapy, the therapeutic use of aromatic substances, has evolved significantly in recent years, integrating innovative approaches that harness the power of scent for healing and wellness. This section explores these advancements, highlighting their theoretical foundations, potential challenges, and real-world applications.

Theoretical Foundations

At the core of aromatherapy lies the interaction between olfactory stimuli and the brain's limbic system, which governs emotions and memory. The theory posits that specific scents can evoke emotional responses and physiological changes. For instance, essential oils like lavender (*Lavandula angustifolia*) have been shown to reduce anxiety and promote relaxation through their influence on neurotransmitters such as serotonin and dopamine.

Recent studies have employed functional magnetic resonance imaging (fMRI) to observe brain activity in response to various scents. Research indicates that pleasant odors can activate the brain's reward pathways, reinforcing positive emotional states. The equation below summarizes the relationship between scent exposure and emotional response:

$$E = f(S, R, T) \tag{184}$$

where E represents the emotional response, S the scent, R the individual's receptiveness, and T the context of exposure. This equation illustrates the complexity of scent perception and its emotional impact, emphasizing the need for personalized approaches in aromatherapy.

Innovative Techniques

1. Scent Diffusion Technology Modern scent diffusion technologies have revolutionized the way essential oils are administered. Devices such as ultrasonic diffusers and nebulizers disperse essential oils into the air, ensuring even distribution and enhancing the olfactory experience. These devices utilize advanced ultrasonic waves to break down the oils into micro-particles, making inhalation easier and more effective.

2. Smart Aromatherapy The integration of smart technology into aromatherapy has led to the development of app-controlled diffusers that can tailor scent experiences based on user preferences and environmental factors. For example, a smart diffuser can adjust the intensity of fragrance in response to changes in mood, time of day, or even biometric feedback from wearable devices. This personalized approach enhances the therapeutic effects of aromatherapy, making it more accessible and effective.

3. Aroma Inhalers Aroma inhalers are portable devices that allow individuals to inhale essential oils directly, providing immediate relief from stress or anxiety. These inhalers can be infused with specific blends tailored to individual needs, such as peppermint (*Mentha piperita*) for mental clarity or chamomile (*Matricaria chamomilla*) for relaxation. The convenience and portability of inhalers make them a popular choice for on-the-go aromatherapy.

4. Synergistic Blending Innovative approaches to aromatherapy also involve the creation of synergistic blends that combine multiple essential oils to enhance their therapeutic effects. Research suggests that certain combinations can produce more significant results than single oils. For instance, a blend of bergamot (*Citrus bergamia*) and ylang-ylang (*Cananga odorata*) has been shown to effectively reduce stress levels while promoting feelings of joy and relaxation.

Challenges and Considerations

Despite the advancements in aromatherapy, several challenges remain. One significant issue is the variability in individual responses to scents, influenced by personal history, cultural background, and even genetic factors. This variability complicates the development of standardized protocols for aromatherapy treatments.

Furthermore, the quality of essential oils can vary widely, affecting their therapeutic efficacy. The lack of regulation in the essential oil industry means consumers must be discerning when selecting products. Research has indicated that adulterated oils can diminish the expected health benefits, leading to skepticism about aromatherapy's effectiveness.

Real-World Applications

Innovative approaches to aromatherapy have found applications across various sectors, including healthcare, wellness, and hospitality.

1. **Healthcare Settings** In hospitals, aromatherapy is increasingly being integrated into patient care protocols. Studies have shown that the use of calming scents, such as lavender and lemon balm (*Melissa officinalis*), can reduce anxiety and improve overall patient satisfaction during procedures. For example, a randomized controlled trial demonstrated that patients undergoing surgery experienced less anxiety when exposed to lavender scent preoperatively.

2. **Workplace Wellness** Employers are recognizing the benefits of aromatherapy in enhancing employee well-being and productivity. Companies are incorporating scent diffusers in office spaces, using invigorating scents like citrus to promote alertness and creativity. Research indicates that workplaces infused with pleasant aromas can lead to increased job satisfaction and reduced stress levels.

3. **Spa and Wellness Centers** Spas are adopting innovative aromatherapy techniques to enhance client experiences. Customized aromatherapy massages using tailored blends allow clients to choose scents that resonate with their personal preferences and therapeutic needs. This personalized approach not only enhances relaxation but also fosters a deeper connection between the client and the treatment.

Conclusion

Innovative approaches to aromatherapy and healing scents represent a dynamic intersection of science and art, offering promising avenues for enhancing well-being. By understanding the theoretical foundations and addressing the challenges associated with scent therapy, practitioners can harness the full potential of aromatherapy. As technology advances and our understanding of olfactory science deepens, the future of aromatherapy holds exciting possibilities for personal and collective healing.

The Emergence of Scented Yoga and Movement Therapies

In recent years, the fusion of scent and physical movement has given rise to a new wave of wellness practices, notably scented yoga and movement therapies. This innovative approach integrates the olfactory senses with physical exercise, creating an immersive experience that enhances both mental and physical well-being. By harnessing the power of scent, practitioners aim to deepen their connection to the body and mind, fostering an environment conducive to relaxation, focus, and emotional release.

Theoretical Foundations

The theoretical basis for scented yoga and movement therapies lies in the profound connection between scent and human emotion, cognition, and memory. Research indicates that the olfactory bulb, responsible for processing smells, is closely linked to the limbic system, the brain's emotional center. This connection suggests that scents can evoke powerful emotional responses and memories, which can be harnessed to enhance the experience of physical movement.

One prominent theory is the *Proustian phenomenon*, named after the French author Marcel Proust, who famously described how the smell of a madeleine cake triggered vivid memories of his childhood. This phenomenon illustrates how scents can transport individuals to different emotional states or memories, making them powerful tools in therapeutic settings. In the context of yoga and movement therapies, specific scents can be used to cultivate desired emotional states, such as calmness, focus, or invigoration.

Challenges in Implementation

Despite the promising potential of scented yoga and movement therapies, several challenges arise in their implementation.

- **Individual Sensitivities:** Scent preferences and sensitivities vary widely among individuals. Some practitioners may have allergies or aversions to certain scents, which can detract from the experience. Therefore, it is crucial to offer a range of scent options and to conduct a preliminary assessment of participants' preferences.

- **Overwhelming Fragrances:** The intensity of scents used can also pose a challenge. Overpowering fragrances may lead to discomfort or distraction, undermining the calming effects that yoga and movement therapies aim to achieve. A delicate balance must be struck to ensure scents are present but not overwhelming.

- **Cultural Considerations:** Different cultures have varying associations with scents, which can influence how individuals respond to them. A scent that is calming for one person may be stimulating or unpleasant for another. Practitioners must be culturally sensitive and aware of the diverse backgrounds of participants when selecting scents.

Practical Applications and Examples

Scented yoga classes typically incorporate essential oils or natural fragrances through diffusers, scented candles, or topical applications. Each session may begin with a brief introduction to the selected scent, explaining its intended benefits and how it relates to the practice.

Example: Lavender and Restorative Yoga Lavender, known for its calming properties, is often used in restorative yoga sessions. Participants may inhale lavender essential oil before beginning their practice, promoting relaxation and stress relief. The soothing scent helps create a tranquil atmosphere, allowing practitioners to focus on their breath and body movements without distraction.

Example: Citrus and Energizing Flow In contrast, citrus scents such as lemon or grapefruit can be employed during more dynamic yoga classes, like vinyasa or power yoga. These uplifting fragrances can invigorate the senses, enhancing energy levels and motivation. Instructors may incorporate citrus-scented sprays or essential oils in the environment to stimulate participants and encourage a lively flow.

Example: Sandalwood and Meditation Sandalwood is another popular scent used in meditation practices, known for its grounding and centering effects.

Participants may use sandalwood incense or essential oil during seated meditation, facilitating a deeper state of mindfulness and connection to the present moment.

The Future of Scented Movement Practices

As awareness of the benefits of scented yoga and movement therapies grows, there is potential for further innovation in this field. Future developments may include:

- **Personalized Scent Profiles:** Utilizing technology to create personalized scent profiles based on individual preferences and emotional responses could enhance the experience. Wearable devices might track physiological responses to different scents, allowing for tailored scent experiences during movement practices.

- **Integration with Virtual Reality:** The combination of scented experiences with virtual reality (VR) could lead to immersive movement therapies that transport participants to serene environments. By pairing visual and olfactory stimuli, practitioners can create a holistic experience that promotes relaxation and well-being.

- **Research and Standardization:** Continued research into the psychological and physiological effects of specific scents on movement practices will be essential for establishing best practices and guidelines. Standardizing the use of scents in yoga and movement therapies can help practitioners optimize their classes for maximum benefit.

In conclusion, the emergence of scented yoga and movement therapies represents an exciting frontier in wellness practices. By harnessing the power of scent, practitioners can create transformative experiences that enhance the mind-body connection, promote emotional well-being, and foster a deeper sense of self-awareness. As this field continues to evolve, it holds the promise of enriching the lives of those who seek a more holistic approach to health and wellness.

Unusual Scented Products for Mind and Body Exploration

In the realm of olfactory experiences, the exploration of unusual scented products offers a unique avenue for enhancing both mental and physical well-being. This section delves into the innovative scented products that challenge conventional perceptions, providing insights into their theoretical foundations, practical applications, and potential benefits.

Theoretical Foundations

The human sense of smell, or olfaction, plays a crucial role in emotional and physiological responses. According to the *Proustian Phenomenon*, scents can evoke vivid memories and emotions, creating a powerful connection between our olfactory senses and psychological states. This phenomenon is rooted in the brain's anatomy, particularly the close proximity of the olfactory bulb to the limbic system, which governs emotions and memory (Herz, 2004).

The use of scented products for mind and body exploration taps into this intricate relationship. By incorporating unconventional scents, we can stimulate sensory experiences that promote relaxation, creativity, and self-awareness. Products designed for this purpose often utilize essential oils, botanical extracts, and even fermented ingredients, which can elicit specific emotional and physical responses.

Innovative Scented Products

1. **Scented Meditation Stones:** These are smooth, tactile stones infused with essential oils that can be held during meditation. The act of touching the stone while inhaling its aroma can enhance focus and grounding. For example, a lavender-infused stone may promote relaxation, while citrus scents can invigorate the mind.

$$\text{Relaxation} \propto \text{Inhaled Aroma} \times \text{Tactile Stimulation} \qquad (185)$$

2. **Aromatic Yoga Mats:** Some yoga mats are embedded with microcapsules containing essential oils that release scents during practice. This feature can enhance the overall yoga experience, providing calming or energizing effects depending on the chosen aroma. A peppermint-scented mat may stimulate alertness, while a chamomile-infused mat may encourage relaxation.

3. **Scented Journals:** These journals come with specially treated pages that release pleasant fragrances when written on. The act of journaling combined with the sensory experience of scent can enhance creativity and emotional expression. For instance, a journal infused with sandalwood may promote introspection, while a floral scent might inspire positivity.

4. **Fermented Scented Candles:** Utilizing the unique aromas from fermentation processes, these candles can create an atmosphere that encourages mindfulness and reflection. The scents of fermented fruits or herbs can evoke feelings of nostalgia and connection to nature, promoting a serene environment conducive to meditation or relaxation.

Practical Applications and Benefits

The integration of unusual scented products into daily routines can offer numerous benefits:
   - **Enhanced Mood Regulation:** Scents like bergamot and ylang-ylang have been shown to reduce anxiety and improve mood. Incorporating these into daily practices can help individuals manage stress more effectively.
   - **Increased Mindfulness:** Engaging with scented products during meditation or yoga encourages a deeper connection to the present moment, fostering mindfulness and self-awareness.
   - **Creative Stimulation:** Unconventional scents can inspire creativity by breaking the monotony of familiar aromas. This stimulation can lead to novel ideas and artistic expression.
   - **Physical Relaxation:** The calming effects of certain scents, such as chamomile or jasmine, can aid in muscle relaxation and stress relief, enhancing overall physical well-being.

Challenges and Considerations

While the benefits of unusual scented products are compelling, there are challenges to consider:
   - **Individual Sensitivities:** Not everyone reacts positively to all scents. Some individuals may experience headaches or allergic reactions to certain fragrances. It is essential to choose products that are hypoallergenic and suitable for sensitive users.
   - **Cultural Perceptions:** Scents can carry different meanings across cultures. A scent that is perceived as pleasant in one culture may be considered unpleasant in another. This diversity necessitates careful consideration when marketing and designing scented products.
   - **Sustainability:** The sourcing of ingredients for scented products must be sustainable and ethical. Consumers increasingly seek products that align with their values regarding environmental impact and social responsibility.

Conclusion

Unusual scented products for mind and body exploration represent a fascinating intersection of sensory experience and personal growth. By harnessing the power of scent, individuals can enhance their emotional well-being, foster creativity, and cultivate mindfulness. As the field of scent innovation continues to evolve, it is essential to remain aware of the challenges and considerations that accompany this exploration, ensuring that the benefits of scent are accessible and enjoyable for all.

Bibliography

[1] Herz, R. S. (2004). *A Natural History of the Senses.* New York: Vintage.

Embracing the Unconventional in Perfume Industry Trends

In recent years, the perfume industry has witnessed a remarkable shift towards embracing the unconventional. This movement is characterized by a departure from traditional fragrance norms, as perfumers explore innovative ingredients, unconventional scent profiles, and unique marketing strategies that challenge the status quo. This section delves into the theoretical underpinnings of this trend, the challenges it presents, and notable examples that exemplify this transformation.

Theoretical Framework

The unconventional approach in the perfume industry can be understood through several theoretical lenses, including postmodernism, consumer culture theory, and the notion of authenticity.

Postmodernism posits that in a world saturated with information and choices, consumers are increasingly drawn to products that defy traditional classifications and expectations. Perfumes that embrace the unconventional often blur the lines between categories, such as combining floral and gourmand notes or incorporating unexpected materials like leather and metal. This creates a sensory experience that resonates with a postmodern audience seeking novelty and complexity.

Consumer Culture Theory suggests that consumers are not merely passive recipients of products; they actively engage in meaning-making processes. As such, the rise of unconventional perfumes reflects a broader cultural shift towards individualism and self-expression. Consumers gravitate towards fragrances that allow them to articulate their identities and values, often seeking scents that reflect their unique experiences and perspectives.

Authenticity has become a key concept in the contemporary fragrance landscape. Consumers are increasingly skeptical of mass-produced products and are drawn to artisanal and niche brands that emphasize transparency and craftsmanship. Unconventional perfumes often highlight their unique sourcing of ingredients, storytelling, and the personal philosophies of the perfumers behind them, thus appealing to the desire for authenticity in a commodified world.

Challenges in Embracing the Unconventional

While the shift towards unconventional perfumes presents exciting opportunities, it also poses several challenges for industry stakeholders:

- **Market Acceptance:** Unconventional scents may initially face resistance from consumers accustomed to traditional fragrance profiles. For instance, a perfume that prominently features the scent of fermented fruits or earthy notes may be perceived as unappealing or off-putting by mainstream audiences.

- **Brand Positioning:** Brands must navigate the delicate balance between being avant-garde and remaining accessible. A fragrance that is too unconventional may alienate potential customers, while one that is overly commercialized risks losing its artistic integrity.

- **Regulatory Considerations:** The use of unconventional ingredients may raise regulatory challenges. For example, certain natural materials may be restricted or require extensive testing before they can be used in consumer products, complicating the development process for innovative perfumes.

- **Sustainability Concerns:** As the industry embraces unconventional ingredients, there is a growing responsibility to ensure that sourcing practices are sustainable and ethical. The use of rare or endangered materials can lead to ecological concerns, necessitating a commitment to responsible sourcing.

Notable Examples of Unconventional Perfumes

Several brands and fragrances exemplify the embrace of the unconventional in the perfume industry:

1. *Byredo's "Mixed Emotions"*   Byredo, a niche fragrance house, launched "Mixed Emotions," a scent inspired by the complexities of human emotions. This fragrance combines notes of weeping willow, birch woods, and black currant, creating a unique olfactory representation of melancholy and joy. Byredo's approach challenges traditional notions of what a perfume should evoke, inviting wearers to embrace the full spectrum of human experience.

2. *Comme des Garçons' "Odeur 53"*   Comme des Garçons is known for its avant-garde approach to fragrance. "Odeur 53" is a prime example of this ethos, featuring a blend of unconventional notes such as metallic, plastic, and synthetic elements. This fragrance challenges the very definition of scent, prompting discussions about what constitutes beauty and desirability in perfumery.

3. *Lush's "Breath of God"*   Lush, a brand celebrated for its ethical sourcing and handmade products, offers "Breath of God," a fragrance that combines both masculine and feminine notes, including incense, rose, and citrus. The scent is designed to evoke a sense of spirituality and connection to nature, appealing to consumers seeking authenticity and emotional resonance in their fragrance choices.

Conclusion

The embrace of the unconventional in the perfume industry signifies a transformative moment that reflects broader cultural shifts towards individuality, authenticity, and complexity. While challenges remain, the innovative spirit of niche brands and forward-thinking perfumers is paving the way for a new era of fragrance that celebrates the beauty of the unexpected. As consumers continue to seek scents that resonate with their identities and experiences, the perfume industry will likely continue to evolve, embracing the unconventional as a cornerstone of its future.

$$S = \sum_{i=1}^{n}(C_i + I_i + A_i) \tag{186}$$

Where:

- S = Overall scent experience
- C_i = Complexity of individual notes
- I_i = Innovation in ingredient sourcing

- A_i = Authenticity in brand storytelling

This equation encapsulates the multifaceted nature of unconventional perfumes, where complexity, innovation, and authenticity converge to create a truly unique olfactory experience.

The Scent-Focused World of Olfactory Healing

In the realm of holistic wellness, olfactory healing emerges as a captivating intersection of scent and therapeutic practice. This approach leverages the profound impact that aromas have on our emotional and physical well-being. The olfactory system, responsible for our sense of smell, is intricately linked to the limbic system, the brain's emotional center. This connection explains why certain scents can evoke vivid memories, alter moods, and even influence physiological responses.

Theoretical Foundations of Olfactory Healing

The theoretical underpinning of olfactory healing is rooted in the notion that scents can stimulate the brain in ways that promote healing and well-being. Research indicates that the inhalation of specific essential oils can trigger the release of neurotransmitters such as serotonin and dopamine, which are associated with feelings of happiness and relaxation. For instance, the scent of lavender (*Lavandula angustifolia*) has been shown to reduce anxiety and improve sleep quality, making it a staple in aromatherapy practices.

The following equation illustrates the relationship between scent, brain activity, and emotional response:

$$E = f(S, B)$$

Where: - E represents the emotional response, - S denotes the scent, - B signifies brain activity.

This function suggests that as the scent (S) is inhaled, it activates specific areas in the brain (B), leading to a corresponding emotional response (E).

Common Problems Addressed by Olfactory Healing

Olfactory healing is employed to address a myriad of issues, including stress, anxiety, depression, and even chronic pain. The therapeutic use of essential oils can provide a natural alternative to conventional treatments, offering relief without the side effects commonly associated with pharmaceuticals.

For example, the use of peppermint oil (*Mentha piperita*) is known to alleviate headaches and enhance cognitive function. A study conducted by Moss et al. (2010) demonstrated that participants exposed to peppermint aroma showed improved alertness and cognitive performance compared to a control group.

Examples of Olfactory Healing Practices

1. **Aromatherapy Diffusion**: This practice involves dispersing essential oils into the air using a diffuser. Scents like eucalyptus and tea tree oil are often used for their invigorating properties, promoting respiratory health and mental clarity.

2. **Inhalation Techniques**: Direct inhalation of essential oils can provide immediate effects. For instance, inhaling the scent of bergamot (*Citrus bergamia*) has been shown to reduce stress levels and improve mood. Users can place a few drops on a tissue or inhale directly from the bottle.

3. **Scented Baths**: Adding essential oils to bathwater can create a tranquil environment, enhancing relaxation. Oils like chamomile (*Matricaria chamomilla*) and ylang-ylang (*Cananga odorata*) are popular choices for their calming effects.

4. **Massage with Essential Oils**: Incorporating essential oils into massage therapy can amplify the benefits of touch. Oils such as frankincense (*Boswellia carterii*) are known for their grounding properties, making them ideal for reducing tension and promoting emotional balance.

Challenges and Considerations in Olfactory Healing

While olfactory healing holds great promise, it is not without challenges. Individual responses to scents can vary significantly, influenced by personal preferences, cultural backgrounds, and even past experiences. This variability necessitates a personalized approach to olfactory therapy, where practitioners consider the unique needs and sensitivities of each individual.

Moreover, the quality of essential oils is paramount. Not all oils are created equal; synthetic fragrances may lack the therapeutic properties of pure, high-quality essential oils. Practitioners should prioritize sourcing oils from reputable suppliers to ensure efficacy and safety.

Conclusion

The scent-focused world of olfactory healing offers a rich tapestry of possibilities for enhancing well-being through the power of smell. By understanding the intricate connections between scent, emotion, and physiological responses, individuals can harness the therapeutic potential of aromas to navigate the complexities of modern life. As research continues to unveil the profound effects of olfactory stimuli, the future of olfactory healing looks promising, inviting us to explore the fragrant pathways to health and happiness.

Scented Mindfulness: The Power of Aromatics in Self-Care

In the fast-paced world we inhabit, the need for mindfulness has never been more pressing. The integration of aromatics into self-care routines offers a unique avenue for cultivating mindfulness, enhancing emotional well-being, and promoting a deeper connection with oneself. This section explores the theoretical foundations, practical applications, and transformative potential of scented mindfulness in self-care practices.

Theoretical Foundations of Scented Mindfulness

Mindfulness, as defined by Jon Kabat-Zinn, is the practice of maintaining a moment-by-moment awareness of our thoughts, feelings, bodily sensations, and surrounding environment. When combined with scent, this practice can be significantly enriched. Aromatherapy, the use of essential oils for therapeutic purposes, operates on the principle that certain scents can evoke emotional responses and influence mental states.

The olfactory system is intricately linked to the limbic system, the part of the brain responsible for emotions and memory. This connection allows for scents to trigger memories and feelings, making them powerful tools in mindfulness practices. For instance, the scent of lavender has been shown to reduce anxiety and promote relaxation, while citrus scents can invigorate and uplift mood.

$$\text{Mindfulness} = \text{Awareness} + \text{Acceptance} + \text{Presence} \qquad (187)$$

Where: - Awareness refers to the conscious recognition of thoughts and feelings. - Acceptance involves acknowledging these thoughts without judgment. - Presence signifies being fully engaged in the current moment.

Problems Addressed by Scented Mindfulness

Incorporating aromatics into mindfulness practices addresses several common issues faced in self-care:

- **Stress and Anxiety:** The daily grind often leads to heightened stress levels. Aromatic compounds like chamomile and bergamot can help mitigate these feelings, promoting a sense of calm and tranquility.

- **Disconnection from Self:** Many individuals experience a disconnect from their bodies and emotions. Engaging the senses through scent can foster a deeper connection to oneself, encouraging reflection and self-awareness.

- **Difficulty in Maintaining Mindfulness:** Traditional mindfulness practices can be challenging to sustain. The introduction of scent can serve as an anchor, helping individuals return to the present moment when their minds wander.

Practical Applications of Scented Mindfulness

Implementing scented mindfulness can be achieved through various methods, each tailored to individual preferences and lifestyles. Here are some effective practices:

1. **Aromatic Meditation:** Create a serene environment by diffusing essential oils such as sandalwood or frankincense during meditation. The scent can enhance focus and deepen the meditative experience.

2. **Mindful Breathing with Scent:** Incorporate scented oils into breathing exercises. For example, inhale deeply while holding a drop of peppermint oil in your palms. The invigorating scent can enhance alertness and clarity.

3. **Scented Journaling:** Combine journaling with aromatherapy by selecting a specific scent to accompany your writing. This practice can create a sensory association with your thoughts and feelings, enriching the reflective process.

4. **Scented Baths:** Elevate bath time by adding essential oils to your bathwater. Scents like ylang-ylang and eucalyptus can transform a simple bath into a luxurious self-care ritual, promoting relaxation and mindfulness.

5. **Aromatherapy in Daily Activities:** Incorporate scents into everyday tasks, such as applying a scented lotion after showering or using a scented candle while cooking. This practice encourages mindfulness in routine activities.

Examples of Aromatic Self-Care Practices

The following examples illustrate the diverse applications of scented mindfulness in self-care:

- **Lavender Eye Pillow:** Create an eye pillow filled with dried lavender and flaxseed. Use it during relaxation or meditation to promote calmness and reduce tension.

- **Citrus Zest Ritual:** Incorporate citrus peels into your morning routine. The invigorating scent can awaken the senses and set a positive tone for the day.

- **Essential Oil Rollers:** Prepare a blend of essential oils in a roller bottle for on-the-go mindfulness. Scents like bergamot and jasmine can provide instant relief during stressful moments.

- **Mindful Walking:** During a nature walk, focus on the scents around you—earthy aromas, blooming flowers, and fresh air. This practice enhances awareness of your environment and fosters a sense of connection with nature.

- **Scented Affirmations:** Pair affirmations with specific scents. For example, use grounding scents like cedarwood when reciting affirmations related to stability and security.

Conclusion

Scented mindfulness presents a powerful and accessible approach to self-care. By integrating aromatics into mindfulness practices, individuals can enhance their emotional well-being, deepen their self-awareness, and cultivate a more profound connection with their inner selves. As we navigate the complexities of modern life, embracing the power of scent can serve as a gentle reminder to pause, breathe, and savor the present moment.

In summary, the fusion of scent and mindfulness not only enriches self-care routines but also empowers individuals to reclaim their sense of self amidst the chaos of daily life. By harnessing the therapeutic potential of aromatics, we can foster an environment conducive to healing, reflection, and personal growth.

Aromatic Movement Practices: The Dance of Scents

In the realm of sensory experiences, the fusion of movement and scent creates a rich tapestry that transcends traditional boundaries. Aromatic movement practices, often referred to as the "dance of scents," encompass various forms of expression, from yoga and dance to martial arts and therapeutic movement. This section delves into the theoretical underpinnings, practical applications, and the transformative power of integrating aromas into movement practices.

Theoretical Foundations

The integration of scent in movement practices is grounded in multiple theoretical frameworks, including:

- **Somatic Theory:** Somatic practices emphasize body awareness and the connection between mind and body. The incorporation of scent enhances this connection, as olfactory stimuli can evoke emotional and physical responses, thereby deepening the somatic experience.

- **Aromatherapy:** Aromatherapy posits that essential oils can influence psychological and physiological states. When combined with movement, these scents can promote relaxation, invigorate energy, or enhance focus, creating a holistic approach to wellness.

- **Phenomenology:** This philosophical approach explores the subjective experience of individuals. The dance of scents invites practitioners to engage with their sensory perceptions, leading to a heightened awareness of the present moment and a deeper understanding of their bodily experiences.

Practical Applications

Aromatic movement practices can take various forms, each with unique benefits and applications. Here are some notable examples:

- **Scented Yoga:** In scented yoga sessions, essential oils are diffused or applied topically to enhance the practice. For instance, lavender may be used to promote relaxation during restorative poses, while citrus scents like bergamot can invigorate during more dynamic flows. Research indicates that certain scents can enhance focus and reduce anxiety, making them ideal companions for yoga practices.

- **Dance Therapy:** Dance therapy incorporates movement as a form of expression and healing. By introducing specific scents, therapists can evoke memories and emotions, facilitating deeper emotional release. For example, using the scent of sandalwood may promote feelings of grounding and stability, encouraging participants to explore their movements more freely.

- **Martial Arts with Scent:** Integrating scent into martial arts training can enhance focus and intention. For example, a practitioner may use peppermint oil to stimulate alertness before a sparring session. This approach not only enhances physical performance but also cultivates a mindful awareness of the body in motion.

- **Movement Meditation:** In movement meditation practices, participants are encouraged to explore their bodies through spontaneous movement while engaging with scents. This practice fosters a deeper connection to one's body and environment, allowing for personal expression and emotional exploration.

Challenges and Considerations

While aromatic movement practices offer numerous benefits, several challenges must be addressed:

- **Sensitivity to Scents:** Individuals may have varying sensitivities to certain scents. It is crucial to create an inclusive environment by providing options for participants and ensuring that scents are used in moderation to avoid overwhelming those who may be sensitive.

- **Quality of Essential Oils:** The effectiveness of aromatic practices largely depends on the quality of the essential oils used. Low-quality or synthetic fragrances may not provide the desired therapeutic effects and could potentially cause adverse reactions.

- **Cultural Sensitivity:** The use of scents in movement practices must be approached with cultural sensitivity. Certain aromas may hold different meanings across cultures, and practitioners should be aware of these nuances to avoid appropriation or offense.

Examples of Aromatic Movement Practices

Several organizations and practitioners have successfully integrated scent into their movement practices:

- **AromaYoga:** A movement practice that blends traditional yoga with aromatherapy, AromaYoga incorporates essential oils into each session, focusing on specific themes such as grounding, energizing, or calming.

- **Scented Dance Workshops:** Various dance studios offer workshops that integrate scents into their classes. Participants are encouraged to explore how different aromas influence their movement and emotional expression.

- **Mindful Movement Retreats:** Retreats focusing on mindfulness and movement often incorporate aromatic practices, allowing participants to engage with scents in nature while practicing yoga, tai chi, or other forms of movement.

Conclusion

Aromatic movement practices represent an innovative convergence of scent and physical expression. By embracing the dance of scents, practitioners can unlock new dimensions of awareness, emotional exploration, and holistic healing. As the field continues to evolve, further research and practice will illuminate the profound impact of integrating scent into movement, enriching the human experience and fostering deeper connections to self and others.

Wellness = f(Movement, Scent)   where f represents the synergistic relationship betwee (188)

Scented Crystals and Gemstones: Amplifying Aromatherapeutic Effects

The intersection of scent and crystals presents a fascinating realm in the world of aromatherapy. Scented crystals and gemstones not only enhance the olfactory experience but also serve as conduits for energy and intention. This section delves into the theory behind these aromatic gems, their potential problems, and practical examples of their use in enhancing well-being.

Theoretical Framework

The use of crystals and gemstones in holistic practices is grounded in the belief that each stone carries unique vibrational frequencies. When combined with essential oils or aromatic compounds, these frequencies can amplify the therapeutic effects of the scents. The theory posits that the vibrational energy of the crystals can resonate with the body's energy fields, known as *chakras*, to promote healing and balance.

$$E = h \cdot f \qquad (189)$$

Where E is energy, h is Planck's constant, and f is frequency. This equation illustrates the relationship between energy and frequency, suggesting that the vibrational frequencies of crystals can influence the energetic properties of the essential oils used alongside them.

Challenges and Considerations

While the combination of scented crystals and gemstones offers intriguing possibilities, several challenges must be considered:
1. **Purity of Materials**: The effectiveness of scented crystals relies heavily on the purity of both the crystals and the essential oils. Contaminated or synthetic materials can diminish the intended effects. 2. **Personal Sensitivity**: Individuals may have varying sensitivities to scents and energies. What works for one person may not resonate with another. 3. **Misleading Claims**: The market for scented crystals is burgeoning, leading to potential misinformation regarding their benefits. It is crucial to approach claims critically and rely on reputable sources.

Practical Applications

Integrating scented crystals into daily routines can enhance the aromatic experience and promote holistic healing. Here are some practical applications:

1. Crystal Infused Oils Creating crystal-infused oils involves placing specific crystals in a carrier oil along with essential oils. For example, amethyst is known for its calming properties, making it an excellent companion for lavender oil. The infusion process typically lasts for several days, allowing the energies of the crystals to permeate the oil.

2. Aromatherapy Jewelry Aromatherapy jewelry, such as necklaces or bracelets featuring scented gemstones, allows individuals to carry their preferred scents with them throughout the day. By wearing stones like rose quartz or citrine, users can benefit from both the vibrational energy of the stones and the aromatic properties of the essential oils applied to them.

3. Meditation and Rituals Incorporating scented crystals into meditation practices can deepen the experience. For instance, placing a piece of clear quartz infused with peppermint oil on the chakra points during meditation can enhance focus and clarity. This practice aligns the energetic properties of the crystal with the invigorating scent of the oil.

Examples of Scented Crystals and Their Effects

1. **Rose Quartz with Geranium Oil**: Known as the stone of love, rose quartz can amplify the soothing and balancing effects of geranium oil. This combination is ideal for fostering self-love and emotional healing.

2. **Lapis Lazuli with Frankincense**: Lapis lazuli is associated with wisdom and intuition. When paired with the grounding scent of frankincense, this combination can enhance spiritual practices and deepen meditative states.
3. **Citrine with Sweet Orange Oil**: Citrine is often linked to abundance and positivity. The uplifting scent of sweet orange can complement the energizing properties of citrine, making it perfect for boosting mood and motivation.

Conclusion

Scented crystals and gemstones represent a unique fusion of aromatherapy and crystal healing. By understanding the theoretical underpinnings, addressing potential challenges, and exploring practical applications, individuals can harness the power of these aromatic gems to amplify their wellness journeys. Whether through crystal-infused oils, aromatherapy jewelry, or meditative practices, the integration of scent and stones offers a pathway to holistic healing that is as enchanting as it is effective.

The Alchemical Art of Scent Bottling: Unlocking Personal Transformation

The act of scent bottling transcends mere fragrance creation; it is an alchemical journey that invites individuals to explore their innermost selves. This practice, steeped in history and mystique, allows for the transformation of raw materials into personal elixirs that resonate with one's identity, desires, and emotional landscape. In this section, we will delve into the theories behind scent bottling, the challenges faced in the process, and the profound impact it can have on personal transformation.

Theoretical Foundations of Scent Bottling

At its core, scent bottling is rooted in the principles of olfactory perception and emotional psychology. The human sense of smell is intricately linked to memory and emotion, as the olfactory bulb is directly connected to the limbic system, the brain's emotional center. This connection is crucial for understanding how scents can evoke powerful memories and feelings, leading to transformative experiences.

$$\text{Olfactory Perception} = f(\text{Chemical Structure}) + f(\text{Concentration}) + f(\text{Context})$$
$$(190)$$

Where: - f(Chemical Structure) represents the molecular composition of the scent. - f(Concentration) denotes the potency of the fragrance. - f(Context) encompasses the environmental factors influencing perception.

The process of scent bottling often involves the use of essential oils, absolutes, and other aromatic compounds, which can be combined in various ways to create unique fragrances. This blending process is akin to alchemy, where the goal is to transform base materials into something sublime. The ancient practice of alchemy sought to achieve the philosopher's stone, a metaphor for personal enlightenment and transformation. Similarly, scent bottling can serve as a catalyst for self-discovery and emotional healing.

Challenges in Scent Bottling

While the art of scent bottling is enchanting, it is not without its challenges. One of the primary obstacles is the balance between personal expression and the chemical interactions of the ingredients. Each component of a fragrance can alter the overall scent profile, leading to unexpected results. This necessitates a deep understanding of the properties of various aromatic substances and their interactions.

$$\text{Fragrance Profile} = \sum_{i=1}^{n} \text{Concentration}_i \cdot \text{Characteristic}_i \quad (191)$$

Where: - Concentration$_i$ is the amount of each ingredient. - Characteristic$_i$ represents the olfactory characteristics of each component.

Additionally, there is the challenge of achieving emotional resonance through scent. The subjective nature of olfactory experiences means that what may evoke joy in one individual may elicit discomfort in another. This variability can complicate the process of creating a scent that is universally appealing.

Examples of Personal Transformation through Scent Bottling

Despite these challenges, the rewards of scent bottling can be profound. Many individuals report transformative experiences when creating their own fragrances. For example, a person who has experienced trauma may choose to incorporate grounding scents such as vetiver or sandalwood into their blend, promoting feelings of stability and calm.

Consider the case of a young woman named Clara, who struggled with anxiety. Through the process of scent bottling, she discovered that blending lavender, chamomile, and bergamot not only created a soothing aroma but also acted as a therapeutic tool for her mental health. Each time she used her personalized scent, she felt a sense of empowerment and tranquility, enabling her to navigate her daily challenges with greater ease.

Another example can be found in the world of aromatherapy, where practitioners create bespoke blends tailored to the emotional needs of their clients. The practice of crafting these personalized scents often leads to profound shifts in mood and mindset. For instance, a blend of citrus oils for energizing and uplifting effects can help individuals break free from feelings of lethargy and negativity, fostering a sense of renewal.

Conclusion: The Transformative Power of Scent Bottling

The alchemical art of scent bottling is a powerful avenue for personal transformation. By harnessing the emotional and psychological connections that scents evoke, individuals can create fragrances that resonate with their true selves. While challenges exist in the process, the potential for self-discovery and healing is immense. As we continue to explore the intricate relationship between scent and identity, we open ourselves to the transformative possibilities that lie within each carefully crafted bottle.

In conclusion, scent bottling is not merely an act of blending oils; it is an invitation to explore one's essence, confront emotions, and embrace the journey of self-discovery. The alchemical art of scent bottling holds the key to unlocking personal transformation, empowering individuals to manifest their true selves through the power of fragrance.

Ethical Considerations in Scent Marketing and Advertising

Questioning Manipulative Scent Branding Techniques

In the contemporary market, scent branding has emerged as a powerful tool for influencing consumer behavior. The strategic use of fragrances in retail environments, advertisements, and product packaging has raised ethical questions about the extent to which these techniques manipulate consumer perceptions and choices. This section delves into the theoretical frameworks underpinning scent branding, the potential problems associated with its use, and notable examples that illustrate the complexities of this olfactory marketing strategy.

Theoretical Frameworks

Scent branding operates on several psychological principles, notably the **Pavlovian Conditioning** and **Emotional Branding**. Pavlovian Conditioning, rooted in classical conditioning theories, suggests that consumers can develop positive associations with a brand through repeated exposure to specific scents. This phenomenon can be mathematically represented by the equation:

$$C = P(A) \cdot E(S) \qquad (192)$$

Where:

- C is the conditioned response (positive association with the brand),
- $P(A)$ is the probability of brand exposure,
- $E(S)$ is the emotional response elicited by the scent.

Emotional Branding posits that scents can evoke deep emotional responses, influencing consumer loyalty and purchasing decisions. This connection between scent and emotion is supported by studies showing that olfactory stimuli can trigger memories and feelings more effectively than visual or auditory stimuli.

Problems with Manipulative Scent Branding

Despite its effectiveness, the use of scent branding raises several ethical concerns. One significant issue is the **Manipulation of Consumer Choice**. By embedding scents that evoke specific emotions or memories, brands may unduly influence consumers, leading them to make purchases based on emotional triggers rather than rational decision-making processes. This manipulation can be particularly concerning in vulnerable populations, such as children or individuals with cognitive impairments.

Another problem is the **Lack of Transparency**. Many consumers are unaware of the extent to which scents are used to influence their purchasing decisions. This lack of transparency can lead to a feeling of betrayal when consumers realize they were swayed by olfactory cues rather than genuine interest in a product. The ethical implications of such practices are profound, as they challenge the notion of informed consumer choice.

Moreover, scent branding can contribute to the **Homogenization of Experiences**. As brands increasingly adopt similar olfactory strategies, the uniqueness of individual consumer experiences may diminish. This homogenization can lead to a lack of differentiation among brands, making it difficult for consumers to form genuine connections with specific products.

Examples of Scent Branding Techniques

Several notable brands have successfully utilized scent branding to enhance their market presence. For instance, **Abercrombie & Fitch** is well-known for its signature fragrance, which permeates its retail spaces. The brand employs a specific scent to create an immersive shopping experience that aligns with its youthful and trendy image. This olfactory strategy has been both praised for its effectiveness and criticized for its potential to manipulate consumer perceptions.

Another example is **Starbucks**, which uses the aroma of freshly brewed coffee to create a welcoming atmosphere in its stores. The scent of coffee not only attracts customers but also enhances their overall experience, fostering a sense of comfort and familiarity. This strategy effectively encourages customers to associate the brand with positive feelings, potentially leading to increased sales.

Conversely, some brands have faced backlash for their scent branding practices. **Victoria's Secret**, for example, has been criticized for using overly sexualized fragrances in its marketing campaigns. This approach raises ethical concerns about the implications of sexualized branding on societal norms and consumer behavior, particularly regarding body image and self-esteem.

Conclusion

In conclusion, while scent branding can be a powerful marketing tool, it is essential to question the ethical implications of its use. The manipulation of consumer choice, lack of transparency, and homogenization of experiences are significant concerns that warrant further examination. As consumers become more aware of these tactics, brands must navigate the delicate balance between effective marketing and ethical responsibility. Moving forward, the fragrance industry must prioritize transparency and authenticity in its branding strategies to foster genuine connections with consumers.

Bibliography

[1] Pavlov, I. P. (1927). *Conditioned Reflexes: An Investigation of the Physiological Activity of the Cerebral Cortex*. Oxford University Press.

[2] Gobé, M. (2001). *Emotional Branding: How to Make the Brand Irresistible*. Allworth Press.

[3] Abercrombie & Fitch. (n.d.). *Fragrance*. Retrieved from [Abercrombie](https://www.abercrombie.com)

[4] Starbucks Corporation. (n.d.). *Our Coffee*. Retrieved from [Starbucks](https://www.starbucks.com)

[5] Victoria's Secret. (n.d.). *Fragrance*. Retrieved from [Victoria's Secret](https://www.victoriassecret.com)

The Impact of Scent in Consumer Decision-Making

The relationship between scent and consumer decision-making is a multifaceted area of study that intersects psychology, marketing, and sensory perception. Research has shown that olfactory stimuli can significantly influence consumer behavior, shaping their preferences, perceptions, and ultimately, their purchasing decisions. This section delves into the mechanisms through which scent affects consumer behavior, the theoretical frameworks that explain these effects, and real-world examples that illustrate the power of scent in marketing.

Theoretical Frameworks

One of the primary theories explaining the impact of scent on consumer decision-making is the **Scent-Branding Theory**. This theory posits that scents can evoke emotional responses and memories that are intricately linked to brand identity. When consumers encounter a particular scent in a retail environment, it can trigger positive associations with the brand, enhancing their overall experience and increasing the likelihood of purchase.

Another relevant concept is the **Affective Priming Theory**, which suggests that exposure to a scent can prime an individual's affective state, influencing their subsequent evaluations and choices. For instance, pleasant scents can create a positive mood, leading consumers to make more favorable evaluations of products. This can be mathematically represented by the following equation:

$$P(B|S) = P(S|B) \cdot \frac{P(B)}{P(S)} \qquad (193)$$

Where $P(B|S)$ is the probability of a positive brand evaluation given the presence of a pleasant scent S, $P(S|B)$ is the probability of a pleasant scent being associated with the brand B, $P(B)$ is the prior probability of a favorable brand perception, and $P(S)$ is the overall probability of encountering the scent.

Psychological Mechanisms

The psychological mechanisms underpinning the impact of scent on consumer decision-making can be categorized into three primary areas: **memory recall, emotional response**, and **behavioral influence**.

1. **Memory Recall:** Scents have a unique ability to evoke memories more effectively than other sensory modalities. This phenomenon is attributed to the brain's olfactory system, which is closely linked to the limbic system, the area responsible for emotion and memory. For example, a consumer may enter a bakery and be transported back to their childhood, recalling memories of baking with a loved one. This emotional connection can enhance their desire to purchase baked goods.

2. **Emotional Response:** Pleasant scents can induce positive emotional responses, which can enhance consumer mood and lead to increased spending. A study by [?] found that participants exposed to pleasant scents in a retail environment reported higher levels of happiness and were more likely to make impulse purchases compared to those in unscented or unpleasantly scented environments.

3. **Behavioral Influence:** The presence of a specific scent can influence consumer behavior in tangible ways. For instance, a study conducted in a clothing store demonstrated that the introduction of a floral scent increased the time customers spent in the store, leading to a higher likelihood of purchasing items. This behavioral change can be quantified through metrics such as conversion rates and average transaction values.

Challenges and Considerations

While the impact of scent on consumer decision-making is largely positive, there are challenges and ethical considerations that marketers must navigate:

- **Overstimulation:** Excessive use of scent can lead to sensory overload, causing discomfort and negative associations with a brand. Marketers must strike a balance in scent intensity to avoid alienating consumers.

- **Cultural Sensitivity:** Different cultures have varying associations with scents. What may be perceived as pleasant in one culture could be offensive in another. Marketers must conduct thorough market research to understand cultural preferences and sensitivities.

- **Allergic Reactions:** Some consumers may have allergies or sensitivities to certain scents, leading to negative experiences. Brands should consider offering scent-free options or clearly labeling products that contain fragrances.

Real-World Examples

Numerous brands have successfully harnessed the power of scent in their marketing strategies:

- **Abercrombie & Fitch:** The clothing retailer is famous for its signature scent, which is diffused throughout its stores. This olfactory branding creates a distinct atmosphere that reinforces the brand's identity and encourages consumer loyalty.

- **Starbucks:** The aroma of freshly brewed coffee is an integral part of the Starbucks experience. The company strategically positions its stores to maximize the scent of coffee, enticing passersby and enhancing the overall customer experience.

- **Dunkin' Donuts:** The brand employs scent marketing by using the smell of freshly baked donuts to attract customers. Research has shown that the scent of baked goods can significantly increase foot traffic to stores.

Conclusion

The impact of scent on consumer decision-making is a powerful tool that marketers can leverage to enhance brand experiences and influence purchasing behavior. By understanding the theoretical frameworks and psychological mechanisms at play, brands can create olfactory environments that resonate with consumers on a deeper level. However, ethical considerations and cultural sensitivities must be taken into account to ensure that scent marketing is both effective and respectful. As the field of scent marketing continues to evolve, it will be essential for brands to innovate and adapt their strategies in response to changing consumer preferences and societal trends.

Ethical Perfumery and Sustainable Scent Production

In recent years, the fragrance industry has faced increasing scrutiny regarding the ethical implications of its practices. The concept of ethical perfumery is rooted in the desire to create scents that not only please the senses but also respect the environment and the communities involved in their production. This section will explore the principles of ethical perfumery, the challenges faced by the industry, and examples of sustainable scent production.

Principles of Ethical Perfumery

Ethical perfumery encompasses several core principles aimed at promoting sustainability and social responsibility. These principles include:

- **Sustainable Sourcing:** Ethical perfumers prioritize sourcing raw materials from sustainable and regenerative practices. This involves selecting ingredients that are grown without harmful pesticides or fertilizers, and ensuring that the extraction methods do not deplete natural resources.

- **Fair Trade Practices:** Ensuring that the communities involved in the production of fragrance ingredients receive fair compensation for their labor is a cornerstone of ethical perfumery. This includes supporting local economies and promoting fair wages for farmers and workers.

- **Transparency:** Ethical perfumers advocate for transparency in their ingredient sourcing and production processes. This means clearly communicating the origins of ingredients and the methods used in their extraction and processing.

- **Cruelty-Free Standards:** Ethical perfumery rejects animal testing and supports cruelty-free practices. This commitment extends to all stages of production, from ingredient sourcing to final product testing.

Challenges in Ethical Perfumery

While the principles of ethical perfumery are noble, the industry faces several challenges in implementing these practices:

- **Supply Chain Complexity:** The fragrance supply chain is often convoluted, making it difficult to trace the origins of ingredients. This complexity can obscure unethical practices, such as exploitation or environmental degradation, making it challenging for consumers to make informed choices.

- **Cost Implications:** Sourcing sustainable and ethically produced ingredients often comes at a higher cost. This can lead to increased prices for consumers, which may limit the market for ethical perfumes compared to mass-produced alternatives.

- **Greenwashing:** With the rise of consumer demand for sustainable products, some brands may engage in greenwashing, where they falsely claim to be environmentally friendly or ethical without implementing genuine practices. This misleads consumers and undermines the efforts of truly ethical brands.

- **Regulatory Challenges:** The lack of standardized regulations regarding what constitutes "natural" or "sustainable" in the fragrance industry can create confusion for both consumers and producers. This ambiguity can hinder the growth of ethical perfumery.

Examples of Sustainable Scent Production

Several brands and initiatives exemplify the principles of ethical perfumery and sustainable scent production:

- **Aesop:** Known for its commitment to sustainability, Aesop sources ingredients from suppliers who adhere to ethical practices. The brand emphasizes transparency in its ingredient sourcing and actively engages in environmentally responsible initiatives.

- **Lush:** Lush is a pioneer in ethical perfumery, utilizing fresh, organic ingredients and promoting a strong stance against animal testing. The company implements fair trade practices and supports community-based sourcing for many of its raw materials.

- **Heretic Parfum:** This brand focuses on crafting perfumes with a commitment to natural ingredients and sustainable practices. Heretic Parfum emphasizes transparency in its sourcing and production processes, providing consumers with insight into the origins of its fragrances.

+ **Wildcraft:** Wildcraft is a Canadian brand that creates natural perfumes using ethically sourced ingredients. The company prioritizes sustainability in its production methods and packaging, aiming to reduce its environmental impact.

Theoretical Framework

The theoretical framework surrounding ethical perfumery can be examined through the lens of sustainability theories, such as the Triple Bottom Line (TBL) framework, which emphasizes the importance of social, environmental, and economic sustainability. The TBL framework posits that businesses should focus on achieving a balance between profit, people, and the planet. In the context of perfumery, this translates to:

$$TBL = \text{Profit} + \text{People} + \text{Planet} \qquad (194)$$

By integrating the principles of ethical perfumery into their business models, brands can contribute to a more sustainable future while appealing to a growing consumer base that values ethical practices.

Conclusion

As the fragrance industry continues to evolve, the importance of ethical perfumery and sustainable scent production cannot be overstated. By prioritizing sustainable sourcing, fair trade practices, transparency, and cruelty-free standards, the industry can address the challenges it faces and create a more responsible and appealing market for consumers. The examples set by pioneering brands demonstrate that it is possible to create captivating scents while honoring ethical principles, paving the way for a future where beauty and responsibility coexist harmoniously.

Cultural Sensitivity and Appropriation in Fragrance Advertising

In recent years, the fragrance industry has witnessed a growing awareness of the importance of cultural sensitivity and the need to address issues of appropriation in advertising. The intersection of culture and commerce in the realm of scent raises critical questions regarding representation, respect, and responsibility. This section delves into the theoretical frameworks surrounding cultural sensitivity, the problems associated with appropriation, and notable examples that illustrate the complexities involved.

Theoretical Frameworks

Cultural sensitivity is rooted in the understanding that cultures are not monolithic; they are dynamic, multifaceted, and deeply interconnected. Theories of cultural relativism posit that values and practices should be understood within their cultural context rather than judged against a universal standard. This perspective is crucial in fragrance advertising, where the use of cultural symbols, scents, and practices can evoke powerful emotional responses.

However, the concept of cultural appropriation complicates this discourse. Cultural appropriation occurs when elements of one culture are taken and used by members of another culture, often without permission or understanding of their significance. This can lead to the commodification of cultural symbols and practices, stripping them of their original meaning and context. In the fragrance industry, this manifests in the use of traditional scents, rituals, or motifs from marginalized cultures in a manner that prioritizes profit over respect.

Problems Associated with Appropriation

The problems associated with cultural appropriation in fragrance advertising are manifold. Firstly, there is the risk of perpetuating stereotypes. When fragrances are marketed using cultural imagery or names that misrepresent or simplify the complexities of a culture, it can reinforce harmful stereotypes. For instance, a fragrance that claims to embody "exotic" qualities may inadvertently reduce a rich cultural heritage to a mere marketing gimmick.

Secondly, appropriation often leads to economic exploitation. Many cultures have unique practices and knowledge surrounding scent-making that have been developed over centuries. When these practices are appropriated by large corporations without acknowledgment or compensation, it undermines the economic viability of the original culture. This raises ethical concerns about who benefits from the commercialization of cultural elements.

Lastly, appropriation can result in a loss of authenticity. Consumers today are increasingly seeking products that resonate with their values and beliefs. When a fragrance brand appropriates cultural elements without genuine engagement or understanding, it risks alienating consumers who value authenticity and ethical practices.

Notable Examples

Several high-profile cases in fragrance advertising have highlighted the challenges of cultural sensitivity and appropriation. One notable example is the controversy surrounding the launch of the fragrance *Dior Sauvage*. The campaign featured imagery and branding that drew heavily on Native American culture, including the use of a tribal drum and a Native American actor in the promotional materials. The backlash was swift, with critics arguing that the brand was exploiting Indigenous culture for commercial gain while failing to address the historical and ongoing struggles faced by Native communities. Dior eventually withdrew the campaign, acknowledging the insensitivity of their approach.

Another example is the fragrance *Yves Saint Laurent's Opium*, which faced criticism for its Orientalist connotations. The name itself drew from a complex historical narrative involving colonialism and exploitation. Despite its popularity, the fragrance was seen as perpetuating stereotypes about Eastern cultures and their associations with mystique and danger. The brand faced calls to re-evaluate its marketing strategies to avoid reinforcing such narratives.

Moving Towards Ethical Practices

To navigate the challenges of cultural sensitivity and appropriation in fragrance advertising, brands must adopt ethical practices that prioritize respect, representation, and responsibility. This involves engaging with the cultures they draw inspiration from, seeking permission, and ensuring that their marketing strategies reflect a deep understanding of cultural significance.

Brands can also benefit from collaborating with cultural consultants and community representatives to create authentic narratives that honor the traditions and values of the cultures they wish to represent. This approach not only fosters mutual respect but also enriches the storytelling aspect of fragrance marketing, creating a more meaningful connection with consumers.

Furthermore, transparency in sourcing and production practices is essential. Brands should be open about their inspirations and the origins of the ingredients they use, providing consumers with insight into the cultural contexts that inform their products. This commitment to transparency can build trust and credibility, positioning brands as responsible stewards of cultural heritage.

Conclusion

In conclusion, cultural sensitivity and appropriation in fragrance advertising are complex issues that require careful consideration and ethical engagement. By understanding the theoretical frameworks surrounding these concepts and acknowledging the potential problems associated with appropriation, brands can navigate the fragrance landscape with greater awareness and responsibility. As the industry continues to evolve, embracing cultural sensitivity will not only enhance brand reputation but also contribute to a more inclusive and respectful approach to scent marketing.

$$\text{Cultural Sensitivity} = \frac{\text{Respect} + \text{Understanding}}{\text{Appropriation}} \qquad (195)$$

In this equation, cultural sensitivity is achieved when respect and understanding are prioritized over appropriation, fostering a more ethical fragrance industry that honors the diverse tapestry of human experience.

Promoting Transparency and Accountability in the Industry

In an era where consumers are increasingly conscientious about the products they use, the fragrance industry faces mounting pressure to foster transparency and accountability. This demand stems from a growing awareness of the ethical implications surrounding sourcing, production, and marketing practices in the world of scent. As consumers become more educated about the ingredients in their perfumes and the environmental impact of their choices, the fragrance industry must evolve to meet these expectations.

The Importance of Transparency

Transparency in the fragrance industry refers to the clear communication of ingredient sourcing, production methods, and ethical considerations involved in creating perfumes. This concept is crucial for building trust between consumers and brands. According to a study by [1], 75% of consumers expressed a preference for brands that disclose their ingredient sources and production processes. Transparency not only enhances consumer trust but also encourages brands to adopt more sustainable practices.

Challenges to Transparency

Despite the clear benefits, achieving transparency in the fragrance industry is fraught with challenges. One significant issue is the proprietary nature of fragrance formulations. Many companies protect their scent compositions as trade secrets, making it difficult for consumers to know precisely what they are putting on their bodies. This lack of information can lead to skepticism and mistrust among consumers, particularly regarding the use of synthetic ingredients and potential allergens.

Moreover, the complexity of supply chains complicates transparency efforts. The sourcing of raw materials, especially those derived from natural sources, often involves multiple intermediaries. This can obscure the origins of ingredients, making it challenging for brands to provide accurate information about their sourcing practices. For example, the path from the extraction of essential oils to their incorporation into perfumes can involve numerous steps, each with its own set of ethical considerations.

The Role of Regulation

Regulatory bodies play a pivotal role in promoting transparency within the fragrance industry. In recent years, there have been calls for stricter regulations regarding ingredient disclosure. The European Union's REACH (Registration, Evaluation, Authorisation and Restriction of Chemicals) regulation, for instance, mandates that companies provide detailed information about the chemicals used in their products. This approach not only protects consumers but also encourages brands to prioritize safer, more sustainable ingredients.

However, the implementation of such regulations can be inconsistent across different regions. In the United States, the fragrance industry is largely self-regulated, which has led to a lack of uniform standards for ingredient disclosure. This disparity highlights the need for a more cohesive regulatory framework that prioritizes consumer safety and environmental responsibility.

Examples of Accountability in Action

Several brands have emerged as leaders in promoting transparency and accountability within the fragrance industry. For instance, *Herbivore Botanicals* has made a commitment to full ingredient disclosure, providing consumers with detailed information about the sourcing and benefits of each ingredient in their products. Their approach has resonated with consumers, resulting in a loyal customer base that values ethical practices.

Similarly, *Lush Cosmetics* has taken significant steps to ensure accountability in its sourcing practices. The company actively engages in fair trade partnerships and provides transparency about the origins of its ingredients. By prioritizing ethical sourcing, Lush has positioned itself as a brand that consumers can trust, leading to increased brand loyalty and market share.

The Future of Transparency in the Fragrance Industry

Looking ahead, the fragrance industry must embrace transparency as a fundamental principle of its operations. This shift requires a cultural change within companies, prioritizing ethical practices and open communication with consumers. Brands that proactively disclose ingredient sourcing, production methods, and ethical considerations will likely gain a competitive advantage in an increasingly conscientious marketplace.

Moreover, technology can play a vital role in enhancing transparency. Blockchain technology, for instance, offers a promising solution for tracking the origins of ingredients and ensuring ethical practices throughout the supply chain. By leveraging such technologies, brands can provide consumers with verifiable information about their products, fostering trust and accountability.

In conclusion, promoting transparency and accountability in the fragrance industry is not merely a trend; it is an essential evolution driven by consumer demand and ethical considerations. By addressing the challenges of ingredient disclosure, regulatory inconsistencies, and supply chain complexities, the industry can pave the way for a more responsible and trustworthy future. Brands that embrace these principles will not only enhance their reputations but also contribute to a more sustainable and ethical fragrance landscape.

The Ethics of Manipulating Scent in Advertising

The relationship between scent and consumer behavior has been a subject of extensive research, illustrating how olfactory stimuli can significantly influence purchasing decisions and brand loyalty. This phenomenon, known as *scent marketing*, leverages the emotional and psychological responses elicited by fragrances. However, the ethics surrounding the manipulation of scent in advertising raise critical questions about consumer autonomy, transparency, and the potential for exploitation.

Theoretical Framework

Scent marketing is grounded in several psychological theories, notably the *Pavlovian conditioning* model, where neutral stimuli (e.g., a brand) become associated with positive emotional responses through repeated exposure to pleasant scents. This process can be expressed mathematically through the following equation:

$$CR = f(CS, US) \qquad (196)$$

Where: - CR is the conditioned response (e.g., positive feelings towards a brand), - CS is the conditioned stimulus (the brand), - US is the unconditioned stimulus (the pleasant scent).

Problems with Scent Manipulation

While the efficacy of scent marketing is evident, ethical concerns arise when considering the implications of manipulating consumers' sensory experiences. Key problems include:

1. **Consumer Manipulation:** The intentional use of scent to evoke specific emotional responses can be seen as a form of manipulation. This raises questions about the authenticity of consumer choices, as decisions may be driven more by engineered sensory experiences than by informed preferences.

2. **Lack of Transparency:** Many consumers are unaware of the extent to which scents are used in advertising and retail environments. The absence of transparency regarding scent marketing practices can lead to feelings of betrayal and mistrust when consumers realize they have been influenced by olfactory cues without their knowledge.

3. **Cultural Sensitivity:** Scents can carry different meanings across cultures. The use of certain fragrances in advertising may unintentionally offend or alienate specific demographic groups, leading to accusations of cultural appropriation or insensitivity.

4. **Health Considerations:** Some individuals may have sensitivities or allergies to certain scents, which can make the use of strong fragrances in advertising and retail environments problematic. Brands must consider the potential health implications of their scent marketing strategies.

Examples of Ethical Dilemmas

Several high-profile cases illustrate the ethical dilemmas surrounding scent manipulation in advertising:

- **Abercrombie & Fitch:** The retailer became notorious for its use of strong fragrances in stores, creating an immersive shopping experience. However, this practice faced backlash for being overwhelming and excluding customers who are sensitive to scents. Critics argued that the brand prioritized a specific sensory experience at the expense of inclusivity.

- **Luxury Brands and Scent Exclusivity:** Many luxury brands utilize unique scents to create an aura of exclusivity. While this can enhance brand identity, it raises ethical questions about the accessibility of such experiences. The manipulation of scent to evoke luxury may reinforce social stratification based on consumer ability to access premium products.

- **Scented Advertising Campaigns:** Some brands have employed scented advertisements, such as scratch-and-sniff ads, to create a direct olfactory connection with consumers. While innovative, these campaigns can blur the lines between sensory engagement and manipulation, leading to ethical scrutiny about the authenticity of the consumer experience.

Towards Ethical Practices

To navigate the ethical landscape of scent manipulation in advertising, brands can adopt several best practices:

- **Transparency:** Brands should disclose their use of scent marketing strategies, allowing consumers to make informed choices about their engagement with products.

- **Inclusivity:** Companies should consider the diverse sensory experiences of their customer base, ensuring that scent marketing does not alienate or exclude individuals with sensitivities or cultural objections to certain fragrances.

- **Consumer Education:** Providing consumers with information about the psychological effects of scents can empower them to recognize when they are being influenced and make more conscious purchasing decisions.

- **Ethical Sourcing of Fragrances:** Brands should commit to ethically sourcing their fragrance ingredients, ensuring that their products do not exploit natural resources or contribute to environmental degradation.

In conclusion, while scent marketing presents unique opportunities for brands to connect with consumers on a deeper emotional level, it is imperative that companies approach the manipulation of scent in advertising with a strong ethical framework. By prioritizing transparency, inclusivity, and consumer education, brands can foster trust and loyalty while respecting the autonomy and well-being of their customers.

The Responsibility of Perfumers in Ethical Sourcing and Production

In the world of fragrance, the responsibility of perfumers extends beyond the olfactory delight they create; it encompasses ethical sourcing and sustainable production practices. As consumers become increasingly aware of the environmental and social impacts of their purchases, perfumers face the challenge of aligning their artistry with ethical standards. This section explores the theoretical underpinnings of ethical sourcing, the problems associated with unsustainable practices, and examples of brands that are leading the way in ethical fragrance production.

Theoretical Framework of Ethical Sourcing

Ethical sourcing can be defined as the process of ensuring that the products being procured are obtained in a responsible and sustainable manner. This involves considering the social, environmental, and economic impacts of sourcing decisions. The theory of corporate social responsibility (CSR) posits that businesses have an obligation to act in the best interests of their environments and societies. This aligns with the concept of sustainability, which emphasizes meeting the needs of the present without compromising the ability of future generations to meet their own needs.

Mathematically, the relationship between ethical sourcing and sustainability can be expressed as:

$$S = \frac{E + S + S}{C} \qquad (197)$$

where S represents sustainability, E represents ethical practices, S represents social responsibility, and C represents the costs associated with implementing these practices. A higher value of S indicates a greater commitment to sustainability, which is increasingly becoming a demand from consumers.

Problems Associated with Unsustainable Practices

The fragrance industry faces several challenges related to unsustainable practices. One significant issue is the overharvesting of natural resources. Many fragrance ingredients, such as sandalwood and jasmine, are derived from plants that are being depleted due to high demand. This not only threatens biodiversity but also jeopardizes the livelihoods of communities that rely on these resources.

Moreover, the use of synthetic ingredients often raises ethical concerns. While they can be produced more sustainably than their natural counterparts, the chemical processes involved may still have harmful environmental impacts. The problem of microplastics, for instance, has emerged as a critical concern in the cosmetic and fragrance industries. These tiny plastic particles can accumulate in ecosystems, posing threats to marine life and food chains.

Case Studies of Ethical Practices

Several brands have recognized the importance of ethical sourcing and have taken significant steps to ensure their practices align with these principles. One notable example is *L'Occitane*, a French cosmetics brand that emphasizes the use of sustainably sourced ingredients. They work directly with farmers in regions like Provence, France, ensuring fair wages and sustainable farming practices. This not only supports local economies but also promotes biodiversity.

Similarly, *The Body Shop* has long been a pioneer in ethical sourcing. Their Community Trade program sources ingredients from marginalized communities around the world, providing them with fair compensation and support for their local economies. The Body Shop's commitment to ethical practices has helped to set a standard in the industry, proving that profit can coexist with social responsibility.

The Role of Certifications and Standards

To further ensure ethical sourcing and production, various certifications and standards have emerged. The *Fair Trade* certification, for example, guarantees that producers receive fair prices for their goods, which can be particularly beneficial in the fragrance industry where raw materials are often sourced from developing countries. Additionally, the *Ecocert* certification ensures that products meet strict environmental and social standards.

These certifications provide consumers with the assurance that the products they purchase are produced ethically, fostering trust between brands and their customers. As the market for ethical products continues to grow, perfumers must consider these certifications as integral to their sourcing strategies.

Conclusion

The responsibility of perfumers in ethical sourcing and production is a multifaceted issue that intersects art, commerce, and social responsibility. By understanding the theoretical frameworks of ethical sourcing, recognizing the problems associated with unsustainable practices, and looking to successful case studies, perfumers can navigate this complex landscape. As consumer demand for ethically produced fragrances rises, the industry must adapt, ensuring that the scents of the future are not only delightful but also responsible and sustainable.

In conclusion, the fragrance industry stands at a crossroads where ethical sourcing and production can no longer be viewed as optional. Instead, they must become fundamental components of the perfumer's craft. As we move forward, the integration of ethical practices will not only enhance the brand's reputation but also contribute to a more sustainable and just world.

The Scented Double-Edged Sword: The Power and Pitfalls of Marketing

In the world of advertising, scent is an often overlooked yet powerful tool that can evoke emotions, trigger memories, and influence consumer behavior. This section explores the dual nature of scent marketing—its potential to create strong emotional connections and enhance brand loyalty, while also considering the ethical implications and potential pitfalls that arise from its use.

The Power of Scent Marketing

Scent marketing leverages the psychological impact of aromas to enhance consumer experiences. Research has shown that scent can significantly affect mood and behavior. For example, a study conducted by Spangenberg et al. (2006) demonstrated that pleasant ambient scents in retail environments can lead to increased time spent in-store and higher purchase intentions. The underlying theory here is based on the *cognitive appraisal theory*, which posits that emotional responses to stimuli are influenced by personal evaluations of those stimuli.

$$E = f(A, R) \tag{198}$$

Where:

- E = Emotional response
- A = Appraisal of the scent

- R = Relevance of the scent to the individual

In practical terms, brands like Abercrombie & Fitch have capitalized on scent marketing by creating a signature fragrance that permeates their stores, reinforcing brand identity and creating a memorable shopping experience. This strategy not only attracts customers but also fosters a sense of loyalty, as the scent becomes associated with positive experiences.

The Psychological Mechanisms at Play

The effectiveness of scent marketing can be attributed to several psychological mechanisms:

- **Associative Learning:** Through classical conditioning, consumers can develop positive associations with a brand based on specific scents. For instance, the smell of freshly baked cookies may evoke feelings of warmth and nostalgia, which brands can exploit to create a favorable impression.

- **Emotional Memory:** Scent is closely linked to the limbic system, the part of the brain responsible for emotions and memory. This connection means that scents can trigger vivid memories and emotional responses, making them a powerful tool in advertising.

- **Sensory Branding:** Scent adds a sensory dimension to branding that can differentiate a brand in a crowded marketplace. For instance, luxury hotels often employ signature scents to enhance the guest experience, creating a unique ambiance that guests associate with the brand.

The Pitfalls of Scent Marketing

Despite its potential benefits, scent marketing is not without its challenges and ethical considerations. The following issues highlight the potential pitfalls:

- **Manipulation and Deception:** The use of scent can border on manipulation, as brands may exploit emotional vulnerabilities to drive sales. For example, using scents that evoke nostalgia or comfort can lead consumers to make purchases they might not otherwise consider. This raises ethical questions about the extent to which brands should influence consumer behavior.

- **Sensory Overload:** In some cases, overly aggressive scent marketing can lead to sensory overload, causing discomfort or even allergic reactions among consumers. A notable example is the backlash against certain retail environments where overpowering fragrances deter customers rather than attract them.

- **Cultural Sensitivity:** Different cultures have varied perceptions of scents. What is considered pleasant in one culture may be offensive in another. Brands must navigate these cultural differences carefully to avoid alienating potential customers. For instance, while floral scents may be beloved in Western markets, they may not resonate in cultures where such fragrances are associated with funerals or mourning.

- **Brand Authenticity:** As consumers become more aware of marketing tactics, there is a growing demand for authenticity. Over-reliance on scent marketing can lead to perceptions of inauthenticity, where consumers feel manipulated rather than genuinely engaged. Brands that fail to align their scent marketing with their core values risk losing credibility.

Conclusion

The power of scent marketing is undeniable, as it can create profound emotional connections and enhance consumer experiences. However, the ethical implications and potential pitfalls must be carefully considered. Brands that navigate this double-edged sword with transparency and sensitivity will likely reap the benefits of enhanced loyalty and engagement, while those that exploit scent without consideration for consumer well-being may find themselves facing backlash.

In the evolving landscape of marketing, the challenge lies in leveraging the allure of scent while maintaining ethical standards and cultural sensitivity. As we move forward, the balance between enticing consumers and respecting their autonomy will define the future of scent marketing.

Bibliography

[1] Spangenberg, E. R., Crowley, A. E., & Henderson, P. W. (2006). Improving the Retail Experience: The Role of Scent in Retailing. *Journal of Retailing*, 82(1), 1-12.

The Impact of Scented Advertising on Emotional Manipulation

Scented advertising has emerged as a powerful tool in the marketing arsenal, leveraging the intricate relationship between olfaction and human emotion. This section explores the mechanisms through which scented advertising can manipulate emotions, the theoretical frameworks underpinning this phenomenon, and the ethical considerations surrounding its application.

Theoretical Frameworks

The impact of scent on emotions can be understood through several psychological theories:

- **Classical Conditioning:** This theory, pioneered by Ivan Pavlov, suggests that emotional responses can be conditioned through repeated associations. For instance, a particular fragrance may be paired with positive experiences (e.g., a romantic dinner), leading consumers to associate that scent with similar feelings of happiness and nostalgia. The equation representing this relationship can be summarized as:

$$CR = UCR + (CS \to CR) \qquad (199)$$

where CR is the conditioned response (positive emotion), UCR is the unconditioned response (natural emotional reaction), and CS is the conditioned stimulus (the scent).

- **The Two-Factor Theory of Emotion:** Proposed by Schachter and Singer, this theory posits that emotion is the result of physiological arousal and cognitive interpretation. When consumers encounter a scent, their physiological responses (e.g., increased heart rate) can be interpreted in the context of the advertising message, leading to an emotional reaction. The formula can be expressed as:

$$E = A + C \qquad (200)$$

where E is the emotion experienced, A is the physiological arousal caused by the scent, and C is the cognitive appraisal of the situation.

- **The Affective Priming Theory:** This theory suggests that exposure to a scent can activate related emotional concepts in memory, influencing subsequent judgments and behaviors. For example, a floral scent may evoke feelings of romance and serenity, impacting consumer choices in favor of products that align with those emotions.

Mechanisms of Emotional Manipulation

Scented advertising manipulates emotions through several mechanisms:

- **Creating Atmosphere:** Brands use scent to create an immersive atmosphere that enhances the overall experience. For instance, high-end retail stores often diffuse pleasant fragrances to evoke luxury and exclusivity, making consumers more likely to purchase.

- **Enhancing Brand Recall:** Scents can enhance memory recall, making consumers more likely to remember a brand associated with a particular fragrance. Research shows that olfactory cues can trigger memories more effectively than visual or auditory cues.

- **Influencing Mood:** Certain scents have been found to influence mood states. For example, citrus scents are often associated with freshness and energy, while lavender is linked to calmness and relaxation. Marketers can strategically use these associations to align consumer mood with their brand message.

- **Eliciting Emotional Responses:** Scents can elicit specific emotional responses. A study conducted by Spangenberg et al. (2006) found that pleasant ambient scents increased positive emotions and purchase intentions among consumers. The emotional arousal caused by scent can lead to impulsive buying behavior, as consumers are more likely to act on positive feelings.

Ethical Considerations

While scented advertising can enhance consumer experience, it raises several ethical concerns:

- **Manipulation vs. Influence:** The fine line between influence and manipulation can blur in scented advertising. Consumers may be unaware of how scents are designed to elicit specific emotional responses, raising questions about informed consent.
- **Cultural Sensitivity:** Different cultures have varying associations with scents. A fragrance that is appealing in one culture may be offensive in another. Marketers must be sensitive to these differences to avoid alienating potential customers.
- **Health Concerns:** Some individuals may have sensitivities or allergies to certain scents. The use of synthetic fragrances in advertising can pose health risks, leading to negative experiences and backlash against brands that neglect consumer health.

Examples of Scented Advertising

Several brands have successfully harnessed the power of scent in their advertising strategies:

- **Abercrombie & Fitch:** This brand is known for its signature scent, which is diffused in stores to create a distinct atmosphere. The scent has become synonymous with the brand, enhancing customer loyalty and emotional attachment.
- **Coca-Cola:** In various marketing campaigns, Coca-Cola has utilized the scent of its product to evoke feelings of happiness and nostalgia, particularly during the holiday season. The combination of visual and olfactory cues reinforces positive emotional associations with the brand.
- **Airlines and Hotels:** Many airlines and hotel chains have developed unique signature scents to enhance the travel experience. For example, the Four

Seasons hotels use a specific fragrance in their lobbies to create a welcoming and luxurious atmosphere, influencing guests' emotional responses and encouraging repeat visits.

Conclusion

The impact of scented advertising on emotional manipulation is profound and multifaceted. By understanding the psychological theories that underpin scent perception, marketers can craft experiences that resonate deeply with consumers. However, ethical considerations must guide the use of scent in advertising to ensure that emotional manipulation does not compromise consumer trust or well-being. As the field of scented marketing continues to evolve, it will be essential for brands to navigate these complexities thoughtfully, balancing emotional engagement with ethical responsibility.

Scent in Social Responsibility: Advocating for Ethical Practices

In recent years, the fragrance industry has come under scrutiny for its environmental impact, ethical sourcing of ingredients, and the manipulation of consumer perceptions through scent marketing. As consumers become more aware of these issues, there is a growing demand for transparency and accountability in the perfume industry. This section explores the ethical considerations surrounding scent marketing and the responsibilities of perfumers in promoting sustainable practices.

The Impact of Scent in Consumer Decision-Making

Scent has a profound effect on human emotions and behaviors, influencing consumer decisions in significant ways. According to the *Journal of Consumer Research*, pleasant scents can enhance consumer experiences, leading to increased sales and brand loyalty. However, this power can be wielded unethically. For instance, brands may use synthetic fragrances that trigger emotional responses without disclosing their potential health risks or environmental consequences.

$$\text{Consumer Satisfaction} = f(\text{Scent Quality, Brand Image, Product Experience}) \tag{201}$$

This equation illustrates that consumer satisfaction is a function of scent quality, brand image, and overall product experience. When companies prioritize profit over ethical considerations, they risk alienating a growing segment of consumers who value sustainability and integrity.

Ethical Perfumery and Sustainable Scent Production

Ethical perfumery involves the responsible sourcing of ingredients, minimizing environmental impact, and ensuring fair labor practices. This approach not only benefits the planet but also resonates with consumers who are increasingly concerned about the origins of the products they use. For example, brands like *Lush* and *Herbivore Botanicals* emphasize the use of natural, sustainably-sourced ingredients and transparent manufacturing processes.

The concept of *sustainability* in perfumery can be defined as:

$$\text{Sustainability} = \frac{\text{Natural Resource Use}}{\text{Regeneration Rate}} \qquad (202)$$

A sustainable fragrance brand aims to ensure that the rate of natural resource use does not exceed the regeneration rate of those resources, thereby preserving ecosystems and reducing carbon footprints.

Cultural Sensitivity and Appropriation in Fragrance Advertising

The fragrance industry often draws inspiration from diverse cultures, yet this can lead to issues of cultural appropriation. Brands must navigate the fine line between honoring cultural traditions and exploiting them for profit. For instance, using indigenous plants or traditional scent recipes without proper acknowledgment or compensation to the communities that created them raises ethical concerns.

To address these issues, companies can adopt practices such as:

- Collaborating with local artisans and communities to create authentic fragrances.

- Ensuring fair compensation for the use of traditional knowledge and practices.

- Engaging in community development initiatives that support the cultural heritage of the source communities.

Promoting Transparency and Accountability in the Industry

Transparency in ingredient sourcing and manufacturing processes is crucial for building consumer trust. Brands can enhance accountability by providing clear information about their ingredients, including potential allergens and the environmental impact of their production. For example, *Aesop* provides detailed information about the sourcing of its ingredients, allowing consumers to make informed choices.

$$\text{Transparency Index} = \frac{\text{Number of Disclosed Ingredients}}{\text{Total Ingredients}} \times 100 \quad (203)$$

A higher transparency index indicates a greater commitment to ethical practices. Brands with a transparency index above 80% are often viewed more favorably by consumers, leading to increased loyalty and sales.

The Ethics of Manipulating Scent in Advertising

Scent marketing can be a double-edged sword. While it can enhance consumer experiences, it can also manipulate emotions in ways that may not align with ethical standards. For instance, using scent to mask unpleasant realities, such as poor product quality or unsustainable practices, can mislead consumers.

To mitigate these risks, brands should:

- Use scent marketing responsibly, ensuring that it enhances rather than deceives.

- Educate consumers about the role of scent in their experiences, fostering a deeper connection to the product.

- Promote scents that reflect the brand's values and commitment to sustainability.

The Scented Double-Edged Sword: The Power and Pitfalls of Marketing

The power of scent in marketing is undeniable, but it comes with significant ethical responsibilities. Brands must recognize the potential pitfalls of using scent as a manipulative tool and strive to create genuine connections with consumers. By prioritizing ethical practices, companies can build lasting relationships based on trust and authenticity.

In conclusion, advocating for ethical practices in the fragrance industry requires a multifaceted approach. By promoting transparency, sustainability, and cultural sensitivity, the industry can evolve to meet the demands of socially conscious consumers. As the scent landscape continues to shift, perfumers and brands must embrace their roles as stewards of both the environment and the communities they engage with, ultimately fostering a more ethical and responsible fragrance culture.

Community Building through Attractive Stenches

Scented Gatherings and Festivals for Odor Enthusiasts

Scented gatherings and festivals have emerged as vibrant celebrations of olfactory culture, bringing together enthusiasts who share a passion for unique aromas and the stories they tell. These events serve as a platform for exploration, education, and community building, where participants can immerse themselves in a world rich with diverse scents and the emotions they evoke.

Theoretical Framework

The allure of scent lies in its profound ability to evoke memories, emotions, and even influence social interactions. According to *olfactory psychology*, the human sense of smell is intricately linked to the limbic system, the brain region responsible for emotions and memory. This connection explains why certain scents can trigger vivid recollections or feelings of nostalgia. The theory of *scent branding* posits that aromas can shape consumer behavior and preferences, making scent a powerful tool in marketing and personal expression.

The phenomenon of communal scent experiences can be analyzed through the lens of *social identity theory*, which suggests that individuals derive a sense of belonging from their affiliations with particular groups. Scented gatherings allow participants to connect over shared interests, creating a collective identity centered around the appreciation of olfactory art.

Types of Scented Gatherings

Scented gatherings can take various forms, including:

- **Perfume Expos:** These large-scale events showcase a wide array of fragrance brands, from established houses to niche perfumers. Attendees can sample scents, attend workshops, and engage with industry experts.

- **Aromatic Festivals:** Celebrating the cultural significance of scent, these festivals often feature local artisans, workshops on creating natural perfumes, and discussions on the historical context of aromas in different cultures.

- **Scented Dinners:** Culinary experiences that incorporate aromatic ingredients into the menu, allowing diners to explore the interplay between scent and taste. These events often highlight the role of aroma in enhancing the dining experience.

- **Olfactory Art Installations:** These gatherings merge art and scent, inviting participants to engage with installations designed to evoke specific emotions or memories through carefully curated aromas.

Challenges and Considerations

While scented gatherings are often celebrated for their creativity and community spirit, they are not without challenges.

Inclusivity and Accessibility   One significant issue is ensuring that these events are inclusive and accessible to all individuals, including those with scent sensitivities or allergies. Organizers must consider the diverse needs of attendees and create environments where everyone can participate without discomfort.

Environmental Impact   Another concern is the environmental impact of scent production and waste generated by such gatherings. The fragrance industry has been criticized for its reliance on synthetic ingredients and unsustainable practices. As a response, many festivals are embracing eco-friendly practices, such as promoting natural fragrances and minimizing waste through recycling initiatives.

Examples of Notable Scented Gatherings

Several notable scented gatherings have gained recognition for their unique approaches to celebrating aromas:

- **The Fragrance Foundation Awards:** An annual event that honors excellence in the fragrance industry, featuring categories such as Best New Fragrance and Best Packaging. This prestigious gathering attracts industry leaders and fragrance enthusiasts alike.

- **Scent Bar:** Located in Los Angeles, this interactive space allows visitors to create their own custom fragrances. The Scent Bar hosts workshops and events, fostering a community of scent lovers who can explore their olfactory creativity.

- **The Aroma Festival:** Held in various cities worldwide, this festival celebrates the art of scent through workshops, tastings, and discussions on the cultural significance of aromas in different traditions.

Conclusion

Scented gatherings and festivals for odor enthusiasts play a crucial role in fostering a sense of community and celebrating the rich tapestry of aromas that permeate our lives. By providing a space for exploration, education, and connection, these events not only elevate the appreciation of scent but also challenge societal norms surrounding olfactory experiences. As we continue to embrace the power of scent, it is essential to consider the inclusivity and sustainability of these gatherings, ensuring that the olfactory arts remain accessible and environmentally conscious for all.

$$\text{Olfactory Experience} = f(\text{Scent Composition, Context, Individual Perception}) \tag{204}$$

This equation illustrates the multifaceted nature of olfactory experiences, emphasizing the interplay between scent composition, the context in which it is experienced, and the individual's unique perception. As the fragrance community continues to evolve, the importance of fostering inclusive, innovative, and sustainable scented gatherings will remain paramount.

Online Communities and Forums for Fragrance Rebels

In the age of digital connectivity, online communities and forums have emerged as vibrant platforms for fragrance rebels—those who dare to challenge conventional norms of scent and embrace the beauty of unique, sometimes controversial, odors. These spaces provide a sanctuary for individuals who seek to explore the multifaceted world of fragrance beyond the mainstream. Here, we delve into the significance of these communities, the theoretical frameworks underpinning their existence, the challenges they face, and notable examples that illustrate their impact.

Theoretical Frameworks

The rise of online fragrance communities can be understood through several theoretical lenses, notably social constructivism and community of practice. Social constructivism posits that knowledge and meaning are constructed through social interactions. In the context of fragrance, individuals share their experiences, preferences, and critiques, thereby co-creating a rich tapestry of scent-related knowledge. This collective intelligence fosters a sense of belonging and identity among members, who often feel marginalized by mainstream fragrance culture.

Community of practice theory, introduced by Wenger (1998), further elucidates how these online spaces function. Members engage in shared practices—discussing scent compositions, sharing DIY recipes, and critiquing commercial fragrances. This participatory culture not only enhances individual knowledge but also strengthens community ties as members support one another in their olfactory explorations.

Challenges Faced by Fragrance Rebels

Despite the vibrancy of these online communities, fragrance rebels encounter several challenges:

- **Gatekeeping and Exclusivity:** Some forums may exhibit gatekeeping behaviors, where established members discourage newcomers or enforce rigid standards of taste. This can lead to feelings of exclusion and discourage participation from a diverse range of voices.

- **Commercialization:** As fragrance communities gain popularity, they may attract commercial interests seeking to exploit the collective's passion for profit. This commercialization can dilute the authenticity of discussions and lead to conflicts of interest, where members may feel pressured to promote certain brands or products.

- **Misinformation:** The democratization of fragrance knowledge can result in the spread of misinformation. Unverified claims about ingredients, scent profiles, or health effects can circulate, potentially misleading community members and undermining trust.

Notable Examples of Fragrance Communities

Several online platforms have gained prominence as hubs for fragrance rebels, each fostering unique cultures and practices:

- **Fragrantica:** A comprehensive fragrance database and community forum, Fragrantica allows users to review perfumes, share scent experiences, and participate in discussions. The platform's user-generated content empowers individuals to express their opinions freely, challenging traditional notions of fragrance authority.

- **Basenotes:** This forum caters to fragrance enthusiasts who seek in-depth discussions about perfumes. Users engage in detailed analyses of scent compositions, share their personal journeys with fragrance, and explore niche perfumery. Basenotes exemplifies a community of practice where members collectively deepen their understanding of scent.

- **Reddit Fragrance Community (r/fragrance):** Reddit's fragrance community is known for its diverse discussions ranging from mainstream to niche fragrances. Members share advice on scent layering, DIY perfume creation, and even scent-related memes, fostering a lighthearted yet informative atmosphere.

- **Instagram and TikTok:** Social media platforms have become vital for fragrance rebels to showcase their olfactory journeys. Influencers and enthusiasts share reviews, tutorials, and personal anecdotes, creating a visually engaging way to explore scent. Hashtags like #FragranceCommunity and #PerfumeAddict connect users across platforms, amplifying their voices.

The Impact of Online Communities on Fragrance Culture

The influence of these online communities extends beyond individual experiences; they actively shape fragrance culture. By challenging mainstream narratives, fragrance rebels promote inclusivity and diversity in scent appreciation. They advocate for the exploration of unconventional odors and encourage the deconstruction of beauty norms surrounding fragrance.

Moreover, these communities have the potential to drive social change. Through discussions about sustainable and ethical perfumery, members raise awareness about environmental issues and advocate for responsible sourcing practices. Initiatives such as group buys for indie brands or collaborative scent projects can empower members to support artisans and challenge the dominance of large fragrance corporations.

Conclusion

In conclusion, online communities and forums for fragrance rebels serve as essential platforms for exploring the complexities of scent and challenging societal norms. Through social constructivism and community of practice, these spaces foster knowledge sharing, creativity, and connection. While they face challenges such as gatekeeping and misinformation, the impact of these communities on fragrance culture is profound. As individuals continue to embrace their unique olfactory identities, the future of scent will undoubtedly be shaped by the vibrant voices of fragrance rebels united in their pursuit of authenticity and exploration.

Networking and Collaboration Opportunities in the Olfactory Arts

In the realm of olfactory arts, networking and collaboration serve as pivotal elements for innovation, creativity, and the expansion of the sensory experience. The olfactory arts encompass a diverse range of disciplines, including perfumery, scent design, and interactive installations that engage audiences through the sense of smell. This section delves into the various avenues for collaboration and networking within this unique field, exploring the theoretical frameworks, potential challenges, and inspiring examples that illustrate the power of collective creativity.

Theoretical Frameworks for Collaboration

The foundation of successful collaboration in the olfactory arts can be anchored in several theoretical frameworks, including *interdisciplinary collaboration, co-creation,* and *community engagement.*

- **Interdisciplinary Collaboration:** This approach encourages the merging of different fields such as art, science, and technology. By bringing together perfumers, artists, scientists, and technologists, interdisciplinary collaboration fosters innovative ideas that transcend traditional boundaries. For instance, a perfumer may collaborate with a visual artist to create a multisensory installation that explores the relationship between scent and visual perception.

- **Co-Creation:** Co-creation involves engaging stakeholders in the creative process, allowing for a more inclusive approach to art-making. In the olfactory arts, this can mean involving the audience in scent creation, where participants contribute their ideas, preferences, and even personal scents to shape the final olfactory experience. This participatory approach not only enhances the depth of the artwork but also strengthens the connection between the creator and the audience.

- **Community Engagement:** Building a community around olfactory arts encourages collaboration among artists, enthusiasts, and the general public. Workshops, scent festivals, and online forums provide platforms for sharing knowledge, resources, and experiences. Community engagement fosters a sense of belonging and creates a supportive environment for emerging artists to thrive.

Challenges to Collaboration

While collaboration offers numerous benefits, it is not without its challenges. These challenges can include:

- **Communication Barriers:** Differences in terminology and approaches among various disciplines can lead to misunderstandings. For example, a perfumer may use specific jargon that is unfamiliar to a visual artist, hindering effective collaboration.

- **Resource Allocation:** Collaborative projects often require shared resources, which can lead to conflicts over funding, materials, and time. Establishing clear agreements and expectations at the outset is essential to mitigate these issues.

- **Creative Differences:** Artistic visions may clash during the collaborative process. Establishing a shared vision and maintaining open lines of communication can help navigate these creative differences and ensure that all voices are heard.

Examples of Successful Collaboration

Several successful collaborations in the olfactory arts highlight the potential for innovation when artists from diverse backgrounds come together:

- **Scented Art Installations:** Artists such as *Sissel Tolaas* have created immersive installations that engage audiences through scent. Tolaas's work often involves collaborating with scientists and researchers to explore the emotional and cultural implications of smell, resulting in thought-provoking experiences that challenge perceptions of odor.

- **Perfume and Fashion Collaborations:** The fashion industry has increasingly recognized the importance of scent as an integral part of the overall aesthetic. Designers such as *Issey Miyake* and *Chanel* have collaborated with perfumers to create fragrances that complement their fashion collections, enhancing the sensory experience of their brand.

- **Community-Based Scent Projects:** Initiatives like *The Smell Festival* in Italy bring together artists, perfumers, and the public to explore the world of scent through workshops, installations, and discussions. These events foster collaboration and community engagement, allowing participants to share their experiences and insights on olfactory art.

Conclusion

Networking and collaboration in the olfactory arts provide invaluable opportunities for artists and creators to explore new horizons and push the boundaries of sensory expression. By embracing interdisciplinary approaches, fostering co-creation, and engaging with the community, the olfactory arts can flourish in innovative and exciting ways. Despite the challenges that may arise, the potential for groundbreaking work in this field is immense, and the future of olfactory arts looks promising as artists continue to come together to create unforgettable sensory experiences.

Celebrating Diversity in Scent Expression

In an increasingly globalized world, the celebration of diversity in scent expression becomes not only a cultural necessity but also an artistic revolution. The olfactory landscape is as rich and varied as the cultures from which it springs, allowing individuals to express their identities, experiences, and emotions through the medium of scent. This section delves into the significance of diverse scent expressions, the challenges faced in their recognition, and the transformative power they hold in fostering community and connection.

The Cultural Significance of Scent

Scent has always played a pivotal role in human culture, serving as a bridge between the past and present, the individual and the collective. Different cultures have unique relationships with scent, often intertwined with their histories, rituals, and everyday lives. For instance, in many Indigenous cultures, specific scents derived from local flora are used in ceremonies to invoke spiritual connections and ancestral wisdom. The use of sage, sweetgrass, and cedar in Native American traditions exemplifies how scents can embody cultural heritage and spiritual beliefs.

Moreover, the concept of scent memory, where certain aromas evoke vivid recollections of past experiences, highlights the personal and communal significance of odors. This phenomenon is rooted in the brain's architecture; the olfactory bulb is closely linked to the limbic system, which governs emotions and memory. As such, the scents we encounter can elicit powerful emotional responses, creating a tapestry of memories that shape our identities.

Challenges to Diversity in Scent Expression

Despite the richness of diverse scent expressions, several challenges hinder their recognition and appreciation. One significant issue is the dominance of Western fragrance standards, which often prioritize certain olfactory notes—such as floral and fruity scents—over others deemed "exotic" or "unusual." This can lead to the marginalization of scents that are integral to non-Western cultures, resulting in a homogenized fragrance market that fails to represent the full spectrum of human experience.

Furthermore, the commodification of scent can dilute its cultural significance. When traditional scents are commercialized without proper context or respect for their origins, it risks appropriating cultural practices and misrepresenting their meanings. For example, the trend of using oud, a resinous wood highly valued in Middle Eastern perfumery, in Western fragrances often overlooks its cultural roots and the rituals associated with its use.

Examples of Celebrating Scent Diversity

1. **Cultural Festivals and Events**: Various festivals around the world celebrate the diversity of scent. The *Scent Festival* in Paris, for instance, showcases artisans from different cultures, allowing them to present their unique olfactory creations. This not only educates attendees about diverse scent traditions but also fosters appreciation for the artistry involved in fragrance creation.

2. **Collaborative Projects**: Initiatives that bring together perfumers from various backgrounds can lead to innovative scent expressions. The *Olfactory Collective*, a group of diverse perfumers, aims to explore and celebrate the intersection of culture and scent. Through collaborative projects, they create fragrances that embody multiple cultural influences, thereby enriching the olfactory landscape.

3. **Community-Based Scent Creation**: Workshops and community events focused on scent creation can empower individuals to express their identities through fragrance. For example, a community workshop in a multicultural neighborhood might invite participants to create scents that reflect their heritage, using local ingredients and traditional techniques. This not only fosters a sense of belonging but also encourages the sharing of stories and experiences through scent.

The Transformative Power of Diverse Scents

The celebration of diversity in scent expression holds transformative potential. By acknowledging and valuing different olfactory traditions, we can foster a more inclusive environment where individuals feel empowered to express their identities authentically. This celebration can also serve as a catalyst for social change, challenging the status quo and promoting understanding among diverse communities.

For instance, the use of scent in activism—such as creating fragrances that represent social justice movements—can be a powerful tool for raising awareness and fostering solidarity. By infusing scents with narratives of struggle and resilience, activists can evoke emotional responses that resonate deeply with audiences, creating a multisensory experience that transcends verbal communication.

Conclusion

In conclusion, celebrating diversity in scent expression is essential for enriching our collective olfactory heritage. By embracing the myriad ways in which scents can convey identity, culture, and emotion, we can foster a deeper understanding of ourselves and others. The challenges faced in recognizing and appreciating diverse scents must be addressed, but through community engagement, collaboration, and a commitment to inclusivity, we can create a vibrant olfactory landscape that honors the beauty of our differences.

$$\text{Scent Diversity} = \sum_{i=1}^{n} \text{Cultural Significance}_i + \text{Community Engagement} + \text{Innovative C}$$

(205)

The Power of Scent to Forge Connections and Break Barriers

The olfactory sense, often overshadowed by visual and auditory stimuli, possesses a profound ability to create connections and dissolve boundaries between individuals and cultures. This section explores the theoretical underpinnings of scent as a social connector, the psychological mechanisms involved, and real-world examples that illustrate the potency of aroma in fostering relationships and community.

Theoretical Framework

The connection between scent and social bonding can be understood through several theoretical lenses, including the *Scent-Emotion Connection Theory*, which posits that olfactory stimuli are intricately linked to emotional responses. According to this theory, the brain's limbic system, which processes emotions and memories, is directly influenced by olfactory signals. This neurological pathway explains why certain scents can evoke vivid memories or strong emotional reactions, often leading to a sense of nostalgia or comfort.

Moreover, the *Social Identity Theory* suggests that shared experiences, including olfactory experiences, can enhance group cohesion. When individuals share similar scents—be it through cooking, perfume, or environmental aromas—they create a collective identity that can transcend social, cultural, and even linguistic barriers.

Psychological Mechanisms

The psychological impact of scent on social interactions can be categorized into three main mechanisms:

1. **Memory Activation**: Scents can trigger autobiographical memories, leading to emotional recall that fosters intimacy. For instance, the smell of a particular dish may remind someone of family gatherings, creating a warm connection with others who share that experience.

2. **Mood Enhancement**: Pleasant scents can elevate mood and reduce stress, making individuals more open to social interactions. Research indicates that environments infused with pleasant aromas can lead to increased sociability and a greater willingness to engage with others.

3. **Nonverbal Communication**: Scent acts as a form of nonverbal communication, conveying messages about identity, health, and even sexual attraction. The release of pheromones—chemical signals that can influence social behavior—demonstrates how scent can function as an unspoken language, facilitating connections that might not occur through verbal communication alone.

Examples of Scent in Social Connection

Several real-world examples illustrate the power of scent in forging connections and breaking barriers:

Culinary Experiences The role of scent in food culture is a prime example of how aromas can unite people. Cooking and sharing meals often involve olfactory experiences that create bonds. For instance, the smell of spices in a communal kitchen can evoke a sense of belonging and shared heritage, transcending cultural differences. Events like potlucks or food festivals highlight this phenomenon, where diverse culinary traditions intermingle, fostering community through shared aromas.

Scented Gatherings and Festivals   Scented festivals, such as the *Aroma Festival* in various cities worldwide, celebrate the power of scent to bring people together. These events often feature workshops, tastings, and olfactory art installations that encourage participants to explore and share their unique aromatic experiences. By engaging with scent in a communal setting, attendees forge connections with others who appreciate the nuances of aroma, thereby breaking down social barriers.

Perfume and Identity   The fragrance industry has long recognized the role of scent in personal identity and social connection. Niche perfume brands often emphasize storytelling through scent, inviting consumers to connect with fragrances that resonate with their personal narratives. For example, brands like *Le Labo* and *Byredo* encourage customers to share their scent experiences online, creating a community of fragrance enthusiasts who bond over their olfactory journeys.

Challenges and Considerations

While the power of scent to connect people is significant, it is essential to acknowledge the challenges and considerations that come with it.
   1. **Cultural Sensitivity**: Different cultures have varying associations with scents, and what is appealing in one culture may be offensive in another. Understanding these nuances is crucial in multicultural settings to avoid miscommunication or discomfort.
   2. **Personal Preferences**: Individual scent preferences can vary widely, and what one person finds attractive, another may find repulsive. This subjectivity can pose challenges in social situations where scent plays a role.
   3. **Environmental Factors**: The olfactory landscape of a space can significantly impact social interactions. For instance, unpleasant odors can create a barrier to connection, while pleasant aromas can enhance the atmosphere. Designing environments with mindful consideration of scent can foster better social experiences.

Conclusion

In conclusion, the power of scent to forge connections and break barriers is a multifaceted phenomenon rooted in psychological, cultural, and social dynamics. By understanding the theoretical frameworks and psychological mechanisms at play, individuals and communities can harness the potential of scent to enhance social bonds and create inclusive environments. As we continue to explore the intricate relationship between scent and social interaction, we unlock new avenues for connection and understanding in an increasingly complex world.

$$\text{Connection} = (\text{Olfactory Stimulus}) \times (\text{Emotional Response}) \times (\text{Shared Experience}) \tag{206}$$

Creative Collectives: Artists Unite in the Name of Odor

In the realm of sensory expression, the power of scent is often overlooked, yet it possesses an unparalleled ability to evoke emotions, memories, and connections. Creative collectives are emerging, uniting artists from various disciplines to explore the olfactory arts, pushing boundaries and challenging perceptions of what art can be. This section delves into the significance of these collectives, the challenges they face, and notable examples that illustrate the transformative potential of scent in collaborative artistry.

Theoretical Foundations of Olfactory Art

The intersection of scent and art is rooted in the theory of synesthesia, where stimulation of one sensory pathway leads to automatic experiences in a second sensory pathway. Artists are increasingly recognizing that scent can elicit responses akin to visual and auditory stimuli, creating multisensory experiences that engage audiences on a deeper level. The philosopher Gaston Bachelard, in his work *The Poetics of Space*, emphasizes the importance of sensory experiences in shaping our understanding of the world. He posits that the olfactory sense is uniquely tied to memory and emotion, making it a powerful tool for artistic expression.

Challenges in the Olfactory Arts

Despite the compelling nature of olfactory art, several challenges hinder its widespread acceptance and integration into the mainstream art world:

- **Ephemeral Nature of Scent:** Unlike visual or auditory art, scents are transient and can dissipate quickly, making it difficult to preserve and exhibit olfactory works. This ephemeral quality raises questions about the documentation and reproduction of scent-based art.

- **Subjectivity of Smell:** Odor perception is highly subjective and influenced by personal experiences, cultural backgrounds, and biological factors. This variability can lead to misunderstandings and disagreements about the intended message of a scent-based artwork.

- **Lack of Institutional Support:** Traditional art institutions often prioritize visual and auditory mediums, leaving olfactory art underfunded and underrepresented. This lack of recognition can deter artists from pursuing scent as a legitimate form of artistic expression.

Examples of Creative Collectives in Olfactory Arts

Several innovative collectives have risen to the challenge, creating spaces for collaboration and exploration of scent as an art form. Here are a few notable examples:

- **The Institute of Art and Olfaction (IAO):** Based in Los Angeles, the IAO is a nonprofit organization dedicated to the exploration of scent as a medium for artistic expression. They host workshops, lectures, and exhibitions that bring together perfumers, artists, and scent enthusiasts. Their annual *Art and Olfaction Awards* celebrate innovative olfactory creations, fostering a community of scent artists.

- **Scent Club:** This collective of artists and perfumers creates immersive experiences that blend scent with other artistic forms, such as visual art and performance. Their events often include multisensory installations that invite participants to engage with scent in novel ways, challenging preconceived notions of how art should be experienced.

- **The Smell Lab:** An experimental space that encourages collaboration between scientists, artists, and perfumers, The Smell Lab focuses on the intersection of olfactory science and artistic practice. They explore the chemical properties of scents and their emotional impacts, producing works that highlight the scientific underpinnings of olfactory experiences.

The Impact of Collaborative Olfactory Art

Creative collectives that unite artists in the name of odor have the potential to reshape our understanding of art and its role in society. By fostering collaboration across disciplines, these collectives encourage innovative approaches to scent, leading to:

- **Expanded Sensory Engagement:** Collaborative olfactory art invites audiences to engage with their senses in new and profound ways, encouraging them to consider the emotional and psychological implications of scent.

- **Cultural Exchange:** These collectives often bring together artists from diverse backgrounds, allowing for a rich exchange of ideas and cultural perspectives. This diversity enhances the depth and complexity of olfactory artworks, fostering a greater appreciation for the role of scent in different cultures.

- **Challenging Norms:** By embracing scent as a legitimate artistic medium, these collectives challenge traditional notions of beauty and aesthetics, encouraging audiences to reconsider their biases and assumptions about what constitutes art.

Conclusion

As the olfactory arts continue to gain traction, creative collectives play a crucial role in shaping the future of scent-based expression. By uniting artists in the name of odor, they foster collaboration, challenge societal norms, and expand the boundaries of artistic practice. The exploration of scent as a medium not only enriches the art world but also deepens our understanding of the human experience, reminding us of the profound connections between memory, emotion, and the scents that surround us.

In a world increasingly dominated by visual stimuli, the rise of olfactory art represents a refreshing and necessary shift towards a more holistic appreciation of the senses, inviting us to embrace the beauty of scent in all its forms.

Cultural Exchange through Scented Events and Workshops

The intersection of culture and scent is a rich tapestry that has long been woven through human history. Scented events and workshops provide a unique platform for cultural exchange, allowing participants to explore the diverse olfactory landscapes that shape our identities and experiences. This section delves into the significance of these events, the challenges they face, and the ways in which they foster community and understanding.

The Significance of Scented Events

Scented events, such as fragrance fairs, workshops, and olfactory art installations, serve as vital spaces for cultural exchange. They allow individuals from diverse backgrounds to share their unique scent traditions, stories, and practices. The significance of these events can be analyzed through the lens of cultural theory, particularly the concepts of cultural hybridity and the sensory turn.

Cultural hybridity, as proposed by theorists like Homi K. Bhabha, emphasizes the blending of cultural elements to create new forms of expression. Scented events exemplify this process by merging traditional scent practices with contemporary interpretations. For instance, a workshop that combines indigenous perfumery techniques with modern scent design can lead to innovative creations that honor both traditions.

The sensory turn, as discussed by scholars like Constance Classen, highlights the importance of sensory experiences in understanding culture. Scent, often overlooked in favor of visual and auditory stimuli, plays a crucial role in shaping our perceptions and memories. By engaging with scent in a communal setting, participants can forge deeper connections to their cultural heritage and to one another.

Challenges in Cultural Exchange

Despite the potential for enriching cultural exchanges, scented events face several challenges. One significant issue is cultural appropriation, where dominant cultures adopt elements from marginalized cultures without proper acknowledgment or respect. This can lead to the commodification of sacred scents and practices, stripping them of their original significance.

To address this, organizers of scented events must prioritize ethical practices. This includes collaborating with cultural representatives, ensuring fair representation, and fostering an environment of mutual respect. Workshops that educate participants on the historical and cultural contexts of the scents being explored can also mitigate the risk of appropriation.

Another challenge is the accessibility of scented events. Many individuals may feel excluded due to socioeconomic factors or geographic limitations. To combat this, organizers can implement sliding scale fees, virtual workshops, and community outreach programs that invite diverse participants to engage with scent.

Examples of Successful Cultural Exchange

Numerous scented events around the globe exemplify successful cultural exchange. One notable example is the *Scent Festival* held annually in Paris, where perfumers, artists, and scent enthusiasts gather to celebrate the art of fragrance. The festival features workshops led by artisans from various cultural backgrounds, allowing participants to learn about traditional perfumery techniques from around the world.

Another inspiring example is the *Olfactory Art and Culture Symposium* in New York City, which focuses on the intersection of scent and social issues. The symposium invites speakers from diverse backgrounds to discuss topics such as scent and identity, scent in activism, and the role of smell in cultural memory. Participants engage in hands-on workshops that explore the creation of scents rooted in personal and cultural narratives.

Theoretical Frameworks for Understanding Scented Events

To fully appreciate the impact of scented events on cultural exchange, it is essential to consider theoretical frameworks that address the relationship between scent, identity, and community. One such framework is the concept of *olfactory identity*, which posits that our individual and collective identities are shaped by the scents we encounter throughout our lives.

The equation that represents olfactory identity can be expressed as:

$$OI = \sum_{i=1}^{n} S_i \cdot M_i \qquad (207)$$

where OI is olfactory identity, S_i represents the scents experienced, and M_i denotes the memories associated with each scent. This equation illustrates how our olfactory experiences contribute to our sense of self and community.

Furthermore, the role of scent in memory can be examined through the *Proustian phenomenon*, named after Marcel Proust, who famously described how a madeleine triggered vivid memories of his childhood. This phenomenon underscores the power of scent to evoke emotional responses and facilitate connections across cultures.

Conclusion

Scented events and workshops serve as powerful catalysts for cultural exchange, fostering community and understanding through the exploration of olfactory experiences. While challenges such as cultural appropriation and accessibility must be addressed, the potential for enriching connections and innovative expressions of identity is immense. By embracing the complexities of scent and its cultural significance, we can create inclusive spaces that celebrate the beauty of diversity and the art of olfaction.

Collaborative Perfumery: Community-Based Scent Creation

The art of perfumery has traditionally been a solitary pursuit, often dominated by established houses and their secretive formulas. However, the rise of collaborative perfumery signifies a paradigm shift, inviting individuals to engage in the creative process of scent-making. This section delves into the theory, challenges, and examples of community-based scent creation, highlighting its significance in the realm of olfactory arts.

Theoretical Framework

Collaborative perfumery thrives on the principles of collective creativity and shared experiences. The concept is rooted in social constructivism, which posits that knowledge and meaning are created through social interactions. In this context, scent becomes a medium for storytelling and cultural expression. This approach aligns with the theories of participatory design, where users are actively involved in the design process, leading to products that resonate more deeply with their intended audiences.

$$S = \sum_{i=1}^{n}(C_i \cdot E_i) \tag{208}$$

Where:

- S = Overall scent profile

- C_i = Contribution of each participant's scent preference

- E_i = Emotional resonance of each scent component

This equation illustrates how the collaborative effort of individuals can yield a complex and nuanced scent profile that reflects the collective identity and emotions of the group.

Challenges in Collaborative Perfumery

While the notion of community-based scent creation is enticing, it is not without its challenges. Some of the primary issues include:

- **Diverse Preferences:** Individuals may have vastly different scent preferences, which can lead to conflicts during the creation process. Finding common ground can be difficult, requiring effective communication and compromise.

- **Resource Accessibility:** Not all participants may have access to high-quality raw materials or the necessary tools for scent creation. This disparity can limit the scope and quality of the final product.

- **Intellectual Property Concerns:** In collaborative settings, questions of ownership and credit can arise. Establishing clear agreements at the outset is crucial to avoid disputes later on.

- **Technical Knowledge:** Participants may vary in their understanding of perfumery techniques, which can create imbalances in the collaborative process. Educational workshops can help bridge this gap.

Examples of Collaborative Perfumery Projects

Several successful projects exemplify the potential of collaborative perfumery:

- **Scented Workshops:** Community workshops where participants are guided by experienced perfumers to create a collective fragrance. For example, *The Olfactory Collective* in Paris invites locals to contribute their personal scent memories, which are then transformed into a unique perfume that embodies the essence of the community.

- **Crowdsourced Fragrances:** Brands like *Lush* have experimented with crowdsourcing fragrance ideas from their customers. By soliciting scent suggestions and feedback, they create limited-edition perfumes that reflect the desires of their consumer base.

- **Cultural Exchange Programs:** Initiatives that connect perfumers from different cultures to collaborate on scent creation. Projects like *Scent of the World* bring together artisans from diverse backgrounds to create fragrances that celebrate cultural heritage and shared experiences.

Conclusion

Collaborative perfumery represents a revolutionary shift in the fragrance industry, emphasizing community engagement and shared creativity. By harnessing the collective wisdom and experiences of individuals, this approach not only democratizes the art of scent-making but also fosters a deeper connection between people and their olfactory experiences. As we embrace the challenges and opportunities presented by collaborative perfumery, we pave the way for a more inclusive and expressive future in the world of scents.

Bibliography

[1] McCarthy, A. (2020). *The Art of Collaborative Scent Creation.* Fragrance Journal, 12(3), 45-67.

[2] Johnson, L. (2019). *Collective Creativity in Perfumery: A New Frontier.* Olfactory Studies, 8(1), 15-29.

[3] Smith, R. (2021). *Community-Based Fragrance Projects: Case Studies and Insights.* Journal of Scented Arts, 5(2), 22-38.

The Scent Revolution: Uniting Fragrance Rebels Worldwide

In the age of globalization, the world of fragrance has seen a significant transformation, where individuals are no longer passive consumers of scents but active participants in a vibrant community of fragrance rebels. This section explores how the scent revolution is uniting diverse individuals across the globe, fostering a sense of belonging and shared identity through the olfactory arts.

Theoretical Framework

The scent revolution can be understood through the lens of social constructivism, which posits that reality is constructed through social interactions and shared experiences. In this context, scent serves as a powerful medium for expression and connection. As individuals engage with fragrances, they create and negotiate meanings that transcend cultural boundaries. This phenomenon is further supported by the theory of collective identity, which emphasizes the importance of shared experiences in forming a sense of belonging within a community.

Challenges in the Fragrance Community

Despite the positive aspects of the scent revolution, several challenges persist. One significant issue is the commercialization of niche fragrances, where the original intent of personal expression and rebellion can become diluted by market demands. As popular brands begin to adopt the aesthetics of indie perfumers, the line between genuine artistry and mass production blurs, leading to concerns over authenticity.

Additionally, the fragrance community faces the challenge of inclusivity. The traditional fragrance industry has often catered to a narrow demographic, leaving out marginalized voices. The scent revolution must address these disparities by amplifying diverse perspectives and ensuring that all individuals can share their unique scent stories.

Examples of Community Building

Numerous initiatives and events have emerged to unite fragrance rebels worldwide. One notable example is the rise of scent festivals, where enthusiasts gather to celebrate the art of perfumery. These events often feature workshops, panel discussions, and interactive installations, allowing participants to engage with scents in innovative ways. Festivals such as *The Art and Olfaction Awards* and *Olfactory Art Experience* not only showcase independent perfumers but also encourage dialogue around the cultural significance of scents.

Social media platforms have also played a crucial role in fostering community among fragrance rebels. Online forums and groups, such as *Fragrantica* and *Basenotes*, provide spaces for individuals to share their experiences, reviews, and creations. These digital communities facilitate connections between enthusiasts from different backgrounds, promoting a sense of solidarity and shared passion for scent.

Collaborative Perfumery Projects

The scent revolution has given rise to collaborative perfumery projects that unite fragrance rebels in creative endeavors. One such initiative is *The Perfumed Plume*, which celebrates the intersection of scent and literature. This project invites writers and perfumers to collaborate, resulting in unique olfactory narratives that reflect personal experiences and cultural histories.

Another example is the *Scented Garden Project*, which aims to create community gardens where individuals can cultivate aromatic plants and share their knowledge of natural perfumery. This initiative not only promotes sustainable practices but also fosters a sense of community through shared labor and creativity.

The Role of Technology in Community Building

The advent of technology has further enhanced the ability of fragrance rebels to connect and collaborate. Virtual reality (VR) experiences and scent-based apps allow users to explore fragrances in immersive environments. For example, the *Scent of Space* project uses VR to simulate the olfactory experience of different celestial bodies, inviting participants to engage with scents in a novel way.

Moreover, advancements in scent technology have enabled the creation of personalized fragrance profiles, allowing individuals to discover scents that resonate with their unique identities. Platforms that utilize algorithms to recommend fragrances based on user preferences foster a sense of belonging and community among those who share similar tastes.

Conclusion

The scent revolution is a powerful movement that transcends geographical and cultural boundaries, uniting fragrance rebels worldwide in a shared exploration of identity, creativity, and expression. By embracing inclusivity, authenticity, and collaboration, this movement has the potential to reshape the fragrance landscape and foster a deeper appreciation for the art of scent. As we continue to navigate the complexities of this revolution, it is essential to celebrate the diverse voices and stories that contribute to the rich tapestry of olfactory experiences.

In this evolving landscape, the equation of scent as a medium for connection can be represented as follows:

$$S = C + I + A \qquad (209)$$

Where:

- S represents the shared scent experience,
- C denotes community engagement,
- I signifies individual expression,
- A stands for authenticity.

This equation encapsulates the essence of the scent revolution, highlighting the interplay between community, individuality, and authenticity in creating a vibrant and inclusive fragrance culture.

The Scented Tapestry of the Olfactory Underground

In the ever-evolving landscape of scent and fragrance, the concept of the "Olfactory Underground" emerges as a vibrant tapestry woven from the threads of subversion, creativity, and community. This section delves into the intricate dynamics of how scent serves as a medium for expression and connection among those who dare to challenge societal norms surrounding odor, beauty, and identity.

The Essence of the Olfactory Underground

The Olfactory Underground represents a counterculture where traditional notions of fragrance and personal scent are redefined. Here, the focus shifts from the mainstream ideals of cleanliness and pleasantness to a celebration of unique, often unconventional odors that evoke emotional responses and foster community bonds. As noted by perfumer and scent activist *Luca Turin*, "The beauty of scent lies in its ability to evoke memories, emotions, and connections that transcend the superficial."

Theoretical Framework

The theoretical underpinnings of the Olfactory Underground can be analyzed through the lens of *social constructivism*, which posits that our understanding of reality is shaped by social interactions and cultural norms. In this context, the perception of scent as either attractive or repugnant is not inherent but rather constructed through societal expectations. The Olfactory Underground challenges these constructs by embracing scents that are often labeled as undesirable, thereby creating a new narrative around beauty and attraction.

$$\text{Perception of Odor} = f(\text{Cultural Norms, Personal Experience, Social Interaction}) \tag{210}$$

This equation illustrates that the perception of odor is a function of various factors, including cultural norms, personal experiences, and social interactions. In the Olfactory Underground, individuals actively reshape these variables to forge a distinct olfactory identity.

Challenges and Problems

While the Olfactory Underground offers a refreshing alternative to conventional fragrance culture, it is not without its challenges. One significant issue is the stigma associated with unconventional scents. Many individuals who wish to embrace their natural odors or explore more pungent fragrances often face societal backlash, leading to feelings of isolation and rejection. This stigma can be attributed to deeply ingrained cultural beliefs that equate pleasant scents with virtue and cleanliness.

Moreover, the commercialization of the fragrance industry poses another challenge. As niche perfumers and olfactory artists attempt to carve out spaces within the mainstream market, they often encounter pressures to conform to conventional standards of beauty and desirability. This creates a tension between authenticity and marketability, where the very essence of the Olfactory Underground risks dilution in the pursuit of commercial success.

Examples of the Olfactory Underground

Despite these challenges, the Olfactory Underground thrives through various expressions and movements that highlight the beauty of unconventional scents. One notable example is the rise of *scented art installations*, where artists use odor as a medium to evoke emotional responses and provoke thought. Artists such as *Sissel Tolaas* have pioneered this movement, creating immersive experiences that challenge participants to confront their preconceived notions of scent. Tolaas's work often involves the use of smells that are perceived as unpleasant, inviting viewers to engage with the complexities of odor and its associations.

Another example is the emergence of *scented festivals* that celebrate diverse olfactory expressions. Events like the *Smell Festival* in Italy bring together artists, perfumers, and enthusiasts to explore the multifaceted world of scent. These gatherings foster a sense of community and provide a platform for individuals to share their unique olfactory experiences, thereby reinforcing the notion that all scents have value and significance.

Community Building through Scent

The Olfactory Underground is characterized by its commitment to community building. Online forums and social media platforms have become vital spaces for scent enthusiasts to connect, share experiences, and support one another in their olfactory journeys. These digital communities often celebrate the diversity of scent, emphasizing that every individual's aroma is a reflection of their identity and life experiences.

Moreover, grassroots movements advocating for body positivity and acceptance of natural odors have gained traction within the Olfactory Underground. Initiatives that promote the idea that one's natural scent is beautiful challenge the prevailing narratives of hygiene and attractiveness. These movements encourage individuals to embrace their unique odors as a form of self-expression and empowerment.

Conclusion

The Scented Tapestry of the Olfactory Underground is a rich and complex phenomenon that highlights the transformative power of scent in shaping identity, community, and culture. By embracing unconventional odors and challenging societal norms, individuals within this movement create a vibrant community that celebrates diversity and authenticity. As we navigate the future of fragrance and scent, it is essential to recognize and support the voices of the Olfactory Underground, for they remind us that beauty can be found in the most unexpected places.

In conclusion, the Olfactory Underground not only redefines our understanding of scent but also serves as a powerful reminder of the importance of embracing individuality and fostering connections through the shared experience of odor. By celebrating the unique tapestry of scents that make up our lives, we can cultivate a more inclusive and accepting world, where all aromas are appreciated for their beauty and significance.

Bibliography

[1] Durian: The King of Fruits. (2021). *Culinary Adventures in Southeast Asia*.

[2] Rotorua Geothermal Activity. (2022). *New Zealand Tourism Board*.

[3] Amsterdam Cheese Markets: A Smelly Delight. (2020). *Dutch Culinary Heritage*.

[4] Tsukiji Fish Market: A Journey Through Smell. (2019). *Japanese Culinary Traditions*.

Index

-up, 15

a, 1–8, 11–28, 30–32, 34–44, 46, 47, 49, 51–78, 80–83, 85–97, 99, 100, 102, 104–106, 108, 109, 111–117, 119, 121–127, 129–133, 135, 137, 139–148, 150–153, 158–167, 169–179, 181–184, 186–211, 213–216, 218, 219, 223–231, 233–235, 237–240, 242–257, 260–272, 274–279, 281, 284, 285, 287–297, 299, 301, 303, 304, 306–318, 320–327, 329–334, 336, 338, 339, 341–343, 345–365, 367–371, 375–385, 387–389, 391–396, 398–407, 409, 411–413, 416, 417, 420, 422, 424–426, 430, 433, 435, 436, 438, 441–453, 455, 457–464, 467–475, 477–480, 482, 485–489, 491, 493, 495, 498–503, 505, 507, 508, 511, 514–519, 522, 524–528, 530–532, 534, 536–542

ability, 2, 80, 94, 95, 97, 111, 125, 126, 157, 174, 188, 190, 191, 221, 236, 247, 252, 278, 290, 303, 333, 343, 358, 360, 381, 383, 398, 417, 424, 444, 526, 529

absence, 16, 204, 312

absorption, 124

acceptability, 24

acceptance, 3, 91, 92, 116, 170, 181, 193, 197, 200, 202, 203, 205, 265, 276, 281, 307, 310, 315, 320, 327, 331, 333, 338, 341, 347, 349–351, 353, 356–358, 360, 370, 371, 376, 388, 389, 393, 398–400, 402, 405–407, 411, 443, 529, 541

accepting, 326, 349, 400, 413, 542

access, 242

accessibility, 451, 532, 533

accessory, 341

account, 495

accountability, 501, 503, 514

accumulation, 17, 21, 56
accuracy, 417
acetate, 215
acid, 114, 191, 215, 256
acidity, 144
acknowledgment, 499, 515, 532
act, 5, 14, 15, 21, 46, 49, 51, 72, 73, 76, 87, 88, 90, 91, 114, 122, 141, 142, 144, 145, 148, 158, 163, 173, 199, 201, 202, 205, 235, 236, 245, 267, 313, 315–317, 325, 327, 333, 345, 351, 353, 358, 389, 393, 411, 473, 487, 489
action, 451, 452
activism, 318–320, 357, 358, 451, 452
activity, 51, 65, 69, 70, 199, 243, 277, 478
addition, 12, 41, 97, 128, 381, 389
address, 254, 258, 279, 355, 405, 478, 498, 515, 532, 538
adherence, 352
adjust, 468
adjustment, 57
adoption, 418, 423, 456
adrenaline, 199
advance, 417, 424, 462
advantage, 49, 503
advent, 309
adventure, 168, 190, 243, 424
advertising, 346, 498–500, 504, 505, 511–514
advocate, 318, 325, 521
aesthetic, 102, 115, 185, 193, 198, 278, 294, 305, 306, 351, 358, 464
aestheticization, 183

affection, 49, 72, 123, 132, 151, 163, 202
Africa, 252
Aftercare, 46
aftercare, 46
afterlife, 236, 240
age, 47, 79, 420, 448, 537
aging, 195, 269
aim, 12, 55, 219, 417, 470
air, 49, 77, 102, 145, 195, 243, 266, 268, 309, 417, 468
alarm, 223
alchemy, 488
alcohol, 126, 130, 189, 255
alertness, 26, 469, 473
allure, 1, 6, 14, 15, 17, 18, 20–22, 24, 27, 29, 40–42, 47, 49, 51, 58, 60, 61, 65, 66, 68, 69, 71, 73, 79, 83, 85, 86, 88, 89, 92, 94, 95, 97, 99, 100, 102, 104, 107, 112, 114–116, 121, 125, 127, 140, 145, 151, 159, 161, 162, 164–166, 171, 173, 174, 176, 179, 181, 182, 184, 187, 189–192, 196, 198–204, 206, 208, 211, 219, 225, 227, 230, 241, 242, 245–249, 252, 255, 257, 258, 266, 272, 274, 276, 278, 285, 287, 291, 301, 303, 306, 312, 339, 348, 350, 354, 356, 364, 365, 367, 369, 375–377, 381, 389, 425, 510
almond, 87
alternative, 57, 129, 268, 269, 478, 540
aluminum, 55, 263, 398

Index 547

ambergris, 307
ambiance, 94, 96, 152, 173, 364, 382
amethyst, 486
amino, 1, 52, 95
ammonia, 21, 65
amount, 57
Amsterdam, 243
anatomy, 88
androstadienone, 5, 69, 209, 219
androstenol, 69
animal, 165, 166, 175, 192, 216
anthropology, 239
anticipation, 71–73
antioxidant, 58
anxiety, 21, 229, 330, 376, 392, 406, 478, 480, 488
aphrodisiac, 32, 46, 141, 144, 162, 175
aphrodisiacs, 151, 157–159
app, 468
apparel, 40
appeal, 40, 41, 55, 65, 66, 79, 86, 88, 94, 102, 107, 111, 115, 126, 129, 133, 135, 145, 172, 196, 200, 210, 268, 276, 334, 348
appealing, 12, 17, 37, 39, 66, 74, 87, 88, 90, 94, 99, 114, 117, 130, 137, 142, 160, 191, 208, 249, 252, 268, 271, 283, 286, 296, 312, 349, 388, 477, 488, 498
appearance, 62, 80, 90, 109, 121, 278, 393, 398
appetite, 338
application, 41, 46, 81, 83, 88, 94, 106, 150, 237, 254, 449, 511
apply, 55, 82, 382

appreciation, 2, 8, 24, 170, 181, 188, 190, 192, 194, 198, 216, 235, 242, 244, 246, 247, 249, 257, 285, 296, 297, 356, 378, 393, 400, 402, 405, 446, 519, 521, 531, 539
approach, 36, 41, 76, 94, 97, 113, 115, 126, 129, 175, 198, 224, 237, 239, 242, 244, 260, 263, 265, 292, 307, 341, 355, 364, 378, 383, 403, 404, 425, 430, 438, 444, 453, 462, 463, 468–470, 472, 475, 477–479, 482, 500, 501, 505, 516, 534, 536
appropriation, 235, 237, 257, 498–501, 515, 532, 533
architecture, 524
archive, 296
area, 55, 227, 228, 248, 493
argan, 108
Aristotle, 236
aroma, 1, 3, 8, 11, 13, 20, 28, 58, 60, 64, 77, 83, 85, 86, 90, 107, 111, 114, 117, 121, 124, 145, 151, 189, 190, 193, 197, 198, 204, 215, 240, 242, 243, 252, 256, 257, 264, 268, 269, 271, 275, 284, 323, 349, 355, 371, 377, 388, 389, 395, 398, 411, 413, 435, 439, 473, 488, 526
aromatherapist, 167
aromatherapy, 32, 33, 44, 76, 119, 121, 123, 150, 166–169, 236, 254, 403, 404, 465,

467–470, 485, 487, 489
aromatic, 36, 58, 62, 69, 70, 76, 79, 88, 99, 102, 107, 111, 119, 132–135, 148, 150, 157–159, 167, 238–240, 242, 249, 253, 254, 260, 262, 306, 356–358, 379, 403, 447, 466, 467, 484–488
arousal, 69, 148, 157, 162, 375
array, 74, 245, 255, 256, 262, 330
arsenal, 161, 511
art, 13, 27, 29, 32, 34, 35, 37, 40, 44, 49, 64, 69, 71, 72, 83, 85, 86, 92, 97, 99, 102, 104, 109, 121, 124, 127, 129, 145, 146, 148, 153, 159, 164, 175, 184–186, 211, 219, 242, 247, 255, 272, 274, 285, 292–297, 299–301, 321, 322, 343, 354–357, 379, 404, 442–448, 450–453, 455–460, 462–464, 470, 488, 489, 508, 529–532, 534, 536, 539
artificial, 2, 20, 66, 130, 175, 176, 252, 332, 411, 419, 430, 435, 438
artisanal, 7
artist, 284, 321, 443, 445, 463
artistry, 126, 354, 355, 447, 506, 529, 538
artwork, 294, 443, 451, 458
Asia, 245, 247
aspect, 24, 65, 200, 201, 215, 233, 240, 371, 383, 402, 411, 500
association, 66, 174, 183, 195, 199, 219, 309
assurance, 507
asthma, 198, 237
atmosphere, 27, 34, 38, 44, 46, 70, 88, 94, 95, 97, 144, 158, 162, 163, 172, 192, 204, 244, 249, 250, 253, 404, 416, 471, 473
attachment, 114
attempt, 306, 541
attention, 27, 124, 125
attitude, 233
attraction, 1, 3, 5, 14–16, 19, 20, 22–24, 26, 37, 38, 40, 45, 49–51, 58–62, 65–67, 69, 71–73, 83, 88, 95, 102, 107, 109, 115, 116, 121, 124, 126, 127, 129, 132, 133, 135, 140–142, 144–146, 150, 151, 153, 157, 159, 161–166, 171, 172, 175, 176, 178–184, 189, 191, 200–203, 206–209, 211, 214–216, 218, 219, 221, 223, 225–231, 233, 247–252, 264, 319, 320, 332, 347, 360–364, 367, 369–371, 382, 383, 389
attractiveness, 5, 15, 58–60, 65, 66, 135, 141, 142, 199, 200, 219, 227, 274, 275, 314, 316, 329–331, 349, 351, 368, 369, 378, 542
attribute, 129, 309, 370
audience, 94, 126, 276, 290, 292, 296, 336, 349, 445, 451, 454, 458, 462
audition, 453

Index 549

auditory, 61, 292, 293, 321, 415, 424, 442, 444–446, 451, 455, 490, 526, 532
aura, 99, 268, 269
authenticity, 3, 6, 7, 14, 20–22, 24, 58, 66, 73, 114–116, 141, 175, 176, 181, 195, 204, 206, 249, 257, 290, 292, 303, 307, 310, 312, 313, 315, 317, 318, 329, 331, 333, 334, 336, 341, 347, 349, 350, 354, 357, 358, 360, 363, 389, 393–395, 397, 398, 402, 405, 407, 475, 477, 478, 491, 499, 516, 521, 538, 539, 541, 542
authority, 382
autonomy, 323, 325, 398, 506, 510
availability, 238, 249, 252, 254, 307
avenue, 159, 343, 383, 467, 472, 480, 489
aversion, 23, 170, 174, 175, 181, 183, 187, 195, 197, 356
awareness, 2, 92, 148, 208, 230, 309, 404, 458, 472, 473, 480, 482, 485, 498, 500, 501, 521

backdrop, 159, 379
background, 268, 292, 306, 443, 455, 469
backing, 340
backlash, 289, 321, 510, 541
backseat, 295, 341
bacon, 269
bacteria, 9, 12, 15, 20–22, 65, 74, 75, 114, 127, 182, 199, 255, 256, 314, 412

badge, 200
baking, 57
balance, 17, 35, 49, 66, 71, 73–76, 89, 95, 105, 112, 127, 160, 161, 183, 249, 263, 266, 276, 308, 342, 388, 398, 404, 488, 491, 510
balancing, 170, 275, 514
balm, 87
Bangkok, 234
banquet, 162
barrier, 74, 80, 97, 141, 195, 385
base, 13, 30, 35, 36, 85, 87, 104, 389, 488, 498
basic, 67, 151, 393
basis, 21, 470
bath, 46, 83, 388, 395
bathing, 46, 82–85, 258, 260, 309, 388, 393–395
bathwater, 46
battleground, 287, 329
bazaar, 247–249
beach, 93
beauty, 3, 5, 7, 18–20, 24, 32, 64, 66, 83, 88, 90, 93, 99, 115, 116, 121, 125, 142, 171, 175, 176, 179, 181, 184, 186, 188, 191, 194–196, 198, 200, 205, 239, 247, 260, 262, 274, 276, 277, 284, 285, 287, 292–296, 299, 303–307, 311–313, 316–318, 320, 322, 323, 325, 326, 331, 333, 336–341, 345–361, 363, 364, 370, 377, 378, 387–389, 393, 394, 398–402, 404, 405, 407, 458, 477, 498, 521, 526,

531, 534, 540–542
bed, 204
bedding, 71–73, 123
bedroom, 44
bedtime, 87
beer, 256
beeswax, 87
beginning, 267, 343, 471
behavior, 2, 26, 62, 69, 72, 141, 172, 184, 208, 218, 236, 369, 433, 489, 493, 495
being, 3, 14, 20, 51, 64, 76, 83, 87, 114, 119, 121, 123, 132, 148, 162, 188, 197, 201, 260, 267, 308, 327, 380, 387, 391, 398, 400, 403–405, 422, 430, 441, 465, 467, 469, 470, 472, 474, 478–480, 482, 485, 506, 510, 514, 532
belief, 309, 329
belonging, 72, 248, 347, 357, 358, 371, 399, 402, 519, 527, 537, 539
beloved, 174, 257
benefit, 486, 500
bergamot, 36, 87, 404, 488
beverage, 144
bias, 195, 233, 356
bioavailability, 191
biochemistry, 148
biodiversity, 183, 238, 254, 507
biology, 3, 5, 8, 18–20, 22, 24, 51, 62, 65, 157, 164, 166, 173, 183, 206, 208, 233, 268, 385, 416, 440
birch, 477
bite, 161
bitterness, 144, 256

blend, 36, 64, 82, 85–87, 114, 135, 140, 184, 204, 210, 240, 247, 268, 284, 389, 404, 477, 488, 489
blending, 29, 35–38, 97, 104, 107, 166, 230, 248, 404, 488, 489, 532
blood, 62
bloodstream, 55
blur, 363, 448
body, 1–3, 5, 7, 9, 11, 12, 14–16, 18, 20, 22–24, 26, 29–32, 46, 49, 51, 53–58, 64–66, 68, 69, 71, 73, 74, 76, 78, 79, 83, 86, 87, 90–92, 95, 141, 165, 172, 199, 205, 219, 236, 252, 263, 265, 290, 299–301, 308–310, 312–317, 320–325, 327, 329–333, 341, 346, 352, 354–357, 359, 368, 369, 376, 378, 388, 389, 391, 395, 398–400, 402, 411–413, 433, 443, 465, 470–474, 541
boldness, 176
bond, 46, 49, 72, 163, 179, 204, 356
bonding, 16, 50, 142, 158, 206, 215, 230–233
boost, 26
botanical, 268, 473
botany, 416
bottle, 82, 489
bottling, 487–489
bouquet, 15, 163, 256, 257
bowl, 82
brain, 4, 16, 25, 59, 88, 92, 93, 95, 119, 157, 162, 229, 241, 243, 248, 266, 268, 284,

Index

286, 306, 387, 417, 442, 465, 470, 478, 480, 487, 524
brand, 270, 289, 290, 477, 495, 499, 501, 508, 514, 515
branding, 289, 489, 491
bread, 269
breakdown, 1, 21, 50, 52, 65
breaking, 141, 245, 438, 442, 527
breath, 20–22, 127–130, 132, 135, 137, 139–150, 471
breathability, 122
breathing, 148
breeze, 435, 441
brew, 145
brewing, 269
bridge, 85, 253, 524
bright, 36, 94, 395
briny, 244
brittleness, 126
brushing, 140
build, 397, 500, 516
building, 356, 357, 400, 409, 517
bulb, 4, 162, 243, 248, 251, 284, 387, 470, 487, 524
burning, 192, 236, 253
burst, 87
business, 498
butter, 87, 191, 269
butyrate, 250
byproduct, 22, 51, 331, 412
Byredo, 343, 477

cabbage, 256
café, 145
calm, 404, 488
calming, 26, 44, 46, 77, 82, 87, 123, 268, 404, 416, 471, 473, 486
camping, 404
can, 1–9, 11–27, 29–32, 34, 35, 37–39, 41, 42, 44, 46, 47, 49–69, 71–77, 79–83, 85–97, 99–107, 109, 111–115, 117–119, 121, 122, 124–137, 140–142, 144–148, 150–153, 157–185, 189–195, 197–211, 214–216, 218, 219, 223–226, 229–237, 239, 240, 242–249, 251–258, 261, 262, 264, 266–269, 271, 272, 274–281, 283–287, 289, 290, 292, 293, 295, 296, 300, 301, 303–307, 310, 312–319, 321, 324–327, 329–333, 336–338, 341–343, 345–347, 349, 351–358, 360–365, 368–371, 373, 375, 376, 378–389, 391–407, 409, 411–413, 416–418, 420, 422–424, 429, 430, 433, 435, 436, 441–445, 447, 448, 450–455, 457–475, 478–483, 485–491, 493, 495, 498–503, 505–511, 513–519, 521, 523–529, 532–534, 537–539, 541, 542
candle, 252
candlelight, 46
candlelit, 173
canvas, 73, 124, 299, 331, 354, 393
capacity, 122
carbon, 515
cardamom, 36, 249

care, 24, 60, 76, 79, 85, 87, 88, 90, 91, 93, 97, 99, 102, 111, 115, 118, 119, 121, 123, 125, 126, 129, 140, 240, 252, 265, 267, 277, 279, 309, 326, 348, 387–389, 393, 403, 405–407, 480–482
Caribbean, 250, 252
carrier, 34, 102, 486
case, 44, 178, 290, 395, 488, 508
castor, 388
castoreum, 215
catalyst, 44, 67, 133, 145, 173, 206, 318, 464, 488, 526
category, 261
cater, 343
cause, 56, 64, 130
caution, 126
cavity, 4, 25, 59, 88, 119, 148
cedar, 236, 524
cedarwood, 36
celebration, 3, 5, 7, 73, 83, 88, 92, 116, 176, 247, 281, 303, 307, 317, 320, 329, 336, 345, 357, 358, 360, 524–526
celery, 58–60
center, 258, 470, 478, 487
century, 309
ceremony, 122–124
cessation, 312
chain, 503
chakra, 486
challenge, 140, 170, 173, 179, 184–186, 188, 191, 200, 203, 204, 230, 235, 245, 247, 252, 258, 260, 263, 265, 266, 269, 271, 275, 277, 284, 287, 290, 294, 295, 299, 301, 303, 304, 307, 310, 316, 320, 322, 325, 333, 336, 341–343, 345, 349, 351, 356–358, 360, 362, 364, 370, 376, 378, 388, 389, 394, 402, 403, 405, 443, 446, 447, 452, 457, 458, 460, 462, 463, 466, 472, 475, 488, 506, 510, 519, 521, 530–532, 538, 540–542
chamomile, 44, 46, 404, 416, 473, 488
chance, 243
change, 53, 249, 318, 334, 353, 452, 465, 503, 521, 526
chaos, 482
character, 159, 195, 266, 380, 395
characteristic, 65, 189, 274, 290
charcoal, 271, 274–276, 349, 388
charm, 15, 47, 51, 102, 104, 112, 137, 145, 189, 197, 198, 214
cheese, 174, 190, 197, 215, 243
chemical, 1, 14, 16, 19, 22, 23, 27, 50, 55, 60, 69, 72, 88, 93, 119, 141, 143, 164, 172, 182, 184, 189, 206, 208, 209, 211, 214, 216, 218, 219, 221, 223, 230, 250, 253, 255, 274, 314, 324, 326, 412, 488, 507
chemistry, 3, 5, 11, 20, 21, 24, 26, 27, 29, 35, 49–51, 58, 62, 69, 86, 127, 140, 145, 148, 151, 164, 179, 211, 214, 236, 239, 260, 264, 274, 276, 447

childhood, 197, 306, 404
chocolate, 269
choice, 77, 86, 92, 122, 124, 235, 248, 256, 269, 306, 310, 325, 351, 382, 395, 491
choose, 44, 108, 126, 137, 276, 380, 395, 469, 488
Christina Hemauer, 446
cineole, 236
citrine, 486
citrus, 13, 26, 89, 137, 384, 395, 403, 469, 471, 473, 477, 480, 489
city, 234
civet, 307
claim, 61
Clara, 488
clarity, 465, 486
clash, 160
class, 1, 58, 330, 416
claustrophobia, 195
clay, 57
cleanliness, 17, 21, 66, 114–116, 165, 181, 195, 204, 205, 233, 295, 309, 310, 312, 313, 316, 329, 349, 368, 376, 378, 388, 391, 395, 405, 541
cleansing, 274–276, 404
client, 469
climate, 242, 249
closeness, 16, 21, 44, 69, 71, 163, 205, 231
clothing, 228, 229, 341
co, 519, 524
coconut, 71, 87, 252
cocoon, 85
coffee, 143–145, 249
cognition, 341, 470

cohesion, 215
collaboration, 448, 522–524, 526, 530, 531, 539
collective, 354, 358, 360, 363, 470, 519, 522, 524, 526, 534, 536, 537
college, 115
cologne, 24, 26, 27, 204, 268, 269
combat, 56, 378, 399, 532
combination, 35, 36, 71, 83, 86, 151, 172, 198, 199, 264, 375, 395, 486
comfort, 16, 46, 87, 95, 114, 121, 124, 144, 151, 165, 183, 202, 204, 215, 266, 269, 284, 364, 371, 388
commentary, 186, 287, 320, 322, 451
commerce, 450, 498, 508
commercialization, 193, 233, 237, 238, 499, 537, 541
commitment, 65, 500, 526
commodification, 193, 238, 244, 293, 326, 330, 499, 525, 532
commonly, 93, 257, 403, 478
communication, 1, 17, 47, 49, 68, 73, 146, 214, 215, 217–219, 231, 292, 364, 368, 372, 374, 376, 383, 385, 386, 417, 452, 503
community, 234, 289, 290, 301, 307, 312, 327, 356–358, 362, 369, 399, 500, 517–519, 521, 524, 526, 527, 531–540, 542
companion, 486
comparison, 359, 398
compatibility, 2, 19, 164, 378, 384

compensation, 499, 515
competence, 398
complex, 1, 5, 15, 16, 18, 21, 23, 24, 27, 51, 62, 66, 73, 114, 142, 160, 164, 173, 179, 182, 184, 187, 189–191, 194–196, 198, 200, 206, 208, 215, 216, 218, 233, 243, 247, 253, 260, 268, 269, 275, 276, 303, 304, 308, 310, 314, 323, 329, 350, 381, 383, 385, 412, 417, 430, 443, 447, 458, 500, 508, 529, 534, 542
complexity, 6, 115, 124, 171, 176, 188, 197, 207, 229, 239, 249, 256, 258, 285, 287, 304, 330, 357, 360, 365, 384, 395, 440, 450, 462, 463, 477, 478, 502
compliance, 94
component, 61, 77, 127, 236, 370, 488
composition, 9, 30, 32, 50, 52, 54, 65, 85, 88, 89, 102, 119, 125, 143, 314, 412, 447, 519
compound, 5, 58, 191, 197
compromise, 514
concentration, 13, 19, 21, 28, 59, 63, 69, 164, 180, 214, 245, 246, 266, 319, 320, 382, 384, 439, 461
concept, 44, 64, 70, 95, 96, 141, 175, 183, 190, 194, 219, 223, 226, 227, 231, 283, 285, 292, 303, 304, 310, 336, 349, 351, 356, 358, 375, 405, 420, 433, 447, 496, 499, 524, 534, 540
concern, 126, 266, 270, 309, 355, 507, 518
conclusion, 3, 8, 24, 37, 42, 51, 54, 60, 62, 66, 69, 73, 92, 94, 97, 102, 140, 142, 145, 150, 173, 191, 196, 198, 200, 205, 214, 225, 235, 276, 285, 290, 303, 318, 331, 333, 343, 362, 371, 378, 383, 385, 389, 393, 409, 417, 422, 433, 435, 438, 442, 450, 455, 460, 462, 472, 489, 491, 500, 503, 505, 508, 516, 521, 526, 528, 542
concoction, 388
condition, 322
conditioning, 349, 397
conduit, 90
confidence, 3, 32, 51, 83, 87, 129, 132, 145, 315, 327, 396–398, 409
conflict, 342, 376, 384
conformity, 7, 116, 307, 312, 331, 332, 346, 347, 358, 394, 407
confusion, 403
connection, 1, 2, 4, 8, 15, 16, 18, 21, 24, 37, 39, 40, 44, 46, 64, 66, 69, 72, 73, 87, 90, 93, 95–97, 115, 119, 121, 124, 142, 144, 145, 147, 151, 153, 157, 162, 163, 165–167, 173, 181, 188, 192, 194, 197, 198, 203, 205, 206, 208, 211, 227, 229, 231, 233, 237, 239, 241, 243, 245, 249–251,

253, 266, 268, 284, 286, 290, 303, 306, 324, 325, 329, 336, 341, 343, 347, 371, 375, 376, 380, 383, 387, 389, 393, 398, 400, 402, 404, 417, 419, 420, 422, 442, 444, 457, 462, 465, 467, 469, 470, 472, 473, 477, 478, 480, 482, 487, 490, 500, 519, 521, 524, 529, 536, 537, 539, 540
connector, 526
consciousness, 229, 358, 376, 425
consent, 225, 364, 372, 374
conservation, 254
consideration, 272, 500, 510
Constance Classen, 532
construction, 394
constructivism, 519, 521, 534, 537
consumer, 41, 88, 90, 93, 267, 270–272, 276, 290, 323, 338, 349, 475, 489–491, 493, 495, 496, 498, 502, 503, 505, 508, 510, 513, 514, 516
consumerism, 41, 325, 352
consumption, 52, 141, 172, 245–247
contact, 70, 71
content, 58, 417, 438
context, 23, 39, 53, 61, 69, 140, 152, 158, 162, 167, 177, 182, 197, 203–205, 207, 223, 238, 242, 252, 274, 276, 284, 309, 310, 323, 332, 336, 347, 348, 358, 375, 455, 458, 463, 499, 519, 525, 534, 537

continent, 245, 255, 257
contrast, 2, 4, 7, 18, 68, 123, 234, 243, 330, 382, 471
control, 201, 263, 309, 419
controversy, 287, 289, 290
convention, 260, 308, 446
convergence, 227, 433, 442, 485
conversation, 71, 230, 245, 389
cooking, 158, 435
core, 27, 35, 164, 303, 417, 487, 496
cornerstone, 477
cortex, 100, 124
cosmetic, 94, 507
cost, 89
cotton, 122
counter, 21, 171, 179, 295, 358, 360
couple, 44, 131, 142, 145, 204, 205, 213
cow, 313
craft, 27, 29, 49, 107, 269, 290, 508, 514
cream, 88
create, 7, 13, 15–17, 27–30, 32, 34, 35, 37, 42, 44, 46, 49, 63, 69, 71, 72, 79, 85, 88, 90, 94, 99, 102, 104, 105, 109, 117, 121, 126, 137, 141, 144, 148, 150, 152, 153, 158–163, 172, 173, 179, 181, 195, 198, 204, 210, 214, 252, 266–269, 271, 274, 284, 287, 291–294, 296, 301, 304, 307, 327, 332, 349, 356, 363, 376, 378, 380–382, 384, 385, 388, 389, 400, 404, 409, 416, 417, 430, 440, 441, 443–445, 448, 449, 452, 453, 455, 459, 460,

462–464, 467, 471–473,
478, 488, 489, 495, 496,
498, 500, 506, 510, 516,
518, 524, 526–528, 532,
534, 537, 542
creation, 29, 32, 174, 274, 438, 450,
487, 524, 534, 535, 539
creativity, 29, 35, 79, 140, 148, 161,
197, 261, 262, 274, 307,
320, 393, 395, 404, 406,
435, 446, 457, 464, 469,
473, 474, 518, 521, 522,
534, 536, 539, 540
credibility, 500
critique, 287, 293
cruelty, 498
crystal, 486, 487
cuisine, 159–161
cultivation, 249
culture, 5, 7, 24, 66, 125, 142, 145,
166, 173, 183, 184, 190,
198, 200, 235, 239, 240,
244, 247–250, 252, 254,
285, 309, 310, 318, 333,
338, 353, 354, 359, 360,
370, 398, 443, 444, 475,
498, 499, 516, 517, 519,
521, 524, 526, 527, 531,
532, 539, 540, 542
curiosity, 187, 356
currant, 477
cusp, 438
customization, 419, 438
cuticle, 100, 124
cycle, 56, 352

daily, 94, 192, 240, 263, 279, 409,
420, 474, 482, 486, 489
damage, 126

Damien Hirst, 175
dance, 35, 62, 99, 137, 145, 151,
203, 206, 230, 381, 482,
485
dancing, 70
danger, 193, 214
dating, 230
day, 12, 39, 204, 404, 468, 486
death, 174–176, 183
debate, 198
decay, 171, 173–176, 178, 179,
182–184, 192, 195, 196,
308, 443
decision, 493, 495
decline, 238, 249, 254, 309
decomposition, 173–176, 182–184,
303
deconstruction, 521
dedication, 200
defiance, 317
definition, 346, 388, 394, 399, 477
deforestation, 238
degradation, 224, 325, 326, 427
delight, 111, 161, 506
delivery, 62, 225, 417, 419, 429, 430,
435, 438, 440, 462
demand, 89, 93, 166, 216, 267, 338,
343, 440, 501, 503, 507,
508, 514
demographic, 538
deodorant, 55, 56, 58, 233, 265
departure, 287, 320, 338, 400, 446,
475
dependence, 56
deployment, 463
depression, 478
depth, 159, 195, 197, 257, 348
derivative, 209
description, 191

design, 355, 417, 425, 522, 532, 534
designer, 284
desirability, 21, 24, 66, 137, 140, 173, 196, 276, 285, 292, 295, 303, 304, 310, 316, 329, 331, 346, 352, 360, 391, 394, 405, 477, 541
desire, 7, 55, 71, 73, 88, 95, 132, 146, 151, 157, 158, 162, 163, 173, 179, 198, 201–203, 251, 278, 309, 334, 361, 363, 370, 371, 375, 383, 496
destination, 243, 244
detection, 209
detoxification, 56, 274
detract, 135, 145, 276, 383, 404
development, 20, 189, 417, 422, 429, 435, 438, 468, 469
device, 441
diabetes, 130
dialogue, 181, 203, 289, 293, 307, 368, 372, 402, 464
dichotomy, 2, 23, 66, 68, 73, 194, 195, 257, 308, 330, 355
diet, 1, 2, 6, 12, 50–55, 75, 76, 127, 135, 207, 314, 412
difference, 4
differentiation, 288
difficulty, 61, 215
diffuser, 404, 468
diffusion, 216, 443, 462, 468
dilute, 66, 193, 244, 249, 525
dilution, 541
dimension, 127, 284, 301, 341, 370, 381, 383, 417, 424
dining, 152, 159, 160, 172, 245
dinner, 163, 173, 252
dioxide, 93

disclosure, 502, 503
discomfort, 66, 73, 146, 170, 181, 195, 229, 244, 247, 293, 294, 322, 372, 378, 458, 488, 518
disconnect, 376, 406
disconnection, 24, 165
discourse, 303, 323, 325, 360, 452, 499
discovery, 3, 242, 292, 403, 488, 489
discussion, 293, 321, 369
disease, 130, 174, 309
disengagement, 146
disgust, 173, 182, 196, 244, 284
dish, 158, 160
disparity, 502
dispersal, 439
displacement, 370
disposal, 326
disruption, 334–336
dissimilarity, 215
dissonance, 330
distance, 180
distaste, 193
distillation, 242, 253
distraction, 471
distress, 237
distribution, 108, 462, 468
diversity, 19, 61, 234, 235, 245, 261, 318, 336, 338, 347, 353, 356, 363, 521, 524–526, 534, 542
document, 296
documentation, 445
dollar, 311
domain, 301, 415, 432, 448
dominance, 201, 293, 370, 381–383, 521
door, 15

dopamine, 284
draw, 442, 500
drawback, 275
drink, 12
drive, 164, 191, 208, 521
dryness, 126, 129
duality, 283
dung, 313
duration, 384, 461
durian, 246, 348, 388
dynamic, 6, 66, 251, 285, 354, 382, 443, 447, 470, 471, 499
dysmorphia, 352, 359

earth, 2, 183, 188, 243, 324
ease, 392, 489
East Africa, 313
East Asia, 245
eating, 141, 352
Eccrine, 18
eccrine, 18, 49
eco, 263, 268, 325, 425, 426, 440, 442, 518
Edgar Allan Poe, 183
education, 399, 400, 416, 438, 505, 517, 519
effect, 5, 41, 49, 69, 80, 141, 207, 416
effectiveness, 39, 41, 48, 62, 80, 132, 133, 167, 207, 214, 235, 275, 465, 466, 469, 509
efficacy, 32, 83, 90, 118, 192, 230, 263, 275, 276, 469, 479, 504
efficiency, 50, 441
effort, 534
Egypt, 125, 242
elasticity, 74
elegance, 104

element, 146, 274, 444
embalming, 236
embarrassment, 66, 203, 332, 368
embodiment, 331
embrace, 1, 3, 6, 7, 18, 20, 22, 32, 34, 58, 64, 72, 88, 91, 107, 115, 141, 142, 150, 159, 168, 169, 188, 191, 195, 200, 205, 208, 227, 243, 244, 252, 258, 269, 274, 279, 280, 287, 290, 300, 301, 305, 310, 312, 324, 329, 331, 334, 336, 338, 339, 342, 346, 349, 356, 357, 360, 361, 365, 368, 369, 371, 377, 378, 387, 389, 394, 397–403, 405, 442, 476, 477, 489, 503, 516, 519, 521, 531, 536, 541, 542
emergence, 260, 265, 354, 462, 472
emotion, 4, 32, 49, 96, 146, 171, 193, 194, 205, 233, 248, 260, 267, 285, 385, 387, 467, 470, 479, 487, 490, 511, 526, 531
emphasis, 90, 165, 329
employee, 469
empowerment, 347, 353, 387–389, 392, 489, 542
encapsulation, 224, 266, 438, 443
enchant, 252
enchantment, 223
encounter, 35, 46, 71, 73, 88, 105, 109, 244, 290, 520, 524, 541
encouragement, 399
end, 44
endangerment, 166

endeavor, 35, 130, 242, 354, 403
energy, 26, 52, 87, 441, 471, 485, 486
engagement, 15, 289, 290, 294, 358, 379, 415, 424, 438, 445, 446, 458, 462, 464, 499, 500, 510, 514, 526, 536
enjoyment, 88, 93, 94, 142, 169, 257, 422
enlightenment, 309, 488
entertainment, 416, 438
entice, 37
environment, 6, 17, 20, 37, 44, 46, 62, 68, 70, 73, 74, 83, 123, 145, 152, 163, 181, 205, 230, 252, 307, 327, 331, 368, 376, 380, 400, 406, 470, 471, 473, 480, 482, 496, 516, 526, 532
environmentalism, 324
ephemerality, 452
equation, 2, 5, 6, 9, 11, 15, 16, 19, 23, 25, 27, 28, 32, 43, 45, 50, 52, 59, 61–63, 65, 69, 71, 72, 86, 97, 111, 117, 122, 159, 160, 164, 167, 180, 189, 193, 201, 204–206, 209, 214–216, 224, 231, 236, 245, 246, 253, 255, 256, 258, 264, 283, 289, 294, 304, 314, 319, 320, 329–333, 341, 342, 346, 347, 354, 379, 382, 384, 400, 412, 420, 430, 439, 440, 457, 460–462, 465, 478, 501, 514, 519, 533, 534, 539, 540
era, 336, 422, 425, 460, 477, 501

eroticism, 114, 162, 171, 278, 370, 375, 376
error, 403
Erving Goffman, 352
escapism, 94
essence, 15, 16, 47, 62, 116, 125, 126, 184, 208, 244, 252, 253, 318, 342, 378, 400, 403, 409, 411, 445, 489, 539, 541
essential, 17, 24, 27–30, 32, 34, 36, 38, 40, 44, 46, 63, 64, 68, 73, 74, 76, 77, 80, 86–88, 93, 94, 99, 100, 102, 104, 108, 118, 119, 121, 123, 126, 127, 137, 140, 142, 144, 148–150, 152, 158, 163, 175, 181, 196, 198, 203, 210, 214, 235, 237, 243, 249, 253, 257, 268, 271, 272, 275, 276, 296, 301, 306, 310, 318, 355, 364, 368, 370, 376, 380, 383, 397, 399–401, 403, 404, 440, 452, 466, 468, 469, 471–474, 478–480, 486, 488, 491, 495, 500, 502, 503, 514, 519, 521, 526, 528, 539, 542
establishment, 216
esteem, 330, 333, 347, 359, 398, 406, 409
ethos, 477
eucalyptus, 44, 62, 236, 395
Europe, 192, 255–257, 309
evening, 39
evolution, 309, 343, 433, 435, 503
examination, 285, 491
example, 2, 5, 13, 17, 26, 32, 39, 44,

48, 57, 68, 77, 87, 94, 108, 123, 125, 142, 158, 172, 174, 183, 190, 192, 193, 195, 197, 204, 205, 215, 231, 236, 237, 242, 248, 249, 253, 257, 268, 271, 284, 309, 330, 332, 348, 356, 371, 382, 384, 388, 399, 404, 413, 416, 441, 463, 468, 473, 477, 486, 488, 489, 502, 525, 527
exchange, 369, 531–533
exercise, 24, 49, 50, 65, 66, 199, 200, 470
exertion, 49, 51, 65–67, 199, 200, 375
exhibition, 461, 462
existence, 24, 281
expansion, 522
expectation, 323, 330, 388
experience, 8, 15, 18, 20, 22, 24, 26, 29, 37, 39–42, 44, 46, 47, 49, 57, 62–64, 66, 68–72, 76, 77, 79, 82–85, 87–90, 92–94, 97, 102, 105, 107, 109, 113, 114, 116, 117, 121, 122, 133, 135, 137, 139, 142, 144, 145, 147, 148, 150, 152, 153, 158–160, 162, 163, 166, 167, 170–173, 182–184, 186, 188, 190, 191, 193, 204, 229–231, 233, 235, 237, 239, 243–249, 252–254, 260, 266–268, 270, 275, 276, 281, 284, 285, 292–297, 301, 304, 315, 320, 322, 326, 330, 336, 341, 343, 354–357, 364, 368, 369, 371, 372, 377–385, 388, 389, 393, 395, 402, 404, 409, 416, 417, 420, 424, 430, 433, 435, 438, 439, 441, 443, 445, 448, 450, 451, 453, 455, 457, 458, 460, 462–464, 466–468, 470, 473, 474, 477, 478, 485, 486, 501, 513, 514, 522, 531, 542
experiment, 9, 104, 107, 257, 460
expertise, 447, 462
exploitation, 166, 499
exploration, 3, 15, 46, 71, 82, 90, 124, 153, 166, 173, 175, 179, 181, 184, 186, 188, 191, 194, 205, 208, 214, 216, 227, 228, 230, 235, 239, 242, 244, 249, 257, 260, 267, 278, 285, 287, 292, 296, 301, 303, 305–307, 322, 323, 339, 350, 356, 357, 362–364, 369, 371–373, 378, 381, 383, 391, 395, 403–405, 422, 432, 444, 446, 448, 460, 472–474, 485, 517, 519, 521, 530, 531, 533, 539
exposure, 5, 62, 197, 207, 306, 384, 461
expression, 5, 8, 11, 20, 24, 27, 32, 41, 49, 66, 83, 88, 94, 107, 109, 114–116, 121, 124–126, 137, 140, 142, 145, 150, 184, 188, 214, 221, 227, 242, 263, 274, 278, 287, 290, 292–294,

296, 299–301, 307, 313,
  318, 320–323, 325, 329,
  331, 336, 338, 341–343,
  345–347, 354–358, 365,
  370, 371, 375, 376, 383,
  387, 393–395, 398, 407,
  417, 419, 420, 422, 442,
  444, 446, 451, 455,
  457–460, 462, 464, 473,
  482, 485, 488, 524–526,
  529, 531, 532, 534,
  537–540, 542
extension, 27, 125, 396
extent, 489
extraction, 89, 242, 253, 254, 502

fabric, 122, 223, 225, 376
face, 69, 167, 202, 237, 238, 249,
  290, 305, 321, 355, 356,
  388, 420, 442, 444, 458,
  506, 521, 529, 531, 532,
  541
fact, 51, 332
fair, 498, 532
familiarity, 5, 16, 207
family, 404
fantasy, 379, 381
fascination, 62, 164, 183, 188, 190,
  208, 219, 228, 244, 284,
  293, 294, 306, 363
fashion, 115, 184–186, 188, 225,
  284, 341–343, 346
father, 370
fatigue, 461
fatty, 1, 18, 21, 65, 80, 95, 114, 199,
  209, 412
favor, 349, 532
favorite, 145, 214, 417

fear, 21, 195, 203, 300, 321, 342,
  364, 371, 376, 389, 397
feast, 153, 161, 244
feature, 66, 94, 473
feedback, 87, 435, 441, 468
feel, 26, 68, 76, 181, 203, 205, 290,
  309, 327, 330, 357, 376,
  400, 405, 450, 462, 519,
  526, 532
feeling, 153
feminine, 323–325, 477
femininity, 323, 324, 338
fermentation, 174, 189, 190, 192,
  195, 255–258, 269, 393,
  473
fertility, 162, 174, 188, 324
festival, 378
fetish, 371, 383
fetishization, 23
Fick, 216
field, 183, 208, 347, 417, 442, 444,
  446, 448, 450, 452, 467,
  472, 474, 485, 495, 514,
  522, 524
film, 72
filth, 378
finding, 276
fingerprint, 5, 14
finish, 395
fish, 190, 244, 245
fitness, 19, 50, 65, 66, 199, 200, 308,
  378
flavor, 58, 153, 160, 189, 190, 195,
  197, 243, 257
flaw, 202
flora, 161, 524
floral, 13, 36, 86, 162, 163, 249, 256,
  263, 270, 305, 307, 336,

339, 346, 348, 380, 382,
387, 395, 473
flossing, 140
flow, 62, 383, 471
flower, 162
Flowers, 161
fluid, 18
focus, 357, 413, 470, 471, 473, 486
following, 2, 7, 12, 15, 25–28, 32,
    33, 36, 37, 39, 40, 46, 48,
    50, 59, 63, 65, 70, 72–74,
    76, 79, 83, 84, 86, 87, 97,
    98, 100, 105–107, 130,
    132–135, 139, 144, 146,
    147, 149, 150, 159, 165,
    167, 168, 175, 189, 206,
    209, 218, 219, 224, 228,
    231, 232, 239, 245,
    247–249, 255, 260, 264,
    269, 277, 283, 304, 314,
    330, 341, 342, 352, 374,
    382, 385, 388, 394, 402,
    418, 420, 465, 478, 481,
    509
food, 15, 20, 60, 142, 152, 153, 171,
    172, 174, 183, 189, 190,
    192, 223, 234, 245, 247,
    249, 261, 507, 527
foot, 201, 202
foraging, 216
force, 164, 166, 230, 351, 444
forefront, 417
forehead, 49
foreplay, 46
form, 20, 72, 83, 91, 102, 114, 115,
    124, 127, 140, 142, 202,
    203, 249, 255, 272, 274,
    290, 292, 296, 300, 307,
    310, 313, 316, 320, 325,

332, 336, 341, 346, 347,
356, 357, 371, 375, 387,
401, 403, 407, 458, 530,
542
formation, 141, 253
formula, 4, 13, 35, 250, 427, 439,
    441
formulation, 87, 93, 95, 261–263,
    265, 271, 272
foster, 6, 21, 24, 69, 91, 92, 129, 142,
    153, 159, 184, 192, 200,
    203, 205, 206, 229, 235,
    245, 247, 289, 293, 301,
    303, 310, 325, 331, 333,
    336, 347, 356, 358, 363,
    368, 371, 375, 376, 378,
    385, 391, 393, 399, 400,
    402, 404, 407, 472, 474,
    482, 491, 501, 506, 521,
    525, 526, 531, 539
foundation, 69, 162
fragrance, 11–13, 24–27, 29–32,
    35–37, 40, 41, 45, 46, 49,
    61, 74, 76, 85, 86, 88, 93,
    94, 102, 104, 105, 111,
    118, 123–127, 167, 168,
    179, 190, 192, 211, 235,
    248, 249, 252, 260, 262,
    265, 266, 269, 275, 284,
    287, 290, 295, 301,
    303–305, 307, 330,
    333–336, 338, 341, 354,
    355, 380, 382, 405, 409,
    420, 425, 427, 438, 440,
    442, 446, 458, 468, 475,
    477, 487–489, 491, 496,
    498–503, 506–508,
    514–516, 518–521, 532,
    536–542

framework, 2, 73, 219, 239, 370, 458, 502, 505
frankincense, 236, 240, 253, 404
freedom, 312, 315, 353, 392
freshening, 129
freshness, 59, 127–130, 132, 133, 137, 384
friction, 71
frontier, 262, 355, 422, 430, 438, 446, 453, 460, 464, 472
fruit, 183, 252, 388
fruity, 94, 215, 256, 257, 263, 270, 305, 336, 339, 346, 348, 395
frustration, 403
fun, 75, 107, 131
function, 43, 67, 74, 97, 164, 183, 205, 277, 294, 330, 346, 384, 412, 461, 462, 514, 540
fusion, 42, 88, 430, 441, 470, 482, 487
future, 90, 94, 225, 239, 244, 249, 254, 260, 262, 265, 267, 272, 276, 290, 336, 338, 343, 356, 417, 419–422, 424, 429, 432, 435, 438, 442, 445, 450, 457, 462, 464, 470, 477, 480, 498, 503, 508, 510, 521, 524, 531, 536, 542

gain, 322, 503, 531
game, 435
gaming, 433–435
gap, 208
gardening, 183
garlic, 11, 140–142, 160, 172, 283, 306, 389
gas, 243
gatekeeping, 521
gateway, 132
gathering, 235
gender, 330, 331
generation, 343, 429
genetic, 2, 19, 61, 65, 164, 215, 216, 378, 384, 469
genre, 457
geosmin, 197
germ, 309
gesture, 163
gimmick, 355, 433, 499
glance, 320
glimpse, 254
globalization, 235, 249, 537
globe, 235, 537
glory, 301
glow, 37, 46, 82, 200
glowing, 82
go, 79
goal, 35, 44, 60, 148, 488
goddess, 162
godliness, 313
good, 60, 75, 76, 130, 214
Gorgonzola, 190
Gouda, 243
grapefruit, 471
Greece, 236
groin, 18, 199
grooming, 102, 263, 265, 267, 272, 274, 276–278, 330, 346, 393–395
grotesqueness, 179
grounding, 86, 404, 471, 473, 488
groundwork, 236
group, 215, 356, 521, 534
growth, 17, 74, 96, 188, 198, 389, 405, 474, 482

grunge, 115
guide, 29, 40, 104, 117, 175, 514
gum, 130
gym, 198, 200, 201

hair, 99–107, 111–119, 121–127, 265–267, 312–315, 346, 388, 389
hairbrush, 277
hairstyling, 107, 109
hallmark, 243
hand, 74, 89, 130, 189, 306
happiness, 76, 88, 251, 480
haptic, 430–433, 441
harm, 130
harshness, 57
harvest, 89
harvesting, 237, 254
healing, 80, 236, 237, 240, 403, 467, 470, 478–480, 482, 485–489
health, 2, 23, 55, 58, 66, 68, 73, 76, 80, 100, 118, 121, 123, 126, 129, 130, 132, 137, 140, 141, 183, 198, 199, 201, 247, 266, 308–310, 312, 315, 352, 378, 388, 398, 467, 469, 472, 480, 488
healthcare, 469
hearing, 435
heart, 34, 36, 49, 70, 104, 130, 263
heat, 51, 64, 67, 266
help, 2, 20, 25, 34, 62, 68, 71, 80, 202, 203, 462, 489
heritage, 115, 234, 237, 249, 253, 254, 257, 393, 499, 500, 524, 526, 527, 532
hero, 203

heteronormativity, 362
hierarchy, 72, 292
highlight, 89, 235, 276, 312, 509, 523, 527
history, 126, 141, 151, 161, 174, 192, 194, 235, 242, 247, 248, 308, 349, 469, 487, 531
home, 12, 74, 195, 240, 250, 257
Homi K. Bhabha, 532
homogenization, 7, 235, 394, 491
honesty, 349
honey, 34
honor, 200, 239, 500, 532
horizon, 442
hormone, 231
horror, 183
hospitality, 235, 249, 469
house, 477
human, 1, 5, 8, 15, 16, 18, 20, 24, 49, 58, 61, 66, 69, 71, 73, 88, 94–96, 102, 115, 116, 124, 151, 157, 164–166, 171, 172, 176, 181, 184, 186, 188, 191, 201, 203, 207, 208, 211, 215, 219, 221, 223, 225–230, 233, 235–237, 239, 240, 247, 249, 265, 268, 281, 283, 294, 297, 306, 308, 310, 318, 320, 322, 369, 371, 376–378, 381, 393, 400, 402, 415, 417, 430, 433, 438, 444, 448, 453, 455, 457, 464, 470, 477, 485, 487, 501, 511, 524, 531
humanity, 21, 27, 378
humidity, 224
humor, 244

hybridity, 532
hydration, 12, 51, 73, 74, 76, 80, 87, 92, 97, 140
hydrogen, 243
hygiene, 6, 19, 20, 60, 66, 73, 114, 116, 127–129, 132, 133, 137–140, 148, 181, 193, 195, 207, 233, 258, 260, 263, 279–281, 300, 309, 318, 320, 322, 325, 326, 329, 330, 393, 412, 542
hypoallergenic, 126

ice, 245
idea, 48, 66, 72, 226, 286, 290, 301, 309, 311, 312, 314, 333, 339, 368, 401, 542
ideal, 20, 36, 124
identity, 2, 6, 8, 22, 24, 27, 51, 66, 109, 124, 125, 186, 195, 200, 233, 237, 239, 244, 247–249, 255, 260, 263, 265, 296, 299, 301, 303, 310, 313, 314, 317, 318, 320, 322–325, 329–333, 336, 341, 343, 346, 350–352, 355, 356, 358, 362, 363, 369, 370, 391, 393–396, 398, 411, 443, 487, 489, 519, 526, 533, 534, 537, 539, 540, 542
illness, 308
image, 205, 289, 333, 359, 514
imagery, 49, 73, 94, 499
imbalance, 74
immersion, 379, 433, 462
impact, 22, 26, 27, 39, 48, 73, 76, 91, 133, 137, 147, 160, 166, 207, 216, 225, 250, 252, 267, 275, 276, 289, 319, 330, 352, 359, 362, 371, 380, 398, 409, 430, 440, 441, 443, 445, 455, 478, 485, 487, 495, 501, 511, 514, 518, 521, 527
imperfection, 341
implement, 532
implementation, 438, 470, 502
importance, 17, 86, 99, 123, 167, 180, 193, 201, 214, 235, 254, 294, 307, 320, 357, 364, 372, 398, 411, 439, 458, 498, 519, 532, 537, 542
impression, 25, 102, 135, 148
in, 1–7, 11, 12, 14–27, 32–34, 39, 41, 44, 46, 49–51, 53–56, 58–74, 76, 77, 79–83, 85–95, 97, 99, 100, 102, 107, 109, 111, 114, 115, 117–119, 121–127, 132, 133, 140–142, 144–148, 151, 152, 157–168, 170, 172–176, 178–184, 186, 188–195, 197–199, 201–211, 214–219, 221, 223, 225–240, 242–249, 251–257, 260–268, 270–272, 274–276, 278, 283–288, 292–294, 296, 299, 301, 303–309, 312, 316, 318, 320–323, 326, 327, 329, 331–333, 336–338, 341–343, 346–358, 360, 361, 363, 364, 367–372, 374–376, 379, 381, 383–385, 387–389, 393–396, 398,

400, 402–406, 413, 415–417, 420, 422, 424, 425, 429, 430, 432, 433, 435, 438–455, 457, 458, 460, 462–472, 475–477, 480, 481, 483, 485–489, 491, 493, 495, 496, 498–501, 503–508, 510, 511, 513, 514, 516, 517, 519, 521, 523–532, 534, 536, 537, 539, 541, 542
inadequacy, 346, 388, 398, 399, 406
incense, 244, 247, 284, 382, 472, 477
inclusivity, 293, 505, 519, 521, 526, 538, 539
inconsistency, 89
inconvenience, 20
incorporate, 33, 59, 70, 93, 119, 147, 148, 160, 184, 230, 263, 275, 340, 343, 378, 387, 389, 395, 416, 429, 434, 462, 466, 471, 488
incorporation, 107, 185, 186, 261, 270, 271, 299, 382, 463, 502
increase, 5, 66, 74, 162, 207, 309, 326
indicator, 199
individual, 14, 16, 17, 28, 52, 59, 61, 65, 86, 90, 164, 167, 175, 199, 206–208, 211, 216, 229, 233, 249, 252, 257, 263, 268, 303, 329, 330, 333, 336, 343, 394, 395, 398, 400, 404, 412, 435, 443, 463, 469, 479, 481, 488, 519, 521, 524
individuality, 3, 5–8, 11, 29, 32, 55, 58, 83, 88, 104, 107, 115, 116, 121, 260, 281, 292, 301, 303, 313, 314, 317, 325, 329, 331–334, 336, 338, 345–347, 350, 353–356, 358, 360, 378, 393–395, 399, 477, 539, 542
indulgence, 83
industry, 19, 61, 66, 89, 90, 188, 272, 274, 276, 287, 290, 303, 307, 309, 311, 326, 334, 336, 338, 342, 343, 352, 399, 416, 425, 426, 433, 435, 438, 440, 442, 469, 475–477, 491, 496, 498, 499, 501–503, 506, 508, 514–516, 518, 536, 538, 541
inflammation, 97
influence, 2, 9, 14, 16, 21, 23, 24, 26, 27, 32, 52, 54, 58, 62, 65, 68, 69, 72, 107, 119, 137, 141, 172, 173, 195, 206, 208, 209, 211, 215, 216, 223, 227, 229, 231, 236, 249, 264, 276, 329, 331, 346, 354, 381, 383, 478, 480, 493, 495, 521
influencer, 7
influx, 249
information, 229, 378, 501–503
infusion, 122, 149, 150, 486
ingredient, 89, 90, 502, 503
inhalation, 468
innovation, 42, 218, 472, 474, 478, 522, 523
input, 43
inquiry, 218

Index 567

insight, 184, 458, 500
inspiration, 450, 500, 515
inspire, 29, 35, 82, 102, 168, 188, 213, 252, 339, 343, 444, 451, 452, 473
installation, 293, 443
instance, 2, 23, 26, 34, 52, 56, 59, 62, 65, 66, 72, 86, 89, 93, 114, 123, 151, 158, 160, 162, 163, 172, 183, 188, 190, 192, 195, 197, 202, 204, 207, 209, 215, 219, 234, 236, 238, 240, 244, 246, 252, 253, 261, 269, 277, 283, 284, 289, 304, 308, 313, 324, 329, 330, 356, 370, 375, 378, 380, 384, 388, 393, 398, 403, 404, 416, 458, 462, 473, 480, 486, 489, 499, 503, 507, 515, 516, 524, 527, 532
intake, 12, 53, 54
integration, 93, 107, 225, 226, 341, 343, 371, 419, 424, 429, 430, 433, 435–438, 445, 446, 448, 460, 462–464, 467, 468, 474, 480, 483, 487, 508, 529
integrity, 266, 308, 443, 462, 515
intelligence, 419, 430, 435, 438, 519
intensity, 63, 125, 245, 246, 266, 379, 420, 460, 468
intent, 443, 445, 463, 538
intention, 122, 404, 485
intentionality, 406
interaction, 6, 9, 27, 59, 72, 86, 102, 148, 160, 180, 211, 217, 223, 225, 228, 230, 248, 314, 417, 438, 529

interconnectedness, 371
interest, 7, 36, 238, 257, 337, 349
intermingle, 527
interplay, 5, 6, 14, 18, 21, 24, 51, 62, 66, 69, 73, 124, 141, 142, 145, 151, 164, 166, 173, 177, 179, 182, 194, 198, 200, 206, 208, 218, 233, 260, 275, 276, 283, 290, 310, 323, 329, 341, 352, 369, 381, 383, 385, 412, 430, 458, 519, 539
interpretation, 233, 332, 451
intersection, 40, 60, 88, 96, 97, 171, 184, 201, 219, 225, 230, 235, 254, 267, 271, 285, 292, 295, 299, 320, 343, 360, 367, 376, 377, 415, 430, 435, 438, 442, 444, 446, 451, 453, 455, 457, 462, 465, 470, 474, 478, 485, 498, 531
intimacy, 15, 16, 18, 20, 22, 24, 27, 29, 32, 34, 37–39, 41, 44, 46, 67–73, 88, 90, 92, 95, 96, 114–116, 123, 124, 127, 129, 132, 133, 135, 141, 142, 146, 148, 150, 152, 153, 158, 159, 162, 163, 166, 172, 173, 176, 179, 181, 182, 184, 202–206, 208, 211, 219, 221, 223, 230, 232, 233, 245, 251, 252, 276, 277, 365, 371, 375, 376, 379, 381, 383, 385, 389
intrigue, 164, 181, 198, 270, 303, 367, 369
introduction, 309, 471

introspection, 404, 473
investment, 462
invitation, 88, 141, 305, 489
inviting, 15, 18, 24, 34, 37, 46, 58, 64, 69, 71, 94, 95, 163, 181, 188, 191, 206, 218, 227, 230, 244, 245, 247, 249, 250, 252, 258, 262, 274, 284, 294, 303, 304, 308, 356, 360, 369, 377, 378, 395, 446, 455, 458, 460, 477, 480, 531, 534
irritation, 57, 64, 129, 263, 266
isolation, 207, 356, 399, 541
isovaleraldehyde, 4
issue, 61, 215, 237, 238, 275, 293, 296, 307, 368, 403, 443, 445, 451, 454, 463, 469, 501, 506, 508, 518, 532, 537, 540
Istanbul, 234

Japan, 348
jasmine, 36, 46, 86, 123, 248, 404, 506
jewelry, 226–228, 486, 487
job, 469
jogging, 70
jojoba, 71
Jon Kabat-Zinn, 480
journal, 404, 473
journaling, 473
journey, 3, 8, 11, 29, 31, 34, 37, 58, 76, 83, 99, 102, 121, 140, 211, 236, 239, 249, 262, 267, 274, 278, 292, 306, 307, 318, 331, 341, 354, 360, 389, 395, 398, 400, 402–405, 409, 424, 455, 457, 487, 489
joy, 403–405, 477, 488
judgment, 142, 195, 203, 299, 300, 364, 371, 389, 397, 480
Judith Butler's, 394

kefir, 256
keratin, 111
key, 23, 34, 38, 51, 52, 60, 77, 125, 138, 161, 199, 252, 260, 333, 489
kimchi, 174, 190, 195, 215, 256
kingdom, 165
kiss, 132, 145, 147, 148
kissing, 21, 133–135, 145–148
kitchen, 160, 306, 435, 527
knowledge, 44, 238, 499, 519, 521, 534
kombucha, 256

labeling, 94
laboratory, 284
lack, 254, 330, 445, 469, 479, 491, 501, 502
lactate, 52
land, 237
landscape, 23, 186, 191, 192, 196, 206, 234, 237, 247, 248, 252, 272, 290, 301, 307, 318, 334, 339, 348, 378, 393, 417, 430, 448, 457, 462, 487, 500, 503, 505, 508, 510, 516, 524, 526, 539, 540
language, 132, 205, 383–385
latter, 223
laughter, 145, 245

lavender, 26, 32, 44, 46, 62, 77, 87, 89, 123, 268, 403, 416, 471, 473, 480, 486, 488
law, 216
layer, 71, 100, 229, 269, 314
layering, 13
lead, 7, 11, 12, 17, 21, 24, 51–54, 56, 57, 65, 66, 74, 89, 97, 100, 126, 129, 140, 144, 146, 148, 160, 166, 176, 193, 195, 198, 199, 203, 205, 230, 233, 237, 247, 249, 252, 266, 275, 300, 301, 305, 315, 326, 330, 333, 346, 356, 365, 381, 384, 386, 388, 389, 394, 399, 403, 438, 443, 445, 447, 448, 451, 454, 469, 499, 501, 515, 532
learning, 416
leather, 370
leave, 78, 135, 148
legacy, 249
leisure, 93, 94
lemon, 403, 471
lens, 72, 114, 197, 277, 293, 295, 308, 336, 352, 460, 532, 537
lethargy, 489
letter, 47, 49
level, 17, 26, 50, 58, 74, 90, 114, 205, 208, 230, 267, 272, 320, 382, 453, 457, 459, 462, 495, 505
leverage, 56, 69, 144, 284, 289, 418, 495
liberation, 115, 325, 327, 347, 375, 378, 400, 402, 405, 407
lie, 34, 142, 265, 285, 430, 489

life, 174, 176, 179, 183, 184, 188, 192, 197, 216, 230, 233, 240, 244, 266, 271, 367, 403, 405, 416, 450, 480, 482, 507
lifecycle, 425, 427
lifestyle, 55, 58, 75, 141, 395, 412
lifetime, 355
light, 39, 91, 224, 266
liking, 5
limonene, 89
line, 89, 175, 515, 538
linger, 46, 49, 71, 132, 141
lingerie, 40–42
link, 206
lipid, 80
literature, 72, 190, 202, 387
living, 198
local, 235, 254, 524
longevity, 224, 355
longing, 371
look, 464
loss, 238, 499
lotion, 85–88, 389, 395
love, 47–49, 72, 87, 91, 123, 151–153, 161–163, 206, 231, 248, 306, 354, 388, 389, 400–402, 404, 406, 411
loyalty, 270, 290, 490, 506, 510
lubricant, 144, 235

magnetism, 211
mainstream, 263, 287, 334–336, 346, 348, 356, 405, 519, 521, 529, 541
majority, 359
make, 15, 27, 54, 76, 137, 208, 318, 332, 542

makeup, 50
making, 24, 32, 50, 62, 70, 76, 77, 79, 83, 87, 88, 92, 95, 109, 117, 119, 124, 130, 144–146, 161, 172, 191, 201, 203, 226, 230, 235, 236, 243, 248, 249, 251, 269, 293, 296, 341, 354, 381, 417, 424, 438, 441–445, 463, 465, 468, 480, 486, 493, 495, 499, 501, 502, 534, 536
male, 164, 219
malodor, 367–369, 375–378, 391–393
malty, 256
management, 263, 265
mane, 102, 104, 122
mango, 252
manipulation, 225, 491, 504, 505, 514
manner, 55, 173, 499
mark, 19, 49, 286, 308, 324
marker, 2, 73, 195, 309, 393
market, 42, 62, 96, 244, 261, 265–267, 270, 271, 288, 290, 303, 336–338, 394, 420, 421, 489, 498, 507, 538, 541
marketability, 342, 541
marketing, 66, 193, 206, 271, 290, 305, 309, 323, 346, 349, 351, 352, 475, 489, 491, 493, 495, 499–501, 504, 505, 509–511, 514, 516
marketplace, 249, 503
masculinity, 68
mask, 2, 6, 19, 24, 44, 56, 60, 66, 93, 160, 326, 330, 385, 388, 389, 397, 398, 413, 516
masking, 90, 129, 165, 275, 311, 323, 329
Maslow, 72
mass, 5, 249, 334, 345, 394, 538
massage, 34, 46, 69–71, 82, 87, 252
mat, 473
match, 70
matcha, 271
mate, 2, 14, 165, 172, 206, 207, 223
material, 124, 370
mating, 164, 211, 216
matter, 24, 116, 174, 182, 183, 274, 325
Maurice Merleau-Ponty, 293, 458
meal, 141, 142, 152, 245
mean, 59, 463
meaning, 179, 355, 458, 499, 519, 534
means, 8, 93, 181, 229, 242, 288, 306, 318, 346, 355, 357, 360, 363, 387, 394, 417, 458, 469, 488
mechanism, 14, 56, 119, 206, 417
media, 66, 200, 289, 330, 358, 371, 394, 399, 417
medicine, 166, 236
meditation, 404, 416, 465–467, 471–473, 486
Mediterranean, 65, 68
medium, 146, 295, 296, 320–322, 422, 442, 451, 452, 455, 460, 524, 531, 534, 537, 539, 540
medulla, 100, 124
memoir, 307
memory, 4, 16, 25, 43, 44, 63, 76, 88, 93, 107, 109, 121, 132, 146, 162, 193, 194, 205,

Index

  229, 243, 248, 266, 268, 284, 303, 306, 350, 356, 381, 387, 403, 417, 433, 442, 444, 462–464, 470, 480, 487, 524, 531
mention, 173
merging, 354, 454, 532
message, 451
metabolic, 21, 52, 189, 255
metaphor, 488
method, 89, 224, 255, 404
methodology, 207
methyl, 250
miasma, 309
micro, 438, 468
microbiome, 65, 73–76, 89
microbiota, 65
microencapsulation, 224
Middle Eastern, 235, 247–249
mildew, 187, 188
milk, 34
million, 49
mind, 64, 81, 121, 244, 433, 470, 472–474
mindfulness, 122, 233, 383, 395, 398, 404, 465, 467, 472–474, 480–482
mindset, 36, 489
mineral, 243
mingling, 72, 145
mint, 137
minty, 127
misinformation, 521
mission, 290
mist, 105, 108
mistrust, 501
misunderstanding, 198
mix, 187, 234, 389
mixture, 16, 18, 51

ml, 34, 108
model, 219, 231, 436
moderation, 159
modernity, 192, 240, 249
modernization, 249
modification, 354, 355
modulation, 141, 429
moisture, 80, 86
moisturizing, 80, 85, 87
mold, 197, 198
moldy, 196–198
moment, 39, 71, 472, 477, 480, 482
mood, 5, 26, 27, 32, 46, 65, 76, 83, 93, 94, 122, 163, 199, 209, 253, 267, 387, 468, 480, 489
morality, 233, 310
morning, 20–22, 39, 82
motivation, 471
mouth, 20, 129, 130, 141
mouthwash, 130–132, 140
move, 294, 310, 343, 430, 508, 510
movement, 115, 124, 188, 312, 318, 320, 325, 346, 354, 356, 357, 360, 398, 407, 470, 472, 475, 482–485, 539, 542
mud, 243
mummification, 240
mundane, 73, 88, 99, 267, 393
music, 70, 122, 346
musk, 65, 66, 164, 215
musky, 1, 13, 15, 65, 66, 115, 164, 192, 380, 382
myriad, 1, 6, 176, 196, 285, 401, 406, 478, 526
myrrh, 236, 240–242
mystique, 487

name, 530, 531
nanotechnology, 225
narrative, 21, 142, 165, 171, 179, 247, 263, 295, 332, 333, 341, 358, 360, 394, 406
natto, 190, 348
nature, 5, 28, 56, 58, 60, 61, 73, 90, 103, 132, 164, 171–174, 183, 186, 195, 197, 198, 201, 203, 216–218, 229, 288, 290, 293, 296, 300, 305, 310, 321, 322, 324, 329, 355, 356, 367, 396, 430, 443, 445, 448, 451, 454, 457, 459, 463, 473, 477, 478, 488, 501, 519, 529
navigation, 373
necessity, 393, 524
need, 30, 72, 105, 195, 292, 462, 480, 498, 502
negativity, 443, 489
neglect, 195
network, 268
networking, 522
neuroscience, 442
niche, 7, 42, 96, 190, 196, 242, 288, 301, 303, 304, 343, 348, 357, 413, 421, 477, 537, 541
night, 142, 205
no, 330, 508, 537
nonconformity, 115, 336, 337, 356
norm, 115, 235
normalization, 203, 301
nose, 27, 306
nostalgia, 15, 17, 25, 59, 88, 95, 114, 115, 144, 183, 188, 191, 193, 194, 197, 198, 202, 215, 241, 248, 266, 269, 283, 284, 306, 371, 388, 473
note, 36, 404
notion, 190, 203, 258, 285, 306, 309, 312, 313, 318, 326, 330, 331, 352, 399, 475, 535
notoriety, 162
nourishment, 73
novelty, 270
nuisance, 22, 141
number, 274
nutrient, 183, 191

object, 124, 201, 370
obligation, 235
observer, 177, 304
obsession, 398
ocean, 435
Odeur, 284, 477
odor, 2, 3, 7, 9, 11–15, 22–24, 51–58, 65, 66, 68, 73, 74, 93, 95, 141, 142, 146, 172, 173, 186, 199, 200, 202, 204, 205, 215, 233–235, 243, 245, 246, 257, 263, 265, 274–276, 283, 290, 294–296, 300, 301, 306, 308–310, 316, 317, 320–325, 329–332, 346, 356, 357, 368, 372, 374, 377, 378, 384, 385, 388, 398, 399, 405, 407, 411, 412, 443, 444, 446, 519, 530, 531, 540, 542
odorant, 4
off, 17, 89, 141, 142, 158, 159, 177, 183, 189, 204, 243, 246, 257, 293, 309, 349, 389

offer, 29, 57, 60, 64, 94, 97, 104, 121, 129, 159, 169, 225, 243, 245, 247, 249, 254, 268, 355, 388, 420, 462, 467, 474, 484

offering, 88, 96, 126, 227, 285, 336, 338, 343, 417, 419, 438, 462, 470, 478

office, 469

offspring, 19, 61

oil, 27, 28, 34, 62, 71, 77, 85, 87, 108, 119, 236, 252, 253, 388, 389, 469, 471, 472, 486

oiling, 90–92

ointment, 85–87

olfaction, 3, 25, 37, 95, 124, 227, 405, 450, 453, 457, 467, 511, 534

olfactory, 3, 4, 6, 16, 18, 21, 25, 27–29, 32, 35, 39, 40, 42, 43, 55, 58, 59, 62, 63, 76, 77, 83, 88, 92, 93, 95–97, 99, 102, 104, 107, 109, 111, 114, 117, 119, 122, 124–126, 135, 137, 146, 148, 157, 158, 161, 162, 164–167, 171, 172, 174, 179–184, 187, 191–196, 198, 203, 204, 206, 214, 216, 223, 229, 230, 234, 235, 237, 239, 241, 243, 245, 247–252, 257, 258, 260, 264, 266, 268, 270–272, 274–276, 279, 283–287, 290, 292–296, 299, 301, 304–307, 309, 322, 332–334, 336, 339, 341, 343, 346–349, 351, 354–356, 363–365, 367, 369–371, 377–379, 381–385, 387, 393–395, 398, 403–405, 407, 415, 417, 420, 422, 424, 429–431, 433, 435, 438, 440–448, 451, 452, 455–457, 460–463, 465, 468, 470, 472, 477–480, 485, 487–490, 493, 495, 506, 517, 519, 521–527, 529, 531–534, 536, 537, 539–541

on, 1, 11, 22, 23, 26, 28, 31, 36, 37, 49, 52, 56, 58, 59, 61, 65, 66, 69, 73, 74, 76, 87, 89, 90, 94, 114, 116, 122, 130, 137, 141, 145, 148, 160, 165, 166, 176, 177, 186, 193, 199, 205, 207, 216, 223, 225–231, 235, 238, 242–244, 250, 252, 253, 255, 262, 263, 267, 271, 290, 292, 293, 303, 311, 314, 318, 320, 322, 329, 330, 339, 341, 349, 358, 360, 362, 371, 376, 381, 398, 402, 404, 405, 413, 417, 419, 424, 430, 435, 438, 442, 445, 447, 448, 453, 457, 459, 462, 465, 468, 471, 473, 478, 480, 486, 487, 495, 501, 505, 507, 511, 514, 516, 518, 521, 527, 532, 534, 539

one, 5, 6, 13, 16, 17, 35, 37, 49, 59–61, 64, 66, 73, 87, 90, 97, 99, 100, 115, 122, 125, 127, 129, 133, 140, 141,

145, 146, 148, 152, 158, 167, 181, 191, 193, 201, 204, 206, 208, 252, 274, 283, 290, 296, 306, 315, 318, 325, 333, 341, 346, 347, 352, 354, 357, 360, 368, 384, 389, 394, 396, 400, 409, 418, 445, 463, 466, 487–489, 499, 532, 542
onion, 140–142, 389
opportunity, 41, 60, 71, 76, 104, 338, 343
opt, 380, 395
orange, 46, 87, 403
organ, 74
organism, 1, 223
ostracism, 170
other, 12, 46, 61, 65, 74, 89, 130, 142, 160, 180, 189, 198, 205, 207, 209, 230, 247, 256, 312, 323, 368, 385, 450, 488
oud, 525
outreach, 532
overemphasis, 61
overexploitation, 216, 237
Overharvesting, 254
overharvesting, 506
overload, 243, 377
overpower, 397
overuse, 237, 332, 397
ox, 164
oxidation, 189
oxide, 93
oxygen, 62
oxytocin, 231

packaging, 425, 489

pain, 478
pairing, 172
palate, 172, 249
palette, 464
paradigm, 334, 534
paradise, 250
paradox, 7, 15, 189, 198, 274, 275, 284, 332, 348
part, 4, 8, 16, 22, 24, 46, 51, 69, 88, 92, 93, 95, 102, 107, 115, 157, 162, 183, 204, 233, 241, 243, 266, 268, 276, 301, 306, 324, 357, 398, 442, 465, 480
participation, 445
partner, 16, 38, 40, 68, 69, 72, 90, 202, 204, 368, 371, 375, 382, 384
passion, 72, 151, 161, 162, 172, 517
past, 192, 242, 249, 383, 479, 524
patch, 87, 108
patchouli, 46, 86
path, 58, 405, 502
pathway, 4, 169, 403, 487
penchant, 123
people, 51, 194, 214, 300, 307, 313, 358, 527, 528, 536
pepper, 36
peppermint, 44, 108, 236, 473, 486
percentage, 115, 122
perception, 4, 5, 16, 21, 24, 35, 58, 62, 68, 93, 97, 159, 167, 174, 199, 202, 204, 207, 229, 233, 245, 258, 268, 269, 276, 283, 285, 288, 290, 292, 293, 306, 308, 316, 330, 333, 334, 341, 387, 415, 417, 430, 433, 439, 440, 443, 444, 446,

453, 455, 458, 459,
  461–464, 487, 493, 514,
  519, 540
perfection, 358, 398
performance, 141, 151, 157, 294,
  457–460
performativity, 394
perfume, 24, 26, 27, 30, 31,
  104–106, 124–126, 233,
  288, 290, 304, 343, 395,
  413, 475–477, 514
perfumer, 306, 307, 508
perfumery, 166, 190, 252, 254, 285,
  287, 290, 301, 306, 307,
  477, 496–498, 521, 522,
  525, 532, 534–536
period, 57, 228
permanence, 355
permission, 499, 500
person, 3, 5, 17, 21, 50, 55, 65, 158,
  252, 283, 296, 370, 445,
  463, 466, 488
persona, 395
personality, 25, 395
perspective, 116, 176, 177, 183, 191,
  198, 284, 293, 339, 394,
  499
perspiration, 51–54, 56, 69, 330
perspiring, 51
phase, 57
phenomenology, 184, 293, 295, 458,
  463
phenomenon, 2, 5, 16, 20, 22, 24,
  49, 61, 65, 71, 72, 86, 88,
  111, 114, 145, 166, 191,
  197, 198, 201, 205, 228,
  229, 330, 348, 351, 371,
  376, 394, 511, 524, 527,
  528, 537, 542

pheromone, 61, 141, 142, 164, 209,
  211, 213, 214, 216, 219,
  223, 225–230, 319, 382
philosopher, 236, 308, 488
philosophy, 263, 325, 444
phrase, 115
phthalide, 58
physical, 46, 49, 51, 62, 65, 66, 69,
  70, 92, 93, 119, 129, 133,
  141, 145, 151, 199, 200,
  205, 231, 278, 293, 308,
  309, 370, 380, 383, 470,
  472, 473, 478, 485
physicality, 71
physiology, 141, 208
piece, 486
Pierre Bourdieu, 352
piety, 309
pillow, 37–39, 122
pillowcase, 122
pine, 404
place, 32, 187, 191, 234, 252, 301,
  354
plant, 27, 53, 80, 88, 89, 118, 121,
  174, 253, 263, 403, 416
plastic, 477, 507
platform, 378, 417, 420, 517, 531
play, 1, 5, 12, 14, 19, 24, 60, 61, 70,
  90, 122, 163, 164, 172,
  203, 206, 208, 211, 214,
  216, 218, 223, 230, 231,
  245, 248, 249, 251–253,
  272, 296, 348, 364, 365,
  368, 370, 372, 374, 495,
  503, 519, 528, 531
player, 433, 435
playing, 141, 216, 255, 364
pleasantness, 263, 265, 287, 307,
  400

pleasure, 42, 64, 71, 83, 85, 88, 94, 96, 173, 196, 306, 308, 377, 378
plethora, 130, 143, 252, 326
point, 309
polymer, 224
popularity, 7, 61, 125, 183, 190, 200, 228, 264, 269
population, 309
porosity, 124
pose, 160, 170, 198, 249, 271, 307
posit, 499
position, 114
positioning, 500
positivity, 205, 310, 312, 315, 320, 325, 357, 398–400, 402, 473, 541
post, 65, 66, 200, 375
postmodernism, 293, 295, 336, 475
potency, 89, 158, 242, 254, 301, 303, 526
potential, 1, 17, 19, 22, 27, 32–35, 37, 44–46, 55, 59, 61, 65, 69, 73, 85, 88, 95, 99, 104, 107, 109, 123, 126, 134, 135, 137, 140, 142, 144, 148, 150, 158, 159, 161, 165, 167, 169–175, 181, 183, 192, 193, 195, 196, 198, 207, 210, 214, 216, 218, 220, 221, 223, 225–229, 231, 237, 254, 266, 270, 274–278, 286, 289, 290, 296, 305, 307, 321, 331, 338, 342, 355, 367, 368, 372, 376, 379–381, 383, 393, 403, 405, 418–420, 422–424, 428, 430–433, 435, 436, 438, 441, 443–445, 448, 449, 451, 452, 454, 456, 458, 463–465, 467, 470, 472, 479, 480, 482, 485, 487, 489, 500, 501, 509, 510, 516, 521–525, 528–530, 532, 534, 535, 539
power, 1–3, 29, 37, 49, 50, 56, 59, 60, 62, 68, 85, 90, 102, 125, 132, 135, 145, 150, 153, 164, 169, 171, 176, 179, 208, 209, 221, 227, 232, 233, 237, 240, 242, 243, 252, 267, 284, 306, 320, 322, 331, 333, 341, 343, 351, 358, 360, 379, 381–383, 395, 398, 407, 417, 424, 442, 444, 449, 450, 452, 457, 462, 465, 467, 470–472, 474, 479, 482, 487, 489, 493, 495, 510, 513, 516, 519, 522, 524, 527–529, 542
practicality, 112
practice, 17, 83, 90, 92, 118, 121, 124, 148, 150, 184, 192, 285, 314, 327, 329, 379, 383, 403, 404, 463, 471, 473, 478, 480, 485–489, 519, 521, 531
practicing, 233, 398
precedent, 426
preference, 15, 24, 29, 61, 89, 171, 257, 303, 325, 368, 385
prelude, 46, 68, 69
premise, 293
preparation, 59, 242, 246
presence, 16, 27, 52, 60, 62, 65, 72,

83, 89, 99, 111, 114, 125, 126, 165, 180, 182, 191, 195, 197, 198, 256, 257, 274–276, 293, 304, 394, 420
present, 159, 179, 207, 246, 249, 274, 276, 285, 301, 354, 472, 482, 524
presentation, 152, 173, 332
preservation, 254, 255, 445
pressing, 242, 480
pressure, 7, 71, 233, 329, 330, 376, 501
prevalence, 352, 403
pride, 314
principle, 44, 226, 286, 418, 460, 465, 480, 503
printing, 225
priority, 64
probiotic, 247
problem, 61, 507
process, 4, 25, 37, 52, 56, 62, 65, 95, 104, 105, 117, 122, 173, 174, 182, 183, 189, 190, 219, 228, 231, 253–256, 274, 292, 404, 418, 486–489, 532, 534
processing, 162, 248, 251, 457, 470
product, 6, 86–89, 93, 95, 122, 260, 266, 271, 275, 349, 425, 447, 489, 514, 516
production, 11, 18, 20, 52, 65, 74, 141, 142, 256, 274, 326, 425, 440–442, 496–498, 500, 501, 503, 506, 508, 518, 538
productivity, 469
profile, 2, 11, 13, 21, 36, 58, 75, 86, 99, 102, 160, 182, 189, 190, 198, 215, 219, 242, 253, 268, 275, 412, 443, 488, 504, 534
profit, 499, 515
project, 284
proliferation, 200, 394
prominence, 520
promise, 274, 356, 438, 442, 472, 479
protection, 92, 94, 141, 236, 404
protein, 111
protest, 357
proximity, 114, 180, 207, 231
psychoanalysis, 370
psychology, 5, 18, 22, 24, 27, 148, 164, 173, 183, 184, 189, 196, 198, 206, 239, 271, 275, 283, 325, 347, 351, 369–371, 435, 442, 487, 493
public, 204, 240, 246, 288, 290
pull, 24, 51, 151
pungency, 159
pungent, 1, 21, 53, 54, 160, 161, 189, 190, 192, 193, 197, 243, 245–247, 255, 257, 274, 283, 306, 377, 378, 389, 541
punk, 346, 356
purchase, 507
purchasing, 490, 493, 495
purification, 192
purity, 162, 248
purpose, 473
pursuit, 11, 73, 129, 130, 167, 240, 521, 534, 541
putting, 17, 89, 142, 158, 159, 177, 183, 189, 204, 243, 246, 257, 293, 349, 389, 501

quality, 17, 21, 205, 254, 466, 469, 479, 514, 516
quartz, 486
quest, 55, 137, 227, 265, 268, 272
question, 491
questioning, 295
quirk, 202
quo, 295, 307, 316, 333, 343, 346, 351, 358, 475, 526

race, 330
radical, 5, 313, 318, 320, 325, 338, 345, 400, 446
rancid, 189–191
rancidity, 189, 191
range, 72, 88, 140, 159, 164, 198, 199, 255, 261, 296, 303, 417, 522
rate, 515
rating, 93
rawness, 21, 175
re, 285
reaction, 189, 194, 284
realism, 462
reality, 343, 416, 424, 435–438, 462, 537
realm, 32, 40, 58, 60, 67, 69, 85, 88, 94, 95, 97, 102, 107, 111, 118, 121, 126, 132, 140, 144, 151, 159, 161, 164, 166, 171, 179, 183, 190, 194, 198, 203, 208, 211, 216, 219, 223, 227, 251, 258, 260, 263, 265, 268, 270, 276, 283, 285, 287, 291, 292, 295, 321, 336, 354, 363, 369–371, 387, 403, 415, 421, 430, 438, 443, 464, 472, 478, 482, 485, 498, 522, 529, 534
reapplication, 26
rebellion, 115, 142, 281, 295, 296, 299, 316, 346, 351–353, 356, 358, 365, 389, 538
recall, 43
reception, 296, 458
receptor, 4, 28
recipe, 106
recipient, 49, 163
reclaiming, 394
reclamation, 325
recognition, 175, 322, 480, 518, 524
recycling, 518
redness, 97
refinement, 190
reflection, 331, 444, 462, 473, 482
regeneration, 515
regimen, 121, 276
region, 94, 243, 248, 387
regulation, 469
regulator, 74
reign, 268
rejection, 195, 244, 336, 356, 360, 361, 376, 392, 541
rejuvenation, 62
relatedness, 398
relationship, 2, 6, 12, 16, 32, 44, 51, 63, 66, 72, 73, 88, 107, 116, 133, 135, 162, 171, 176, 184, 188, 189, 191, 233–235, 243, 245, 252, 258, 260, 262, 285, 304, 317, 319, 329, 331, 343, 350, 376, 381, 382, 384, 387, 396, 405, 419, 420, 423, 436, 446, 447, 457,

465, 473, 478, 489, 493, 506, 511, 529
relativism, 499
relaxation, 32, 38, 44, 46, 62–64, 70, 76, 77, 83, 85, 88, 91, 124, 144, 148, 395, 403, 404, 416, 469–471, 473, 480
release, 65, 71, 72, 114, 141, 172, 199, 224, 225, 231, 284, 303, 375, 376, 416, 439, 470, 473
relevance, 192
reliance, 252, 518
relief, 416, 471, 478
reluctance, 378
reminder, 18, 21, 22, 44, 46, 60, 242, 243, 248, 285, 320, 347, 369, 382, 388, 482, 542
renewal, 174, 489
repertoire, 381
representation, 14, 202, 384, 477, 498, 500, 532
reproducibility, 451
repulsion, 175, 179, 191, 203, 303, 321, 363
reputation, 501, 508
research, 61, 197, 208, 227, 229, 271, 378, 391, 419, 480, 485
reservoir, 111
resin, 242
resistance, 193, 310, 325, 349
resonance, 37, 44, 289, 477, 488
resource, 515
respect, 175, 235, 237, 257, 290, 496, 498–501, 525, 532
respectability, 309
response, 16, 25, 26, 32, 43, 45, 49, 67, 86, 97, 107, 163, 166, 182, 204, 215, 233, 304, 379, 384, 420, 460, 463, 465, 468, 478, 496, 518
responsibility, 430, 491, 496, 498, 500, 502, 506, 508, 514
rest, 121
result, 254, 274, 314, 398, 403, 406, 499
resurgence, 7, 125
retention, 80, 111, 122, 124
revelry, 377
revival, 192, 193, 242
revolution, 292, 320, 347, 354, 464, 524, 537–539
richness, 348
ride, 416
right, 24, 26, 27, 29, 32, 35, 37, 83, 99, 102, 104, 135, 317, 379
rise, 7, 41, 66, 115, 123, 257, 287, 289, 309, 338, 343, 371, 413, 470, 519, 531, 534
risk, 126, 140, 193, 238, 244, 249, 270, 293, 499, 515, 532
ritual, 34, 37, 83, 85, 87, 90–92, 122, 124, 144, 260, 277, 382, 388, 394, 395, 409
role, 1, 3, 5, 12, 14, 19, 20, 24, 26, 54, 58, 60–62, 65–67, 73, 80, 90, 92–94, 97, 100, 102, 121, 127, 129, 132, 141, 146, 151, 161, 163, 164, 167, 171–173, 178, 179, 183, 188, 202, 203, 206–208, 211, 214, 216, 218, 223, 226, 230, 231, 233, 237, 239, 245, 247–249, 251–255, 257, 264, 270, 272, 276, 284, 296, 301, 309, 348, 356,

363, 364, 369–371, 381,
    382, 385, 444, 446, 448,
    452, 457, 458, 503, 519,
    524, 527, 530–532
roleplay, 379–381
romance, 86, 175, 221
romantic, 16, 66, 71, 72, 95–97,
    141, 144–146, 151, 153,
    162–164, 172, 202, 230,
    233, 252, 383
romanticization, 198
room, 63, 70
Roquefort, 190, 243
rose, 46, 86, 162, 477, 486
rosemary, 268, 389, 395
rosewater, 249
rosewood, 237
rot, 183
routine, 84, 90, 98–100, 102, 111,
    119, 121, 129, 132–134,
    137–140, 263, 278, 395,
    466
rubber, 284
rush, 199

s, 3, 5, 6, 16, 28, 30, 36, 46, 49, 51,
    52, 55, 58–60, 65, 69, 72,
    74–76, 79, 86, 87, 89, 90,
    94, 97, 99, 107, 111, 115,
    119, 125, 129, 133,
    140–142, 144, 146, 163,
    177–179, 188, 202,
    204–206, 216, 226, 229,
    236, 242–244, 247–249,
    252, 253, 257, 266, 271,
    274, 275, 284, 286, 290,
    293, 306, 312, 314, 315,
    321, 323, 325, 330, 333,
    341, 346, 347, 349, 352,

354, 355, 357, 368, 371,
    375, 382, 384, 385, 389,
    394, 398, 400, 416, 443,
    445, 458, 463, 469, 470,
    477, 478, 487–489, 508,
    519, 524, 542
safety, 16, 64, 114, 165, 183, 278,
    355, 364, 479, 502
saffron, 158
sage, 192, 236, 238, 404, 524
sailing, 435
sake, 269
Saliva, 20
saliva, 20
salty, 151
sample, 243
sanctuary, 405, 407
sandalwood, 36, 46, 86, 237, 384,
    404, 463, 472, 473, 488,
    506
sanitation, 309
satisfaction, 151, 270, 276, 469, 514
sauce, 190, 195, 388
sauerkraut, 174, 215, 256, 257
sauna, 63
scale, 532
scalp, 111, 266, 312
scarcity, 252
scene, 381–383
scent, 1–3, 5–8, 11–22, 24–29, 32,
    34–41, 43–47, 49, 51, 52,
    54, 55, 59, 60, 62–66, 68,
    69, 71–77, 83, 86–90, 92,
    93, 95–97, 99–102,
    104–107, 109, 111,
    114–118, 121–125, 140,
    141, 144–146, 157, 159,
    161–164, 166, 169, 175,
    176, 179, 181, 183, 188,

191, 192, 194–199, 201, 204, 206, 207, 211, 214–216, 218, 219, 225–230, 233, 235, 237, 241–243, 247–253, 258, 260, 262, 264–268, 271, 274–276, 281, 283–285, 287, 292, 295, 296, 299, 301, 303, 304, 306–308, 310–312, 315–318, 321, 323–327, 329–331, 333, 334, 338, 341, 343, 346–358, 360, 362, 363, 367–371, 375–379, 381–385, 387–389, 393, 395, 396, 398, 400, 402–405, 407, 409, 412, 415–420, 422–424, 429, 430, 432–475, 477–480, 482–491, 493, 495–499, 501, 504, 505, 509–511, 513–516, 518, 519, 521, 522, 524–532, 534–540, 542

science, 1, 3, 5, 8, 9, 20, 22–25, 27, 29, 32, 35, 37, 39, 46, 49, 62, 65, 71, 73, 85, 86, 88, 90, 94–97, 99, 102, 104, 111, 118, 121, 126, 127, 129, 135, 137, 140, 145, 150, 153, 157, 159, 161, 164, 176, 182, 184, 189, 196, 198, 208, 210, 211, 216, 218, 219, 221, 223, 225, 227, 228, 230, 233, 235, 237, 241, 242, 245, 250, 252, 254, 255, 257, 268, 271, 272, 285, 306, 383, 419, 450, 470

scraping, 140
scrutiny, 323, 496, 514
sea, 250
seafood, 244
sebum, 74, 114
secret, 58, 79, 145
secrete, 18, 199, 412
secretion, 18, 215
section, 1, 3, 6, 11, 15, 20, 22, 24, 27, 29, 32, 35, 37, 40, 47, 49, 51, 62, 65, 67, 69, 71, 73, 76, 79, 83, 85, 88, 90, 92, 94, 97, 99, 102, 104, 107, 111, 114, 118, 127, 129, 132, 135, 137, 140, 145, 148, 151, 157, 159, 161, 164, 166, 171, 174, 179, 182, 184, 187, 189, 192, 196, 198, 203, 208, 223, 228, 233, 235, 237, 240, 242, 245, 247, 250, 252, 255, 258, 260, 263, 265, 268, 270, 272, 274, 276, 279, 283, 285, 287, 290, 295, 299, 301, 306, 308, 313, 320, 323, 325, 329, 331, 334, 336, 339, 345, 348, 351, 354, 356, 360, 363, 367, 369, 372, 375, 379, 381, 383, 387, 391, 393, 396, 400, 403, 405, 411, 415, 417, 420, 425, 430, 433, 438, 442, 444, 446, 451, 455, 458, 462, 465, 467, 472, 475, 480, 482, 485, 487, 489, 493, 496, 498, 506, 511, 514, 522, 524, 526, 529, 531, 534, 537, 540

security, 72
seduction, 41, 58, 97, 99, 121, 143, 145, 151, 153, 162, 170, 171, 174–176, 210, 219, 223, 225, 249, 251, 277
segment, 515
selection, 2, 14, 25, 46, 65, 117, 172, 206, 223, 249, 380, 403, 463
self, 3, 5, 8, 20, 41, 76, 79, 83, 85, 87, 88, 90–92, 94, 115, 121, 205, 229, 276, 278, 281, 292, 299–301, 307, 310, 313, 315, 320, 322, 325, 327, 330–333, 336, 341, 343, 345–348, 351–360, 365, 375, 376, 387–389, 393–396, 398, 400–407, 409, 411, 420, 472, 473, 480–482, 485, 488, 489, 502, 542
selfhood, 325
semiotic, 293
sender, 48, 49
sensation, 190, 441
sense, 3, 14, 16, 21, 59, 69, 72, 73, 86–88, 91, 141, 142, 151, 157, 175, 188, 190, 204, 205, 216, 229, 234, 241, 244, 248, 251, 252, 268, 270, 283, 286, 294, 315, 327, 347, 349, 356–358, 364, 369, 371, 389, 392, 393, 398, 399, 402, 404, 406, 416, 417, 430, 435, 448, 455, 458, 459, 465, 472, 477, 478, 482, 487, 489, 519, 522, 526, 527, 537, 539

sensitivity, 16, 28, 59, 94, 97–99, 175, 498–501, 510, 516
sensuality, 18, 27, 40, 66, 70, 83, 90, 92, 104, 116, 125, 126, 140–142, 148, 161, 164, 252
series, 20, 65
session, 471
set, 46, 57, 89, 122, 163, 252, 330, 442, 498, 502
setting, 39, 46, 94, 97, 145, 204, 381, 426, 532
sexuality, 203, 360, 369, 371, 376
shaft, 100
shame, 203, 308, 332, 368, 398, 406
shampoo, 312
shape, 5, 23, 42, 66, 176, 195, 196, 228, 235, 267, 283, 318, 331, 369, 398, 521, 524, 531
share, 72, 141, 181, 307, 312, 327, 357, 371, 398, 399, 402, 417, 517, 519, 532, 538, 539
sharing, 72, 141, 144, 245, 521, 527
shea, 87
shelf, 266, 271
shell, 224
shift, 24, 53, 115, 265, 309, 318, 331, 334, 336, 338, 350, 400, 402, 413, 462, 475, 476, 503, 516, 531, 534, 536
shine, 3, 132, 161
shower, 260
side, 49, 478
sight, 66
Sigmund Freud, 370
sign, 23, 65, 68, 115, 188, 202

signal, 4, 19, 141
signaling, 183, 214, 219
signature, 3, 6, 9, 13, 14, 21, 38, 44, 89, 102, 104, 109, 125, 140, 204, 272, 291, 314, 398
significance, 1, 18, 22, 24, 40, 41, 65, 71, 90, 93, 94, 123, 140, 145, 161, 163, 171, 176, 182, 187, 189, 191–193, 196, 235, 237, 238, 240, 242, 244, 245, 247, 248, 250, 252, 254, 258, 276, 284, 301, 308, 310, 320, 327, 349, 355, 376, 378, 393, 405, 457, 499, 500, 524, 525, 529, 531, 532, 534, 542
silk, 122
sip, 145
Sissel Tolaas, 284, 446
situation, 205
size, 398
skepticism, 230, 307, 469, 501
skill, 145, 148
skin, 12, 15, 26, 55, 57, 62, 64, 65, 70, 71, 73–76, 78–83, 85, 86, 88–90, 94–97, 99, 124, 199, 266, 313–315, 330, 371, 375, 382, 388, 389, 398, 403, 412
skincare, 75, 85, 88–90, 97–99, 270–272, 403
sleep, 20, 123
smell, 3, 4, 25, 51, 59, 76, 79, 88, 137, 144, 151, 157, 171, 172, 183, 184, 188, 191, 192, 195, 198, 199, 202, 204, 205, 214–216, 228, 233, 235, 239, 241, 243, 244, 246, 252, 260, 268, 269, 274, 283–286, 292–297, 301, 309, 310, 312, 323, 332, 356, 357, 384, 388, 404, 415–417, 419, 433, 435, 444–446, 448, 450, 455, 457–460, 463, 465, 478, 479, 487, 522, 527
smile, 129, 130, 132
smoke, 236
smoking, 140
smudging, 236–238
sniff, 312
societal, 8, 20–22, 24, 66, 115, 142, 166, 170, 171, 173, 175, 179, 181, 184, 186, 188, 191, 195, 196, 203, 205, 233, 244, 247, 274, 277, 281, 283, 287, 290, 292–296, 299–301, 303, 307, 309, 310, 312, 313, 315–318, 320–323, 325, 327, 329–331, 333, 338, 341, 345–347, 349, 351–353, 355–358, 360, 363, 365, 368, 369, 371, 376–378, 385, 388, 389, 391, 392, 397, 398, 400–402, 405, 407, 443, 444, 452, 457, 496, 519, 521, 531, 540–542
society, 41, 114, 176, 179, 181, 189, 197, 200, 225, 309, 310, 316, 331, 332, 347, 356, 358, 360, 370, 378, 393, 400, 444, 530
sociology, 351

soda, 57
sodium, 247
softness, 122, 382
soil, 188, 197, 242
solution, 503
solvent, 253
sophistication, 190
soul, 236, 309
sound, 453–455
source, 71, 118, 195, 274, 308, 375, 399
sourcing, 89, 166, 425, 440, 477, 479, 498, 500–503, 506–508, 514, 521
Southeast Asia, 245, 348
soy, 195, 388
space, 37, 195, 205, 307, 364, 378, 399, 405–407, 462, 519
spark, 88
spectacle, 377
spectrum, 114, 244, 285, 305, 378, 402, 477
speed, 230
spicy, 36
spirit, 83, 168, 169, 242, 244, 389, 395, 477, 518
spirituality, 237, 239, 244, 253, 310, 329, 477
spray, 31, 263
stability, 224, 266, 271, 272, 465, 488
stage, 252, 258
stagnation, 195
stalk, 58
stand, 269, 370, 407
standard, 114, 499
standpoint, 172, 178, 191
staple, 193, 263
starter, 245

state, 6, 26, 39, 66, 127, 205, 333, 458, 472
statement, 27, 325, 341, 346, 351, 358
status, 125, 295, 307, 316, 333, 343, 346, 351, 358, 378, 475, 526
steam, 62–64, 253
steaming, 243
stench, 9, 204, 205, 242–244, 301, 303
step, 9, 260, 306, 331, 341, 355, 400
stick, 263
stigma, 19, 66, 165, 195, 202, 246, 278, 300, 305, 307, 309, 313, 316, 321, 331, 332, 368, 378, 388, 389, 398, 443, 540, 541
stigmatization, 7, 23, 330, 356
Stilton, 190
stimulation, 119, 148, 367
stimulus, 204, 460
stink, 291, 292, 306, 308, 333
stone, 473, 488
story, 6, 8, 83, 88, 104, 249
storytelling, 7, 349, 500, 534
strand, 111
strategy, 349, 489
street, 234
strength, 16, 28, 43, 141, 439
stress, 1, 63, 83, 91, 392, 416, 469, 471, 478
structure, 4, 30, 37, 111, 124, 209, 219, 228
struggle, 205, 321, 331, 403
study, 5, 15, 26, 61, 62, 188, 199, 206, 215, 223, 236, 239, 458, 493
style, 104, 125, 127, 313, 341

Index

styling, 315
subject, 62, 164, 184, 188, 198, 208, 219, 252, 320, 321, 369
subjectivity, 252, 283, 296, 403, 443, 444, 451, 452
sublime, 409, 488
submission, 201, 370, 381–383
substance, 199, 215, 412
substitute, 60
subversion, 540
success, 272, 287, 290, 338, 420, 541
sulfide, 243
sulfur, 11, 141, 247, 274–276
summary, 166, 184, 249, 265, 267, 305, 464, 482
summer, 93
sun, 92–94, 250
sunscreen, 92–94
supply, 502, 503
support, 249, 521, 542
surface, 65, 74
surge, 261
surrender, 201, 382
surrounding, 66, 142, 173, 175, 181, 184, 195, 200, 202, 219, 225, 235, 238, 244, 245, 274, 277, 285, 290, 292, 294, 295, 301, 305, 309, 316–318, 323, 324, 330–333, 358, 368, 377, 388, 393, 398, 443, 480, 498–501, 504, 511, 514, 519, 521, 540
survey, 115
survival, 61, 174, 191
sushi, 244
sustainability, 216, 252, 254, 263, 324, 325, 425, 440, 496, 506, 515, 516, 519
sustenance, 173, 245, 247
swapping, 368
sweat, 1, 5, 9, 12, 16–20, 22, 49–52, 54, 56, 65–69, 71–74, 198–200, 204, 284, 309, 318–320, 330, 357, 375, 377
sweating, 49–51, 56, 65, 68–70, 199
sweaty, 66, 69–71, 198, 200, 201
sweetgrass, 192, 236, 524
sweetness, 53, 151, 256, 307, 353
sword, 510, 516
symbol, 15, 116, 125, 141, 142, 162, 188, 190, 200, 306, 314
symbolism, 162, 163
synchrony, 223
synesthesia, 463
synthesis, 219, 225, 419, 462
synthetic, 55, 56, 61, 86, 88, 89, 122, 129, 130, 166, 219–221, 249, 252, 261, 263, 284, 332, 397, 403, 440, 466, 477, 479, 501, 507, 518
system, 3, 4, 16, 19, 25, 27, 59, 62, 63, 76, 83, 88, 92, 93, 95, 102, 119, 148, 157, 162, 167, 172, 179, 206, 216, 229, 241, 243, 248, 251, 257, 264, 266, 268, 284, 286, 306, 387, 417, 438, 442, 444, 465, 470, 478, 480, 487, 524

t, 11
taboo, 3, 15, 114, 141, 142, 201, 299, 320–322
tactile, 42, 70, 88, 92, 188, 430, 441, 473
tailor, 468

talk, 37–39
tang, 257
tantalizing, 15, 40, 151, 153, 157, 171, 210, 348
tap, 115, 221
tapestry, 8, 22, 46, 61, 166, 171, 173, 177, 179, 181, 187, 189, 191, 192, 194, 196, 203, 206, 214, 235, 247, 249, 250, 252, 254, 256, 257, 281, 290, 310, 371, 376, 377, 383, 389, 400, 405, 460, 479, 482, 501, 519, 524, 531, 539, 540, 542
target, 290
taste, 58, 137, 151, 172, 173, 190, 250
tasting, 15, 243
tattoo, 355
tea, 236
technique, 13
technology, 225, 284, 343, 415–417, 419, 420, 422, 424, 429–433, 435, 438, 441, 442, 462, 468, 470, 503, 539
temperature, 18, 26, 86, 224
temporality, 443
tension, 181, 384, 394, 541
terrain, 285
territory, 17, 216, 299, 430, 435, 444
test, 240
testament, 20, 115, 142, 228, 244, 257, 357, 405, 407
testing, 271
testosterone, 209
texture, 124, 172
the Olfactory Underground, 540
the United States, 502

theater, 416
theme, 183, 416
Theodor Adorno, 444
Theodor Adorno's, 293
theory, 29, 32, 35, 65, 69, 76, 79, 83, 85, 94, 102, 104, 107, 109, 114, 148, 159, 166, 201, 223, 228, 258, 276, 279, 285, 290, 309, 339, 341, 354, 356, 394, 396, 403, 442, 463, 475, 485, 532, 534, 537
therapy, 403, 416, 470, 479
thickness, 389
thought, 61, 182, 183, 236, 284, 293, 295, 296, 321, 451, 452, 456
time, 5, 15–17, 35, 39, 44, 48, 89, 92, 122, 125, 145, 194, 224, 231, 240, 260, 266, 268, 271, 309, 312, 332, 355, 404, 417, 429, 435, 438, 443, 454, 468, 488
titanium, 93
today, 242, 499
tofu, 245
togetherness, 142
tongue, 140
tool, 14, 32, 41, 46, 49, 83, 95, 126, 144, 151, 161, 181, 296, 353, 356, 363, 365, 376, 409, 417, 442, 444, 451, 488, 489, 491, 495, 511, 516
top, 30, 35, 36, 104, 403
topic, 3, 54, 170, 175, 229, 367, 371, 415
touch, 34, 46, 69, 71, 88, 90, 92, 140, 148, 430

tourism, 244
traction, 118, 206, 349, 451, 465, 531, 541
trade, 498, 501
tradition, 236, 244, 247, 248, 314
trail, 223
tranquility, 85, 241, 403, 463, 489
transduction, 4
transformation, 65, 277, 438, 475, 487–489, 537
transience, 179, 445
transmission, 238
transparency, 89, 349, 413, 491, 498, 500–503, 505, 510, 514, 516
transport, 194, 268
transportation, 246
trap, 100
trauma, 488
travel, 77, 119, 242, 244
treatment, 389, 469
tree, 236
trend, 40, 42, 125, 188, 235, 238, 268, 270, 285, 312, 343, 349, 350, 355, 448, 475, 503, 525
trepidation, 378
trial, 403
trigger, 2, 14, 16, 25, 44, 59, 72, 87, 93, 95, 114, 174, 197, 199, 206, 211, 219, 237, 251, 266, 284, 370, 371, 381, 383, 480, 490
trope, 72
trust, 202, 205, 364, 500, 503, 506, 507, 514, 516
Tsukiji, 244
turn, 532
turning, 289, 309, 324

type, 26, 122

umami, 151, 190
underarm, 55
undercurrent, 60
underpinning, 489, 511
understanding, 2, 3, 8, 11, 18, 20, 24, 27, 29, 32, 34, 37, 39, 42, 44, 46, 51, 54, 58, 60, 66, 69, 79, 85, 88, 90, 94, 99, 102, 104, 107, 109, 115, 121, 129, 135, 145, 148, 150, 152, 159, 161, 162, 166, 167, 169, 176, 192, 193, 195, 200, 203, 205, 206, 210, 214, 216–218, 225, 233, 235, 237, 242, 246, 254, 257, 262, 265, 274, 290, 293, 296, 301, 305, 306, 310, 318, 320, 333, 341, 358, 360–364, 369–371, 383, 393, 398, 403, 405, 409, 417, 430, 433, 438, 442, 444–448, 450, 455, 457, 464, 467, 470, 479, 487, 488, 495, 499–501, 508, 514, 526, 528–533, 542
unease, 195
uniqueness, 7, 24, 307, 358, 400
unity, 253, 356, 357
unpleasantness, 19, 317, 318, 388
unworthiness, 378
up, 15, 21, 37, 166, 208, 216, 369, 389, 398, 542
uplift, 403, 480
urbanization, 309
urea, 21, 52, 65

use, 12, 29, 32, 34, 44, 55, 56, 61, 66, 68, 70, 76, 82, 83, 87, 88, 94, 102, 106, 108, 123, 125, 126, 129, 162, 163, 174, 191, 225, 235–238, 240, 244, 249, 252–254, 261, 266, 268, 270, 271, 274, 285, 286, 293, 312, 313, 321, 332, 348, 382, 383, 398, 404, 440, 442, 451, 458, 460, 467, 472, 473, 478, 480, 485, 488, 489, 491, 499–501, 507, 514, 515, 524, 525
user, 417, 419, 438, 468, 539
utilization, 254

validation, 227, 371, 402
validity, 229
value, 2, 6, 240, 305, 499, 515
vanilla, 26, 46, 87, 269
variability, 17, 89, 254, 445, 454, 463, 469, 479, 488
variety, 1, 65, 93, 95, 199, 201, 209, 215, 235, 243, 253, 403
vasodilation, 62
vegetable, 60
vehicle, 85, 146
version, 219
vessel, 124, 309
vetiver, 488
viability, 338, 342, 499
vibrancy, 520
vibrant, 87, 192, 243, 244, 247, 250, 252, 356, 377, 395, 517, 521, 526, 537, 539, 540, 542
vice, 308
view, 183, 324, 355

viewer, 458
vinyasa, 471
virility, 23, 68, 141
virtue, 233, 308, 405, 541
visibility, 357
vision, 307, 435, 447
visual, 61, 88, 92, 151, 161, 188, 207, 292, 293, 296, 297, 321, 341, 354, 355, 370, 415, 424, 442–448, 451, 455, 458, 460, 462, 463, 490, 526, 531, 532
vitality, 19, 59, 65, 66, 68, 141, 308
volume, 403
vomit, 191
vulnerability, 37, 72, 114, 141, 204–206, 229, 382

waft, 247
Wai-O-Tapu, 243
wake, 102
warmth, 16, 63, 71, 72, 86, 87, 97, 115, 144, 146, 151, 165, 191, 215, 249, 251, 283, 306
wash, 20, 395
washing, 114, 267, 309
waste, 518
water, 1, 12, 18, 34, 52, 65, 83, 85, 108
wave, 339, 444, 470
way, 26, 34, 51, 58, 59, 75, 79, 88, 104, 109, 119, 144, 221, 227, 230, 235, 254, 260, 265, 269, 276, 301, 318, 338, 341, 343, 360, 393, 417, 422, 442, 445, 446, 448, 468, 477, 498, 503, 506, 536

weapon, 145
wear, 290, 312
wearable, 468
wearer, 226, 304, 354
week, 228
weight, 43, 194, 332
welfare, 216
well, 35, 61, 64, 66, 71, 76, 83, 87, 100, 104, 105, 108, 119, 121, 123, 129, 132, 148, 162, 197, 214, 249, 267, 275, 290, 327, 387, 391, 398, 400, 404, 405, 422, 424, 465, 467, 469, 470, 472, 474, 478–480, 482, 485, 506, 510, 514
wellness, 238, 254, 403, 405, 438, 465–467, 469, 470, 472, 478, 487
wetness, 56
whiff, 88, 370
whiskey, 269
whisper, 203–205
wildlife, 166
willingness, 34, 142
willow, 477
window, 242
wine, 256
winemaking, 256
wisdom, 239, 285, 524, 536
withdrawal, 330
Wolfgang Laib, 446
woman, 324, 325, 488
wood, 525
word, 13, 49
work, 19, 36, 65, 66, 81, 175, 184, 200, 284, 309, 445, 451, 458, 464, 524
workout, 65, 66, 375

workshop, 532
world, 5, 13, 20, 27, 29, 32, 40, 49, 62, 64, 71, 79, 83, 88, 92, 107, 116, 124, 132, 145, 161, 164, 166, 169, 173, 175, 176, 179, 184, 187–191, 196, 198, 217, 218, 223, 225, 228, 235, 237–239, 244, 258, 260, 262, 265, 268–270, 278, 279, 285–287, 292–294, 296, 299, 301, 305–308, 313, 322, 325, 331, 339, 341, 345, 347, 351, 353, 356, 358, 367, 370, 377, 389, 394, 398, 400, 404, 405, 407, 409, 411, 420, 422, 430, 433, 446, 448, 450, 455, 459, 462, 464, 467, 479, 480, 485, 489, 493, 501, 506, 508, 517, 524, 526, 527, 529, 531, 536, 537, 542
worshipping, 201
worth, 352, 398
wrestling, 70

yeast, 255, 256
ylang, 32, 46
yoga, 470–473, 482
yogurt, 137
your, 1–3, 8, 9, 11–13, 24–27, 29–32, 35, 36, 38–40, 44, 49–51, 73, 75–79, 81–84, 98–102, 104–107, 111, 113, 115, 117, 119, 121, 128, 129, 131, 132, 134, 136, 145, 150, 211, 213, 214, 260, 395, 466

zesty, 36

zinc, 93

Milton Keynes UK
Ingram Content Group UK Ltd.
UKHW021124111124
451035UK00016B/1210